JAPANESE

AMERICANS

JAPANESE
AMERICANS

THE HISTORY AND CULTURE OF A PEOPLE

Jonathan H. X. Lee, Editor

ABC-CLIO ™

An Imprint of ABC-CLIO, LLC
Santa Barbara, California • Denver, Colorado

Library of Congress Cataloging-in-Publication Data

Names: Lee, Jonathan H. X., editor.
Title: Japanese Americans : the history and culture of a people / Jonathan H.
   X. Lee, editor.
Description: Santa Barbara, California : ABC-CLIO, 2018. | Includes
   bibliographical references and index.
Identifiers: LCCN 2017042053 (print) | LCCN 2017042430 (ebook) |
   ISBN 9781440841903 (eBook) | ISBN 9781440841897 (hardcopy : alk. paper)
Subjects: LCSH: Japanese Americans—History. | Japanese Americans—Social
   conditions. | Japanese Americans—Biography.
Classification: LCC E184.J3 (ebook) | LCC E184.J3 J339 2018 (print) |
   DDC 973/.04956—dc23
LC record available at https://lccn.loc.gov/2017042053

ISBN: 978-1-4408-4189-7 (print)
      978-1-4408-4190-3 (ebook)

22 21 20 19 18   1 2 3 4 5

This book is also available as an eBook.

ABC-CLIO
An Imprint of ABC-CLIO, LLC

ABC-CLIO, LLC
130 Cremona Drive, P.O. Box 1911
Santa Barbara, California 93116-1911
www.abc-clio.com

This book is printed on acid-free paper ∞

Manufactured in the United States of America

I dedicate this volume to my son,
Owen Edward Jinfa Quady-Lee.

Contents

Part II

Political Activity and Economic Life: Business Endeavors and Involvement in American Politics

Part III

Cultural and Religious Life: People, Institutions, and Organizations

Part IV

Literature, the Arts, Popular Culture, and Sports: People, Movements, and Expressions of Identity

Preface

Japanese American history is rich: it is a narrative of dreams, triumph, loss, injustice, and the struggle to be rightly and fully American. It is a relatively short history of 150 years. However, at this moment in the history of the United States, it is critical that Americans reflect on and relearn the history of the Japanese American experience so as to not repeat past injustices, and prepare ourselves to meet the challenges that lay ahead. To be more exact, I wish to invite readers to examine Executive Order 9066, issued on February 19, 1942, by President Franklin D. Roosevelt. Executive Order 9066 authorized the secretary of war to delegate a military commander to designate military areas "from which any and all persons may be excluded." On March 18, 1942, President Franklin D. Roosevelt passed Executive Order 9102, creating the War Relocation Authority that forcefully relocated Japanese Americans from their homes to internment camps. Our government claimed that these orders were passed in the interest of public safety following the Japanese attack of Pearl Harbor on December 7, 1941. These two orders were chiefly enforced against Japanese Americans, though thousands of Italian and German Americans were also affected and interned. In total, nearly 62 percent of Japanese American citizens were interned without due process.

Similarly, on January 27, 2017, President Donald Trump issued Executive Order 13769, "Protecting the Nation from Foreign Entry into the United States" otherwise, known as the "Muslim Ban" to protect America from the potential of terrorist attacks by foreign nationals. In effect, Executive Order 13769 bans travel to the United States from seven Muslim countries: Iran, Iraq, Libya, Somalia, Sudan, Syria, and Yemen. The "Muslim Ban" was met with immediate protest and challenged by the American Civil Liberties Union in the courts, and on March 6, 2017, President Trump reissued a revision of the "Muslim Ban" with Executive Order 13780. Iraq was eliminated from the list of banned countries. However, the executive order continues to target migrants from Muslim countries. Besides the systematic attack on Muslim Americans and their communities, President Trump is also attacking undocumented Americans and wishes to make his priority the construction of a wall to keep "Mexicans out." *Japanese Americans: The History and Culture of a People* offers comprehensive coverage of the Japanese American experience, and reveals the long, hard, and aching struggling of Japanese Americans to be treated as Americans. The internment of Japanese Americans during World War II is not just mere history, but rather, very much a core dimension of Japanese American subjectivity. It is a wound on the community, the scar on the psyche of Japanese Americans that is still painful. Thus, recent political scapegoating of Muslim Americans, LGBTQQI Americans, American women, and undocumented Americans in the realm of civil and equal rights, painfully tells us that the lessons of history, just some 75 years ago, have not been learned. Sadly, history is repeating itself, but we can stop it. The cycle of oppression can be prevented, and it begins with learning.

If we learn from *Japanese Americans: The History and Culture of a People*, we may see hope, and progress, albeit slow, is achievable, as is the case with Japanese Americans seeking redress and an apology for the unlawful injustice and unconstitutional internment, nay, incarceration of American citizens without due process of law during World War II. *Japanese Americans: The History and Culture of a People* contains four sections: Part I tells the story of Japanese emigration to the United States: where Japanese migrants came from, why they came, and what they experienced and encountered as foreign migrants in America. Moreover, it documents their history of oppression and fight to be rightly and fully American. Part II documents Japanese American economic life and political/civic engagement. Again, it documents Japanese Americans becoming American in every aspect of American polity and economy. Part III shifts to the realm of culture and religious life and offers a multitude of examples of Japanese American contributions to the mosaic of American culture and religious pluralism. Last, Part IV explores Japanese American expressions of identity through the arts, popular culture, and sports. Besides covering major historical moments and figures, this volume also documents everyday history makers, such as community activists and religious leaders.

Japanese Americans: The History and Culture of a People provides a chronology of Japanese American history that is comparative and pays attention to international and global contexts of being Japanese Americans. This volume also includes 19 primary documents that are useful archival sources that connect to the major themes of the articles. In addition, a useful bibliography on the subjects covered in the volume as well as general subject index.

I wish to express sincere gratitude to Senior Editor Michael Millman at ABC-CLIO /Greenwood/Praeger who graciously approved several requests for extensions. I also wish to thank Sidney C. Li, my research assistant; my students at San Francisco State University; and colleagues in the Asian American Studies Department at San Francisco State University. Moreover, I wish to acknowledge the work of the Editorial Board, for ensuring the academic rigor of the volume.

I hope *Japanese Americans: The History and Culture of a People* will be a useful resource for students who wish to learn about the contribution and history of Japanese Americans. May we remember our history and use it to guide our future as a country of immigrants, a place where liberty, freedom, and the pursuit of happiness is available to all.

Jonathan H. X. Lee
San Francisco, California

Chronology of Japanese American History

With contributions by Sidney C. Li

1543   Japanese encounter Europeans for the first time when some Portuguese land on a small island off the southern tip of Kyushu Island in southwestern Japan.

1549   Jesuit Francis Xavier starts Christian proselytizing in Japan. The Catholic missionaries convert about 300,000 Japanese by the end of the 16th century.

1560   Oda Nobunaga (1534–1582) begins the unification drive of Japan, ending Ahikaga rule in 1573.

1592–1598   Japan invades Korea with the ultimate goal of conquering China. This military aggression ends with the death of the powerful warrior Toyotomi Hideyoshi, leaving Korea in ruins.

1638   Japan begins a period of seclusion, triggered by a rebellion involving about 20,000 Japanese Christians in 1637 and 1638.

1790   The first U.S. Naturalization Act allows only "free White persons" to become U.S. citizens.

1806   Eight Japanese sailors on board an American ship arrive in Hawai'i. They are the first recorded Japanese who land on the Hawai'ian Islands.

1841   While commanding a whaling ship, the *John Howland* in the Pacific, Capt. William Whitfield rescues five shipwrecked Japanese sailors. In November 1841, four of the rescued Japanese sailors disembark at the port of Oahu. Manjiro Nakahama stays on board and goes with Whitfield to Fairhaven, Massachusetts. On May 6, 1843, the *John Howland* sails into New Bedford harbor. Manjiro Nakahama attends school in New England and adopts a Western name: John Manjiro. Later on, John Manjiro will serve as an interpreter for Commodore Matthew Perry. John Manjiro indirectly influenced the treaty negotiations between Japan and Commodore Perry, which ended the 250 years of Japanese isolation from the world.

1843   The first Japanese arrive in the United States.

1848   James W. Marshall discovers gold on Gen. John A. Sutter's property at Coloma, California.

1850   The California State legislature passes a law that imposes a $20 per month tax on foreign miners.

1852   A Buddhist-Daoist temple to the Empress of Heaven Tien Hau is founded in San Francisco.

1853   American commodore Matthew Perry sails into Edo (Tokyo) Bay, representing the United States on his second expedition to open up Japan to the outside world.

1854   The Treaty of Kanagawa is signed between the Japanese government and Commodore Matthew Perry, establishing formal relations between the two countries and ending 200 years of Japanese isolation. Americans gain privileges similar to those they have in China.

1858   Joseph Heco (1837–1897) is the first Japanese national to become a naturalized citizen, and the first to publish a Japanese language newspaper. Heco was a fisherman from the province of Sanyodo, Japan, who was shipwrecked and brought to California in February 1851 along with sixteen other survivors.

1862   In his inaugural address as the eighth governor of California, Leland Stanford promises to protect the state from "the dregs of Asia."

1868   Meiji Restoration takes place in Japan, ending its feudal system. The teenage Emperor Meiji is restored as a symbolic figure to paramount status, and reform measures are taken to Westernize and modernize the nation. A conscription law is enacted soon thereafter.

1868   Japan-based American businessman Eugene M. Van Reed illegally ships 150 Japanese laborers to Hawai'i and another 40 laborers to Guam to work on sugar plantations. This unlawful recruitment of Japanese laborers, known as the *gannen-mono*, meaning "first year people," marks the beginning of the global Japanese labor migration overseas. However, for the next two decades, Japan's Meiji government bans Japanese laborer migration due to the "slave-like" treatment that the first Japanese migrants encountered in Hawai'i and Guam.

1869   Several hundred Japanese laborers are brought to Hawai'i, Guam, and California by Americans and others. The 148 Japanese are treated poorly in Hawai'i's sugar plantations. The Japanese government will bring 40 of them home and ban emigration.

1869   A group of 22 samurai and their families arrive at Gold Hill region 1,200 feet above the Sacramento Valley. There, with the help of a benefactor, John Henry Schnell, the Japanese purchase the land from Charles Graner and establish the Wakamatsu Tea and Silk Farm Colony.

1870   The Naturalization Act of 1870 is signed into law by President Ulysses S. Grant. The act limits immigration and naturalization to "aliens of African nativity and to persons of African descent" and "whites" thus excluding all Chinese and other non-whites from receiving citizenship. The Act also bans the entry laborers' wives.

1870   California passes law against the importation of Chinese, Japanese, and "Mongolian" women for the purposes of prostitution.

1875   The Page Law is enacted, which bars Asian women suspected of prostitution and attempts to regulate contract labor from China. It also bars entry of Chinese, Japanese, and "Mongolian" felons and contract laborers.

1875   The United States and Hawai'i sign a Reciprocity Treaty. The treaty is a free-trade agreement between the United States and the Kingdom of Hawai'i starting in September 1876. In return, the United States gains lands in the area known as Pu'u Loa that will later house the Pearl Harbor naval base. The treaty encourages increase investment by Americans in Hawai'i's sugar plantations.

1876   Japan forces Korea to sign the Treaty of Kanghwa, gaining privileges similar to those China and Japan were forced to give to Western powers.

1877   Several Japanese Christian students residing in San Francisco assemble and organize the Fukuinkai, or Gospel Society for Bible study, which encourages mutual support for one another. This is the first immigrant association formed by the Japanese.

1880   Section 69 of California's Civil Code prohibits issuing of licenses for marriages between whites and "Mongolians, Negroes, mulattoes and persons of mixed blood."

1881   Hawai'ian King Kalakaua takes a trip around the world. He meets with rulers, perhaps to find more laborers for Hawai'i's plantations. He also wants to learn the ways of other rulers to better protect his own people. He first went to San Francisco, then Japan, China, Siam (now Thailand), Burma, India, Egypt, Italy, Belgium, Germany, Austria, France, Spain, Portugal, and England. In Japan he tries to persuade Japan to lift emigration restrictions, but the Japanese emperor is not moved.

1882   President Chester A. Arthur signs the Chinese Exclusion Act, which bans immigration of laborers and their wives from China for 10 years. It also bans Chinese immigrants from becoming naturalized citizens. As a result, there is an increase in Japanese immigration to replace Chinese laborers.

1882   The United States and Korea sign the Treaty of Peace, Amity, Commerce and Navigation, establishing diplomatic relations between the two countries.

1885   The first Japanese migrants to be officially admitted to a U.S. state or territory arrive in Hawai'i as sugar plantation laborers on the *City of Tokio* freighter. Assisted by the Hawai'ian government's assisted passage scheme, they comprise 676 men, 159 women, and 108 children.

1886   American Robert Walker Irwin, the Kingdom of Hawai'i's minister to Japan, reaches an agreement with the Japanese government to allow its subjects to go abroad. This is known as the Irwin Convention, which remains in force until 1894. A total of 28,691 (23,071 men, 5,487 women, 133 children) government-sponsored Japanese laborers go to work on sugar plantations during this time on three-year contracts. After 1894, emigration business is turned over to private companies.

1889   Jodo-Shinshu priest Soryu Kagai, arrives in Honolulu, surveys the situation, and, eventually, establishes Buddhist groups among the Japanese laborers on the plantations.

1889	Katsu Goto, a prominent merchant and interpreter, is lynched in Hawai'i. He is murdered for his advocacy work on behalf of Japanese plantation workers.
1890	Tsunetaro Jo and Tadoyoshi Sekine's shoemaking business is forced to close by the Boot and Shoemakers' White Labor League. In response, 20 Japanese American shoemakers in San Francisco form the Nihonjin Kutsuko Domeikai, the Japanese Shoemakers' League, the first Japanese trade association in the United States. They shift from shoemaking to shoe repair to avoid competing with white shoemakers.
1892	Ellis Island opens in Upper New York Bay. It will be the gateway to America for European immigrants until 1954.
1892	The first Japanese-language newspaper in Hawai'i appears in Honolulu.
1893	Queen Lili'uokalani, the last native ruler of an independent Hawai'i, is deposed in a bloodless coup d'état by five American nationals, one English national, and one German national. All were living and doing business in Hawai'i and opposed her efforts to establish a new constitution. President Grover Cleveland refuses to annex Hawai'i because he feels the Americans in the sugar industry engineered the overthrow, and that the Hawai'ian people did not want revolution.
1894	Shebata Saito, a Japanese man, applies for U.S. citizenship, but the U.S. circuit courts decide that he should not be granted citizenship because he is not "white" nor "black." This case predates the Takao Ozawa case (1922) by nearly three decades.
1894	Japanese immigrant Namyo Bessho, a U.S. Navy veteran of the Spanish-American War and World War I, files for naturalized U.S. citizenship under the Act of July 26, 1894, which granted citizenship to "any alien" over 21 years of age who served five consecutive years in the Navy or Marine Corps. Bessho finally becomes a U.S. citizen through a measure signed by President Franklin D. Roosevelt in June 24, 1935, granting Asian veterans citizenship rights.
1894	The Sino-Japanese War (1894–1895) starts in Korea in response to the presence of Chinese military called in by Korean government to suppress the Tonghak Rebellion. Japan wins the war.

1895	The Planters' Labor and Supply Company reorganizes under the name Hawai'ian Sugar Planters' Association (HSPA). Its goal is the "advancement, improvement and protection of the sugar industry of Hawai'i, the support of an Experiment Station, the maintenance of a sufficient supply of labor for the sugar plantations of Hawai'i and the development of agriculture in general."
1896	Japanese in Hawai'i start the first Japanese-language school in Honolulu.
1896	The U.S. Supreme Court upholds the "separate but equal" concept in its decision on *Plessy v. Ferguson*. The decision legalizes "Jim Crow" laws for nearly 60 years.
1896	Ulysses Shinsei Kaneko, a Japanese businessman and labor contractor in Riverside, California, becomes a naturalized citizen. He becomes the first Issei to buy land in Riverside in 1897.
1898	U.S. Commodore George Dewey captures Manila Bay in the Philippines.
1898	Spain cedes the Philippines and Guam to the United States with the Treaty of Paris, which ends the Spanish-American War. This is the start of Filipino migration to the United States.
1898	The first Japanese-language newspaper in the mainland United States, the *Nichibei Shimbun*, is published in San Francisco.
1899	The Philippine-American War begins. The war is officially declared over on July 4, 1902.
1900	Twenty-seven men from the Japanese island of Okinawa arrive in Hawai'i aboard the SS *City of China*. They are taken to the Ewa Plantation, where they work.
1900	The Hawai'ian Organic Act makes all U.S. laws applicable to Hawai'i, thus ending contract labor in the islands.
1900	The first large-scale anti-Japanese protest takes place in San Francisco, organized by various labor groups.
1900	San Francisco orders the quarantine and compulsory inoculation of all Japanese and Chinese upon discovery of a bubonic plague victim in Chinatown.
1900	The Hawai'ian Islands officially become a U.S. territory, and all islanders become American citizens. President William McKinley appoints Sanford B. Dole the first governor.

1900   In response to the growing anti-Japanese sentiments, the Japanese Foreign Ministry stops issuing passports to laborers headed for the United States and Canada.

1901   Peter Ryu, the first recorded Korean immigrant to Hawai'i, arrives on a Japanese ship, the *Kongkong Maru*.

1901   Satori Kato, a Japanese American chemist, invents the first stable and soluble coffee powder in Chicago, earning a patent in 1903. This becomes a seminal breakthrough for mass-market instant coffee.

1902   President Theodore Roosevelt declares the end of the Philippine-American War.

1902   Hawai'ian Sugar Planters' Association hires David W. Deshler in Korea to recruit Korean laborers.

1902   The first novel authored by a Japanese American, *The American Diary of a Japanese Girl*, is published by Yone Noguchi with the help of editor and lover Léonie Gilmour.

1902   The U.S. Senate passes the Philippine Organic Act, which sets up terms for the civil government established in 1901 under the governorship of President William Howard Taft. The act allows for "self-government" while maintaining U.S. control.

1902   Several Japanese businessmen found the Japanese American Industrial Corporation (JAIC), one of the largest labor contracting firms in California.

1903   Five hundred Japanese and 200 Mexican laborers become the charter members of the Japanese Mexican Labor Association in Oxnard, California. Kozaburo Baba serves as president. This is the first farmworkers' union in California, but the American Federation of Labor refuses to recognize a nonwhite union.

1903   In *Yamataya v. Fisher* (also known as the Japanese Immigrant Case), the U.S. Supreme Court sets a precedent for allowing deportation to be challenged in courts by attacking the legitimacy of predeportation procedures. Kaoru Yamataya, a Japanese girl, is deported.

1903   Thirty-five Okinawans arrive in Honolulu aboard the SS *Hongkong Maru*.

1904   The Russo-Japanese War (1904–1905) is fought in Korea. Japan defeats a Western colonial power and emerges as the dominant military power in Asia.

1904	The Chinese Exclusion Extension Act makes Chinese exclusion permanent.
1904	Hawai'i Sugar Planters' Association's trustees adopt a resolution stating that all skilled positions on the plantations will be filled by "American citizens, or those eligible for citizenship."
1904	Two thousand plantation laborers go on strike at Waialua.
1905	The *San Francisco Chronicle* front-page headline reads "The Japanese Invasion: The Problem of the Hour."
1905	With the Japan-Korea Treaty, Japan declares Korea its virtual protectorate.
1905	A Japanese and Korean Exclusion League is established.
1905	The Asiatic Exclusion League is established in San Francisco by 67 labor unions. Eventually more than two hundred labor unions join the league to restrict Asian immigration to the United States.
1906	Hawai'i Sugar Planters' Association (HSPA) begins recruiting workers from the Philippines after access to Chinese, Japanese, and Korean labor is limited by immigration legislation. Fifteen laborers are sent to Ola'a Plantation on the Big Island (Hawai'i). In 1909, 554 Filipino laborers arrive in Hawai'i, followed by 2,653 in 2010; 1,363 in 1911; 4,319 in 1912; and 3,258 in 1913. By 1930, about 100,000 Filipino workers have migrated to Hawai'i.
1906	San Francisco Board of Education passes a resolution that orders Japanese and Korean children to be placed in a segregated school with already segregated Chinese children.
1906	Abiko Kyutaro (1865–1936), the founder of the *Nichibei Shimbun* newspaper, establishes the American Land and Produce Company and builds a farm community—Yamato Colony—near Livingston, California.
1907	President Theodore Roosevelt's administration persuades the San Francisco Board of Education and mayor to rescind the segregation order.
1907	The Gentlemen's Agreement between the United States and Japan is concluded in the form of a Japanese note agreeing to

deny passports to laborers who want to migrate to the United States.

1907   President Theodore Roosevelt signs Executive Order 589 prohibiting Japanese with passports from Hawai'i, Mexico, or Canada reentry to the United States.

1907   A mob of 400 to 500 white working men in Bellingham, Washington, gather on September 4 to drive a community of South Asians out of the city. By the end of the day, 125 South Asians have been driven out of town, six hospitalized, and roughly 400 held in jail for "protective custody." Shortly after the Bellingham riot, the Japanese and Korean Exclusion League was renamed the Asiatic Exclusion League to include the growing South Asian immigrant community.

1907   A riot against Asians in the Chinese and Japanese section of Vancouver, British Columbia, erupts.

1908   Japanese "picture brides" set foot on the United States. Selected by Japanese Americans through a matchmaking service, these native Japanese women are paired using no more than photographs and input from family members. The women's reasons for participating vary, including the pursuit of financial support for their families back home, familial obligation, new freedoms, and escape from traditional familial responsibilities.

1908   The Gentlemen's Agreement between the United States and Japan is fully effective.

1908   Chang In-hwan, a Korean independence activist, shoots and kills Durham Stevens, who supported Japanese occupation of Korea.

1909   Japanese plantation workers strike for four months on the island of Oahu, but Hawai'i plantation owners refuse to negotiate.

1910   The Gentlemen's Agreement of 1907 stops the issuance of passports to Japanese laborers wanting to go to America or Hawai'i. However, a loophole in the agreement allowed wives and children of Japanese laborers already residing in the United States to emigrate. As a result of the loophole, many Japanese picture brides are able to continue to migrate to Hawai'i and the United States.

1910   The U.S. government opens Angel Island Immigration Station on Angel Island in the San Francisco Bay.

1910   Korea is formally annexed by Japan through the Japan-Korea Annexation Treaty.

1912   The Republic of China (Taiwan) is established, and Sun Yat Sen of the Kuomintang (the KMT or Nationalist Party) is proclaimed provisional president.

1913   California State legislature passed the Webb-Haney Act, or Alien Land Law, following fears among white farmers that their independent ventures were at risk against Japanese success. This act prohibits "aliens ineligible to citizenship" from buying land or leasing it for longer than three years.

1914   World War I begins. It lasts until 1918. In spite of racial discrimination against Asian Americans, many serve in the war and are awarded naturalization for their military service.

1914   Japanese American landscape designer Makoto Hagiwara invents the fortune cookie, which becomes a staple dessert in many Chinese American restaurants.

1914   Sessue Hayakawa, a Japanese stage actor, appears in two movies during his first year in the United States.

1917   The Immigration Act of 1917 restricts immigration of anyone born in a geographically defined "Asiatic Barred Zone," excluding Japanese and Filipinos. The Gentlemen's Agreement already restricts immigration of Japanese laborers, and because the Philippines is an American colony Filipinos were considered American nationals and have unrestricted entry. On December 14, 1916, President Woodrow Wilson vetoed the act, but Congress overrode his veto. The act prohibits immigration from all of Asia and India by drawing an imaginary line from the Red Sea in the Middle East all the way through the Ural Mountains: people living east of the line are not allowed entry to the United States. The act also includes a literacy test requirement.

1917   President Woodrow Wilson asks Congress to declare war on Germany. The United States formally enters World War I on April 6.

1918   The Treaty of Versailles formally ends World War I on November 11.

1918   Judge Horace W. Vaughn of the U.S. District Court for Hawai'i rules that Japanese, Chinese, and Korean veterans of World War I are eligible for naturalization under the Act of May 8, 1918. As a result, 398 Japanese, 99 Koreans, and 4 Chinese are granted citizenship by November 14, 1919. Unfortunately, their citizenship is revoked by the *Toyota v. United States* decision on May 25, 1925.

1919   Koreans in Korea protest Japanese occupation with a nationwide nonviolent demonstration.

1919   One hundred fifty Koreans attend the first Korean Liberty Congress in Philadelphia to advocate Korean independence and make public the plight of Koreans under Japanese occupation.

1920   Pablo Manlapit, head of the Filipino Labor Union, unilaterally issues an order for Filipinos to strike and urges the Japanese to join them. By February 1, a united strike that includes 8,300 Filipinos and Japanese strikers, 77 percent of the entire plantation workforce on Oahu, brings the plantation to a stop. The strike lasts six months.

1920   The 1913 California Alien Land Law is amended to close a loophole that permitted Asian immigrants to own or lease land under the names of their native-born children.

1920   The Japanese Foreign Ministry stops issuing passports to picture brides. Only women who are accompanying their husbands to the United States are issued passports.

1921   Arizona, Texas, and Washington State pass alien land laws.

1921   President Warren G. Harding, pressured by the Immigration Restriction League, signs the Johnson Act, also known as the Emergency Quota Act of 1921, or the Immigration Act of 1921, into law. It is the first quota immigration act that limits the annual number of immigrants to 3 percent of the number of foreign-born persons of most nationalities living in the United States in 1910.

1921   White vigilantes force 58 Japanese laborers from Turlock, California, driving them out by truck at gunpoint.

1922   The U.S. Congress passes the Cable Act, which strips any women of European or African ancestry of their citizenship if they marry an "alien ineligible to citizenship." A woman can regain her citizenship through the naturalization process if she divorces her alien husband or if he dies. The Cable Act is repealed in 1936.

1922   The U.S. Supreme Court in *Takao Ozawa v. U.S.* upholds the 1790 Naturalization Act and rules that Japanese (and other Asians) are ineligible for naturalized citizenship: naturalization is limited to "free white persons and aliens of African nativity."

1922   New Mexico passes an alien land law.

1923   Idaho, Montana, and Oregon pass alien land laws.

1923   The U.S. Supreme Court in *U.S. v. Bhagat Singh Thind* upholds the 1790 Naturalization Act and declares South Asians ineligible for naturalized citizenship.

1923   The U.S. Supreme Court in *Terrace v. Thompson* upholds the constitutionality of Washington's Alien Land Law.

1923   The U.S. Supreme Court in *Porterfield v. Webb* upholds the constitutionality of California's Alien Land Law.

1923   The U.S. Supreme Court in *Webb v. O'Brien* rules that cropping contracts between a citizen with legal rights and a noncitizen with no legal rights are illegal because they are a ploy that allows Japanese to possess and use land in California.

1923   The U.S. Supreme Court in *Frick v. Webb* forbids aliens "ineligible to citizenship" in California from owning stocks in corporations formed for farming.

1924   President Calvin Coolidge signs the Immigration Act of 1924 into law, establishing a national origins quota, which limits the number of immigrants by country and excludes all immigrants from Asia, except for Filipinos who are "nationals" because the Philippines was a U.S. protectorate.

1924   Nevada passes an alien land law.

1925   Kansas passes an alien land law.

1925   The U.S. Supreme Court in *Hidemitsu Toyota v. U.S.* rules that a "person of the Japanese race, born in Japan, may not legally be naturalized."

1927   The U.S. Supreme Court in *Weedin v. Chin Bow* rules that a person born abroad of an American parent or parents who has never lived in the United States cannot be a citizen of the United States.

1927   The U.S. Supreme Court in *Gong Lum v. Rice* rules in favor of separate but equal facilities for Mongolian children in Mississippi.

1927   A group of white workers drives out Filipino farm laborers from Yakima Valley, Washington.

1927   James Sakamoto (1903–1955) becomes the first Nisei boxer to fight professionally at Madison Square Garden in New York.

1927   The first Japanese mayor of a U.S. city, Kinjiro Matsudaira, is elected in Edmonston, Maryland, at the time one of the most diverse U.S. municipalities. Matsudaira's father was Japanese and his mother white, and he was born in Pennsylvania. His father was descended from a Nipponese noble family.

1929   Stock market crash, known as "Black Thursday," triggers the Great Depression.

1931   Japan invades Manchuria in northeastern China on September 18.

1931   An amendment to the Cable Act declares that no American-born woman who was stripped of her citizenship (by marrying an alien ineligible to citizenship) can be denied the right of naturalization at a later date.

1934   Eight second-generation Japanese baseball teams form the Nisei Central Japanese League in California.

1937   Japan invades China.

1937   Japan and Nazi Germany sign Anti-Comintern Pact directed at the Soviet Union.

1940   Japan is granted rights to station troops in Indochina from the Vichy French government. By 1941, Japan extends its control over the whole of French Indochina.

1940   Germany, Italy, and Japan sign the Tripartite Pact, which is known as the Axis alliance.

1941   Japan's civilian government of Prince Fumimaro Jonoye is taken over by a military cabinet led by Gen. Hideki Tojo.

1941   On December 7, Japan attacks U.S. military bases at Pearl Harbor, Hawai'i. More than 3,500 U.S. service men are wounded or killed.

1941   President Franklin D. Roosevelt brings declaration of war on Japan to Congress; Congress passes it.

1942	President Franklin D. Roosevelt passes Executive Order 9066 authorizing the secretary of war to delegate a military commander to designate military areas "from which any and all persons may be excluded." Executive Order 9066 is chiefly enforced against Japanese Americans.
1942	President Franklin D. Roosevelt passes Executive Order 9102, which creates the War Relocation Authority that forcefully relocates Japanese Americans from their homes to internment camps.
1942	Congress passes Public Law 503 to punish anyone defying orders to carry out Executive Order 9066.
1942	Japanese American attorney Minoru Yasui turns himself in for arrest at the Portland, Oregon, police station to test the discriminatory curfew policies issued by Gen. John L. DeWitt.
1942	State of California fires all Japanese Americans in the state's civil service.
1942	One hundred forty-one South American civilians of Japanese ancestry arrive at San Francisco aboard a U.S. vessel at the request of the U.S. government who wants to employ them for future prisoner exchanges. By 1944, a total of 2,100 persons, mostly from Peru, have been transported into U.S. custody.
1942	Japanese American University of Washington student Gordon Hirabayashi turns himself in to the authorities to test the constitutionality of the curfew and detention orders.
1942	Japanese American Fred Korematsu is arrested in Oakland, California, for violating orders to report for detention.
1942	The U.S. Army completes its transfer of all Japanese American detainees from 15 temporary centers to 10 permanent War Relocation Authority detention camps: Manzanar, Poston, Gila River, Topaz, Granada, Heart Mountain, Minidoka, Tule Lake, Jerome, and Rohwer.
1942	Second War Powers Act repeals the confidentiality of census data, allowing the FBI to use this information to round up Japanese Americans and change naturalization restrictions to allow persons serving the U.S. military during World War II to become naturalized.
1942	Japanese American detainees protest at the Poston War Relocation Center in Arizona.

1942   James Ito and James Kanagawa are killed when military police fire into a crowd during a protest at the Manzanar War Relocation Center in California.

1942   The 100th Infantry Battalion is formed by Japanese soldiers from Hawai'i and sees its first battle in Europe only a year later.

1943   The U.S. Supreme Court rules in *Hirabayashi v. United States* that the curfew law imposed on persons of Japanese ancestry is constitutional.

1943   The U.S. Supreme Court rules in *Yasui v. United States* in favor of Congress in enacting Public Law 77-503, authorizing the implementation of Executive Order 9066 and providing criminal penalties for violation of orders of the military commander.

1943   The War Relocation Authority designates Tule Lake, California, as a segregation center for Japanese American detainees who will not sign the loyalty oath.

1943   The Magnuson Act is signed into law. This act repeals the Chinese Exclusion Act, allows Chinese to become naturalized citizens, and allows China a quota of 105 immigrants per year.

1944   The Western Defense Command issues Public Proclamation No. 24, revoking exclusion orders and military restrictions against Japanese Americans.

1944   In *Korematsu v. United States*, the U.S. Supreme Court rules that, based solely on one's ancestry, one group of citizens may be singled out and relocated from their homes and imprisoned for several years without trial.

1944   In *Ex Parte Mitsuye Endo*, the U.S. Supreme Court rules that the War Relocation Authority has no authority to detain a "concededly loyal" American citizen.

1944   Ben Kuroki, the first and only Japanese American in the U.S. Army Air Force during World War II, serves in combat operations in the Pacific.

1945   The War Department announces that the exclusion orders are withdrawn after the U.S. Supreme Court rules in *Ex Parte Mitsuye Endo* that "loyal" citizens cannot be detained without trial.

1945   Nazi Germany surrenders unconditionally to the Allies; Japan fights on alone.

1945   The United States drops the first atomic bomb on Hiroshima, Japan, on August 6. The United States drops the second atomic bomb on Nagasaki, Japan, on August 9.

1945   Japan formally surrenders to the Allies on board the battleship USS *Missouri* on September 2. After the capitulation of Japan to Allied forces, Ho Chi Minh and his People's Congress establish the National Liberation Committee of Vietnam to create a provisional government. Japan transfers all power to Ho Chi Minh and the Viet Minh. Thirty thousand Japanese Americans are stranded in Japan. Korea is divided at the 38th parallel: the Soviet Union with military presence in the North, and the U.S. military forces in the South.

1945   All War Relocation Authority Internment camps are closed except for Tule Lake Center.

1945   Congress enacts the War Brides Act, signed into law by President Harry S. Truman. This act allows 722 Chinese and 2,042 Japanese women (as well as European women) who married American servicemembers to come to the United States between 1946 and 1953.

1945   The 442nd Regimental Combat Team, which includes the Hawai'i-based, all-Japanese U.S. Army 100th Battalion, receives 18,143 decorations. The team is awarded 9,486 Purple Hearts. It becomes the most decorated unit in the military history of the United States.

1946   Tule Lake "Segregation Center" closes.

1946   Congress enacts the Alien Fiancées Act, also known as the G.I. Fiancées Act, which grants fiancées of American servicemembers during World War II a special exemption from immigration quotas to enter the United States.

1946   The War Relocation Authority program officially ends.

1946   President Harry S. Truman signs the Luce-Celler Act into law, which grants naturalization rights to Filipinos and South Asians.

1946   The Philippines gains independence from the United States. This had been promised by the passage of the Tydings-McDuffie Act of 1934.

1946   First Indochina War starts when Viet Minh forces attack French forces at Hanoi.

1947	President Harry S. Truman grants full pardons to 267 Japanese American draft resisters who violated the Selective Training and Service Act of 1940.
1948	President Truman signs into law the Japanese Americans Evacuation Claims Act on July 2, enabling World War II Japanese American internees to file claims for their financial losses.
1948	In *The People v. Oyama*, the Supreme Court declares that California's escheat action, which allows the state to seize land of Japanese Americans, is unconstitutional.
1950	North Korea invades South Korea, initiating the Korean War.
1950	First U.S. ground troops are deployed in Korea.
1951	The San Francisco Peace Treaty between Japan and 55 other nations is signed in September, allowing Japan to gain independence when U.S. occupation of Japan ends in 1952.
1952	The California Supreme Court finds California's Alien Land Law of 1913 unconstitutional.
1952	The Immigration and Nationality Act of 1952, also known as the McCarran-Walter Act, revises and consolidates all previous laws regarding immigration and naturalization. The act upholds the national origins quota system, which limits the number of immigrants allowed to enter the United States annually by country. It eliminates the Asiatic Barred Zone, and allots each Asian country a minimum of 100 visas annually, and creates a preference system that determines eligibility based on skills and family ties in the United States.
1953	Japanese American Monica Sone publishes *Nisei Daughter*, an autobiographical account of the author's life growing up in Seattle, Washington.
1954	Japanese American sergeant Hiroshi Miyamura, a veteran of World War II, receives the Congressional Medal of Honor from President Dwight D. Eisenhower for his service in the Korean War.
1956	California Proposition 13 is repealed in California's 1913 Alien Land Law by popular vote.
1957	Japanese American John Okada publishes *No-No Boy*.
1959	Daniel K. Inouye, initially an at-large representative from the new state of Hawai'i, is elected as the first Japanese American

in Congress. He serves in the House of Representatives for more than three years, before becoming a member of the Senate for the rest of his life.

1960   John F. Kennedy barely defeats Richard M. Nixon in the presidential election.

1961   Seiji Ozawa, a world-class music conductor from Japan, is appointed as assistant director of the New York Philharmonic.

1962   Daniel K. Inouye becomes U.S. senator and Spark Matsunaga becomes U.S. representative from Hawai'i.

1962   Japanese American Minoru Yamasaki's Yamasaki Associates is commissioned to design the twin towers of the World Trade Center in New York City. Yamasaki is the first Japanese American architect of an American supertall skyscraper.

1963   President John F. Kennedy is assassinated in Dallas, Texas.

1964   Patsy Takemoto Mink becomes the first Japanese American woman and woman of color to serve in Congress as a representative from Hawai'i.

1964   Lyndon B. Johnson wins the presidential election in a landslide victory over Republican Barry Goldwater of Arizona.

1964   Japan hosts the 18th Summer Olympic Games in Tokyo, the first Olympic Games in Asia.

1964   Japanese American photographer Yoichi R. Okamoto becomes the head of the White House Photo Office for President Lyndon B. Johnson.

1965   The U.S. Congress passes the Immigration and Nationality Act, which eliminates national origins quotas. Twenty-thousand people per country are allowed entry annually. Priority is given to those with skills and/or family residing in the United States.

1966   Japanese American actor Mako Iwamatsu is nominated for an Academy Award for best supporting actor.

1967   Japanese American boxer Paul Fujii wins the junior welterweight boxing championship.

1967   In *Loving v. Virginia*, the U.S. Supreme Court declares antimiscegenation laws unconstitutional.

1968   President Lyndon B. Johnson declines running for reelection.

1968	Dr. Martin Luther King Jr. is assassinated at the Lorraine Motel in Memphis, Tennessee.
1968	The Black Student Union and the coalition of other student groups known as the Third World Liberation Front lead a strike at San Francisco State University to demand the establishment of ethnic studies programs and classes.
1968	Republican Richard M. Nixon is elected president of the United States.
1969	Yuji Ichioka, an adjunct professor of history at UCLA, coins the term "Asian American." He opens the first "Asian American Studies" course at the university. Beforehand, those with Asian ancestry commonly had been referred to as "Oriental" or "Asiatic."
1969	The student-led protest at San Francisco State University ends with a settlement to establish the country's first and still only School (now College) of Ethnic Studies. Asian American Studies is one of the programs, along with American Indian Studies, Black Studies (now Africana Studies), and La Raza Studies (now Latina/o Studies).
1970	The Japanese American Citizens League resolves to seek redress for Japanese Americans interned during World War II, signifying the beginning of the redress movement.
1971	Norman Y. Mineta is elected the mayor of San Jose, California, the first Japanese American mayor of a major U.S. city.
1972	*Manzanar*, the first personal documentary about Japanese internment during World War II, is produced by Robert A. Nakamura. The documentary wins honors from the San Francisco Museum of Art and the Los Angeles Museum of Contemporary Art.
1972	Japanese American Ken Kawaichi and Dale Minami found the Asian Law Caucus.
1973	Japanese American writer Jeanne Wakatsuki Houston, with her husband James Houston, publishes *Farewell to Manzanar*, a recollection of their memories during World War II.
1973	All warring parties in the Vietnam War sign a cease fire. It is signed in Paris by Henry Kissinger and Le Duc Tho.
1974	George R. Ariyoshi becomes Hawai'i's first Japanese American governor.

1974	President Richard M. Nixon resigns.
1974	The U.S. Supreme Court in *Lau v. Nichols* rules that school districts with children who speak little English must provide them with bilingual education. The Court says, "The failure of the San Francisco school system to provide English language instruction to . . . students . . . who do not speak English, or to provide them with other adequate instructional procedures, denies them a meaningful opportunity to participate in the public educational program and thus violates 601 of the Civil Rights Act of 1964."
1975	Fall of Saigon.
1975	Ann Kiyomura, a Japanese American, and Kazuko Sawamatsu of Japan win the women's doubles title at the Wimbledon tennis championship in England.
1976	Japanese American S. I. Hayakawa from California wins a U.S. Senate seat; "Spark" Masayuki Matsunaga from Hawai'i wins a seat in the U.S. Senate after seven consecutive terms in the U.S. House of Representatives; native Hawai'ian Daniel K. Akaka is elected to the U.S. House of Representatives from Hawai'i.
1976	President Gerald Ford rescinds Executive Order 9066, 34 years after World War II.
1978	Ellison Shoji Onizuka, a Japanese American, becomes the first Asian American astronaut in the United States. He later dies as a mission specialist when the *Challenger* space shuttle explodes.
1978	Japanese American Robert Matsui of California wins a seat in the U.S. House of Representatives.
1980	President Jimmy Carter signs the Refugee Act into law. Under this act, the Office of Refugee Resettlement is established. It adopts the definition of "refugee" used in the United Nations Protocol and provides regular and emergency admissions of refugees.
1980	Congress creates the Commission on Wartime Relocation and Internment of Civilians. The Commission is charged with investigating World War II internment programs.
1982	Japanese American sculptor and architect Isamu Noguchi receives the Edward MacDowell Medal for outstanding lifetime contribution to the arts.

1983   The Commission on Wartime Relocation and Internment of Civilians reports that Japanese American internment was not justified by military necessity and that internment was based on "race prejudice, war hysteria, and a failure of political leadership." The commission recommends an official government apology redress payments of $20,000 to each of the survivors; and a public education fund to help ensure that this will not happen again.

1983   The Federal District Court of San Francisco reverses Fred Korematsu's original conviction and rules that the U.S. government had no justification for issuing the internment orders.

1986   The U.S. Congress enacts the Immigration Reform and Control Act, which includes civil and criminal penalties for employers who knowingly hire undocumented "aliens."

1986   Japanese American Ellison Shoji Onizuka (1946–1986) from Hawai'i is the first Asian American astronaut, and one of the members of the Space Shuttle *Challenger* who died.

1987   President Ronald Reagan issues proclamation of Asian/Pacific American Heritage Week.

1987   The U.S. Congress enacts the Amerasian Homecoming Act, which eases immigration of Amerasian children born, or war babies, during the Vietnam War—mostly the offspring of American fathers and Vietnamese mothers. By 2009, about 25,000 Vietnamese Amerasians and 60,000 to 70,000 of their relatives entered the United States under this law.

1987   Japanese American Patricia Saiki is elected to Congress representing Hawai'i.

1987   Charles J. Pedersen (1904–1989), born in Korea to a Norwegian father and Japanese mother, is awarded the Nobel Prize in Chemistry.

1988   The Civil Liberties Act is signed into law by President Ronald Reagan. This act provides for individual payments of $20,000 to each surviving Japanese American internee and a $1.25 billion education fund among other provisions.

1988   Japanese American Eric Sato wins Olympic gold medal in volleyball.

1990	The Immigration Act is enacted and increases the annual visa cap to 700,000 annually. The act also created the Diversity Immigrant Visa program.
1990	The first nine redress payments are made at a Washington, D.C., ceremony. Rev. Mamoru Eto of Los Angeles, who by this time is 107 years old, is the first to receive his check.
1990	Japanese American golfer David S. Ishii wins the Hawai'ian Open PGA tournament.
1991	Japanese American Bob H. Suzuki is selected as president of California State Polytechnic University, Pomona.
1992	Japanese American Kristi Yamaguchi wins a gold medal for women's figure skating at the 1992 Winter Olympics in Albertville, France.
1994	Isamu Akasaki and Hiroshi Amano from Japan and Shuji Nakamura, a Japanese American, provide the experimental groundwork for the first commercially sold LED (light-emitting diode), the blue LED. They win the Nobel Prize for Physics for this achievement in 2014.
1995	Japanese baseball player Hideo Nomo becomes a Major League Baseball player in the United States as a pitcher for the Los Angeles Dodgers.
1996	A. Wallace Tashima is appointed by President Clinton to the U.S. Court of Appeals for the Ninth Circuit, with jurisdiction over states in the western United States, Alaska, and Hawai'i. He is the first Japanese American appointed to a judgeship on a court of appeals.
1997	At midnight on July 1, 1997, Hong Kong is returned to China and becomes a Special Administrative Region.
1998	Chris Tashima wins an Academy Award for his role in the film *Visas and Virtue*. He is the first U.S.-born Japanese American actor to attain this honor.
1999	Gen. Eric Shinseki of the U.S. Army becomes the first Asian American to serve as a chief of staff in the U.S. armed forces. A decade later, he is appointed by President Barack Obama to be the first Asian American secretary of veterans affairs.
2000	Norman Y. Mineta, former mayor of San Jose, California, becomes the first Asian American appointed to the U.S. Cabinet

as the secretary of commerce for the Clinton administration. He remains as the secretary of transportation for the George W. Bush administration, where he is the only Democratic cabinet member.

2000 The U.S. Census records 1,152,324 Japanese in the United States, and the majority of the population (61 percent) is native born.

2001 Dr. Kenneth Matsumura, a Japanese American scientist at the Alin Foundation in Berkeley, California, invents a working bioartificial human liver. The manufacturing technique for the liver has since been used to treat liver cancer.

2001 Japanese American Mike Honda is elected to the U.S. House of Representatives from California.

2002 Japanese American Apolo Anton Ohno wins a gold medal in 1,500-meter short-track speed skating at the Salt Lake Winter Olympics.

2007 Japanese American Mike Honda is named House Democratic senior whip.

2008 Japanese American Bryan Clay wins Olympic gold in the decathlon in Beijing.

2008 Japanese American scientist Yoshiro Nambu is awarded the Nobel Prize in Physics; Japanese American scientist Osamu Shimomura and Chinese American scientist Roger Tsien share a Nobel Prize in Chemistry with American biologist Martin Chalfie.

2010 Daniel K. Inouye, the first Japanese American member of Congress, becomes president pro tempore of the U.S. Senate. Third in succession to the presidency, Inouye becomes the highest-ranking Asian American politician in U.S. history.

2010 U.S. Census records 1.3 million Japanese residing in the United States.

2012 Asians surpass Hispanics as the largest group of new immigrants in the United States. An estimated 18.2 million Asians are recorded as residing in the United States, making them the fastest-growing racial-ethnic group in the country.

2012 Republican Mazie Hirono, a Japanese American, becomes the first female Asian American U.S. senator. She is also Hawai'i's first female senator.

2012   Japanese American Mark Allan Takano, a Democrat, wins a seat in the House of Representatives, representing California's redrawn 43rd Congressional District in Riverside, California.

2013   A comprehensive immigration reform act (the "Dream Act") is introduced in the U.S. Congress. If enacted, the bill will create a path toward naturalization for undocumented persons living in the United States who entered as children (15 and under).

2017   President Donald Trump issues Executive Order 13769, "Protecting the Nation from Foreign Entry into the United States," otherwise known as the "Muslim Ban."

PART I

CONTEXT OF JAPANESE EMIGRATION: COMING TO AMERICA

HISTORICAL OVERVIEW

Japanese Americans are descendants of immigrants who came from Japan, or Nippon, meaning "source of the sun." There are also many who are from Okinawa and self-identify as Okinawan instead of Japanese American. Since they follow on the heels of Chinese immigrants, their experience reveals many similarities, yet, because of Japan's rapid industrialization and modernization during the Meiji period (1868–1912), it was also very different from the Chinese American experience. On the U.S. mainland, Japanese communities formed around agriculture. Japanese immigrants entered the United States in the greatest numbers from 1886 to 1908, with a second wave of mostly woman immigrants peaking between 1916 and 1920. Until the 1970s, Japanese Americans were the largest single ethnic group among Asian Americans and their history in Hawai'i was longer, more sustained, and more significant than anywhere else in America.

Factors of Japanese Migration

During the Meiji period, thousands of people were displaced because their land was taken out of cultivation or their homes were taken away. By 1870, the U.S. Census indicates that 55 Japanese immigrants were living in the United States. In 1880, the U.S. Census shows 148 Japanese immigrants living in the United States, 86 of whom resided in California. Most of this early immigration was considered illegal by Japanese law. Pressure from its growing displaced population resulted in the Japanese government lifting its ban on emigration and allowed Japanese laborers to go to Hawai'i to work on sugar plantations starting in 1884. On January 8, 1900, the first group of 27 Okinawans arrived at the shores of Honolulu on the SS *China*. The Japanese laborers went to Hawai'i and the United States as contract laborers. They signed contracts for agricultural employment in exchange for passage. As such, they were like the

A group of first generation Japanese immigrants gathered at a garden club meeting, Oregon, July 1924. (Underwood Archives/Getty Images)

Chinese who were mostly *dekaseginin*, or "sojourners," who were young men who intended to work for a limited time and then return to Japan with their earnings from abroad.

Since Chinese laborers were excluded from immigration with the passage of the 1882 Chinese Exclusion Act, businesses on the mainland United States were in need of cheap laborers as well. Eight years after Chinese exclusion, there were 2,039 Japanese living in America: two decades later, there were 72,257 Japanese in America. San Francisco, Seattle, and Portland were major ports of entry for Japanese immigrants. Roughly 76 percent of the Japanese immigrants settled along the Pacific coast: this trend continued for four decades. There were sizable populations of Japanese immigrants in Colorado, Utah, and New York.

Early Japanese immigrants remained primarily single and male. In the 1900 U.S. Census, 23,916 of 24,326 Japanese immigrants were male and only 410 were female. The ratio of women to men shifted when, after 1908, the United States and Japan signed the Gentlemen's Agreement that restricted the migration of unskilled laborers from Japan to the United States, but it did not cut off the migration of wives or family members of permanent residents. The period from 1908 to 1924 was dominated by the arrival of "picture brides." These were women who migrated to join husbands they had married either during a return trip to Japan or by proxy. This period also initiated the rapid growth of the second generation of Japanese Americans their communities.

Though the Japanese immigrants were aware of the experience of the Chinese before them and hence attempted to do things differently, they inherited much of the resentment directed toward the Chinese because both were Asian, and nonwhite. Even so, the Japanese transitioned from *dekaseginin* to citizens, in light of nativist perceptions that to be American is to be "white."

Japanese Immigration, Exclusion, and Citizenship

Japanese American communities faced increasing restrictions against immigration, citizenship, property rights, and basic civil rights over the first four decades of the 20th century. First, as Japanese immigrants first entered the United States, they found a society already ordered by racial hierarchies, segregation, and the recent passage of the 1882 Chinese Exclusion Act. It did not take long for Japanese immigrants to become targets of race-based attacks and for exclusionist efforts to cut off immigration from Japan. In 1902, white workers successfully got the Chinese Exclusion Act of 1882 extended, and they wanted to include the Japanese.

On October 11, 1906, the San Francisco municipal school board directed all school principals to send Chinese, Japanese, and Korean students to "Oriental Schools." This action lead to an international geopolitical event as the government of Japan voiced their protest to Washington. Washington was careful in its dealing with Japan because it was a rising military power in Asia. President Theodore Roosevelt forced the San Francisco municipal school board not to segregate Japanese American children, which allowed them to attend school with white children. However, President Roosevelt agreed to the Gentlemen's Agreement, signed in 1907 and implemented in 1908, which restricted the migration of unskilled laborers from Japan. Furthermore, President Roosevelt prohibited Japanese laborers holding passports for Hawai'i, Mexico, or Canada from remigrating to the U.S. mainland. The State of California agreed not to pass overtly anti-Japanese legislation in the future. Roger Daniels points out that the Gentlemen's Agreement was "sold" to Californians as "tantamount to exclusion" but it was not. Instead, under its terms, the Japanese American population would double in less than 20 years because Washington agreed that Japanese already residing in America could send for their wives and family members left behind. However, by 1924, the immigration policy changed banning entry to all aliens ineligible to become citizens, which ended all Japanese immigration. The Immigration Act of 1924 is considered to be the ultimate triumph of the Native Sons of the Golden West.

Laws and discriminatory policies were passed that further politically racialized the Japanese as "Other" and noncitizen. In 1913 the California legislature passed a law that denied Japanese residents the ability to own property. Japanese immigrants were able to subvert that law by purchasing property in their children's names because they were born in America and were thus American citizens according to the 14th Amendment and *United States v. Wong Kim Ark*, 169 U.S. 649 (1898). Many Issei parents purchased land in their children's names. When tested in court, the California State Supreme Court upheld the right of even the youngest Nisei, second generation child, to own property as a right of citizenship (*Estate of Tetsubumi Yano* [1922] 188 Cal. 645, 648). This only angered many white Californians and fueled a call for a total ban on Japanese immigration. By 1920, however, a new anti-Japanese legislation corrected that loophole. The right to own property, to establish a home, a business, or a farm, was directly tied to the rights of the Issei to become naturalized citizens.

Japanese American Experience and World War II

The bombing of Pearl Harbor by Japanese forces on the morning of December 7, 1941, marked a bitter turning point in Japanese American history. President Franklin D. Roosevelt signed Executive Order 9066 in February 19, 1942, authorizing the exclusion of Japanese—including Okinawan—Americans from the West Coast. The order granted the federal government ability to create military zones, including the authority to remove individuals—mostly American citizens and residents of Japanese descent—from areas that there deemed threats to national security. Immediately after Pearl Harbor, the Federal Bureau of Investigation (FBI) identified and captured Japanese American community leaders from California, Oregon, and Washington—states that were designated critical zones of national security. These early detainees, arrested by the FBI as early as December 1941, were sent to facilities such as the Department of Justice internment camps in Santa Fe, New Mexico, Crystal City, Texas, and Fort Missoula, Montana. They were held without bail, without being formally charged, and without knowing what crime they were being accused of committing.

On March 18, 1942, President Roosevelt issued Executive Order 9102, establishing the War Relocation Authority (WRA) for the purposes of relocating Japanese Americans named in Executive Order 9066. In total, 112,000 Japanese Americans were forced to leave their homes and property and move into government detention facilities euphemistically called "Assembly Centers" and "Relocation Centers." They were sent to 10 camps located in far-flung regions, each housed 10,000 to 20,000 Japanese Americans: Rohwer and Jerome, Arkansas; Gila River and Poston, Arizona; Manzanar and Tule Lake, California; Amache, Colorado; Minidoka, Idaho; Topaz, Utah; and Heart Mountain, Wyoming. The relocation began in the summer of 1942 and was completed by November. All facilities were surrounded by barbed wire and military guard towers. The WRA described the relocation centers as "pioneer communities" that offered inhabitants basic housing and federal government protection. Remarkably, Executive Order 9066 did not relocate Hawai'ian Japanese, who made up nearly one-third of the population of the islands where the attack took place. In total, nearly 62 percent of American born Japanese Americans were interned.

Some individuals were placed under government control in a variety of other facilities ranging from Department of Justice Internment Centers to segregation facilities and even federal penitentiaries. Additionally, 2,264 individuals of Japanese ancestry were sent by 12 countries in Latin America for detention in the United States during the war: 1,800 of them were Japanese Peruvian. Although the exact purpose of this international transfer of individuals was unclear, common speculations include a plan to use Japanese Latin Americans for hostage exchange purposes.

Several years after the initial relocation, public opinion began to shift concerning the need for incarcerating Japanese Americans who never demonstrated any disloyalty to the United States. Secretary of War Henry Stimson, who approved the proposal to organize an all-Nisei combat team in 1943, withdrew his support of Executive Orders 9066 and 9102 in 1944 claiming that the relocation program was based on misinformation and public hysteria.

To date, scholars still debate the terminology that best describes the facilities used to detain Japanese Americans. Although the word *internment* is commonly used to refer to the confinement of all Japanese Americans, only those aliens arrested by the FBI and held under the authority of the Department of Justice were housed in internment camps. During the war, some had already begun using the term "concentration camp" to describe the facilities that held the majority of Japanese Americans, but today the use of this term is less common because of its close association with the concentration camps that housed Jews and other groups targeted by Nazi Germany for extermination in the death camps. Other common terms are detention facilities, confinement centers, or virtual prisons, but none are precisely accurate. What scholars can agree on is the power that the government wielded by creating facilities that were extralegal and outside the boundaries of U.S. constitutional law.

Fighting in the Courts

Japanese Americans challenged their treatment during World War II in formal ways by disputing the discriminatory laws in the courts. Four cases made it all the way to the Supreme Court: *Yasui v. United States* (1943), *Hirabayashi v. United States* (1943), *Korematsu v. United States* (1944), and *Ex Parte Mitsuye Endo* (1944). Minoru Yasui was born in Oregon to Issei parents. On March 28, 1942, Yasui deliberately broke the curfew by walking around downtown Portland after hours and presenting himself to the police station. Yasui was a member of the Oregon bar and was an army second lieutenant in the infantry reserve. Executive Order 9066 limited the movement of Japanese Americans to home and work by establishing a curfew between 9:00 p.m. to 6:00 a.m. Through Public Proclamation Number 3 issued on March 24, 1942, the curfew was justified as a means of securing the country from risk of espionage and acts of sabotage. Yasui waived his rights to a trial by jury and was found guilty: he was fined $5,000 by a federal judge and sentenced to one year in the Multnomah County Jail in Portland. He was transferred to the Minidoka War Relocation Center in 1944. While serving his sentenced, he filed an appeal to the Ninth Circuit Court. In May 1943, the Supreme Court heard the case, and on June 21, 1943, it issued its ruling. The ruling, authored by Chief Justice Harlan Fiske Stone upheld the constitutionality of the curfew and the War Powers Act.

In a similar case, a student in Seattle named Gordon Hirabayashi was arrested for breaking the curfew and challenging exclusion from the West Coast. Hirabayashi claimed his Fifth Amendment rights to "due process under the law" were violated by the exclusion and curfew orders. Hirabayashi's case would be the first case to test the laws in May 1943. Moreover, it was the first case to challenge the laws based on race because it only applied to one ethnic group—Japanese Americans. Hirabayashi's lawyer argued that he was a citizen of the United States, was born in the United States, had no ties to Japan, had never been to Japan, and had no relations with anyone living in Japan. However, the court ruled that national security was paramount during times of war. The curfew, the court argued, was a "protective measure." The court was able to avoid more complex legal issues with exclusion, registration, and relocation by focusing their ruling on Hirabayashi's violation of the curfew law.

Fred Korematsu challenged the exclusion from the West Coast as well. Korematsu refused to obey the relocation order and was arrested for violating the Civilian Exclusion Order No. 34. He was found guilty in federal court on September 8, 1942. His conviction was upheld on January 7, 1944, by the Ninth Circuit Court of Appeals. Korematsu then appealed to the U.S. Supreme Court. Korematsu's case completed Hirabayashi's case by forcing the court to address the constitutionality of force relocation and exclusion. On December 18, 1944, the court issued its ruling. Five justices affirmed the lower court's ruling. Justice Hugo Black wrote the majority opinion and said that national security concerns outweighed Korematsu's constitutional rights. Three justices—Owen Roberts, Frank Murphy, and Robert Jackson—wrote dissenting opinions. Justice Roberts argued that relocation was akin to imprisonment. Furthermore, without evidence of disloyalty and because there were no trials, Japanese Americans' Fifth Amendment rights had been violated. Justice Murphy concurred with Justice Roberts but went on to add that the policies were acts of racism against Japanese Americans. Justice Jackson dissented on the grounds that because the relocation orders only targeted Japanese Americans whose parents were born in Japan, the order was unconstitutional because it was based on "inherited guilt."

Mitsuye Endo was a Japanese American woman who was born in Sacramento. On May 15, 1942, she was forced to leave her home and job as a stenographer for the California State Highway Commission in Sacramento. She was relocated to Tule Lake Relocation Camp in northern California. Sacramento is the capital of the state of California, so under Public Proclamations Numbers 1 and 2, it was classified as a sensitive military zone. Hence, any person of Japanese descent within the zone was put under strict curfew or ordered to be relocated to less sensitive areas. At the time of her relocation, Endo was an American citizen and her brother was a member of the U.S. Army. In July 1942, Endo filed a writ of habeas corpus demanding that the government present evidence for her arrest. She asked that the court grant her freedom and release her from Tule Lake Relocation Camp. Endo lawyers argued that her detention was illegal due to the length of time she had been detained without being charged. The lack of due process, they argued, was a federal abuse of the War Powers Act, which violates the 14th Amendment "equal protection under the law" clause because Italian Americans and German Americans were not targets of relocation or curfew and their home countries were officially at war with the United States.

Only Endo's case received a favorable ruling during the war. The Supreme Court agreed with her on all counts. Before the Supreme Court's ruling was able to be put in effect, Endo was released from camp on the basis of a citizenship review. In 1983, Korematsu had his conviction overturned under a writ of error called *coram nobis* at the federal court level. The *Korematsu* case in particular remains unchallenged at the Supreme Court level and continues to be used as precedent for cases that require "strict scrutiny" because they have the potential of affecting only a specific population of people. Hirabayashi's conviction on the exclusion count was overturned in 1986. Then in 1988 his conviction for curfew violation was overturned, also under *coram nobis*. His attorney argued that the court had made an error based on inaccurate information regarding the scope of disloyalty among Japanese Americans in the state of Washington. The federal appeals court agreed and issued Hirabayashi a formal apology for the original convictions.

After World War II, Japanese Americans worked hard to restore their lives and recover from the devastation of having been imprisoned without due process and being charged with any crimes. Many did not want to talk about their experiences. Nisei became notorious for keeping their wartime experiences from their Sansei children. However, it is the Sansei generation who will fight for their rights and the rights of their elders to be recognized and treated as fully American!

ALIEN LAND LAW (1913)

The Alien Land Law (1913), alternatively known as the California Alien Land Law and the Webb-Haney Act, was legislation passed by Governor Hiram Johnson (1866–1945, governor 1911–1917), which directed that foreign aliens and immigrants were ineligible for citizenship and by extension restricted from leasing and owning land. Although not explicitly discriminatory toward a particular group, the intention and focus of the law was directed at Chinese and Japanese immigrants in the United States who faced increasingly anti-Asian sentiment in most western American states. Although Japanese American persons utilized a range of legal means to circumvent the land lease and ownership stipulations in the Alien Land Law of 1913, subsequent state legislation was eventually enacted to further restrict the rights of Asian immigrants. This legislation was reflective of the anti-immigrant and anti-Asian public sentiment expressed in discriminatory state laws of the period, and indicative of the general treatment of Japanese Americans throughout the late 19th and early 20th centuries. Though the California Alien Land Law was eventually found unconstitutional by the U.S. Supreme Court (1948, 1952), it nonetheless had a lasting impact upon Japanese Americans by limiting the economic and social opportunities available to them in the United States.

California's Alien Land Law, passed on May 19, 1913, legislated that aliens, foreign citizens, and immigrants were ineligible for citizenship. By extension, this law meant that immigrants were also ineligible to own land in California. In addition, the Alien Land Law restricted the leasing of agricultural land by foreigners to a set duration. Although such laws were broadly framed, their specific focus was directed at Japanese immigrants who were excluded based on the Naturalization Act (1790), which restricted American citizenship to white persons, and laws such as the Page Act (1875) and the Chinese Exclusion Act (1882). Despite being officially opposed by the U.S. federal government, under pressure by the Japanese government who sought to protect its citizens, California's Webb-Haney Act was passed and influenced similar legislation in other western states including Arizona, New Mexico, Washington, and Oregon.

Passage of the Alien Land Law was the result of a number of culminating factors including an economic recession, increasing competition for work in western states, the rising availability of cheap immigrant labor, concern for foreign ownership and control throughout the region, and the growing anti-Asian sentiment promoted by organizations such as the Asiatic Exclusion League, who falsely maintained that Japanese persons were incapable of blending into American society given their different physical features, clothing, and language. Much of this situation had arisen following passage of the Chinese Exclusion Act, which had effectively halted Chinese immigration to America, leading to increasing numbers of Japanese immigrants settling on the West

Coast. Attempts to limit Japanese immigration into America had been made with the Gentlemen's Agreement (1907) between the U.S. and Japanese federal governments, wherein laborers were effectively excluded from immigration. As a result, Japanese immigration during the period shifted to increasing numbers of individuals seeking to start businesses and own agricultural land, which in turn reinvigorated American concerns about foreign ownership. Like the Chinese Exclusion Act, the varying Alien Land Laws (1913, 1920, 1923) were part of a process that sought to limit Asian immigration and citizenship and thereby prohibit property ownership in America by foreigners.

In response to the passage of California's Alien Land Law, Japanese Americans utilized a number of inventive means to legally evade the exclusionary state laws of the period, and even eventually sought to challenge the legality of the law. A typical example of community action against the Alien Land Laws developed when many first-generation Japanese immigrants and Japanese Americans, also known as Issei, registered their property and land as being owned by their American born children, who were second-generation American citizens, or Nisei. However, the legislative response to such resistance led to increasingly restrictive legislation, including the Alien Land Law of 1920, which imposed stronger limitations on Asian property ownership, banned Japanese Americans from leasing agricultural land, and increasingly limited who land could be transferred to. As a result, the anti-Asian sentiment in many states persisted for decades throughout the early 20th century.

Ultimately, the Alien Land Law of 1913 was found unconstitutional by ruling of the U.S. Supreme Court in the cases of *Oyama v. State of California* (1948) and *Fujii Sei v. State of California* (1952). The passage of the Immigration and Nationality Act (1952) during this period, codifying national immigration policy, eliminated racial restrictions on citizenship requirements and effectively supplanted state Alien Law Acts. Regardless, the influence of the Alien Land Law has been vast. Aside from California's Alien Land Law, the terminology used became symbolic of the anti-Asian sentiments of the period, and was the name given to the general range of legislation passed in varying states to restrict foreign immigration, citizenship, and land ownership. Furthermore, the sentiments that directed the passage of such policies in the early 20th century subsequently influenced and shaped popular sentiment regarding Japanese loyalty during World War II (1939–1945), making it increasingly publicly and politically acceptable to relocate and intern Japanese Americans. Finally, such legislation also impacted the early Japanese American immigration experience, limited employment opportunities as well as reduced Japanese Americans' ability to establish businesses and communities, undermined their ability to garner capital or pursue higher education opportunities, and has hindered the acceptance of Japanese and Asians into American society.

See also: Anti-Japanese Movement; Japanese American Exclusion; Japanese Americans in Farming and Agriculture

Further Reading

Barkan, Elliot. *From All Points. America's Immigrant West, 1870–1952.* Bloomington: Indiana University Press, 2007.

Daniels, Roger. *The Politics of Prejudice: The Anti-Japanese Movement in California and the Struggle for Japanese Exclusion.* Berkeley: University of California Press, 1999.

Sean Morton

ANTI-JAPANESE MOVEMENT

The Anti-Japanese Movement can be described as the widespread reaction in the late 19th and early 20th century against Japanese immigrants, laborers, and business owners in the western Pacific states of America. These sentiments were also evident at the federal level of the government, which sought to limit the ability of Asians to gain American citizenship, establish families, build communities, purchase property, access educational opportunities, and defend their civil rights. In particular, the Anti-Japanese Movement restricted Japanese migration though legislation such as the Alien Land Laws, business ordinances, and limitations on the immigration of family members as a means of controlling the influx of foreign labor. The movement was driven by the public sentiment of the period and included individuals, small businesses, newspapers, social organizations, labor unions, state legislators, and federal officials. In addition, anti-Asian exclusionary organizations such as the American Legion Native Sons and Daughters of the Golden West, Japanese Exclusion League of California, and California Joint Immigration Committee were founded to foster anti-Japanese sentiment. Such groups, though concerned about labor and wages, based their position on arguments that Japanese persons could not be assimilated into American culture and that they were untrustworthy and morally degenerate. Focused in states such as California, Oregon, Washington, Arizona, and New Mexico, the Anti-Japanese Movement was ultimately successful in prompting the passage of various pieces of anti-Japanese legislation and in negatively portraying Japanese immigrants and citizens to the American public for decades. As a result, not only were those of Japanese ancestry discriminated against by the American public but such anti-immigrant ideas propelled national racist sentiments for years, culminating in passage of the Immigration Act (1924), which prohibited the immigration of Japanese into the United States and provided the legislative and popular basis for the internment of Japanese Americans during World War II (1939–1945).

In many ways, American discrimination against Japanese persons is rooted in both regional and national approaches to groups such as Native Americans,

Africans, non-European immigrants, and Hispanics, which have been reflected and legitimized in the passage of legal restrictions throughout the nation's history. Laws such as the Naturalization Act (1790), which confined American citizenship to white persons, the Page Act (1875), which restricted immigration by undesirables or Asians, and the Chinese Exclusion Act (1883), which historically prevented a specific ethnic group from immigrating to the United States, serve as the legislative precedents for anti-Japanese attitudes. Indeed, later legislation such as the Alien Land Laws (1913, 1920), Immigration Act (1924), and Executive Order 9066 (1942) in their attempt to restrict immigration and limit property ownership, and business opportunities for Japanese persons must be seen as extensions of this process of discrimination.

Japanese immigration into the American west was primarily the result of the decline of Chinese immigrant laborers following rising anti-Chinese tensions and passage of the Chinese Exclusion Act, which led to a shortage of low-wage workers on the Pacific coast in rail, forestry, and agricultural industries. However, declining economic conditions, combined with increasing numbers of immigrants, who were perceived as accepting lower wages and therefore taking American employment opportunities throughout the 1890s, led to rising anti-Japanese sentiments in western states. As a result, labor unions and anti-Asian groups such as the Asiatic Exclusion League, the Native Sons and Daughters of the Golden West, the American Legion, California State Federation of Labor, Japanese Exclusion League of California, California Joint Immigration Committee, Anti-Japanese League, Veterans of Foreign Wars, and Washington State's Veterans Welfare Commission advocated against Japanese immigrant rights. In response, state legislation was passed restricting immigration, the types of labor obtainable, landownership possibilities, and business opportunities available to Japanese persons. In addition, the Anti-Japanese Movement promoted exclusion of Japanese persons and the boycotting of Japanese businesses, and began disseminating the idea that those of Japanese dissent were unable to assimilate into American society, were untrustworthy and morally degenerate, and represented a "yellow peril," which threatened Caucasian authority.

International affairs at the outset of the 20th century, including the Japanese victory over Russia in the Russo-Japanese War (1904–1905), increased American concerns about the Empire of Japan's intentions throughout the Pacific, and propelled Theodore Roosevelt (1858–1919, president 1901–1909) to arrange the Gentlemen's Agreement (1907) restricting the immigration of laborers into the United States. Moreover, a combination of rising public sentiment and lobbying led the state of California to pass the landmark Webb-Haney, or Alien Land Law (1913, 1920), limiting foreign property ownership. This law in turn led to the adoption of similar measures by state legislatures in Washington, Oregon, and Arizona. Similarly, following World War I (1914–1918), anti-Japanese sentiments propelled national debates, suggesting that Japanese immigrants were taking jobs away from American veterans and that Japanese businesses were undermining American industries. As a result, national anti-immigrant policies, which had previously focused on Eastern Europeans, were expanded to include Japanese applicants. By 1924, the Immigration Act, proposed by congress member Albert Johnson (1869–1957) and considered the culmination of the Anti-Japanese Movement, was passed into law, resulting in the near complete exclusion of Japanese immigrants from the United States for four decades. Passage of the Immigration Act served as the legal legitimization of the Anti-Japanese Movement and had a lasting and profound impact upon the Japanese American experience throughout the rest of the 20th century. Indeed, bills such as the Alien Land Laws and Immigration Act served as the legislative basis for Franklin D. Roosevelt's (1882–1945, president 1933–1945) signing of Executive Order 9066, which authorized the relocation and internment of over 120,000 Japanese American citizens during World War II (1939–1945) and led to the loss of property, businesses, and possessions and the disruption of communities.

Despite Supreme Court decisions in 1948 and 1952 ruling that such legislation was unconstitutional and the passage of the Immigration and Nationality Act (1965), which ended immigration on the basis of national origin and race, the Anti-Japanese Movement nonetheless had a lasting influence. The discrimination fostered in western states throughout the late 19th century, which had in turn given way to the formation of anti-Japanese organizations, had also proliferated racism throughout American society. As a result, similar discrimination again emerged in the depiction of Asians during the Korean War (1950–1953), throughout the Vietnam War (1954–1975), and in the 1980s when Japan became an economic power rivaling American industry. The longevity of such discrimination reveals how both Asian Americans and Japanese Americans were framed within the American mind-set from the late 19th-century onward. It is also noteworthy that the Anti-Japanese Movement fostered the formation of stronger Japanese communities and led to the creation of Nisei Japanese American political advocacy organizations such as the Japanese American Citizens League (JACL).

See also: Alien Land Law (1913); Executive Order 9066; Gentlemen's Agreement (1907–1908); Immigration Act of 1924; Japan Bashing; Japanese American Exclusion; Native Sons of the Golden West

Further Reading

Azuma, E. *Between Two Empires: Race History, and Transnationalism in Japanese America.* New York: Oxford University Press, 2005.

Daniels, R. *The Politics of Prejudice: The Anti-Japanese Movement in California and the Struggle for Japanese Exclusion.* Berkeley: University of California Press, 1977.

Sean Morton

DRAFT RESISTERS

Some 300 Japanese Americans refused to be inducted into the U.S. Army from internment camps during World War II. The largest numbers of resisters came from Poston, Arizona, and Heart Mountain, Wyoming. A wide range of motivations led these Nisei men to refuse induction. Some resisted the draft because of their obligation to look after their families in the camps. Others found the conscription notice as the ultimate violation of constitutional rights after enduring numerous acts of injustice by the U.S. government. The draft resisters were convicted for sedition under the Selective Training and Service Act of 1940, and most of them served time in federal prison. After the war, President Harry S. Truman pardoned all of them.

The Nisei draft resisters were ostracized from the Japanese American community and eventually forgotten for decades after the war. Those who believed in Nisei's assimilation to the white mainstream society—represented by the views of the Japanese American Citizens League (JACL)—saw the draft resisters as troublemakers, pro-Japanese fanatics, or cowardly "draft dodgers." The JACL instead glorified the achievements and sacrifice of Nisei soldiers as the ultimate proof of their loyalty to the United States. Many Japanese Americans

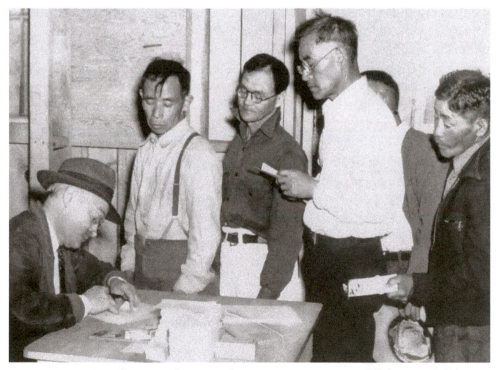

Japanese internees from Pacific Coastal regions at Manzanar, California, 1942, were included in the nationwide draft registration. Around 300 Japanese Americans refused for various reasons, including being betrayed by their own government. (AP Photo)

also confused the draft resisters with the so-called No-No Boys. The latter refer to draft-age men who answered "no" to two crucial questions in the questionnaire handed out by the War Relocation Authority testing Japanese Americans' loyalty to the United States. The questions asked whether they would be willing to serve in the U.S. Army and whether they would forswear any allegiance to the Japanese emperor. Not all of the draft resisters answered "no" to the initial question of induction. Although the questionnaire and the subsequent registration process triggered some tensions and resentments among Japanese Americans, it was not until the conscription notices were actually reinstated that resistance to these orders entailed serious consequences: charges of a federal crime.

The reception of draft resisters started to change in the 1970s, when some revisionist historians such as Roger Daniels and Douglas Nelson for the first time shed light on the responses of Japanese Americans in the internment, saying that they were not just about silence and resignation. Soon, some Asian Americans found inspiration in their stories of standing up against racial discrimination. In particular, Chinese American writer Frank Chin wrote extensively about the draft resisters, especially those representing the only organized draft resisters' group, the Heart Mountain Fair Play Committee. As the stories of draft resisters gradually came to attract wider attention, they also caused conflicts and controversies in the Japanese American community. Critics of the JACL's accommodationist stance during the war demanded that the JACL officially apologize to the draft resisters for stigmatizing those who did not conform to their version of Americanism. Some older Japanese Americans were critical of the way young people with little or no direct wartime experience hailed the draft resisters as heroes and dismissed the contribution of Nisei soldiers. After much heated debate, in 2000 the JACL finally adopted the resolution officially apologizing to the World War II draft resisters.

The wartime act of Nisei draft resisters continues to inspire people beyond the Japanese American community in the aftermath of the September 11, 2001, terrorist attacks. With the passage of the USA Patriot Act of 2001, the government gained wide-ranging powers to limit civil liberties in the name of a fight against terrorism, and discussion ensued about whether the act provided federal protection or violated civil rights. In this context, the Nisei resisters have attracted renewed attention as "resisters of conscience," who challenged the government's racist policies 60 years ago.

See also: Commission on Wartime Relocation and Internment of Civilians; No-No Boys; World War II

Further Reading

Chin, Frank. *Born in the USA: A Story of Japanese America, 1889–1947.* Lanham: Rowman & Littlefield, 2002.

Muller, Eric L. *Free to Die for Their Country: The Story of the Japanese American Draft Resisters in World War II.* Chicago: University of Chicago Press, 2001.

Nelson, Douglas W. *Heart Mountain: The History of an American Concentration Camp.* Madison: State Historical Society of Wisconsin for the Department of History, University of Wisconsin, 1976.

Aiko Takeuchi-Demirci

EX PARTE MITSUYE ENDO (1944)

In the case of *In re Mitsuye Endo* 323 U.S. 283 (1944), announced in December 1944, the U.S. Supreme Court ruled that the federal government could not confine concededly loyal citizens of Japanese ancestry. This case was fundamental in reshaping the wartime trajectory of Japanese Americans, as it led to the opening of the camps and the mass return of inmates to the West Coast before the end of the war.

The fact that the *Endo* case was brought at all, let alone appealed before the Supreme Court, was in some sense a matter of chance given its importance. Mitsuye Endo, a stenographer at the Department of Motor Vehicles in Sacramento, was one of a small group of Nisei state employees who were dismissed from their positions in early 1942. Following her removal to the Tanforan Assembly Center, Endo was contacted by ACLU lawyer James Purcell, who sought to challenge the arbitrary dismissal of the Nisei state employees. Although Endo either never met her lawyer or did so only on one occasion, she agreed to serve as a test case. Purcell's original intent was not to challenge confinement as such but for Endo to regain the civil service job from which she had been arbitrarily dismissed. Purcell determined, however, that the most rapid legal means to achieve this goal was by the circuitous route of challenging her confinement via a habeas corpus petition. Thus, Purcell charged the federal government with unlawful detention that deprived Mitsuye Endo of her right to return to her job.

In bringing his petition, Purcell was supported not only by the ACLU, but by the Japanese American Citizens League, which had earned the enmity of many Nisei by declining to oppose mass wartime removal. Unlike the other challenges to Executive Order 9066, Endo's case did not involve a challenge to the initial removal but rather a larger question of liberty from arbitrary confinement.

In July 1942, Endo's habeas corpus petition was argued before Judge Michael Roche. Although a habeas corpus petition is supposed to be an expedited proceeding, Judge Roche deliberately stalled his decision for over one year following the hearing, during which time Endo remained arbitrarily confined, first at Tanforan and then at the Tule Lake camp. (Some time later, Endo was once more removed to the Topaz camp in Utah. In theory, this removed her from the jurisdiction of the California court, but Judge Roche neither acted to freeze her location nor withdrew from the case.) Finally, in July 1943, after the Supreme Court decisions in the *Hirabayashi* and *Yasui* cases were issued, Roche issued an order summarily dismissing Endo's petition but did not offer any explanation or grounds for his action.

Purcell appealed Endo's case to the U.S. Court of Appeals for the Ninth Circuit. Government lawyers recognized that they had little chance of prevailing on appeal, especially because Mitsuye Endo had filled out a leave clearance questionnaire and had been adjudged "loyal." Government officials nevertheless feared the consequences of opening the camps. Thus, the War Relocation Authority (WRA)'s chief attorney, WRA Solicitor Philip Glick, traveled to see Endo and tried to persuade her not to continue, offering her an immediate "leave permit" to resettle outside the West Coast if she would abandon the case. Endo refused and remained in confinement as her appeal was perfected.

In March 1944, as the Ninth Circuit prepared to hear Endo's appeal, the Supreme Court agreed to hear the *Korematsu* case. James Purcell and the ACLU lawyers defending the *Korematsu* case hoped that the two would be argued together, as the arguments presented in defense of Mitsuye Endo might influence the justices to rule in favor of Fred Korematsu as well. In turn, the fact that both cases were forthcoming might push the government to take rapid action to lift West Coast exclusion to avoid being put in the position of acting illegally. Ninth Circuit appellate judge William Denman, who hoped for a rapid resolution to the *Endo* case, certified questions for the Supreme Court in April 1944, so that it could be brought before the court before its summer recess. Although the court did decide in the end to hear the cases together, it reached an opposite conclusion as to time—instead of hastening action in *Endo*, already prolonged immoderately for a habeas corpus case, the justices decided to put off arguments on both cases until its fall 1944 term. The court justified the delay by reference to the needs of the lawyers involved in the cases. However, it was surely not coincidental that it saved the court from being forced to rule on the cases during the fall 1944 electoral season.

In October 1944, the *Endo* and *Korematsu* cases were both argued before the U.S. Supreme Court. On December 18, 1944—also the same day as it announced its ruling in the *Korematsu* case—the Supreme Court unanimously ordered the executive branch to release Mitsuye Endo from confinement. In contrast to the sharp exchanges between the justices in *Korematsu*, Justice William O. Douglas's opinion in *Endo* was brief and almost offhanded. In the interests of maintaining unity among the fractious justices, Douglas evaded all constitutional questions regarding the arbitrary race-based imprisonment of American citizens and the essential question of the government's power to issue military orders against citizens. Instead, he merely found that nothing either in Executive Order 9066 or in the congressional legislation enforcing it granted the WRA or any agency the power to detain a concededly loyal citizen such as Endo. So cautious were Justice Douglas and the court that the opinion did not even explicitly state whether Endo might return to her home and job on the West Coast.

In essence, then, Douglas took the demonstrably absurd position that the WRA had acted as a rogue agency in pursuing mass confinement without approval. Justice Owen Roberts rejected Douglas's logic in a concurrence, stating that the president had confirmed the action in his messages to Congress, and Congress had approved incarceration by funding the agency. Justice Frank Murphy added his own concurrence, explicitly connecting the confinement in *Endo* with the mass removal that the court had just upheld in *Korematsu*.

The *Endo* decision capped a long struggle within government circles over whether to permit Japanese Americans to return to the West Coast. The court's unanimous ruling provided political cover not only for the executive branch to open the camps, but for the War Department to lift exclusion. Beginning in early 1944, the War Department had quietly allowed various categories of Japanese Americans, such as the wives and children of Nisei soldiers, to return to the West Coast, but it had retained its overall policy and enjoined silence on the returnees. The *Endo* case provided constitutional sanction for the former inmates to return home, and the War Department lifted exclusion as of January 2, 1945. Within 12 to 18 months after the *Endo* decision, the majority of the mainland Japanese population had resettled in the former excluded zone.

Paradoxically, despite its vital impact on the lives of confined Japanese Americans, the *Endo* case was little cited in subsequent rulings by the court and remains comparatively little known. In contrast, the *Korematsu* decision, which had little or no actual influence in the shaping of government policy toward Japanese Americans, has achieved classic status in the history of American constitutional law. In a further irony, even after her long-sought victory, Mitsuye Endo (later Mitsuye Tsutsumi) did not return to the West Coast and the job she had left. Instead, she settled permanently in Chicago, where she took a job as an assistant to the city's Human Rights Commission. She died in May 2006.

In the decades after her case was decided, Endo shied away from public scrutiny and did not actively participate in the protests and commemorations of the Japanese American redress movement (although she did produce a short oral history for John Tateishi's 1984 anthology *And Justice for All*). Because of the fact that Endo won her initial case—and perhaps also in view of her retiring nature—she was not associated with the *coram nobis* petitions through which her fellow wartime Supreme Court plaintiffs challenged their convictions during the 1980s, and in the process she achieved renewed celebrity. (She likewise fit awkwardly, both on gender and ideological grounds, into popular celebration of the "resisters" who had stood up against official oppression.) Her obscurity is unfortunate, as Endo's actions, in their quiet way, were at least as heroic as those of the others. First, she was prepared to challenge her arbitrary dismissal from a California civil service job—itself an unusual achievement for a Nisei woman in the prewar days when discrimination was the rule. In addition to her desire to hang on to such a prized position for herself, she was surely inspired to defend her rights on behalf of the larger group. Furthermore, her refusal to accept a "leave permit" and moot her case, and her willingness to remain in confinement for some 18 months to ensure that her case was heard, demonstrated Endo's courageous dedication to principle.

See also: Executive Order 9066; *Hirabayashi v. United States* (1943); Internment, World War II; Korematsu, Fred (1919–2005)

Further Reading

Gudridge, Patrick. "Remember Endo?" *Harvard Law Review* 116 (2003): 1933–1970.

Greg Robinson

EXECUTIVE ORDER 9066

Signed by President Franklin Delano Roosevelt on February 19, 1942, Executive Order 9066 was written under the supervision of Assistant Secretary of War John J. McCloy, with the assistance of Allen W. Gullion, provost marshal general of the U.S. Army; Maj. Karl R. Bendetsen, chief of the Aliens Division in the provost marshal general's office; and Lt. Gen. John L. DeWitt, commanding general of the Fourth Army and the Western Defense Command.

The order "authorize[d] and direct[ed] the Secretary of War, and the Military Commanders whom he may . . . designate . . . to prescribe military areas . . . from which any or all persons may be excluded, and with respect to which, the right of any person to enter, remain in, or leave shall be subject to whatever restrictions the Secretary of War or the appropriate Military Commander may impose [at] his discretion." The War Department's draft order effected a federal military police power—in the absence of martial law—over aliens and citizens alike.

Executive Order 9066 "supersede[d] designations of prohibited and restricted areas by the Attorney General under [three previous Presidential] Proclamations of December 7 and 8, 1941, [as well as] . . . supersede[d] the responsibility and authority of the Attorney General under the . . . Proclamations [with] respect [to] such prohibited and restricted areas." The earlier Proclamations had authorized the attorney general of the United States "with the duty of executing all . . . regulations . . . regarding the conduct of [Japanese, German and Italian] alien enemies within the continental limits of the United States, Puerto Rico, the Virgin Islands and Alaska."

By "direct[ing] all Executive Departments, independent establishments and other Federal Agencies, to assist the Secretary of War or the said Military Commanders in carrying out this Executive Order, including the furnishing of medical aid, hospitalization, food, clothing, transportation, use of land, shelter, and other supplies, equipment, utilities, facilities, and services," the order set in motion a series of subsequent military and executive department actions to create and administer 16 assembly centers from Puyallup, Washington, in the north, to Pomona, California, in the south, and 10 internment camps located in Arkansas, Arizona, California, Colorado, Utah, and Wyoming. Following the removal from assembly centers to relocation camps, the military agency initiated by the War Department on March 11, 1942, to effect removal from the West Coast—the Wartime Civil Control Administration (WCCA)—relinquished control to the War Relocation Authority (WRA), created under Executive Order 9102 on March 18, 1942. The WRA was terminated on June 26, 1946.

Although the order made no ethnic differentiation in its applicability, the genesis of Executive Order 9066 was wartime hysteria following the Japanese Empire's attack on the American naval base at Pearl Harbor, the subsequent rapid and startling Japanese military successes in the Pacific Ocean theater of war, countless false reports of Japanese citizen and alien sabotage and espionage, and an acute rekindling of decades of racial animosity directed toward Japanese American citizens and resident aliens on the West Coast.

When the first inquiry report on the circumstances surrounding the December 7, 1941, attack on Pearl Harbor was made public on January 24, 1942—erroneously implicating Japanese consular officials and local Japanese in the Hawai'i attack—the fevered cry for the removal of all Japanese from the states of California, Oregon, Washington, and Arizona was a chorus joined by elected officials, journalists, and citizens. Demands for removal reached the Department of Justice and the War Department. For Atty. Gen. Francis Biddle, removal of Japanese American citizens was not constitutional under any circumstances, and any mass evacuation of aliens was not possible under the resources of the Department of Justice. When Biddle learned that Roosevelt supported the War Department plan to remove all Japanese from the West Coast, he accepted the proposed executive order presented by the War Department.

Executive Order 9066 subsequently authorized the removal of 111,155 Japanese citizens and resident aliens from the three Pacific coast states and Arizona. On March 21, 1942, Public Law 503 gave congressional approval to the order by making a crime punishable by a $5,000 fine and one-year imprisonment for any violation against an order issued by a designated military commander. The order was rescinded by presidential proclamation on February 19, 1976, by Gerald R. Ford. In 1983, the Commission on Wartime Relocation and Internment of Civilians concluded that Executive Order 9066 and the subsequent removal of Japanese American citizens and resident aliens was in part "a failure of political leadership."

See also: Commission on Wartime Relocation and Internment of Civilians; *Ex Parte Mitsuye Endo* (1944); 442nd Regimental Combat Team/100th Infantry Battalion; Internment, World War II; Pearl Harbor; World War II

Further Reading

Conn, Stetson. *The Decision to Evacuate the Japanese from the Pacific Coast.* Washington, DC: Center of Military History, U.S. Army, 1990.

The Evacuated People: A Quantitative Description. Washington, DC: U.S. Government Printing Office, 1946.

Personal Justice Denied: Report of the Commission on Wartime Relocation and Internment of Civilians. San Francisco, CA: Japanese American Citizens League, 1983.

David Alan Rego

442ND REGIMENTAL COMBAT TEAM/100TH INFANTRY BATTALION

The 442nd Regimental Combat Team's performance in the field challenged military and political leaders' ban on the enlistment of Japanese American soldiers and provided entry for their large-scale military service. The 442nd consisted for two distinct units: the 442nd Regimental Combat Team (RCT) and the 100th Infantry Battalion (IB). The 100th IB formed before World War II and consisted almost entirely of Japanese Americans from Hawai'i. The 100th IB was the first U.S. Army unit of Japanese Americans activated in World War II and the first to see combat. Upon deployment, the 100th IB was granted permission to use its chosen slogan, "Go for broke," which reflected the battalion's reputation as a no-holds-barred, fearless fighting unit.

The 442nd RCT was activated in 1943 at Camp Shelby, Mississippi, where the 100th IB also completed basic training. The 442nd RCT was composed of Japanese American volunteers from the internment camps, Hawai'i, and states outside of the West Coast exclusion zone as well as Japanese American soldiers who were already serving in the U.S. Army. During training, the 442nd RCT—like the 100th IB—encountered racial prejudice from white soldiers. A factsheet from the U.S. Army noted that "there have been occasional clashes with White American soldiers, but brought on by some unthinking individual who referred to them as 'Japs,' or 'yellow-bellied so and sos.' Such difficulties, however, never last . . . Of these are many American divisions that have the highest regard for the men of this unit both as individuals and as a group." Negotiating the Jim Crow American South was a racial balancing act for the 100th IB and 442nd RCT. Officers instructed the Japanese Americans to act "white," that is,

The 442nd Regional Combat Team was composed of Japanese American volunteers from the internment camps, Hawai'i and states outside of the west coast exclusion zone as well as Japanese American soldiers who were already serving in the U.S. Army. (Library of Congress)

drink from white water fountains, use white bathrooms and sit in the front of the bus. Despite occupying more privileged position than blacks, Japanese Americans continued to face anti-Japanese sentiment.

In combat, the 442nd RCT, fortified by the 100th IB, rescued the "Lost Battalion" of Texas soldiers pinned down by German troops near the French/German border. Two previously dispatched units failed. After five days of brutal battle, the 442nd saved the Texas battalion while suffering heavy casualties. Wallace Tasaka, a Nisei from Kaua'i, recalled that only one out of every three men survived the mission. Along with rescuing the battalion, the 442nd liberated the towns of Bruyères, Belmont, and Biffontaine. In March 1945, Gen. Clark requested the 442nd lead the effort to break the Gothic Line, a heavily fortified German defense that repelled Allied forces for six months. By April 23, 1945, the 442nd broke through, allowing other Allied troops to pursue the German army until its surrender on May 2, 1945.

The 442nd RCT was the most decorated unit for its size and length of service in the history of American warfare. The 4,000 men who initially came in April

1943 had to be replaced nearly 2.5 times. In total, about 14,000 men served, earning 9,486 Purple Hearts, 8 Presidential Unit Citations, and 21 Medals of Honor.

See also: World War II

Further Reading

Duus, Masayo. *Unlikely Liberators: The Men of the 100th and the 442nd.* Honolulu: University of Hawai'i Press, 1987.

Masuda, Minoru. *Letters from the 442nd: The World War II Correspondence of a Japanese American Medic.* Seattle: University of Washington Press, 2015.

Tanaka, Chester. *Go for Broke: A Pictorial History of the Japanese American 100th Infantry Battalion and the 442nd Regimental Combat Team.* Novato, CA: Presidio Press, 1997.

Lauren S. Morimoto

GENTLEMEN'S AGREEMENT (1907–1908)

Under the leadership of President Theodore Roosevelt, the United States and Japan established what has been commonly referred to as the Gentlemen's Agreement in 1907 and 1908, severely restricting Japanese immigration. This agreement was not represented by a formal treaty, or even a single written document signed by two parties. Rather, it was composed of a series of letters and telegram cables between Washington and Tokyo, the contents of which were not fully disclosed to the public. It did, however, respond to public appeals for the curbing of Japanese migration to the United States.

The agreement emerged at a time of strong anti-Japanese sentiment in the United States, particularly in California, similar to that against the Chinese in previous decades. Racist attitudes toward the Chinese combined with fears that inexpensive Chinese labor was undermining the potential for gains by native-born workers resulted in the passage of the Chinese Exclusion Law by Congress in 1882. Although not preventing Chinese immigration entirely, it succeeded in severely restricting it. However, Japanese immigration increased notably and new arrivals took the place of Chinese in California. Discrimination grew, and tensions flared after the San Francisco school board's decision to segregate elementary-level students of Japanese descent to the Oriental Public School for Chinese, Japanese, and Koreans. The board rationalized its action by pointing to recent damage to school buildings and the destruction of municipal records caused by the 1906 earthquake, as well as the 1896 U.S. Supreme Court ruling in *Plessy v. Ferguson*, which defended and expanded "separate but equal" policies regarding education. Still, the move was clearly grounded in racism, representing a growing animosity toward the Japanese population and contributing to further deterioration of U.S.–Japanese relations. Though comparatively low in numbers, certainly in contrast to European immigrants in eastern cities during the same period, the Japanese in California were seen as a threat. Furthermore, they did not tend to self-segregate and remain primarily in distinct neighborhoods of San Francisco as the Chinese had. Instead, Japanese immigrants dispersed throughout San Francisco and into other regions of California and, through engagement in farming and other enterprises, made it clear that they intended to take up permanent residency in the United States.

Californians' demands for Japanese immigration restriction intensified by 1905 and were articulated strongly by labor union leaders, the Asiatic Exclusion League, and opinion writers for the *San Francisco Chronicle* describing the "yellow peril." However, Roosevelt found himself in a diplomatic position that differed from that with the Chinese. Though race theories of prominent academics and policy makers of the day placed both Chinese and Japanese populations into Asian categories of inferiority, and thereby potentially detrimental to the future of the United States, Japan was posing a significant political force in the Pacific region. U.S. actions against the Japanese could meet with far greater resistance than those against the Chinese. Newcomers to the imperialist global stage at the turn of the 20th century, the United States and Japan were treading carefully in their actions toward one another and this situation would affect the manner in which Roosevelt approached Japanese immigration. His successful negotiation of peace at the end in 1905 of the Russo-Japanese War—in which Japan proved itself a competitive military power and rising global force as with victory in the Sino-Japanese War in 1895—earned him the Nobel Prize for peace, but the segregation of San Francisco's schools tarnished the nation's image in the eyes of Japanese leaders, and he viewed continued attacks on California's Japanese as further damaging relations. Roosevelt and Secretary of State Elihu Root invited San Francisco's mayor and school board members to Washington, where they were convinced to rescind the segregation mandate with the assurance that Japanese immigration would be addressed at the federal level.

Much of the controversy regarding Japanese immigration surrounded the issuance of passports. Where Chinese immigrants had been barred unilaterally in 1882, Washington officials decided to grant Japan a greater degree of privilege and negotiate with the Japanese government through more diplomatic measures. In 1894, Japanese officials recognized that immigration caused concern in the United States and agreed to stop issuing passports to Japanese laborers in search of work in the United States, at the U.S. government's request. However, many laborers who secured passports to Mexico, Canada, or Hawai'i were subsequently able to enter the United States via border crossings after 1894. In February 1907, the United States began restricting entrance to Japanese who sought passports to other countries with the United States as their intended ultimate destination. In turn, the Japanese government safeguarded the right to issue passports to nonlaborers, returning laborers, and family members who had already resided in the United States. It prohibited new laborers from entering the continental United States but did allow them in Hawai'i, now a territory of the United States and under development. Due to the protection of Japanese wives and daughters, population grew in the United States, particularly in California, as they bore children, even though the number of immigrants decreased.

Similar to the ways in which Japanese population grew after Chinese immigration was restricted, Filipino immigrants served as replacements when Japanese immigration was curbed. This movement was facilitated as West Coast developed with Filipino labor and by the Philippines having become a U.S. territory in 1898. Regulations outlined in the Gentlemen's Agreement remained in effect until new immigration laws were enacted in 1924 and Japanese immigration was prohibited. It resumed once again following passage of the Immigration and Nationality Act of 1952.

See also: Anti-Japanese Movement; Immigration Act of 1924

Further Reading

Patterson, David S.. "Japanese-American Relations: The 1906 California Crisis, the Gentlemen's Agreement, and the World Cruise." In *A Companion Guide to Theodore Roosevelt*, edited by Serge Ricard, 391–416. Oxford: Wiley-Blackwell, 2011.

Kathleen A. Tobin

HARADA HOUSE

The Harada House is a National Historic Landmark located in downtown Riverside, California, and reflects the struggle of early Asian immigrants. The California Alien Land Law of 1913 prohibited immigrants ineligible for citizenship from buying land or property. This law was a sign of the strong anti-Asian sentiment present in California at the time. Jukichi and Ken Harada were pioneers as they worked to make Riverside their home. Jukichi first emigrated from Japan to the United States in 1898. He had worked on a U.S. navy ship as a food service worker, which spurred his migration to the United States and his later work in restaurants. His wife Ken and young son Masa Atsu would arrive a few years later, and he would go on to manage and operate the Washington Restaurant in downtown Riverside, which prided itself for serving American food.

Years later, his next three children were born. He was determined to provide housing that was safe and sanitary following the death of his first American-born son. Knowing that as an immigrant he was unable to purchase a home, Jukichi was able to purchase a home at 3356 Lemon Street under the names of his American-born children Mine, Sumi, and Yoshizo. Located in a middle-class neighborhood at the time, the neighbors vehemently opposed their presence. Even in her old age, Sumi would recall the hatred, harassment, and prejudice that their family continually faced. Neighbors had wanted them to leave their neighborhood and even tried to buy them out. Jukichi refused stating that the house was owned by his American-born children. Over

60 neighbors signed a petition calling for the family's eviction. Eventually charges through the attorney general of California were filed alleging violation of the California Alien Land Law.

On December 14, 1916, the trial of *The People of the State of California v. Jukichi Harada, et al.* began and the case gained national notoriety because it was the first case to test the constitutionality of the Alien Land Law. The suit claimed that an immigrant, Jukichi Harada, was ineligible for citizenship and therefore was not allowed to possess, acquire, transfer, or enjoy any real property in the state of California. On September 17, 1918, Judge Hugh Craig of the Riverside County Superior Court ruled in favor of the Harada family. Because the three children were American citizens, he ruled that Mine, Sumi, and Yoshizo, who were born in the United States, were entitled to equal protection as any other U.S. citizen no matter their parentage. Appeals to the decision were not pursued and that allowed other immigrants that followed to acquire property under their children's names. The Alien Land Law was modified over time to close various loopholes, and it was not officially overturned until after World War II.

Through the 1910s to the 1930s, the Harada family expanded with the births of Harold and Clark and the adoption of Roy Hashimura. In these two decades, they continued to raise their family and operate their family restaurant and boarding house business. By the 1940s, many of the children had grown up and moved out of the home with the exception of Sumi and Harold.

The Harada family experienced their next great challenge with the bombing of Pearl Harbor in 1941. On February 19, 1942, the family's life was again interrupted. President Franklin D. Roosevelt signed an executive order ordering all people of Japanese descent residing in the designated area of the West Coast to be placed in internment camps. By May 23, 1942, the Harada family was evacuated to Poston, Arizona, and later to Topaz, Utah. During the years the family was interned, the Harada family would face the death of father Jukichi and mother Ken.

During the internment, Harold had gone on to serve in the 442nd Regimental Combat Team and after the internment went on to complete his dental education. After the internment, Sumi Harada spent time in Chicago and was eventually able to return to her Riverside home after the war in 1945, thanks to the Harada's family friend Jess Stebler, who cared for their home during their internment. This was not often the case for many other Japanese Americans, who were not able to return home. With the passing of her parents and with the restaurant being closed, Sumi opened the Harada home to others by turning the house into a boarding home for many other Japanese Americans who were returning from internment. When there was no longer a need for a boarding home for Japanese Americans, Sumi found work as a housekeeper and worked for many years.

In honor of her parents' fight against the 1913 California Alien Land Law, she had saved everything including old photographs, letters, documents such as passports and birth certificates, letters, photographs, and newspapers pertaining to their immigration, their legal fight, their incarceration, their restaurant business, and other key moments in the Harada family. She was a keeper of all her family's memories. She kept all of it, which would later be shown after her passing in a curated exhibition at the Riverside Metropolitan Museum in 2009.

Sumi lived to see her parents' efforts recognized nationally and locally. In 1977, the City of Riverside recognized the home as a city landmark. In 1990, President George Bush designated the home as a National Historic Landmark. She also received several awards within the Southern California Japanese American community for her family's fight against the 1913 Alien Land Law.

Until a few years before she passed, Sumi Harada was active in speaking about her experiences to local college and high school students. She was poignant and direct about the racism that her family suffered during her family's fight to keep their home on Lemon Street and their later subsequent evacuation and incarceration during World War II. She was a long-standing member of the local Riverside Japanese American Citizens League and First Congregational Church in Riverside. She was also continually recognized in the Asian American community as an advocate and fighter for civil rights for all. At the University of California, Riverside, an annual award, the Sumi Harada Award, which reflects the work of the Harada family in their fight against the 1913 Alien Land Law, is given out to this day to a student, staff, or faculty member who has been an advocate of Asian American issues.

Sumi Harada passed away in 2000 at the age of 90. The house was passed on to her brother, Harold Harada, who died in 2003. The family donated their home, artifacts, and archives to the City of Riverside under the stewardship of the Riverside Metropolitan Museum in 2004. The Riverside Metropolitan Museum curated an exhibit "Reading the Walls: The Struggles of the Haradas, A Japanese American Family" in 2009–2010, which focused on 100 years of history of the Harada family. The museum, in partnership with the Riverside Unified School District, developed a history curriculum for 11th graders focused on Riverside's stories of internment and return. Currently, the house is being restored by the city with future plans for a civil rights museum and education center. The museum is also cataloging the extensive Harada collections, enhancing the Web site information, and developing plans for the long-term preservation and interpretation of the National Historic Landmark Harada House.

See also: Japanese American Communities

Further Reading

Rawitsch, Mark, with afterword by Lane Ryo Hirabayashi. *The House on Lemon Street: Japanese Pioneers and the American Dream.* Boulder: University Press of Colorado, 2012.

Rawitsch, Mark Howland. *No Other Place: Japanese American Pioneers in a Southern California Neighborhood.* Riverside: Department of History, University of California, 1983.

Grace J. Yoo

HAWAI'IAN SUGAR PLANTATIONS

From 1835 to 1946, the sugar plantations came to dominate the Hawai'ian economy, dramatically altering the ethnic, social, and economic fabric of the islands. In 1835, Ladd & Company dispatched William Hooper to Koloa, Kaua'i, to establish the first sugar plantation and cultivate sugar cane as a cash crop. Throughout the next decades, increased demand for sugar on the

Sugar workers at the Hawaiian Agriculture Company walk a picket line for better wages and working conditions in one of the many strikes leading to "The Great Sugar Strike of 1946." (AP Photo)

mainland, reliable transportation for the product, and laws displacing native Hawai'ians, fueled the rise of the plantation economy. Displaced from their lands, Hawai'ians worked on the new plantations and lived in plantation housing, purchased commodities from the plantation store, and visited a plantation doctor. Hooper established a form of paternalistic capitalism, similar to company towns like Pullman, which informed the labor–plantation relationship until the demise of the Hawai'ian sugar economy.

During the next century, the sugar plantations transformed the ethnic makeup and economy of Hawai'i. Hawai'ian natives comprised almost 100 percent of the population when Hooper first set foot on Kaua'i. By 1920, Hawai'ians made up only 16.3 percent of the population, while whites and Japanese represented 19.2 percent and 42.7 percent, respectively. The 8,000-pound shipment of sugar and molasses, in 1836, from the Koloa plantation morphed into a 556,871-pound industry that dominated the Hawai'ian economy by 1920.

Early on, "The Big Five" controlled the plantations. The Big Five, consisting of American companies, expanded its reach to banking, shipping, and importing. King Kamehameha III, Hawai'i's longest reigning monarch whose power was usurped by the plantation owners, made concessions regarding land and religion. The Big Five supported the successful 1893 overthrow of the Hawai'ian kingdom, hoping for its annexation by the United States.

As sugar production increased, plantations began importing labor to augment and, eventually, replace most of the Hawai'ian workers, whom Hooper found impossible to transform into an obedient, effective workforce. By the late 1830s, he began importing Chinese labor. In 1850, other plantations followed suit. As a strategy to prevent workers from organizing, the plantations created an ethnically diverse workforce. Starting in 1868, Japanese migrated to Hawai'i, followed by the Portuguese, Koreans, and Filipinos. The plantations perpetuated ethnic divisions among workers by creating a caste system that played out in work assignment, physical structure, and salary. For instance, the plantations created housing camps segregated by ethnicity, with the optimal housing structures and locations occupied by those higher on the ethnic hierarchy such as the Portuguese lunas (overseers). Additionally, the plantations paid ethnic groups different wages for the same work.

The plantation economy and culture began dismantling after the Great Sugar Strike of 1946, which followed smaller, successful strikes from 1920. The 1946 strike succeeded through interethnic organizing and won major salary and work condition concessions from the plantations. The success of the strike weakened the paternalistic, capitalistic model. The demise of the old plantation culture, in tandem with sugar imports from Cuba, the Philippines, and Puerto Rico, made it difficult for Hawai'ian sugar to compete on the market.

The declining demand, along with the expanding tourist industry, eventually led to the closure of the Hawai'ian plantations.

See also: Japanese Americans in Farming and Agriculture

Further Reading

Beechert, Edward D. *Working in Hawaii: A Labor History.* Honolulu: University of Hawai'i Press, 1985.

Takaki, Ronald. *Pau Hana: Plantation Life and Labor in Hawaii, 1835–1920.* Honolulu: University of Hawai'i Press, 1983.

Lauren S. Morimoto

HIRABAYASHI V. UNITED STATES (1943)

The initial trial *Gordon Kiyoshi Hirabayashi v. the United States of America* was held in the U.S. District Court in Seattle, Washington, May 1942. The charges were: violation of Public Law No. 503, Curfew Act, and violation of Civilian Exclusion Order No. 57. Gordon Hirabayashi was found guilty of each offense charged in the two-count indictment.

The District Court decision was appealed in February 1943 and transferred to the Circuit Court of Appeals, which passed the case on to the U.S. Supreme Court on March 27, 1943. *Gordon Kiyoshi. Hirabayashi v. United States, United States Supreme Court:* Curfew 320 U.S. 81, 638 S.Ct. 1375; Exclusion 105, 63 Supreme Court, 1387. On June 21, 1943, the court upheld the validity of Hirabayashi's conviction on the curfew order alone.

In *Gordon Kiyoshi Hirabayashi v. United States of America, writ of coram nobis* (regarding U.S. District Court ruling in Seattle, May 18, 1944) the court denied the government motion to dismiss and set a hearing on the *writ of coram nobis* for June 1985.

In *Gordon Kiyoshi Hirabayashi v. United States of America,* U.S. Court of Appeals for the Ninth Circuit, March 2, 1987, the judgment of the district court as to the exclusion conviction was reexamined. The judgment as to the curfew conviction was reversed, and the matter was remanded with instructions to grant Hirabayashi's petition to vacate both convictions.

Gordon Kiyoshi Hirabayashi

Gordon Hirabayashi, a Nisei, second-generation Japanese American, was born in Seattle in 1918 and raised in the small rural community of Thomas just south of Seattle. It was a closely knit Japanese American community with supportive Euro-American neighbors. Hirabayashi's youth revolved around relationships not only in the Japanese American community but also with the American society. Hirabayashi's interests included Japanese American and Euro-American networks and elementary school, religious, Boy Scout, and sports activities. As such, Hirabayashi's childhood entailed the merging of both Japanese American and American experiences. At the University of Washington, Hirabayashi continued his religious affiliations. He became a student leader in the University YMCA and joined the University Quaker meeting. He also joined the Japanese American Students Club.

World War II

On February 19, 1942, President Franklin D. Roosevelt, acting under his emergency war powers, issued Executive Order 9066. The order enabled the secretary of war and the military commanders under him to carry out any necessary steps to protect national security, including removal of any suspicious individuals from military areas. A proclamation issued March 24, 1942, that was essentially a curfew order, restricted the movement of certain individuals including persons of Japanese ancestry, whether citizens or not. Gen. John L. DeWitt's order confined all enemy aliens: Germans, Italians, and Japanese—including U.S. citizens of Japanese ancestry—to their homes between 8:00 p.m. and 6:00 a.m. The same curfew order also restricted travel to a radius of five miles from a given individual's home.

The government soon posted an official proclamation on telephone poles and Post Office bulletin boards: NOTICE: TO ALL PERSONS OF JAPANESE ANCESTRY, BOTH ALIEN AND NONALIEN, ordering all Japanese and Japanese Americans into camps run by the military and then civilian authorities.

American Citizenship

Because of his American citizenship and Christian religious principles, Gordon Hirabayashi believed that both curfew and mass detention were unnecessary, discriminatory, and unjust. He decided to resist both orders, on principle, and retained a lawyer. Hirabayashi's decision caught the attention of progressive Seattle community leaders, and quickly his stand garnered the status of a test case with support on the part of religious and political sympathizers.

Hirabayashi and his Quaker lawyer, Art Barnet, presented themselves at the Seattle FBI office on May 13, 1942, with Hirabayashi's written statement, "Why I Refuse to Register for Evacuation." In the statement, Hirabayashi wrote:

> Over and above any man-made creed or law is the natural law of life—the right of human individuals to live and to creatively express themselves. No man was born with the right to limit that law . . . This order for the mass evacuation of all persons of Japanese descent denies them the right

to live . . . Over sixty percent are American citizens, yet they are denied on a wholesale scale without due process of law the civil liberties which are theirs . . . If I were to register and cooperate under those circumstances, I would be giving helpless consent to the denial of practically all of the things which give me incentive to live. I must maintain my Christian principles. I consider it my duty to maintain the democratic standards for which this nation lives. Therefore I must refuse this order for evacuation.

With the support of the Gordon Hirabayashi Defense Committee, made up of progressive supporters in the University District, the initial trial proceeded. Lawyer Frank Walters argued the Fifth Amendment right of due process was violated by the exclusion order, emphasizing that Hirabayashi had never been accused of posing a danger in terms of espionage or sabotage, the two ostensible reasons for the exclusion proclamation. He moved that the court dismiss the indictment on the grounds that the defendant had been deprived of liberty and property without due process of law. Furthermore, Hirabayashi and his lawyer charged that Executive Order 9066, Proclamations 2 and 3, and Civilian Exclusion Order No. 57 of the military commander, as well as Public Law No. 503, were all unconstitutional and void. The judge pronounced Hirabayashi guilty of each offense charged in the two counts of the indictment. His trial lasted just one day.

Hirabayashi and his lawyers pursued judicial review at the U.S. Supreme Court. In May 1943, his case was given a hearing, and in the following month his convictions were upheld. In an interesting twist of fate, the justices decided to hear only the curfew aspect of Hirabayashi's case, and ultimately upheld the right of the president and Congress to take any necessary measures needed, in times of crisis, to defend national security. Although the case generated judicial debate, all of the Supreme Court justices ended up concurring with the majority ruling in regard to the legality of the imposed curfew.

Implications of the *Hirabayashi* Case

There are at least three reasons to revisit *Hirabayashi v. the United States* today. First, it illustrates a situation where the standard principle of checks and balances broke down. Instead, that is, of fully tackling the issue of mass removal and mass incarceration of an entire ethnic/racial group, the Supreme Court justices dodged a key constitutional issue by focusing only on the wartime need for curfew regulations.

Second, given the partial success of Hirabayashi's *coram nobis* case in 1986, it has now been demonstrated that the War Department manipulated evidence and essentially lied to the Supreme Court in making its case. Using the government's own documentary record, that is, Hirabayashi's legal team was able to demonstrate that military leaders and federal officials knew full well that Japanese Americans did not constitute a wholesale threat to national security, and that there were means in place to identify and contain those persons inside of the community who may indeed have constituted a potential threat. This point would have reinforced Hirabayashi's claim that the Fifth Amendment was being violated by the federal government's actions.

Third, as legal historian and scholar Eric Muller has pointed out, in a post-9/11 world, the domestic use of a wholesale curfew against an identifiable segment of the U.S. population—such as Middle Eastern, or Muslim, Americans—is a much more likely scenario should any site on the lower 48 states be subject to a large, violent attack. In this sense, the Supreme Court's *Hirabayashi* ruling could take on a new relevance, especially because the mass incarceration of a domestic population would be relatively unlikely, not only because of the expense but also because the public at large would probably not support such a measure.

See also: Commission on Wartime Relocation and Internment of Civilians; *Ex Parte Mitsuye Endo* (1944); Internment, World War II; Korematsu, Fred (1919–2005); World War II

Further Reading

Irons, Peter. *Justice at War: The Story of the Japanese American Internment Cases.* New York: Oxford University Press, 1983.

Muller, Eric. "Hirabayashi and the Invasion Evasion." *North Carolina Law Review* 88 (2010): 1333–1389.

Lane Ryo Hirabayashi and James A. Hirabayashi

IMMIGRATION ACT OF 1924

The culmination of two decades of effort to restrict immigration from "undesirable" nations of the world, the Immigration Act of 1924 was coauthored by Rep. Albert Johnson (R-Wash.) and Sen. David Reed (R-Pa.). It was signed into law on May 19, 1921, by President Calvin Coolidge, a Republican and former governor of Massachusetts. The act created an immigrant admissions policy whereby future immigration to the United States was determined by a quota system based on the historical origins of the foreign-born population as counted in the 1890 federal census. The quotas ended open and unlimited immigration into the United States from the Western Hemisphere. Favoring immigration from England, Ireland, and Germany, the act substantially limited immigration from Southern and Eastern Europe.

Importantly, the act also required that any quota immigrant entering the United States must be eligible for citizenship by naturalization. Because citizenship was open only to "white persons or persons of African nativity or African descent," the law barred the Japanese from even the minimum yearly allowance of 100 quota immigrants per year. Where United States/Japanese relations involving immigration had been addressed previously through channels of diplomacy, the Immigration Act of 1924 voided an 1894 treaty between the two nations that had guaranteed the Japanese the right to immigrate, and abrogated the 1907–1908 Gentlemen's Agreement through which the Empire of Japan agreed to restrict the immigration of laborers to the United States. What had been the purview of United States foreign policy for three-quarters of a century was transformed into a domestic policy issue. That transformation damaged relations between the two nations, leading to World War II.

See also: Japanese American History before 1945; Native Sons of the Golden West

Further Reading

Hunt, Rockwell D. "Fifteen Decisive Events of California History: Part IV." *The Historical Society of Southern California Quarterly* 40, no. 4 (December 1958): 363–367.

David Alan Rego

INTERNMENT, WORLD WAR II

Japanese internment refers to the forced relocation of approximately 120,000 individuals of Japanese ancestry during World War II. Anti-Japanese sentiment, nativism, and xenophobia—already persistent features of local communities especially on the West Coast—galvanized around the attack on Pearl Harbor and America's declaration of war against Japan. As the West Coast was declared a military zone, Japanese American communities in the region were uprooted and concentrated in 10 "relocation camps," all located inland and in barely habitable environments. Estimates suggest that two-thirds of those incarcerated were legal citizens of the United States, and internment would be the most fundamental feature of the Japanese American experience of World War II.

Racism

Prior to World War II, approximately 260,000 people of Japanese ancestry resided in the United States. The foreign-born, first-generation Japanese Americans who had immigrated from Japan, primarily for opportunities in West Coast agriculture, were called Issei. By the interwar period, a growing group of second-generation Japanese, called Nisei, were assimilating more broadly with mainstream American culture but would still find themselves treated as foreign and alien. These generational divides would become even more fracturing

THE 10 INTERNMENT CAMPS

The long-term incarceration of Japanese Americans took place in 10 "War Relocation Camps," which are the most famous features of Japanese internment:

- Manzanar, California, 10,046 incarcerees
- Tule Lake, California, 18,789 incarcerees
- Poston, Arizona, 17,814 incarcerees
- Gila River, Arizona, 13,348 incarcerees
- Granada, Colorado, 7,318 incarcerees
- Heart Mountain, Wyoming, 10,767 incarcerees
- Minidoka, Idaho, 9,397 incarcerees
- Topaz, Utah, 8,130 incarcerees
- Rohwer, Arkansas, 8,475 incarcerees
- Jerome, Arkansas, 8,497 incarcerees

This list does not include the various other kinds of incarceration facilities that held Japanese Americans during World War II, such as the assembly centers and those that housed "problem cases," which were run by the U.S. Justice Department, the Federal Bureau of Prisons, and the U.S. Army.

during internment, as the community struggled to come to terms with its place in America.

Even though Japanese Americans had served in World War I, and Japan had been an ally of the United States, the virulence of anti-Japanese sentiment was in many ways enmeshed in the overall anti-Asian racism common in the United States. Fears of "yellow peril," stoked up by sensationalist "journalism," further exacerbated the anti-Japanese and anti-Asian sentiment.

This sentiment was especially pernicious on the West Coast, where concentrations of Japanese immigrants found themselves after the Chinese Exclusion Act of 1882 had cut off the supply of cheap labor for farms. As a result, Japanese immigrants filled in the agricultural labor niche previously held by Chinese immigrants, primarily through tenant farming. In response to the growing role of Japanese Americans in the vital agricultural sector of the West Coast, local discriminatory laws explicitly prevented "aliens ineligible for citizenship" from owning land. California's Alien Land Law of 1913 is but one example of specifically anti-Japanese practices.

Pearl Harbor and Executive Order 9066

It was against this domestic backdrop that the Japanese surprise attack on Pearl Harbor on December 7, 1941, set events in motion. Soon after Pearl Harbor, President Franklin D. Roosevelt signed Executive Order 9066, which authorized the deportation and forced relocation of the Japanese from "exclusion zones" in the United States as determined by "military commanders."

One such commander was Lt. Gen. John Lesesne DeWitt, who coordinated the defense of the West Coast as head of what would become the Western Defense Command (WDC). DeWitt and his superior, Secretary of State Henry L. Stimson, were influential in Roosevelt's decision to enact Executive Order 9066. DeWitt's "Public Proclamation No. 1" designated the entire Pacific coast (and 100 miles inland) as "Military Area No. 1." Although some Japanese voluntarily relocated out of Military Area No. 1, several months later, the exclusion zone was expanded again, and those families that had not moved far enough away were forced to move again or be interned.

Although military necessity was the primary justification for internment, in reality, internment was unfounded: There was not a single documented instance of espionage, sabotage, or other fifth column activity on the part of either American-born Japanese or resident Japanese noncitizens. At other times, U.S. authorities and internment advocates rationalized Japanese internment as a public safety measure to "protect" Japanese against vigilantes.

Evidence of the low strategic value of internment can be found in Hawai'i. Hawai'i, which had by some accounts nearly 160,000 residents of Japanese ancestry (35 percent of its population), did not undertake forced relocation, which would have caused complete economic and social collapse locally. However, Hawai'i's geographic insecurity, high strategic value, and high concentration of Japanese Americans should have made it a prime candidate for internment. Yet, despite the lack of internment, Japanese Americans remaining in Hawai'i did not engage in acts of sabotage, and, in fact, Hawai'i was one of the few places where a person of Japanese descent could serve in the military, albeit in noncombat roles and often in segregated units until 1943.

Further, German Americans and Italian Americans, even though they were far more numerous and more dispersed geographically in the United States were not subject to internment on the same scale or in the same way. Some 11,000 Germans and 2,000 Italians were interned, but these numbers represent but a small portion of the estimated 1.2 million Germans and 700,000 Italians residing in the United States. Comparing the numbers, it is clear that, while other "enemy races" would be judged on a case-by-case basis, only the Japanese were considered universally dangerous.

Thus, the Japanese American experience after Pearl Harbor was far from uniform but was distinctly Japanese. Although the vast majority were forced into internment, in Hawai'i and also along the East Coast (where there were relative few) Japanese Americans were not incarcerated, and some would continue to serve in the armed forces.

Life Interrupted

In March 1942, President Roosevelt signed the executive order to create the War Relocation Authority (WRA), headed by Milton Eisenhower, brother of Dwight D. Eisenhower. Eviction and forced relocation to camp facilities soon began in earnest. Collected first in makeshift "assembly centers" like the Santa Anita Racetrack in California, the Japanese were deprived of their property and uprooted, taking with them only whatever personal property they could carry. Their family businesses were forcibly abandoned, and their remaining assets and personal property left vulnerable to theft. Families were labeled with numbered tags to keep them together as the family unit was the basic unit of organization in camp.

But, the assembly centers were only meant as temporary holding camps for the internees while more permanent "relocation centers" were built. By August 1942, the majority of West Coast Japanese Americans were in 10 camps, all located in desolate areas in Arkansas, Arizona, California, Colorado, Idaho, Utah, and Wyoming. Selecting sites for relocation centers was extremely difficult, as inland states fought against becoming "'a dumping ground' for California's problem." After assuring state governments that the incarcerees' movements would be strictly controlled, these receiving states would agree to housing Japanese internment camps.

Perhaps the most famous camp was Manzanar, now a National Historic Landmark, located in the foothills of the Sierra Nevada Mountains in California. Previously occupied by Native Americans and ranchers, the town of Manzanar was abandoned when the City of Los Angeles purchased the water rights there. Originally called the "Owens Valley Reception Center" and operated by the U.S. Army Wartime Civilian Control Administration (WCC), it was the first internment camp established. Later, the camp was transferred to the WRA in June 1942 and renamed the "Manzanar War Relocation Center."

At its height, the population of the camp was over 10,000 individuals, most of which were from the Los Angeles area. The first incarcerees built the camp, which consisted of residential blocks of tar-paper barracks; each residential block included common facilities, like latrines, laundry rooms, and mess halls. The lack of privacy was a particularly common complaint in the poorly built barracks. Barracks were overcrowded and divided with walls that did not extend to the ceiling.

The rush to build relocation centers taxed the already scarce labor and construction materials supply, much of which had to be redirected to the war effort as well. The hastily built camps could barely provide shelter against the harsh environment, especially in the winter. For example, at Manzanar, summer daytime temperatures could top 100°F, while winter nights were cold. Low rainfall meant that the dust was ever present and kicked up by the high winds of the plateau.

Over the course of incarceration, internees worked to re-create the lives they had had before. They built houses of worship, general stores, beauty parlors, and banks, even ran newspapers and raised livestock to supplement their diets. Other inmates worked for the camp: Even though incarcerees were not required to do so, it was expected that they would participate in administering the internment camps, at first for no pay but eventually for nominal wages significantly lower than their Caucasian counterparts. The wages were paltry: around $12 per month for unskilled labor and $19 per month for professionals, such as doctors and nurses. Two centers experimented with work programs to involve inmates in the war effort, such as Santa Anita's camouflage netting factory.

While adults either worked or created new social circles from the vestiges of their old lives, schools and activities were set up to give the children some semblance of normality, such as baseball teams, Boy and Girl Scouts, and the like. Many of the autobiographies that appeared after the war recount childhood experiences, such as Jeanne Wakatsuki Houston's *Farewell to Manzanar* and Yoshiko Uchida's *The Invisible Thread*. A whole generation of young Japanese Americans would be shaped by the experience. For example, actor George Takei would go on to interpret his childhood experience of internment into a Broadway musical, *Allegiance*.

Life during internment was far removed from mainstream society, and little information about camp life reached the outside world because of media suppression. For example, famed photographer Dorothea Lange, whose poignant style had so captured the spirit of the Great Depression, had been hired by the WRA to document the camps. However, Lange found her movements restricted to presenting a rosy view of the internment experience. Only recently were these photographs rediscovered in the archives. A contrasting collection of photographs from Manzanar comes from famed naturalist photographer Ansel Adams, who visited the internment camp as a private individual and was able to capture somewhat more candid images.

But, perhaps the most extensive and true collection of photographs are those of Tōyō Miyatake, himself photographed by Adams. An Issei photographer based in Los Angeles before internment, Miyatake smuggled a camera lens into the camp and constructed a camera body out of wood. His collection of photographs is preserved at the Japanese American National Museum in Los Angeles.

Resistance
Naturally, some reacted to their internment with feelings of despair and betrayal, while others kept their faith in the U.S. government, such as the Japanese American Citizens League (JACL) headed by Mike Masaoka (1915–1991).

The JACL had been formed in the late 1920s from various Nisei organizations and had fought bans against citizenship for Japanese Americans during the interwar period. By specifically focusing on naturalization, the JACL largely excluded Issei from its ranks, and its position on internment was controversial. Wanting to be portrayed as "loyal Americans," the JACL leadership encouraged members to report suspected "disloyalty" to American authorities, such as the Federal Bureau of Investigation.

At the camps, in addition to several civil disturbances protesting specific injustices such as wages, these ideological rifts around loyalty and citizenship further exacerbated the generation gap between foreign-born Issei and U.S.-born Nisei. Tensions would boil over in the December 1942 riot at Manzanar: When JACL official Fred Tayama was beaten after returning from a JACL meeting in Utah, Harry Ueno was arrested for the beating. Several hundred incarcerees marched in protest to Ueno's arrest, and the guards responded with tear gas and bullets, killing two inmates.

Still, small numbers of Japanese Americans would be vetted and allowed to leave the camps, either to attend college or to work in agriculture, especially after war turned in the United State's favor. Others would be labeled "disloyal" and segregated from the larger community either by formal criminal charges, which would bring them into custody outside the internment camp system, or by removal to the Tule Lake Segregation Center.

Also, because of the ongoing need for soldiers, the U.S. War Department began to assess whether Japanese Americans would be "suitable" for military service. In 1943, it sent a 28-question survey, called the "Statement of United States Citizen of Japanese Ancestry," to all Japanese American men, both interned and free, that were of eligible age for military service. Although many questions were fairly banal, such as questions about religion or hobbies, the final two questions of the "loyalty questionnaire" evoked strong emotions. Question 27 asked whether the respondent would be willing to serve in the armed forces, while Question 28 asked whether the respondent would renounce their loyalty to the emperor of Japan.

Both questions caused consternation among Japanese internees. The first question made inmates wonder whether or not military service would guarantee citizenship for them. The second question was offensive because it presumed that persons of Japanese descent were loyal to the emperor, regardless of place of birth or upbringing, such that this loyalty had to be explicitly renounced in order to become American. Although many did fill out the questionnaire, those who answered "no" to both questions would be called the No-No Boys and would find themselves under suspicion and segregated from the rest of the interned population.

In response to the "loyalty questionnaire," several instances of protest occurred, despite the threat of 20 years in prison as well as fines. At the Heart

Mountain Relocation Center in Wyoming, the loyalty questionnaire was questioned by the Heart Mountain Fair Play Committee, organized by Kiyoshi Okamoto, Frank Emi, and Paul Nakadate. The committee urged young men to refuse to answer the questionnaire unless the government specifically clarified whether service would restore their rights. When draft orders were extended to incarcerees, the Heart Mountain Fair Play Committee urged inmates to refuse to serve. As a result, over 60 Heart Mountain incarcerees were prosecuted for felony draft evasion. In all, over 300 draft resisters from across the 10 camps were prosecuted, while the organizers at Heart Mountain faced conspiracy charges.

Relative to its size, Tule Lake had the highest concentration of No-No Boys, and Tule Lake became a segregation center, bringing in "problematic" internees from other camps, while "less problematic" incarcerees would be moved to other camps. For example, Joseph Yoshisuke Kurihara (1895–1965) was a Nisei born in Hawai'i, where his family worked on the sugar plantations. When World War I broke out, Kurihara volunteered and was shipped to France with the 85th Division, 328th Field Artillery. Even though he was a veteran of World War I, Kurihara was originally incarcerated at Manzanar. The experience would inspire Kurihara to renounce his American citizenship, and some, like him, chose to relocate to Japan after the war. At the end of the war, as the other camps closed, Tule Lake would become a holding center for these cases.

Life after Internment

As the United States made gains against the Japanese in the Pacific, the imagined threat of the Japanese in America became even less real, and continued internment gradually lost credibility among those in power. In December 1944, the Supreme Court ruled on two cases: In *Korematsu v. United States*, the exclusion order that established internment was declared constitutional, while *Ex Parte Mitsuye Endo* ruled that continued incarceration was unnecessary, and the camps were closed.

But the end of internment did not mean the end of displacement and hardship for many Japanese families. After all, the forced relocation of the Japanese on the West Coast decimated the communities that they had established, like Los Angeles's Little Tokyo, which became the predominantly African American and Latino neighborhood of Bronzeville (and later site of the Zoot Suit Race Riots).

When the camps closed, Japanese families were left largely to their own fates, with little to no assistance to return to their former lives or to relocate and start new lives in new communities. Some detainees tried to stay at the camps because they had nowhere to go, only to be forcibly removed again as the federal government divested itself from internment camp-related properties. In

1948, the Japanese-American Evacuation Claims Act allowed Japanese Americans to claim damages from the government for their loss of property during internment.

Throughout the 1970s, leaders of the Japanese American community—such as the JACL, the National Coalition for Redress and Reparations (NCRR), and the National Council for Japanese American Redress (NCJAR)—began the call for reparations. Some considered seeking justice through a class action lawsuit. Japanese American members of Congress, including veteran senator Daniel Inouye of Hawai'i, spearheaded the initiative in Congress.

In 1980, Congress authorized the bipartisan Commission on Wartime Relocation and Internment of Civilians to investigate Japanese internment and its legacy. Over 750 testimonies were heard, and the commission's final report recommended several forms of redress, including a public apology from Congress, presidential pardons for curfew violators, and reparations. In 1988, the Civil Liberties Act was signed by President Ronald Reagan offering a formal apology and reparations in the form of $20,000 for each survivor.

In attempting to recover from and understand the phenomenon and its place in American and Japanese American history, a debate in the 1990s touched on whether the term "concentration camp" could or should be used to describe Japanese internment. Although some objected to the use of the term, it has largely accepted that the parallels between the Japanese American internment experience and the experience of the Jewish people in the Holocaust are unavoidable.

Today, little remains of the 10 relocation camps, as after the war, the federal government divested itself of the properties, and building materials were salvaged. Memorials and/or remnants of facilities exist at all the locations, some of which are maintained by the National Park Service, the most well kept being Manzanar. Instead, the memorialization of Japanese internment resides in the people who were impacted by the atrocity. Ways of remembering Japanese internment include books (both fiction and nonfiction), films, and pilgrimages to Manzanar and Tule Lake, which continue to this day.

See also: Commission on Wartime Relocation and Internment of Civilians; Draft Resisters; Executive Order 9066; 442nd Regimental Combat Team/100th Infantry Battalion; Japanese American Citizens League; Kooskia Internment Camp; Manzanar Children's Village (1942–1945); Masaoka, Mike Masaru (1915–1991); National Japanese American Memorial; No-No Boys; Pearl Harbor

Further Reading

Inada, Lawson Fusao. *Only What We Could Carry: The Japanese American Internment Experience.* Berkeley, CA: Heyday Books, 2000.

Uchida, Yoshiko. *Journey to Topaz: A Story of the Japanese-American Evacuation.* Berkeley, CA: Heyday Books, 2005.

Wakatsuki Houston, Jeanne. *Farewell to Manzanar: A True Story of Japanese American Experience during and after the World War II Internment.* Boston, MA: Houghton Mifflin, 1973.

Yvette M. Chin

JAPANESE AMERICAN COMMUNITIES

First-generation Japanese immigrants coming to the United States from the late 19th to the early 20th centuries, called Issei, established and developed relatively self-sufficient ethnic communities. These communities—called "Japan Towns" or *nihonmachis*—consisted of residences, businesses, and a variety of community organizations such as temples, churches, and social associations. Such communities, or ethnic enclaves, served as refuges to protect Japanese immigrants and their children from racial discrimination and prejudice of the mainstream society, provided them with cultural commodities and services, and nurtured ties within and between communities across the western United States. Internment at camps in the interior of the country during World War II resulted in the dispersion of many Issei and their families throughout the United States and damaged the social networks that Japanese communities had built. Although nearly 90 percent of Japanese on the U.S. mainland lived on the West Coast in the prewar period, the concentration had dropped to 55 percent in 1947. Yet, returnees from internment camps devoted themselves to rebuilding their communities, and many of the communities had regained their prewar liveliness by the early 1950s.

Decline of Historic Communities and Urban Renewal

The postwar prosperity of Japanese American communities was short lived because of changes in the social and economic status of the subsequent generations and external forces including urban renewal movements. First, Nisei and Sansei (second- and third-generation Japanese Americans, respectively) achieved upward mobility in the postwar period. In the prewar period, few Japanese Americans could find mainstream white-collar jobs even if they had university degrees. However, as racial discrimination in U.S. society lessened in the postwar period, Nisei and Sansei became increasingly able to find jobs with higher socioeconomic status outside their ethnic communities. Japanese Americans who joined the military had opportunities to receive higher education in universities through the G.I. Bill, which made them more competitive in the mainstream job market. Nisei and Sansei became less interested in taking over small, family-owned businesses, which had constituted the socioeconomic basis of Japanese American communities. In addition, more Nisei and Sansei married non-Japanese, particularly Caucasians. As a result, many Nisei and Sansei moved out of urban ethnic enclaves to suburban areas where there were fewer Japanese Americans. When Japanese Americans, along with Chinese Americans, "attained" model minority status in the eyes of mainstream society by the mid-1960s, their urban ethnic enclaves had already begun to show decline.

Also, urban renewal programs conducted in major cities from the 1950s to the 1970s greatly impacted several Japanese American neighborhoods that were located in or near central business districts. City officials, with the support of the federal government, sought to revitalize deteriorated central business districts and encourage investment in these areas. Although downtown residents and businesses first welcomed redevelopment plans, their optimism faded when urban renewal resulted in mass evictions that were often coercive and rarely provided sufficient compensation for relocation. Japanese Americans often call this forced removal the "second relocation."

Examples of historic urban Japanese American communities that were strongly affected by urban renewal include San Francisco's Japantown and Los Angeles's Little Tokyo. The redevelopment projects in the 1950s and 1960s essentially converted San Francisco's Japantown from an ethnic residential area to a tourist attraction. The project led to the removal of about 8,000 residents, including many African Americans and Japanese Americans, and the demolition of 6,000 units of low-rent housing. The city offered a section of the project area to Japan-based corporations, which were experiencing rapid growth in Japan and were also eager to establish themselves in the United States. Residents and young Japanese American community activists established the Committee against Nihonmachi Evictions (CANE) in response. However, in the end, these Japan-based corporations managed to open luxury hotels, a Japanese theater, and shopping malls. The malls not only provided a showcase for both traditional and modern Japanese cultural products such as foods, consumer electronics, and automobiles for domestic and international tourists but also housed overseas branch offices of many Japanese companies.

However, CANE activists argued that making Japantown into a tourist destination commodified their community and degraded their culture.

The fate of Los Angeles's Little Tokyo was similar to that of San Francisco's Japantown. Expansion of the police administration building, Parker Center, led to evictions of about 1,000 residents in the early 1950s. Ironically, in the following decades, foreign investment in redevelopment from Japan resulted in the removal of a number of local residents and forced many Japanese American family businesses to close. Amid the growing Asian American Movement, younger Japanese Americans established the Little Tokyo People's Rights Organization (LTPRO) to protest evictions and demolitions of facilities with historic and cultural significance to their community. Nevertheless, the redevelopment greatly changed the physical appearance of Little Tokyo. Although Japanese capital supported the completion of the luxurious

New Otani Hotel and the Weller Court shopping mall, it also sponsored the construction of a couple of low-income housing units and the Japanese American Cultural and Community Center, which houses several community organizations. The latter are considered the fruits of the LTPRO-led community protests.

Preservation of Historic Communities

The success of the redress movement in the 1970s and 1980s, which sought an apology and compensation from the U.S. government for the wartime internment, illustrates the growing political power and strength of Japanese American communities. However, nothing could reverse the exodus of younger Japanese Americans from old urban enclaves to the suburbs. Moreover, despite the large influx of Asian immigrants into the United States after the Immigration and Nationality Act of 1965 that have contributed to rejuvenation of existing communities and established a number of new Asian communities, the number of immigrants from Japan since 1965 remains relatively low. These factors account for the continued decline of Japanese American communities. For example, although Japanese Americans constituted the largest Asian American group until 1970, they fell to sixth largest in 2010, behind Chinese, Filipinos, Asian Indians, Vietnamese, and Koreans.

In the late 1990s, the preservation movement of historic urban Japanese American communities was initiated by community leaders who were worried about the unstable economy and the fading sense of Japanese American ethnicity. Long-time Japanese American residents were aging and Japanese American family-owned shops were closing one after another because they could not find anyone to take over their businesses. Accordingly, these businesses were purchased by others, particularly Korean American and Chinese American merchants, who transformed the properties into businesses reflecting their own ethnicities. The economic recession in Japan in the early 1990s caused the withdrawal of Japan-based companies from San Francisco's Japantown and Los Angeles's Little Tokyo, as well as a decrease in the number of tourists from Japan. Japanese American community leaders in San Francisco, Los Angeles, and San Jose acknowledged preservation and revitalization of historic urban communities as a common issue and began collaborating. They held the first nationwide community conference "Ties That Bind" in Los Angeles in 1998 and a second one, "Nikkei 2000," in San Francisco in 2000. The coalition of these communities claimed that Los Angeles's Little Tokyo and the Japantowns in San Jose and San Francisco were the only remaining Japantowns in the United States and emphasized their historical significance. Their efforts resulted in

California Senate Bill 307, approved in 2001, which provided $450,000 for the preservation of those historic Japantowns.

Each community also sought public recognition of the historical value of these communities. Los Angeles's Little Tokyo was designated as a National Historic Landmark District in 1995. The Japanese American National Museum that opened in the heart of Little Tokyo in 1992 has played an important role in educating young Japanese Americans and the general public about the experiences of previous generations of Japanese Americans. San Francisco's Japantown was designated as a Special Use District in 2005, which provided Japanese American communities the power to control land use within the neighborhood to some degree, so that the place retained a sense of Japanese cultural and historic identity.

New Suburban Japanese Communities

Although urban Japanese American enclaves continued to decline, an increase in the number of Japanese companies in the United States has led to the development of new suburban Japanese communities that are primarily composed of postwar Japanese immigrants and nonimmigrants such as business expatriates and their families. These communities developed in suburban cities such as Torrance and Costa Mesa in Southern California and Santa Clara in northern California, where a number of Japanese companies are concentrated. Unlike prewar Japanese immigrants, who lived in urban ethnic enclaves, contemporary Japanese business expatriate families tend to avoid living close to other Japanese families, preferring instead to live in suburbs that have low crime rates and high-quality schools for their children.

New suburban Japanese communities are usually composed of several clusters of commercial facilities close to major Japanese companies rather than having a central location for residences and community organizations. Each cluster usually includes a supermarket, a bookstore, several Japanese restaurants, and other services such as travel agents, real estate agents, law offices, clinics, and cram schools. Most of these businesses are operated by long-term Japanese residents and not by Japanese Americans. They were designed to primarily serve Japanese business expatriates and their families, who stay only temporarily in the United States and return to Japan eventually. Thus, they try to create a very similar environment to contemporary Japan by providing commodities and services of the same type and quality as are available in Japan. In this sense, these new communities provide comfort and cultural continuity to contemporary Japanese transnationals who are not accustomed to English language and American culture in a similar way that prewar Japanese communities did for immigrants. However, as many of those who constitute new communities are transient employees of global corporations who work outside of their residential areas, the sense of community is not very strong.

These new communities have few connections to historic urban communities or Japanese American communities under the leadership of the Sansei and increasingly Yonsei (fourth generation). The old and new Japanese communities have been separate, mainly because most Sansei and subsequent generations lack fluency in Japanese. Even though they share common cultural roots, they have different historical experiences and different perspectives and interpretations of Japanese culture. As long as contemporary Japanese immigrants and nonimmigrants enjoy the comforts and conveniences found in the cultural "bubble" of their suburban communities, they have few opportunities to interact with Japanese Americans even in areas like California, which has a large Japanese American population.

The growth of these new suburban Japanese communities presents a sharp contrast to the recent decline in historic urban Japanese communities. Japanese foreign capital, once directed to redevelopment of old Japanese communities, changed course and has been used to relocate Japanese businesses to suburban communities. Many Japanese companies consider investment in Japanese suburban communities as more lucrative than investments in historic urban communities, despite continuous efforts to revitalize the latter.

Contemporary Japanese American communities lack geographic centers as Japanese Americans disperse to the suburbs and are more residentially and socially integrated into the mainstream. Historic urban Japanese communities are no longer residential neighborhoods with small ethnic businesses like those that existed in the prewar period; rather, the areas in which these prewar communities existed, despite their renovations, have become largely symbols of Japanese American ethnicity today. They are still a hub of many community organizations and home to Japanese American churches and temples, and they serve as the stage for traditional community events like summer Bon festivals and New Year's celebrations. Japanese Americans living in the suburbs occasionally visit for these events to remind themselves of their ethnic heritage.

See also: Little Tokyo

Further Reading

Fugita, Stephen S., and David J. O'Brien. *Japanese American Ethnicity: The Persistence of Community.* Seattle: University of Washington Press, 1991.

Tatsuno, Sheridan. "The Political and Economic Effects of Urban Renewal on Ethnic Communities: A Case Study of San Francisco's Japantown." *Amerasia Journal* 1 (1971): 33–51.

Yoko Tsukuda

JAPANESE AMERICAN EXCLUSION

In American history, the period of Japanese immigrant exclusion is typically associated with the years between 1924 and 1945. The legal exclusion of Japanese immigrants from the United States actually commenced in 1907 and occurred in stages. The key restrictions on Japanese immigration were the Executive Order of March 14, 1907 (Executive Order 589), the Gentlemen's Agreement of 1907–1908, the termination of the picture bride practice in 1920, and the Japanese exclusion clause to the Johnson-Reed Act (Immigration Act of 1924).

The Executive Order of March 14, 1907, which President Theodore Roosevelt issued, prohibited the migration to the United States of skilled and unskilled laborers who were citizens of Japan and held passports to Hawai'i, Canada, or Mexico. The purpose of the order was to stop the flow of Issei (Japanese immigrants; literally, "the first generation") plantation laborers from Hawai'i to California. Between 1900, following the enactment of the Hawai'ian Organic Act that made Hawai'i a territory of the United States, and 1907, more than 68,000 Issei plantation laborers migrated from Hawai'i to the U.S. mainland in search of jobs that paid higher wages.

In the Gentlemen's Agreement of 1907–1908, the Japanese Foreign Ministry agreed in a series of six written notes exchanged with the U.S. Department of State to cease issuing passports to Japanese skilled and unskilled laborers for entry into the United States. The agreement exempted former legal residents of the United States, farmers who owned their crops, wives, children under 20 years old, parents, and siblings of Issei resident laborers. Although the agreement did not bind it to do so, the Japanese Foreign Ministry imposed similar restrictions on Japanese immigration to Hawai'i and Mexico. The Foreign Ministry acceded to the Executive Order of March 14, 1907, and the Gentlemen's Agreement to bring resolution to a crisis that the San Francisco Board of Education had instigated in 1906. In October of that year, the Board of Education ordered ethnic Japanese and Korean students to attend the racially segregated Chinese School. The segregation order affected 93 Issei and Nisei (American-born children of Japanese immigrants; literally, "second generation"). With two exceptions, Issei parents declined to send their children to the Chinese School, which was situated in Chinatown, a district that the 1906 San Francisco earthquake and fire had devastated. Some parents also retained an Issei attorney to file a legal challenge to the segregation order in federal district court. Desiring to defuse the crisis to maintain cooperative relations with the United States without harming Japan's international standing, the Japanese Foreign Ministry agreed to the immigration and migration restrictions only after the rescission of the segregation order. The Theodore Roosevelt administration had pressured the Board of Education to rescind the segregation order for all ethnic Japanese students who were not overage for their grade levels. The rescission meant that Issei and Nisei students could resume attending racially integrated public schools in San Francisco. Although excluding the immigration of laborers the Gentlemen's Agreement also indirectly enabled the immigration of picture brides. The Gentlemen's Japanese Exclusion Agreement required all Issei residents of the United States to register with the Japanese Foreign Ministry. With the assistance of Japanese consular general officials, Issei community leaders established organizations named Japanese Associations to process registration applications and other forms, including applications to bring Japanese women into the United States as picture brides of Issei men whom they knew, in most cases, only through letters and photographs. There were four central bodies on the Pacific coast—in Los Angeles, San Francisco, Portland, and Seattle—and 86 local associations across America.

Although Issei picture bride marriages date back to the late 19th century, the Japanese Foreign Ministry had imposed various restrictions that prohibited picture brides of most laborers from entering the United States after the Gentlemen's Agreement. Beginning in the summer of 1915, the Foreign Ministry opened picture bride marriage eligibility to all Issei males provided that they met financial, age, and health requirements. Picture bride marriages were crucial to Japanese American society. Until the 1910s, Japanese America had been predominantly a bachelor society. Picture brides altered community demographics, enabling substantive family formation and the growth of the Japanese American population.

Family formation enabled some Issei resident alien farmers to circumvent the California Alien Land Act of 1913 (Webb-Haney Act). The law prohibited the purchase of agricultural land and the leasing of agricultural land for more than three years to "all aliens ineligible to citizenship." Although the law was unsettled at the time on the question of whether Japanese and Asian Indian aliens were "white persons" and thereby eligible for naturalized citizenship pursuant to the Revised Statutes of 1875, the majority view was that both groups were aliens ineligible for citizenship. The U.S. Supreme Court finally resolved the questions in *Ozawa v. United States*, 260 U.S. 178 (1922), holding that Japanese aliens were not Caucasian and therefore ineligible for American citizenship, and in *United States v. Bhagat Singh Thind*, 261 U.S. 204 (1923), holding likewise that Asian Indians were not "white" and therefore ineligible for citizenship. To avoid the constraints of the alien land law, Issei farmers purchased or transferred title to agricultural lands in the names of their Nisei children. Nisei were American citizens by virtue of their birth on American soil. This maneuver combined with race-based fears about the expanding ethnic Japanese population in California helped revive the Japanese exclusion movement shortly after the end of World War I, a war in which the United States and Japan had been allies.

At the behest of the Japanese Foreign Ministry, which desired to appease the Japanese exclusion movement, the executive board of the Japanese Association of America, a central body that was based in San Francisco, called for the termination of the picture bride practice in late October 1919. The three other central bodies of the Japanese Association, along with many local associations, denounced the position of the Japanese Association of America. Four weeks later, the entire executive board resigned under pressure from local affiliates. Despite the overwhelming opposition of Issei to the termination of the picture bride practice, the Japanese Foreign Ministry halted the issuance of passports to picture brides for travel to the United States as of March 1, 1920.

By terminating picture bride marriages, the Japanese Foreign Ministry delayed Japanese exclusion. The Chinese Exclusion Act of 1882 had made Chinese ineligible to American citizenship and had excluded Chinese immigrants with exceptions for merchants engaged in international trade pursuant to treaty obligations, students, educators, religious ministers, and spouses and children of the excepted categories. With similar exceptions, the Immigration Act of 1917 (Asiatic Barred Zone Act; Dillingham-Burnett Act) contained a latitude and longitude clause that established a barred zone, excluding immigrants from countries in Southeast Asia, South Asia, and parts of Central Asia. By 1923, along with Filipinos, ethnic populations in the Japanese empire—Japanese, Koreans, Ainu, Okinawans, and Taiwanese—were among the few remaining Asian populations whom the United States had not yet excluded en masse.

Japanese exclusion became a national issue in 1924 during debate on an immigration bill in the U.S. House of Representatives. The primary purpose of the Johnson bill was to restrict immigration from Southern and Eastern Europe. To accomplish this Japanese exclusion objective, the bill proposed a national origins quota system, limiting immigration from each foreign nation to an annual quota of 2 percent of the nation's foreign-born population residing in the United States as determined in the 1890 U.S. Census. Mass immigration from Southern and Eastern Europe to the United States did not begin until the 1890s. By utilizing the 1890 U.S. Census to determine immigration quotas, the Johnson bill ensured low quotas from nations in Southern and Eastern Europe. In both intent and effect, the bill imposed racial quotas to maintain the Anglo-Saxon, Nordic, Germanic, and Celtic racial majorities in the United States and inhibit growth of the "darker" European races.

The ethnic Japanese population in the United States was likewise small in 1890. Based on the 2 percent formula, the 1890 U.S. Census, and the existing Gentlemen's Agreement, Japan would receive an annual immigration quota of 146 persons. Despite the paltry number of Japanese immigrants admissible pursuant to these criteria, Japanese exclusionists in the U.S. House of

Representatives sought tighter restrictions. They added a clause to the bill in March 1924 that prohibited the admission to the United States of any "alien ineligible to citizenship" except for aliens admissible as nonquota immigrants. The exceptions included merchants engaged in international trade, students, legal residents returning from visits abroad, religious ministers, college and university educators, spouses, and unmarried minor (under 18 years) children of excepted persons.

Charles Evans Hughes, the U.S. secretary of state, asked U.S. Rep. Albert Johnson (R-Wash.), the chairman of the House Committee on Immigration and Naturalization and the primary sponsor of the Johnson bill, to remove the Japanese exclusion clause from the bill. After Johnson declined to do so, Secretary Hughes asked Masanao Hanihara, the Japanese ambassador to the United States, to write a note addressed to Hughes that summarized and supported the retention of the Gentlemen's Agreement. In his note of April 10, 1924, Ambassador Hanihara wrote that although the exclusion of an additional 146 Japanese per year was inconsequential, the unilateral method of exclusion was at variance with America's "high principles of justice and fair play in the intercourse of nations." Hanihara further stated, "I realize, as I believe you do, the grave consequences which the enactment of the measure retaining that particular provision [Japanese exclusion] would inevitably bring upon the otherwise happy and mutually advantageous relations between our two countries." Two days later, the House approved the Johnson bill with the exclusion clause by a vote of 323–71.

After reviewing Ambassador Hanihara's note, Secretary Hughes sent copies of the note to the chairs of the House and Senate immigration committees. In early April, before receipt of Hanihara's note, Hughes had convinced a majority of the members of the Senate Committee on Immigration to support an amendment to the Johnson bill that would continue the Gentlemen's Agreement and subject Japan to the 2 percent immigration quota based on the 1890 U.S. Census, and thereby permit Japan to have 146 quota immigrants per year. Hughes believed that Hanihara's letter would help ensure Senate passage of the amendment.

On April 14, Sen. Henry Cabot Lodge (R-Mass.), during debate on the Senate version of the immigration bill, motioned on the Senate floor for a closed executive session to discuss Hanihara's note. After returning from the session, Sen. Lodge declared on the Senate floor that the phrase "grave consequences" in the note was a "veiled threat" against the United States. Lodge then stated that he would not support the amendment to remove the Japanese exclusion clause from the bill. Sen. David Aiken Reed (R-Pa.), the chairman of the Senate Committee on Immigration, next took the floor and said that the "veiled threat" had also "compelled" him to vote against the amendment. When in executive session, Senators Reed and Lodge convinced most of their Senate colleagues to reject the amendment. Later that day, the Senate voted 76–2 against the amendment.

The Senate's reaction to Hanihara's note surprised both Secretary Hughes and Ambassador Hanihara. On April 17, in a letter to Hughes, Hanihara explained that the phrase "grave consequences" was not a threat but referred to the damage that an exclusion law would have on "the otherwise happy and mutually advantageous relations" between Japan and the United States. The next day, the Senate approved its version of the immigration bill, which included the Japanese exclusion clause ("aliens ineligible to citizenship"), by a vote of 62–6. President Calvin Coolidge signed the bill into law on May 26, 1924, attaching a written statement that faulted Congress for the method utilized to achieve exclusion. The resulting Johnson-Reed Act made Japanese exclusion effective as of July 1, 1924.

The immigration restrictions coincided with the peak years of Japanese emigration. As a consequence of the restrictions that became effective between 1907 and 1924, and similar restrictions in Canada, Australia, and New Zealand, hundreds of thousands of Japanese instead immigrated to Brazil between the 1910s and late 1930s and again during the 1950s and early 1960s, Manchuria during the 1930s and early 1940s, and other locales in East Asia and Latin America. Although the United States technically ended Japanese exclusion with the enactment of the War Brides Act of 1945 and the McCarran-Walter Act of 1952, the War Brides Act applied only to Japanese spouses and children of American-citizen military servicemembers, whereas the McCarran-Walter Act (Immigration and Nationality Act of 1952) capped other Japanese immigration at 185 per year. By the time the Hart-Celler Act (Immigration and Nationality Act of 1965), which abolished the quota system and relaxed immigration restrictions, became effective in July 1968, increasing affluence and robust economic growth in Japan had curtailed emigration.

See also: Alien Land Law (1913); Anti-Japanese Movement; Executive Order 9066; Immigration Act of 1924; Internment, World War II

Further Reading

Bailey, Thomas. *Theodore Roosevelt and the Japanese-American Crises.* Stanford, CA: Stanford University Press, 1934.

Daniels, Roger. *The Politics of Prejudice: The Anti-Japanese Movement in California and the Struggle for Japanese Exclusion.* Los Angeles: University of California Press, 1962.

Ichioka, Yuji. *The Issei: The World of the First Generation Japanese Immigrants, 1885–1924.* New York: The Free Press, 1988.

Daniel H. Inouye

JAPANESE AMERICAN HISTORY BEFORE 1945

In 1841, Manjiro Nakahama was shipwrecked and rescued by an American ship. He eventually chose to remain on board, and would later settle in Massachusetts and adopt the name John Manjiro. Although Manjiro was not the first Japanese individual to reach the United States, he set the stage for subsequent migration and was perhaps the most significant of the early 19th-century Japanese castaways.

On March 31, 1854, Commodore Matthew C. Perry sailed to Japan and by 1858 coerced the ruling Tokugawa shogunate to sign the Treaty of Kanagawa and open Japan's international borders. Manjiro served as Commodore Perry's interpreter. This moment marked the beginning of relations between Japan and the United States of America. Ten years later, the Meiji emperor came into power, ended the feudalistic Tokugawa rule, and began an overhaul of the entire country's social structure in hopes of modernizing to compete with the United States and other Western nations.

The Earliest Japanese Settlers

By the start of the Meiji Era in 1868, members of the samurai class faced a peculiar predicament with the erosion of the social class system. One specific group of 22 defeated samurai from Aizu Wakamatsu province (present-day Fukushima Prefecture) feared retribution from the Meiji government and chose to relocate with their families to California. On May 20, 1869, these Japanese immigrants arrived in San Francisco with plans to establish the Wakamatsu Tea and Silk Farm in the Sierra Nevada foothills. This venture faced several obstacles and essentially failed within two years.

Meanwhile in Japan, the children of the former elite samurai class were able to partake in the earliest stages of Japanese modernization by studying at newly established American-run mission schools. As the Meiji government pushed for the modernization of Japan during the early 1870s, it sponsored young males to travel abroad in hopes of one day returning with a new set of skills and mentalities to transform Japan into a global industrialized leader. These individuals represented the official start of legal Japanese immigration to the United States of America. Many found housing in San Francisco and employment as "schoolboys" who tended to the households of wealthier white Americans.

By the late 1870s, anti-Chinese agitation in California was reaching its boiling point. As white immigrants and their descendants organized throughout the country to fight for labor rights, Chinese immigrants were crossing picket lines and taking their jobs for lower wages. In response to the greater public's blatant anti-Chinese sentiment, President Chester A. Arthur signed the Chinese Exclusion Act in 1882, which effectively stopped all Chinese immigration. To fill the need for cheap labor, American business owners began to search for a new source of immigrant labor. It is in this context that large-scale Japanese immigration to the United States began.

The First Japanese Immigration Wave

During the first major wave of Japanese immigration between 1882 and 1924, over 450,000 Japanese settled in the United States and Hawai'i (at that time, a sovereign kingdom) to work in the railroad, mining, lumber, fishing, and agricultural industries with dreams of making a fortune and eventually returning to Japan. However, they soon experienced the same level of persecution as their Chinese predecessors.

In the late 19th century, Chinese in San Francisco faced a considerable amount of segregation, including in schools. Due to pressures from the Asiatic Exclusion League, the San Francisco Board of Education voted to force all Japanese students to attend the segregated Chinese school instead of the public schools for white students. The Japanese American community of San Francisco protested, and word soon traveled to the Japanese government. Eventually this issue reached President Theodore Roosevelt. President Roosevelt, having just witnessed Japan's military defeat over Russia in the Russo-Japanese War, did not want this debate to lead to further incident and convinced the San Francisco school board to rescind the segregation order.

In exchange for rescinding the order, Japan agreed to new immigration guidelines. The Gentlemen's Agreement of 1907 was an informal agreement between Japan and the United States in which Japan agreed to stop issuing passports to prospective laborers. This effectively stopped male Japanese laborers from immigrating to the United States and taking jobs from American citizens.

Although the Gentlemen's Agreement stopped the incoming flow of Japanese laborers, family reunification by Japanese into the United States was still allowed. Most of the early Japanese immigrants were single men and unable to marry white American women due to the antimiscegenation laws of the time. Many men found wives instead through the picture bride practice of selecting spouses across long geographic distances only through photographs supplied by a matchmaker. These partnerships played an instrumental role in the growth of second-generation Niseis.

Anti-Japanese Legislation

The California Alien Land Law of 1913 prohibited non-American citizens from owning land. At the time, it was impossible for a Japanese immigrant to become a naturalized American citizen, thus it was assumed the growing Japanese American community would forever remain branded as a group of outsiders within the United States and eventually be forced to leave the country. In 1915, Jukichi and Ken Harada registered their house in Riverside, California, under the names of their children who possessed American citizenship by birth. This legal maneuver was challenged unsuccessfully in *The People of California v. Jukichi Harada*, and thus presented Japanese American families with a loophole for long-term settlement. The irony in the Alien Land Law is that it indirectly encouraged Japanese immigrants to raise families and create long-term plans.

Also in 1915, a Japanese American immigrant named Takao Ozawa applied for naturalization. Although Ozawa was born in Japan, he spent the majority of his life in the United States. He attended the University of California, Berkeley, worked for an American company, and spoke to his fellow American-educated wife in English. In his application for American citizenship, Ozawa argued that despite his Japanese ethnicity, he should be classified as a "free white person." On November 13, 1915, the Supreme Court case *Takao Ozawa v. United States* ruled against Ozawa's petition, thus eliminating any path to citizenship for him and all other Japanese immigrants. Citizenship would not be made possible for Japanese immigrants until the passage of the McCarran-Walter Act in 1952.

In 1924, the U.S. Congress instituted a new immigration act that effectively ended immigration from all Asian countries (not including the Philippines, which was an American territory at the time). This virtual ban on Asian immigration remained in effect until the Immigration Act of 1965, and it dramatically changed the demographics of Japanese America by eliminating the flow of immigrant culture and thus increasing the rate of cultural assimilation.

On December 7, 1941, Pearl Harbor was attacked by the Imperial Japanese Navy, marking the start of American involvement in World War II on the Pacific front against Japan. 2,403 Americans were killed in the surprise attack, and 1,178 were wounded. Following this incident, many Americans fell victim to war hysteria and believed that Japanese Americans would partake in subversive plots against the United States. Several Japanese American community leaders were arrested immediately. Within months, President Franklin D. Roosevelt signed Executive Order 9066, ordering the forced incarceration of all 110,000-plus Japanese Americans living on the West Coast into concentration camps for the duration of the war. The majority of Japanese American incarcerees were American citizens, and all were targeted solely due to their ethnic heritage. Many would in fact volunteer for the U.S. Army to prove their loyalty. Regardless, this clear violation of civil rights permanently altered the trajectory of Japanese America.

See also: Japanese American Population Trends; Japanese Immigration to Hawai'i

Further Reading

Daniels, Roger. *The Politics of Prejudice: The Anti-Japanese Movement in California and the Struggle for Japanese Exclusion.* Berkeley: University of California Press, 1962.

Ichioka, Yuji. *The Issei: The World of the First Generation Japanese Immigrants, 1885–1924.* New York: The Free Press, 1990.

Dean Ryuta Adachi

JAPANESE AMERICAN POPULATION TRENDS

Japanese population trends in the United States have reflected historical policies and international relations between the two countries. In many ways, those policies and relations were similar to those with regard to East Asia in general, but they also represented circumstances unique to Japan. Economic, infrastructural, and agricultural development in the late 19th century drew East Asian immigrants into the United States as the growing nation was coming to depend on foreign labor. With increases in Asian immigration, including that from Japan, there emerged resistance from the native U.S. population, due to racism and concerns over secure employment access to resources. However, diplomatic relations, attitudes, and legislation influenced population trends among the Japanese in the United States in ways that were distinct within the Asian population as a whole.

The first significant migration of Japanese was initiated also as a result of the Meiji Restoration beginning in 1868, which expanded relations with the West. In these early years, most Japanese emigrants traveled to the Hawai'ian Islands and the West Coast to work as laborers. The Japanese government initially banned emigration to Hawai'i, as this work was viewed as demeaning and unrepresentative of Japan's noble character, but it lifted that ban in 1885, opening the door for Japanese labor on sugar and pineapple plantations. In addition, congressional legislation restricting Chinese immigrants in 1882 forced U.S. businesspersons and landowners to encourage increased immigration from Japan to replace them. Japanese immigration continued until the Gentlemen's Agreement between the governments of the United States and Japan placed new restrictions on the flow of male laborers in 1907. The migrants during this period were not solely farm laborers, however. Many started enterprises of their own, including farms, and engaged in fishing. The Gentlemen's Agreement allowed for immigration of spouses of Japanese men already living in the United States, as well as that of students and businesspersons, resulting in the establishment of families and rates of population growth that surpassed those of the Chinese. The Chinese were not permitted the same privilege at the turn of the 20th century.

Japanese immigration was prohibited under the Immigration Act of 1924, which established quotas favoring immigrants from Northern and Western Europe, causing a generational division in population. Japanese immigrants in the United States born in Japan were referred to as Issei, a group generally distinguished from their U.S.-born descendants by language and cultural traditions, but also citizenship, as the Naturalization Act of 1790 had limited citizenship to free whites, and thereby excluded the Japanese-born. Japanese Americans born in the United States were referred to as Nisei, and they would essentially constitute the U.S. Japanese population after the ban on immigration in 1924. Animosity and military conflict in the 1930s and 1940s further disrupted relations and the movement of Japanese. Within the borders of the United States during World War II, the Japanese population was relocated into internment camps. In the postwar period, revised immigration policies would provide access to the United States once again.

Though Japanese population dispersed throughout the United States, more than 70 percent of Japanese Americans remain in the West, with more than 60 percent in Hawai'i and California alone. The overall population of Japanese Americans has more than doubled since 1970, with some decline noted in the 2000 U.S. Census. That decline is due to some decline in immigration rates, as well as comparatively small family size and increases in intermarriage. Until 1960, the U.S. Census included categories for only Chinese, Japanese, and Other in enumerating the Asian population. In 1960, the bureau added Filipino and, in 1970, Korean and Hawai'ian. By 1990, the categories of national origin were much more diverse. This process may have influenced some shifts in the numbers of Japanese counted, as an increasing number of Japanese intermarried with either other Asians or non-Asians in the second half of the 20th century, and their descendants self-identified as Japanese or part Japanese. Census analysts were careful to distinguish more "purely" Japanese from those with mixed ancestry in an effort to provide consistency in reports from decade to decade. Today there are fewer self-identifying as Japanese in the United States but more claiming partial Japanese heritage. Significant increases in Japanese population after 1950 reflected a surge in immediate postwar migration, as well as the granting of statehood for Alaska and Hawai'i in 1959, making them officially part of the United States. Economic growth within Japan in the 1960s and 1970s provided more opportunities at home. Recent declines in Japanese fertility have contributed to smaller family size in Japan and coinciding social and economic consequences of an aging population. An additional result is a decline in need, as well as desire, for Japanese to migrate to the United States.

See also: Japanese American Communities

Further Reading

Ichihashi, Yamato. *Japanese in the United States: A Critical Study of the Problems of the Japanese Immigrants and Their Children.* Stanford, CA: Stanford University, 1932.

Jones, Nicholas A. "The Asian Population in the United States: Results from the 2010 Census." U.S. Bureau of the Census. https://www.census.gov/newsroom/releases/pdf/2012-05-02_nickjones_asianslides_2.pdf. Accessed August 1, 2017.

Wilson, Robert A., and Bill Hosokawa. *East to America: A History of the Japanese in the United States.* New York: William Morrow and Company, 1980.

Kathleen A. Tobin

Table 1   Japanese Population in the United States (Japanese and U.S. Born)

Year	Total	Male	Female
1870	55	47	8
1880	148	134	14
1890	2,039	1,780	259
1900	24,326	23,341	985
1910	72,157	63,070	9,087
1920	111,010	72,707	38,303
1930	138,834	81,771	57,063
1940	126,947	71,967	54,980
1950	141,768	76,649	65,119
1960	260,059	124,323	135,736
1970	591,290	—	—
1980	716,331		
1990	847,562		
2000	796,700		
2010	763,325		

Source: Compiled from *United States Census Reports* 1870–1970. Numbers between 1970 and 2010 vary due to changing trends in self-identification.

Table 2   Distribution of Japanese Immigrants, 1901–1910

Year	Total	Continental United States	Alaska	Hawai'i
1901	5,249	4,908	3	338
1902	14,445	5,325	5	9,125
1903	20,041	6,990	6	13,045
1904	14,382	7,776	16	6,590
1905	11,021	4,319	10	6,692
1906	14,243	5,178	14	9,051
1907	30,824	9,948	11	20,865
1908	1,418	7,250	15	9,153
1909	3,275	1,593	3	1,679
1910	2,798	1,552	7	1,239
Total	132,706	54,839	90	77,777

Source: *Annual Reports of the United States Superintendent and Commissioner-General of Immigration,* 1901–1910.

Table 3   Distribution of Japanese Residents (Japanese and U.S. Born), 1880–1930

Geographic Division	1880	1890	1900	1910	1920	1930
New England	14	45	89	272	347	352
Middle Atlantic	27	202	446	1,643	3,226	3,662
East North Central	7	101	126	482	927	1,022
West North Central	1	16	223	1,000	1,215	1,003
South Atlantic	5	55	29	156	360	393
East South Central	—	19	7	26	35	46
West South Central	—	42	30	428	578	687
Mountain	5	27	5,107	10,447	10,792	11,418
Pacific	89	1,532	18,269	57,703	93,490	120,251
Total	148	2,039	24,326	72,157	111,010	138,834

Source: Compiled from *United States Census Reports* 1880–1930.

JAPANESE AMERICAN WAR BRIDES

Japanese war brides (soldier brides) are Japanese women who immigrated to the United States from 1947 through the 1960s as spouses of American military personnel. Approximately 40,000 to 50,000 Japanese war brides entered the United States from 1947 to 1959. Although the exact numbers vary depending on the sources cited by scholars, these women comprised a sizable Asian immigrant group to the United States in the postwar period. The 1947 War Brides Act amendment enabled American servicemembers to bring their Japanese wives to the United States. This was the first legislation to permit immigration from Japan since 1924, when the Immigration Act prohibited immigration from Asia. The McCarran-Walter Act (the Immigration and Nationality Act of 1952) repealed restrictions on naturalization for Japanese and permitted a quota of only 100 Japanese per year. However, Japanese war brides, as spouses of American citizens, were exempt from the quota.

Postwar occupations by the Allied Powers in Europe and Asia led to a large number of marriages between American servicemembers and women from countries such as Italy, Germany, China, Korea, the Philippines, and Japan. In war-devastated Japan, many Japanese women of marriageable age had difficulty finding partners, as a large proportion of young Japanese men had lost their lives or were severely injured in the battlefields. To support their families, many Japanese women had to find jobs rather than spouses and were often the family breadwinners. Many were drawn to opportunities to work in the service industry for the Occupation Forces and later the U.S. military. Such jobs included employment as housemaids, office clerks, typists, and waitpersons in facilities for military personnel. Many couples met and were married through

Servicemen jam the consular office in Tokyo on March 19, 1952, to get married in time to beat the 2:00 p.m. deadline to benefit from a law that enabled them to bring their Japanese brides to the United States. Soldiers, sailors, and marines stood with their mates and went through the simple and very brief ceremony. (AP Photo/Max Desfor)

contact at such jobs. Such marriages, however, often aroused strong opposition from family members because marriage was considered a family matter rather than an individual decision in Japanese society at the time.

Stereotypes and Representations

Japanese war brides had long been marginalized within Japanese American communities because of the negative stereotypes that have been rampant in both Japan and the United States. Japanese women who married American service-members were falsely associated with images of prostitutes called *panpan*, who mainly served the foreign soldiers. The Japanese media often criticized Japanese women who had affairs with American soldiers, characterizing them as shameless women who lost not only their individual pride but also faith in their country. Some Japanese men saw romantic relationships between Japanese women and American soldiers as insults to Japanese masculinity: they could do nothing to stop "their" women from being attracted to their former enemies, who embodied wealth, democracy, and freedom as "the liberators." From the American point of view, on the other hand, Japanese women needed to be rescued and liberated from male-dominated and impoverished postwar Japanese society.

Many Japanese people have assumed that Japanese war brides lived unhappy lives in the United States that were characterized by loneliness and isolation and often culminated in divorce. It is true that those women faced difficulties adjusting to American culture as participants in not only international but also often interracial marriages. Some were shocked to find that their American husbands were from very poor families in rural areas, far from the glittering images of the United States promoted in Japan. Others encountered blatant prejudice because hatred of Japanese as wartime enemies was still intense in the United States. However, in fact, many Japanese war brides had happy married lives with their American husbands.

Japanese war brides were also objects of attention in the American media. Their entry into the United States and subsequent acculturation was regarded as a type of test as to the assimilability of a foreign, but unthreatening, Japanese figure at the same time that interned Japanese Americans were being resettled. Romance between Japanese women and American soldiers gained popularity in novels and movies: the most notable is James Michener's novel *Sayonara* (1954) and the movie by the same title (1957), which reemphasized exotic, geisha-like images of Japanese women through a love story between a Japanese actress and an American serviceman in postwar Japan.

A substantial number of Japanese war brides married Japanese American servicemembers. Compared to those who married non–Japanese Americans, such war brides suffered less from isolation and loneliness because spouses and their families had a shared sense of culture and couples could be part of Japanese American communities. However, they were not necessarily free from the negative stereotypes that were imported from Japan within the community.

Japanese War Brides Today

As memories of World War II fade, few use the term war brides today; rather, these marriages fall under the term kokusai kekkon, or international marriages. However, Japanese war brides' distinctive role as "grassroots cultural ambassadors" in postwar U.S.–Japan relations has recently begun to receive positive attention from Japanese American communities and academics. Their descendants, who often have interracial heritages, have emerged as leading Japanese American figures. Velina Hasu Houston, whose mother married an African American serviceman, produced *Tea* (1985), a play depicting the lives of Japanese war brides in the Midwest. More recently, Jero has gained popularity as an enka (a traditional Japanese music genre) singer in Japan. Born and raised in Pittsburgh, and the grandson of a Japanese war bride and an African American serviceman, Jero represents inheritance of an ethnically blended traditional culture to the contemporary interracial generation. Additionally, the first national convention of Japanese war brides was held in 1988 and drew more than 300 participants from around the country. Rejecting the past negative stereotypes, many Japanese war brides have started to tell their unique stories with pride.

See also: Japanese American Women; Japanese American Women in the 1930s; World War I; World War II

Further Reading

Glenn, Nakano Evelyn. *Issei, Nisei, War Bride: Three Generations of Japanese American Women in Domestic Service.* Philadelphia: Temple University Press, 1986.

Simpson, Chung Caroline. "'Out of an Obscure Place': Japanese War Brides and Cultural Pluralism in the 1950s." *Differences: A Journal of Feminist Cultural Studies* 10, no. 3 (1998): 47–81.

Yoko Tsukuda

JAPANESE AMERICAN WOMEN

The first Japanese women came to Hawai'i with their husbands around 1885 where they worked as field hands in the sugar industry. The first wave of female migrants to the mainland between 1909 and 1924 brought over 33,000 women to the United States. This period spans the time between the Gentlemen's Agreement—which limited labor migration from Japan but allowed wives to join their husbands in the United States—and the 1924 Immigration Act, which made immigration from Asia illegal. The second wave of female migration from Japan consisted of approximately 45,000 war brides who entered the United States after World War II between 1950 when immigration restrictions were lessened and the mid-1960s when the marriage between American servicemembers and Japanese women became less common.

Issei Women

By 1923, women accounted for almost two-fifths of Japanese immigrants. The vast majority of them were from small-town entrepreneurial or farming families in southern Japan. A substantial number of, especially, early female migrants were prostitutes from impoverished families. They were shunned by their community and attacked by propaganda marking Japanese immigrants as a moral problem. Most, however, came as daughters or wives and played a crucial part in building and maintaining the culture and cohesion of the community. Many Issei women were not only solely responsible for housework and childrearing but also engaged in paid work (mostly domestic labor) and unpaid labor for the family's farm or small business to support the family income. Migration tended

A group of young Japanese American women, all Nisei, limber up in a gymnasium in the Japanese section of Los Angeles, 1941. Within months the Unites States became involved in World War II, and Japanese Americans would be forced to relocate to internment camps. (AP Photo)

to increase women's workload in a society in which they could not own land or become naturalized; but their situation also improved because they did not live under the supervision of a mother-in-law (which was common practice in Japan) and they gained power in the family by contributing money.

Picture Brides

Picture brides experienced additional struggles. Often their husbands—whom they only knew from photos and letters because the men did not have the money to travel to Japan or feared being drafted—did not live up to prior expectations; in many cases, husbands did not match the photos they had sent or they could not provide their wives with the living standards that they had promised. For some picture brides, life with their husband and the daily hardship proved too disappointing, and they decided to run away. It was not uncommon to find pictures of and bounty offers for wives in Japanese-language newspapers, which functioned as a social control tool. Because the arrival of picture brides marked the shift of Japanese immigrants from temporary sojourners to a permanent community, anti-Japanese agitation increased in the United States. In 1921, the Japanese government stopped issuing passports to picture brides who tended to work outside of the home, which was seen as violating the Gentlemen's Agreement.

Nisei

Most Nisei, second-generation Japanese American, women were born between 1915 and 1940. The majority of them were raised bilingual and bicultural, which posed challenges. Despite the fact that they were American citizens, the Nisei were relocated to internment camps during World War II where they attended school in barracks. Camp conditions were harsh. But being in the camps freed Issei women from many day-to-day housewife responsibilities, which gave them the opportunity to engage in crafts or take classes. For the Nisei, internment eroded political and economic patriarchal elements as fathers were often unable to function as the head of household due to their foreigner status and language barriers.

During World War II, many young female Nisei volunteered for the Nisei Women's Army Corps and U.S. Cadet Nursing Corps. One-third of the first students allowed to leave camp for college were women. To afford school, many young women served as domestic workers in European American households. Despite some occupational mobility for them after the war, it proved generally hard for Japanese American women to find employment due to gender discrimination and racism against people of Japanese descent. In contrast to their mothers, most female Nisei chose their own husbands, and the vast majority married Nisei men. During the 1970s and 1980s, Nisei women became involved in the women's and redress movements and the Japanese American Citizen League and started to strive for more independence and political involvement. In 1964, Patsy Takemoto Mink (1927–2002) of Hawai'i became the first woman of color elected to Congress.

War Brides

Because of immense economic need after World War II, many young Japanese women started working on U.S. military bases. A shortage of young Japanese men of marriageable age and the prospect of an egalitarian relationship enticed thousands of Japanese women to marry U.S. servicemembers. Once these war brides, *sen'soo hanayome*, arrived in the United States, they often underwent a harsh adjustment period because of language barriers and being seen, by the wider American public, as submissive war trophies. War brides have a higher divorce rate than Issei and Nisei because they experienced more powerlessness due to a lack of resources and feelings of isolation.

Sansei and Yonsei

Third- and fourth-generation Japanese American women continue to cope with issues of identity, cultural values, and prejudice. Sansei and Yonsei are becoming more likely to marry outside their own community. Like women in other demographic groups, they are reaching higher corporate and political levels than ever before. Famously, Kristi Yamaguchi (1971–), a Yonsei, received international attention when she won an Olympic gold medal in figure skating in 1992.

See also: Japanese American Women in the 1930s; Picture Brides/Shashin Hanayome

Further Reading

Glenn, Evelyn Nakano. *Issei, Nisei, War Bride. Three Generations of Japanese American Women in Domestic Service*. Philadelphia: Temple University Press, 1986.

Matsumoto, Valerie. "Japanese American Women during World War II." In *Unequal Sisters. A Multicultural Reader in US Women's History*, edited by Vicki L. Ruiz and Ellen Carol DuBois, 3rd ed., 478–491. New York: Routledge, 2000.

Nakano, Mei T. *Japanese American Women. Three Generations 1890–1990*. Berkeley, CA: Mina Press, 1990.

Ina C. Seethaler

JAPANESE AMERICAN WOMEN IN THE 1930s

During the 1930s, young Japanese American women played significant roles as workers, ethnic community representatives, and cultural agents. Drawing on the values and customs of their immigrant parents, elements of mainstream American society, and the practices of friends and neighbors from other racial-ethnic groups, Nisei (U.S.-born second-generation) women helped to shape ethnic culture. In the difficult years of the Great Depression, the work of girls as well as boys was important to the family economy, whether tending crops on a farm or sweeping a hardware store. Facing racial barriers to participation in extracurricular activities in some districts, Nisei girls formed their own network of lively organizations, particularly in urban areas. Through membership in clubs affiliated with churches, such as the Young Women's Christian Association (YWCA), and the Girl Scouts USA, they gained access to recreation and leadership training, provided community service, and socialized with young men. Called upon to wear kimonos and perform traditional Japanese songs and dance at civic events, Nisei girls also served as highly visible representatives of the ethnic community.

Family Formation and the Emergence of the Nisei

Japanese American youths were the largest group of second-generation Asian Americans in the prewar period. In Hawai'i, families grew up on the sugarcane plantations where Japanese men and women had been recruited as an early part of the labor force. In the continental United States, Japanese American settlements primarily took shape in the West, where many Issei (first-generation immigrants) engaged in farming or urban small business. The Gentlemen's Agreement implemented in 1908 between the United States and Japan ended the immigration of Japanese laborers, but a loophole permitted the entry of family members of Japanese already residing in the United States. By the time the Immigration Act of 1924 stopped most Asian immigration to the United States, many Japanese women had arrived: some rejoined husbands who had immigrated earlier, some accompanied men who had returned to Japan to marry, and others came as picture brides to meet new spouses. As families formed, the numbers of Nisei grew steadily. They quickly became the majority in the Japanese American population—of the approximately 120,000 Japanese immigrants and their children incarcerated during World War II, two-thirds were U.S. citizens by birth.

The majority of the Nisei were born between 1910 and 1940; because of their wide age range and the diversity of their experiences in different rural and urban areas, it is hard to generalize about them. Prewar interracial relations varied by neighborhood and region. However, Japanese Americans, like many Asian Americans and people of color, faced prejudice and discrimination in the workforce, housing, recreational facilities, and businesses such as restaurants and theaters.

The Issei valued education and encouraged their children to be disciplined, hard-working students. Besides attending public school, many Nisei were sent to Japanese school to gain grounding in Japanese language and culture. Girls were taught domestic skills such as sewing and knitting, and, when families could afford lessons, were expected to learn Japanese cultural arts such as odori (traditional dance) and ikebana (flower arranging).

The second generation grew up integrating the values and holidays of their Issei parents with mainstream customs as well as other ethnic cultural practices of friends and neighbors. Indeed, many families—whether Buddhist or Christian—not only celebrate New Year's with special foods but also now observe Christmas and Thanksgiving. Like their non–Japanese American peers, the Nisei played baseball and basketball, listened to music on the radio, enjoyed movies, and learned to waltz and foxtrot.

Daughters and sons contributed significantly to the family economy, whether living on a farm or in the city. Rural children hoed, irrigated, and picked crops, nailed boxes, and tended farm animals. Their city peers helped clean and run small family businesses such as tofu shops, grocery stores, and restaurants. Girls were responsible for domestic duties, from which their brothers were usually exempt, supervising younger siblings and doing household chores such as ironing, cooking, and cleaning. However, urban Nisei were more likely than their rural cousins to have free time and access to leisure pursuits.

Constructing a Nisei Social World

In the early 20th century, shifting gender dynamics, embodied by the "New Woman," spurred debate about appropriate roles for women in ethnic enclaves as well as in the larger society. Although remaining dutiful economic contributors to their families, many young Nisei women sought more freedom to socialize with their peers and to choose their own spouse. Urban Japanese American daughters wore flapper fashions, applied makeup, and learned to jitterbug. Like their Chinese American and Chicana sisters, they tried to negotiate between mainstream ideas of modernity and the values of the immigrant community. Their participation in popular culture was complicated not only by racial barriers and economic limitations during the Great Depression, but also by Issei parents' expectations regarding proper female behavior. Because daughters' chaste reputations were markers of families' standing in the ethnic community, girls were subject to greater surveillance and control than their brothers.

In the face of such pressures, many of the second generation formed peer networks for camaraderie and recreation.

Girls' clubs proliferated throughout the 1920s and 1930s, especially in cities like Seattle, San Francisco, and Los Angeles. Often affiliated with Buddhist and Christian churches, or with organizations such as the Girl Scouts USA, these groups constituted a parent-approved vehicle for youth activities. Clubs offered girls opportunities to compete in team sports, to hear educational speakers, to develop leadership skills, to learn handicrafts, to organize parties, and to socialize with Nisei boys. They also provided community service through fund-raising and other charitable efforts. Excluded from college fraternities and sororities, Nisei students established their own organizations, including Chi Alpha Delta, the first Asian American sorority, founded at the University of California, Los Angeles, in 1929. The wide array of Japanese American youth club activities filled the pages of the English-language sections of newspapers such as the Shin Sekai in San Francisco and the Rafu Shimpo in Los Angeles.

Through their clubs, city girls both reinforced and pushed gender-role boundaries. For example, in joint activities with Nisei boys' clubs, girls were often responsible for bringing the refreshments for hikes and socials; this underscored expectations of young women's domestic role. By organizing club socials and engaging in couples dancing, Japanese American women expanded the sphere of activities their immigrant parents deemed acceptable for young females.

Japanese American women also took active roles in prewar artistic and literary endeavors. Writers such as Chiye Mori, Mary Oyama Mittwer, Toyo Suyemoto, and Hisaye Yamamoto participated in a Nisei literary movement, submitting poetry, fiction, and essays to the ethnic press. Gyo Fujikawa began a long, successful career as a painter and children's book illustrator, including a stint working for the Disney Studios. Despite the obstacles faced by women of color seeking to enter the performing arts and entertainment industry, a few Nisei persevered, such as dancer Dorothy Takahashi Toy.

In the prewar period, young Nisei women often served as representatives of the Japanese American community, dancing in kimonos and singing Japanese songs. Girls were called upon to perform at celebrations in the ethnic community, at school festivals, and in parades and other civic events. Issei parents took pride in their daughters' accomplishments in ethnic cultural arts. Some Nisei enjoyed ethnic-cultural performance, but others felt uncomfortable about a role that, in the view of mainstream society, could seem to present them as foreign. By the eve of World War II, this role had grown increasingly complicated.

Courtship and Marriage

Like youths across the nation, second-generation Japanese Americans were influenced by mainstream films, music, magazines, and radio programs. Notions of romantic love, purveyed on the silver screen by stars like Clark Gable and Carole Lombard, colored their dreams. As courtship moved from the private to the public sphere in the United States, the urban Nisei were more likely to participate in peer socializing and dating, with dancing becoming highly popular.

Competing ideals of womanhood became particularly visible in the tensions regarding romance and marriage. Like their mothers, Nisei women expected that their future would revolve around marriage and family, but their notions of marriage differed from those of their parents. The Issei's marital partnerships had been arranged by their families; the Nisei, however, wanted to choose their own spouses and expected a union based on romantic love. Throughout the 1930s, the second generation increasingly moved away from arranged marriages. Mindful of the endogamous preferences of the ethnic community as well as of the antimiscegenation laws applying to people of Asian descent in California and 13 other states, most expected to marry other Japanese Americans.

Of necessity, most Nisei women also expected their futures to include entering the workforce. The older Nisei who came of age during the Great Depression faced limited opportunities and racial discrimination. A tiny minority of women succeeded in becoming professionals, such as doctors and nurses, often serving an ethnic clientele. Others vied for positions as secretaries and clerks within the Japanese American community, or continued working in family businesses. According to sociologist Evelyn Nakano Glenn (1986), agricultural labor and domestic service were the largest arenas of work for Issei and Nisei women during the prewar period. Given the dearth of choices, a small number set their sights on Japan, where they hoped to utilize their language skills to find positions.

During the World War II uprooting and incarceration, Issei and Nisei women and men in the western United States endured enormous losses and hardship. Young women as well as men left the camps as soon as possible; barred from returning to the Western Defense Zone until after the war, they sought education and jobs in the East and Midwest. Working as domestic servants and factory operatives, they continued to play a role in the family economy as much as their circumstances permitted. Their labor and organizational experience would prove valuable in rebuilding postwar communities, as many Japanese Americans returned to the U.S. West. In the 1970s and 1980s women's organizational skills would also help fuel the Japanese American movement for World War II redress.

See also: Japanese American History before 1945; Japanese American Women

Further Reading

Glenn, Evelyn Nakano. *Issei, Nisei, War Bride: Three Generations of Japanese American Women in Domestic Service*. Philadelphia: Temple University Press, 1986.

Lim, Shirley Jennifer. *A Feeling of Belonging: Asian American Women's Public Culture, 1930–1960*. New York: New York University Press, 2006.

Nakano, Mei. *Japanese American Women, Three Generations, 1890–1990*. Berkeley, CA: Mina Press, 1990.

Tamura, Eileen. *Americanization, Acculturation, and Ethnic Identity: The Nisei Generation in Hawaii*. Urbana and Chicago: University of Illinois Press, 1994.

Yoo, David. *Growing Up Nisei: Race, Generation, and Culture among Japanese Americans of California, 1924–49*. Urbana: University of Illinois Press, 2000.

Valerie J. Matsumoto

JAPANESE IMMIGRATION TO HAWAI'I

Located in the middle of the Pacific Ocean between the East and the West, Hawai'i had shared a special connection to Japan even prior to the 19th century. Before British explorer Capt. James Cook and his crew landed in Kealakekua Bay on Hawai'i Island in 1778, travelers from the East, rumored to be Japanese, were believed to have arrived in the Islands hundreds of years earlier. These reputed Japanese visitors came not as migrants or adventurers, but rather as drifters, arriving on boats blown off course within the vast expanse of the Pacific. Those who did not perish at sea were picked up by foreign sailing vessels or wrecked on the Hawai'ian archipelago.

Cook's arrival initiated changes that forever altered traditional ways of life. Foreigners who came to Hawai'i transformed the self-sustaining indigenous economy with the development of sandalwood trade, then whaling, and finally sugar cane production. During the American Civil War, the price of sugar increased eightfold, making sugar production extremely profitable. The demand for sugar, which continued even after the end of the war, established the prestige of several island families, including the Baldwins, Castles, Cookes, Rices, and Wilcoxes. However, as the plantations flourished, the need for labor increased given its short supply. Measles, small pox, and venereal disease had significantly reduced the indigenous population, and, by 1860, only approximately 22 percent (66,984) of the original 1778 Hawai'ian population remained. The number of native Hawai'ians available to work as laborers would have been insufficient even if they had been inclined to work in the sugar industry, which they were not.

After unsuccessful experiences with Chinese workers, planters tried to lure Japanese overseas as early as the closing years of the Tokugawa period. During the last days of the civil war that marked the end of the Tokugawa shogunate and the establishment of the new Meiji government, Japanese officials received several requests from foreigners to send Japanese workers abroad. These included overtures made by the Hawai'ian Foreign Ministry to the Japanese government. After a series of diplomatic negotiations, Eugene Van Reed, the Hawai'ian representative in Tokyo, received permission in 1868 to send a group of Japanese to work on sugar plantations in Hawai'i. Japanese were subsequently recruited off the streets of Yokohama to work on the plantations in Hawai'i. In 1868, or Meiji One, the British ship *Scioto* set sail out of Yokohama under Van Reed's order on May 17. On board were 153 Japanese, including 146 men, 5 women, and 2 teenagers. These first-year men, called *Gannenmono*, represented an initial effort to determine the feasibility of further Japanese labor migration. However, predictions for Japanese tractability proved unfounded as Japanese laborers quickly became disillusioned with plantation work. Many quit working in the cane fields and headed to Honolulu in search of other employment. Complaints about their treatment and letters of appeal for help soon reached Japan and officials recalled the *Gannenmono* from Hawai'i.

This 1868 episode of the *Gannenmono* forestalled large-scale Japanese migration for the next 17 years. However, the diplomatic relationship between the Kingdom of Hawai'i and Japan began to improve after the signing of the Treaty of Commerce and Friendship in 1871. Moreover, the demand for large-scale migration increased after the Hawai'ian government successfully negotiated the Reciprocity Treaty with the United States. Beginning in 1876, 15 Hawai'ian products, including sugar, entered American markets duty-free. With sugar production a booming industry, Hawai'ian sugar planters were determined to expand the amount of acreage under cultivation. Workers were needed for this growing industry, a fact recognized by plantation owners closely aligned with government officials. Between 1864 and 1886, sugar planters incurred over $850,000 in expenditures and the Hawai'ian government spent over $1 million to attract foreign workers. Despite the failure of the *Gannenmono* in 1868, sugar planters continued to look to Japan as a source for potential plantation workers, assisted by the Hawai'ian government.

During the 1880s, Hawai'ian officials made three important visits to Japan. The reigning monarch of the Hawai'ian Kingdom, King Kalākaua, visited Japan in 1881 during a trip around the world. Although Kalākaua mentioned the need for Japanese workers in Hawai'i, the Japanese government did not take any action at this time. The following year a diplomatic mission headed by John M. Kapena arrived in Tokyo with a specific labor proposal for Japanese authorities, and finally in 1884 government representative Col. Curtis Piehu Iaukea presented to Japanese officials another set of proposals for the resumption of Japanese migration to Hawai'i. As a result of these collective efforts, the Japanese government decided to send Japanese to Hawai'i on a regular basis, if under strict government supervision. The first group was composed of 676 males, 150 females, and 110 children, for a total of 936 migrants sent to Hawai'i.

This period of government-sponsored migration lasted from 1885 to 1894, and 26 ships carrying Japanese migrants landed in Honolulu, bringing approximately 29,000 Japanese to Hawai'i's shores. The passage of the Organic Act in 1900 that ended labor contracts, however, dramatically opened up options for Japanese who were no longer bound to labor on the plantations. Many departed to become shopkeepers, salespersons, carpenters, and general laborers in the various villages and towns. By 1907, over 40,000 had left for employment on the U.S. mainland where there was a labor shortage and the promise of higher wages. During this period, however, white efforts to control the Japanese on the plantations similarly intensified. The signing of the 1907 Gentlemen's Agreement severely limited the mobility of Japanese workers who were now forced either to accept contract terms or face unemployment. Anti-Japanese sentiment culminated in the 1924 Exclusion Act that effectively banned Japanese migration to Hawai'i and the United States and prohibited travel to America. These events reflected growing concerns of economic and political leaders in Hawai'i and federal officials in Washington to control the Japanese threat that stretched across the Pacific to seize control of the territory.

See also: Hawai'ian Sugar Plantations; Japanese American History before 1945; Japanese Immigration to Latin/South America; Japanese Immigration to Peru

Further Reading

Hazama, Dorothy Ochiai, and Jane Okamoto Komeiji. *Okage Sama De: The Japanese in Hawai'i 1885–1985.* Honolulu: Bess Press, 1986.
Okahata, James H. ed. *A History of the Japanese in Hawaii.* Honolulu: The United Japanese Society of Hawaii, 1971.

Kelli Y. Nakamura

JAPANESE IMMIGRATION TO LATIN/SOUTH AMERICA

The migration of Japanese to Latin America began in the 16th century when Spain laid claims to territory both in the Western Hemisphere and in East Asia. Japanese–Latin American relations were established between 1542 and 1592, a period during which Spain created transport and trade routes between Manila in the Philippines, China, and Japan. By the early 17th century, there were thousands of Japanese in Manila and many served as crew members on Spanish galleons traveling between holdings on both shores of the Pacific Ocean. After 1592, Japanese traders under the Tokugawa government hoped to initiate business connections in Latin America, but strict mercantilist policies instituted by the Spanish crown created barriers to commerce. In addition, Spanish efforts to spread Catholicism through evangelization among Asians were rejected by the Japanese, further slowing intercultural relations. Progress in relations that might have expanded Japanese immigration into Latin America ended when Japan closed its doors to Europeans, except for Dutch traders, from the mid-17th century to the mid-19th century.

The opening of Japan to the West in the 1850s and the Meiji Restoration in 1868 paved the way for more interaction between Latin America and Japan. By this time, Latin American nations had become independent from the Spanish and Portuguese empires and were investing in their own systems of economic development. With this came the need for labor. As the African slave trade came to an end, Latin American nations turned to Asia as a source of labor. Latin American landowners and businesspersons advertised employment opportunities, and immigration, including that from Japan, began. Many 19th-century Asian migrants were destined for the United States. However, when Chinese immigration into the United States was severely restricted by the Chinese Exclusion Act of 1882, Japanese workers saw an increase in opportunities there. Once the trend of Japanese migration to the Americas began, many looked beyond the United States to Latin America.

An initial wave of Japanese immigrants entered Mexico and Peru between 1885 and 1912, as part of the first phase of migration. The Japanese arriving in this period were largely agricultural laborers. They had been promised a good life, adequate wages, and a temperate climate with far milder winters than those they experienced in Japan. However, the treatment of laborers was harsh, contracts were often violated, and many did not survive. The experiences of surviving Japanese immigrants in Mexico and Peru differed in a number of ways. First, those who did survive in Mexico tended to assimilate better and integrate more fully into Mexican society. This was possible because their numbers were smaller, they dispersed more readily, and they often married Mexican nationals. Japanese living in Peru, however, largely separated themselves from the rest of Peruvian society.

Migration patterns from Japan to Latin America transitioned into a second phase between 1912 and 1926, a period noted for significant economic expansion in the region and immigration expansion that accompanied it. This growth in Japanese migration occurred for a number of reasons. First, Japanese leaders were experiencing the long-term effects of the Gentlemen's Agreement between the United States and Japan in 1907, which had significantly restricted Japanese immigration there. Latin American countries provided alternative opportunities. In addition, Japan was experiencing a surge in population growth, with inadequate employment opportunities at home. Though Japan was modernizing rapidly, the standard of living for the rural population and labor class did not increase significantly. As a result, large sectors of the Japanese population could not fully participate in or benefit from the economy. On the other hand, World War I expanded Latin American economies, which supplied raw materials, some finished products, and food to belligerent nations in Europe, and labor demands and economic opportunities were flourishing there. In this phase, the majority of immigrants from Japan traveled to Peru and Brazil. Migration policies and practices in Spanish America differed from those in Brazil, which gradually offered more incentives for Japanese migration. Brazilian and Japanese interests inspired capital investment and substantial subsidization. Japanese laborers were needed on Brazil's coffee plantations, but migrants were also offered opportunities in colonization. Brazil had an abundance of land and resources, and subsidies helped Japanese begin their own enterprises there.

Japanese migration to Latin America peaked during the third phase, between 1926 and the early 1930s. Though economic opportunities declined with the onset of the Great Depression, Japanese emigration policies continued to encourage migration as a means to ease population pressures and mass unemployment, which continued. The Overseas Emigration Societies Act of 1927 and the founding of the Kobe Emigration Center in 1927 provided support for Japanese seeking employment abroad, as well as the purchase of land in other countries for the purpose of establishing farms. In addition, the Overseas Development Company provided direct financial assistance for the cost of travel. Associations for Japanese immigrants were founded in Latin American countries, as well. They facilitated settlement with education, housing, and employment assistance. Although Japanese were encouraged to assimilate into Latin American society in order to offset racism and racist attacks, associations often created circumstances that kept them connected to one another. Familial relationships and continued experiences in Latin America also contributed to expanding migration. Patterns of chain migration, with one family member following another, aided in building communities and increasing numbers of newcomers, as well as children born through Japanese marriage.

Although Japanese immigrants initially intended to serve as plantation laborers for a limited period of time before returning home (often under contract), many fled to urban areas and established businesses. This was true especially for the Japanese living in Peru. They tended to form close-knit communities in ways that kept them separate from Peruvian nationals, displaying a strong work ethic and support of newcomers from Japan with financial support and education assistance. They were also able, as were many Japanese living in other Latin American countries, to save enough to send remittances to their family members in Japan. The success of Japanese immigrants and descendants living in Peru, in addition to their internalization and segregation, added to suspicions, fears, and attacks based on race and discrimination.

Peru was not the only Latin American nation exhibiting tensions related to Japanese population during the 1930s. As Japan rose to military prominence and displayed imperialist behavior, concerns regarding Japanese residing throughout North and South America grew. The weakening of the economy during the Great Depression added to social and political conflict, and the Japanese became targeted in ways similar to the Jews living in Europe. These tensions fueled nationalism and the rise of new political factions with undertones of racial identity, which contributed to anti-Japanese sentiment. Migration of Japanese to the largest receiving countries in Latin America was heavily restricted (Brazil in 1934 and Peru in 1936) and prohibited completely following the Japanese attack on Pearl Harbor in 1941. Latin American nations allied themselves with the United States, and U.S. military bases were constructed in Brazil, Peru, Panama, and other Latin American countries. Thousands of Japanese and their descendants were deported to the United States to live in internment camps. In addition, their businesses and land were confiscated and financial assets frozen. Many met with physical attacks. By this time, there were approximately 235,000 Japanese living in Latin America, including nearly 190,000 in Brazil. The majority of Japanese immigrants had arrived in Brazil between 1908 and 1941. The Mexican government under President Lazaro Cardenas refused to cooperate with the United States in military expansion and the deportation of Japanese.

Restrictions against the Japanese in Brazil and Peru during the Great Depression and World War II caused many to flee to other countries of South

America, including Paraguay and Bolivia. The reestablishment of relations following the war initiated Japanese immigration once again in 1951, but actual numbers were limited. The Japanese worked to rebuild their own country in the postwar years and, by the 1960s, were experiencing economic growth beneficial to Japan. Japanese employment opportunities increased, reducing the incentive for people to emigrate. Some 2,000 Japanese emigrated to Argentina and the Dominican Republic during the postwar years, with a comparative few to other Latin American countries. The majority of Japanese who did migrate were destined primarily for Brazil, and between 1952 and 1962 Brazil became home to nearly 50,000 new Japanese. Many of these migrants were from Okinawa, which had been devastated by war and was claimed for military base expansion by the United States. The United States encouraged Okinawans to leave for Brazil to facilitate the acquisition of land. Plans were also under way to transplant Japanese to Bolivia and Paraguay for the purpose of creating rural *colonias* there. The Japanese supported colonization efforts with land purchases, infrastructure development, and loans. There was some initial success in Brazil, but less in Bolivia and Paraguay.

By the early 1970s, Japanese migration to Latin America all but came to an end, and the vast majority of Japanese living there were now second and third generation. As such, they were considered more established in their countries and in their communities and began holding more prominent positions in business and politics. At the same time, Japan's population has been aging and declining, resulting in reverse migration patterns. The countries to which Japan sent migrants in the 1930s, including those in Latin America, are now sending migrants back to Japan to meet labor shortages. It is unlikely that significant portions of the Japanese Latin American population will relocate to Japan, as they have few cultural and traditional ties with Japanese natives. Through generations, they have become far more Latin American. In addition, there is no guarantee that their children would become Japanese citizens, as Japanese law does not guarantee citizenship to those born there.

See also: Hawai'ian Sugar Plantations; Japanese American History before 1945; Japanese Immigration to Hawai'i; Japanese Immigration to Peru

Further Reading

Baily, Samuel L., and Eduardo Jose Miguez, eds. *Mass Migration to Modern Latin America*. Wilmington, DE: Scholarly Resources, 2003.
Endo, Toake, *Exporting Japan: Politics of Emigration toward Latin America*. Urbana: University of Illinois, 2009.

Kathleen A. Tobin

Table 1 Japanese Remittances from Immigrants Residing in Latin America, 1937

Country	Yen
Brazil	1,730,372
Peru	911,134
Mexico	302,139
Argentina	199,557
Chile	18,023
Panama	11,815
Colombia	11,300
Cuba	8,769
Bolivia	1,939
Uruguay	1,380
Venezuela	750
Total	3,197,178

Source: Japan, Ministry of Foreign Affairs and Tigner, James L. "Japanese Immigration into Latin America: A Survey," *Journal of Interamerican Studies and World Affairs* 23, no. 4 (November 1981): 462.

Table 2 Japanese Migration to Latin America (Phases 1–3: Imperial Eras)

Country of Destination	Meiji (1898–1912)	Taisho (1913–1926)	Showa (1927–1941)	Total
Mexico	11,099	1,197	2,270	14,566
Panama	0	182	233	415
Cuba	4	419	249	672
Brazil	4,573	44,046	139,062	187,681
Peru	9,106	15,134	8,827	33,067
Argentina	22	1,321	4,055	5,398
Chile	135	189	174	498
Colombia	0	5	224	229
Bolivia	0	24	178	202
Venezuela	0	0	12	12
Uruguay	0	0	18	18
Paraguay	0	0	521	521
	24,939	62,517	155,823	243,279

Source: Gaimusho Ryoji Iiju-bu, *Waga kokumin no kaigai hatten: Iiju hyakunen no aymi* (Tokyo: Ministry of Foreign Affairs, 1971), 142–143. In *The Japanese in Latin America,* edited by Daniel M. Masterson and Sayaka Funada-Classen, 113. Urbana: University of Illinois Press, 2004.

JAPANESE IMMIGRATION TO PERU

Economic and agricultural development in Peru during the 19th century demanded an increased labor supply and inspired immigration from Asia, including Japan. Advertisements assured prospective migrants that Peru was a paradise with a temperate climate, no epidemics, rich farming soil, and an abundance of gold. The first Japanese immigrants served as contract laborers and arrived in Peru in 1899 to work on sugar plantations, permitted by way of Peruvian presidential decree. They were followed by 80 additional groups arriving between 1900 and 1923. Though married couples were encouraged to migrate, these early immigrants were primarily men—upward of 85 percent—who were promised wages higher than they could earn in their home country. The majority intended to return to Japan once they had earned sufficient money. In the plantation system, they met with harsh working conditions, severe punishment, and often violation of their labor contracts. Many went on strike and eventually fled the plantations in search of more rewarding work. A significant portion moved to urban areas and started businesses of their own.

Despite migration within Peru, the Japanese remained an essentially homogeneous group. Although they recognized differences among themselves, based primarily on the various Japanese regions from which they originated (most notably between the Okinawans and the Naichi-jin, or mainland Japanese), they were set apart in many ways from the rest of Peruvian society. Contract immigration ended in 1923; however, a family reunification policy was instituted and the flow of immigrants continued. Between 1924 and 1930, nearly 8,000 new Japanese immigrants arrived in Peru. Patterns of assistance emerged, with settled Japanese encouraging newcomers from their native villages and towns and aiding in language learning, education, employment, and association membership. Among the post-1924 migrants were Japanese women who intended to marry once they were in Peru. This differed significantly from early migration, when just over 230 women arrived in the 10-year span between 1899 and 1909. The increased presence of women among Japanese immigrants would facilitate population growth in Peru through the stabilizing forces of marriage and family and increased birth rates. At the same time, immigration continued, and, by the late 1970s, census findings showed there were 4,998 Japanese immigrant men and 5,650 Japanese immigrant women in Peru.

Many Japanese arrived in Peru before the late 1930s. Social and political reforms, as well as the rise of militarism, shaped Japanese relations with the rest of the world, and, though the country experienced economic growth, much of the Japanese population did not benefit from this strong economy and many left in search of better opportunities. Economic growth was slow in Peru during the global Depression of the 1930s, with little positive impact for the middle class. As a result, Japanese immigrants were blamed and racist anti-Japanese sentiment surged. They brought into and maintained within Peru a strong work ethic and group solidarity intent on achieving success, and native Peruvians accused them of monopolizing business and finance much in the same way Jews had been in other parts of the world during the same period.

The Japanese suffered discrimination under a Peruvian immigration law in 1936, which threatened the loss of citizenship to children whose births were not registered with the government, and a 1940 law, which threatened the loss of citizenship to those who left the country and attempted to return. Though the laws did not target Japanese explicitly, the group was nonetheless targeted. First, the Japanese population was a close-knit one, with customs, practices, and behaviors kept traditionally apart from the majority of Peruvian society. It was not uncommon for Japanese childbirth there to go unnoticed by the outside community. Second, although the majority of Japanese immigrants remained in Peru, their intention was to return to Japan or at least maintain close ties. They often sent their offspring to study there, which would have resulted in the loss of citizenship. Additional laws reflected the economic tensions of the Great Depression and restricted Japanese-owned businesses in a number of ways. One of the most blatant restrictions was the requirement that 80 percent of employees in all businesses be Peruvian.

Peru ended diplomatic relations with Japan during World War II, when it allied with the United States and Japan became an enemy nation. Japanese community and business leaders were blacklisted by the U.S. Embassy in Peru and approximately 1,800 Japanese were deported from Peru to U.S. internment camps. Japanese were deported from other countries in Latin America at this time for the same reason, but the proportion from Peru was greater. Japanese businesses in Peru were also appropriated and Japanese bank assets were frozen. Anti-Japanese practices in Peru led the population to integrate more into Peruvian society. The devastation of Japan in World War II prevented them from returning home, and the loss of businesses and financial assets in Peru forced them to begin their lives again.

Japanese migration to Peru began again in the late 1950s, but never reached the same levels as that before 1937. Among the most famous Japanese Peruvians was President Alberto Fujimori, the son of Japanese immigrants elected to office in 1990. Many Japanese refused to vote for him for fear of discrimination and retaliation if he performed poorly. His administration was not without controversy; however, he served until 2000.

See also: Hawai'ian Sugar Plantations; Japanese American History before 1945; Japanese Immigration to Hawai'i; Japanese Immigration to Latin/South America

Further Reading

Hirabayashi, Lane Ryo, Akemi Kikumura-Yano, and James A. Hirabayashi, eds. *New Worlds, New Lives: Globalization and People of Japanese Descent in the Americas and from Latin America in Japan*. Stanford, CA: Stanford University Press, 2002.

Masterson, Daniel M., and Sayaka Funada-Classen. *The Japanese in Latin America*. Urbana: University of Illinois Press, 2004.

Kathleen A. Tobin

KOOSKIA INTERNMENT CAMP

The Kooskia (pronounced KOOS-key) Internment Camp is an obscure and virtually forgotten World War II detention facility that was located in a remote area of north central Idaho, 30 miles from the town of Kooskia, and six miles east of the hamlet of Lowell, at Canyon Creek. The U.S. Immigration and Naturalization Service (INS) administered the Kooskia Internment Camp for the U.S. Department of Justice. Over time, the camp held some 265 men of Japanese ancestry who were termed "enemy aliens," even though most of them were long-time U.S. residents denied naturalization by racist U.S. laws.

Immediately following Japan's bombing of Pearl Harbor, Hawai'i, on December 7, 1941, numerous Japanese, German, and Italian aliens were arrested and detained on no specific grounds, without the due process guaranteed to them by the U.S. Constitution. They were sent to INS detention camps at Fort Missoula, Montana; Bismarck, North Dakota; and elsewhere. The INS camps were separate and distinct from the 10 major War Relocation Authority (WRA) camps, including Minidoka, at Hunt, in southern Idaho. The WRA camps are often called "internment camps" also, but that term for them is misleading; they should actually be called incarceration camps.

Although there were a number of INS-run Justice Department internment camps throughout the United States during World War II, the Kooskia Internment Camp was unique because it was the only camp of its kind in the United States. Its internees had volunteered to go there from other camps and received wages for their work. Besides the Japanese aliens, 24 male and three female Caucasian civilian employees; two male internee doctors, one Italian and one German; and one male Japanese American interpreter occupied the Kooskia Internment Camp at various times between May 1943, when the camp opened, and May 1945, when it closed. Whereas some of the internees held camp jobs, most of the men were construction workers for a portion of the Lewis-Clark Highway, the present Highway 12, between Lewiston, Idaho, and Missoula, Montana, parallel to the wild and scenic Lochsa River.

The Japanese internees at the Kooskia camp came from Alaska, California, Colorado, Connecticut, Florida, Hawai'i, Idaho, Illinois, Louisiana, Maryland,

Massachusetts, Minnesota, Montana, Nevada, New Jersey, New Mexico, New York, Ohio, Oregon, Pennsylvania, Texas, Utah, and Washington. Well-known internees at the Kooskia camp included Reverend Hozen Seki, founder of the New York Buddhist Church, and Toraichi Kono, former employee of Charlie Chaplin. The Kooskia Internment Camp also housed Japanese from Mexico, as well as other Japanese Latin Americans whom U.S. government agencies had kidnapped from Panama and Peru in collusion with the governments of those countries. "Digging in the documents" has produced INS, Forest Service, Border Patrol, and University of Idaho photographs and other material. These records, combined with internee and employee oral and written interviews, shed light on the internees' experiences, emphasizing the perspectives of the men detained at the Kooskia Internment Camp.

According to the terms of the Geneva Convention, a 1929 document specifying how prisoners of war should be treated, later extended to cover detainees, internees could not be forced to do this kind of work; therefore, they were all volunteers. Road workers were paid $55 or $65 per month, with a $10 deduction for special clothing, whereas camp workers, in the kitchen, laundry, and so on, received only 80 cents per day. Consequently, there were few volunteers for camp work. By early May 1943, 104 men from the Santa Fe Internment Camp had definitely committed to Kooskia and had solved the camp operation problem. After the men decided to distribute all the income equally, 25 of them agreed to perform the required kitchen, laundry, and other support tasks.

At first, the men appreciated their scenic surroundings and the lack of the usual barbed-wire fence. Soon, however, they realized that conditions were not as had been promised. The Kooskia camp superintendent was a former prison administrator, and the Kooskia internees especially resented his treatment of them as prisoners rather than internees. The disgruntled internees prepared a lengthy petition detailing their complaints. They requested eyeglasses, adequate clothing, wage adjustments, better dental care, and better emergency medical and first aid facilities, and they asked that they be treated as internees, not prisoners.

Because the volunteer internees were crucial to the success of the road-building project, the next few months saw many changes and improvements at the Kooskia camp in response to their petition. In mid-November 1943, morale was helped considerably when the superintendent resigned and was replaced with a career INS officer, who treated the internees with respect and compassion. Only one other group of internees, at the Lordsburg, New Mexico, Internment Camp, had earlier used their knowledge of the Geneva Convention to such great advantage. Following a successful strike, the Lordsburg camp superintendent was ultimately replaced. Some of the Kooskia internees had previously been at the Lordsburg camp so were doubtless aware of their rights under the Geneva Convention. Their successful petition allowed them to regain some control over their lives.

Because of the Geneva Convention requirements, the men at the Kooskia Internment Camp were better fed and housed than the Japanese Americans who were in the WRA incarceration camps. The Kooskia internees could even get beer. This especially made for some hard feelings with local Caucasian American residents, who, because of shortages, could not get beer themselves.

The Kooskia Internment Camp was a successful experiment in using Japanese alien internees as volunteers for building a portion of the Lewis-Clark Highway between Idaho and Montana. Besides helping a much-needed road progress toward completion, the project enabled the unconstitutionally incarcerated internees to again become productive members of society. Once their early grievances were resolved, they became exemplary workers, earning praise and respect from their Caucasian supervisors and from INS personnel. Although the work was tiring, difficult, and sometimes even dangerous, the men appreciated the opportunity to receive fair wages in exchange for performing useful work, thus allowing them to regain much of the self-respect that many of them must have lost through the humiliation of having been so unjustly interned.

See also: Commission on Wartime Relocation and Internment of Civilians; Internment, World War II; Manzanar Children's Village (1942–1945); World War II

Further Reading

University of Idaho Library Digital Collections. "Kooskia Internment Camp Scrapbook." http://contentdm.lib.uidaho.edu/cdm4/browse.php?CISOROOT=/spec_kic. Accessed March 29, 2010.

Wegars, Priscilla. *Imprisoned in Paradise: Japanese Internee Road Workers at the Kooskia Internment Camp*. Moscow, ID: Asian American Comparative Collection, University of Idaho, 2010.

Wegars, Priscilla. "Japanese and Japanese Latin Americans at Idaho's Kooskia Internment Camp." In *Guilt by Association: Essays on Japanese Settlement, Internment, and Relocation in the Rocky Mountain West*, edited by Mike Mackey, 145–183. Powell, WY: Western History Publications, 2001.

Priscilla Wegars

MANZANAR CHILDREN'S VILLAGE (1942–1945)

The Manzanar Children's Village is part of the Japanese American internment story but told from the viewpoint of individuals who were a part of a camp inside a camp. The Children's Village cared for children who were interned without their families, and they spent the duration of the war under the care of

Preschool children walk home to their barracks after school at Manzanar Relocation Center in California. While not well-known in the Manzanar Internment narrative, there were both orphans and lone children kept in a "Children's Village" in the camp. (National Park Service)

trained staff. This is a different experience than what is most frequently told as the internment history, which is told as a family narrative. Much of the remaining historical record of the Children's Village exists as oral history interviews, gathered from the California State University Fullerton's Oral History Program archives.

Japanese American Internment Camps

The Japanese American internment during World War II is arguably one of the worst infringements on civil liberties in the history of the United States since the enslavement of African Americans. President Franklin D. Roosevelt issued Executive Order 9066 on February 19, 1942, giving the military the power to imprison roughly 120,000 Japanese Americans during World War II, two-thirds of whom were American citizens, and none who were guilty of any crimes besides being of Japanese descent. Most Japanese Americans lived along the West Coast where they had established farms, businesses, and other community organizations. Japanese Americans residing in the military zone were considered threats and relocated to one of 10 concentration camps scattered across the United States for the duration of the war. Of the 10 Japanese internment camps during World War II, only one of them had an orphanage for Japanese American children.

Orphanages in the Japanese American Community

At the time World War II broke out, there were three orphanages in existence that cared for children of Japanese descent as well as mixed race Japanese children. These orphanages served the needs of the Japanese American communities in Los Angeles (the Shonien and Maryknoll Catholic Home) and in San Francisco (the Salvation Army Children's Home). Both the Shonien and the Salvation Army were built by Issei who had converted to Christianity and had a passion for improving social services in the Japanese American community. As the Japanese American community became more established in the United States, their needs for social services increased.

Masasuke Kobayashi was born in Japan in 1883 and migrated to San Francisco in 1902. He was involved with the YMCA and was baptized as a Presbyterian in Ogden, Utah. Kobayashi returned to Japan in 1918 and joined the Japanese Salvation Army, where he became a major. He obtained donations for a home for "helpless Japanese girls" in Japan, and also worked to build the Salvation Army Children's Home in San Francisco; he received donations from many sources, namely the Issei in the community and even the Japanese emperor.

The founder of the Shonien, Rokuichi Kusumoto, was born in Beppu, Japan, in 1873. Prior to coming to the United States in 1908, he worked in Osaka as the director of education at the Episcopal Benevolent Children's Home. In 1912, he came to Los Angeles and was involved in social welfare activities; he worked with the community to organize the Japanese Humane Society to protect young women. Shortly thereafter he founded the Shonien, the first Japanese children's home and day care center in Los Angeles.

The Shonien, the Salvation Army Children's Home, and the Maryknoll Catholic Home served the needs of the Japanese American community prior to internment. The circumstances by which the children came to the orphanages before the internment, and to Manzanar after internment, vary widely. It is thought by some of the former residents and staff that the Manzanar Children's Village was not an orphanage but a village full of children, because not all of the children who lived there during the internment were orphans. By the 1940s, there was a rise in the number of children's homes because of economic reasons, parental illness, and death. For some of the children, they lost one or both of their parents to diseases like tuberculosis, polio, or mental illness, some died because of childbirth or suicide. For others, their single mothers or single fathers simply did not have the economic means to support their children, or they had gone to Japan and could not return to the United States because of the war. For others their parents worked full-time, and rather than be placed for adoption, these children were put in the temporary guardianship of the children's home staff and would later be cared for by the surviving parent when economic situations improved. At the time, many Japanese Americans in the United States did not have large extended families or grandparents to rely on to care for their minor-aged children. The children's homes were the best alternative for these struggling families.

After Executive Order 9066, the Japanese Americans residing on the West Coast made preparations for relocation. With great dignity, the Japanese American community arrived on time at the relocation meeting points dressed in their best clothing with the exact number of suitcases and required items, and boarded the trains or buses to their destination. Included in the logistics for relocation were the three orphanages. The War Relocation Authority (WRA) appointed Henry and Lillian Matsumoto as the superintendent and assistant superintendent of the Children's Village. They had both received graduate education in business and social welfare, respectively, and had worked at the Shonien with Rokuichi Kusumoto. Before their relocation to Manzanar, the State of California Department of Welfare had recommended to the WRA that the Matsumotos be in charge of the children when they arrived at camp.

The Staff at the Children's Village

The Matsumotos were aware that they would have to relocate the orphanage to the internment camps and were able to go to Manzanar before moving to make suggestions about the Children's Village facilities. The layout was slightly different than the other housing areas because of the recommendations, such as having indoor toilets, prior to construction. One difference between the Children's Village and the other barracks housing area at Manzanar was that there was a grassy lawn and a gazebo in front of the Children's Village.

This made their arrival at Manzanar on June 23, 1942, much later than many of the other families. The Matsumotos and other staff members of the Children's Village were in a unique position because they chose to work at the village and live there rather than be private citizens living in their own barracks. In addition to the Matsumotos, many of the staff at the Children's Village were Nisei, second-generation Japanese Americans, because one generation had passed after the Issei founded the orphanages. Most of the staff were already working for the Shonien and just directly transferred with the children to Manzanar. Rather than enter the camps with their families, all of the staff continued their jobs from the Shonien and relocated as staff members of the Children's Village. In addition, three staff members from the Salvation Army Home worked at the Children's Village. The staff of the Children's Village worked under the Matsumotos, whose supervisors were Margaret D'Ille, the director of Community Affairs, and Ralph Merritt, the director of the Manzanar Relocation Center. It is most certain that the staff members had a great impact on the daily care and supervision of the children.

Many Children's Village former residents recalled Sohei Hohri as one of the most memorable staff members. Hohri had lived in the Shonien during the 1930s as a child when both of his parents had contracted tuberculosis and were placed in a sanitarium. After they recovered, he and his siblings were reunited with his parents. When he was in high school he relocated with his family to Manzanar and did odd jobs. At Manzanar, he was hired by the Matsumotos to work at the Children's Village. Many of the former residents recall his special talent as a storyteller at the Children's Village. The stories he told were from *Les Miserables* about the characters Jean Valjean and Cosette, as well as Homer and stories from the *Odyssey*. Hohri recalled that there was very little entertainment at Manzanar, with the exception of the radio after five o'clock in the evening; so when he told the stories, the children listened intently with their eyes and mouths open.

The sudden change to a structured institutional life behind barbed wire was one of the most difficult adjustments for the Japanese American internees. However, in the case of most of the children who came to Manzanar from the orphanages, they were already exposed to and familiar with institutionalized life, where they had a schedule, and rules for living were enforced without question. According to Lillian Matsumoto, the children from the Shonien were much younger, whereas the children from the Salvation Army Home were slightly older, and many of them were teenagers when they came to Manzanar. Twenty-four were from the Shonien, and 19 were from Salvation Army Orphanage.

The Internment from Their Eyes

The children ranged from infants and toddlers to 18 years old, and certainly their experiences of Manzanar varied greatly. Prior to departure, the children did not have to prepare for the move or pack their own clothes or belongings because many of them were unable to do so as children. Children's Village residents were unaware of the politics behind the internment at the time, because most of them were too young to understand. Many had few belongings and did not have property to lose. As did other internees, the residents of the Children's Village had to sleep in the barracks on straw bedding that was placed on top of cots. There was no privacy: no doors on the toilets or showers, and there were many beds lined up in a large room. The barracks were divided by age: the infants, younger boys, older boys, younger girls, older girls, and the staff. Like many Japanese Americans, this was the first time that they were around a concentration of primarily Japanese Americans. The children were in an environment where they could play with many other children. The former residents of the Children's Village recalled playing with children from private families, but those children rarely went to the Children's Village to play.

They attended school at Manzanar outside of the Children's Village with students from private families; after school, they had to return straight home to the Children's Village. They already had exposure to living in an institution with a regimented schedule, so when they were interned, the pace of life was a routine similar to the one they had before: they had to get up at a certain time, do chores in the morning, eat breakfast, go to school, and return home. They all had chores to complete, and the older children mainly helped with the laundry. Their schedules were structured by time and enforced with rules.

There were several rules about eating that stood out for many of the residents. One of the rules of the Children's Village, which was different from the experience of many of the other internees, was that all residents of the Children's Village had to have their meals together in the Village dining room. Other Japanese Americans in the camps did not have this rule, and during mealtimes at the mess halls, many families ate separately where the children would eat together with their friends away from their parents and families. Many interned families discuss the overall breakdown of the nuclear family within the Japanese American community because they did not eat together.

Another rule for the Children's Village was that they had to eat all of their food. They had to eat everything that was on their plate before they could leave the table, even if they were full. In the oral histories of Children's Village residents, they frequently mentioned that the quality of the food at the Children's Village was better than the other blocks at Manzanar. This difference had to do with the fact that they had a different cook than the other blocks, namely the chef from Clifton's Cafeteria in Los Angeles.

The Manzanar Children's Village was home to a little over 100 children both Japanese American and multiracial Japanese American during the course of the World War II internment. Although the Children's Village itself was ephemeral, the influences of the staff left a solid foundation for the residents so they could get on with their lives after their release from the internment camps.

See also: Commission on Wartime Relocation and Internment of Civilians; Executive Order 9066; Internment, World War II; Kooskia Internment Camp

Further Reading

Irwin, Catherine. "Twice Orphaned: Voices from the Children's Village of Manzanar." Fullerton: California State University, 2008.

Nobe, Lisa. "The Children's Village at Manzanar: The World War II Eviction and Detention of Japanese American Orphans." *Journal of the West* 38 (1999): 65–71.

Whitney, Helen. "Care of Homeless Children of Japanese Ancestry during Evacuation and Relocation." MSW thesis, School of Social Welfare, University of California, Berkeley, 1948.

Lily Anne Yumi Welty

MANZANAR RIOT (1942)

The Manzanar "Riot" or "Resistance" occurred on December 5–6, 1942, when Japanese Americans prisoners incarcerated at the Manzanar War Relocation camp openly resisted the policies of the War Relocation Authority (WRA). This violence was a culmination of an intergenerational struggle predating incarceration. After Pearl Harbor, in an attempt to curry favor with authorities and secure power, Nisei (second generation) members of the Los Angeles branch of the Japanese American Citizens League (JACL) began reporting to federal agents on alleged activities in the camp. During incarceration, some felt deeply betrayed by the JACL calling them *inu* (literally translated as dog). On the night of December 5, 1942, six masked assailants attacked Fred Tayama, a JACL leader, in his barracks sending him to the hospital. The next morning, the WRA arrested Hawai'ian Kibei (Nisei educated in Japan), Harry Ueno, who was perceived as a dissident because of early challenges to WRA policies. He organized kitchen workers into the Mess Hall Union to protect their rights and accused Assistant Project Director Ned Campbell of stealing rationed sugar and meat from Japanese inmates to sell on the black market. Despite the lack of physical evidence or proof of involvement, Ueno was removed from Manzanar and jailed in nearby Independence, California.

Ueno was respected for his stance of fighting for prisoners' rights. His arrest and removal sparked a demonstration of an estimated 2,000 to 4,000 prisoners demanding Project Director Ralph Merritt release him or at least give him a fair trial at the Manzanar Center—Merritt agreed to the trial. Militant Japanese prisoners then staged a second rally later that day when Ueno returned to the camp reading a death list of *inus* and making several additional demands. From this rally, two groups with separate goals formed, one to release Ueno from the Manzanar jail and the second to kill Tayama at the hospital. Drs. Morris Little and James Goto saved Tayama's life by hiding him. Ueno refused to leave his cell until Merritt released him.

As the situation deteriorated, Merritt and Capt. Martyn Hall ordered the army to launch tear gas on the unarmed Japanese prisoners. As they dispersed, one MP opened fire on the crowd and killed two Nisei bystanders and injured a dozen; all but one were shot in the back or the side, indicating the victims were moving away from the shooter. Capt. Hall decreed martial law throughout the center. All forms of communication were censored and the army imposed a curfew. Troops remained in the camp until after Christmas. Consequently, Fred Tayama and 64 others, predominantly members of the JACL, were transferred to Death Valley National Monument before attaining indefinite leaves. Numerous Issei and Kibei, including Harry Ueno, were arrested by the military police and sent to a Civilian Conservation Corps camp near

Moab, Utah. WRA officials attempted to downplay this "incident" by blaming a handful of dissidents. The national press misinformed the American public that the riots were Japanese Americans celebrating the anniversary the Pearl Harbor attack.

The Manzanar riot and the Poston strike were the first demonstrations of Japanese American resistance to WRA. These demonstrations eventually led to the controversial "loyalty questionnaire" and later the Tule Lake Segregation Center for those "disloyal" and "unpatriotic" prisoners, including Harry Ueno.

See also: Commission on Wartime Relocation and Internment of Civilians; Executive Order 9066; Internment, World War II; Kooskia Internment Camp; Manzanar Children's Village (1942–1945)

Further Reading

Harth, Erica. *Last Witnesses: Reflections on the Wartime Internment of Japanese Americans.* New York: Palgrave Macmillan, 2003.

Kashima, Tetsuden. *Personal Justice Denied: Report of the Commission on Wartime Relocation and Internment of Civilians.* Seattle: University of Washington Press, 1997.

Lyon, Cherstin. *Prisons and Patriots: Japanese American Wartime Citizenship, Civil Disobedience, and Historical Memory.* Philadelphia: Temple University Press, 2012.

Terumi Rafferty-Osaki

NATIVE SONS OF THE GOLDEN WEST

A fraternal society organized in July 1875 to celebrate the 25th anniversary of California statehood, the Native Sons of the Golden West (NSGW) was incorporated on March 1876 to preserve and promote the history of California. From its earliest days, the NSGW was the most important financial backer of history scholarship at the University of California, providing funds for scholars to travel to archives around the world to collect documents related to the early history of the state. From the 19th century to the mid-20th, NSGW funded graduate student scholarship and research on the history of California. Through the financial support of the NSGW, the state university at Berkeley funded its first lectureship on the history of California. The Native Sons of the Golden West have placed at least 1,300 monuments and commemorative plaques along roadsides and on buildings, trees, and cemeteries and gravesites throughout California. Despite its admirable contributions to the history of

California, the NSGW's organizational history is marred by its anti-Japanese agitation in the first half of the 20th century.

In 1905, the NSGW joined nativist organizations in California to form the Japanese and Korean Exclusion League. In 1906, the NSGW's support for segregation of the San Francisco public schools led to a diplomatic conflict between the United States and Japan culminating in the informal Gentlemen's Agreement between the administration of President Theodore Roosevelt and the Empire of Japan in 1907. The NSGW and its nativist allies successfully agitated for California's Alien Land Law of 1913, prohibiting the ownership and long-term leasing of property by aliens ineligible for U.S. citizenship. NSGW's official publication, the *Grizzly Bear*, was so vitriolic and so influential with the Hearst and McClatchy newspaper syndicates in anti-Japanese sentiment that prior to America's entry into World War I, American journalist Edward Lyell Fox (an agent of the Kingdom of Germany), recommended to Fritz von Papen, military attaché at the German Embassy in Washington (and later German chancellor and then vice-chancellor under Adolf Hitler), that Germany provide surreptitious financial support to promote the anti-Japanese press in California to counter the failure of pro-German propaganda in the United States.

By the eve of World War I, the NSGW's political power made membership in the organization a de facto requirement for anyone with local, state, or national political aspirations in California. In 1918, the NSGW formed a Committee on Asiatic Matters. In 1920, the NSGW joined the American Legion, the California State Federation of Labor, the California Grange, and other organizations to form the Japanese Exclusion League of California. With the complete legal prohibition of Japanese immigration under the federal Immigration Act of 1924, NSGW and its allies in the exclusion league regrouped under the California Joint Immigration Committee (CJIC) in a concerted effort to denounce the lives and culture of Japanese aliens and citizens. After Pearl Harbor, NSGW's agitation against the Japanese in the United States contributed to Franklin Roosevelt's Executive Order 9066, culminating in the removal and incarceration of Japanese American aliens and citizens during World War II. In 1942, NSGW members resolved to support a federal constitutional amendment stripping U.S.-born Japanese Americans of citizenship. From 1943 through 1945, the NSGW was instrumental in the passage of laws limiting Japanese American and alien employment and landownership rights (later found unconstitutional by the U.S. Supreme Court), opposed statehood for Hawai'i, and argued that Japanese who returned to the state after the war be reconfined at internment camps to alleviate the postwar housing shortage in California

An organization that in its earliest efforts supported and promoted scholarship on California history, the NSGW found itself in an increasingly untenable position when World War II gave way to the Cold War. Due in part to the efforts of political scientist David Prescott Barrows, former president of the

University of California and founder of the Northern California Committee on Fair Play for Citizens and Aliens of Japanese Ancestry (founded 1941), NSGW returned to historic preservation as its primary mission in the 1950s.

See also: Alien Land Law (1913); Anti-Japanese Movement; Immigration Act of 1924; Japanese American History before 1945

Further Reading

Chapman, Charles E. "The Native Sons' Fellowships." *The Southwestern Historical Quarterly* 21, no. 4 (April 1918): 389–394.

Hirobe, Izumi. "American Attitudes toward the Japanese Immigration Question, 1924–1931." *The Journal of American–East Asian Relations* 2, no. 3 (Fall 1993): 275–301.

Hurtado, Albert L. "Herbert E. Bolton, Racism, and American History." *Pacific Historical Review* 62, no. 2 (May 1993): 127–142.

David Alan Rego

NO-NO BOYS

During World War II, the No-No Boys challenged the U.S. government's Executive Order 9066 and being subject to the draft while detained at internment camps. In early 1943, the War Relocation Authority required all interned Japanese American adults to complete a form that included two questions (Nos. 27 and 28) aimed at distinguishing the "loyal" from the "disloyal." Although the majority of respondents replied "yes" to both, a significant number (approximately 12,000 out of 78,000) answered "no" or offered a qualified "yes." Internees who failed to answer "yes" were segregated and sent to Tule Lake.

Young Japanese American males who responded "no" to the following questions became known as the No-No Boys:

Question 27: "Are you willing to serve in the armed forces of the United States on combat duty, wherever ordered?"

Question 28: "Will you swear unqualified allegiances to the United States of America and faithfully defend the United States from any or all attack by foreign or domestic forces, and forswear any form of allegiance or obedience to the Japanese emperor, or other foreign government, power or organization?"

The No-No Boys had various reasons for refusing to answer "yes." Many argued that the U.S. government had no right to demand military service from them—individuals whose civil liberties had been so openly disregarded and disrespected. As for question 28, some of the No-No Boys believed that a "yes" implied that they had previous allegiance to Japan or were torn between two countries. While not all who responded "yes" enlisted when drafted and not all who responded "no" refused enlistment, No-No Boys were often conflated with draft resisters.

Upon receiving his draft notice, Frank Emi, an internee at Heart Mountain, helped form the Fair Play Committee. Fair Play Committee members asserted their loyalty to the United States and its principles of freedom and justice, but refused to enlist in light of the government's trampling of their rights. Emi, along with 300 internees/draft resisters, was prosecuted, convicted of a felony and incarcerated at a federal penitentiary.

Along with their punishment by the U.S. government, the No-No Boys experienced backlash from the Japanese American community. For instance, the leadership of the Japanese American Citizens League (JACL) criticized the No-No Boys and draft resisters, labeling them dishonorable and cowardly. Additionally, the JACL contended that the No-No Boys raised questions in Americans' minds about the loyalty and patriotism of Japanese Americans.

Although stigmatized during World War II, the No-No Boys were seen positively in later years. In the 1970s, younger Japanese American activists framed the No-No Boys as courageous individuals asserting their rights without support from the American public and Japanese American community. The No-No Boys illuminated the tensions within the Japanese American community during the internment as well as those between individual rights and the welfare of the collective in American society.

See also: Draft Resisters; Executive Order 9066; Internment, World War II; Okada, John (1923–1971); World War II

Further Reading

Mura, David. "No-No Boys: Re-X-Amining Japanese Americans." *New England Review* 15 (1993): 143–165.

Okada, John. *No-No Boy.* Rutland, VT: Charles E. Tuttle, 1957. Reprint. Seattle: University of Washington Press, 2014.

Lauren S. Morimoto

OKINAWA AND OKINAWANS

Home to 1.4 million people—about 1 percent of Japan's population—the prefecture of Okinawa encompasses 160 of the islands of the Ryūkyū Archipelago, the nation's southern and westernmost chain, with the largest, Okinawa Island, hosting the capital, Naha. Scattered in the East Asian Sea, midway between Shanghai, Taiwan, and Kyushu, the location of the Okinawa Islands has had both positive and negative impacts. Long an important trading hub with commercial connections both to neighboring countries and to the rest of Japan, Okinawa has also been a target for intrusive foreign involvement, including occupation by the United States from 1945–1972. The region had already developed a rich culture encompassing elements of indigenous tradition alongside influences from various trading partners. Okinawa's distinctive cultural heritage, cuisine, and history, along with its subtropical climate and natural beauty, attract many visitors, particularly from the Japanese mainland and nearby countries, making tourism the prefecture's main industry. Yet its "exotic" location on the Japanese periphery has also contributed to the sociopolitical marginalization of Okinawa, which has suffered invasion and aggression from mainland Japan. Forcibly placed in a subservient position, Okinawa's relationship with the center of Japanese power has long been delicate, contributing to the strong group identity for which Okinawans are known.

The Ryūkyū Kingdom and the History of Okinawa

Although some argue that the reference includes present-day Taiwan, most scholars agree that the mention of "Lewchew" in the Chinese compendium *Zuisho* (636 CE) is the first historical reference to Okinawa. Nonetheless, little record exists until the 14th century, when the court of the Ryūkyū Kingdom began recording events and customs. After King Shō Hashi (1371–1439) of the Shō Dynasty (1429–1879) unified Okinawa's three major regions into a single kingdom in 1429, the island society flourished through trade with Sumatra, Java, Malacca, Siam, Korea, Ming China, and the Malay Peninsula and functioned as a valuable commercial conduit for Japan. Its advantageous trading position, however, drew unwanted attention. In 1609, the Satsuma fiefdom invaded Okinawa and imposed a poll tax. During Japan's seclusion in the 17th to 19th centuries, the kingdom continued to communicate with Japan, but its position as a critical trading hub weakened as Europe extended its trading activities into Southeast Asia, the Ming Dynasty removed its ban on maritime activities and began trading directly with Japan and Korea and Holland opened trade with the mainland via designated ports in the 17th century.

In 1879, as part of the nationwide modernization process, Japan abolished the Ryūkyū Kingdom and annexed it as Okinawa Prefecture under an appointed governor. Late in World War II, Okinawa's geographic position again changed the course of the islands' history when it became the site of the Battle of Okinawa, in which many Okinawans died. When the imperial forces surrendered, Okinawa was removed from Japanese governance and constituted as a U.S. Occupied Territory. During the Korean War and Cold War political tensions caused the occupation to shift toward greater military presence. Occupation finally ended with the Reversion Agreement of 1972, which returned Okinawa to Japan. Nonetheless, the U.S. military base still occupies 10 percent of

Okinawan land, leading to a tense relationship in which broad public outcry for the removal of the base coexists with large-scale economic dependence on the provision of services to the U.S. military presence.

Okinawa, Uchinanchū (Okinawans), and Japan

The *jōmon* people who resided in Okinawa during prehistoric times show genetic relation to the people of the Japanese mainland, yet the history of occupation and marginalization has left Okinawans tepid in their identification with mainland Japan. They distinguish themselves as *uchinanchū* from the people of the mainland, the *yamatonchū*. At the end of the 19th century, when Japan was undergoing modernization, conflicting movements could be observed. On the one hand, a prominent Okinawan scholar promoted a legend that the 12th-century Okinawan King Shōten had a blood relationship with the high-ranking samurai Minamoto clan as proof of Okinawans' allegiance to the mainland and to advance their sociopolitical position. On the other, the former Ryūkyū ruling class and other groups campaigned for Okinawan independence, an effort that failed partly because an important potential supporter, Qing China, was defeated in the First Sino-Japanese War of 1895. Subsequently, in the 20th century, the discrimination encountered by economic migrants to mainland Japan and the islands' experience of World War II served to further strengthen Okinawans celebration of their *Uchinanchū* heritage.

Okinawan Emigration and Diaspora

Spurred by a scarcity of natural resources and poor soil that could not support robust agriculture, the islands experienced considerable emigration during the so-called Okinawan modern era (1879–1945), leading to a diaspora estimated—as of 2008—at around 360,000 emigrants and their descendants. Qing China and mainland Japan were important early destinations, but in 1890 Toyama Kyūzō (1868–1910), known as the "Father of [Okinawan] Emigrants," facilitated the first organized group of 26 contract labor migrants to work on a plantation in Hawai'i, which to this day has the world's largest population of Okinawan émigrés. Records from 1899–1938 show that Okinawans emigrated primarily to Hawai'i (20,000), the Philippines (16,000), and Brazil (15,000), and the number coming to the United States would have been larger if not for Hawai'i's request for immigration restraint in 1908 and the passage of the U.S. Immigration Act in 1924.

From the beginning, Okinawans abroad formed close communities. The first known association of Okinawan expatriates was formed in San Francisco in 1902, and since then Okinawan associations in many countries have helped émigrés to keep their identity, heritage and language alive, maintained ties with Okinawa, and provided relief support in times of hardship.

Cultural Heritage of Okinawa

Okinawa's ethnographic, linguistic, and cultural heritage continues to be a topic of debate and an area for new discoveries. The primary cultural forms have developed in the 15th and 16th centuries with a mixture of elements through regional trade and have matured in the context of court culture in the 17th and 18th centuries. The Ryūkyū language has traces of early Japanese, but differs significantly from the standardized Japanese of today. The early Okinawans used pictures, knots, and signs to express numbers and words until Japanese kana scriptures were introduced in the 14th century, and they have a strong and distinctive tradition of songs and folklore that have been passed down through oral tradition.

Shinto and Buddhism were introduced to Okinawa in the 15th century, but they were considered imported culture and did not spread widely. Instead, the indigenous religion persisted, including ceremonial dances and songs dedicated to a rich harvest. Meanwhile, classical court and folk performing arts assimilated influences from China and Japan, as did the native string music performed on the *jamisen* and *sanshin*. Around the same time, Okinawa's textile producers developed vivid and colorful dyes, unique designs and weaving techniques (notably *bingata-zome* and *kasuri*) as their craft evolved from traditional jute weaving to weaving fibers from Southeast Asia and, once the material became available from China, to silk weaving.

When the Japanese government annexed the Ryūkyū Kingdom, it promoted early education and learning of standardized Japanese, and for a time banned the use of the Okinawan dialect. Later, Okinawan writers began to use a mixture of local expressions with Japanese, but such native traditions as the head-dress, topknot, and robe once donned by men of higher social standing and the tattooing of married women's hands have largely disappeared.

See also: Japanese Immigration to Hawai'i; Okinawan (Ryūkyūan) Spiritual Culture

Further Reading

Hook, Glenn D., and Richard Siddle, eds. *Japan and Okinawa: Structure and Subjectivity.* London and New York: Routledge, 2003.

Kerr, George. *Okinawa: The History of an Island People.* Tokyo: Tuttle Publishing, 2000.

Matsumura, Wendy. *The Limits of Okinawa.* Durham and London: Duke University Press, 2015.

Midori Tanaka Atkins

PEARL HARBOR

Pearl Harbor has been the site of a major U.S. naval base since 1875. In that year, the Hawai'ian Kingdom granted the United States the right to construct

Rescuers pull a seaman from the water as the 31,800-ton USS *West Virginia* burns at Pearl Harbor on December 7, 1941, the Japanese attack that initiated the United States' involvement in World War II. (Library of Congress)

and maintain a coaling and repair station in the harbor of the Pearl River. During January 17–21, 1893, U.S. naval marines supported a cabal who overthrew the monarchy, despite U.S. recognition of Hawai'ian sovereignty. But newly elected president Grover Cleveland (1893–1897) slowed the rush to annexation. And an annexation treaty during the presidency of his successor, William McKinley (1897–1901), also failed to gain sufficient support in the U.S. Senate.

Despite antiannexation petitions signed by most adult native Hawai'ians, U.S. congressional approval of the Newlands Resolution (July 1898) facilitated U.S. seizure of territory held by the rebel republic in July 1898, solidifying U.S. control of Pearl Harbor. By then, the United States was using the harbor to resupply naval ships during the Asian phase of the Spanish-American War (1898). This continued during the subsequent Philippine-American War (1899–1902).

In the 1930s and early 1940s, mutual provocations between the United States and Japan led to Japan's attack on Pearl Harbor on December 7, 1941. Led by Adm. Isoroku Yamamoto (1884–1943), the air attack sunk 9 U.S. ships, damaging 21 others. The combined military–civilian death toll exceeded 2,300 with almost 1,200 injured. Although successful military tactics include stealth, the bombing of Pearl Harbor was disdainfully described as a "sneak attack"—a phrase that has persisted in folklore. Nonetheless, Japan's attack was not strategically disastrous. It missed three aircraft carriers assigned elsewhere that day. And a strategic petroleum depot was overlooked. The surprise attack led to declarations of war against Japan and the other Axis powers.

Calls for relocating and interning local Issei and Nisei Japanese would have dislocated the economy. However, about 1,000 Japanese Buddhist priests, community leaders, and other suspects were interned. This was a relatively small percentage of the Japanese population compared to the forced evacuations of about 120,000 Japanese Americans from communities in California, Oregon, and Washington. Also, Germans and other European nationals were interned. Martial law lasted until 1944.

Unsurprisingly, many Japanese felt the need to prove their loyalty to the United States and that they were not collaborators in intelligence gathering for the attack on Pearl Harbor. Nisei (second-generation) Japanese perceived military service as a chance to redeem the community. This sentiment gave rise to the 100th Infantry Battalion, the first all-Nisei combat unit in World War II. It became one of three units composing the famed 442nd Regimental Combat Team, U.S. Army, which fought valorously against Italian and German armies. But racism against Japanese also had a negative impact. In the then-continental United States, 10,000 No-No Boys in the internment camps refused to be inducted into the Armed Forces.

During the Cold War, Pearl Harbor was an important part of a global network of U.S. military bases, facilitating U.S. involvement in the Korean and Vietnam Wars. In 1964, U.S. secretary of the interior Stewart L. Udall designated the Pearl Harbor Naval Base as a National Historic Landmark District embracing five National Historic Landmarks. A metaphor for surprise attack, Pearl Harbor resonated in media reaction to the September 11, 2001, attack on the World Trade Center.

Twelve decades of environmental damage to the land and water led to the formation of the military–civilian Pearl Harbor Restoration Advisory Board in the 1990s. A tourist attraction, Pearl Harbor is the site of the U.S. Pacific Command.

See also: Commission on Wartime Relocation and Internment of Civilians; Executive Order 9066; 442nd Regimental Combat Team/100th Infantry Battalion; Internment, World War II

Further Reading

Masters, Patricia Lee. "Warring Bodies: Most Nationalistic Selves." *East–West Film Journal* 7 (1993): 137–148.

Osorio, Jonathan Kamakawiwo'ole. *Dismembering Ka Lahui: A History of the Hawaiian Nation to 1887*. Honolulu: University of Hawai'i Press, 2002.

Vincent Kelly Pollard

PICTURE BRIDES/SHASHIN HANAYOME

"Picture bride" marriages originated with arranged marriages that had their origins—within aristocratic circles and in the samurai class during feudal times—before the modern Meiji Era (1868–1912) in Japan. The practice became accepted even among peasants in rural communities. With the introduction of photography from the West, exchanging photos introduced couples when it was difficult to meet in person. This also allowed the go-between, or "nakodo," to bring a photograph. This could save embarrassment if one party were rejected; the matter could then be quietly resolved.

Japanese immigration to Hawai'i, in the earliest period between 1885 and 1910, included four times as many men as women. When the men in Hawai'i wanted to start families, they returned to their villages and had their families arrange marriages. But the trip was long and expensive, and many wrote their parents to find suitable wives or asked nakodo for assistance. Go-betweens generally conducted research to ensure a good match in the socioeconomic status, educational backgrounds, and family histories of the intended couple. The peak period for this picture bride practice was after the Gentlemen's Agreement of 1905–1906, which restricted laborers from entering the United States until 1924, when the United States banned immigration from Japan.

During this restricted immigration period, there was a significant increase in the number of Japanese women who came to Hawai'i. Over 20,000 picture brides were married to Japanese men in Hawai'i in absentia through families back home or nakodo, and the years from about 1910 to 1924 are often referred to as the "picture bride period." The influx of brides marked the transition from a society of largely single male transients to communities of permanent residents. In 1900, out of the total population of 24,326 Japanese immigrants in the United States, there were only 985 females (24 males for every female). By 1910, the female population had climbed to 9,087; by 1920, there were 22,193 women.

Of course, not all the arranged marriages succeeded. In some cases, men sent photos from years earlier to disguise their ages or even photos of younger friends. Some grooms never showed up at the immigration station. In other cases, women arrived as kari-fufu (temporary spouse) simply to gain entry into the United States. Many immigrants then remarried. The system allowed adventurous women to join the workforce at a time when labor immigration was restricted but spouses were still allowed. The Exclusion Act of 1924 closed this loophole almost entirely until well after World War II ended in 1945. In the meantime, the picture bride system permitted a large and flourishing community of Japanese American families to develop in the United States.

See also: Japanese American History before 1945; Japanese American Women; Japanese American Women in the 1930s

Further Reading

Sunoo, Sonia Shinn. *Korean Picture Brides: 1903–1920: A Collection of Oral Histories.* Bloomington, IN: Xlibris Corporation, 2002.
Uchida, Yoshiko. *Picture Bride: A Novel.* Seattle: University of Washington Press, 1987.

Noriko Sanefuji

POST-1965 JAPANESE IMMIGRATION

The mid-1960s marked a turning point in U.S. immigration history that would affect numbers of Asian immigrants, including those from Japan. Japanese immigration patterns in the early decades of the 20th century had been influenced by diplomatic relations with the United States, economic trends, and issues of racism. Those factors shifted in the late 20th century, resulting in an increase in newcomers from Japan. After restrictive barriers had been put into place in 1924 and the Japanese American population was devastated by internment policies and practices during World War II, politics promoting democracy, more open borders, and antiracial discrimination were ushered in during the late 1940s. Cold War fears of the 1950s made enemies of the Soviets and Chinese, but had little impact on U.S. attitudes toward Japan, which was viewed as a fledgling democracy both militarily and economically. Legislation promoting diversity in the United States during the 1950s and 1960s encouraged further immigration from Japan and paved the way to citizenship for "nonwhite" people of the world, including the Japanese.

The 1965 Immigration Act, also known as the Hart-Celler Act and sponsored by Rep. Emanuel Celler of New York and Sen. Phillip Hart of Michigan, changed U.S. immigration trends and patterns significantly. Where decades of immigration law, reaching back to the Chinese Exclusion Act of 1882, had restricted immigration based on race and eventually instituted racial quotas, the 1965 policy would open doors to the Japanese and other immigrants in unprecedented ways. In 1952, the McCarran-Walter Act had nullified racial restrictions on naturalization outlined in 1790, allowing Issei to become naturalized citizens. The 1965 Immigration Act went further in welcoming immigrants from Africa and Asia and emphasized family reunification and scarce professional skills. These policies inspired growth in the U.S. Japanese population from 260,000 in 1960 (both U.S. and Japanese born) to nearly 600,000 in

1970 (both U.S. and Japanese born), 716,000 in 1980, and nearly 850,000 in 1990. From that point, the U.S. Japanese population began to decline, largely due to a decline in Japan's population, an aging population, Japanese economic strength, and therefore less incentive for emigration to the United States.

Although Japanese immigration patterns following the 1965 Immigration Act have been studied from a perspective shaping Japan's comparatively long history of sending migrants to the United States, they have also been studied in the context of changing immigration patterns of all Asians. Immigration policies between 1924 and 1965 had affected Japanese migration in ways similar to what were considered other traditional Asian groups—Chinese and eventually Korean—but restrictive legislation and historical relations had essentially barred immigration from other Asian countries after immigrants from the traditional sending regions arrived. That would change after 1965. Between 1965 and 1980, the Japanese maintained their position as the largest Asian group; however, Japanese immigration to the United States did not increase as rapidly as that of other Asian countries. U.S. Census researchers noted particular growth from Asian India (now designated as a specific category), as well as the Philippines, and from Laos, Cambodia, and Vietnam following the fall of Saigon in 1975, in addition to China, beginning in 1980 when U.S.–Chinese relations improved.

The demographics of Japanese immigrants did distinguish them from some other Asian immigrant groups, however. First, the majority were female, creating the potential for population growth through childbearing, even as intermarriage with non-Japanese Asians and non-Asians increased. Second, Japanese immigrants were dispersed beyond the state of California in greater percentages than those of differing Asian ancestry. In 2010, the Japanese population remained among the top five Asian groups in 6 out of 20 metropolitan areas, all of which were located in the West, yet the concentration of other Asians in the West was greater. There is some indication that World War II internment of California's Japanese inspired this dispersal, but it should not be forgotten that the Japanese had often moved great distances from their entry point of San Francisco beginning in the 19th century. In addition, Japanese immigrants after 1965 were more likely to be college graduates, work as professionals, and hold positions as executive managers. This trend was related to Japan's own economic growth and expansion in manufacturing and the corporate world by the 1970s.

This economic growth had a significant negative impact on Japanese emigration to the United States while numbers of other Asian immigrants increased, as the new economy saw increased demands for Japanese labor at home. Fewer than 95,000 Japanese entered the United States between 1965 and 1984, and they represented only 3 percent of all Asians. Though the 1965 Immigration Act allowed for 20,000 per year, Japan was sending an average of only 4,000 annually, and, by the first half of the 1980s, they comprised only 1.7 percent of total Asian immigration. Between 2000 and 2010, the Japanese population within the United States experienced the slowest growth of all Asian (alone or in any combination) groups that had a minimum population of one million, with an increase of only 14 percent. In contrast, the Indian population grew the most rapidly at 68 percent, the Filipino population grew 44 percent, Vietnamese 42 percent, Korean 39 percent, and Chinese 40 percent. As a result of the decline in Japanese immigration, Japanese Americans have become largely a native-born population with few ties to Japan and little knowledge of Japanese language, culture, or traditions.

See also: Japanese American History before 1945; Japanese American Population Trends

Further Reading

Chin, Gabriel J., and Rose Cuison Villazor. *The Immigration and Nationality Act of 1965: Legislating a New America.* Cambridge: Cambridge University Press, 2015.

Daniels, Roger. *Asian America: Chinese and Japanese in the United States since 1850.* Seattle: University of Washington Press, 1988.

Wong, Morrison G. "Post-1965 Asian Immigrants: Where Do They Come from, Where Are They Now, and Where Are They Going?" *The Annals of the American Academy of Political and Social Science* 487 (September 1986): 150–168.

Kathleen A. Tobin

Table 1   Japanese Immigration 1965–1980

Year	Total	Women	Men
1965	3,180	2,727	453
1966	3,394	2,687	707
1967	4,125	2,921	1,025
1968	3,613	2,726	887
1969	3,957	2,958	999
1970	4,485	3,291	1,194
1971	4,457	3,295	1,162
1972	4,757	3,403	1,354
1973	5,461	3,893	1,568
1974	4,860	3,380	1,480
1975	4,274	2,810	1,464
1976	4,258	2,702	1,556
1977	4,178	2,579	1,599
1978	4,010	2,595	1,415
1979	4,048	2,608	1,440
1980	4,225	—	—

WORLD WAR I

With the breakdown of the uneasy balance of power in Europe, World War I (1914–1918) embroiled the great powers in total war. Extensive imperial and colonial interests throughout the world involved not just the major European powers but also the Japanese Empire in competition over various holdings in Asia as the disintegrating Qing Empire caused a power vacuum in the region.

Japan had been an ally of the United Kingdom since the turn of the century and found itself part of the Triple Entente as war erupted. During the war, Japan took over Germany's Asian colonies, such as Qingdao, a strategic port located on the Shandong Peninsula on mainland China. At the end of the war, Japan's military predominance in the region, especially through its navy, secured its place as a great imperial power as it expanded and consolidated its sphere of influence during the interwar period.

Already tense because of domestic U.S. sentiment against Japanese immigration, relations with the United States at this time were exacerbated by Japanese imperial designs on mainland China, manifested in the Twenty-One Demands of 1915 that would have made China a Japanese protectorate. In contrast, American interests had long favored an independent, open China to balance power in the region. This tension was somewhat alleviated by the Lansing-Ishii Agreement of 1917 but came to the forefront again in U.S.–Japan relations with the outbreak of World War II in the Pacific.

During World War I, Japanese Americans were involved in the war effort, both through military service and on the home front. The high concentration of people of Japanese descent in Hawai'i meant that many volunteered for Hawai'i's territorial militia and, from there, went on to be mobilized into the regular armed forces to fight in Europe.

Some hoped that military service would create a path for assimilation, especially because citizenship had been denied to Japanese Americans because of exclusionary policies against Asian immigration and naturalization. Although a 1918 law had made foreign-born veterans eligible for American citizenship, a series of legal setbacks prevented the law from being applied equally to all Asian veterans, such as the Supreme Court case *Hidemitsu Toyota v. United States*. Emigrating to the United States in 1913, Hidemitsu Toyota had served honorably in the U.S. Coast Guard during the war. When he petitioned for citizenship under the 1918 law, his request was granted by a lower court but then rescinded by a higher court. Ultimately, the Supreme Court decided in 1925 that the law for foreign-born veterans was intended specifically for Filipino veterans and did not apply to Japanese veterans.

Through litigation, organization, and personal advocacy, Japanese American veterans sought national legislation to extend U.S. citizenship to veterans of all backgrounds. A key figure in this movement was Tokutaro Nishimura Slocum (1895–1974), who had been born in Japan but emigrated to the United States as a child. Slocum interrupted his education at Columbia University Law School to fight in World War I. As part of the 82nd Division, 328th Infantry, Slocum participated in the Meuse-Argonne Offensive and the Battle of St. Mihiel in France. After the war, Slocum was an active force in winning Japanese American veterans the right to naturalize, also a cause for the nascent Japanese American Citizens League, and their efforts culminated in the Nye-Lea Act, which President Franklin D. Roosevelt signed into law in 1935.

However, even though these steps would allow some modicum of assimilation for Japanese American veterans, this progress was diluted by the pervasive anti-Asian and anti-Japanese racism of the time, especially on the West Coast, which would take an even darker turn in World War II, especially now with Japan itself an enemy Axis power.

For example, after the attack on Pearl Harbor, decorated Japanese American veterans were not immune from classification as enemy aliens and incarceration in internment camps. Slocum himself would be interned in Manzanar. Another veteran, Joseph Yoshisuke Kurihara (1895–1965) was a Nisei born in Hawai'i, where his family worked on sugar plantations. When World War I broke out, Kurihara volunteered and was shipped to France with the 85th Division, 328th Field Artillery. During World War II, Kurihara was incarcerated at Manzanar. Internment would result in Kurihara renouncing his American citizenship, as would others, who, like him, chose to relocate to Japan after the war.

In all, the Japanese American experience of World War I only somewhat tempered pervasive anti-Japanese sentiment in the United States, even though Japan was America's ally in the war. Part of this stemmed from competing national interests in Asia, but much of the Japanese American experience was shaped by racism at home, even while brave Japanese Americans served during World War I.

See also: Japanese American Citizens League; World War II

Further Reading

Chuman, Frank F. *The Bamboo People: Japanese Americans, Their History and the Law.* Chicago, IL: Japanese American Citizens League, 1976.

Keegan, John. *The First World War*. New York: Vintage Books, 2000.

Tamura, Eileen. *In Defense of Justice: Joseph Kurihara and the Japanese American Struggle for Equality*. Urbana: University of Illinois Press, 2013.

Yvette M. Chin

WORLD WAR II

The Japanese American experience of World War II was marked by great heroism and great disappointment. During World War I, Japan had been allied with the victors, and Japanese Americans had served in the armed forces, but pervasive anti-Asian sentiment prevented their assimilation into broader society. The attack on Pearl Harbor, and the United States' subsequent entry into World War II, lit the powder keg of anti-Japanese sentiment, most notably resulting in the forced relocation and incarceration of Japanese Americans in a policy known as internment.

The March to Total War in the Pacific

Since the 19th century, Japan had pursued expansionist policies on the Asian mainland, gaining much territory after successful wars against both China and Russia. After World War I, Japan further expanded its sphere of influence on the Asian mainland, extending beyond some of the territorial gains won from allying with the winning side against Germany. For example, Japan took over the German base at Qingdao, a strategic port located on the Shandong Peninsula in northeast China.

Japan's naval strength greatly enhanced its imperial dominance of the region, exacerbating relations with the United States who had long had special interests in maintaining a strong, independent China. In 1931, the Japanese Kwantung Army staged the Mukden Incident as a pretext to invade China. Moving south, Japan had invaded French Indochina in 1940 after France was invaded by the Germans.

The United States responded to Japan's imperialist expansion by halting shipments of important war matériel to Japan, such as gasoline, oil, and machine parts, but this made the Japanese Army desperate for more local resources to fuel its war effort. Now with a military presence in southern China and Southeast Asia, Japan was poised to take the resource-rich Dutch East Indies. However, American sentiment against becoming involved either against Germany in Europe or Japan in Asia meant that the United States made diplomatic overtures to Japan to de-escalate hostilities in the region; that is, until the Japanese attack on Pearl Harbor on December 7, 1941.

The 90-minute surprise attack resulted in the loss of over 2,400 Americans killed and another 1,000 wounded. In the two waves of air attacks, over twenty ships were sunk or damaged. The USS *Arizona*, one of the eight battleships attacked that day, exploded and sank to the bottom, where, to this day, it continues to leak oil, which rises to the surface. American aircraft also suffered heavy losses before having the chance to take off, but, fortunately, the aircraft carriers had been sent out and were spared from the attack.

The next day, President Franklin D. Roosevelt requested a declaration of war in his famous "Infamy" speech before bringing the United States to war against Japan's allies, Germany and Italy. The American war machine mobilized quickly to defend its remaining presence in the Philippines, but the Japanese offensives were too powerful. American forces in the Philippines surrendered to the Japanese at Corregidor in April 1942, and these prisoners of war would be tortured on the famed Bataan Death March.

"Enemy Aliens" in Our Midst

The reaction to the surprise attack at Pearl Harbor was swift, and all Japanese Americans were classified as "enemy aliens." Even those born in the United States (the Nisei) and/or prominent in their communities would come under suspicion. Sanje Abe (1895–1982), for instance, was a Nisei born in Hawai'i who entered the Hawai'i National Guard during World War I. After the war, Abe was elected to Hawai'i's territorial senate, after renouncing his Japanese citizenship. Soon after Pearl Harbor, Abe was arrested for possessing a Japanese flag, which was not a crime when he was arrested. Martial law declared it illegal several days after his arrest.

By far, however, the most egregious American policy during World War II was internment, which resulted in the incarceration of approximately 120,000 individuals of Japanese ancestry from 1942–1945. Japanese Americans from the West Coast, which had been declared an "exclusion zone," were concentrated in 10 "relocation camps," all located inland and in barely habitable environments. Estimates suggest that two-thirds of those incarcerated were legal citizens of the United States.

Entire families were uprooted and moved into these poorly built camps, taking only what personal property they could carry, and internees were expected to contribute to their own imprisonment. Makeshift schools, sports activities, and even the Scouts were set up to give the children some semblance of normality, even while the only country these children had known treated them as dangerous enemy aliens.

Nor were decorated Japanese American veterans immune from incarceration as enemy aliens in internment camps. For example, Tokutaro Nishimura Slocum had volunteered for the army in World War I, although attending Columbia University Law School at the time. Serving in the 82nd Division, 328th Infantry, Slocum participated in the Meuse-Argonne Offensive and the Battle of St. Mihiel in France.

Internment would be the apex of anti-Japanese war fears during World War II and caused severe rifts in Japanese American society. Naturally, some reacted to their internment with feelings of despair and betrayal, while others put their faith in the United States, such as the Japanese American Citizens

League headed by Mike Masaoka (1915–1991). These rifts further exacerbated the generation gap between foreign-born Issei and U.S.-born Nisei. These tensions would boil over in the December 1942 riot at Manzanar, when JACL official Fred Tayama was beaten and Harry Ueno was arrested for the beating. Approximately 4,000 incarcerees marched in protest to Ueno's arrest, and the guards responded with tear gas and bullets, killing two incarcerees.

However, the Japanese American experience after Pearl Harbor was far from uniform. Because those of Japanese descent had constituted such a high proportion of Hawai'i's population (some estimates claim 40 percent), Hawai'i was not declared an exclusion zone. As a result, Hawai'ian Japanese Americans continued to serve in some capacity in the armed forces and were not subject to internment as those on the West Coast had been.

Japanese Americans in the Armed Forces

Because Japanese American men were classified as "enemy aliens," they were largely excluded from military service. Some, however, had volunteered earlier or had been drafted when Selective Service was established in 1940 (after Pearl Harbor, Japanese Americans did not fall under the draft). As a result, an estimated 5,000 Japanese Americans had been serving in the U.S. military before Pearl Harbor. Immediately, these soldiers found themselves under suspicion, often relieved of duty, sometimes segregated from the rest of their units, and generally banned from combat roles.

And, yet, these soldiers would become among the most decorated of the war. Hawai'i in particular became the key organizational point for the Japanese Americans who had volunteered to serve before the outbreak of war, primarily through the Hawai'i National Guard. Although the Hawai'i National Guard was vital after Pearl Harbor, fears about internal security and the security of the army grew, resulting in a battalion of Nisei being sent to the mainland for training.

For local Hawai'ian defense, the Hawai'i Territorial Guard was formed in the immediate aftermath of Pearl Harbor, using troops drawn from Reserve Officers' Training Corps (ROTC) students. In January 1942, its Japanese members were dismissed; however, they petitioned Gen. Delos Emmons to continue to contribute to the war effort and formed the Varsity Victory Volunteers.

In 1943, military authorities decided to allow combat training to the Japanese American soldiers already serving and called for volunteers, even among those interned in camps. This call to arms in the internment camps further fractured Japanese American communities, as authorities circulated an infamous "loyalty questionnaire" to men throughout the camps. Although incarcerees did answer the call to arms, the sending of draft orders to inmates led to conflict and several cases of draft evasion.

From these segregated Japanese American units in the army, and some former internees that enlisted, the all-Nisei 442nd Infantry Regiment was formed. The 442nd was deployed to Italy in 1944, taking first the town of Belvedere and then moving toward the Arno River, eventually defeating the German unit stationed north of Rome. Then, the regiment was redeployed to northeastern France, continuing to fight with distinction. After liberating the towns of Bruyères and Biffontaine, the 442nd was then tasked with rescuing the "Lost Battalion," part of an infantry division trapped by German soldiers in the Vosges Mountains in October 1944.

For its size (approximately 14,000 men), the 442nd Infantry Regiment is one of the most decorated units in U.S. military history. Perhaps the most well-known member of the 442nd Infantry Regiment was Daniel Inouye (1924–2012), future Democratic senator from Hawai'i, who volunteered in 1943. While with the 442nd in Italy, Inouye's singular bravery broke through the heavy German defensive line, which resulted in the amputation of his right arm. Although decorated with the Purple Heart and other medals, it was not until 2000 that Inouye, along with 19 other Nisei soldiers, received the Medal of Honor from President Bill Clinton.

The ranks of the 442nd Infantry Regiment included 21 Medal of Honor winners, over 50 Distinguished Service Cross recipients, and a high number of Purple Hearts awarded for wounds sustained during battle. Of those 21 Medal of Honor winners, only one had been awarded immediately after the war, to Private First Class Sadao Munemori (1922–1945), killed in action in Italy.

Two Japanese American soldiers were captured by the Japanese and held as prisoners of war. Born in Japan but raised primarily in Oklahoma, Sgt. Frank Fujita (1921–1996) joined the Texas National Guard, and along with 550 others in his unit, he was captured after the fall of Java and was imprisoned by the Japanese for three and a half years.

Richard Mosoto Sakakida (1920–1996) had enlisted in the U.S. Army in 1941, and because of his language skills, he was assigned to the Counter Intelligence Corps (CIC). While stationed in the Philippines, Sakakida was tasked with posing as a civilian to spy on the Japanese community. He was captured during the Battle of Bataan and the army's surrender at Corregidor in May 1942. While imprisoned, Japanese authorities branded him a traitor on account of his ancestry and tortured him, but he was also treated differently from the Filipino and non-Asian prisoners of war. Somehow convincing the Japanese that he had been a civilian, they put him into service as a translator, which allowed him to gather intelligence.

After the War and Today

In the Pacific theater, the tide turned at the Battle of Midway in June 1942, just six months after Pearl Harbor, when the Japanese navy suffered heavy casualties. Over the course of the next three years, American forces moved north toward Tokyo and, by March 1945, had taken back the Philippines and were poised for invading Japan after the bloody, five-week Battle of Iwo Jima. With the dropping of the atomic bombs on Hiroshima and Nagasaki, and the subsequent surrender of Japan in August 1945, World War II was over.

In addition to serving in combat roles during the war, Japanese American soldiers assisted in the American occupation of Japan after the war. Often, even those former internees that had renounced their American citizenship and moved to Japan found themselves employed by the occupation forces in administrative roles, especially during the Tokyo War Crimes Tribunal.

As they demobilized, Japanese American veterans, however, often found that their valor in battle did not translate to acceptance at home. Their contributions were forgotten and pushed aside, all the more painful because of the policy of internment, and it was not until the 1990s that bravery and loyalty of Japanese American veterans would be recognized. Soldiers were conferred with medals and official recognition decades after they had served. The "Go for Broke" memorial in Little Tokyo, inspired by the motto of the 100th Infantry Battalion, was dedicated in 1999, the National Japanese American Memorial was dedicated in 2000 in Washington, D.C.

World War II was, in many ways, a watershed moment for the Japanese American community. The experience of being "enemy aliens" was all-encompassing and fractured the community. Soldiers suffered extreme discrimination and marginalization even in service to country, while the all-encompassing civilian experience of internment fractured communities and families for decades to come.

See also: Commission on Wartime Relocation and Internment of Civilians; Draft Resisters; Executive Order 9066; 442nd Regimental Combat Team/100th Infantry Battalion; *Hirabayashi v. United States* (1943); Inouye, Daniel Ken (1924–2012); Internment, World War II; Japanese American Citizens League; Korematsu, Fred (1919–2005); Masaoka, Mike Masaru (1915–1991); No-No Boys; Pearl Harbor; World War I; World War II

Further Reading

McNaughton, James. *Nisei Linguists: Japanese Americans in the Military Intelligence Service during World War II*. Washington, DC: U.S. Army Center of Military History, 2007.

Odo, Franklin. *No Sword to Bury: Japanese Americans in Hawai'i during World War II*. Philadelphia, PA: Temple University Press, 2004.

Sakakida, Richard, as told to Wayne S. Kiyosaki. *A Spy in Their Midst: The World War II Struggle of a Japanese-American Hero*. Ann Arbor, MI: University of Michigan Press, 1995.

Yvette M. Chin

PART II

POLITICAL ACTIVITY AND ECONOMIC LIFE: BUSINESS ENDEAVORS AND INVOLVEMENT IN AMERICAN POLITICS

HISTORICAL OVERVIEW

Japanese immigrants were needed as laborers in Hawai'i. Because fertile land was owned by the "Big Five" corporations, and small business opportunities such as retail stores were operated by the plantations, the Japanese population in Hawai'i focused on unionization and organized labor strikes to improve their social and economic standards of living. Japanese workers saw themselves in class terms and recognized that their strength lay in collective action. Japanese American labor organizations led to the island's largest sugar strikes in 1909 and 1920.

Things were different over on the mainland. The Japanese discovered certain possibilities that existed on the mainland to a greater extent than on the islands: opportunities for small businesses and small farms. The first Japanese-owned farm in California was established May 27, 1869. Followers of Lord Matsudaira Katamori established the Wakamatsu Tea and Silk Farm Colony on 600 acres on the Sacramento River at Placerville. They introduced mulberry trees, silk cocoons, tea plants, and bamboo roots to California. In less than two years, the colony failed because the dry California weather was not conducive to their cultivation.

Over in California, the Japanese immigrants were aware that the Chinese immigrants attempted to be a part of the general economy, in manufacturing and trade occupations, which provoked anti-Chinese violence, policies, and ultimately exclusion. The Japanese therefore withdrew from manufacturing and entered instead into related enterprises. So, instead of shoe manufacturing, they were into shoe repair. Thus the Japanese focused on entrepreneurial opportunities such as restaurants, barbershops, billiard halls, saloons, and groceries and

Japanese American farmer harvesting cauliflower on a ranch near Centerville, California. Japanese Americans pursued careers in farming initially due to industrialization and the efficiency created by refridgerated train car transport. (Library of Congress)

operated buses and delivery wagons because labor unions were one of the staunchest opponents of Japanese inclusion. In fact, their members belonged to anti-Japanese organizations such as the Asiatic Exclusion League whose mission is to protect white workers by excluding all Japanese and Koreans from coming to the United States. Other nativist groups, like the Sons of the Golden West, the Grange Association, and the American Legion pressured politicians to deport Asian immigrants and to segregate them into ghettos of laboring underclass. Despite the racial economic exclusion, the Japanese immigrants focused on ethnic enterprises and by extension ethnic solidarity as a viable means of livelihood. However, their success only fueled anti-Asian, anti-Japanese sentiments even though they developed ethnic communities and economies for survival. Even more frustrating is the nativist conclusion that the Japanese immigrants were unassimilable because they develop ethnic communities and economies.

The Japanese immigrants faced a lot of racism and social prejudice. Some were called "chinks," revealing they inherited the anti-Chinese sentiments. Additionally, they were also called "Yellow Jap" or "Dirty Jap" and were told to "go home." They were refused service at restaurants and barbershops and found it difficult to rent homes or buy houses. The real issue was not the number of Japanese immigrants in the United States at the time but rather the assumption that they are cheap labor that would undermine the standard of living for white workers, propelling American society into a downward spiral of economic, moral, and racial degeneration.

Japanese farming in the late 19th century was fueled by industrialization coupled with the nationalization of the railroad, and modernization as exemplified by the refrigerated car, which resulted in an increased need for fresh agricultural produce. In addition, the development of California's irrigation system with water from Colorado also spurred Japanese farming. By the first years of the 20th century, fully two-thirds of the Japanese in California (about 16,000 individuals) earned a living as farm laborers. In 1900, the federal census recorded that only 29 Japanese leased land in California, by 1910, that number jumped to 1,816. Japanese farmers belong to prefectural associations known as *kenjinkai,* and agricultural associations, or *nogyo kumiai,* who pooled their resources together to form *tanomoshi,* or a credit-rotating system that allows members to have the capital needed to start a small business or farm. One big factor in transforming the Japanese population from *dekaseginin,* or sojourners, to settlers was their entry into agriculture and utilization of mutual-support systems, which allowed them to coordinate crop production, fix prices, exchange information, provide financial assistance, arbitrate disputes, stabilize rent, and establish marketing organizations.

On October 11, 1906, the San Francisco municipal school board directed all school principals to send Chinese, Japanese, and Korean students to "Oriental Schools." This action lead to an international geopolitical event as the government of Japan voiced their protest to Washington. Washington was careful in its dealing with Japan because it was a rising military power in Asia. President Theodore Roosevelt opposed the segregation of Japanese American children by the San Francisco municipal school board, allowing them to attend school with white children. However, President Roosevelt agreed to the Gentlemen's Agreement, signed 1907 and implemented in 1908, which restricted the migration of unskilled laborers from Japan. Furthermore, President Roosevelt prohibited Japanese laborers holding passports for Hawai'i, Mexico, or Canada from remigrating to the U.S. mainland. The State of California agreed not to pass overtly anti-Japanese legislation in the future. The Gentlemen's Agreement was "sold" to Californians as "tantamount to exclusion" but it was not. Instead, under its terms, the Japanese American population would double in less than 20 years because Washington agreed that Japanese already residing in America could send for their wives and family members left behind. However, by 1924, the immigration policy changed, banning entry to all aliens ineligible to become citizens, which ended all Japanese immigration. The Immigration Act of 1924 is considered to be the ultimate triumph of the Native Sons of the Golden West.

Laws and discriminatory policies were passed that further politically racialize the Japanese as "Other" and noncitizen. In 1913, the California legislature passed a law that denied Japanese residents the ability to own property. Japanese immigrants were able to subvert that law by purchasing property in their children's names because they were born in America and were thus American citizens according to the 14th Amendment and *United States v. Wong Kim Ark,* 169 U.S. 649 (1898). Many Issei parents purchased land in their children's names. When tested in court, the California State Supreme Court upheld the right of even the youngest Nisei, second-generation child to own property as a right of citizenship (*Estate of Tetsubumi Yano* (1922) 188 Cal. 645, 648). This only angered many white Californians and fueled a call for a total ban on Japanese immigration. By 1920, however, a new anti-Japanese legislation corrected that loophole. The right to own property and establish a home, a business, or a farm was directly tied to the rights of the Issei to become naturalized citizens. The relocation of Japanese American families after Pearl Harbor marked an end to Japanese American farmers. The Western Growers Protective Association supported the order as it meant the elimination of competition. In their absence, Japanese American land and property were simply taken over by other farmers and families. After the war, only a few were able to return to their property and restore their farms and reestablish their businesses.

Civil Rights and Redress

The social and political climate during the postwar period was one of civil rights and ethnic pride. Although the Japanese American Citizens League (JACL) was disparaged for cooperating with the U.S. government in all of their policies during World War II, lawyers and lobbyists for the JACL worked diligently to overturn laws banning interracial marriage, legalizing segregation, and restricting rights to citizenship and immigration based on race. The end of race-based immigration quotas following the passage of the 1965 Immigration Act allowed immigration from Japan to be restored, yet the number of new Japanese immigrating remained low due to a booming postwar economy in Japan. Those Japanese who did immigrate to the United States after the war often came because of family ties, such as marriage to a U.S. soldier, and became the first generation of Japanese immigrants no longer barred from naturalized citizenship due to racial discrimination and restrictions.

From the late 1960s through the 1970s, the JACL, National Coalition for Redress/Reparations, National Council for Japanese American Redress (NCJAR), and Japanese American politicians, such as Sen. Daniel Inouye, Sen. Spark Matsunaga, congress member Norman Mineta, and congress member Robert Matsui, lawyers, and activists worked unstintingly to achieve redress for Japanese Americans interned during the war. After years of hard work, the U.S. Senate passed the Civil Liberties Act on April 20, 1988, by a vote of 69–27. The act acknowledged that the U.S. government had committed a grave injustice against all those who were interned. Each surviving individual received a tax-free payment of $20,000 as a token payment for the losses incurred because of their internment. Some people returned the checks out of protest, arguing that money could never repay them for all that they had suffered and lost. One of the most significant outcomes of redress was the resurgence of stories about internment camp experiences from the Nisei generation. Oral history projects boomed as people began talking more openly about what really happened during the war, including conflicts over the draft resisters, the loyalty questionnaire, those who answered the loyalty questionnaire "no-no," those who renounced their citizenship, and the collaboration between the JACL and the government. Having achieved redress, many Japanese Americans felt vindicated and could finally tell their stories to their children and to the public without feeling shame or guilt. As well, the redress campaign brought the generations together.

ABIKO, KYUTARO (1865–1936)

Kyutaro Abiko was an early Japanese immigrant to the United States best known as an influential community leader and publisher of the *Nichibei Shimbun* newspaper.

Early Life in Japan and California

Abiko was born in Niigata Prefecture, Japan, in 1865. At the age of 17, he moved to Tokyo to learn English and, soon after, converted to Christianity. In 1885, he immigrated to the United States under the sponsorship of the San Francisco–based *Fukuinkai* (Gospel Society). Upon settling in California, Abiko worked as a schoolboy and attended the Lincoln Grammar School and, later, the University of California, Berkeley. He quickly became a leader in the Fukuinkai, and helped to establish the Japanese Methodist Episcopal Church in San Francisco, which was the first independent Japanese American religious institution.

In 1897, Abiko purchased the *Soko Nihon Shinbun* newspaper in San Francisco. By 1899, he would merge it with the *Hokubei Nippo* to create the *Nichibei Shimbun*, which would eventually become the leading Japanese-language newspaper in the western United States with approximately 25,000 readers. By the 1920s, the *Nichibei Shimbun* added a Los Angeles edition, as well as an English-language section for American-born Niseis. In addition to sharing current events in both Japan and the United States, the newspaper listed employment and housing opportunities and wrote on many issues relevant to the early Japanese American community.

Some of the articles included advice on American etiquette and editorials on social and political causes. Abiko encouraged his readers to search for Japanese wives through the "picture bride" system. He also spoke out and protested against anti-Japanese legislation such as the Alien Land Laws and Immigration Act of 1924. He was a major proponent of proper "moral" behavior to improve the Japanese American community as well as its outward reputation.

Community Involvement

Beyond his newspaper duties, Abiko also invested time and resources toward the development of a utopian Japanese American Christian agricultural community in Central California. In order to achieve this vision, he first established the *Nichibei Kangyosha* (Japanese American Industrial Company) in 1902 to handle contract labor of Japanese immigrants and acquire farmland throughout central California. This organization encouraged immigration of Japanese laborers from both Japan and Hawai'i. Abiko subsequently created a savings and loan company to seed Japanese American farms, known as the

Nichibei Kinyusha. In 1906, he founded the *Beikoku Shokusan Kaisha* (American Land and Produce Company) to purchase undeveloped land in Livingston, California.

By 1907, Abiko invited several Issei families to become farm owners and begin developing the Yamato Colony on 2,450 acres of land in Livingston. He would eventually form two additional Japanese colonies in nearby Cressey, California, in 1918 and Cortez, California, in 1919. After some initial struggles with the natural terrain, as well as financial hardships of Abiko's land company, these colonies successfully grew a number of important agricultural crops.

Abiko died in 1936, before the unfortunate events of World War II. Although the mass incarceration of all West Coast Japanese Americans eventually led to the closure of the *Nichibei Shimbun* and the abandonment of the colonies he formed, Abiko's influence on Japanese America remains unmistakable.

See also: Nichibei Shimbun (Japanese American News)

Further Reading

Azuma, Eiichiro. *Between Two Empires: Race, History, and Transnationalism in Japanese America*. New York: Oxford University Press, 2005.

Ichioka, Yuji. *The Issei: The World of First Generation Japanese Immigrants 1885–1924*. New York: The Free Press, 1988.

Matsumoto, Valerie. *Farming the Home Place: A Japanese American Community in California, 1919–1982*. Ithaca, NY: Cornell University Press, 1993.

Dean Ryuta Adachi

AISO, JOHN FUJIO (1909–1987)

John Fujio Aiso was a second-generation Japanese American best known for his legal career as both a lawyer and a judge. He also served as an instructor at the Military Intelligence Service Language School during World War II.

Early Life and Education

Aiso was born on December 14, 1909, in Burbank, California, to Japanese immigrant parents. Although he was a very good student and popular among his classmates, he faced considerable discrimination due to his Japanese ethnicity. During junior high school, he was elected student body president, but the student government was suspended until his graduation, due to protests by other parents. In 1926, he won his high school's oratorical contest on the U.S. Constitution but was forced to withdraw by the school principal in order to coach the runner-up, who was of European descent.

After high school, Aiso attended Brown University, where he would graduate as class valedictorian in 1931. He then attended Harvard Law School, which he graduated from in 1934. By 1935, Aiso established his first successful law practice in New York. He also studied legal Japanese and Japanese law, which enabled him to do numerous translation and interpretation jobs for prominent Japanese, American, and even British companies.

Military Career

In 1941, Aiso was conscripted into the American army. Intelligence specialists in the U.S. War Department's Military Intelligence Division decided to create a secret language school for Japanese Americans called the Military Intelligence Service Language School (MISLS). Their primary training was as translators, interpreters, interrogators, and propaganda writers.

Although Aiso was originally assigned to the MIS Language School as a student, his linguistic aptitude caught the attention of the leaders, and he quickly became head instructor, and ultimately, director of training. Over the course of World War II, Aiso graduated over 6,000 military intelligence specialists, each of whom played a pivotal role in saving lives and shortening the war. He was the highest-ranking Nisei in the U.S. Armed Forces during World War II.

Return to Legal Career

After retiring from the army in 1947, Aiso established a new law practice in Los Angeles. He became the first Nisei judge when he was appointed to the Los Angeles Municipal Court in 1952. He became a superior court judge in 1957 and was appointed associate justice of the California court of appeal, Second Appellate District in 1968 by Governor Ronald Reagan.

In 1965, Aiso was awarded the Legion of Merit by President Lyndon Johnson, and, in 1984, he was awarded the 3rd Class Order of the Rising Sun by Japanese emperor Hirohito in honor of his contributions to understanding and friendship between the United States and Japan. He retired in 1983.

In December 1987, Aiso was attacked at a gas station during a mugging attempt. He suffered a severe head injury and was transported to a Burbank, California, hospital, where he would die later that month.

See also: Ito, Lance Alan (1950–)

Further Reading

Bess, Demaree. "California's Amazing Japanese." *Saturday Evening Post* 227, no. 44 (April 3, 1955): 38–83.

Ichinokuchi, Tad, ed. *John Aiso and the M.I.S: Japanese-American Soldiers in the Military Intelligence Service, World War II.* Los Angeles: The Club, 1988.

Morrision, Patti, and Santiago O'Donnell. "John Aiso, Prominent Nisei and Jurist, Dies after Mugger's Attack." *Los Angeles Times,* December 31, 1987. http://articles.latimes.com/1987-12-31/local/me-7802_1_john-aiso. Accessed August 1, 2017.

Dean Ryuta Adachi

AOKI, RICHARD (1938–2009)

Born November 20, 1938, in San Leandro, California, Richard Aoki was a civil rights activist and member of the Black Panther Party. Aoki was born to Japanese parents and later interned at the Topaz War Relocation Center in Utah from 1942 to 1945. Following World War II, Aoki and his family moved to West Oakland in a predominantly black neighborhood. After graduating from high school, he served in the U.S. Army on active duty for the first six months, followed by seven and a half years on reserve duty. After his active duty service, Aoki held a number of working-class jobs, in which he met fellow workers who were labor organizers, socialists, and communists who exposed him to Marxist–Leninist literature. In the early 1960s, Aoki joined the Socialist Workers Party (SWP) and the Young Socialist Alliance. As a student at Oakland City College (now Merritt College), he cofounded the Socialist Discussion Club in 1964. Through his group, he began working with the Soul Students Advisory Council and one of its leaders Bobby Seale, who eventually introduced Aoki to Huey Newton. Through their friendship, Aoki expanded his study to include Black Nationalism. When Seale and Newton organized the Black Panther Party for Self-Defense (BPP) in 1966, they consulted Aoki with their Ten-Point Program, the organization's set of guidelines, and Aoki was actively involved with the BPP from its onset, becoming the only Asian American in the organization to hold a leadership position.

In 1968, Aoki became involved in the early Asian American Movement in the San Francisco Bay area. He was a founding member of the Asian American Political Alliance (AAPA) at the University of California, Berkeley, advocating for ethnic studies programs on campus. In 1969, Aoki was one of four teaching assistants for the first Asian American studies program at UC Berkeley. He also was the chair of AAPA and the Asian American spokesperson for the Third World Liberation Front (TWLF) who pushed for ethnic studies. Aoki was one of the first Asian American Studies coordinators and taught many of its first classes. In 1972, Aoki moved on to the Peralta Community College District in the East Bay for the next 26 years as a counselor, instructor, and administrator.

Based on documents released by the Federal Bureau of Investigation (FBI) and after suing the FBI fives times, journalist Seth Rosenfeld gained access to over 300,000 pages of heavily redacted documents, which revealed Aoki as a paid informant from 1961 to 1977. When Rosenfeld interviewed Aoki in 2007, he denied having worked with the FBI.

Aoki died on March 15, 2009, originally reported to have died from complications from dialysis; however, it was later revealed that he had committed suicide by a self-inflicted gunshot wound. Before shooting himself, he laid out two sets of clothing: his U.S. Army uniform and his Black Panther uniform.

See also: Ichioka, Yuji (1936–2002)

Further Reading

Fujino, D. C. "The Black Liberation Movement and Japanese American Activism: The Radical Activism of Richard Aoki and Yuri Kochiyama." In *Afro Asia: Revolutionary Political and Cultural Connections between African Americans and Asian Americans,* edited by F. Ho and B. V. Mullen. Durham, NC: Duke University Press, 2008.

Fujino, D. C. *Samurai among Panthers: Richard Aoki on Race, Resistance, and a Paradoxical Life.* Minneapolis: University of Minnesota Press, 2012.

Cynthia Mari Orozco

ARATANI, GEORGE (1917–2013)

George Tetsuo Aratani was a second-generation Japanese American businessperson and philanthropist. He was best known for founding Mikasa chinaware and Kenwood electronics in the United States.

Early Life

Aratani was born in Gardena, California, on May 22, 1917. As a child, his parents moved their family to Guadalupe, a small agricultural community located in Santa Barbara County on the California central coast. George's father, Setsuo Aratani, became a successful farmer and entrepreneur. George was a talented high school athlete, and especially excelled in baseball.

Although George hoped to attend Stanford University, his parents convinced him to instead attend Keio University in Tokyo, where he could pursue a degree in Japanese law, while also learning the Japanese language and culture of his parents and ancestors. George's mother died in Tokyo in 1935, and his father died of tuberculosis in 1940. George decided to return to Guadalupe to help operate his father's businesses and never completed his undergraduate degree.

Following his father's death, George assumed leadership of the Guadalupe Produce Company in 1940 at the age of 22. In less than two years, Pearl Harbor was attacked by the Japan, leading to the incarceration in concentration camps of all Japanese Americans on the West Coast. Aratani was first sent to the Tulare Assembly Center, and eventually to the Gila River War Relocation Center. While at Gila River, he was forced to sell the Guadalupe Produce Company to repay his father's loan to the Superintendent of Banks, which had assumed the assets of Sumitomo Bank that were frozen at the outset of the war.

In 1944, Aratani joined the Military Intelligence Service Language School (MISLS), where he used his bilingual skills to teach Japanese to American soldiers. Before leaving for the MIS school at Camp Savage, Minnesota, he married Sakaye Inouye, a second-generation Japanese American incarcerated at the nearby Poston Relocation Center.

Successful Business Career

Following the end of World War II, George and Sakaye Aratani settled in Hollywood, California. He reached out to his former employees from the Guadalupe Produce Company and colleagues from the MIS to start a new imports company named American Commercial, Inc. The company's earliest widespread commercial success was with a line of Japanese-made chinaware introduced in late 1957 under the Mikasa brand. Mikasa eventually went public in 1994 and was sold to Arc International in 2000. At the time of its sale, Mikasa had $400 million in annual sales. Some of Aratani's other business ventures included a medical equipment export company founded in 1951 named AMCO, as well as Kenwood Electronics in 1961.

Philanthropy

George and Sakaye donated generously to many Japanese American organizations, especially in Southern California. They helped found the Keiro Nursing Home for Japanese American senior citizens, which currently operates as Keiro Senior HealthCare. In honor of their support, their name is quite visible in the Japanese American community, from the Japanese American National Museum's George & Sakaye Aratani Central Hall to the George and Sakaye Aratani Community Advancement Research Endowment grants at UCLA for research projects that strengthen ties between the Japanese American community and UCLA students, staff, faculty, and alumni. In 2004, he estimated that he had donated $10 million to various Japanese American organizations.

See also: Japanese Americans in Farming and Agriculture

Further Reading

Hirahara, Naomi. *An American Son: The Story of George Aratani, Founder of Mikasa and Kenwood.* Los Angeles: Japanese American National Museum, 2001.

Trounson, Rebecca. "George Aratani dies at 95; L.A. philanthropist who funded Japanese American causes." *Los Angeles Times*, February 21, 2013. http://articles.latimes.com/2013/feb/21/local/la-me-george-aratani-20130221. Accessed March 1, 2017.

Dean Ryuta Adachi

ARIYOSHI, GEORGE (1926–)

George Ariyoshi served as governor of Hawai'i from (1973–1986). He was Hawai'i's first Japanese American governor and the first elected governor of Asian descent in the United States. Ariyoshi, known for his quiet effectiveness, participated in the 1954 Democratic Revolution in Hawai'i, which saw the Democratic Party gain majorities in the house and senate in the territorial election. The 1954 Revolution was driven, in large part, by returning Japanese American military veterans (like Ariyoshi) unwilling to accept second-class status at home. Ariyoshi began his political career in the territorial House in 1954, followed by terms in the territorial Senate. Ariyoshi was elected as lieutenant governor in 1970; he was appointed acting governor when Gov. John A. Burns fell ill. Residents of Hawai'i reelected him to second and third terms. Throughout his political career, Ariyoshi never lost an election and continues to serve as an elder statesman for the Democratic Party in Hawai'i.

Ariyoshi, born in Honolulu to Japanese immigrants, recognized how his Japanese identity shaped his approach to public service. In his autobiography, Ariyoshi shared that serving as the first Japanese governor sometimes felt like a burden as he felt an obligation to succeed. In particular, he cited the concept of haji (shame) in Japanese American communities, where there is no greater wrong than to bring shame upon one's family and culture.

As governor, Ariyoshi promoted policies that optimized Hawai'i's development and strategic position on the Pacific Rim. He guided the state through its first poststatehood economic recession and wrestled with the challenges of land development and population growth and their impact on Hawai'i's limited natural resources. For example, he guided Hawai'i in its transition from an agricultural economy reliant on sugar and pineapple to diversifying land use. He advocated agricultural production of food crops that would advance the islands' self-sustainability. He also supported nonagricultural land development that helped Hawai'i transition to a tourism-based economy.

After term limits prevented him from seeking additional terms as governor, Ariyoshi accepted various corporate and nonprofit positions that continue his work expanding Hawai'i–Asia connections to advance trade and technological advancement. For instance, he serves on the board of the East West Center and is president of the Pacific Basin Development Council and founder of the Pacific International Center for High Technology Research. He remains with the law firm of Watanabe, Ing, and Komeiji, specializing in international, Hawai'i, and U.S. business consulting.

See also: Hirono, Mazie Keiko (1947–); Honda, Mike (1941–); Inouye, Daniel Ken (1924–2012); Matsui, Doris O. (1944–); Matsui, Robert T. (1941–2005); Matsunaga, "Spark" Masayuki (1916–1990); Mineta, Norman (1931–); Mink, Patsy Takemoto (1927–2002)

Further Reading

Ariyoshi, George R. *Hawai'i: The Past Fifty Years, the Next Fifty Years.* Honolulu: Watermark Publishing, 2009.

Ariyoshi, George R. *With Obligation to All.* Honolulu: Ariyoshi Foundation, distributed by University of Hawai'i Press, 1997.

Phillips, Paul C. *Hawaii's Democrats: Chasing the American Dream.* Washington, DC: University Press of America, 1982.

Lauren S. Morimoto

COMMISSION ON WARTIME RELOCATION AND INTERNMENT OF CIVILIANS

The Commission on Wartime Relocation and Internment of Civilians (CWRIC) was established by President Jimmy Carter (1924–, president 1977–1981) in 1980 to investigate and review the justification, implementation, and consequences of Executive Order 9066 (1942). This document was signed by Franklin D. Roosevelt (1882–1945) on February 19, 1942, and, on the basis of military necessity, it created the War Relocation Authority (WRA) and authorized the relocation and internment of over 120,000 Japanese American citizens during World War II (1939–1945). Once established, the CWRIC assessed the impact of the relocation, internment, and detention of American citizens and resident foreigners and recommended viable legislative remedies and financial redress for those individuals and families affected. Ultimately the commission resulted in publication of *Personal Justice Denied* (1982), passage of the Civil Liberties Act of 1988, an official government apology, survivors being awarded reparations, and establishment of a public education fund dedicated to discouraging similar actions and attitudes in the future.

Though the CWRIC was a bipartisan federal commission that was created through passage of the Commission on Wartime Relocation and Internment of Civilians Act, it also had roots in the activism of the Asian American community, as well as in the efforts of organizations such as the Japanese American Citizens League (JACL) and the National Council for Japanese American Redress (NCJAR). The nine-member commission held public hearings in various locations throughout the United States during 1981, during which they collected the testimony of over 750 persons, including interred Japanese Americans, Aleut Alaskans, elected officials, scholars, and other interested parties. In addition, the commission also reviewed government documents, military assessments, archived material, scholarly analysis, and personal testimonies.

The conclusions and recommendations of the CWRIC, published as *Personal Justice Denied*, stated that the relocation and internment of Japanese Americans had not been justified by security concerns or military necessity, and

In 1981 Senator Daniel K. Inouye of Hawai'i, spoke before the Commission on Wartime Relocation and Internment of Civilians. Inouye lost his right arm fighting for the United States in Europe during World War II, and told the panel that its report should haunt the nation "so that we will never forget that we are capable of such an act" as the holding without charge or crime of 120,000 Japanese Americans during that war. (AP Photo/ Dennis Cook)

highlighted the fact that prior to the government's actions there was little documented evidence to suggest cases of Japanese American espionage or sabotage. Instead, the report maintained that the actions taken by the American government in 1942 were the result of racial prejudice, public hysteria arising in the aftermath of the attacks on Pearl Harbor, and the failure of political leadership. Furthermore, the commission cited that the government policies of the period promoted racial exclusion and led to losses in property, finance, education, employment, and the division of Japanese American families and communities.

The comprehensive and influential nature of CWRIC's report led to issuance of an official government apology, passage of the Civil Liberties Act of 1988, authorization of compensation and redress payments of $20,000 each to survivors and their relatives, as well as the establishment of a public education fund. In addition, both the commission and its recommendations heightened the American public's understanding of Japanese American culture and the unjust internment of American citizens during World War II. Subsequently, several war relocation camps were designated either as state historical landmarks or as National Historical Sites, which means they are listed on the National Register of Historic Places and are under the direction of the U.S. National Park Service.

See also: Executive Order 9066; Internment, World War II; Kooskia Internment Camp; Manzanar Children's Village (1942–1945); Pearl Harbor; World War II

Further Reading

Commission on Wartime Relocation and Internment of Civilians. *Personal Justice Denied: Report of the Commission on Wartime Relocation and Internment of Civilians.* Seattle: University of Washington Press; and Washington, DC: Civil Liberties Public Education Fund, 1997.

Hatamiya, Leslie T. *Righting a Wrong: Japanese Americans and the Passage of the Civil Liberties Act of 1988.* Stanford, CA: Stanford University Press, 1993.

Shimabukuro, Robert Sadamu. *Born in Seattle: The Campaign for Japanese American Redress.* Seattle: University of Washington Press, 2001.

Sean Morton

FUKUHARA, HARRY KATSUHARU (1920–2015)

Harry Katsuharu Fukuhara was a Nisei linguist in the U.S. Military Intelligence Service and worked as an interpreter, translator, and interrogator during World War II and the occupation of Japan. Born in Seattle, Washington, Fukuhara moved back to his mother's hometown of Hiroshima when he was 13 years old. After five years, Fukuhara returned to the United States and moved to California where he received an associate's degree in June 1941 from Glendale Junior College. Following the signing of Executive Order 9066, resulting in the removal of Japanese to incarceration centers, authorities sent Fukuhara to Gila River, Arizona. To prove his loyalty, Fukuhara enlisted in the U.S. Army in November 1942 and was sent to training at the Military Intelligence Service Language School (MISLS) at Camp Savage, Minnesota.

Upon graduation in May 1943, Fukuhara was sent to Australia, New Guinea, and then the Philippines as part of the Allied Translator and Interpreter Service (ATIS). Fukuhara eventually became the chief of a 10-man interrogation/interpreting team that was composed of Australian, Dutch, and American military personnel. Fukuhara's team had great success obtaining critical information from seized documents and prisoners of war. They were also critical in preparing surrender leaflets, participating in reconnaissance missions, persuading Japanese soldiers to surrender, and serving on U.S. Navy patrol torpedo missions. For his accomplishments, authorities promoted Fukuhara to master sergeant and awarded him a Bronze Star with two oak leaf clusters. He later received a battlefield commission to second lieutenant on August 10, 1945.

The conclusion of the war was bittersweet for Fukuhara, who, like other Nisei linguists, had relatives residing in Japan including his mother, two brothers, and an aunt who were in Hiroshima when the United States dropped the atomic bomb. Ultimately, he accompanied the occupation forces as part of the 33rd Division and on his days off searched for his family members in the remnants of Hiroshima. His mother and aunt survived the bomb by hiding

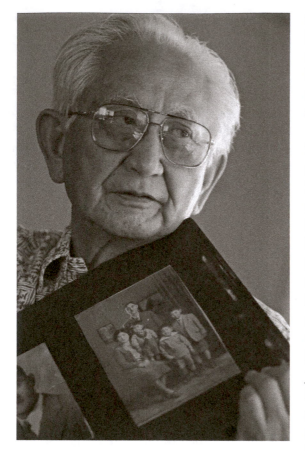

Harry Fukuhara, 75 years old, poses with a family portrait from his childhood taken in Hiroshima, Japan, in 1927, at his home in San Jose, California, in 1995. (AP Photo/Lacy Atkins)

in an underground shelter but his older brother, Victor, was traveling to work when the bomb exploded and died from acute radiation sickness within a year.

Fukuhara continued to serve in the army until his retirement as a colonel in 1971. For the next 20 years, he served as a Department of the Army civilian focusing on counterintelligence. For his work during World War II, Fukuhara was inducted into the Military Intelligence Hall of Fame in 1988 and also received the Order of the Rising Sun 3rd Class, Gold Ray with Neck Ribbon from the emperor of Japan. Fukuhara died on April 8 in Honolulu at the age of 95 and was survived by sons Brian and Mark, daughters Shary Fukuhara-Hashimoto and Pam Tsuzaki, and eight grandchildren. Services were held in San Jose, California, and in Honolulu.

See also: Draft Resisters; 442nd Regimental Combat Team/100th Infantry Battalion; No-No Boys; World War II

Further Reading

Fukuhara, Harry. "The Return," *Nikkei Heritage: National Japanese American Historical Society* VII, no. 3 (1995): 12.

Ishimaru, Stone S. *Military Intelligence Service Language School, U.S. Army, Fort Snelling, Minnesota.* Los Angeles: Tec Com Production, 1991.

Kelli Y. Nakamura

HAYAKAWA, SAMUEL ICHIYÉ (1906–1992)

Samuel Ichiyé "S. I." Hayakawa was a Canadian-born scholar and U.S. senator. He is best known for his contributions to the field of linguistics as well as his controversial tenure as president of San Francisco State College (now San Francisco State University).

Early Life and Career

Hayakawa was born to Japanese immigrant parents in Vancouver, Canada, although as a child his family would later settle in Winnipeg. Hayakawa earned his bachelor's degree from the University of Manitoba in 1927. He also went on to receive graduate degrees in English from McGill University and the University of Wisconsin–Madison. Hayakawa would go on to become an English lecturer and professor at the Armour Institute of Technology (currently Illinois Institute of Technology), the University of Chicago, and San Francisco State College. Hayakawa's most significant literary contribution, *Language in Action* (1941) expanded on the General Semantics movements led by Alfred Korzybski.

Because he was living in Illinois at the outbreak of World War II, away from the forced incarceration of Japanese Americans living in the western United States, Hayakawa was not sent into a concentration camp. Although he expressed sympathy toward the incarcerated Japanese Americans, Hayakawa generally avoided discussing anti-Japanese discrimination. His strong conservative beliefs often clashed with the prevailing attitudes of Japanese American communities during the mid-20th century. In fact, he later spoke out against the McCarran-Walter Act of 1952 that would create a path toward naturalization for Isseis.

Political Involvement

In 1968, the president of San Francisco State College resigned amid the campus-wide student protests of the Third World Liberation Front. Hayakawa became the acting university president and rose to public awareness due to his defiant stance against the student protesters. Perhaps his height of notoriety was when he personally jumped onto a sound truck to rip speaker wires during a live televised student demonstration, leading many to refer to him as "Samurai Sam."

Following his tenure in higher education, Hayakawa pursued a career in politics. In 1976, his reputation as a political outsider helped him win the Republican primary over more established political opponents, and eventually he defeated the incumbent Democratic senator John Tunney. During his single term in office, he supported a bill to create the Commission on Wartime Relocation and Internment of Civilians. Although this commission's findings eventually led to redress and reparations for all Japanese Americans sent to concentration camps during World War II, Hayakawa personally stated that the camps ultimately were advantageous for the Japanese American community by taking them away from "their ghettoized Japan-town existence into the main-stream of American life."

Hayakawa spent his later years in Mill Valley, California. Some of his other diverse personal interests included fencing, African artwork, Chinese ceramics, and jazz music. In 1992, he died of a stroke at the age of 85, after being hospitalized for bronchitis.

See also: Japanese American Citizens League; University Presidents and Chancellors

Further Reading

Haslam, Gerald W., and Janice E. Haslam. *In Thought and Action: The Enigmatic Life of S.I. Hayakawa*. Lincoln: University of Nebraska Press, 2011.

Robinson, Greg. *After Camp: Portraits in Midcentury Japanese American Life and Politics*. Berkeley: University of California Press, 2012.

Dean Ryuta Adachi

HIRONO, MAZIE KEIKO (1947–)

Mazie Keiko Hirono is a U.S. senator for Hawai'i. She was previously lieutenant governor of Hawai'i for eight years and served in both the Hawai'i and U.S. Houses of Representatives. Hirono is the first female senator for Hawai'i and the first Asian American female senator in the United States.

Hirono was born in Mutsuai (now Koori), Fukushima Prefecture, Japan, on November 3, 1947. She states that her father, Matabe Hirono, was an alcoholic gambler, and that her mother Laura fled with her three children to escape the marriage. In 1955, Mazie moved to Hawai'i with her mother and her brother Roy. Mazie's other brother, Wayne, joined them two years later. Mazie Hirono became a naturalized U.S. citizen in 1959. Although she could not read English at first, Hirono graduated with honors from Kaimuki High School in 1966 and then completed a bachelor of arts degree in Psychology at the University of Hawai'i, Mānoa. She was inspired by visits to a mental health facility and Vietnam War protests to become involved in the public life to serve others. Hirono completed her law degree at Georgetown University in 1978 and returned to Honolulu, where she served as the state's deputy attorney general before beginning her career as a lawyer.

Encouraged by friends to enter politics, Hirono ran as a Democratic candidate for the Hawai'i House of Representatives in 1980. She won her seat and served in the House from 1981 to 1994, where she chaired the House Consumer Protection and Commerce Committee. She left the position in 1994 when she was elected as the state's lieutenant governor, a title she held until 2002. In this role, she focused her attention on education, tourism, and insurance laws. She ran unsuccessfully for governor in 2002 before winning a seat in the U.S. House of Representatives in 2006. She took office as the first Asian-born woman to serve in the House. She was part of the Committee on Education and the Workforce as well as the Committee on Transportation and Infrastructure. She was reelected to her seat in the 2008 and 2010 elections before deciding to run for the vacated U.S. Senate seat of fellow Democrat Daniel Akaka. She faced Linda Lingle, who had beaten her in the gubernatorial race but was successful this time, receiving 68 percent of votes.

Hirono is the first Japanese-born senator, the first woman of Asian ancestry to be elected to the Senate, and the first Buddhist senator. She is a member of the Congressional Asian Pacific American Caucus. She serves on several committees, including the Committee on Armed Services, Committee on Energy and Natural Resources, and the Select Committee on Intelligence. Hirono is known for a strong liberal voting record and her focus on issues related to youth, Hawai'i's heritage, and assistance for immigrants. In March 2015, she helped introduce the Filipino Veterans Family Reunification Act, which aims to help Filipinos who fought for the United States in World War II receive visas for their children.

Hirono lives in Honolulu with her husband Leighton Kim Oshima.

See also: Ariyoshi, George (1926–); Inouye, Daniel Ken (1924–2012); Honda, Mike (1941–); Matsui, Doris O. (1944–); Matsui, Robert T. (1941–2005); Matsunaga, "Spark" Masayuki (1916–1990); Mineta, Norman (1931–); Mink, Patsy Takemoto (1927–2002)

Further Reading

Joint Committee on Printing. *Official Congressional Directory: 113th Congress.* Washington, DC: U.S. Government Printing Office, 2014.

Weatherford, Doris. *Women in American Politics: History and Milestones.* Los Angeles: CQ Press, 2012.

Kevin Hogg

HONDA, MIKE (1941–)

Mike Honda is a currently serving Democratic congressman from California's 15th District. Geographically, Honda's district encompasses western San Jose and the Silicon Valley, which he has represented since 2001. Honda is of Japanese descent. Michael Makoto Honda was born on June 27, 1941, in California. Like many others of Japanese ancestry, Honda spent considerable time with his family in an internment camp in Colorado during World War II. Honda's family eventually returned to their native California and Honda graduated in 1968 with bachelor's degrees in Biological Science and Spanish from San Jose State University. During college, Honda took time away from his studies and served in the Peace Corps between 1965 and 1967 in El Salvador. He would later earn a master of arts from San Jose State University in 1974. Before Honda's political career, he was a science teacher and later served as a principal in public schools.

In 1981, Honda won his first election and started his political career from the San Jose Unified School Board. He was later elected to the Santa Clara County Board of Supervisors in 1990 and served in the California State Assembly between 1996 and 2000.

In 2000, Honda, a staunch Democrat, was successful in his bid for the House seat after defeating his moderate Republican competitor. Since then, Honda has so far been up for reelection six times without any serious challenge. He was reelected in 2010 and 2012 and is currently serving his district in Congress. As a representative for the Silicon Valley, Honda has emphasized his commitment to high-tech industries as well as the infrastructure accommodations of a fast-growing region. Since his election, Honda has served on the Science Committee and the Transportation and Infrastructure Committee and was later appointed to join the influential Appropriations Committee in 2007. Honda also sits on various subcommittees. In terms of his role within the Democratic Party, Honda was selected as House Democratic senior whip in 2007 and works closely with the Democratic Caucus to promote Democratic agendas.

Honda, a champion of civil rights, has served for many years as the chair of the Congressional Asian Pacific American Caucus and is the founder and the chair of the Congressional Ethiopia and Ethiopian American Caucus.

True to his commitment to civil rights, Honda voted for the Local Law Enforcement Hate Crimes Prevention Act of 2009, which will provide assistance to law enforcement agencies in the prevention as well as prosecution of hate crimes.

Honda is also adamant about protecting voting rights for all Americans, especially those serving in the military or residing overseas. It is Honda's belief that unnecessary bureaucratic red tape prohibits or deters those Americans living abroad from exercising their voting rights. Moreover, Honda's personal experience from serving in the Peace Corps as a young man made him sympathetic to the plight of those who try to vote from outside the United States.

In response to the aforementioned problem, Honda cosponsored the Overseas Voting Practical Amendments Act of 2009, which he hopes will help eliminate voting restrictions for Americans overseas based on state residency or other state-enforced requirements (such as having the ballot printed on a certain type of paper). This bill will also provide funding for the dissemination of voting information to those living abroad. As of August 2017, the Overseas Voting Practical Amendments Act of 2009 was still under consideration in the U.S. Congress.

On a similar note, Honda maintains that all Americans should have the right to vote regardless of race, ethnicity, or English proficiency. In response to the growth of language minorities in the United States, Honda supports the renewal and provisions under the Voting Rights Act that states English proficiency cannot become a criterion in determining whether one has the right to vote. For Honda, language minorities should not and cannot be disenfranchised because of their potentially lower levels of English proficiency.

Honda is one of the few Asian Americans who have served in the U.S. Congress since the inception of the United States of America. His commitment to civil rights, particularly fighting inequality in the education system, has earned him the Civil Rights Award from the National Education Association (NEA).

See also: Ariyoshi, George (1926–); Inouye, Daniel Ken (1924–2012); Hirono, Mazie Keiko (1947–); Matsui, Doris O. (1944–); Matsui, Robert T. (1941–2005); Matsunaga, "Spark" Masayuki (1916–1990); Mineta, Norman (1931–); Mink, Patsy Takemoto (1927–2002)

Further Reading

Honorable Michael Honda, Member of Congress. 2013. *Who's Who of Asian Americans.* http://www.asianamerican.net/bios/Honda-Mike.html. Accessed September 16, 2013.
The Washington Post. 2009. "The U.S. Congress Votes Database: Members of Congress/ Mike Honda." http://projects.washingtonpost.com/congress/members/H001034/. Accessed September 14, 2012.

Jeanette Yih Harvie

ICHIOKA, YUJI (1936–2002)

Yuji Ichioka was born in San Francisco as a son of Japanese immigrants. Having interned at the Topaz internment camp in Utah during the Pacific War at the age of six, Ichioka returned with his parents and siblings to Berkeley, where he stayed until high school graduation in 1954. Ichioka then served in the U.S. Army and was stationed in Germany; after his discharge, he attended University of California, Los Angeles (UCLA) and graduated in 1962. Intending to pursue modern Chinese history with a fellowship, Ichioka moved to New York City to enroll in a Columbia University graduate program, which he quit soon after. It was during this period that he became deeply involved in social justice and civil rights issues in collaboration with African American and other minority activists. After leaving the intellectual ivory tower, Ichioka worked as a youth guidance counselor in predominantly minority neighborhoods of New York City. His commitment to minority empowerment soon led to a strong interest in the history of Asian Americans, providing a background for his first trip to Japan in the winter of 1966. As he often discussed later, Ichioka's encounter on a Yokohama-bound ship with aged Japanese immigrants from Brazil peaked his interest in migration history and the migrant experience.

After returning from Japan, where he established lifelong friendships with progressive-minded Japanese, Ichioka enrolled in the Asian Studies graduate program at the University of California, Berkeley, to write a master's thesis on a Japanese nationalist of the Meiji era, titled "Takayama Chogyu and His Nihonshugi: Its Nature and Significance" (1968).

Ichioka's contribution to the Asian American Movement and Asian American Studies took place during his graduate education at UC Berkeley. Along with his partner Emma Gee, who he had met at Columbia, Ichioka played a central role in forming the Asian American Political Alliance—an organization of mainly college-age radical Asian activists in the area, who participated in the interracial civil rights and anti–Vietnam War movements. Ichioka is credited with coining of the term "Asian American" to bring different Asian groups under a panethnic political coalition for the causes of racial equality, anti-imperialism, and social justice. Along with Gee and other activists/students, Ichioka was involved in the development of the first Asian American studies courses at UC Berkeley. When students at UCLA successfully demanded a course on Asian Americans in 1969, Ichioka was selected as the first instructor, thereby beginning his lifelong affiliation with UCLA. Ichioka and Gee served as founding members of the Asian American Studies Center there. When taking part in curriculum building and other administrative matters, Ichioka promoted research and archival development relating to Japanese immigration history. His role as an archivist, cataloger, and custodian of the Japanese American Research Project (JARP) Collection was illustrative of his multifaceted contribution to historical scholarship on Japanese Americans.

Committed to producing scholarship for the benefit of social justice and community empowerment, Ichioka made himself available for off-campus lectures and other nonacademic speaking engagements. This same activist-scholar impulse, however, also turned Ichioka rather critical of recent Asian American scholarship that tended to overindulge in the use of theoretical jargon and abstraction.

At the same time, Ichioka was ahead of an academic trend in Asian American studies. For example, he was among the first to break new ground in transnational studies as early as the mid-1980s despite his refusal to depart from empirical historical research. Before such studies became popular in the field, Ichioka advocated comparative studies of Japanese in the Western Hemisphere. He pioneered in the critical analysis of immigrant nationalism and transnationalism, albeit without relying on fashionable theoretical formulations. These developments coincided with another notable shift in Ichioka's scholarship from research on leftists, common laborers, and immigrant women to an analysis of the "second-generation problem" and other controversial subjects, like Nisei "disloyalty." At the time of his death in September 2002, he was preparing a manuscript for his second book, and he was contemplating a major conference and research on Kibei. When he passed away, Ichioka was research associate and adjunct associate professor of history at UCLA. He was married to Emma Gee, a scholar of Asian American women and history as well as a writer and labor activist.

During his career as a professional historian, Ichioka traveled numerous times to Japan for research and teaching while publishing two major monographs: *The Issei: The World of the First Generation Japanese Immigrants, 1885–1924* (The Free Press, 1988), and *Before Internment: Essays in Japanese-American History*, edited by Gordon H. Change and Eiichiro Azuma (Stanford University Press, 2005). Other publications include: two edited volumes: Karl G. Yoneda, *Ganbatte: Sixty-Year Struggle of a Kibei Worker* (1983), and *Views from Within: The Japanese American Evacuation and Resettlement Study* (1989); two major annotated bibliographies: *A Buried Past* (1974), and *A Buried Past II* (1999); and dozens of path-breaking journal articles in *Amerasia Journal*, *Pacific Historical Review*, *Agricultural History*, and *California History*, among others. His personal papers and research materials are available at UCLA's Special Collections.

See also: Aoki, Richard (1938–2009); Japanese Transnational Identity

Further Reading

Ichioka, Yuji. *Before Internment: Essays in Prewar Japanese American History*, edited by Gordon H. Chang and Eiichiro Azuma. Stanford, CA: Stanford University Press, 2006.

Eiichiro Azuma

IIJIMA, KAZU IKEDA (1918–2007)

The youngest of three daughters, Kazu Ikeda Iijima was born in West Oakland's Chinatown. Her father, Kando Ikeda, was an avowed Issei nationalist who published a local Japanese language newspaper, and her mother, Tsukiko, worked as a domestic in neighboring Piedmont County. The Ikeda children were rooted, but not limited, to the Oakland Japanese American community. Kazu Ikeda, like many young Bay Area Nisei, participated in ethnic Japanese activities. She visited Buddhist Temple and attended Japanese Language School. She also played on integrated sports teams and wrote several stories for her high school literary journal. However, the onset of the Great Depression, the tragic passing of her mother in 1933, and her decision to enroll at UC Berkeley in 1935 ended this sheltered life and exposed Ikeda to radical ideas for the first time.

The 1930s witnessed a dire economic downturn, entrenched U.S. racism, and rising Fascist movements in Europe and Japan. Yet Ikeda remained largely unaware of the severity and interconnectedness of these crises until introduced to Marxist analyses by her older sister Nori, who was by then a Communist Party (CPUSA) member. It was the Communist Party's antiracist principles and

Marxist approach to tackling racism in particular that won Ikeda over to the Party, which she joined in 1938. As she later recalled, "we couldn't understand why everyone hated us [Japanese Americans] so much. So when my sister talked about communism and socialism we responded to that." Furthermore, the multiracial Berkeley chapter of the Young Communist League (YCL), the "only place where we didn't face racism" according to Ikeda, carried out their socialist ideals in their everyday interactions, a stark contrast to the anti-Asian discrimination the Ikeda sisters experienced in Oakland.

Ikeda's activism within the YCL brought her into contact with like-minded Japanese Americans in the East Bay Area, with whom she formed the Oakland Nisei Democratic Club in 1938. Created as a political outlet for working-class Japanese Americans, many of whom were close to the CPUSA, the Oakland Nisei Democrats attempted to recruit Niseis to progressive causes and provide a counterweight to the more conservative JACL. Yet the impact of the Nisei Democrats extended beyond local Japanese American communities. For instance, the Club supported picketing GM workers in Oakland and helped to pass a resolution at the 1938 Young Democrats convention that committed the California Democratic Party to ending racial discrimination.

Shortly after the attack on Pearl Harbor, however, the Communist Party revoked the membership of West Coast Japanese Americans, including Ikeda's, under the pretext of an anti-Fascist alliance with President Roosevelt. This betrayal was compounded by the CPUSA's silence on the unconstitutional internment of Japanese Americans under Executive Order 9066, which Ikeda and the Nisei Democrats protested in defiance of the party. These setbacks inadvertently set the stage for Ikeda to focus on her personal life and establish herself as an independent radical. In 1942, she married Tak Iijima, a member of the 442nd Army unit in the Topaz, Utah, concentration camp. After the war, the couple resettled to New York City, where they had two children, Chris and Lynne. In New York, Ikeda, now Iijima, joined the Japanese American Committee for Democracy (JACD), a left-wing, anti-imperialist organization where she served as editor of their newsletter. Her involvement with the JACD was the exception to an otherwise apolitical period, however, as she put activism on the backburner, until the 1960s, to concentrate on raising her children.

Inspired by the Black Power's penetrating critique of U.S. racism and instillation of cultural pride, Iijima and her friend Minn Matsuda created Asian American for Action, or Triple A, one of the first East Coast pan-Asian organizations, in 1968. Triple A's primary focus was the Vietnam War. According to Triple A, U.S. imperialism in Southeast Asia was facilitated by American dehumanization of the Vietnamese, which mirrored the racism encountered by Asian Americans, and an imperialist drive for the region's natural resources. As an experienced organizer, Iijima helped mobilize weekly Triple A meetings and demonstrations along with her two children, including two large anti-imperialist rallies in Washington, D.C., and mentored a new generation of Asian

American activists, who appreciated her flexible approach to the changing political environment. Iijima later became recognized as the "Mother of the Movement" and continued to be politically active until she passed in 2007. Today, Kazu Ikeda Iijima is remembered not only as a tireless advocate for social justice but also as a caring mother, wife, and community member.

See also: Aoki, Richard (1938–2009); Ichioka, Yuji (1936–2002); Japanese American Citizens League

Further Reading

Ishizuka, Karen L. "Flying in the Face of Race, Gender, Class and Age: A Story about Kazu Iijima, One of the Mothers of the Asian American Movement." http://www.onyxfoundation.org/static/uploads/2008/essaycontest/ishizuka.pdf. Accessed December 10, 2012.

Megan White

INOUYE, DANIEL KEN (1924–2012)

Daniel Ken Inouye was a Democratic senator from Hawai'i who reached the status of President pro tempore of Congress, third in line to the U.S. presidency; a distinguished army officer in the famed 100th/442nd Regimental Combat Team during World War II; and a member of the campaign for Hawai'i statehood, which culminated in a congressional ratification in 1959. Inouye, at the time of his death, was and remains the only Asian American to lay in state in the U.S. Capitol.

Daniel Ken Inouye was a senator and army officer in the famed 100th/442nd Regimental Combat Team during World War II. Inouye also served as chairman of the U.S. Senate Committee on Appropriations. (AP Photo)

Early Life in Hawai'i, World War II, and Military Participation

Born in Honolulu of the Territory of Hawai'i, Inouye, the eldest of four children and whose parents were Hyotaro and Kame Inouye, grew up on Honolulu and attended McKinley High School. After the bombing of Pearl Harbor, United States' entry into World War II, and the incarceration of Japanese and Japanese Americans on the West Coast, the War Department in cooperation with the Japanese American Citizens League called for volunteers for a Japanese American military unit, which later became known as the 442nd Regimental Combat Team. Inouye enlisted, trained at Camp Shelby, Mississippi, and participated in the European campaign where he rose to the rank of captain, sustained an injury that claimed his right arm, and distinguished himself on the battlefield, which garnered him several military accolades. On June 21, 2000, then-president Clinton upgraded his Distinguished Service Cross to the Medal of Honor.

Postwar Hawai'i and Congressional Experience

In the aftermath of World War II, Inouye returned back to Hawai'i and rather than pursue a medical degree, due the loss of most of his right arm during war, he graduated from the University of Hawai'i with a BA in political science in 1950 on the G. I. Bill. After marrying Margaret "Maggie" Awamura, Inouye applied to George Washington University Law School in Washington, D.C., and received his JD in 1952. After law school, Inouye's political career as a representative of Hawai'i began in 1954 when he was elected to Hawai'i's territorial House of Representatives. His desire to participate in politics stemmed from his wartime experiences where he and others from the 100th/442nd Regimental Combat Team wanted to change Hawai'i to benefit the nonwhite population. After the passage of Hawai'i statehood in 1959, Inouye was elected as a U.S. representative and later senator in 1962 of Hawai'i.

Throughout the 1970s and 1980s, Sen. Inouye was involved in some prominent political issues such as serving on the Senate Watergate Committee and chairing a special committee during the Iran-Contra investigations. Inouye was also influential in the passage of the Civil Liberties Act of 1988, which relied on the Commission on Wartime Relocation and Internment of Civilians that revealed that Japanese American incarceration was not a military necessity but premised on racial prejudice and discrimination.

During the 1990s and 2000s, while as senior Democratic senator of Hawai'i, Inouye championed Native American rights not only for native tribes of the continental U.S. but also Kanaka Maoli (native Hawai'ians). Inouye was instrumental in the passage of the 1988 Native Hawai'ian Education Act, which supported native Hawai'ian students with education tuition assistance, and, in 1990, Inouye sponsored the Native American Language Act in order to preserve, protect, and promote the rights of native peoples to practice, develop, and conduct business in their native languages. In spite of Inouye's congressional record, native scholars and activists of Hawai'i have contested that

Inouye served as an extension of the U.S. empire by the increased support of and resources for U.S. militarism around the world and especially for military bases, exercises, equipment, and personnel in Hawai'i. In the 2000s, Inouye reached the top echelons in U.S. national politics by becoming President pro tempore of the U.S. Senate and the chairman of the U.S. Senate Committee on Appropriations.

See also: Ariyoshi, George (1926–); 442nd Regimental Combat Team/100th Infantry Battalion; Hirono, Mazie Keiko (1947–); Honda, Mike (1941–); Japanese Immigration to Hawai'i; Mink, Patsy Takemoto (1927–2002); World War II

Further Reading

Inouye, Daniel K. *Go for Broke.* Englewood Cliffs: Prentice-Hall, 1967.
Inouye, Daniel K. *Journey to Washington.* Englewood Cliffs: Prentice-Hall, 1967.

Jeffrey T. Yamashita

ITO, LANCE ALAN (1950–)

In 37 years of professional life as corporate lawyer, assistant district attorney, judge, proponent of television cameras in the courtroom, and advocate for the rights of foreign nationals and non-English speakers in the courts of California, Lance Alan Ito is most remembered as the presiding judge in *People v. Orenthal James [O.J.] Simpson*, a double homicide trial in which Simpson, a famous former athlete, television sportscaster, actor, and advertising pitchman, was acquitted in 1995 of the brutal murders of his former wife, Nicole Brown Simpson and her friend, Ronald Lyle Goldman. The most significant criminal proceeding in the last quarter of the 20th century, Ito's decision to allow cameras in the courtroom during the Simpson trial brought to the surface issues of racism and class privilege in America.

The second child and only son of public school teachers Toshi Nagamori Ito and James Osamu Ito, Lance Ito was born on August 1, 1950, in Los Angeles, California, five years to the day that his maternal grandfather Seiichiro Nagamori committed suicide. Born in Japan, Nagamori was a successful salesman for the Sun Life Insurance Company of Canada, enjoying a solidly middle-class professional life at a time when few such opportunities existed for any Japanese—alien or native born—in the United States. One of only 98 insurance sales agents of Japanese ethnicity in the entire United States, he worked alongside five colleagues in an office in Los Angeles's Little Tokyo, until Executive Order 9066 and subsequent military proclamations forced Nagamori, his wife, and his teenage daughter to the Santa Anita Racetrack Assembly Center in March 1942 and their later removal to the Heart Mountain, Wyoming, Internment camp, where he and his wife remained until December 1945. Financially ruined by internment and unable to find work, Seiichiro Nagamori's death was emblematic of the psychological impact of internment on the lives and fortunes of the Issei (first generation). In her memoir, Toshi Ito wrote that Lance's maternal grandmother Kei Hiraoka Nagamori believed her only grandson was the reincarnation of his grandfather.

Lance Ito and his sister Chrislyn were raised in the Silver Lake neighborhood of Los Angeles. At John Marshall High School, Ito was elected student body president and played varsity tennis. Entering the University of California, Los Angeles, in 1968, he majored in political science, graduating with honors. Graduating from the School of Law at the University of California, Berkeley, in 1975, Ito decided to pursue a career in corporate litigation. Joining the law firm of Irsfeld, Irsfeld, and Younger, he grew impatient with the slow pace of his apprenticeship. Determining that work as a public prosecutor offered unparalleled opportunity to gain the experience in litigation he needed for a senior position in corporate practice, he joined the Office of the Los Angeles District Attorney as an assistant in 1977. He never returned to the private sector.

At the Office of District Attorney, Ito's work focused primarily on criminal gang activity. As assistant district attorney, he authored California Penal Code Section 171 (making it a felony to carry a weapon into a California courthouse) and Penal Code 600 (making it a felony to harm a police dog or police horse). It was his work in gang activity that brought him to the attention of then California attorney general George Deukmejian. Elected governor of California in 1983, Deukmejian appointed Ito to the Municipal Court in 1987, and then to the Superior Court in 1989, where he served as an elected judge until his retirement in 2015.

Prior to his 1994 assignment as judge in the Simpson murder trial, Ito was presiding judge in California's 1991 prosecution of Charles Keating for fraud, racketeering, and conspiracy in the failure of 1,043 savings and loan associations in the United States. Keating's state and federal convictions were overturned by the U.S. Court of Appeals in 1996. In the state case, the federal court ruled that Ito had erred by giving the jury faulty instructions. In 1999, Keating entered a plea agreement with the federal government. In the California case, Ito famously quoted American songwriter Woody Guthrie, telling Keating, "More people have suffered from the point of a fountain pen than from a gun." Ito's work in the savings and loan scandal led the Los Angeles Bar Association to name him trial judge of the year in 1992.

Ironically, although the arrest, trial, and acquittal of O. J. Simpson from 1994 to 1995 became a narrative of race relations in the United States at the end of the 20th century, the black/white conflict revealed a simplification of racism beyond the black/white divide. Throughout the trial, Ito was the subject of scorn and ridicule, much of it centered on racialized stereotypes of Asian

American speech and mannerisms. From the lowest reaches of shock jock radio personalities, to the mocking derision of U.S. senator from New York, Alfonse D'Amato, Lance Ito maintained his personal dignity throughout. To this day he has never made a public comment about the Simpson trial.

Ito lives in Pasadena, California, with his wife of 35 years, retired chief of Los Angeles County Police, Margaret York.

See also: Aiso, John Fujio (1909–1987)

Further Reading

Ray, Don. "Lance A. Ito, Judicial Profile." *Los Angeles Daily Journal*, December 10, 2008. http://web.archive.org/web/20081210030442/http://www.donray.com/LanceIto.htm. Accessed March 1, 2017.

Toobin, Jeffrey. *The Run of His Life: The People v. O.J. Simpson.* New York: Random House, 1996.

JAPAN BASHING

Japan bashing refers to anti-Japanese sentiment caused by U.S.–Japan trade friction during the 1970s and 1980s. Despite severe damage to its land and infrastructure during World War II, Japan experienced rapid economic growth from the mid-1950s to the early-1970s, a phenomenon called the "Japanese economic miracle." During the U.S. occupation of Japan and up until the early 1950s, most Americans regarded products made in Japan as cheap and low quality. However, vast improvements in manufacturing led to a rapid increase in product quality and, subsequently, an increase in exports, particularly to the United States. By 1968, these economic developments had improved the Japanese economy so much that Japan's Gross National Product was second only to that of the United States. However, the U.S. economy had been suffering from a deep recession, and its trade balance slipped into deficit in the 1970s. America's trade deficit with Japan grew from $1.2 billion in 1970 to $43.5 billion in 1985.

The massive trade imbalance between the United States and Japan developed into a serious political issue. The United States placed restrictions on the importation of Japanese textiles, consumer electronic goods, and steel in the 1960s to 1970s, and on automobiles in the 1980s. American manufacturers complained that competition with Japan was "unfair"—politicizing the issue and refusing to recognize that American products were becoming less competitive as Japanese imports became increasingly affordable and higher in quality. The U.S. government demanded that Japan voluntarily limit exports to the United States and open its closed domestic market to U.S. agricultural products. It imposed a high tariff on particular Japanese imports, enacted a series of trade sanctions, and accused several Japanese manufacturers of "dumping" products in the U.S. market.

On the other hand, many Americans became curious as to why Japan had been able to achieve such rapid economic success. Several books about Japanese business management systems became popular, including Ezra Vogel's *Japan as Number One: Lessons for America* (1979) and William Ouchi's *Theory Z: How American Management Can Meet the Japanese Challenge* (1981). These books disseminated several key concepts and terms of Japanese management such as *kaizen* (continuous improvement), *keiretsu* (a group of closely interconnected companies), and *kanban* (the just-in-time system of efficient production).

Anger and Fears Regarding Japan's Economic Power

Strong anti-Japanese sentiment quickly spread throughout the United States in the 1980s and the early 1990s. Many blue-collar workers in manufacturing blamed Japan for their unemployment and showed their anger publicly: members of United Automobile Workers destroyed Japanese automobiles with hammers in large demonstrations, and images of such displays were widely circulated by U.S. media outlets. Additionally, several members of the U.S. Congress smashed Toshiba radios in front of Capitol Hill in 1987 to show their anger when Toshiba and a Norwegian company sold submarine technology to the Soviet Union, a violation of an agreement among Western bloc nations. In the early 1990s, many activists, politicians, and labor union representatives led "Buy American" campaigns to boycott Japanese products. To calm anti-Japanese sentiments in the United States, Japanese manufacturing corporations adopted a strategy of "localization": they moved sites of production to the United States and employed American workers rather than exporting finished products.

Many Americans also felt threatened by Japanese corporations' substantial investments in the U.S. market during Japan's bubble economy from the late 1980s to the early 1990s. They were shocked to find that Japanese companies purchased companies or real estate properties considered to be important American cultural icons. For example, Sony purchased CBS Records in 1987 and Columbia Entertainment Pictures in 1989; Mitsubishi Estate Company became the primary owner of Rockefeller Center in 1989. The cover of *Newsweek* on October 9, 1989, carried the headline "Japan Invades Hollywood" and an image of a Japanese geisha, mimicking the logo of Columbia; it implied fears that all precious American cultural assets might be bought and remade by Japanese corporations. The *Newsweek* issue also included a poll indicating that Americans feared Japan's economic power more than the Soviet Union's military power. Such views of Japan were also reflected in Hollywood movies in the 1980s and 1990s. One of the most popular movies of this genre was *Rising Sun* (1993), which portrays a conspiracy led by a fictional Japanese company in California with connections to Japanese criminal gangs.

Influence on Asian American Communities

Anti-Japanese sentiment rarely resulted in physical violence against Japanese nationals living in the United States, but it did trigger a brutal hate crime against a non-Japanese man in 1982. Vincent Chin, a Chinese American, was beaten to death in Detroit, Michigan, by two Caucasian autoworkers—Ronald Ebens and Michael Nitz. Nitz had been recently laid off. Mistaking Chin for Japanese, Ebens and Nitz blamed their job losses on "Japanese like him" and killed him with a baseball bat on the streets of Detroit. Despite finding the men guilty of manslaughter, the court sentenced them to just three years' probation and fined them $3,780 each. This verdict outraged Asian American communities and led them to file a lawsuit against Ebens and Nitz, charging that they violated Chin's civil rights; however, the murderers still served no jail time.

Fear and anger regarding Japan's economic power from the 1980s through the early 1990s rekindled racial hatred of Japan felt during World War II. The U.S. media revived "yellow peril" with imagery of "trade war" and "economic Pearl Harbor." Moreover, the term "Japan bashing" appeared in major U.S. newspapers most frequently around the 50th anniversary of Japan's attack on Pearl Harbor. However, anti-Japanese sentiment dwindled as Japan's bubble economy burst in the mid-1990s and its economic power declined just as China emerged as a new source of America's economic anxiety. Japan bashing serves as a reminder of how economic competition can cause widespread hostility especially when mixed with racialized images.

See also: Alien Land Law (1913); Anti-Japanese Movement; Immigration Act of 1924; Native Sons of the Golden West

Further Reading

Johnson, Sheila. *The Japanese through American Eyes*. Stanford, CA: Stanford University Press, 1998.

Morris, Narrelle. *Japan-Bashing: Anti-Japanism since the 1980s*. New York: Routledge, 2010.

Ouchi, William. *Theory Z: How American Management Can Meet the Japanese Challenge*. New York: Perseus Books Group, 1981.

Vogel, Ezra. *Japan as Number One: Lessons for America*. Lincoln, NE: iUniverse.com Inc., 1979.

Yoko Tsukuda

JAPANESE AMERICAN CITIZENS LEAGUE

The Japanese American Citizens League (JACL) is a Nisei organization founded in 1929 with the initial goal of lobbying for Japanese American civil rights

Fred Tayama, chairperson of the Southern District Council of the Japanese American Citizens League, explaining curfew and travel laws to two fellow Japanese Americans in 1942. (Library of Congress)

while promoting the integration of citizens into American culture. Since its inception, the JACL has expanded its mandate to focus on lobbying for the civil rights of all Asian American citizens and protecting the Japanese American cultural heritage. The JACL is considered one of the oldest and most influential national organizations promoting social justice and equality throughout the country. The actions of the JACL have frequently been shaped by historical events, as well as both public prejudice and political attitudes. As a result, the organization has, at times, been both critiqued by the Asian American community for its support of racist government policies and praised for its opposition of legislative discrimination. In particular, the organization has been criticized for its complacency during World War II (1939–1945) with the federal government's discriminatory internment of Japanese American citizens.

The origins of the JACL reside in the large number of Asian immigrants who came to the United States at the end of the 19th century and the beginning of the 20th century and who typically took up residence in regions along the American West Coast. Despite being earnest laborers, entrepreneurs, and American citizens, people of Asian ancestry were frequently targets of racial discrimination and exclusionary legislation stemming from the rising anti-immigrant sentiment of the period. During this period, Asian immigrants increasingly experienced the racism of the American public, as well as institutionalized segregation legislated in bills such as the Chinese Exclusion Act (1882), Alien Land Laws (California Alien Land Law, 1913), and Immigration Act (1924). As a result, the community sought to organize as a means of asserting their national loyalty and defending their rights as citizens in the political and legal forums of states such as California, Oregon, and Washington. In addition to their lobbying activities, the JACL promotes legislative reform, supports educational programs, and produces a regular newspaper, originally titled the *Nikkei Shimin* (Japanese American Citizen) and later named the *Pacific Citizen*.

In its early years the JACL began advocating for the rights of Japanese American World War I (1914–1918) veterans, which led to passage of the Nye-Lea Act (1935). In addition, the JACL campaigned to have the Married Women's Citizenship Act, also known as the Cable Act (1922), which had revoked citizenship from any woman married to an Asian migrant, amended. Despite these early successes, however, the JACL was challenged by the attitude of the American government and the Federal Bureau of Investigation (FBI) during World War II, especially after the bombing of Pearl Harbor on December 7, 1941. This event led President Franklin D. Roosevelt (1882–1945, president 1933–1945) to sign Executive Order 9066 (1942) authorizing the relocation and internment of over 120,000 Japanese American citizens. During this process, the JACL was pressured by the American government to cooperate and assist in removing and interning citizens of Japanese descent. The JACL assisted the federal government in the belief that cooperation rather than opposition would convince Americans of the loyalty of the Japanese American community to the United States. Given the internment of many of their members and the ongoing anti-Japanese atmosphere of the period, the JACL was unable to accomplish many of its goals during this time. However, despite such limitations, the JACL lobbied the American government to improve conditions for those being detained and to allow Japanese American citizens to demonstrate their loyalty by serving in the armed forces. As a result, the U.S. government created a separate military division known as the 442nd Regimental Combat Team, which subsequently earned notoriety as one of the most decorated units of the conflict and in American history. Pointedly, however, those Nisei in the Japanese American community who resisted JACL cooperation with the U.S. government during this period were condemned as disloyal by the organization. Understandably, therefore, as a result of their support for the government's discrimination, the JACL was soon critiqued by the Japanese American community as collaborators.

Following World War II, the JACL resumed lobbying both state and national governments for the repeal of discriminatory policies and legislation. In particular, the organization became involved in the repeal of California's Alien Land Law (1913) and passage of the Civil Rights Act (1964). During this period the JACL also promoted the political involvement of individuals within the Japanese American community on matters of segregation and racial discrimination. In addition, during the 1970s, the JACL became committed to keeping the issue of the wartime internment of Japanese American citizens and the possibility of government redress in both the public consciousness and the political forum. As a result of their lobbying efforts, President Jimmy Carter (1924–, president 1977–1981) established the Commission on Wartime Relocation and Internment of Civilians (CWRIC) in 1980. This commission ultimately concluded that the internment of Japanese Americans had not been undertaken out of military necessity, advocated that the government formally apologize for its actions, led to the passage of the Civil Liberties Act (1988), and mandated that payments to detainees and their survivors be issued.

In recent decades, the JACL has broadened its mandate to include lobbying for all Asian Americans victimized by racial injustice while remaining dedicated to promoting the preservation of civil liberties for all who face racial, religious, and cultural discrimination. In addition, the JACL has also lobbied for the reform of national immigration policy, promoted gender equality, endorsed same-sex marriages, and supported the rights of members of the gay and lesbian community in America. In the early 21st century, the organization has continued its work striving to protect the heritage of the Japanese American community and civil rights of all Americans. To achieve these goals the JACL continues to regularly organize national conferences, supports community programs, promotes youth leadership within the Asian American community, and offers student assistance, including national scholarships.

See also: Commission on Wartime Relocation and Internment of Civilians; Post–World War II Redress

Further Reading

Spickard, Paul. "The Nisei Assume Power: The Japanese [American] Citizens League, 1941–1942." *Pacific Historical Review* 52, no. 2 (May 1983): 147–174.
Takahashi, J. *Nisei/Sansei: Shifting Japanese American Identities and Politics*. Philadelphia: Temple University Press, 1997.

Sean Morton

JAPANESE AMERICANS IN FARMING AND AGRICULTURE

During the late 19th and early 20th centuries, many Japanese American immigrants to the United States and Hawai'i were employed in the agriculture industry. As immigrant laborers, agricultural work provided them with opportunities to make more than they could in Japan. Also, they introduced several new techniques to the American farming industry and quickly became quite successful in the United States.

In 1885, 153 Japanese immigrants arrived in Hawai'i as contract laborers, primarily at sugarcane and pineapple plantations. Soon after, Japanese migrants set off for California and other western states in search of jobs with higher pay. These farmers became a vital part of California's—and ultimately America's—agricultural economy, successfully growing all varieties of fruits, vegetables, and flowers.

Japanese plantation labor in Hawai'i also played an important role in the O'ahu Sugar Strike of 1920. This multiracial strike with Filipino American laborers highlighted the unique divisions of racial and ethnic stratification in Hawai'i. After over six months of protesting, the unions' demands for pay raises were met.

On the mainland, many of the early Japanese American farmers specialized in labor-intensive crops on small, leased plots of land. The Issei and Nisei farmers were well known for an intense work ethic, working long hours seven days a week. Also, many of the wives and children helped out with work on the farm. Over time, many became successful enough to purchase substantially larger farms and exponentially increase the scale of their productions. By the early 1940s, Japanese Americans farmed more than 200,000 acres, accounted for 30 percent of California's truck farmers, and dominated the specific industries of strawberries, celery, and peppers. In fact, as anti-Japanese rhetoric escalated at the onset of World War II, some Americans feared that the large Japanese American fields and orchards could even be used to signal Japanese fighter pilots.

Farming behind Barbed Wire

When all West Coast Japanese Americans were sent into concentration camps during World War II, the farmers were forced to abandon their fertile farmland and relocate into unfamiliar, desolate regions. Despite these obstacles, they persisted in raising livestock and growing produce, and ultimately established shipping operations to exchange produce between the different concentration camps. Some of their crops included spinach, cabbage, daikon radish, burdock root, and potatoes.

For their hard work, most were paid $12 each month, which was a fraction of what they would have made on their own. After World War II, the former camp sites had become more valuable due to functional irrigation systems and region-specific skills developed by the Japanese American incarcerees.

Following the end of World War II, many Japanese Americans chose to return to their agricultural roots. Many became sharecroppers, since it was the easiest way to start over from scratch. Through considerable struggle and determination, many of these farmers once again found considerable success. In 1966, sociologist William Petersen highlighted Japanese American farmers in his article "Success Story, Japanese-American Style" that introduced the concept of Japanese Americans as the new model minority.

By the end of the 20th century, developments in the agricultural industry facilitated several mergers and acquisitions, especially among family-owned Japanese American farms. Also, increasing numbers of Sanseis and Yonseis have chosen to pursue nonagricultural careers. Nevertheless, the impact of

Japanese Americans on the nation's fruits, vegetables, and flowers cannot be understated.

See also: Alien Land Law (1913); Hawai'ian Sugar Plantations; Japanese Immigration to Hawai'i; Seabrook Farms (New Jersey); Yamato Colony of California

Further Reading

Commission on Wartime Relocation and Internment of Civilians. *Personal Justice Denied: Report of the Commission on Wartime Relocation and Internment of Civilians.* 1997.

Lukes, Timothy J., and Gary Y. Okihiro. *Japanese Legacy: Farming and Community Life in California's Santa Clara Valley.* San Jose: California History Center, 1985.

Matsumoto, Valerie. *Farming the Home Place: A Japanese American Community in California, 1919–1982.* Ithaca, NY: Cornell University Press, 1993.

Petersen, William. "Success Story, Japanese-American Style." *New York Times,* January 9, 1966, p. 180. http://inside.sfuhs.org/dept/history/US_History_reader/Chapter14/modelminority.pdf. Accessed August 1, 2017.

Dean Ryuta Adachi

JAPANESE AMERICANS IN JAPAN

"Japanese Americans" refers to people of Japanese ancestry who are citizens or residents of the United States. Most Japanese Americans reside in the United States, but they also migrate to other places, including Japan. The broader definition of Japanese Americans used in the United States becomes problematic when talking about Japanese Americans in Japan. "Japanese Americans in Japan" includes U.S. citizens of Japanese ancestry living in Japan whereas Japanese nationals residing in the United States who return to Japan would be considered "Japanese returnees." As of 2011, I estimated the number of Japanese Americans living in Japan to be about 7,000, which is approximately 13 percent of the 52,149 registered U.S. citizen residents. There are no official demographic data on this population because the U.S. and Japanese governments do not keep ethnic or racial information regarding U.S. citizens residing outside the United States.

Most Japanese Americans living in Japan were born and raised in the United States and moved to Japan as adults for a variety of reasons and lengths of time. Younger (in their 20s to early 30s), single Japanese Americans who have not yet established careers tend to go to Japan for shorter periods of time—up to a year or two. These Japanese Americans are more likely to migrate to Japan because of an interest in connecting with their heritage culture and society.

Those living in Japan as long-term residents tend to be married with Japanese spouses. These Japanese Americans are usually older (typically in their late

30s, 40s, and 50s) and, although culturally interested in Japan, tend to migrate primarily for work-related reasons. Most Japanese Americans in Japan migrate temporarily, many as college exchange and language students, as members of the Japan Exchange and Teaching (JET) Program, and as white-collar workers on limited contracts. Some Japanese Americans have "permanently" settled in Japan, though many who have the resources still have plans to return to the United States after retiring.

Similar to other U.S. citizens in Japan, most Japanese Americans can be found in urban areas. They are a highly educated population in general, almost all college-educated or in the midst of attaining their college degrees; many have graduate and professional degrees. Japanese Americans in Japan work predominantly in white-collar occupations, in contrast to far more numerous Japanese from Latin America (particularly from Brazil) who are mainly found working in factories doing unskilled work.

Similar to the U.S. Japanese American population, Japanese Americans in Japan include people with diverse backgrounds. They vary in citizenship status, have been raised in a variety of places, are multigenerational and are multiethnic and multiracial. If defined as U.S. citizens of Japanese ancestry, the Japanese American population in Japan includes Japanese emigrants who naturalized in the United States then return migrated back to Japan. Most Japanese Americans in Japan have been raised in Hawai'i or the continental United States, with a small portion raised in Japan and internationally. Some were raised on U.S. military bases and few now work or are stationed in them. Japanese Americans have parents from the United States and Japan. Many have parents who are of Japanese ancestry but of differing generations (e.g., one Japanese immigrant parent, one second-generation Japanese American parent). Others have one parent who claims Japanese ancestry and one who does not. Experiences in Japan are shaped by these characteristics—generations removed from Japan, exposure to Japanese language, and citizenship.

U.S. Japanese American migration to Japan can be organized into various periods, highlighting variations in generations, historical contexts, and motivations.

Nisei Educated and Socialized in Japan (1920s–1940s)

From the 1920s, as soon as there was a Nisei (second generation) born in the United States, some of these American-born Japanese migrated to Japan. University of Pennsylvania historian Eiichiro Azuma estimates between 40,000 and 60,000 Nisei to have been living in Japan in the 1930s. The majority of them eventually returned to the United States, although some of them remained in Japan.

According to Azuma, these Nisei in Japan can be divided into three categories. One group went to Japan as children and assimilated into Japanese society (some eventually returned to the United States). Some had moved to Japan with their parents, whereas others were sent by parents in the United States to live with their relatives in Japan temporarily. The second group consisted of a few hundred highly educated bilingual men and women who took on important positions in media, academia, government, and business in Japan. Ironically, Azuma notes, it was their racial exclusion from the United States that led them to search for opportunities in Japan. The third group was composed of college and language students who planned to return to the United States after receiving their academic and cultural educations in Japan.

The Nisei who lived in Japan as children and then returned to the United States are referred to as "Kibei Nisei." In Japanese, "Ki" means "to come" and "bei" refers to the United States. Most, if not all, Nisei in Japan were dual nationals. Some remained in Japan for the duration of World War II and were drafted by the Japanese military. In doing so, they lost their U.S. citizenship. Many Kibei Nisei returned to the United States and were drafted into the U.S. military as Military Intelligence Service (MIS) language specialists. Anecdotally, there are stories of Kibei Nisei who were in Japan when World War II began and were drafted by the Japanese military, then upon returning to the United States after the war ended, they were again drafted by the U.S. military and, in many cases, sent back to Japan as MIS specialists. This double drafting dramatizes the dual pressures placed on Japanese Americans during the war.

Nisei Linguists and Nurses in Occupied Japan (1945–1952)

Once World War II ended, many Nisei men were stationed in Japan as part of the Allied Forces occupying Japan from August 1945 to April 1952. As language specialists, these members of the MIS were in charge of translating and interpreting documents between English and Japanese:

> One Japanese American in the MIS was responsible for translating for the emperor. Most effective members of the MIS were Kibei Nisei who were born in the United States, sent to Japan for few years as children, then returned to the United States, and were drafted specifically as linguists because of their strong Japanese skills. Other Nisei raised only in the United States ranged greatly in their Japanese skills; the U.S. government provided language training before sending them to Japan and other parts of Asia and the Pacific.

During this period, some Japanese American women and children were also living in Japan. According to Brenda L. Moore, in 1946, 13 members of the Women's Army Corps graduated from the Military Intelligence Service Language School and went to Japan. The women were told that when they arrived in Tokyo, they would be discharged and would work as civil servants; they were all assigned to the Allied Translator and Interpreter Section (ATIS) of the U.S. Army as clerks, secretaries, and translators. In addition, some Japanese American women were recruited as civilian nurses supporting the occupation. Some members of the MIS brought their families with them, meaning that Sansei children were stationed in Japan with their Nisei parent(s).

Many Japanese Americans were able to reconnect with family members who had survived the war in Japan. The conditions for Japanese in the postwar period were harsh, most lived in poverty and struggled to make ends meet. Most stories of their experiences in Japan during this period told by Japanese Americans include giving food and supplies to Japanese relatives and those in need, though research has also shown that some Nisei mistreated Japanese, abusing their power as part of the occupying forces.

Sansei Searching for Cultural Roots and Language Study (1960s–1970s)

During this period, as a result of the Asian American Movement in the United States, many later generation Asian Americans, including Japanese Americans, were reclaiming their roots and asserting cultural and ethnic pride. As a way to assert ethnic pride, many Sansei (third-generation Japanese Americans) were interested in learning Japanese, because most Nisei stressed Americanization in the aftermath of internment and did not send their children to Japanese language schools. Many of these Sansei migrated to Tokyo as language and exchange students. International Christian University (ICU) in Mitaka City located in the western part of Tokyo Prefecture, was host to many of these students. As a Christian university established by American missionaries in Japan, ICU already had a history of bilingual language education in English and Japanese; to this day it continues to host the University of California Education Abroad Program Center as well as individual exchange students who intend to improve their Japanese language skills and take academic classes on Japanese society and culture.

Attracted by Japan's Economic Bubble and the JET Program (1980s–)

With the development of the Japanese bubble economy (an overinflated economy that eventually "burst" in the 1990s) and the strong Japanese yen, people from all over the world were attracted to seek their fortunes in Japan. Japanese Americans were among these migrants who found jobs teaching English and working for various companies, especially those looking to expand their international employees and clientele.

In the late 1980s, the Japanese government, partly because of its economic strength, established the Japan Exchange and Teaching (JET) Program, bringing in foreign nationals to teach English, with the larger goal of "internationalizing" Japanese society. In addition to English and other foreign language teachers, the program also brings in college-educated foreign nationals to work in Japanese governmental offices, to organize international events, to interpret, to translate, and to advise on sports education.

Even after the bubble burst at the end of the 1990s, the establishment of Tokyo as a global city has drawn international businesspeople and professionals such as lawyers and doctors who serve this expatriate community. Many college-educated, working Japanese Americans are pulled by a powerful combination of economic opportunity and cultural affinity to Japan.

Japanese Traditional and Popular Culture

Many Japanese Americans have also migrated to Japan to learn about Japanese traditional and popular culture. For decades, Japanese Americans (as well as others outside of Japan) have been interested in Japanese kimonos, tea ceremonies, religions, flower arranging, calligraphy, martial arts, and other forms of traditional arts and culture.

Since at least the 1980s, Japanese American interest in taiko has risen in the United States and, as a result, many Japanese Americans have gone to Japan to learn about Japanese styles of training and drumming. Kenny Endo, a Nisei/Sansei from Los Angeles now based in Honolulu, is one of the most famous Japanese American taiko artists. He trained in Japan for over a decade, developing his own style of drumming that he now teaches and for which he is world famous.

In more recent years, younger- and later-generation Japanese Americans have been attracted to live in Japan to study martial arts and to learn more about Japanese society generally because of a growing global interest in manga and anime. This interest in martial arts may actually be traced back to the 1960s and 1970s.

See also: Japanese Transnational Identity

Further Reading

Hawaii Nikkei History Editorial Board. *Japanese Eyes, American Heart: Personal Reflections of Hawaii's World War II Nisei Soldiers.* Honolulu: Tendai Educational Foundation, distributed by University of Hawai'i Press, 1998.

Moore, Brenda. *Serving Our Country: Japanese American Women in the Military during World War II.* New Brunswick, NJ: Rutgers University Press, 2003.

Mura, David. *Turning Japanese: Memoirs of a Sansei.* New York: Anchor Books, 1992.

Tomita, Mary Kimoto, and Robert G. Lee. *Dear Miye: Letters Home from Japan, 1939– 1946.* Stanford, CA: Stanford University Press, 1995.

Yamashiro, Jane. "Racialized National Identity Construction in the Ancestral Homeland: Japanese American Migrants in Japan." *Ethnic and Racial Studies* 34 no. 9 (2011): 1502–1521.

Jane H. Yamashiro

KOCHIYAMA, YURI (1921–2014)

Yuri Kochiyama was a prominent human rights activist, advocating for civil rights causes across black, Latino, Native American, and Asian American communities with heavy involvement in the Black Power movement and in securing reparations for Japanese Americans subjected to internment during World War II. Born Mary Yuriko Nakahara on May 19, 1921, in San Pedro, California, Kochiyama was one of three children of parents who had immigrated from Japan. Although her political consciousness developed much later in life, Kochiyama engaged in early community involvement through student government and playing tennis at San Pedro High School, as a sports writer for the San Pedro News Pilot, and as a Sunday school teacher. Kochiyama graduated from high school in 1939 and from Compton Junior College in 1941.

Prior to internment, Kochiyama's father was taken away and detained by the Federal Bureau of Investigation (FBI) agents for six weeks, being one of 1,300 Japanese Americans detained within the first 48 hours of the attack on Pearl Harbor. Upon his return and due to aggravated health problems from detainment, he died on January 21, 1942, the day after his release. Kochiyama and her family were forced to leave their home in San Pedro to the Santa Anita Assembly Center before being relocated to the Jerome War Relocation Center in Arkansas for three years. In camp, Kochiyama organized a large-scale letter-writing campaign, sending holiday cards to 3,000 Nisei soldiers fighting in World War II overseas. After the war, she married fellow Jerome internee and war veteran Bill Kochiyama in 1946 and moved to New York City in 1948, living in public housing. The couple had six children.

In the 1950s, the Kochiyamas hosted open houses each weekend with up to 100 attendees, both friends and strangers, and invited political speakers. In 1960, the family moved from midtown Manhattan to Harlem, which further drove her radical transformation, being at the center of the civil rights movement in Harlem and witnessing injustices in the community, from the quality education for inner-city children to labor rights in the community. Kochiyama met Malcolm X in 1963 and they had a close friendship and mutual respect for one another. Kochiyama was present at his assassination in 1963, captured in a famous *Life* magazine photograph of her cradling the head of the slain leader.

Over the years, Kochiyama dedicated herself to many causes, including support of black nationalist organizations, political prisoners, the prison industry, and nuclear disarmament. Her engagement across civil rights platforms launched her as a leader in the Asian American Movement in the late 1960s. In the 1980s, Kochiyama was heavily involved in the Redress Movement, seeking reparations for those interned during World War II. She was nominated for the Nobel Peace Prize through the "1,000 Women for the Nobel Peace Prize 2005" project.

Kochiyama died of natural causes at 93 on June 1, 2014.

See also: Aoki, Richard (1938–2009); Ichioka, Yuji (1936–2002); Japanese American Citizens League

Further Reading

Fujino, D. C. "The Black Liberation Movement and Japanese American Activism: The Radical Activism of Richard Aoki and Yuri Kochiyama." In *Afro Asia: Revolutionary Political and Cultural Connections between African Americans and Asian Americans*, edited by F. Ho and B. V. Mullen. Durham, NC: Duke University Press, 2008.

Fujino, D. C. *Heartbeat of Struggle: The Revolutionary Life of Yuri Kochiyama*. Minneapolis: University of Minnesota Press, 2005.

Cynthia Mari Orozco

KOREMATSU, FRED (1919–2005)

Fred Korematsu emerged as a civil rights leader for the Japanese American community during World War II. In 1942, at age 23, he refused to relocate to the government internment camps. When the government incarcerated Korematsu and convicted him of disobeying Executive Order 9066, he appealed his conviction all the way to the Supreme Court of the United States. He argued that removing Japanese Americans from their property and relocating them was unconstitutional. The 1944 Supreme Court decided to uphold the legality and constitutionality of the internment, arguing it constituted a military necessity.

In 1983, legal researchers discovered key documents that government intelligence agencies had hidden from the Supreme Court in 1944. The hidden documents showed that Japanese Americans had committed no acts of treason and thus dismantled the rationale for mass incarceration. With new evidence in hand, a pro bono legal team that included the Asian Law Caucus reopened Korematsu's 40-year-old case on the basis of government misconduct. On November 10, 1983, Korematsu's conviction was overturned in a federal court in San Francisco.

When Franklin D. Roosevelt signed Executive Order 9066 in February 1942, authorizing the removal and relocation of individuals of Japanese descent, Korematsu defied the order. In an effort to remain free, he underwent plastic surgery on his eyes to appear less Japanese, changed his name to Clyde Sarah and claimed Hawai'ian and Spanish ancestry. Despite these evasive actions, Korematsu was arrested in 1942. While in jail, he collaborated with lawyer Ernest Besig to serve as a test case for the constitutionality of the executive order. The California court convicted Korematsu for his failure to obey military orders. Korematsu filed appeals that both the Court of Appeals and Supreme Court of the United States ultimately rejected.

Although hailed by some, others criticized Korematsu's actions. Many Japanese American residents living on the West Coast cooperated with the internment order, hoping to prove their loyalty as Americans. As a result, some Japanese Americans expressed disdain for Korematsu and viewed him as a threat to other Japanese Americans. When Korematsu's family relocated to the internment camp in Topaz, Utah, Korematsu would later describe feeling isolated because people who recognized him worried about being identified as "troublemakers" if seen conversing with him.

After World War II and the 1983 vacating of his conviction, Korematsu continued to fight against racial prejudice and profiling. He spoke out after September 11, 2001, cautioning Americans to prevent people of Middle Eastern descent from experiencing what Japanese Americans previously experienced. When Korematsu believed the U.S. government detained Guantanamo Bay prisoners for too long, he filed two *amicus curiae* briefs with the Supreme Court and warned the government not to repeat the mistakes of the Japanese internment.

To commemorate his civil rights activism, California observed "Fred Korematsu Day of Civil Liberties and the Constitution" on January 30, 2011. This was the first such commemoration for an Asian American in the United States.

See also: Ex Parte Mitsuye Endo (1944); *Hirabayashi v. United States* (1943); Post–World War II Redress

Further Reading

Bannai, Lorraine K. *Enduring Conviction: Fred Korematsu and His Quest for Justice*. Seattle: University of Washington Press, 2015.

Daniels, Roger. *The Japanese American Cases: The Rule of Law in Time of War*. Lawrence: University of Kansas Press, 2013.

Lauren S. Morimoto

LITTLE TOKYO

Little Tokyo is the Japanese American ethnic enclave in Los Angeles, California. It is one of three remaining historic Japantowns in the United States. The Little Tokyo Historic District was declared a National Historic Landmark District in 1995.

Founding

The earliest significant Japanese immigration to the mainland United States began during the 1870s. Due to the housing discrimination practices that were prevalent at the time, these early Japanese immigrants often resided in or around the Chinatowns that were created by this earlier group of Asian immigrants. As Chinese immigration to the United States was outlawed by the Chinese Exclusion Act of 1882, and as Japanese immigration rose sharply after 1885, many of these Chinatowns faded into the shadows of growing Japantowns.

Little Tokyo is the commonly used nickname for Los Angeles's Japantown. From the late 19th century until World War II, it was the center for Japanese American commerce in Southern California. Its proximity to railroad and agricultural jobs was ideal for immigrant laborers, and Little Tokyo soon became a thriving Japanese American ethnic economy consisting of grocery stores, restaurants, hotels, bathhouses, churches, and much more. Its location near downtown Los Angeles was central and easily accessible to several Japanese American communities throughout Southern California, from coastal fisherman to valley farmers. It is estimated that roughly 30,000 Japanese Americans were living in Little Tokyo at the outset of World War II.

Bronzeville

When all Japanese Americans on the West Coast were forced into concentration camps during World War II, Little Tokyo was virtually transformed into a ghost town overnight. Meanwhile, many African Americans from the segregated American South were moving west to work in California's rapidly growing war defense industry. This movement is often referred to as the Second Great Migration. Because these African American migrants sought accommodations that did not defy the racially discriminatory housing covenants of the time, they quickly settled in empty Little Tokyo. As the community's demographics changed, Little Tokyo became known as Bronzeville, and its population soon increased to roughly 80,000 individuals.

Post–World War II Significance

When Japanese Americans were allowed to return to the West Coast after World War II, several tried to reclaim their previous houses and businesses in Little Tokyo, with varying degrees of success. As the war came to an end, so too did many of the wartime jobs for Bronzeville residents, and Little Tokyo once again became a center for Southern California's Japanese Americans, who were now scattered much more widely across the region.

In the late 1970s and early 1980s, many Japanese corporations began expanding to the United States and established offices in or around Little

Tokyo, also bringing a new wave of Japanese immigrants to Los Angeles. In 1992, the Japanese American National Museum opened its doors at the historic Honpa Hongwanji Buddhist Temple; it would later relocate one block over to a state-of-the-art facility. Also nearby is the Go for Broke Monument commemorating Japanese American army veterans.

Although Southern California is home to the largest Japanese American population in North America, the majority of this community no longer lives in Little Tokyo. Nevertheless, Little Tokyo remains a cultural center through its historical sites, annual festivals such as Nisei Week, and its many social, cultural, and religious institutions.

See also: Japanese American Communities

Further Reading

Kurashige, Lon. *Japanese American Celebration and Conflict: A History of Ethnic Identity and Festival in Los Angeles, 1934–1990.* Berkeley: University of California Press, 2002.

Kurashige, Scott. *The Shifting Grounds of Race: Black and Japanese Americans in the Making of Multiethnic Los Angeles.* Princeton, NJ: Princeton University Press, 2010.

Dean Ryuta Adachi

MASAOKA, MIKE MASARU (1915–1991)

Mike Masaru Masaoka was a community organizer, political advocate, businessperson, veteran, and lobbyist. He became known within the Japanese American community through his leadership as the national secretary and field executive of the Japanese American Citizens League (JACL), a second-generation Japanese American organization that aimed to Americanize the Japanese American population and cooperated with the U.S. government's mass incarceration of Japanese and Japanese Americans. These actions made Masaoka a controversial figure within the Japanese American community.

Early Life in Utah, JACL, and World War II

Born in Fresno, California, Masaoka grew up in Salt Lake City, Utah, and became a member of the Church of Jesus Christ of Latter-day Saints. Raised by a single mother at a young age with seven siblings, Masaoka attended the University of Utah, where he was deeply influenced by Utah's political science professor and later elected senator, Elbert D. Thomas, who supported his political consciousness and growth. After graduating the University of Utah, Masaoka moved to San Francisco where he began to work for the JACL. Before the war, Masaoka penned a manifesto, the "Japanese-American Creed," which became a pro-American pledge to dispel any suspicion of disloyalty among the Japanese Americans.

Following the attacks on Pearl Harbor that ushered the United States formally into World War II, Masaoka used the JACL as an organization to shape pro-American ideologies and encourage active assimilation within the Japanese American community. Masaoka's leadership within JACL propelled him to be a liaison between the War Relocation Authority (WRA), the U.S. governmental agency charged to oversee the incarceration of Japanese and Japanese Americans, and the Japanese American community. Although Masaoka advocated for the incarceration, he has defended his controversial position in his autobiography by articulating that some form of cooperation was needed to prevent further governmental transgressions during the war. In addition, Masaoka helped lead the call for the formation of the 442nd Regimental Combat Team (RCT), an all-segregated Japanese American military unit that was composed of Japanese American men from Hawai'i, the incarceration camps, and non–West Coast cities. Masaoka served in a public relations role and transmitted the accolades and military heroism of the 442nd RCT across the U.S. nation to combat anti-Japanese racism.

Postwar Political Activism and Lobbying

In the postwar era, Masaoka served as a lobbyist on behalf of Japanese Americans in order to advocate for their civil rights. Masaoka played a role in the passage of the Japanese American Evacuation Claims Act of 1948, which was the first attempt to compensate Japanese and Japanese Americans for their material losses from the incarceration. He was also involved in legislation to help first-generation Japanese immigrants become naturalized citizens, which materialized into the McCarran-Walter Immigration and Naturalization Act of 1952. This was a repeal of the Immigration Act of 1924, which officially barred Japanese immigration into the United States between 1924 and 1952. In 1972, Masaoka left the JACL and began his own consulting firm assisting both Japanese and American agricultural and commercial enterprises. Masaoka was married to Etsu Mineta Masaoka, the elder sister of former secretary of transportation Norman Mineta. Masaoka lived in Washington, D.C., until his death in 1991.

See also: Aoki, Richard (1938–2009); 442nd Regimental Combat Team/100th Infantry Battalion; Ichioka, Yuji (1936–2002); Japanese American Citizens League

Further Reading

Dudley, William, ed. *Asian Americans: Opposing Viewpoints*. San Diego: Greenhaven Press, 1997.

Hosokawa, Bill. *Nisei: The Quiet Americans*. Boulder: University Press of Colorado, 2002.

Imai, Shiho. "Mike Masaoka." *Densho Encyclopedia*. http://encyclopedia.densho.org
/Mike_Masaoka/. Accessed December 20, 2016.

Masaoka, Mike, with Bill Hosokawa. *They Call Me Moses Masaoka: An American Saga*.
New York: William Morrow, 1987.

Jeffrey T. Yamashita

MATSUI, DORIS O. (1944–)

Doris Matsui is a Japanese American politician who has represented California's Fifth Congressional District since 2005. Before her tenure in Congress, Matsui had been involved in local Sacramento politics and she also served in various posts in the William J. Clinton administration.

Doris Matsui was born Doris Okada at an internment camp in Poston, Arizona, on September 25, 1944. As a person of Japanese descent, the internment experience was commonly shared by many Japanese Americans during World War II. Matsui later grew up on a farm in Dinuba, California, and attended the University of California, Berkeley. When she was at Berkeley, Matsui met her future husband, the late congress member Robert T. Matsui. They married in 1965.

Matsui's attorney husband was elected to the Sacramento City Council in 1971 and to Congress in 1978 (representing California's Fifth District); meanwhile Matsui herself also became active in public life. She was known as an early supporter of Bill Clinton's bid for the Arkansas gubernatorial seat. Furthermore, when Clinton was elected to the White House, Doris Matsui was a member of the Clinton transition team. She later served as deputy assistant to the president in the White House Office of Public Liaison under Alexis Herman during President Clinton's first term. Her tenure in the White House extended between 1993 and 1998.

Although for many years after her time in the White House, Matsui did not hold public office, she was nonetheless active in community organizations in Sacramento and Washington, D.C. Some of the projects and positions she was involved with included president and chairperson of the board for the KVIE public television station in Sacramento. She was also actively involved in the Sacramento Children's Home, the Woodrow Wilson Center Board of Trustees, Arena Stage, and many other organizations.

A major change came for Matsui in 2005 when her husband passed away after serving in Congress for over 26 years. Matsui announced her decision to run for her husband's vacant seat on January 9, 2005, and the special election was held on March 8, 2005. In the short three months of her campaign, Matsui gained the support of the Democratic Party as well as many local leaders in the Sacramento area. The result was that Matsui beat out 11 other candidates

Democratic Representative Doris Matsui at a rally at Sacramento City College in Sacramento, California, 2016. (AP Photo/John Locher)

and was elected to replace her husband with 72 percent of the overall vote and 88 percent of the Democratic vote. At the same time, Matsui became the first Asian American woman from the U.S. mainland to be elected to Congress. She was clearly the favorite in the special election. She has since then been reelected, in 2006, 2008, 2010, and 2012.

One of the major points of Matsui's initial campaign was that she would carry on the work and important agendas of her late husband. One of the most important issues that Matsui has focused on since taking office is flood protection in her district. She was able to garner the support of others in Congress and obtain $700 million in authorized funds for flood control projects in the Sacramento area. Flood control was also an issue that her late husband cared deeply about and worked extensively for.

Matsui also focused her efforts on renovating the transportation infrastructure to address the rising cost of gas as well as the toll of carbon emissions on the environment. Her efforts have included the planning of an intermodal transportation center in downtown Sacramento. Her plan took into account the rising cost of transportation as well as the growing population in the Sacramento area. In May 2009, Matsui also sponsored and spoke on behalf of the Smart Planning for Smart Growth Act. This is a piece of legislation that would require states and metropolitan planning organizations to plan according to emission reduction guidelines by reducing per-capita vehicle miles traveled. This bill echoes Matsui's other work on the Committee of Energy and Commerce. She also serves on the subcommittee on Commerce, Trade, and Consumer Protection; the Subcommittee on Communications, Technology, and the Internet; and the Subcommittee on Energy and Environment.

Aside from transportation and environmental issues, Matsui has been committed to promoting community service. She has helped garner and preserve funding for AmeriCorps programs, which organize and promote community service around the country. Matsui is also the cochair of the National Service Caucus.

Matsui is a member of the House Committee on Rules. Her caucus membership includes the Congressional Asian Pacific American Caucus. She was appointed to the Smithsonian Institution's Board of Regents in 2007 by House Speaker Nancy Pelosi.

Matsui has a good relationship with the Democratic leadership cultivated during her husband's tenure as a representative. She is a very active member of the Democratic Party and served as Parliamentarian at the 2008 Democratic National Convention in Denver, Colorado.

See also: Ariyoshi, George (1926–); Hirono, Mazie Keiko (1947–); Honda, Mike (1941–); Inouye, Daniel Ken (1924–2012); Matsui, Robert T. (1941–2005); Matsunaga, "Spark" Masayuki (1916–1990); Mineta, Norman (1931–); Mink, Patsy Takemoto (1927–2002)

Further Reading

Govtrack.us. Rep. Doris Matsui (D-CA5). 2009. http://www.govtrack.us/congress/person .xpd?id=400663. Accessed September 18, 2012.

The Online Office of Congresswoman Doris Matsui. The Honorable Doris O. Matsui. 2009. http://www.matsui.house.gov/index.php?option=com_content&task=view. Accessed December 20, 2016.

Jeanette Yih Harvie

MATSUI, ROBERT T. (1941–2005)

Robert Matsui was an American politician of Japanese descent. He was a member of the House of Representatives and served for 13 terms and represented California's Third and Fifth Congressional Districts. During his lifetime, Matsui served for 26 years in the U.S. Congress.

Robert Takeo Matsui was born on September 17, 1941, to Japanese American parents in Sacramento, California. He was third-generation Japanese American. However, like many Japanese Americans during World War II, Matsui, who was merely six months old at the time, and his family were sent to an internment camp at the Tule Lake Camp, which was located near the California and Oregon border. Matsui and his family would move briefly to Caldwell, Idaho, for work and eventually return to their native Sacramento when he was four years old. After graduating from high school in 1959, Matsui went on to continue his education at the University of California, Berkeley, where he majored in political science.

During his time at Berkeley, Matsui met his future wife, Doris Okata, whom he married in 1965. After graduation from college in 1963, Matsui went on to the University of California, Hastings College of the Law in San Francisco. After law school, Matsui and his wife moved back to his native Sacramento and he started his own law practice.

Matsui's political career started when he was elected to the Sacramento City Council in 1971. He was reelected in 1975 and became the vice-mayor in 1977. After working in local politics, Matsui decided to move on to national politics when congress member John E. Moss announced his retirement. Matsui ran for Congress in 1978 and was elected to office, representing California's Third Congressional District.

One of Matsui's main efforts as a political leader concerned the reparations of the treatment of Japanese Americans during World War II. Along with other congressional members such as Sen. Daniel Inouye (D-Hawai'i), Sen. Masayuki "Spark" Matsunaga (D-Hawai'i), and Rep. Norman Mineta (D-Calif.), Matusi advised the national Japanese American Citizens League (JACL) on an appropriate course for the emerging movement concerning the past incarceration of Japanese Americans. In 1985, Matsui also gave a speech on the floor of the U.S. House of Representatives on the aforementioned issue and called for reparations on the part of the U.S. government. Finally, after a decade of effort from many, including Robert Matsui, the Japanese American Redress Act (known as the Civil Liberties Act of 1988) passed through Congress and provided monetary compensation and government apology for those Japanese Americans interned during World War II. This act was signed into law on August 10, 1988, by President Ronald Reagan.

Also in his effort to educate and seek reparation for incarcerated Japanese Americans, Matsui was crucial in having Manzanar (an internment camp during World War II) set up as a national historic site. Moreover, Matsui helped to procure land on the National Mall in Washington, D.C., for the National Japanese American Memorial to Patriotism during World War II.

During Matsui's tenure in Congress, he served on the Judiciary Committee and was also a high-ranking member of the House Ways and Means Committee by the time of his death. Although Matsui spent a wealth of time and effort advocating for Japanese Americans, he was also known for his work on important issues of the day, including policies related to international trade, taxes, health care and welfare reform as well as social security.

Also, as a member of the Democratic Party, Matsui chaired the Democratic Congressional Campaign Committee during the 2004 election cycle and served in various positions on the Democratic National Committee.

Robert Matsui served in the U.S. House of Representatives until his passing on January 1, 2005, because of complications from a prior health condition. In a special election later that year, his wife, Doris Matsui, was elected to fill his vacant seat in California's Fifth District. Doris Matsui is a member of the Democratic Party and had served as a deputy director of public liaison in the Clinton administration up until 1998. A lifelong public servant and leader from the Sacramento area, the city of Sacramento dedicated a waterfront park in Robert Matsui's name in October 2008.

See also: Ariyoshi, George (1926–); Hirono, Mazie Keiko (1947–); Honda, Mike (1941–); Inouye, Daniel Ken (1924–2012); Matsui, Doris O. (1944–); Matsunaga, "Spark" Masayuki (1916–1990); Mineta, Norman (1931–); Mink, Patsy Takemoto (1927–2002)

Further Reading

CNN.com. "Congressman Dies of Rare Disease." CNN.com, January 3, 2005. http://www.cnn.com/2005/ALLPOLITICS/01/02/obit.matsui/index.html. Accessed February 12, 2017.

Matsui, Robert T. Foundation for Public Services. Official Biography of Hon. Robert T. Matsui. 2009. http://www.rtmfoundation. Accessed February 12, 2017.

Jeanette Yih Harvie

MATSUNAGA, "SPARK" MASAYUKI (1916–1990)

"Spark" Masayuki Matsunaga was a Japanese American politician from the state of Hawai'i. He served in the U.S. House of Representatives from 1971 to 1977 and the U.S. Senate from 1977 to 1990. Matsunaga originally got the nickname "Sparky" because he was slow. The name comes from the character "Sparkplug," an old nag in a popular comic strip during Matsunaga's youth. After World War II, Matsunaga had his name changed legally to Spark Masayuki Matsunaga.

Spark Masayuki Matsunaga was born on October 8, 1916, to poor Japanese immigrant parents in Kaua'i, Hawai'i. Coming from humble beginnings, Matsunaga's father worked on a sugar plantation and was killed in a work-related accident. Matsunaga had to work his way through school but eventually graduated with honors from the University of Hawai'i in 1941. He not only majored in education but participated in the ROTC (Reserve Officer Training Corps) program.

After the attack on Pearl Harbor and the start of World War II for the United States, Matsunaga volunteered for active duty with the U.S. Army. During the war, Matsunaga was a member of the famed 100th Infantry Battalion of the 442nd. He was wounded twice in a minefield in Italy, which earned him the Bronze Star, the Purple Heart, the Legion of Merit, and the Army Commendation Medal. Highly decorated, he was honorably discharged in 1945 with the rank of a captain. After leaving the army, Matsunaga worked as a veterans' counselor. He would also go on to earn a law degree from Harvard University Law School in 1951.

After law school, Matsunaga returned to Hawai'i to work as an assistant public prosecutor in the city of Honolulu between 1952 and 1954. His political career took shape in Hawai'i's territorial House, where he served from 1954 to 1959. During his time in the territorial House, Matsunaga demonstrated his commitment to helping those in need in his community and served as the majority leader between 1957 and 1959.

Although Matsunaga was unsuccessful in his bid as lieutenant governor, he was elected to the U.S. House of Representatives in 1962 and would serve through 1976 with seven consecutive terms. Matsunaga was sympathetic to the injustice suffered by many Japanese Americans during World War II. He cosponsored a bill to repeal Title II of the Emergency Detention Act/Internal Security Act, which had allowed the imprisonment of anyone seen as a security risk during time of war. This repeal was signed into law by President Richard Nixon. When Matsunaga was a member of the House, he served on the influential Rules Committee and the Agriculture Committee. He was also the deputy majority whip.

Matsunaga opted not to run for reelection in 1976 for his House seat but instead was elected into the Senate. He ran against fellow Hawai'ian Patsy Mink for the seat Hiram Fong left vacant when he announced his retirement. During his time in the Senate, Matsunaga played important roles in the passing of civil rights legislation, the support for space programs, and the quest of reparations for Japanese Americans that were wrongly imprisoned during World War II. He sponsored the Civil Liberties Act of 1988, which provided for reparation to Japanese Americans. This legislation was signed into law by President Ronald Reagan. Aside from Matsunaga's work on minority issues, he was also concerned with environmental issues and advocated for additional research and awareness of our environment. In fact, his last major act as a senator was the support of the Clean Air Act.

Matsunaga would serve three terms as a U.S. senator. He was chair of the International Trade and Aging Subcommittees and also had membership on the Veterans' Affairs as well as Labor and Human Resource subcommittees. He continued his work as a leader in the Democratic Party, serving as the Senate Democratic chief deputy whip until 1988.

In January 1990, Matsunaga told the public that he had prostate cancer and was seeking treatment. He passed away on April 15, 1990, in Toronto, Canada, at the age of 73 as a result of his illness. He was succeeded by Daniel Akaka in the U.S. Senate.

One of Matsunaga's many accomplishments during his lifetime was the instrumental role he played in the establishment of the Institute for Peace at the University of Hawai'i, which was renamed the Matsunaga Institute for Peace.

See also: Ariyoshi, George (1926–); Hirono, Mazie Keiko (1947–); Honda, Mike (1941–); Inouye, Daniel Ken (1924–2012); Matsui, Doris O. (1944–); Matsui, Robert T. (1941–2005); Mineta, Norman (1931–); Mink, Patsy Takemoto (1927–2002)

Further Reading

Flint, Peter. "Spark M. Matsunaga Dies at 73; Senator Led Fight for Reparations." *New York Times,* April 16, 1990. http://www.nytimes.com/1990/04/16/obituaries/spark-m -matsunaga-dies-at-73-senator-led-fight-for-reparations.html. Accessed March 1, 2017.

Glosserman, Brad. "A Practical Politician with His Eyes Fixed Firmly on the Stars." *The Japan Times Online,* December 29, 2002. http://search.japantimes.co.jp/cgi-bin /fb20021229a2.html.

Kim, Hyung-Chan, ed. *Distinguished Asian Americans.* Westport, CT: Greenwood Press, 1999.

University of Hawai'i at Mānoa. 2005. The Sen. Spark M. Matsunaga Papers. http:// libweb.hawaii.edu/libdept/archives/congressional/matsunaga/index.htm. Accessed March 1, 2017.

Jeanette Yih Harvie

MINETA, NORMAN (1931–)

Norman Mineta is an American politician of Japanese ancestry. He served as secretary of transportation for six years (2001–2006) during the George W. Bush administration and six months as the secretary of commerce for the Clinton administration (2000–2001). Mineta also served for 20 years in the U.S. House of Representatives (1975–1995).

Norman Yoshio Mineta was born on November 12, 1931, in San Jose, California, to Japanese immigrant parents. The Mineta family operated a prosperous insurance business and were well regarded in the local community. However, like many individuals of Japanese descent, Mineta and his family were forced to shut down the family business and were sent away from their native California to an internment camp during World War II. Mineta spent two years of his youth as a detainee at Heart Mountain, Wyoming. The Minetas would eventually return to San Jose to restart their lives.

In 1953, Mineta graduated from the University of California, Berkeley, with a degree in business administration. Upon college graduation, Mineta joined the U.S. Army and served as a military intelligence officer in Japan and Korea between 1953 and 1956. After serving in the military, he returned home to work for his father, who had reopened their insurance agency.

Well regarded in the San Jose community, Mineta was appointed to fill a vacancy on the San Jose City Council Human Relations Commission in 1967. In 1969, he went on to win the San Jose City Council election and in 1971 became the mayor of San Jose. Mineta was the first Asian American to serve as the mayor of a major American city.

After working in San Jose local politics, Mineta was elected as a representative to the U.S. Congress in 1974 and began his 20-year tenure in the House. As one of the few Asian Americans in Congress, Mineta cofounded and served as chair of the Congressional Asian Pacific American Caucus. Moreover, Mineta dedicated a great deal of effort to redress the harsh treatment of Japanese Americans during World War II. The Commission of Wartime Relocation and Internment of Civilians was established in 1978, and Mineta was persistent in pushing the commission investigation. Ultimately, Mineta sponsored the Civil Liberties Act of 1988 with Wyoming's Republican senator Alan K. Sampson, who Mineta had first met as a detainee in Wyoming. The two politicians became friends and have remained friends since. The Civil Liberties Act, which granted reparation to Japanese Americans interned during World War II, was signed into law by President Ronald Reagan in 1988.

In terms of committee work in Congress, Mineta was a prominent member (chair between 1992 and 1995) of the Public Works and Transportation Committee and chaired the Aviation Subcommittee between 1981 and 1988. Mineta played important roles in most transportation legislations in the 1980s and 1990s. In particular, he worked to increase funding for the Federal Aviation Administration (FAA) and sponsored the Intermodal Surface Transportation Efficiency Act of 1991 (ISTEA). Mineta's work on ISTEA was important because it changed the process of transportation planning and policies and gave local government control of highways and other mass transit decisions.

After serving 10 terms as representative, Mineta resigned his seat in 1995 and the Democrats lost his seat to Republican Tom Campbell in the subsequent special election. Between 1995 and 2000, Mineta worked mainly in the private sector. In fact, Mineta had left Congress to join Lockheed Martin as a vice president. Also, drawing upon his expertise in transportation, Mineta also served as the chairman of the National Civil Aviation Review Commission.

In July 2000, with only six months left in his term, President Clinton asked Mineta to serve as the secretary of commerce. Upon Senate confirmation, Mineta became the first Asian American to serve on a president's cabinet.

As the Clinton administration transitioned to the Bush administration, Mineta was asked to stay and serve as the secretary of transportation. This was a job that Mineta was extremely well suited for, considering the wealth of experience that he had accumulated as a congress member. Norman Mineta was sworn in on January 25, 2001, and became the 14th secretary of transportation. During the eight years of the Bush administration, Mineta would be the only Democratic cabinet member.

As secretary of transportation, Mineta was in charge of more than 100,000 employees, managed a budget of well over $60 billion, and was responsible for the country's major roadways, waterways, public transit, harbors, and airports. On September 11, 2001, in the wake of the terrorist attack, Mineta issued an order for all flights to land immediately and grounded all air transportation. Furthermore, his order to divert all incoming international flights to Canada was made possible with the help of the Canadian government.

Although Mineta received praise for his swift decisions during the September 11 emergency, the pressing need to provide higher levels of airport and inflight security fell on his shoulders. Mineta played a crucial role in the establishment of the Transportation Security Administration (TSA).

In 2006, Mineta put in his resignation as secretary of transportation. After serving for over five years, he was also the longest serving secretary in the history of the Transportation Department. Later that year, Mineta was awarded the Presidential Medal of Freedom, the nation's highest civilian honor, by President George W. Bush.

Although in his 70s when he retired from public service, Mineta took a position as vice chairman of the Washington-based public relations firm of Hill and Knowlton. To honor his hard work and dedication, especially to the transportation infrastructure in this country, the Norman Y. Mineta San Jose International Airport in San Jose was named after him. Highway 85 in California was also named after Mineta.

See also: Ariyoshi, George (1926–); Hirono, Mazie Keiko (1947–); Honda, Mike (1941–); Inouye, Daniel Ken (1924–2012); Matsui, Doris O. (1944–); Matsui, Robert T. (1941–2005); Matsunaga, "Spark" Masayuki (1916–1990); Mink, Patsy Takemoto (1927–2002)

Further Reading

ABCNews. "Profile: Transportation Secretary Norman Mineta." ABCNews, January 13, 2005. http://abcnews.go.com/Politics/Inauguration/story?id=122140. Accessed September 18, 2012.

Academy of Achievements. "Norman Mineta Biography." http://www.achievement.org /autodoc/page/min0bio-1. 2008. Accessed September 18, 2012.

Hill and Knowlton. "Norman Mineta." http://www.hkstrategies.com/company/leader ship/norman-mineta-0. 2009. Accessed September 18, 2012.

Jeanette Yih Harvie

MINK, PATSY TAKEMOTO (1927–2002)

Patsy Takemoto Mink, a third-generation Japanese American, served in the U.S. Congress from 1965–1977 and again from 1990–2002, representing Hawai'i's First and Second Congressional Districts. The first woman of color and first Asian American woman elected to Congress, she worked tirelessly for civil rights, women's rights, and economic justice. On November 24, 2014, Mink was awarded a posthumous Presidential Medal of Freedom, the nation's highest civilian honor.

Mink was born in Paia, Hawai'i to Nisei (second-generation) Japanese Americans. Her political career started in high school, where she won the student body presidential election about a month after the Japanese attack on Pearl Harbor. Mink successfully addressed fellow students' unease with all things Japanese. After high school, Mink attended the University of Hawai'i to prepare for medical school. However, in 1948, none of the 20 medical schools to which she applied accepted women. Believing that the judicial processes would be most successful in changing medical school policies, Mink attended law school at the University of Chicago.

After law school, Mink was elected to a number of prestigious positions in the following order: territorial House of Representatives, territorial Senate, Hawai'i State Senate, and finally U.S. Congress. Mink became known as an outspoken defender of women's rights and challenger to the culture of Congress. She supported the successful effort to allow female members of Congress to use the heretofore all-male House gym. Later, she forced the resignation of Dr. Edgar F. Berman from a national subcommittee after he asserted that "raging hormones" made women unsuitable for executive positions in government and business.

During her terms in the U.S. House of Representatives, Mink coauthored Title IX of the Higher Education Act Amendments, known as the Equal

Portrait of Patsy T. Mink, Democratic U.S. representative from Hawai'i, (1965–1977, 1990–2002). (U.S. House of Representatives)

Opportunity in Education Act. Passed in 1972, Title IX is landmark legislation prohibiting gender discrimination in educational institutions receiving federal funding. Title IX dramatically increased opportunities for females in higher education and both high school and collegiate athletics. Mink also introduced the first comprehensive Early Childhood Education Act and Women's Educational Equity Act. These laws that Mink authored/coauthored were critical legislation for the advancement of equal rights in the United States.

Reelected in 1972 and 1974, Mink continued to champion social causes and oppose the Vietnam War. The following year, she coauthored the Surface Mining and Reclamation Act, which brought federal regulation to the strip mining of coal and provided for related environmental cleanup and repair. Additionally, she coauthored the Mineral Leasing Act, which restricted mining on public lands. Both laws are considered milestones in the modern American environmental movement.

In 2002, Mink announced her candidacy for reelection to the House and easily won the Democratic primary. Late that summer she contracted chicken pox and was hospitalized. She contracted pneumonia, leading to her unexpected death. However, it was too late to remove her name from the ballot and she was posthumously reelected. A month after her death, House colleagues paid tribute to her memory by renaming Title IX the Patsy T. Mink Equal Opportunity in Education Act.

See also: Ariyoshi, George (1926–); Hirono, Mazie Keiko (1947–); Honda, Mike (1941–); Inouye, Daniel Ken (1924–2012); Matsui, Doris O. (1944–); Matsui, Robert T. (1941–2005); Matsunaga, "Spark" Masayuki (1916–1990); Mineta, Norman (1931–)

Further Reading

Arinaga, Esther K., and Renee E. Ojiri, "Patsy Takemoto Mink." *Asian-Pacific Law & Policy Journal* 4 (2003): 571–597.

Davidson, Sue. *A Heart in Politics: Jeannette Rankin and Patsy T. Mink.* Seattle, WA: Seal Press, 1994.

Matsuda, Mari J., ed. *Called from Within: Early Women Lawyers of Hawai'i.* Honolulu: University of Hawai'i Press, 1992.

Lauren S. Morimoto

NATIONAL JAPANESE AMERICAN MEMORIAL

The National Japanese American Memorial, also commonly known as the Japanese American Memorial to Patriotism, is located in Washington, D.C., at the intersection of Louisiana Ave., New Jersey Ave., and D Street. The landscaped site features a pathway bordered by curved and inscribed granite walls that leads to an open central courtyard in which stands a bronze sculpture of Japanese cranes, as well as a memorial temple bell. The site was initially conceptualized as a monument to the loyalty, patriotism, and contribution of Japanese American veterans who served during World War II (1939–1945) in the highly decorated 100th Infantry Battalion and the 442nd Regimental Combat Team units. However, the memorial has subsequently come to symbolize the sacrifice of all Japanese American persons who were relocated and detained in internment camps from 1942 until 1945 and who have since tirelessly defended civil rights.

The creation of a memorial to the military contributions of Japanese Americans was originally proposed in 1988 with the establishment of the "Go for Broke" campaign, which was named after the wartime slogan of the Japanese American 100th Battalion and was led by the National Veterans Association Foundation, later known as the National Japanese American Memorial Foundation (NJAMF). The memorial's construction was authorized by federal statute PL 102-502 and signed into law by President George H. W. Bush (1924–, president 1989–1993) on October 24, 1992, following passage of the Civil Liberties Act (1988) and a formal federal apology to the Japanese American community for the unlawful wartime internment in the 1940s. The structure of the memorial was designed by architect Davis Buckley, while the memorial court's central statue of bronze cranes trapped in barbed wire was created by the Japanese American artist Nina A. Akamu (1955–). The site was dedicated in November 2000, turned over to the national government in 2002, and has since been maintained and cared for by the National Parks Service.

Physically the structure of the memorial is designed to mirror the historic experiences of the Japanese American community, moving visitors through the process of their exclusion, internment, release, and formal apology. To this end, the structure of the memorial consists of a long narrow curved walkway that directs visitors into an open circular plaza that is engraved with the names of the American internment camps (Amache, Gila River, Heart Mountain, Jerome, Manzanar, Miniddoka, Poston, Rohwer, Topaz, Tule Lake), as well as panels listing the names of those Japanese Americans who perished fighting as American soldiers during World War II. Set at the center of the memorial court, a pair of bronze cranes, traditionally symbols of happiness, are depicted entangled in barbed wire and struggling, which represented the need for community cooperation to overcome the social circumstances and political limitations placed upon individuals and groups. Also incorporated into the memorial is a large temple bell, designed by Paul Matisse (1933–), whose tone resonates throughout the site.

See also: 442nd Regimental Combat Team/100th Infantry Battalion; World War II

Further Reading

National Japanese American Memorial Foundation, *Patriotism, Perseverance, Posterity: The Story of the National Japanese American Memorial.* Washington, D.C.: National Japanese American Memorial Foundation, 2001.

Sean Morton

NICHIBEI SHIMBUN (JAPANESE AMERICAN NEWS)

Published in San Francisco, the *Nichibei Shimbun*, or *Japanese American News*, had its official beginning on April 4, 1899. Its origins, however, can be traced to two earlier vernacular papers called the *Hokubei Shimpo* (1898) and the *Soko Nihon Shinbun* (*Japan Herald* 1897). Organized by a group of immigrant students ("school boys") and writers, the *Soko Nihon Shinbun* came into the hands of Abiko Kyutaro, a Christian entrepreneur who had come to the United States as an indigent student, by 1898. The *Hokubei Shimpo* was a product of ongoing disputes between Christian converts and other factions of the early Japanese immigrant community in San Francisco. Whereas non-Christians seized editorial control of the preexisting *Shin Sekai Shimbun* (*New World Daily* 1894) to turn it into something of their political organ, some Christian Issei cut their ties from the newspaper to form the *Hokubei Shimpo*. Thus, for a short period around 1898, the San Francisco Japanese community had three major vernacular newspapers; however, under the support of nationalist-minded immigrants and working-class newcomers, the *Shin Sekai* increased its readership rapidly. Sharing a similar political support base, the *Soko Nihon Shinbun* and *Hokubei Shimpo* were thus soon compelled to merge into a new paper called the *Nichibei Shimbun*. Abiko served as its publisher and editor whereas such immigrant intellectuals as Yamato Ichihashi (later a Stanford University professor) and Yoneda Minoru (later a renowned diplomatic historian in Japan) participated in the operation of the *Nichibei Shimbun* in its inceptive years. By a few years later, Abiko became the sole proprietor of the *Nichibei Shimbun*, as others moved back to Japan or onto other ventures in the United States.

Throughout the prewar years, the *Nichibei Shimbun* remained one of the most important Japanese vernaculars in San Francisco. The old politico-ideological conflict between the *Nichibei Shimbun* and *Shin Sekai* resurfaced time and again, which often reflected deep-seated religious divides in early Japanese America. The *Nichibei Shimbun* represented aspects of Japanese immigrant political thinking and practice that sought harmony with white America, valorized social assimilation and permanent settlement over immigrant sojourning, and aspired to adapt to America's Christian traditions. Yet, for that very reason, the newspaper sometimes found itself under severe attacks by more nationalistic segments of early Japanese America that had close ties to the *Shin Sekai* and Buddhist churches, as well as some leftist elements. In 1911–1912, for example, the *Nichibei Shimbun* was accused of being traitorous to the Japanese emperor, for it refused to criticize an Issei Christian minister in Bakersfield who had exhibited his serious "disrespect" for the throne. Some eight years later, the *Nichibei Shimbun* came under fire by the *Shin Sekai* again, when the former supported the Japanese government's decision to suspend the issuance of passports to "picture brides" bound for the United States. Given the *Nichibei Shimbun*'s proassimilation stance, it made perfect sense that the newspaper embraced Tokyo's policy, because white exclusionists had singled out the picture-marriage practice as an example of Issei's "un-American" character. But the *Shin Sekai* was upset by its support for Tokyo's decision to make it impossible for ordinary Issei to get married without having to go to Japan. In this way, the rivalry between the two San Francisco vernaculars illuminated a major political fault line within early Japanese America. As historian Yuji Ichioka argued, it is important to note that Abiko's advocacy for permanent settlement contributed to the emergence of stable settlement Japanese communities during the 1910s. And Abiko's desire to reform Japanese immigrant society through the *Nichibei Shimbun* compelled him to extend its reach to Southern California. In 1922, he purchased a bankrupt local vernacular and renamed it the *Rafu Nichibei (Los Angeles Japanese American)*.

Abiko's quest of interracial harmony unfolded in tandem with his belief in the intermediary role of second-generation Japanese Americans (Nisei) in U.S.–Japan relations. The concept of Nisei as a bridge of understanding thus became a main underpinning of *Nichibei Shimbun*'s editorial policy, especially after the completion of racial exclusion of Issei by the mid-1920s. His dream of inclusion into white America was untenable as far as the immigrant generation was concerned because of the denial of naturalization rights and the 1924 Immigration Act. Yet, Nisei U.S. citizens were free from existing legal discrimination against "aliens ineligible for citizenship." Although Abiko optimistically predicted that Nisei would be able to blend into white America on account of their outstanding racial character, he also believed that the youngsters were saddled with the mission to improve bilateral relations between the country of their birth and their ancestral country by dispelling white American misunderstanding about the Japanese—both Issei and people of Japan. Abiko used the *Nichibei Shimbun* to disseminate this idea, stressing the importance of teaching Nisei about Japan with an eye to enabling them to serve as a bridge of mutual understanding between the United States and Japan. In 1925 and 1926, the newspaper sponsored "kengakudan," or "study tours" of selected Nisei men and women to Japan. Abiko Yonako, Kyutaro's wife, accompanied these study tours, which received red carpet welcomes by upper echelons of Japanese society. In the ensuing years, many other community organizations dispatched similar Nisei study-tour groups to Japan on the basis of the bridge ideal espoused by Abiko. The *Nichibei Shimbun*'s pioneering role in the edification of Nisei also entailed its new policy of inserting English-language Nisei sections—the practice that began in 1925 and was subsequently imitated by all major Japanese press in the continental United States and Hawai'i.

During the early 1930s, the *Nichibei Shimbun* was engulfed in serious financial problems and labor strife. In 1931, a dispute over editorial policy and unpaid wages led to an all-out strike by the *Nichibei Shimbun* staff, which resulted in the liquidation of the *Rafu Nichibei*, the dismissal of many workers and reporters, and the establishment of the *Hokubei Asahi* by the dismissed *Nichibei* employees. That newspaper and the *Shin Sekai* merged in 1935. The bitter rivalry between the *Nichibei Shimbun* and *Shin Sekai* continued until the outbreak of the Pacific War. In the same decade, the *Nichibei Shimbun* underwent other significant changes as well. The death of Abiko Kyutaro in 1936 resulted in the transfer of the business operation to his wife Yonako. Three years later, the *Nichibei Shimbun* suffered a devastating fire, reducing its building to ashes. Although a new building and equipment were acquired by 1940, Japan's attack on Pearl Harbor caused the newspaper to permanently cease its operation in April 1942. After the wartime internment of Japanese Americans, former employees of the *Nichibei Shimbun* formed the *Nichibei Jiji* (*Nichi Bei Times*) under the control of Yasuo William Abiko, Nisei son of Kyutaro and Yonako. The newspaper is still in operation out of San Francisco as an English weekly and online-based news outlet.

See also: Abiko, Kyutaro (1865–1936); Japanese Immigrant Press

Further Reading

Ichioka, Yuji. *The Issei: The World of the First Generation Japanese Immigrants, 1885–1924*. New York: Free Press, 1988.

Eiichiro Azuma

POST–WORLD WAR II REDRESS

After World War II, Japanese Americans worked hard to restore their lives and recover from the devastation of having been imprisoned without due process and charged with any crimes. Many did not want to talk about their experiences. Nisei became notorious for keeping their wartime experiences from their Sansei children. However, it is the Sansei generation who will fight for their rights, and the rights of their elders, to be recognized and treated as fully American!

The social and political climate during the postwar period was one of civil rights and ethnic pride. Although the Japanese American Citizens League

(JACL) was disparaged for cooperating with the U.S. government in all of their policies during World War II, lawyers and lobbyists for the JACL worked diligently to overturn laws banning interracial marriage, legalizing segregation, and restricting rights to citizenship and immigration based on race. The end of race-based immigration quotas following the passage of the 1965 Immigration Act allowed immigration from Japan to be restored, yet the number of new Japanese immigrating remained low due to a booming postwar economy in Japan. Those Japanese who did immigrate to the United States after the war often came because of family ties, such as marriage to a U.S. soldier, and became the first generation of Japanese immigrants no longer barred from naturalized citizenship due to racial discrimination and restrictions.

From the late 1960s through the 1970s, the JACL, National Coalition for Redress/Reparations, National Council for Japanese American Redress (NCJAR), and Japanese American politicians, such as Sen. Daniel Inouye, Sen. Spark Matsunaga, congress member Norman Mineta, and congress member Robert Matsui, lawyers, and activists worked unstintingly to achieve redress for Japanese Americans interned during the war. Some, like the NCJAR, sought redress through the courts while others lobbied Congress. On April 20, 1988, after years of hard work, the U.S. Senate passed the Civil Liberties Act by a vote of 69–27. The act acknowledged that the U.S. government had committed a grave injustice against all those who were interned. Each surviving individual received a tax-free payment of $20,000 as a token payment for the losses incurred because of their internment. Some people returned the checks out of protest, arguing that money could never repay them for all that they have suffered and lost. One of the most significant outcomes of redress was the resurgence of stories about internment camp experiences from the Nisei generation. Oral history projects boomed as people began talking more openly about what really happened during the war, including conflicts over the draft resisters, the loyalty questionnaire, those who answered the loyalty questionnaire "no-no," those who renounced their citizenship, and the collaboration between the JACL and the government. Having achieved redress, many Japanese Americans felt vindicated and could finally tell their stories to their children and to the public without feeling shame or guilt. As well, the redress campaign brought the generations together.

See also: Draft Resisters; Executive Order 9066; *Ex Parte Mitsuye Endo* (1944); 442nd Regimental Combat Team/100th Infantry Battalion; *Hirabayashi v. United States* (1943); No-No Boys; Pearl Harbor; World War II

Further Reading

Hosokawa, Bill. *JACL in Quest of Justice: The History of the Japanese American Citizens League.* New York: William Morrow, 1982.

Lyon, Cherstin. *Prisons and Patriots: Japanese American Wartime Citizenship, Civil Disobedience, and Historical Memory*. Philadelphia, PA: Temple University Press, 2011.

Jonathan H. X. Lee

SAIKI, PATRICIA F. (1930–)

Patricia "Pat" Fukuda Saiki is a Japanese American politician and educator from the state of Hawai'i. She represented Hawai'i's First Congressional District for four years (1987–1991) and served as the administrator of the Small Business Administration under President George H. W. Bush (1991–1993). She is a Republican.

Patricia Fukuda Saiki was born on May 28, 1930, in Hilo, Hawai'i. She graduated from high school in 1948 and then from the University of Hawai'i in 1952 with a bachelor's degree. After graduation from college, Saiki got married and taught history in Hawai'i's public and private schools for many years. She began her political career by working in local party politics and would later become the vice chair of the state Republican Party (1966–1968). She was a very active member of the Hawai'ian Republican Party organization. Her first

President George H. W. Bush meets with Small Business Administration Administrator Pat Saiki in the Oval Office of the White House, 1992. (AP Photo/J.Scott Applewhite)

public office was in the Hawai'ian House of Representatives. Saiki was elected in 1968 and served for six years.

In 1974, Saiki was elected to the Hawai'ian State Senate and enjoyed an eight-year tenure. During her time in the Hawai'ian State Senate, she rose to occupy the position of assistant GOP floor leader. However, she left in 1982 and made an unsuccessful bid for the position of lieutenant governor.

During her time out of public office, Saiki returned to her political roots by working for the Republican Party. In her position as party chair (1983–1985), she played an instrumental role in reviving the Republican Party in Hawai'i's Democrat-dominant political climate. In 1984, President Ronald W. Reagan was able to become the second Republican presidential candidate to carry the Hawai'ian Electoral College during the presidential election.

In September 1986, Saiki was unsuccessful in the special election for the vacant seat of U.S. representative Cecil Heftel, which he left behind when he entered the Hawai'ian gubernatorial race. She lost the race to Democrat Neil Abercrombie. However, as Heftel's original term ended, Saiki once again faced her Democratic opponents. In the same year (1986), Saiki ran a second time for the representative seat from Hawai'i's First Congressional District, but this time against Democrat Mufi Hannemann (Neil Abercrombie had lost the primary to Mufi Hannemann). She was successful the second time around and was elected to Congress, thus becoming the only Hawai'ian Republican to ever hold a House seat. She would serve for two consecutive terms, extending her tenure in Congress between 1987 and 1991.

Although Saiki served in Congress, she also took up important positions in the Republican Party. She served as a delegate and secretary of the Republican National Convention (RNC) in 1988.

Saiki was known for being fiscally conservative on economic issues. She was also a staunch supporter of the foreign policies of President Ronald Reagan and President George H. W. Bush. During her time in the House, she voted in support of funding for the Strategic Defense Initiative as well as aid for the Nicaraguan Contras. However, she was much more moderate when it came to social issues. She believed that women should have control of their own reproductive choices. This issue position stemmed from her own experience as a woman who had to work hard to prove herself professionally in a male-dominant field. Saiki also had a deep interest in the protection and preservation of life in the ocean as well as offshore habitat. As a representative from Hawai'i, it is perhaps unsurprising that the protection of the ocean environment was an issue that she felt deeply about. In addition, as a person of Japanese descent, Saiki cosponsored the Civil Liberties Act of 1988, which provided monetary reparation and official government apologies for Japanese Americans who were interned during World War II. She was one of the few Republicans who broke rank to vote in favor of this bill. This landmark piece of legislation was signed into effect by President Ronald Reagan.

During her time in the House, Saiki served on the Committee on Banking, Finance, and Urban Affairs, the Committee on Merchant Marine and Fisheries, as well as the Committee on Aging.

In 1990, Saiki decided to enter the special election to fill the senatorial seat that was left vacant when Sen. Spark Matsunaga passed away unexpectedly. She was able to beat out other Republican hopefuls to win the GOP nomination but fell short of her efforts when she faced her Democratic opponent, Daniel K. Akaka, during the special election. She was succeeded in her congressional seat by Democrat Neil Abercrombie.

After departure from Congress, Saiki continued to serve in the government, but this time as the director of the Small Business Administration working under President George H. W. Bush between 1991 and 1993. In 1994, she also made an unsuccessful bid for the Hawai'ian gubernatorial race, losing to her Democratic opponent Ben Cayetano.

During her long and distinguished political career, Saiki had assumed many leadership roles. Some of those include the chairman of the National Women's Business Council, a delegate to the emperor of Japan's funeral, a member on the President's Advisory Council on the Status of Women and the President's National Commission on the Observance of International Women's Year.

Saiki returned to her educator role after retiring from public life. She taught in Hawai'i and briefly at Harvard University's Institute of Politics at the John F. Kennedy School of Government in 1993.

See also: Ariyoshi, George (1926–); Hirono, Mazie Keiko (1947–); Honda, Mike (1941–); Inouye, Daniel Ken (1924–2012); Matsui, Doris O. (1944–); Matsui, Robert T. (1941–2005); Matsunaga, "Spark" Masayuki (1916–1990); Mineta, Norman (1931–); Mink, Patsy Takemoto (1927–2002)

Further Reading

Biographical Directory of the United States Congress. Saiki, Patricia Fukuda (1930–). http://bioguide.congress.gov/scripts/biodisplay.pl?index=S000014. 2009. Accessed September 20, 2012.

Harvard University Institute of Politics. Former Fellow: Patricia Saiki. http://www.iop.harvard.edu/former-fellows/all?page=17. 2009. Accessed September 20, 2012.

Jeanette Yih Harvie

SEABROOK FARMS (NEW JERSEY)

During World War II, approximately 120,000 persons of Japanese ancestry (almost two-thirds were American citizens) were incarcerated in 10 internment camps throughout the United States. Executive Order 9066 (EO 9066) was signed by President Franklin D. Roosevelt on February 19, 1942—the order that was the basis for the incarceration. All persons of Japanese ancestry in designated areas on the West Coast of the United States were targeted by EO 9066 to be removed and relocated to mostly desolate areas of the United States.

One notable exception to the implementation of EO 9066 was the "voluntary" resettlement program. Persons of Japanese ancestry who lived on the West Coast were given the opportunity to leave Washington, Oregon, and California and move to the interior states. Approximately 5,000 persons chose this option and voluntarily relocated to Nevada, Utah, Colorado, and numerous other sites throughout the United States. This short-lived program was terminated when the political leaders of the states impacted by the movement eastward by persons of Japanese ancestry voiced their opposition to allowing further "voluntary" resettlement.

In the fall 1943, the War Relocation Authority and the FBI granted a small number of Japanese American men (who were no longer deemed to be a threat to national security) to travel beyond the internment camps to search for employment on the East Coast. During the process of looking for employment, several Japanese Americans became aware of a company in New Jersey that was seeking workers. Seabrook Farms, located in Seabrook, a small town in a farming district just north of the city of Bridgeton in Cumberland County, was the site that became the haven for approximately 3,000 persons of Japanese ancestry (600 family units) who moved from the 10 internment camps to southern New Jersey beginning in late 1943 and stayed until the end of World War II, when most returned to the West Coast, or Chicago and New York City.

Seabrook Farms

Albert P. Seabrook started the Seabrook Farms Company in 1870. His son, Charles Franklin Seabrook, assumed the operation of Seabrook Farms and demonstrated an unwavering passion and initiative that led to the company becoming one of the largest farms with significant acreage in America. He succeeded in his endeavors by introducing new technologies and building power plants and an irrigation system that facilitated the growing of crops at Seabrook Farms. In addition, he constructed an infrastructure that allowed for transportation of his products to a burgeoning customer base throughout Pennsylvania and New York.

In the 1930s, Charles Seabrook partnered with Birds Eye and General Foods to quick-freeze vegetables, which enabled Seabrook Farms to be an innovator in the food-processing industry. At one point, the company operated the largest processing plant of its kind, supplying 20 percent of the nation's packaged frozen food. The company's moment of real expansion came with World War II, becoming a major food supplier to the U.S. military during World War II. Seabrook Farms had long struggled with labor shortages and difficulties prior to World War II, and the wartime labor market heightened their need for a new labor source. The recruitment of persons of Japanese ancestry who were incarcerated at 10 internment camps was a strategy employed by an entrepreneurial industrialist to fill his workforce needs. In addition to Japanese Americans from the internment camps, Latin Americans of Japanese ancestry (primarily from Peru and Panama), who had been rounded up and transported to American internment camps run by the U.S. Justice Department (via Crystal City, Texas), became coworkers. In addition, displaced Europeans, including Germans, Estonians, Latvians, Ukrainians, and other refugees were recruited to work at Seabrook Farms. Also, German prisoners of war joined the Europeans, albeit they were closely supervised and lived in a separate housing unit at Seabrook Farms. These individuals joined a workforce that already included African American workers from the South, Scots-Irish from Appalachia, and contract farm workers from Jamaica, Puerto Rico, and other parts of the Caribbean. Seabrook Farms was described as a global bootstrap village, where downtrodden yet hardy peoples of diverse cultures, including Japanese Americans and other displaced people, were given a chance to regenerate their lives. At its peak in 1947, Seabrook Farms employed about 5,000 workers speaking more than 30 different languages.

In the years that followed, the company town of Seabrook had a taste of economic hard times. By the 1960s, the Seabrook family had sold the plant and its operations. The site passed through a number of corporate hands. In the late 1970s, James M. Seabrook, grandson of the founder, reopened the business as Seabrook Brothers and Sons.

Incarcerated Japanese Americans Depart for Seabrook Farms

The lives of persons of Japanese ancestry, from the time they entered the 10 internment camps in 1942 until the U.S. government decided to allow men to leave to seek employment on the East Coast in 1943, were days of humiliation created by the living conditions, divisiveness among families regarding loyalty questions, and living life through *gaman* (Japanese term for perseverance). So, when the information about a frozen food company (Seabrook Farms) in New Jersey that was recruiting for workers, with the blessing of the War Relocation Authority, made its way to the internment camps, there were mixed reactions by the internees. One segment of the internment population was risk-adverse, feeling that moving out of a segregated community to an unknown and uncertain geographic area in New Jersey was problematic (fearing hostility by East Coast citizens), and although the life in an internment camp was barely tolerable, it was still a preferred place to remain until they were released from the internment camps. However, there were internees who were persuaded by "scout teams," who had visited the Seabrook Farms plant in New Jersey, that leaving the internment camps would grant them freedom and independence, away from a confined, barbed-wire existence, to seek employment at Seabrook Farms.

Adaptation, Acculturation, Assimilation, and Incorporation at Seabrook Farms

The concept of relocation from one environment to another has a common process. First, there is the adaptation phase, where people begin to make efforts to adjust to the new surroundings. The next phase is acculturation, where people take up the culture of the dominant group. The third phase is assimilation, where the objective is to achieve equal footing in the new environment's primary groups and social institutions. And, finally, there is the incorporation stage where people earn incomes comparable to their counterparts in the community.

The Japanese Americans who moved to Seabrook experienced every stage of the relocation process. Their adaptation from living in a concentration camp to relocating to unrestricted freedom, and living in company housing at Seabrook Farms, was a welcome change to their livelihood. The East Coast culture was significantly different from both their internment experience and their original homes on the West Coast, most notably the impact of the weather on daily lives and coexisting with a homogeneous Caucasian community in the town of Seabrook. Their assimilation was a challenging one because the "accepting" culture of New Jersey had not been exposed or introduced to an Asian culture and peoples, prior to the Japanese Americans arriving in 1944 in their neighborhoods and environment, and thus assimilation was possible, only if the "accepting" culture chose to do so. There was never a commitment to staying at Seabrook Farms, beyond the six-month contract that was a condition of employment, and some left, after earning enough money at Seabrook Farms, to begin their new lives elsewhere at the end of the war. Thus, there were about 500 Japanese Americans who successfully incorporated into the local community to stay in Seabrook, who chose to stay there immediately after the war ended.

Further examples of positive and negative acculturation and assimilation by Japanese Americans in Seabrook have been articulated in several oral histories that have been conducted. Several people shared the constant internal family struggles of relocating to New Jersey, and how they appreciated the existence of a benevolent paternalism whereby the Seabrook family safeguarded the workers from any local harassment as "enemy aliens." Some depicted the harsh conditions they faced, especially in the housing accommodations. Anti-Japanese incidents were rare, however, and the public schools and local Scout troops, while assimilating the children of these diverse cultures, started a tradition in the 1940s of multicultural fairs long before they began to be popularized in other American towns.

Current Status of Japanese Americans in Cumberland County, New Jersey

At its peak in 1947, there were almost 3,000 Japanese Americans living in the Seabrook Village section of Upper Deerfield Township, whose families were affiliated with Seabrook Farms. Today several hundred remain, scattered about southern New Jersey, including Bridgeton and Vineland in Cumberland County.

The current Japanese American community in the Seabrook area is multigenerational. These include several Nisei (second generation) and older Sansei (third generation—children of the camps) who moved from the internment camps to New Jersey in 1944. Also, there are numbers of a cohort of Sansei, who were born in New Jersey to Nisei parents, Yonsei (fourth generation and the children of Sansei) and Gosei (fifth generation and children of Yonsei). The multicultural elements of the Japanese American experience remain in several ways. There are some tombstones, engraved with traditional Japanese family crests, at the Deerfield Presbyterian Church Cemetery on Route 77 and at Overlook Cemetery in nearby Bridgeton. The Seabrook Buddhist Temple, said to be the only Buddhist temple in the state of New Jersey, has on its grounds a Japanese garden and a small gong that rings during church services and festivals. Also, the Japanese American community is centered by a museum, the Seabrook Educational and Cultural Center, which was built in 1994, to preserve a shared identity among the Seabrook Japanese Americans, while providing a platform for presenting their story and the stories of other former Seabrook workers to museum visitors.

See also: Alien Land Law (1913); Japanese Americans in Farming and Agriculture; Yamato Colony of California

Further Reading

Harrison, Charles H. *Growing a Global Village: Making History at Seabrook Farms*. New York: Holmes & Meier Publishers, 2003.

New Jersey Committee for the Humanities. "The War at Home: Oral Histories from Japanese Americans at Seabrook Farms." *Humanities* 16, no. 2 (March–April, 1995): 32–35.

Noguchi, Paul H., Noguchi, Rei R., and Seabrook, John M. *Seabrook Village New Jersey: Oral Histories of a Community*. Seabrook, NJ: Seabrook Educational and Cultural Center, 1997.

Michael M. Ego

UNIVERSITY PRESIDENTS AND CHANCELLORS

In November 2005, the Committee of 100, a national Chinese American Leadership Organization, chose to examine executive leadership in higher education among Asian Pacific Americans (APAs). The study concluded that although APAs are the most widely represented minority group within faculty ranks, the lack of APAs serving as presidents, vice presidents, and executive management positions demonstrates that APAs are "egregiously under-represented in executive decision-making roles."

The following information provides the backgrounds of Japanese American university presidents and chancellors. There have been a total of eight Japanese Americans presidents and chancellors since the inception of higher education in the United States at Harvard University in 1636—all of whom served beginning in 1968 to the present. A biographical sketch is provided for each of these individuals.

S. I. Hayakawa

Samuel Ichiyé "S. I." Hayakawa was a naturalized American citizen who was born in British Columbia, Canada, and received an undergraduate degree from the University of Manitoba and graduate degrees in English from McGill University and the University of Wisconsin–Madison.

Dr. Hayakawa was an instructor at the University of Wisconsin from 1936 to 1939 and at the Armour Institute of Technology (now Illinois Institute of Technology) from 1939 to 1948. He was a lecturer at the University of Chicago from 1950 to 1955, and English professor at San Francisco State College (now called San Francisco State University) from 1955 to 1968. He was president of San Francisco State College during the period of 1968 to 1973. Dr. Hayakawa turned to politics after his presidency at San Francisco State College and he was elected to the U.S. Senate representing California in 1976 and served from 1977 to 1983.

Roy Saigo

Roy H. Saigo was born in the state of California, and spent part of his childhood in an internment camp in Arizona during World War II—a period in American history where 120,000 persons of Japanese ancestry were incarcerated without due process and at a loss of their constitutional rights. He earned his undergraduate degree in Biological Science at University of California, Davis, and his PhD in Botany and Plant Physiology at Oregon State University.

Dr. Saigo has served in multiple academic assignments: professor of Biology at the University of Wisconsin–Eau Claire (1967–1984); adjunct associate professor of Botany, University of Wisconsin–Madison (1975); internship in Academic Affairs, University of Wisconsin System Administration (1976–1977);

director of the Special Project on Undergraduate Teaching Improvement, University of Wisconsin System Administration (1976); assistant to the dean, School of Arts and Sciences, University of Wisconsin–Eau Claire (1976–1981); assistant dean, School of Arts and Sciences, University of Wisconsin–Eau Claire (1981–1984). His senior executive positions include dean of the College of Natural Sciences at the University of Northern Iowa (1984–1990), and vice president for Academic and Student Affairs at Southeastern Louisiana University (1990–1994). Dr. Saigo has served as the CEO of three universities: chancellor of Auburn University Montgomery (1994–2000); president of St. Cloud State University (2000–2007); and president of Southern Oregon University (2014–present).

Bob Suzuki

Bob H. Suzuki was born in State of Oregon, and spent his childhood in the Japanese American internment camp in Idaho during World War II, along with 120,000 other internees who were incarcerated at 10 concentration camps throughout the United States. He received his BS degree and his MS degree in Mechanical Engineering at the University of California, Berkeley, and his PhD from the California Institute of Technology in Pasadena. From 1961 to 1963, Dr. Suzuki was a research engineer for the Boeing Company in Seattle, Washington. He taught for more than four years in the Department of Aerospace Engineering at the University of Southern California. Dr. Suzuki began his academic administrative career in January 1981 when he assumed the position of dean of Graduate Studies and Research at California State University, Los Angeles. Since July 1985, he served as vice president for Academic Affairs at California State University, Northridge. From 1991–2003, Dr. Suzuki served as the fourth president of California State Polytechnic University, Pomona.

Gene Awakuni

Gene I. Awakuni was born in the state of Hawai'i and earned a master's degree in Clinical Social Work and a bachelor's degree in Political Science from the University of Hawai'i, Mānoa, and a doctorate in Counseling and Consulting Psychology from Harvard University. Dr. Awakuni's focus in higher education was in student affairs, and he served as director of the Counseling and Psychological Services Center at the University of California, Irvine, and then as special assistant to the vice chancellor for Student Affairs at the University of California, Irvine. He then served as assistant vice chancellor for Student Academic Services at the University of California, Santa Barbara, and also as vice president for Student Affairs and University Advancement at California State Polytechnic University. He followed these administrative assignments as vice president of Student Services at Columbia University and vice provost for

Student Affairs at Stanford University (2000–2005). In 2005, Dr. Awakuni was appointed as the chancellor of the University of Hawai'i, West O'ahu, and he served in this position until 2013.

Leroy Morishita

Leroy M. Morishita was born in the state of California and holds a bachelor of arts in Psychology from the University of California, Berkeley, and a master of science in Counseling from San Francisco State University. He also earned a doctorate in Education in Administration, Planning and Social Policy from the Harvard Graduate School of Education. Dr. Morishita began his academic career as counseling coordinator and counselor for the Educational Opportunity Program San Francisco State University (1978–1981), with subsequent appointments as freshmen testing programmer/analyzer, Salem State College and director, Asian Student Programming, Tufts University (1983–1984). He returned to San Francisco State University in 1984 where he served as assistant to the director, Admissions and Records; director of University and Budget Planning and executive assistant to the vice president for Administration (Concurrent Appointment); interim executive director of Enrollment Planning and Management (Concurrent Appointment); associate vice president of Budget Planning and Resource Management; vice president of Physical Planning and Development; and vice president/chief financial officer, Administration and Finance. In 2011, Dr. Morishita was appointed president of California State University, East Bay, where he serves as its fifth president.

University of Cincinnati president Santa J. Ono has his head shaved following an NCAA college basketball game between Cincinnati and Notre Dame, in Cincinnati. Ono was making good on a bet he would shave his head if the Cincinnati basketball team won 10 games in a row, 2013. (AP Photo/Al Behrman)

Santa J. Ono

Santa J. Ono is a naturalized American who was born in British Columbia. Canada. Dr. Ono earned his BA at the University of Chicago and PhD at McGill University. Prior to assuming executive leadership in higher education, Dr. Ono served in a variety of teaching, research, and administrative positions at the Johns Hopkins School of Medicine, Harvard Medical School, and the Schepens Eye Research Institute, University College London (UCL), and Moorfields Eye Hospital in London. He has served at Emory University as vice provost for Academic Initiatives and deputy to the provost and then senior vice provost for Undergraduate Academic Affairs. His career at the University of Cincinnati has progressed from holding faculty appointments as professor of Pediatrics in the College of Medicine and professor of Biology in its McMicken College of Arts and Sciences; senior vice president and provost; and as president from 2012 to present.

Clyde Sakamoto

Clyde Sakamoto was born in the state of Hawai'i, and earned his bachelor's and master's degrees from the University of Hawai'i, Mānoa, and his doctorate at George Washington University. Dr. Sakamoto has committed his entire academic career at the University of Hawai'i, Maui campus, where he has served as its dean of students (1973–1980), dean of instruction (1980–1984), provost (1988–2001), and chancellor (2003–2014). He also served as director of international services at the American Association of Community Colleges (1984–1987).

Judy H. Sakaki

Judy H. Sakaki was born in the state of California and earned both a bachelor's degree in Human Development and a master's degree in Educational Psychology from California State University, Hayward, now known as California State University, East Bay, and received a PhD in Education from University of California, Berkeley, in 1991. Dr. Sakaki has dedicated her career to higher education and to developing, leading, and implementing best practices in access, affordability, inclusion, diversity, and student success. From 1976 to 1994, she served in a variety of capacities focused on students at California State University, Hayward (now California State University, East Bay), including executive director of student academic services and special assistant to the president for educational equity. During the period 1995 to 2002, she served first as dean of students and then as vice president and dean for student affairs at California State University, Fresno, and subsequently served as vice chancellor of student affairs at University of California, Davis (2002–2005). Prior to her appointment as president of Sonoma State University in 2016, she was the vice president for student affairs from 2005 to 2016 at the Office of the President of the University of California. She holds the distinction of being the first

Japanese American woman to serve as a president of a four-year university in the United States.

See also: Hayakawa, Samuel Ichiyé (1906–1992)

Further Reading

The Committee of 100's Asian Pacific American (APAs) in Higher Education Report Card. New York: Committee of 100, 2005.

Michael M. Ego

YAMATO COLONY OF CALIFORNIA

Between 1906 and 1917, Japanese immigrants made three separate efforts to establish intentional settlements in the United States: one in Florida (1904), one in California (1906), and another in Texas (1917). All were named the "Yamato Colony." Of the three, only the colony in California survived.

An examination of the history of California's Yamato Colony provides insight into the impact of prejudice and anti-Japanese legislation on one community. It gives a view of a people whose tenacity, strategic thinking, and ability to cooperate with one another made it possible to establish themselves and thrive.

Founding (1906–1914)

California's Yamato Colony began as 3,214 acres of undeveloped land south of Sacramento between the cities of Modesto and Merced. The community's founder, Kyutaro Abiko, was an idealist and entrepreneur who believed in America as a land of freedom and opportunity—a place where the Japanese could make major contributions and where they should put down roots.

Abiko was born in 1865 in the village of Suibara, Niigata Prefecture. In 1885, he was able to make his way to San Francisco. After trying his hand at a restaurant and a laundry, he founded a major newspaper (the *Nichibei Shimbun*), the Japanese American Bank (the Nichibei Ginko), and the Japanese American Industrial Corporation (the Nichibei Kangyosha labor-contracting firm). At its peak, between 1904 and 1907, Abiko's contracting firm supplied Japanese workers to American mines, farms, and railroads in Wyoming, Idaho, Nevada, California, and Utah (where it had a statewide monopoly on contracts with sugar beet owners).

In 1906 and 1907, using capital from the bank and labor contracting firm, his personal resources, and money from investors, Abiko, with a handful of colleagues, financed the purchase of three contiguous tracts of empty land near the town of Livingston, California. The area offered several advantages.

The Southern Pacific Railroad linked it to major markets in San Francisco and Los Angeles, the land was inexpensive, and prior plantings of vegetables and berries testified to the soil's fertility. The first settlers were truly "pioneers"; however, the colony consisted of empty sand, overrun by thousands of jack-rabbits and seared by the desert sun.

Between 1906 and 1908 approximately 32 people moved to the Yamato Colony. As has been the case throughout its history, the community's greatest strength lay in its people. Most of the original settlers could speak some English. Two were fluent and played important roles as intermediaries with the town. Most were older. Several were upper class and highly educated, including a civil engineer, a college professor of agriculture, a writer, a high school teacher, and two graduates of a farming school. Some who bought land were already wealthy and functioned as both settlers and financial backers of the colony project. About 16 were Christian. Three families, including four women and seven children, brought additional stability to the group.

As anti-Japanese prejudice intensified throughout the West Coast, the new community benefited from several advantages. Given their age, class, education, and in many cases their Christianity, the earliest settlers could not be easily demonized or dismissed by the people of the nearby town. Livingston also had a natural interest in the successful establishment of the farms as a potential boon to the local economy. Equally important, the Japanese adopted a cautious approach. There has never been a Japanese store inside or near the community, and community members have always attributed this to a promise of no competition made by their earliest leaders. Friendly relations were quickly cultivated, notably with the editor of the town's newspaper.

On the land, the colonists survived by endurance, hope, and collaboration. They planted grapes and orchards for the long-term future, stubbornly replanting whenever their crops were eaten by rabbits or buried by sandstorms. In 1908, they formed a Colony Association for discussion of community-wide issues. The organization of a purchasing cooperative for bulk foods was followed by the establishment of a cooperative marketing association, popularly called the kumiai. The community hired the kumiai's first manager in 1914 and celebrated the building and opening of a community hall that year.

Establishment (1915–1919)

Despite the strength of anti-Japanese forces in California, the passage of the state's Alien Land Laws, and the Gentlemen's Agreement of 1908, the Yamato Colony took shape as a notably successful settlement, benefiting from a period of national prosperity.

The colony's survival depended upon the ability of would-be settlers to circumvent the Alien Land Laws, which prohibited the Japanese from owning or leasing land. Like Japanese throughout California, many early and later colonists bought land and protected their holdings through corporations created in the names of trusted friends or, increasingly, their own American-born children. Even a partial list of the colony's farm companies rings with poetry and hope: Delicious Fruit, Belle Terre, Eagle, Lucky, Mercy, Grace, Paradise, Peace, Sunnyside, Truth.

Marriage became another issue as the colony's crops reached maturity and provided means enough for workers to buy their own land and to marry. Again like many of their countrymen, the colony settlers found a way around government restrictions. In Japan, marriage is accomplished when a woman's name is added to the registry listing of the man's family. Once the men settled on their own farms in the colony, they found brides, some by returning home and others by shashin kekkon (with the help of intermediaries, an exchange of photographs and family information that led to an arranged marriage finalized in Japan).

As Abiko had hoped, the colony gave the Japanese settlers roots. Reconstructing the population growth between 1915 and 1919, old timers later remembered the arrivals of 15 brides and the start of 16 new farms (seven in the contiguous colony of Cressey, which had been bought by Abiko and his associates in 1918).

A more complex community developed as the colony's population expanded and its farms reached full production. In 1916, with more fruits than it could sell in the San Francisco area, the colony's kumiai joined the California Fruit Exchange, a statewide cooperative with access to national markets. At about that time, the organization legally incorporated as the Livingston Cooperative Society and built a $10,000 packing shed by the railroad tracks in town.

New organizations emerged. In 1917, 46 community members officially founded the Livingston Church of Christ. That year, the settlers dragged the old colony hall to 10 acres they purchased in the heart of the colony. Through donations, they built a modern parsonage, expanded the hall, and hired a minister, probably through the Methodist Conference. Church groups and programs took stronger shape, and, in 1918, the Colony Association and church created the area's first kindergarten. A white woman, hired to prepare the Japanese children for grade school, offered English and religious instruction and taught the children the Pledge of Allegiance and patriotic songs.

Maturity (1920–1940)

During the 1920s, anti-Japanese prejudice intensified. California passed two more alien land laws, Japan stopped issuing passports to picture brides, and in

1924 a national exclusion act halted any further immigration from Japan. The colony offered Issei and Nisei a haven, but external prejudice and the stress of the Depression affected every individual, every farm, and the community as a whole.

As recalled by Issei elders, between 1920 and 1922, approximately 23 families and couples moved to the Yamato Colony or to land next door in Cressey. Somewhere around that time, almost 10 men also found brides. Reacting to the population growth and influenced by anti-Japanese agitation in nearby towns, Livingston's Farm Center and Board of Trade endorsed an anti-Japanese resolution drafted by the newly formed California Exclusion League, calling, among other measures, for the removal of citizenship from American-born children. In 1920, for several months, two signs on the highway at either side of town proclaimed "No More Japanese Wanted Here."

Anti-Japanese sentiment among people in the town was far from universal. The colonists still had some allies and friends, but life changed. The vast majority of the colony's children grew up aware of anti-Japanese feelings in the town. Though they participated in high school sports teams and the boys joined the Boy Scouts, interracial dating was unthinkable and visits to the homes of white school friends happened rarely, if ever. The children of the earliest settlers had experienced no apparent barriers to relationships with their high school classmates. They left the community for college, but several returned home after graduation, forced back by prejudice and the bad economy of the Depression.

The mature Yamato Colony was far too complex to be described as "a family," a term often used by the original settlers to indicate the intimacy of the early settlement. Years later, entering a community known as a Christian one, non-Christian settlers had to adjust. Informal separations emerged as people drew nearer to those who had come to the United States from their own prefectures. Financial pressures intensified the differences between larger, more established settlers and those who had come later, buying smaller plots and facing a bad economy that made it difficult for them to establish themselves. Probably reflecting these strains, in 1927 the kumiai divided into two separate organizations: the Livingston Fruit Exchange (dominated by members of the original kumiai) and the Livingston Fruit Growers Association.

Like any other community, the colony was no utopia, but it offered a rich life to all its members. The church served as a social center for men and women, young and old. In 1934, the colonists built a church social hall, which was used for Japanese language lessons, classes for kendo (a martial art), and occasional Japanese movies. Tennis courts were installed and open land made available for baseball games. Looking back, the Nisei remember growing up in what they describe as a haven.

War (1941–1945)

The bombing of Pearl Harbor and the "evacuation" of all Japanese Americans from the West Coast could have ended the Yamato Colony. Instead, utilizing friendships, business connections, and the strength of their cooperatives, the colonists were able to maintain ownership of all but a few farms, and the community regrouped after the war.

Like all other Japanese Americans throughout the West Coast, those in the Livingston area had little time to prepare for the evacuation. The final order for imprisonment was given on April 30, 1942, setting a deadline of May 13 for incarceration. In less than two weeks, workers put up an "assembly center" on the Merced County Fair Grounds. Intended for approximately 4,500 people—all the Japanese Americans in seven counties—the site was to include the Issei and Nisei of the Yamato Colony, their neighbors in Cressey, and those from nearby Cortez, a third colony opened by Abiko and his colleagues in 1919.

Preparing to leave, the families from all three colonies were confronted with the immediate need to arrange for the harvest of thousands of acres of fruit. They also had to find someone who could be trusted to manage the farms during their absence. The decision to define these as community problems proved critical. Members of the two kumiai from the Yamato and Cressey colonies, and the kumiai in Cortez, met to discuss options. Because of their fluency in English and their status as citizens, older Nisei took the lead. Ultimately, they made it possible for kumiai members to place their lands under the care of a joint trusteeship of three: a local lawyer and one representative each from the California Fruit Exchange and the Pacific Fruit Exchange (statewide marketing groups to which the kumiais belonged). The combined acreage and income from the three colonies enabled the group to hire G. A. Momberg, a manager who had handled foreclosed land for the Bank of America. With a legally binding agreement and trusted allies in key positions as advisors, trustees, and, in one case, as an employee, the farmers had done all they could to protect their interests. All but a few of the families in the Yamato, Cressey, and Cortez colonies chose to place their land under the joint trusteeship.

On May 13, 1942, the Issei, Nisei, and a handful of children born to Nisei couples entered the Merced Assembly Center under armed guard. Three months later, they were moved to the Amache Relocation Camp in Granada, Colorado. From there, the young people of the community dispersed. Some found jobs outside the camp. The National Japanese American Student Relocation Council, a group spearheaded by the Quakers, advocated for the Nisei and helped many of them enroll in colleges and universities far from the West Coast. Over two-thirds of the community's draft age men served in the military, either as members of the 442nd combat team or in the

Military Intelligence Service. Three young Nisei from the community lost their lives on battlefields in Europe.

When the exclusion orders were revoked on January 2, 1945, the Japanese Americans whose land had been managed by Momberg had the option to return to California. Care of the ranches varied according to individual renters, but none of the trust's farms were lost. Reentry was not easy, but in spite of open hostility, shunning, and, in several cases, drive-by shootings, many chose to return.

The Nisei/Sansei Era

The community that reassembled following the war was smaller, but it again grew strong. The elderly Issei retired, and under the care of their Nisei children, the farms flourished. In 1957, the two kumiai merged to form the Livingston Farmers Association (LFA). Expansion became possible, and between 1958 and 1959, the group modernized its town packing shed, put up an almond shelling plant, constructed a new office building, and began constructing space for cold storage.

The church again became the center of community life. A new chapel was dedicated in 1950, and the church was renamed Grace Methodist. Though Issei, Nisei, and the Nisei's Sansei children met regularly with their contemporaries and worshipped in their own languages, services and events drew all three generations together. With time, the number of Issei decreased, and, in 1968, the colony and town churches merged. Unified worship continued in the colony church.

By the 1960s and 1970s, the colony had fulfilled its founder's dream. It provided the base for a good life rooted in America, and it served as a springboard for opportunities far beyond its borders, particularly for the community's Sansei children, who entered a world in which all professions were open to them and interracial relationships and marriages were possible.

Afterword (the Colony Today)

Changes in agriculture and the economy have made life challenging for anyone who wants to sustain a family on a small farm. Nonetheless, the community once known as the Yamato Colony still exists with surprising strength today. Though the majority of Nisei have died or moved away, 22 Nisei households may be found in or near the colony. Eleven Sansei children have returned home, nine of whom are running the family farms (either themselves or through a spouse). The kumiai (still the Livingston Farmers Association) handles over $6 million in business and includes a few of the original Nisei among its members.

The city of Livingston has encroached on the family farms, but the colony exerts a powerful hold on the hearts of its members, many of whom now live thousands of miles away. In 2007, advised by a small group of Nisei, a committee of Sansei planned a two-day celebration honoring the 100th anniversary of the colony's founding. This drew more than 500 people, some of whom traveled from the East Coast and Japan. A committee of Nisei and Sansei also created and in 2010 dedicated a memorial on the Merced Fairgrounds to recognize and warn against the kind of hatred that led to the community's imprisonment during the war.

Year in and year out, the church still unifies the community. Nisei and Sansei gather annually for a church fund-raiser that has roots in the Japanese celebration of the New Year. Working together, they steam, pound, and form 500 pounds of sweet rice into the mochi that is traditionally eaten on New Year's Day. Sansei parents are also drawn back to the community every summer from far distances for Tomodachi Gakko, a one-week program introducing their children to the songs, language, and crafts of Japan.

During its height, the Yamato Colony robustly nurtured three generations of Japanese Americans and, later, the children of the small number of Sansei who returned to the farms. It is a community treasured by those who trace their roots there.

See also: Alien Land Law (1913); Seabrook Farms (New Jersey)

Further Reading

Masumoto, David Mas. *Harvest Son: Planting Roots in American Soil.* New York: W. W. Norton & Co., 1998.

Masumoto, David Mas. *Wisdom of the Last Farmer: Harvesting Legacies from the Land.* New York: The Free Press, 2009.

Matsumoto, Valerie. *Farming the Home Place: A Japanese American Community in California.* Ithaca, NY: Cornell University Press, 1993.

Noda, Kesa. *Yamato Colony: 1906–1960.* Livingston, CA: Livingston-Merced JACL Chapter, 1981.

Kesaya E. Noda

PART III

CULTURAL AND RELIGIOUS LIFE: PEOPLE, INSTITUTIONS, AND ORGANIZATIONS

HISTORICAL OVERVIEW

Immigrants from Japan arrived in the United States with their rich cultural heritage and religious faiths. Japanese cultural and religious faith traditions have contributed to the rich mosaic of American civil society and American pluralism. Japanese Americans practice several world religious traditions, including faiths unique to Japan. The religions include Japanese forms of Mahayana Buddhism—Jodo Shinshu, Jodo Shu, Nichiren, Shingon, and Zen—in addition to the Japanese indigenous tradition known as Shinto and various forms of Christianity. The majority of first- and second-generation Japanese Americans observe Buddhist and Shinto ritual activities, although some observe Christian rituals, and others appear to be secular in terms of their religious beliefs and practices, as they participate in rituals only on occasion such as at the Lunar New Year or times of birth, marriage, and death.

Japanese American communities flourished in the 1920s and 1930s. Communities built Japanese language schools and both Christian congregations and Buddhist temples, and they established judo clubs. The Buddhist Missions of North America, later called the Buddhist Churches of America, epitomized the emergence of a distinctly Japanese American religious culture as the interior of Buddhist temples resembled the interior of American protestant churches. This structural transformation occurred during the post–World War II period as a means to make Japanese Americans and Buddhism resemble mainstream Euro-American society. As such, they called their Buddhist place of worship a "church" instead of a "temple," incorporated pews for seating, adapted Sunday services, published hymnals, created Sunday school for the children, and called their "monks" "priests." These adaptations were a systematic attempt to emphasize their "American" identity in light of the fear and xenophobia they experienced during World War II. The Buddhist Churches of America and the Honpa Hongwanji Mission of Hawai'i are Buddhist associations and represent two Japanese imports that have thrived within the United States.

Berkeley Higashi Honganji Buddhist Temple was established in 1925. It is affiliated with Shinshu Otani-ha, also called Higashi Honganji Temple, in Kyoto, Japan. (Courtesy of Jonathan H. X. Lee)

Besides observing various world religious faiths, the Japanese American religious landscape includes "new religions" that developed in Japan, such as Mahikari, Oomoto, Soka Gakkai, and Tenrikyo. Of these four new religions, Soka Gakkai is perhaps the most integrated faith-based institution within Japanese American society. Derived from Nichiren Buddhism in the early 20th century, Soka Gakkai made its international expansion in 1975 forming the Soka Gakkai International group (SGI). Today, the SGI's American branch, Soka Gakkai nternational United States, has over 2,600 neighborhood discussion groups, nearly 100 centers, as well as an academic institution known as Soka University of America, in Aliso Viejo, California.

The presence of these temples and shrines associated with Buddhist and Shinto traditions, respectively, provide Japanese Americans a venue for rites of passage (e.g., marriage and funerals), rituals (e.g., blessings and purifications), and celebrations (e.g., memorials). For example, such rites of passage and rituals include *omiyamari*, a purification practice; *yakubarai*, an official cleansing of the soul; and *kigan*, a prayer-based ceremony where a variety of items are blessed including automobiles, businesses, and even one's preperformance set of skills for passing major exams.

Besides using religion and rituals to express themselves as Japanese and American, Japanese Americans also relied on cultural traditions and festivals. For instance, Japanese Americans celebrate the traditionally Buddhist Obon festival, which, over time developed into an expression of community identity. The Obon festival is celebrated in the fall to honor the ancestors and the dead who have no living relatives. Many consider it the most popular cultural-religious celebration within the Japanese American community. For three days, participants of the Buddhist tradition honor their deceased ancestors by cleaning their places of burial and celebrating their memory. This celebration also includes a dance known as the *bon-odori*, performed to a variety of traditional Japanese music. Over time, this festival transformed into a secular tradition that included Buddhist and non-Buddhist community members and emphasized the celebration of Japanese American culture and identity. In Los Angeles, Japanese American community leaders developed Nisei Week in 1934 to support Japantown businesses and inculcate a sense of pride among the second-generation Japanese Americans of their ancestral cultural heritage and to encourage community solidarity. The Obon festivals, Nihonmachi, or Japantown Street Fairs, and Nisei Week remain important events in Japanese American communities today.

At these community festivals, Japanese American folk dances and performances will be highlighted. Folk dance and performance in Japanese America generally ranges between audience-directed performance and personal expression. One popular audience-directed performance is traditional Japanese percussion known as *taiko*. Originating from China between BCE 500 and 300 CE, taiko is often performed by groups of drummers in a variety of religious, as well as secular, festivals. In the United States, taiko groups, such as the San Francisco Taiko Dojo and San Jose Taiko, are well-known practitioners of this art. In addition, a Los Angeles–based group made up of several young Japanese Americans known as the TAIKOPROJECT, have crafted an innovative form of taiko that blends Japanese and American themes to create a unique transnational performance. Several foundations serving the Japanese American community within the United States are frequent sponsors of organized festivals featuring performances and dances that reinforce Japanese cultural traditions in America. Each year in the Los Angeles area of Little Tokyo, for example, the Nisei Week Foundation offers various activities including a Queen and Court contest, cultural exhibitions, and taiko drumming.

AIKIDO IN AMERICA

Aikido is a Japanese martial art that is practiced in the United States and throughout the world. It is primarily a complementary and defensive style of combat that uses an attacker's own energy to dispel an oncoming attack. In practice, it is about learning to blend and work together with one's opponent for reciprocal benefits. The word *aikido* loosely translates to "the way of harmony and spirit." Physical strength and size are not integral to the practice of aikido, thus it can be performed and effectively used by almost everyone. The throws and falls that are common in aikido practice can be executed by students of almost any size or weight as they are based on being centered and grounded and emphasize hip rotation, motion, and getting off of the line of attack. Aikido differs from many other martial arts in that it is almost exclusively used for practice, functional application, and mental and physical benefits and is not a competitive art/sport.

Aikido was created by Morihei Ueshiba (1883–1969), who is also known as o-sensei (great teacher). Aikido was born out of Ueshiba's training in the older art of daito-ryu aiki jujitsu and his proficiency with multiple weapons and spiritual beliefs that focused on being harmonious and at one with the surrounding universe. It is an early mixed martial art form with diverse roots. Aikido is thus not only an empty hand style of combat and self-defense but it also combines the use of joint locks, nerve manipulation, and weapons including the jo (wooden stick), bokken (wooden sword), and tanto (wooden knife). The use of breath, meditation, and mind–body awareness are also vital to the art.

Aikido was first brought to the continental United States and the territory of Hawai'i in 1953. The first aikido dojo outside of Japan was established in Honolulu, Hawai'i, and is still in use seven days a week. Though there are aikido dojos throughout the United States, the art is especially popular in the Hawai'ian Islands perhaps because of the large local Japanese population and its close ties to Japan.

Currently, there are several styles of aikido that are practiced and passed down. One of the primary motivators for multiple styles emerging was a conflict that occurred after o-sensei's death between his son, Kisshomaru Ueshiba, and one of his students, Koichi Tohei. The younger Ueshiba continued to teach his father's style whereas Tohei founded a new style with a differing governing organization. Today, the most common forms of aikido practiced include aikikai (Ueshiba's traditional style), ki aikido (which derived from Tohei), and the Iwama style that emerged from Kisshomaru Ueshiba's student, Morihiro Saito. Many high-ranking sensei teaching in the United States today are only two generations removed from the founder.

Twenty-first-century aikido in America adheres to many of the traditions that were in use when it was first brought over from Japan over 60 years ago.

Students begin as white belts and over the course of several years take promotional tests (kyu tests) to achieve the rank of Shodan (first-degree black belt). Shodan is really the beginning of the students' own personal training where they begin to merge their years of aikido education with their own understanding of the practice.

There are several degrees of black belts that are awarded and each additional degree requires years of training. Unlike many martial arts where a student can accumulate ranks and belts in a relatively short period, aikido is known for being an art where promotions are given at a slower rate and students must practice for a longer period between each belt.

Advancement in aikido requires a student to be conversant with the Japanese language as tests are given in Japanese. Students must also have a firm grasp of dojo etiquette. Aikido has no preference for age, gender, culture, ethnicity, or nationality but it adheres strongly to respect for rank. Junior students are expected to take direction from senior students and all dojo members are expected to follow instruction from their sensei.

Because it is based on movements that are not in opposition but rather complement each other, Aikido is sometimes criticized for being not brutal or effective enough as a fighting art. However, as students progress, they are expected to be able to execute techniques at a faster pace and to fend off multiple attackers and attackers brandishing weapons. Though aikido is a noncompetitive martial art, many of its forms have the potential to cause serious to fatal injuries. A competitive form of the art would require eliminating many of the techniques.

See also: Judo in America; Martial Arts

Further Reading

AikiWeb: The Source for Aikido Information. "Eric Sotnak." http://www.aikiweb.com/. Accessed June 11, 2012.

Gengo, Stevan. Sensei, Aikido of Noe Valley, in discussions with the author, June 2006–April 2012.

Valerie Lo

BUDDHIST CHURCHES OF AMERICA

The Buddhist Churches of America (BCA) is an incorporated faith organization affiliated with the Jōdo Shinshū Honganji-ha (sect) headquartered in Kyoto, Japan. Jōdo Shinshū or Shin Buddhism was founded on the teachings of Shinran (1173–1262), a Japanese cleric active during the Kamakura period (1185–1333). The BCA administers and directs its denominational activities in the continental United States from its headquarters in San Francisco, California.

This entry gives an overview of the doctrines and beliefs that guide the BCA, its history, and its institution.

Beliefs and Doctrines

Jōdo Shinshū Buddhists hold that Shinran's thoughts contained in the *Kyōgyōshinshō*, *Tan'nishō*, *Mattōshō*, and other writings crystallize the spiritual vision articulated in the *Muryōjukyō* (*Larger Sukhāvatīvyūha-sūtra*), *Kammuryō-jukyō* (*Amitāyurdhyāna-sūtra*), and *Amidakyō* (*Smaller Sukhāvatīvyūha-sūtra*). The *Muryōjukyō* details 48 vows that Bodhisattva Dharmākara fulfilled to become Amida Buddha and to establish the Pure Land with the intent to save all beings. Of these 48, the 18th vow is central.

> If sentient beings hear [Amida's] name and quicken faith and joy, with even a single thought [of the Amida Buddha]; and if they offer their spiritual merit to others with a sincere heart; and if they desire to be born in [Amida's] Pure Land, they will attain birth there and reside in the stage of nonretrogression. Only those who commit the five damning offenses or slander the true teaching will be excluded.

Over the course of the development of Japanese Pure Land thought, Buddhist thinkers expanded the embrace of Amida Buddha's compassion to include all beings. The expression "a single thought" evolved to mean uttering Amida's name in the form *Namu Amida Butsu*—I take refuge in Amida Buddha. The *Amidakyō* states that sentient beings can be born in the Pure Land by simply hearing and by being sincerely mindful of Amida's name. Carrying this idea further, the *Muryōjukyō* expounds that even evil persons on their deathbeds who utter Amida Buddha's name with utmost sincerity will be received in Pure Land.

The insights from these three *sūtras* provided Shinran with the rationale for dispensing with rigorous spiritual discipline and highlighting the centrality of *shinjin*, true or sincere faith espoused by Nāgārjuna (ca. 150–250), Vasubandhu (ca. fifth century), and others. The centrality of faith assures spiritual release when the devotee appreciates his or her inadequacies and surrenders to the absolute Other Power (*tariki*) of Amida Buddha. *Shinjin*, the prime condition for birth in the Pure Land, is a gift from Amida Buddha; and the sincere utterance of the *nembutsu* is an invocation of gratitude and joy for Amida's compassion. Birth in the Pure Land is the most conducive way station for the ultimate realization of enlightenment (bodhi) or Nirvāṇa.

History

The Buddhist Churches of America celebrated its centennial in 1999. During the previous century the teachings of Shinran and its American institutional incarnation have had to respond and adapt to the American experience. This adventure began with the arrival of the Revs. Sonoda Shuye (1863–1922) and Nishijima Kakuryō (1873–1942) in San Francisco on September 1, 1899; this date marks the official beginnings of the BCA. Their arrival was prompted by a personal plea in 1896 by Hirano Nisaburō to the Honpa Hongwanji Sect headquartered in Kyoto to dispatch priests to minister to the growing Japanese immigrant community. Two years later the Revs. Honda Eryū and Miyamoto Ejun traveled to the United States to survey the spiritual needs of the Japanese community. During their visit they assisted Dr. Kaida (a.k.a. Hirakida) Katsu-gorō, who was in the process of setting up a medical practice in San Francisco, and others to establish the Bukkyō Seinenkai (Young Men's Buddhist Associa-tion—YMBA), the first Jōdo Shinshū Buddhist organization in the continental United States. After visiting Sacramento, Seattle, Vancouver, and other areas with sizable Japanese communities, they returned to Kyoto and recommended that priests be sent. The U.S. government census figures note that the number of Japanese immigrants had grown tenfold from 2,039 in 1890 to 24,327 in 1900.

Because most of the early immigrants were Jōdo Shinshū devotees, they naturally appealed to the Honpa Hongwanji authorities. In addition to serv-ing their constituents, the leadership viewed this invitation as an opportunity to propagate Shinran's teaching to an English-speaking community. Although Japanese is still integral in its rituals, in the intervening 100 years English has gradually become the lingua franca for conducting services and temple affairs.

Uchida Kōyu (1896–1960), who arrived in 1905 with his wife Seto, laid the institutional foundation of the Buddhist Mission of North America, the fore-runner of the BCA. During their 18 years, Rev. and Mrs. Uchida witnessed the establishment of 13 temples and a number of fellowships in the western states of California, Oregon, and Washington. Temples were also established in Salt Lake City and Denver. Recognizing the growing number of temples and the administrative complexity, the BCA officially appointed Uchida *sōchō* (bishop) in 1918. Prior to receiving this new designation, Uchida held the title of *kan-toku* (director).

The sixth *sōchō*, Masuyama Kenjū (1887–1968), arrived in 1930 and quickly surmised that the Buddhist mission would require ministers who could com-municate fluently in English. Shortly thereafter he established the Buddhist Society of America to reach English speakers, as well as second-generation Japanese Americans. He enlisted the assistance of Robert S. Clifton (1886–1963), Julius A. Goldberg (1908–2011), Sunya Pratt (1898–1986), and other Euro-Americans. He also encouraged American-born and -educated Tsunoda Noboru (1913–2005) and Kumata Masaru (1908–1989), the first Japanese Americans to undertake ministerial training in Kyoto. The bishop created the Young Buddhist Association, moved to sponsor Boy Scout groups, encouraged

Dharma (Sunday) School expansions, and promoted English publications. He left to his successor, Matsukage Ryōtai (1890–1948), 48 temples and fellowships that extended from Vancouver, Canada, to the north and New York City to the east.

The outbreak of World War II and the subsequent internment of the Japanese community along the Pacific Coast marked an important milestone in the American Pure Land experience. President Franklin Delano Roosevelt's 1942 Executive Order 1099, the Civilian Exclusion Orders, legalized the removal and relocation of persons of Japanese ancestry from their homes, farms, and businesses. U.S. authorities closed all of the Buddhist temples and arrested and sent most of their clerics and lay leaders to various internment centers throughout the United States.

Bishop Matsukage Ryōtai relocated to the Topaz Relocation Center in Utah. Government officials allowed Buddhist groups to carry on their religious activities in the centers. In 1944 a general meeting of ministers and lay leaders from the various centers and from other noninterned communities gathered at Topaz, Arizona, to adopt the articles of incorporation that officially changed the name from Buddhist Mission of North America to the Buddhist Churches of America.

Ironically, the internment provided new opportunities. In lieu of entering the internment centers, the government allowed the Japanese to settle away from the Pacific Coast states. Many found their way to such cities as Chicago, Detroit, St. Louis, New York, Philadelphia, and Seabrook, New Jersey, where they established Buddhist fellowships, many of which eventually evolved into full-fledged temples. The arrest and internment of the largely Japanese-speaking leadership thrust the younger American-born English-speaking clerics into leadership positions. After the war, great efforts were made to change the temple-related activities from Japanese to English and to nurture a new generation of leaders and devotees. English became the primary language for conducting services and other temple-related meetings. In 1954, the BCA established the Buddhist Study Center in Berkeley, California, to provide instruction in English for ministerial aspirants. The center was renamed the Institute of Buddhist Studies (IBS) in 1966; and in 1985 the IBS became an affiliate of the Graduate Theological Union (GTU).

Beginning in 1959, Bishop Hanayama Shinsho (1898–1995) and his Canadian-born successor Kenryū Tsuji (1919–2004) centralized and transformed BCA into a modern American institution through innovative educational, outreach, ministerial, and financial programs. The BCA created a scholarship fund to assist ministerial aspirants, a ministerial disability income and accidental death benefits program, a financial foundation, and other institutional reforms. Rev. Kenryū Tsuji's bishop's accession ceremony was the first to take place in the United States. On his watch the Hongwanji accredited the ministerial program at the Institute of Buddhist Studies. Ministerial training was now possible in English. Ordination, however, is still done in Kyoto.

Like other mainline U.S. denominations, from the mid-1970s the BCA's vitality began a slow decline, due in part to declining membership, financial difficulties, an aging clergy, and uninspiring leadership. In an attempt to reverse this decline, the BCA initiated the Campaign for Buddhism in America in 1982 with the goal of raising $15 million. Funds from this capital campaign were intended to establish a more secure financial base for Buddhist education and to expand the capacity of the IBS, which was about to become part of the GTU, to improve ministerial pensions, and other programs. The campaign raised $10 million. Once again in 2003 the BCA embarked on a capital campaign, this time to raise $31 million for Buddhist education, ministerial benefits, and to secure a permanent facility for the IBS in Berkeley.

Since peak in the mid-1970s the BCA has steadily lost devotees and has had to trim its administrative staff. The department of Buddhist Education and Sunday (Dharma) School that produced many innovative programs and publications was eliminated. Many temples are without ministers. The IBS's 1985 affiliation with the GTU was seen as a way to revitalize the tradition by training a new generation of ministers. It began with much fanfare; but eight years into its affiliation in 1993 the IBS began to systematically reduce its faculty and staff; it sold its newly acquired facility on Addison Street in 1997 and moved to Mountain View, California. The IBS eventually returned to Berkeley in 2006 to a newly remodeled Jōdo Shinshū Center on Durant Street. Ironically, the new facility was not designed to house its substantial Buddhist library. The IBS shares the facility with the Center for Buddhist Education that was established in 2005. Unable to sustain the BCA archives that were begun with a grant from the National Historical Publications and Records Commission, the BCA transferred its archives to the Japanese National Museum in Los Angeles, California, in 1998.

The racial-ethnic makeup of the membership is becoming increasingly diverse. Many non-Japanese have been attracted to the faith through interest in Jōdo Shinshū teachings and in Japanese culture and by marrying into the faith. A cursory review of the BCA's 2011–2012 directory reveals that many non-Japanese have assumed leadership roles. There are a number of non-Japanese clerics.

Administrative Structure

From its headquarters in San Francisco, the BCA oversees 61 temples and 5 fellowships with approximately 16,000 dues paying members throughout the contiguous United States. Administratively, the BCA consists of eight geographic districts, six of which are concentrated on the Pacific Coast. The Mountain

States District serves devotees in Colorado, Wyoming, and Nebraska. The Eastern District includes the temples and fellowships east of the Rocky Mountains. This far-flung scattering of temples is governed by a board of directors composed of the bishop, the board president, the Ministerial Association chair, district-elected board members, board members at large, and representatives of BCA-affiliated organizations. Its annual meeting is held in February.

Although the BCA and the office of the bishop administer national programs, the individual temples maintain separate budgets and administrations. The individual temples support the operations of the BCA by forwarding monies based on an annual assessment of the dues-paying membership. The bishop's office appoints ministers to the local temples and mediates disputes. In addition to the overarching national organization, there are a number of affiliated organizations such as the Federation of Buddhist Women's Association, Western Adult Buddhist League, Federation of Dharma School Teachers' League, California Young Adult Buddhist League, and Western Young Buddhist League. These affiliates have local chapters.

The American Shin Buddhists in the state of Hawai'i have a separate jurisdiction and administration. The Honpa Hongwanji Mission of Hawai'i traces its beginnings to 1899. At the time of its founding, the kingdom of Hawai'i was not part of the United States. It is headquartered in Honolulu, Hawai'i. Like Hawai'i, the Canadian Shin Buddhists have a separate organization. Pure Land Buddhists arrived there in 1905. Its national headquarters is in British Columbia, Canada.

Contributions

The Buddhist Mission of North America (BMNA) and its successor organization, the BCA, have made significant contributions to American spiritual experience. In 1915, the BMNA hosted the World Buddhist Conference in San Francisco. This first international Buddhist conference in the United States was held in conjunction with the International Exposition. In 1935, Bishop Matsuyama and Rev. Shodo Tsunoda (1913–2005) traveled to Siam (now Thailand) to receive a portion of the corporeal remains of Śākyamuni Buddha from the royal family. The remains were unearthed in the late 19th century in Piprahwa in northern India. Bishop Matsukage carried the relics to the Topaz War Relocation Center. Spearheaded by the Young Buddhist Association of Hawai'i and the continental United States, BCA lobbied the U.S. Department of Defense to recognize Buddhism as a legitimate faith tradition. During World War II only Japanese American Christian ministers were allowed to accompany Japanese American combat troops. At the time the U.S. government recognized only three faith traditions; accordingly military personnel dog tags were imprinted with "C" for Catholic, "P" for Protestant, and "O" for Jewish. Additionally, the

Department of Defense now allows the Buddhist (Dharma) wheel on grave markers.

See also: Higashi Honganji; Honpa Hongwanji Mission of Hawai'i; Japanese American Religions; Jōdo Shū (Pure Land Sect); Nichiren Shōshū

Further Reading

Dobbins, James C. *Jōdo Shinshū, Shin Buddhism in Medieval Japan*. Bloomington: Indiana University Press, 1989.

Kashima, Tetsuden. *Buddhism in America: The Social Organization of an Ethnic Religious Institution*. Westport, CT: Greenwood Press, 1977.

Tuck, Donald R. *Buddhist Churches of America, Jōdo Shinshū*. Lewiston, NY: Edwin Mellon Press, 1987.

Ronald Y. Nakasone

CHANOYU/TEA CEREMONY

The vitality of *chanoyu* (*ocha, chado,* or *sado*) as an artistic folk practice comes from it being the transmitter of a time-honored tradition that reflects patterns of life to people inside and outside Japan. The terms *chanoyu, chado, sado, temae, chaji,* and *chakai* are all translated as "tea ceremony." Chado is simply the making of tea for a guest. Chanoyu refers to hot water for tea. Chado and sado refer to the discipline or path of study. Temae refers to a specific preparation of tea for a guest. There are many ways of preparation depending on the season and utensils used. Chaji refers to a series of temae done for a guest or guests, usually lasting three to four hours. Chakai refers to a meeting for tea, either private or public, that is for multiple guests. Studying chanoyu is encouraged for anyone who wants to learn and understand Japanese culture, especially those of Japanese ancestry living in other countries. Therefore, it has become part of American Japanese practice and adds to the folkways of Japanese Americans.

The original home of the custom of drinking tea is China. Early records indicate Shomu Tenno (724–749 CE) was the first to offer tea ceremonially in Japan. Although several important individuals contributed to the creation of a unique art form using tea, a particularly influential person in its development was Sen Rikyu, whose innovations have indelibly stamped the character of modern chado. Although chado began in the Kyoto area, as a result of its popularity, it is practiced all over Japan. The practitioner is not only a person who takes or teaches lessons (keiko) or conducts chaji (four-and-a-half hour meeting for tea) and chakai (public gatherings for tea) but also may be a person who collects students and makes a living from their fees (ocha no sensei). Learning the history, arts, and stories of the development of the art is part of learning what it means to be Japanese American.

The 14th Urasenke Grand Master Tantansai and his son, Hounsai, have promoted chanoyu study in many countries of the world, especially the United States. They were the first to invite nonelite and non-Japanese participation. Chanoyu was taught in Japanese communities in the United States until World War II. Many teachers were discouraged from teaching Japanese cultural arts at this time. The internment of Japanese and Japanese Americans interrupted the teaching and practice of chado. While young, the Urasenke Grandmaster studied at the University of Hawai'i and with local teachers founded the Hawai'i Shibu and the Tea Ceremony Club. Several chashitsu (tea houses) were built in Hawai'i for lessons. A chashitsu was built for the 1964 World's Fair in New York and also for the Montreal Expo of 1976. Urasenke and Omotesenke teachers give lessons in major U.S. cities, such as Honolulu, San Francisco, New York, Los Angles, Chicago, and Seattle. Urasenke has spent the most energy and resources to teach chado all over the world as part of Grandmaster Hounsai's "Peace through a Bowl of Tea" crusade.

See also: Floral Arrangements/Ikebana; Japanese American Foods and Foodways

Further Reading

Austin, Lewis. *Saints and Samurai: The Political Culture of the American and Japanese Elites.* New Haven: Yale University Press, 1975.

Sadler, Arthur L. *Cha-No-Yu: The Japanese Tea Ceremony.* Tokyo: Charles E. Tuttle, 1962.

Sen, Soshitsu. *Tea Life, Tea Mind.* Tokyo: Weatherhill, 1979.

Barbara Lynne Rowland Mori

CHERRY BLOSSOM FESTIVAL

The Cherry Blossom Festival (CBF) in the United States is a Japanese cultural festival celebrating the blooming of cherry blossom trees, which signals spring. Produced in American cities with large, tradition-conscious Japanese American populations, the festival aims to display and promote Japanese culture and heritage to the public, and to recognize the contributions of the Japanese American community to American life. The festivals, staged by volunteers, vary in length from two days (Los Angeles), to two weeks (San Francisco), to two months (Honolulu).

The community-wide festival typically schedules performances and demonstrations of Japanese cultural arts, foods, and talent, such as traditional dancing, taiko drumming, flower arranging, tea ceremonies, and the martial arts. The festivals sponsor scholarships and contests for designing a festival poster, or writing an essay on Japanese cultural contributions, and are forums for announcing leadership or community service awards. These events are often

With pink blooms in full splendor, participants march down Constitution Avenue in Washington, D.C., during the National Cherry Blossom Festival Parade, 2002. The festival has been celebrated every year since 1912, when the cherry blossom trees were first given as a gift from the Japanese as a symbol of friendship. (AP Photo/J. Scott Applewhite)

showcased free at street fairs, which also feature celebrity appearances and vendors peddling ethnic foods, arts, and crafts. In Los Angeles and San Francisco, the festival climaxes with a street parade of floats, marching bands, dancers, CBF pageant winners, and dignitaries.

Other festival events that involve cost, sometimes for charity, may include fashion shows, golf tournaments, receptions, concerts, beauty pageants, and coronation balls. The Cherry Blossom Queen Pageant is a prominent feature in some festivals such as northern California's and is central to the one in Honolulu. Organized by the Honolulu Japanese Junior Chamber of Commerce in 1953, the Hawai'i Japanese CBF is the oldest in the United States and was constructed around the Queen Pageant.

As a beauty competition, the Queen Pageant generates public excitement and interest in the festival. The public appearances of the contestants at shopping malls and festival events and their visits to convalescent homes all draw press coverage. The queen represents the Japanese American community as a model of their values and gender ideals (there was never a swimsuit competition). She also links the Japanese American community to its ethnic homeland. One of the pageant prizes is the goodwill tour to Japan. The queen, her court, and their entourage are treated as dignitaries during their publicized trip, the highlight of which is the Pageant Queen's audience with a member of the Japanese royal family.

The requirements for the Cherry Blossom Queen have changed to reflect the increasingly diverse multiethnic Japanese American community. Prior to 1998, the contestants had to be of 100 percent Japanese ancestry; now it is 50 percent. To encourage contestants with leadership and community service accomplishments, the CBF raised the age limit to 26, which fostered a candidate profile of college coeds or graduates.

Ethnic festivals galvanize a community by refocusing on its heritage. The first northern California CBF in San Francisco in 1967 brought community groups together amid the social turbulence and dissensions over the Vietnam War. In Hawai'i, the CBF created a positive image of Japanese culture and of Japanese Americans as civic-minded citizens in the aftermath of World War II. They unified the Japanese community, instilling it with cultural pride.

See also: Chanoyu/Tea Ceremony; Floral Arrangements/Ikebana; Matsuri; Taiko Performance

Further Reading

Yano, Christine. *Crowning the Nice Girl: Gender, Ethnicity, and Culture in Hawai'i's Cherry Blossom Festival.* Honolulu: University of Hawai'i Press, 2006.

Linda Sun Crowder

FLORAL ARRANGEMENTS/IKEBANA

Ikebana literally translates to "living flowers." The whole spiritual basis for floral arrangement within Japanese American culture suggests the unity of mind, body, and soul. Practitioners of this traditional art, which incorporates the use of natural stems of plants and flowers in a minimalist arrangement, often focus on developing their appreciation for nature. The goal is to capture the true essence of nature within the arrangement and to utilize certain techniques that produce a realistic representation of flowers found blooming during each of the four seasons. Thus, there is a cycle of seasons that may be perpetuated through the spirituality of live flowers within Japanese American homes on a year-round basis.

Japanese American flower arrangement practices are continuous and find their origins in ancient Japan. For centuries, the Japanese people have developed a long and deep affinity for plants and flowers. The *Nihon Shoki* (*The Chronicles of Japan*, 720 CE) is the oldest and official historical documentation of Japanese history and has been quoted as a reliable source for all things Japanese. In this document, it states, "all plants can speak to us." Thus, it was interpreted by some, if not all, of the early Japanese immigrants to the United

States that trees and flowers in nature talk to us using the same spiritual "language" as human beings.

The ancient Japanese had revered every element of nature as the "divine" and developed the notion of yorishiro (summoning divinities) through the talk between human beings, flowers, and plants. This spiritual belief continues to be passed down through the generations by Japanese Americans in the United States. In this regard, many Japanese Americans believe that by making votive offerings in home shrines and community-based religions centers, one can experience a sense of communion with nature. There are special ceremonies and festivals known as *kami mukae* (deity welcoming) during certain times in a given season. To guide these deities to the landmark shrine, tall plants are used as a sort of antennae to "catch" these floating divinities for prayer sessions. This is to ensure the presence of these divinities for certain ceremonies held at the shrines such as weddings.

Generally speaking, plants such as evergreens are utilized as a fitting shelter for divinities whose appearances are honored at a given shrine and even at home through a simple floral arrangement called kuge. This type of arrangement consists of evergreen branches and a few flowers with their stems. It represents the beginning stages of ikebana as part of a religious offering to the divinities in home shrines and shrines at local community Buddhist/Shinto centers.

For Japanese Americans, the practice of flower arranging thus originated with a sacred act of welcoming the spirits of nature and one's deceased ancestors' to one's home. Through ikebana, these cultural traditions retained some aspects of these religious practices from Japan. The sacredness of offering flowers to the divinities to communicate with them is the source from which the world of ikebana has developed over the past 500 years of Japanese history. This simple act of offering flowers to a home-based shrine continues to flourish in Japanese American communities today. As an example, the way of kado, or "plant arrangement," is a common practice for the Japanese to erect pine boughs called kadomatsu at the entryway to their homes. The cultural understanding garnered in this offering is to welcome the shichifukujins, or the "Seven Gods," especially on New Year's Day.

Flower arrangement practices were first imported to the United States by early Japanese immigrants who came after the start of modern political reformation during the Meiji period (1868). The first-known Japanese immigrants were from the town of Aizu-Wakamatsu, Fukushima Prefecture. A small group of 21 members started a silkworm colony in Coloma, California, in 1869, just after the Boshin Wars. Subsequent immigration patterns from Japan established a stronger basis for the proliferation of these floral arrangements as part of preserving Japanese-styled cultural traditions at local Buddhist churches and/or Japanese American community centers throughout the United States.

Moreover, this type of floral arrangement has changed over time and developed into new schools of thought in response to the changing circumstances of Japanese Americans' everyday lives.

As established from tradition, the ideas generated from early Japanese history, the cultural essence of Japanese flower arrangements is the employment of minimalism. Most arrangements consist of only a few stalks and leaves and a few full-blossomed flowers that provided a hint of seasonal reference. Generally, the structure of Japanese American flower arrangement is based on a scalene triangle and organized by three main points, and this is done with twigs and branches that symbolize the heaven, earth, and humankind.

The organic elements combined in this triangular pattern must inspire a naturalism that is preserved through various techniques of cutting, trimming, and placement within a container. The use of various pottery containers is the key focus of composition for Japanese American floral arrangements, but what inspires the creator is the desire to experience a deeper connection with nature itself.

In sum, the contemporary use of the art of floral arrangement has moved toward an appreciation of nature in a self-contained expression that must evoke a naturalness to be complete. As a result, the various schools that teach this form of floral arrangement believe that there can be some source of communion with nature itself.

See also: Cherry Blossom Festival

Further Reading

Kawase, Toshiro. *The Book of Ikebana*. Tokyo: Kodansha International, 2000.

Ruby Toshimi Ogawa

HIGASHI HONGANJI

Jōdo Shinshū Buddhism's second-largest denomination, called Higashi Honganji, has nine temples in the United States. Higashi Honganji, whose formal name is Shinshū Ōtani-ha, traces its roots to a samurai battle in 17th-century Japan, the effect of which more than 400 years ago split the powerful Honganji organization in half, creating two giant temples just blocks away from each other in the city of Kyoto, which, due to their location, resulted in the names *"Nishi"* (West) and *"Higashi"* (East) Honganji. Over the years, Higashi has become known for its influential and progressive thinkers who helped interpret Jōdo Shinshū in the modern era and eventually to the Western world.

Near the end of the 16th century, Honganji had followers throughout Japan and a fortresslike headquarters in Osaka surrounded by a town of supporters that symbolized power and influence. The temple stood at the site where Osaka Castle stands today. In 1570, military leader Oda Nobunaga (1534–1582), in an attempt to conquer other warlords and unify the country, launched a battle against Honganji, whose followers rushed to its defense, resulting in a 10-year standoff. After Oda was assassinated by one of his own generals, his successor, Toyotomi Hideyoshi (1536–1598), negotiated a truce with Honganji's abbot, who agreed to leave the compound, a move his eldest son Kyōnyo (1558–1614) opposed. A new temple was built in Kyoto, where a younger son eventually became abbot. The next ruler, Tokugawa Ieyasu (1542–1616), in a move that further weakened Honganji's political influence, offered Kyōnyo his own temple just east of his younger brother's temple. Higashi Honganji temple in Kyoto today is one of the largest wooden structures in the world and one of Japan's largest Buddhist temples. The denomination claims a membership of about 5.5 million followers in Japan.

Shortly after Japan ushered in the modern era in the 1860s, leaving behind centuries of feudalism, Japanese immigrants began venturing west, initially finding work in the fields of Hawai'i. Higashi ministers from Japan traveled to the islands and established the denomination's first temples in the early 1900s, several in rural areas in new Japanese communities. Many of those temples closed in the following decades as those workers and communities disappeared. Today five Higashi temples remain on the islands of O'ahu, Hawai'i, and Kaua'i.

Japanese immigrants continued to move westward, establishing other communities on the West Coast, particularly in the San Francisco Bay Area and Los Angeles. Unlike its Nishi counterpart, the Higashi denomination made no concerted effort to establish temples on the mainland United States, although priests were sent to Brazil, which today has two dozen temples. In the United States, Higashi's development was characterized more by serendipity.

In Los Angeles, Nishi minister Izumida Junjō (1866–1951) switched to the Higashi denomination after a dispute with temple leaders. In 1904, he founded a temple that eventually became the first Higashi temple in California and later the central temple of Higashi Honganji's North America District. The temple is located in Los Angeles's Little Tokyo district. In Berkeley, California, a single Nishi Hongwanji temple served a vibrant Japanese community during the early 1900s until a rift occurred among members over its Japanese-language school. In 1926, a group of families left to start a temple headed by a Higashi minister, making it Higashi's second mainland temple.

Today in addition to Los Angeles, Berkeley, and Hawai'i, Higashi temples are also found in the Southern California cities of West Covina and Newport Beach. Membership ranges from 400 families at its largest temple in Los Angeles to far fewer at its smallest temples.

Although all Jōdo Shinshū denominations trace their teachings to the 13th-century priest Shinran, the way those teachings were interpreted varies. Fundamental Jōdo Shinshū teachings are rooted in Pure Land Buddhist *sutras,* which are full of arcane and abstract concepts and references that primarily focus on a symbolic Buddha named Amida who resides in the Pure Land, a place of peace and bliss, having vowed to save all living beings. The core expression of worship is reciting the name of this Buddha. Consequently, over the centuries, Jōdo Shinshū seemed to incarnate into a form increasingly dissimilar from the original Buddha's teachings, resembling more a form of prayer and deity worship.

A reformation of Jōdo Shinshū thought occurred at the turn of the 20th century led by Kiyozawa Manshi (1863–1903), a Higashi scholar whose controversial career includes teaching, protests, expulsion from the organization, reinstatement, founding the Higashi denomination's first university, illness, poverty, and the tragic deaths of his wife and two sons. An early student of Western philosophy, Kiyozawa vehemently spoke out against the denomination's emphasis on fund-raising while sacrificing spiritual study and practice. At one point, he adopted an extremely harsh lifestyle, only wearing Buddhist robes, living a threadbare existence, and eating a subsistence diet that ultimately contributed to his contracting tuberculosis. However, he came to see the fallacy of belief in a "self," instead describing ultimate reality as "power beyond self." His writings and focus on spiritual understanding through personal experience using the language of Western rationality set the tone for a number of subsequent Higashi teachers, several of whom became influential in their own right, such as Akegarasu Haya (1877–1967), Kaneko Daiei (1881–1976), and Soga Ryōjin (1875–1971). That philosophical lineage influenced the founders of the Chicago Buddhist Temple and the Maida Center for Buddhism in Berkeley, California.

Although Higashi Honganji follows a progressive interpretive approach to teaching Jōdo Shinshū, it adheres to traditional rituals in ceremony and services. Such practices may be found at its American temples, evident in an emphasis on ritualistic chanting of Buddhist *sūtras* and reciting melodic poems of Shinran, performed by priests wearing traditional Japanese-style robes.

In the United States, the temples served dual roles since their founding as spiritual centers and as de facto preserves for Japanese language, food, and culture where Japanese immigrants could feel welcome. Temples typically sponsored clubs specializing in flower arranging, bonsai, martial arts, Japanese poems, singing, and so forth. As each succeeding generation became more "Americanized," and in many cases intermarried with other races and ethnicities, and as non-Japanese people joined the temples, much of the Japanese culture aspect faded or disappeared, especially the Japanese language. Still, some clubs remain, Japanese food commonly is served, and certain activities continue to be popular such as summer bazaars and the *Obon* dance, a kind of Japanese group folk dance.

The most important function of the Higashi Honganji temples remains spiritual. They continue to be places where people go for services, weddings, and funerals and to listen to Buddhist teachers. Though relatively small in number, Higashi Honganji in the United States represents a denomination of the largest Japanese Buddhist sect and an influential force in the development of Buddhist thought.

See also: Buddhist Churches of America; Honpa Hongwanji Mission of Hawai'i; Japanese American Religions

Further Reading

Ama, Michihiro. *Immigrants to the Pure Land: The Modernization, Acculturation, and Globalization of Shin Buddhism, 1898–1941.* Honolulu: University of Hawai'i Press, 2011.
Rogers, Minor, and Ann Rogers. *Rennyo: The Second Founder of Shin Buddhism.* Fremont, CA: Asian Humanities Press, 1991.

Ken Yamada

HONPA HONGWANJI MISSION OF HAWAI'I

Honpa Hongwanji Mission of Hawai'i (HHMH) is a Buddhist organization affiliated with the Jōdo Shinshū Honganji-ha (Nishi Hongwanji) sect centered in Kyoto, Japan. Its 35 temples throughout the state of Hawai'i, base their spiritual life on the Jōdo Shinshū (True Pure Land) teachings of Shinran (1173–1262). HHMH serves as the central administrative hub of Nishi Hongwanji temples in Hawai'i from its headquarters in Honolulu. This entry provides an overview of HHMH with emphasis on its history and contributions to Buddhist education and to society.

Beliefs and Practices

The Jōdo Shinshū school of Buddhism (Shin Buddhism), of which HHMH is a part, arose through the insight and experience of Shinran and is a sectarian development within the larger tradition of Pure Land Buddhism, based on the *Muryōjukyō* (Larger *Sukhāvatīvyūha-sūtra*), *Kammuryōjukyō* (*Amitāyurdhyāna-sūtra*), and *Amidakyō* (Smaller *Sukhāvatīvyūha-sūtra*).

Pure Land Buddhist teachings emphasize the Mahāyāna Buddhist ideal in which salvation for oneself cannot be separated from that of others. Hence, in the mythological story of Bodhisattva Dharmākara becoming Amida Buddha through the fulfillment of 48 aspirations or "vows"—described in the *Larger*

Sukhāvatīvyūhasūtra—the salvation of all beings is the fundamental condition for Dharmākara's own acceptance of Buddhahood. The content of the 48 vows is epitomized by the 18th vow, which voices the aspiration that all beings everywhere will reach enlightenment when, hearing and thinking about the name "Amida," they awaken aspirations to be born in Amida's Pure Land and are thus assured of birth in that land in the next life. In the Pure Land tradition, aspirants are encouraged to recite the *nembutsu*, that is, to say the name of Amida Buddha (*Namo Amida Butsu*) as the means to actuate Amida's saving power and thus guarantee birth in the Pure Land. Even ordinary people who are unable to live virtuous lives or perform difficult Buddhist practices can achieve birth in the Pure Land and ultimate enlightenment through the easy practice of reciting the *nembutsu*.

Shinran, however, brought a unique perspective to this view. Based on his own experience, he realized that the desire to recite the *nembutsu* (or to perform any practice) to save himself remained an expression of human self-centeredness and ego. He realized that true and real "birth" occurs when one awakens to oneself as a being filled with blind passion, totally lacking in virtue and unable to save oneself. Only then is one able to hear the *nembutsu* as Amida's voice calling out, assuring salvation. The practitioner thus awakens faith in the reality of already being saved though Amida's Vow. In his personal insight, Shinran inverted the ordinary view of religion and reenvisioned the act of religious practice, particularly that of reciting the *nembutsu*, as a sign of salvation—and an expression of gratitude for that salvation—rather than as a means to an end.

This insight had radical implications for society in that the attainment of salvation became a matter of "grace" rather than something earned. Thus, religious or state authorities could no longer use fear of punishment in the afterlife as a means to threaten people or to enforce conformity. Existentially, for ordinary people, Shinran's teaching removed anxiety about the next life because, for the adherent of Shin Buddhism, trust in Amida's saving power was the central focus of his life. Total reliance on Amida meant that one felt accepted "just as I am," and that life could be lived with gratitude and joy. Thus, for Shin Buddhists, there is no act or practice that need be performed.

However, in the historical development of Shin Buddhism in Japan, institutionalization brought with it a large degree of conformity with generally accepted religious rituals in Japan, most of which catered to the respect for ancestors and to the family piety that were the norm in a Confucian society. As a result, the tradition of obligatory memorial observances at prescribed days and years after the death of a family member became a mainstay of Shin Buddhist life for most people, as well as the main financial support of the temple, just as it was in every other Buddhist sect. Even today, the performance of these rituals is a large part of the occupation of temple ministers and of the involvement of temple members.

In HHMH, the fulfillment of family ritual obligations still forms a large part of the work of each temple, though the numbers of members who most value and request such observances have been diminishing as the older generations have passed away. At the same time, the younger generations who have rekindled an interest in Buddhism, as well as non-Japanese persons who have been attracted to Shin Buddhism, are not satisfied with family piety and are seeking a spiritual path that can help them understand and find meaning in their lives in this confusing modern world. The teaching of Shinran, which emphasizes self-acceptance and appreciation of life as it is, is finding a truly receptive audience today amid the disturbing uncertainty of these times. For HHMH, this has been an opportunity to share Shinran's message of hope through various educational programs and by responding to the needs of society in new and creative ways.

Historical Developments

The arrival of Buddhism in Hawai'i began with the need for cheap labor to work the booming sugar plantations of the 1870s and 1880s. Recruiters searched for workers in Japan, where crop failures and problems of modernization beset Japan at the time of the Meiji Restoration. An early group of migrants arrived in Hawai'i in 1868, the first year of the Meiji period (*Gannenmono*). However, Japanese immigration formally began in 1885 with an agreement between the Japanese and Hawai'ian governments. They were designated *Kanyaku Imin*, which means contract immigrant (laborer). Reportedly, over 200,000 Japanese came to Hawai'i between 1885 and 1924, when limits were placed on the numbers permitted entry. The immigrants were mainly single males who intended to make their fortunes in Hawai'i, fulfill their contracts, and return home to live on their savings. However, many workers could not afford to return and so established roots in Hawai'i. They were largely Buddhist in background, from areas in western Japan where the Nishi (West) Hongwanji branch of the Jōdo Shinshū Buddhist school was strongest.

The immigrants repeatedly requested authentic clergy from the mother temple. As a minority group, they experienced various forms of discrimination and Christian evangelism. Nevertheless, they held on to their traditional customs, faith, and loyalties. The Nishi Hongwanji responded in 1889 by sending Rev. Kagahi Soryu (1855–1917). Although his visit was short, Kagahi established Dharma centers (*fukyojo*) in Honolulu and in Hilo on the island of Hawai'i. He perceived that the people of Hawai'i, apart from the Japanese, would not accept Buddhism, and suggested to the Hongwanji in Japan that the Christian

God should be equated with the Eternal Buddha, since Christianity was the dominant religion. This view was quickly rejected and Kagahi never returned to Hawai'i.

Satomi Honi (1853–1922) assumed leadership of the mission in 1898. He established a Shin Buddhist temple on Fort Street in downtown Honolulu where he started the Fujinkai (later Buddhist Women's Association). Yemyō Imamura succeeded him in 1900. Imamura's contributions and influence as a Buddhist and community leader in Hawai'i were wide ranging. He was suited for this role, receiving a high level of education in the Hongwanji, including a broad understanding of religion together with knowledge of English. He was also inspired by his association with the famous modern educator Fukuzawa Yukichi (1833–1901), the founder of Keio University, who stressed the study of English. Further, Imamura participated in the Hanseikai (Society for Self-Reflection), a reform and temperance movement, and was editor of the *Hanseikai Zasshi* (magazine).

With his strong interest in education, cultural enlightenment, and religious reform, Imamura, confronting community opposition, embarked on a mission to implant Buddhist roots deep in the soil of Hawai'i. Imamura began the Young Men's Buddhist Association in 1900, cooperating with the YMCA in its citizen's education campaign, promoting democracy and the wartime food conservation effort. In 1902, Imamura established an independent elementary school, Hongwanji Fuzoku Shogakko, to counter the anti-Buddhist environment of the zealous minister Takie Okumura's (1865–1951) Nuuanu Nihonjin Shogakko. In 1907, Imamura opened the Hawai'i Chugakko (Junior High School) to provide a higher level of education.

The purpose of these schools was to teach English and Japanese to the youths and also to Americanize them. Okumura's approach to Americanization was to convert the students to Christianity, maintaining that this was the only basis for democracy and good citizenship. Imamura taught loyalty as American citizens, while retaining Japanese culture, values, and relationships. Establishing the Giseikai or Legislative Assembly in 1908, HHMH itself became more democratic, following the example set earlier by Hongwanji in Japan. In addition, Imamura called for justice and equality in the face of discrimination by the dominant society. While educating the youths in Buddhism and extolling democratic ideals, he exposed the hypocrisy of a "democratic" society that claimed that only Christians could be good citizens.

The Hongwanji schools flourished as a result of Imamura's effectiveness in mediating and ending the 1904 sugar strike, instigated by a cruel overseer. Stressing Buddhist principles of gratitude and compassion, Imamura persuaded the workers to return to work, leading the planters to view Buddhism more favorably as a force for peace and stability. As a result, the planters donated land for temples and Imamura became the recognized leader of the Buddhist community. During the 1920 sugar strike, Imamura sided with workers who were evicted from their homes and suffered financially. Earning only 77 cents a day, they were asking for a wage increase to improve their living conditions. Imamura and other Buddhist clergy attempted to convince the sugar planters to accept the workers' demands, and thereby earned the planters' ire. This situation resulted in later efforts to limit or abolish language schools (an attempt that failed in the U.S. Supreme Court), to restrict immigration, and to support intensive efforts at "Americanization."

In 1917, as a result of a gift of land to Hongwanji by Mary Foster (1844–1930), an ardent Buddhist, Imamura constructed the Honpa Hongwanji Hawai'i Betsuin. The building had an eclectic architecture that combined Western, Indian, and Buddhist elements to suggest the universality of Buddhism. He termed temples as "abodes of light and love." Light is a symbol for wisdom and temples were to be centers for education. He set up what he called "education homes," where English was taught to first-generation (Issei) immigrants and Japanese to the second (Nisei), to avoid divisions in families over language and matters of citizenship. In 1921, Imamura and Thomas Kirby initiated the Hongwanji English Department. In 1924, they engaged the assistance of Ernest (Kaundinya-Shinkaku) Hunt and his wife Dorothy (Shinkoh), who were the first Caucasian priests, to compose the first English service book, *Vade Mecum*, for use by Nisei youth.

Through immigration, the Hongwanji quickly became the largest religious body and the largest Buddhist sect in Hawai'i. Imamura's progressive leadership set the direction for Hongwanji's future, integrating both the Japanese immigrants and Buddhism itself into Hawai'ian society. He introduced pews and pulpits in temples, assembled *gatha*-hymn books, and even installed a pipe organ, the first in any Buddhist temple, at the Hawai'i Betsuin in 1918. In addition, the first Hawai'i Betsuin choir was organized. In 1929, inspired by the visiting Chinese monk Tai Xu, Imamura established the nonsectarian International Buddhist Institute to spread Buddhism.

With the onset of the war in 1941, Issei Japanese and their citizen Nisei children found their loyalty and patriotism under great suspicion. However, those suspicions were dispelled with the valor of the highly decorated Japanese American 100th Battalion and the 442nd Regimental Combat team, which fought bravely in Europe. Some 374 youths of the Hongwanji died, unrecognized by the military as Buddhists. It was not until after the war—and partly due to the exemplary service of these soldiers—that Buddhism was finally recognized as a religious identity by the military.

During the war, ministers were incarcerated in concentration camps under martial law and soldiers occupied temples. Services were carried on largely by laypeople, thereby limiting the efforts of the temples. With the end of the war in 1945, the members of the HHMH set about reestablishing their closed temples and reorganizing for a new era. In this new era, laypeople assumed more control of temples, initially electing bishops from among the clergy. The English language was emphasized. At this time, the Hongwanji Mission School was established and the YMBA (now YBA) was reactivated. A new hymn book, *Praises of the Buddha*, replaced the *Vade Mecum* and English services and Dharma schools increased. In 1954–1955 the *Shinshu Seiten* (*Shinshu Sacred Texts*), an English anthology of Pure Land and Shinran's writings, was published by Yamamoto Kosho, sponsored by the HHMH. However, demographic changes also affected Hongwanji and other Buddhist sects. Membership in neighboring islands decreased as people moved to O'ahu and Honolulu. In 1965, under Ohara Shojitsu (1897–1979), lay study groups and radio broadcasts were initiated. Most outstanding was the construction of the new Hongwanji Mission School building.

In 1967, Rev. Kanmo Imamura (1904–1986), the son of Yemyō Imamura, became the first elected Nisei bishop in Hawai'i, after a dedicated ministry in Berkeley. Education became a focus for Imamura with the opening of the Buddhist Study Center adjacent to the University of Hawai'i in 1974, on the occasion of HHMH's 85th anniversary. It was intended to be a student center to carry on research and translation, as well as ministerial training. Soon after, for health reasons, Kanmo Imamura resigned and returned to Berkeley. On the occasion of the 100th anniversary of the Hongwanji in Hawai'i, a new and modern Buddhist Study Center facility was opened.

With changing demographics, marked by the passing of the first generation and the aging second generation, HHMH temples witnessed a decline in membership, largely through attrition, while few new members were added. Further, the third (Sansei), fourth (Yonsei), and fifth (Gosei) generations have shown little interest in the temples. This was partly due to the growing success and respect enjoyed by Japanese Americans (due both to the bravery of the Nisei veterans and to greater political participation in the Hawai'ian community after statehood in 1959). Thus, the youths have had greater mobility to develop their lives without depending on temples for encouragement and social recognition. On the other hand, the growing acceptance of Buddhism in contemporary Western society has encouraged rediscovery and renewal of declining ethnic traditions.

Despite an aging and declining membership, the HHMH developed new congregations in Kailua, in Mililani, a new community with younger families, and in Kapolei, an emerging community in west O'ahu. In 1989, becoming aware of the reality of an aging community, the farsighted leaders, Mrs. Shimeji Kanazawa and Mrs. Rose Nakamura, organized an interfaith volunteer organization called Project Dana. *Dana* is a Buddhist concept meaning "selfless giving," and Project Dana serves to aid the increasing numbers of those in the community who find themselves as caregivers of parents and spouses, providing volunteer help to aid them in surmounting the difficulties of this role. The effort has grown throughout the islands, has spread to the mainland, and has been nationally recognized.

The Hongwanji Mission School is a respected Buddhist elementary school, but offered instruction only to the eighth grade. With the launch of the Pacific Buddhist Academy in 2003, HHMH now has an accredited Buddhist school system.

Growing recognition of the importance of education for the future of the HHMH, as well as for the spread of Buddhism, has given rise to lecture programs such as the Futaba Annual Memorial Lecture, a meditation program, and the Dharma Light Project, an adult educational program, providing courses in Buddhism for members and the general community. These programs are centered at the Honpa Hongwanji Hawai'i Betsuin, but they serve a much wider segment of the HHMH, as well as the general community.

The development of HHMH's social awareness and involvement has recently became evident though the success of Pacific Buddhist Academy students and Junior YBA youths in gaining legislative approval for an annual Peace Day commemoration. Further, the public support of HHMH for civil union legislation represents a significant turning point in its political involvement with—and in relation to—the general society.

Through its 120-year history, influenced by the progressive spirit of Yemyō Imamura, the HHMH has shown flexibility and adaptability in meeting new challenges. The title of Ruth Tabrah's book marking the 100th centennial commemoration, *A Grateful Past, a Promising Future*, remains an apt description of Hongwanji's path in history.

HHMH has made significant contributions to the spiritual life of the Hawai'ian Islands and the well-being of society. Yemyō Imamura's views on democracy, religious equality, and pluralism were way ahead of their time and paved the way for the current diversity and mutual respect among religions that is characteristic of Hawai'i today. Moreover, his willingness to intervene in the sugar strikes of 1904 and 1920 set a precedent for Buddhist social engagement and involvement in society.

See also: Buddhist Churches of America; Japanese American Religions

Further Reading

Ama, Michihiro. *Immigrants to the Pure Land: The Modernization, Acculturation, and Globalization of Shin Buddhism, 1898–1941*. Honolulu: University of Hawai'i Press, 2011.

Bloom, Alfred. *Strategies for Modern Living: A Commentary with the Text of the Tannisho*. Berkeley, CA: Numata Center, 1992.

Williams, Duncan Ryuken, and Tomoe Moriya, eds. *Issei Buddhism in the Americas*. Urbana: University of Illinois Press, 2010.

Alfred Bloom and Richard Tennes

JAPANESE AMERICAN CHRISTIANITY

In 1885, the Meiji government of Japan began to allow large-scale emigration of laborers to Hawai'i and the United States. These immigrants, who were raised with a combination of Buddhist and Shinto teachings from their homeland, encountered a new society where Christianity was the dominant religion. For many of the Isseis that were struggling in their new surroundings, the practical lessons offered by Christian churches became especially appealing. Within the next decade, several Japanese American Christian churches had been established throughout the West Coast and Hawai'i. In fact, it was not until 1899 that the first Japanese American Buddhist temple was built. For this earliest wave of Japanese immigrants, Christian organizations played a pivotal role in their acculturation to the United States.

However, stepping foot on American soil was not necessarily the immigrants' first encounter with Christianity. Christianity in Japan can actually trace its history back to the 16th century, when Jesuit and Franciscan missionaries reached Japan and converted up to an estimated 10 percent of the population to Catholicism. However, in the early 17th century, the Tokugawa Shogunate expelled all foreign missionaries, and what little Christianity remained was forced underground into what are now referred to as Kakure Kirishitan, or "Hidden Christian," communities.

Early Japanese America and the Christian Church

On March 31, 1854, Commodore Matthew C. Perry sailed to Japan and, by 1858, coerced the ruling Tokugawa Shogunate to sign the Treaty of Kanagawa, thus ending Japan's three centuries of seclusion. This moment marked the beginning of trade between Japan and United States and also enabled Christian missionaries to proselytize within Japanese borders. By the start of the Meiji Era in 1868, American and Canadian missionaries from several Protestant denominations had established a number of mission schools throughout Japan. Many of the earliest students at these mission schools were shizoku, or members of the former samurai class, which had previously been abolished by the Meiji emperor.

In the early 1870s, a shizoku student from Yamaguchi Prefecture named Kanichi Miyama made his way to Tokyo, where he opened a clothing store. It was in the early years of the Meiji Era, when the Japanese government encouraged wealthy young men to travel abroad to Europe and the United States to learn and bring back skills to help modernize Japan. Miyama was a perfect candidate to heed this call, and would eventually travel to San Francisco in 1875 at the age of 27. Before departing, he met Rev. George Cochrane, who was one of the earliest Canadian Methodist missionaries in Japan. Rev. Cochrane wrote Miyama a letter of introduction to his Methodist colleague in San Francisco, Rev. Thomas Guard.

Soon after arriving in San Francisco, Miyama and two other young Japanese men visited Rev. Guard at the Powell Street Methodist Episcopal Church. Apparently unsure of what to do with these Japanese immigrants, Guard instead directed them to the nearby Methodist Episcopal Chinese Mission, just about one mile away in Chinatown. Christian missionaries such as Rev. Otis Gibson had been in Chinatown since at least 1852 in response to the over 25,000 Chinese laborers living and working there. Despite the large Chinese population, there were likely only about 200 Japanese in San Francisco at the time.

Rev. Gibson of the Methodist Episcopal Chinese Mission allowed these young Japanese men to study English and have regular Bible study sessions in the basement of his Chinatown church. On February 22, 1877, Kanichi Miyama became the first legal Japanese immigrant to the United States to be baptized, and soon was instrumental in creating the Fukuinkai (Gospel Society), which was the first voluntary Japanese organization in the United States. In addition to promoting Christian teachings and values, the Fukuinkai also hosted English lessons and several secular workshops to help the Japanese immigrants settle into their new surroundings.

The Initial Growth of Japanese American Christianity

By 1881, the Fukuinkai had split into two different factions, with one remaining under the guidance of Rev. Gibson and the Methodist Episcopal Church, whereas the other moved under the influence of the Presbyterian Church. In 1885, this Presbyterian group, known as the Tyler Fukuinkai, organized the earliest Japanese American church, the First Japanese Church of San Francisco (present-day Christ United Presbyterian Church). That same year, the Methodist Episcopal Church California Conference officially allocated a budget of $2,100 for a Japanese mission in San Francisco, which led to the establishment of the Japanese Methodist Episcopal Church (present-day Pine United Methodist Church) under the leadership of Bishop Merriman Colbert Harris and his now ordained assistant, Rev. Kanichi Miyama. In 1887, the Methodist Episcopal Church California Conference became aware of the large masses of Japanese laborers immigrating to Hawai'i (which at the time was still an independent kingdom). Rev. Miyama joined with Congregationalist minister Dr. C. M. Hyde of the Hawai'i Evangelical Association and created the Japanese Methodist Church in Hawai'i (present-day Harris United Methodist Church) and Nu'uanu Congregational Church.

By the 1890s, Japanese American communities throughout California, Hawai'i, and several other western and Rocky Mountain states had their own Christian churches. Although the Methodists and Presbyterians were the earliest denominations to specifically reach out to the Japanese immigrant community, several other groups soon followed, such as the Congregationalists,

Baptists, and Episcopalians. In fact, some of the different denominations even worked with one another to focus on specific geographic areas for practical reasons. For example, in 1901, Methodist bishop M. C. Harris and Presbyterian superintendent Dr. Earnest Sturge created an agreement so that the Methodists would focus on Santa Clara County, whereas the Presbyterians would take care of Santa Cruz and Monterey counties. This led to certain churches changing their denominational affiliations, such as Westview Church in Watsonville, California, which switched from Methodist to Presbyterian.

Throughout the early decades of the 20th century, Japanese American Christianity continued to grow, especially as increasing numbers of Japanese laborers married and started their own families. During this period, it is estimated that 15 to 20 percent of all Isseis were Christians, with even higher numbers for their Nisei children, who greatly contributed to the exploding new church memberships. In 1920, many of the different Japanese American Christian churches began to work together to host a conference for high school and college-aged Niseis. The Young People's Christian Conference (YPCC) became extremely popular and would eventually bring upward of 500 young Japanese Americans together from various churches to socialize as Japanese American Christians. Although YPCC stopped because of World War II, several subsequent Japanese American Christian youth summer camps such as the Lake Sequoia Retreat, Japanese Evangelical Missionary Society (JEMS), Mt. Hermon Conference, and the United Methodist Asian American Summer Camp trace their roots to these early annual meetings.

Japanese American Churches and World War II

On December 7, 1941, Pearl Harbor was bombed by the Imperial Japanese Navy. Due in part to the combination of war hysteria and a general distrust of Japanese Americans, President Franklin D. Roosevelt signed Executive Order 9066, which led to the forced incarceration of more than 110,000 individuals of Japanese descent living on the West Coast into concentration camps scattered throughout the United States. The Japanese American churches in the affected regions, some of which were now over 50 years old, were forced to shut their doors for the duration of the war.

Even though the churches closed, Japanese American Christians continued to actively practice their faith throughout their stay in temporary assembly centers and more permanent concentration camps. The Pacific Japanese Provisional Conference of the Methodist Episcopal Church, which had just been formed in 1940, was forced to hold their annual meeting in 1942 at the Santa Anita Racetrack Assembly Center under armed supervision. All 10 of the concentration camps had regularly scheduled Christian worship services, as well as Sunday schools for the children. In many cases throughout the different camps, Christians received preferential treatment over Buddhists, who were viewed as "less American."

In the years immediately following World War II, Japanese Americans resettled throughout the country. Although many would eventually return to their former West Coast hometowns such as San Francisco and Los Angeles, a significant number chose to start over in cities such as Chicago and Minneapolis. As new Japanese American communities sprouted in these cities, Japanese American Christian churches were also formed there during the late 1940s and early 1950s.

For the Japanese American Christians that chose to reopen their churches on the West Coast, a series of new issues began to affect the direction of their respective congregations. During World War II, Japan was clearly the enemy of the United States. In response to constant villainization of Japan by the American media, it is understandable that many of the young Japanese Americans (who were most likely born and raised in the United States) began to distance themselves from culturally Japanese signifiers such as language and customs. Instead, many Japanese Americans chose to adopt a much more patriotic identity, as can be seen in the thousands of Japanese Americans who volunteered for the highly decorated 100th Battalion and 442nd Regimental Combat Team.

By the 1950s, Niseis began to take senior leadership roles within many of the Japanese American Christian churches. For the first time, the ethnically Japanese leaders of these churches were native English speakers who could better serve their increasingly English-speaking congregations. As the Sansei generation was generally born during and immediately following World War II, it is possible that many were raised in households that chose to ignore much of their Japanese heritage. Perhaps not coincidentally, these years line up chronologically with the dissolution of the Methodist Pacific Japanese Provisional Conference in 1964. This dissolution, which sought to create a more "color-blind" church, caused all Japanese American Methodist churches to be removed from an ethnic grouping and instead be placed under the supervision of geographic-based leadership. This is particularly significant because it occurred during the civil rights movement when many ethnic minority groups took the opposite route and instead chose to proudly embrace their heritage.

Recent Developments of Japanese American Christianity

By the 1980s and 1990s, most of the original Issei founders had passed away, and Japanese American Christian churches encountered an entirely new set of issues. Some of the churches have disappeared, and many have distanced themselves from their historically Japanese American identity to several different degrees. Ontario Community United Methodist Church in Eastern Oregon, for example, currently has an aging Nisei and Sansei population, whereas the younger church members are almost exclusively white. Meanwhile, some churches such as Buena Vista United Methodist Church in the San Francisco Bay Area now have an increasingly panethnic congregation that reflects its local neighborhood. In 1990, the Japanese Congregationalist and United Methodist churches in Fresno, California, merged to create the United Japanese Christian Church. Evergreen Baptist Church in Los Angeles, which is now one of the largest and most well-known pan-Asian congregations, developed from a specifically Japanese congregation. At the other end of the spectrum, Wesley United Methodist Church in San Jose Japantown is one of the last remaining Japanese American churches to employ a full-time Japanese-speaking minister, specifically to serve the significant shin-Issei community.

A recent survey has estimated that 43 percent of all Japanese Americans claim a Christian identity. Although this number is less than the nearly 80 percent of all Americans that identify as Christian, it is significantly larger than the 1 percent Christian population in Japan. Although it is true that many Japanese American Christians have since joined mainline Christian congregations and are no longer members of Japanese American churches, the historical significance of Japanese American Christian churches remains. In fact, only a couple generations prior, it would have been impossible for Japanese Americans to worship anywhere else. From their humble roots inside a Chinatown basement, Japanese American Christian churches have persevered in the face of injustice and are now well into their second century of ministry. Today, they lead the way for the next generation of church members that are increasingly diverse ethnically, generationally, and geographically.

See also: Japanese American Religions

Further Reading

Hayashi, Brian Masaru. *For the Sake of Our Japanese Brethren: Assimilation, Nationalism, and Protestantism Japanese American Christianity among the Japanese of Los Angeles, 1895–1942.* Stanford, CA: Stanford University Press, 1995.

Suzuki, Lester. *Ministry in the Assembly and Relocation Centers of World War II.* Berkeley, CA: Yardbird Publishing, 1979.

Dean Ryuta Adachi

JAPANESE AMERICAN FOODS AND FOODWAYS

Perhaps the most familiar image of Japanese cuisine is its distinctive use of raw seafood and seaweed. However, Japanese cuisine also makes extensive use of grains (especially rice), beans, vegetables, fruits, and chicken. Although salads can be found on the Japanese dining table, Japanese tend to prefer their vegetables stir-fried rather than raw and cold. Buddhism—perhaps the single most

A woman eats from a selection of Japanese dishes. Japan has one of the longest-living populations in the world, in part due to a healthy traditional diet of fish and seafood, vegetables, and tofu. (PhotoTalk/iStockphoto.com)

influential religious heritage in Japan—traditionally frowns on eating meat, and so Japanese cuisine even today maintains a notable vegetarian component. Postwar Japanese have learned to appreciate wheaten products and have increasingly been eating meat due to Western influence. Indeed, the younger generation of Japanese these days probably appreciates hamburgers almost as much as do their American counterparts. Nonetheless, the Portuguese were the first to introduce the grilling of meats in Japanese cuisine during the 15th century, and the familiar meat dish known as sukiyaki (as well as some related dishes such as shabushabu) is probably of Portugese origin.

Seasoning stock is often made from sea tangle (a type of thick seaweed) and dried small sardines. Soy sauce, miso (soybean paste), sake, sweet sake (mirin), starch syrup, and rice vinegar are also used for seasoning. Compared to other cuisines, only a limited amount of oil is utilized, and the kinds of spices and herbs used are also limited. Japanese food is generally high in salt and low in fat.

A Japanese meal is served all at once, with each selection served in small dishes. The custom is to sample each dish in turn rather than finishing one dish and going to another. The first course is typically miso soup made of fermented soybean paste and a broth. More informal meals consist of rice, soup, condiments (e.g., pickles), and fish or meat.

Japanese foods were introduced to the United States in the late 19th century when Japanese immigrants began settling in California for mining, agriculture, and domestic service. At that time, Japanese food was consumed primarily by Japanese communities in part due to the unfamiliarity (or limited availability) of its raw ingredients. It was not until the 1980s that Japanese foods began to be found throughout the United States. Today the freshness, healthiness, exotic taste, and interesting textures of Japanese cuisine have gained popularity among American diners who traditionally did not eat raw fish and had little appetite for tofu.

The most typical Japanese foods that are served in the contemporary United States include sushi, sashimi (thinly sliced raw fish), teriyaki (thinly cut strips of chicken or fish served with its own special sauce), yakitori (baked chicken with sweet or salty sauces), tempura (sea food and vegetables dipped in a special batter and deep fried), ramen (wheat noodles and always served hot), zaru soba (noodles made with buckwheat and served cold with a unique sauce), and oden (a soup with many ingredients including soy sauce, sugar, and sake).

Japanese foods in the United States have gone through major changes in style and taste, so that new ingredients and seasoning have been incorporated into the traditional recipes. For example, Japanese American sushi contains many ingredients that are never used in original sushi, such as crawfish, avocado, spicy sauce, and cream cheese. Japanese American foods now also include different sorts of deep-fried meats. Some traditional Japanese ingredients (e.g., shiitake mushroom and tofu) are widely used for other cuisines. As such, Japanese American dishes have been well assimilated into the American diet.

In turn, most Japanese people coming from Japan would probably find that Japanese American foods have hardly maintained any substantial degree of authenticity. In fact, Japanese American foods are often served at other Asian restaurants. Many Japanese and Americans probably realize that Japanese American foods are being prepared by chefs without any serious training or proper knowledge of traditional Japanese cuisine. Thus, Japanese American food is often modified or mixed together with Chinese and Korean styles of cooking.

See also: Chanoyu/Tea Ceremony

Further Reading

Booth, Shirley. *Food of Japan.* New York: Interlink Books, 2002.

Hosking, Richard. *A Dictionary of Japanese Food: Ingredients and Culture.* North Clarendon, VT: Tuttle Publishing, 1997.

Isao Takei

JAPANESE AMERICAN NATIONAL MUSEUM

The Japanese American National Museum (JANM) is headquartered in the Little Tokyo Historic District east of downtown Los Angeles in the heart of one of the nation's oldest Japanese American communities. It is a member of the Smithsonian Institution Affiliation program and one of the world's most prominent museums that specifically pays tribute to Japanese American contributions and experiences. Its mission is to "promote understanding and appreciation of America's ethnic and cultural diversity by sharing the Japanese American experience." The JANM became a nonprofit organization in 1985 and officially opened its doors in May 1992, nearly 50 years after President Franklin D. Roosevelt ordered the incarceration of Japanese Americans and only days after the Los Angeles riots dissipated. The museum was first located in the historic Nishi Hongwanji Buddhist Temple in Little Tokyo. Major renovations eventually led to the opening of facilities exceeding 100,000 square feet in 1999. The JANM houses over 60,000 collections including artworks, documents, films, photographs, and other artifacts. The museum regularly sponsors exhibitions and programs related to Japanese American culture, experiences, and histories but also supports events that highlight the Japanese American community's interracial connections. As a nonprofit organization, the JANM's structure includes a board of directors, curators, general members, and volunteers. The museum's board of directors include prominent Japanese American businesspeople, politicians, and professionals from across the United States as well as leaders from other ethnonational groups that support JANM's mission.

Establishing the JANM took several years of careful planning. Initial discussion began when prominent entrepreneurs in Little Tokyo and World War II veterans discussed plans to institutionalize the Japanese American legacy. Bruce T. Kaji, a prominent Japanese American banker, along with esteemed war veterans Yoshio "Buddy" Mamiya and Col. Young Oak Kim are the three founders of the JANM. Initial funds to build the museum came from the City of Los Angeles and the State of California, as well as corporate and personal donations. During the 1980s and 1990s, the museum was partially funded by wealthy Japanese corporations.

At the start of strong anti-Japanese sentiment during the rise of the Japanese automobile and electronic industries, the Japanese government was seeking to rehabilitate negative images of Japan and saw the JANM as a crucial educational space for attaining this goal. The transnational ties between the JANM and Japanese businesses also allowed the Japanese American community to serve as a symbolic cultural broker between Japan and the United States. Clearly central to the decision-making process were collaboration and interracial coalitions; that is, multiple stakeholders were invested in sustaining the JANM as a major cross-cultural and educational institution.

The JANM was initially a volunteer-based community organization that was run mostly by second-generation and third-generation Japanese American activists. However, to gain legitimacy as an educational public institution, the founding leaders agreed that the organization needed an annual budget, operational procedures, and a trained staff. To help establish the museum's credibility, key leaders pushed to hire academicians who specialized in areas such as Asian American studies and historical research to assist with program building.

The JANM initially focused its programming on narratives of assimilation and patriotism, particularly highlighting the contributions of Japanese American war veterans. The museum now hosts a variety of public awareness events including educational tours, exhibits, film screenings, national conferences, and workshops. Preserving the legacy of Japanese American history, especially the Japanese American experience during World War II, is central to the organization's strategic plan. The stories are mostly told from Japanese American perspectives, which is a significant milestone given the reality that the community's history has frequently been distorted or misrepresented by outsiders. Further, since many Japanese American families had their property destroyed, sold, or stolen, restoring cultural artifacts and personal documents has been a significant means for the JANM to help the community revive its collective memory of their turbulent past.

Although the JANM's programming still centers on promoting an awareness of Japanese American history, the museum has recently focused on building multiracial coalitions and situating the Japanese American experience within comparative and transnational perspectives. For instance, *Looking Like the Enemy*, a 52-minute documentary that won critical acclaim, highlights the racism that Japanese Americans and other servicemembers of color confronted in their service during World War II and the Vietnam War. In the aftermath of the September 11, 2001, terrorist attacks, the JANM board collaborated with Arab American, Muslim American, and South Asian American communities to host public events on the problems of maintaining homeland security and civil liberties concurrently in times of wartime hysteria.

The JANM has become a major source of preserving Japanese American narrative and visual culture. Lost stories have been revived through artwork, exhibitions, and oral history projects. The museum has also sponsored cultural awareness events showcasing the Japanese aspects of Japanese American culture. For instance, the JANM has sponsored events including obon (dance) festivals and taiko (drum) demonstrations. Common Japanese cultural motifs are displayed or sold at events including Japanese teapots, kokeshi dolls, and the Maneki Neko (lucky cat).

See also: Japanese American Artists; Japanese American History before 1945; Post-1965 Japanese Immigration

Further Reading

Kikumura-Yano, Akemi, Lane Ryo Hirabayashi, and James A. Hirabayashi. *Common Ground: The Japanese American National Museum and the Culture of Collaboration.* Boulder: University Press of Colorado, 2005.

Rachel Endo

JAPANESE AMERICAN RELIGIONS

The religious history of the Japanese American community has been shaped by the experience of migration, adaptation to a foreign environment, resistance to bigotry and discrimination, and social interaction with other religious and ethnic groups. As with other immigrant communities, the first generation of Japanese in Hawai'i and North America suffered from poverty, social instability, and political alienation. And, as with other immigrant communities, they brought their customs, cultures, and religious traditions. But Japanese religious practices were harshly scrutinized. As non-Christians, Japanese Americans were doubly marginalized, for their race and for their religious faith.

Buddhism dominates Japanese American religious history. The majority of Japanese immigrants who arrived in Hawai'i and North America came from rural prefectures in Japan where Jōdo Shinshū Buddhism prevailed. Of the two branches—Nishi and Higashi Hongwanji—Nishi Hongwanji established the most missionary branches in Hawai'i, Canada, and the continental United States. Other Buddhist sects—Shingon, Nichiren, Tendai, and Sōtō Zen— were also established by the first generation of Japanese immigrants (Issei). A minority of immigrants were Christians, converted by Presbyterian, Congregational, Methodist, and Baptist missionaries.

It is estimated that prior to World War II, more than 50 percent of Japanese Americans were members of a Buddhist sect; nearly 30 percent were affiliated with a Christian denomination. Three overseas districts—the Buddhist Churches of America, Hongpa Hongwanji Mission of Hawai'i, and the Jōdo Shinshū Buddhist Temples of Canada—claim over 100 temples in their jurisdiction. These are still the largest Buddhist denominations in North America, representing more than 30 percent of those who claim Buddhist affiliation.

The religious culture of Japanese American communities is adaptive, creative, and syncretic. Japanese American congregants and congregations adjusted to a hostile social atmosphere by consolidating resources to protect the community. They made imaginative use of space and location, acculturating without conceding to wholesale assimilation. And they collaborated across denominational, generational, and ethnic boundaries, innovating syncretic and lively spiritual traditions that helped to sustain and strengthen their communities.

Issei Adjustment

Issei immigrants were, by and large, agricultural workers who labored on sugar and pineapple plantations in Hawai'i and in the farming and fishing industries along the Pacific Coast of North America. Jōdo Shinshū ministers and missionaries arrived first in Hawai'i and San Francisco, responding to requests by Japanese immigrants for help in coping with their hardships.

Kagahi Sōryū (1865–1917), a Jōdo Shinshū priest who arrived in Hawai'i in 1889, conducted the first Buddhist service there and subsequently established the Great Imperial Japan Hongwanji Denomination, Hawai'i Branch (Dai Nippon Teikoku Hongwanji-ha, Hawai'i), Kagahi was not an official representative of Nishi Hongwanji; he took it upon himself to investigate the social and spiritual conditions of Japanese plantation workers. As a result of his efforts, several small Buddhist temples were erected in plantation camps and served by itinerant priests. In 1897, an official representative of Nishi Hongwanji, Miyamoto Ejun (1853–1919), was sent to Hawai'i and Yamada Shoi (1879–1945) was made the first *kaikyoshi* or missionary priest. By 1899, six official temples were established; within five years there were 14 more throughout the islands.

Miyamoto was later dispatched to California on a similar mission, arriving in San Francisco in July 1898. He was met by the small community of Issei men who had already formed a Young Men's Buddhist Association (YMBA). One year later, two priests, Sonoda Shuye (1863–1922) and Kakuryo Nishijima (1873–1942), arrived in San Francisco and founded the North American Buddhist Mission, later to be known as the Buddhist Churches of America (BCA).

Hawai'i's Japanese population grew rapidly, requiring extensive outreach by Buddhist ministers. Japanese workers were the largest ethnic group in Hawai'i from 1900 to 1942, ultimately representing over 40 percent of the island's population by World War II. Imamura Yemyō (1867–1932) arrived in Hawai'i in 1899 and served there until his death in 1932. During his tenure, he built nearly one temple a year on every island, often in and around plantation camps rather than in nearby towns and villages. Because of their isolation, Buddhist temples became an essential link between Japanese workers throughout the islands, acting as a social and communication network.

Christianity was an important part of the religious life of the Issei generation as well, especially for those early immigrants who came to the United States as students between 1868 and 1880. Although some had converted to Christianity before leaving Japan, many others became members of Protestant congregations through the efforts of missionaries in California. Methodists, Baptists, Presbyterians, and Congregationalists reached out to Japanese immigrants, offering housing, food, language instruction, and help securing employment. A small group of San Francisco Issei Christians founded their own Bible study group, the Fukuinkai ("Gospel Society") in 1877 and, a year later, the Presbyterian Japanese Gospel Society. These groups formed the basis of Japanese

American Christian congregations such as the First Japanese Presbyterian Church in San Francisco in 1885. Christianity spread rapidly in California, which had the largest Japanese population outside of Hawai'i. Between 1885 and 1942, 46 Japanese congregations were founded in Southern California alone. In northern California, 30 congregations and as many as 6,000 members comprised the northern California Japanese Christian Church Federation.

There were far fewer Japanese Christian churches in Hawai'i. With some exceptions such as the Rev. Takie Okumura's Makiki Christian Church (1904), there were few large Japanese Christian congregations. Okumura (1865–1951) established the first Japanese-language school in Hawai'i and opened his home to students who traveled to Honolulu to further their education or to take jobs. But in communities where Buddhism was strong, Christian conversion was much less prevalent.

Other religious organizations were brought to Hawai'i and North America by Issei. In Hawai'i where the Japanese population was more than twice the size it was in North America there was greater religious diversity. Temples and shrines were built by Sōtō Zen, Nichiren, Tendai, and Shingon Buddhists and followers of Shinto, Tenrikyō, and Konkōkyō. The greatest number of temples and shrines were built in California and Hawai'i. Forty-eight Shinto shrines were built in this era, indicating the importance of indigenous cultural practices and traditions for the Issei.

Religious groups utilized many adaptive strategies as they integrated into the American religious landscape. Japanese Christians formed their own churches, responding to the racial hostility of white Americans. Buddhists adopted the denominational structures and English terminology such as "church" and "bishop." They created a Sunday worship schedule, installed pews, and sang hymns. Architectural forms represented an attempt to find a balance between tradition and modernity. Congregations sometimes opted for a traditional Western façade with signage in kanji and English. Takie Okumura's Makiki Christian Church was built to resemble Kochi Castle in Japan, symbolizing Christianity as a refuge. Yemyō Imamura's Hawai'i Hongwanji headquarters resembles a traditional Indian Buddhist *stūpa*, suggesting the universalism of Buddhism.

Buddhist leaders also responded to the challenge of establishing a new religion in a Christian country by making explicit outreach to white Americans. Within a year of his arrival, Kakuryo Nishijima began publishing *Light of Dharma*, which featured writing by prominent Japanese Buddhists. Yemyō Imamura invited the public to services and celebrations and created an "English Department" to oversee these efforts. He, too, published and distributed English-language materials on Buddhism. In both cases, Buddhist ministers found it necessary and advantageous to cultivate the curiosity and goodwill of white Americans. Through these efforts, Jōdo Shinshū institutions became incubators for American Buddhism.

For the Issei, religious institutions provided a needed connection to home. In many towns, a church or temple was the only site available for community gatherings. Churches and temples hosted religious services, but also cooperated in staging seasonal celebrations that in Japan would have involved an entire village. New Year's celebrations, which involved symbolic representations of Shinto and Buddhist customs, were not restricted to specific faith traditions. Denominational affiliations were less important than a sense of common ethnic identity and ancestry. In that way, Japanese religious communities were far more syncretic than was common in the United States.

Nisei Adaptation

For the Nisei generation, religious faith played the paradoxical role of encouraging their independence as Americans and reinforcing their ties to their families. Buddhist and Christian religious leaders were challenged by the demands placed on the Nisei whose status as American citizens did not protect them from bigotry and institutional discrimination. Nisei relied on their association with religious organizations to help them negotiate the border between adapting and assimilating.

Churches and temples often functioned as a bridge between Issei and Nisei. The Nisei generation, who possessed American citizenship, were under much greater pressure to assimilate. As noncitizens, their parents had little incentive to abandon their language and customs. The Nisei, however, were often forced to choose between the false dichotomy of loyalty to their country and devotion to their families. Buddhist and Christian ministers recognized the precarious position Nisei were placed in. As Japanese, they were obliged to offer respectful obedience to their parents. But, as Americans, they were encouraged to express themselves as individuals. Religious institutions were a space where Japanese values and filial bonds were reinforced through religious idioms and the shared experience of worship.

Christianity and Buddhism offered Nisei opportunities to socialize, organize, and develop leadership skills. Individual churches had youth organizations, but the YMCA and YBA (Young Buddhist Association) were the largest religious confederations for Nisei. These religious organizations provided important opportunities for Nisei men and women to meet and socialize, opportunities that did not exist anywhere else, particularly in places where Japanese Americans were a visible minority. Attending youth conferences, participating in sports leagues, organizing fund-raisers, and dances were opportunities to socialize and make friends but also a chance to exercise their leadership skills, opportunities that might not have been available to them in typical white American high schools or colleges. These organizations provided a sense of solidarity and a way to share their common faith and their common struggles.

World War II Incarceration

The mass incarceration of the entire Japanese community was an egregious betrayal of the constitutional rights of Nisei citizens and the human rights of their Issei parents. Although the evacuation, resettlement, and incarceration were traumatic experiences, it forced Issei and Nisei, Buddhist and Christian to reevaluate their religious faith and national loyalty. Christians who may have assumed their faith might protect them from suspicion were no less vulnerable than Buddhists.

In the years leading up to the war, federal agencies engaged in surveillance of Japanese American communities. Issei leaders—religious clergy and language school teachers—were suspected of being agents of the Japanese government. Buddhist priests and institutions were targeted because Americans did not understand the differences between Buddhism and Shinto, nor did they make any clear distinction between state Shinto propagated by the Japanese government and Shinto as the religion that was indigenous to Japan. Therefore, in the days and weeks following the bombing of Pearl Harbor, Buddhists priests were immediately rounded up by agents of the U.S. government. As noncitizens, they were classified as "enemy aliens." They were incarcerated by the Department of Justice and many were later deported. Those who remained in the United States were isolated from the rest of the Japanese American community.

Consequently, Christian ministers outnumbered Buddhist priests in War Relocation Authority (WRA) camps. Buddhists consolidated their congregations, working together to sustain Buddhist practices across sectarian lines. Christians and Buddhists also worked together in camps, cooperating in efforts to run schools and social programs. Religious activity in the camps was limited and proscribed. Because use of Japanese was prohibited, Buddhists texts, prayers, and songs had to be translated into English. With no altars, statues, or other material manifestations of faith, internees improvised, fashioning religious objects from locally available materials. However, religious institutions became all the more important because they helped to preserve community values. In spite of efforts to more fully Americanize the Nisei, incarceration strengthened their ties to their parents, reinforcing filial values. Religious faith supported rather than undermined community cohesion.

The internment has shaped subsequent generations of the Japanese American community. Some have sought to recover the experiences of their parents and grandparents, imbuing these painful events with spiritual meaning. The Tule Lake Pilgrimage, for example, brings together survivors and their families and supporters to embark upon a sacred journey of return. The pilgrimages, which began in 1969, return to several internment sites where participants gather, listen, teach, learn, and reflect. Similarly, the annual Day of Remembrance, which commemorates the signing of Executive Order 9066, has become a sacred occasion and catalyst for community cohesion and celebration.

Postwar Developments

The postwar years saw both expansion and retraction for Japanese American congregations. Newly established branches of the Buddhist Churches of America were opened in Cleveland and Chicago in 1944. Nisei who left the camps to return to college established Young Buddhist Associations providing a seed for the growth of future temples. The reestablishment of temples that had been closed before the war was an important milestone for many communities, but in several cases, new temples were built to replace those that had been lost or to serve congregations in new locations.

The postwar years also witnessed an increased interaction between Japanese Americans and white Americans who became interested in Buddhism. Conversion to Buddhism was limited before World War II, but many of those who did convert became affiliated with the BCA. After the war, Buddhist temples hosted Dharma study and meditation groups for the growing number of Americans who had been introduced to Buddhism while serving in Japan or who were attracted by visiting monks such as D. T. Suzuki. When the Berkeley Buddhist Church reopened in 1946, Kanmo Imamura (1904–1986) (the son of Yemyō Imamura) and his wife Jane Matsuura Imamura (1920–2011) provided dormitory space and other services to students from the University of California. They reached out to Nisei and Sansei, reviving the Young Buddhist Association, but also to white students who were curious about Buddhist practices. The poet Gary Snyder, who would go on to intensive Buddhist study in Japan, began his education with the Imamuras. They also helped to launch a long-running series of lectures by religious leaders, which came to be known as the Pacific Seminar. The activities of the Berkeley Buddhist Church signal the importance of the already established institutions like the BCA in launching a new phase of American Buddhism.

In the late 20th century, the expansion of religious choices and religious diversity in the United States has affected Japanese American religious culture. The introduction of new religious movements from Japan such as Soka Gakkai have influenced how Japanese and Japanese American religious traditions are perceived. Buddhism has spread and become more diverse as Japanese Americans intermarry at greater rates and as more non-Japanese join the church and become ministers. Internet access has also vastly influenced the shape and direction of religious organizations, promoting interreligious dialogue and facilitating virtual links between faith communities. As Buddhism has become more mainstream and accessible, Japanese American religious culture is exposed to greater and more diverse influences, adapting to new demands and challenges.

See also: Buddhist Churches of America; Higashi Honganji; Honpa Hongwanji Mission of Hawai'i; Japanese American Religions; Jōdo Shū (Pure Land Sect); Mahikari (True

Light); Nichiren Shōshū; Obon (Urabon); Okinawan (Ryūkyūan) Spiritual Culture; Rinzai Zen; Shinto; Soka Gakkai; Sōtō Zen

Further Reading

Kashima, Tetsuden. *Buddhism in America*. Westport, CT: Greenwood Press, 1977.

Williams, Duncan Ryuken. "Complex Loyalties: Issei Buddhist Ministers during the Wartime Incarceration." *Pacific World: Journal of the Institute of Buddhist Studies* 3, no. 5 (2003): 255–274.

Yoshida, Ryo. "Japanese Immigrants and Their Christian Communities in North America: A Case Study of the Fukuinkai, 1877–1896." *Japanese Journal of Religious Studies* 43, no. 1 (2007): 229–244.

Lori Pierce

JAPANESE AMERICAN RELIGIOUS FEDERATION

The Japanese American Religious Federation (JARF) is an interfaith consortium of Buddhist, Christian, and independent faith traditions. Its origins date to 1948 when leaders of Japanese faith congregations in the city of San Francisco established the Shukyōka kondankai (religious leader's discussion group) to coordinate the immediate housing needs of Japanese Americans returning from the internment camps. The churches and temples served as hostels until 1954. This informal gathering incorporated in 1968 as Nichibei shukyō renmei (Japanese American Religious Federation) as a nonprofit entity.

This early experience of providing housing for the Japanese community galvanized JARF to incorporate the Japanese American Religious Federation Housing (JARF Housing) in 1975 to partner with the Department of Housing and Urban Development (HUD) to build and operate Nihonmachi Terrace and Hinode Towers, a 245-unit low-income housing facility for low-income seniors. The housing needs of frail low-income elders prompted members of the Pine Street Methodist Church to explore the possibility of securing a suitable facility. JARF took up the cause and incorporated the JARF Assisted Living Facility (JALFI) in 1996. The San Francisco Redevelopment Agency awarded JALFI a contract in 1977 to develop the 54-unit Kokoro Assisted Living Facility for moderate- to low-income seniors on the former site of Ohabai Shalom Synagogue on 1881 Bush Street. JARF and JALFI launched a capital campaign in 1999, broke ground in 2001, and welcomed its first residents two years later.

Interestingly, the clerical and lay leadership of JARF insisted that spiritual and cultural components be integral to the design of the Kokoro facility, staff training, services, and administrative policy, not an afterthought. This insistence was the result of years of experience with the cultural and spiritual insensitivity of the American health care system toward Japanese cultural and spiritual values. Such sensitivity is particularly critical during a resident's later and last stages of life, and in helping families cope with grief and mourning. To this end JARF commissioned the Stanford University Geriatric Education Center and the Graduate Theological Union to offer a six-unit graduate course, Aging and Spirituality in the Japanese Experience, during the 1999–2000 academic year to heighten awareness of the cultural and spiritual needs of Kokoro's intended residents. The year-long course also helped to galvanize community support for the project and for raising funds.

In addition to its housing projects, JARF sponsors the annual interfaith community-wide Memorial Day, Thanksgiving, and Atomic Bombing Commemorative services. JARF also sponsors a monthly interfaith radio program, *Kurashi no shirabe* (Wisdom of living), provides monthly services at Kokoro Assisted Living Facility, Kimochi Home, and participates in other community-wide activities.

The founding congregations of JARF were the Buddhist Church of San Francisco, Christ Episcopal Church, Gedatsu Buddhist Church of America, Christ United Presbyterian Church, Konkōkyō Church of San Francisco, Nichiren Buddhist Church of America, Pine United Methodist Church, St. Francis Xavier Catholic Church, San Francisco Independent Church, Seventh-Day Adventist Japanese Church, and Sōkōji Zen Temple of San Francisco. The Gedatsu Buddhist Church, Seventh-Day Adventist Church, and the San Francisco Independent Church are no longer part of JARF. Hokkeshū Hon'nōji Buddhist Temple, Risshō Kōsei Kai Buddhist Church, and Tenrikyō–America West are now part of the organization. The membership roster is current as of 2011.

See also: Japanese American Christianity; Japanese American Religions; Selma (California) Japanese Mission Church

Further Reading

Japanese American Religious Federation Assisted Living Facility. *Japanese American Religious Federation Assisted Living Facility, Inc. By-laws.* San Francisco: American Religious Federation Assisted Living Facility, 1998.

Nakasone, Ronald Y. "Teaching Religion and Healing: Spirituality and Aging in the San Francisco Japanese Community." In *Teaching Religion and Healing*, edited by Linda Barnes and Inez Talamantez, 277–291. Oxford: Oxford University Press, 2006.

Ronald Y. Nakasone

JAPANESE EVANGELICAL MISSIONARY SOCIETY

On February 19, 1942, President Franklin Roosevelt signed Executive Order 9066, which sent over 120,000 Japanese Americans to 10 concentration camps in the western United States. About 73 percent of the internees were American citizens, and many who were not able to become citizens by law were the parents of citizens. Much has been written about the dilemma of the

Japanese Americans, the injustice of the government, and the later admissions by successive presidents that the internment was a "mistake." When peace was declared in August 1945, the camps were closed, and the imprisoned Japanese Americans were released. JEMS, the Japanese Evangelical Missionary Society, was initiated because of the need for fellowship, their common experience of internment, and their seeking their prewar status of equality and justice in resettlement. For the Christian leaders, this was the challenge for the future. It was hoped that the victimization, injustice, racism, poverty, and suffering would work together for good. Two urgent missions confronted the Japanese Americans: one was the strengthening of bonds within our Japanese American community; and the other was salvation—salvation meaning finding peace, purpose, security, and hope for the future, as well as faith in God.

Rev. Dr. Paul Nagano was called by Rev. Dr. Ralph L. Mayberry of the Los Angeles Baptist City Mission Society in the autumn of 1945 even before the camps were officially closed and the captives released, to come to Los Angeles and help the bewildered Japanese Americans to settle into civilian life after their captivity of two to four years. Rev. Nagano was able to develop an ecumenical worship service in East Los Angeles (Boyle Heights) and help people get resettled and find places to live and jobs. In February 1946 he was able to initiate the Nisei Baptist Church (conveniently named "Nisei" to encourage the English-speaking, second-generation Japanese Americans to find a place of refuge, fellowship, and support) located on East Second Street and Evergreen Avenue. Soon afterward, the Japanese Free Methodist Church began a church nearby and the pastor for that church was Rev. Hideo Aoki. Being lonely and in need of companionship and prayer, Rev. Aoki and Rev. Nagano met together for prayer once a week. It was not long after that the prayer meeting grew and became a breakfast-prayer fellowship with over 20 Japanese American ministers attending. The spirit of these prayer meetings and breakfasts was great! The longing for mutual strength and affirmation was something to behold! A similar group was developed in central and northern California. For more fellowship and prayers, the combined groups met together at Mount Hermon in the Santa Cruz Mountains where eventually the JEMS Mount Hermon Conference, the largest Japanese American Conference, was developed (now approximately 1,500 people of all ages meet together each year).

The founding of JEMS came at the Wee Boys' Lodge in Palos Verdes, California, in 1950. Ernest Ono, a dedicated Los Angeles schoolteacher and counselor, was editor of *Vision and Faith*, the publication of JEMS. In 1985, the issue that celebrated the 35th anniversary of JEMS remembered the steps in the inspired experience of the birth of JEMS:

The group was in its second day of its retreat, spending much time in deep, earnest prayers. The requirements for leadership had been thoroughly altered; a person with vision, enthusiastic [*sic*], dedication, an initiator, an innovator, a polished speaker, a capable organizer, and administrator, one with a flare and zeal for evangelizing. Seeking guidance from God in selecting their first leader. The prayers finally ended. Silence followed. Then came what the Vision of Faith calls "The electric moment": Breaking the agonizing silence, Rev. Paul Nagano addressed the group. "If the Evergreen Baptist Church feels with me that this is the direction of our Lord, and after discussing this with my family, we feel this is the direction of God for our lives, and if you feel that I am the person of God's choice, I will be willing to give myself to this ministry."

The ministers confirmed that God had called Rev. Paul Nagano to be their first executive secretary. They supported the first executive secretary of JEMS by pledging $10 per month from their limited salaries. Looking back over the years, the Vision of Faith could not identify with certainty who the 21 members of that prayer meeting were, but the best attempt at such identification yielded the following:

Hideo Aoki, Llewellyn Davis, Harry Hashimoto, Eishi Hirose, George Hirose, Roy Ishihara, Ren Kimura, William Kobayashi, Akira Kuroda, John Miyabe, Harry Murakami, Paul Nagano, John Nagayama, Harumi Nishimoto, Harper Sakauye. Dan Shinoda, Joseph Sakakibara, George Takaya, Roy Takaya, Howard Toriiumi, and Paul Waterhouse.

Having experienced imprisonment in the concentration camps, there was a deep unity and love among the Japanese American ministers. The mission of JEMS was shared throughout California and other parts of the United States, as well as Canada, Japan, and South America. On May 1, 1953, Dr. Hideo Aoki was officially appointed as the JEMS radio missionary. He broadcast the Gospel in the United States and Canada, with one broadcast going to Japan via the Philippines.

During 1951, Gospel teams composed primarily of college students traveled over 10,000 miles ministering at churches, camps, conferences, retreats, and special rallies. One year the team conducted its summer schedule by traveling to Palacio, Texas, to minister and have fellowship with Nisei Christians there. Those who traveled for JEMS included David Shigekawa, Hiro Yoshida, Saburo Masada, Roy Sano, George Inadomi, and, in time, Ray Narusawa. Five of the Gospel team members became ministers in Japanese American churches. Roy Sano became a bishop of the United Methodist Church and Hiro Yoshida became an administrator of a Christian enterprise in the Midwest. Rev. Akira Hatori, the first missionary JEMS staff member from Japan, took over the radio ministry of Hideo Aoki and the Japanese-language ministry, first in the United States and later in Japan as part of the Pacific Broadcasting Association (PBA).

A JEMS Gospel team went to New York, Chicago, and Texas. Later two teams went to Hawai'i. The Hawai'i teams consisted of Masumi Toyotome, Bill Tamagi, Art Tsuneishi, and Herbert Murata. After one of these trips in 1952, he was asked to consider the pastorate of the Makiki Christian Church of Honolulu. He left word with the Makiki Christian Church that he would ask the JEMS Board, as well as my family, if they believed this was the will of God, the same process as when he accepted the position as the executive secretary of JEMS in 1950. With the consent of the JEMS board and his family, in March 1954 he left the position with JEMS and became the English-speaking pastor of the Makiki Christian Church in Honolulu, serving from March 1954 until August 1962. Executive directors of JEMS that followed him from January 1954 included Hideo Aoki, Roy Takaya, Ray Narusawa, and Masumi Toyotome. Upon his return from Hawai'i in September 1962, Dr. Nagano was asked to resume as executive director and served until 1971. Sam Tonomura, who originally was from Canada and served as associate pastor of the Gardena Valley Baptist Church, became the executive director in September of that year (1970), but continues to serve under the present leadership of Rev. Richard "Rick" Chuman, former pastor of the English section of the Los Angeles Holiness Church.

JEMS is one of the truly indigenous organizations that is not sponsored by any particular Christian denomination, but has existed primarily with the Japanese American churches and has a three-story building near Little Tokyo, Los Angeles. Its primary ministry has been among Japanese Americans since 1950. It is amazing that the Japanese American Christian community has initiated and continued to serve our mostly Japanese churches, missionaries, and community for over 64 years at this writing! The question is asked, why was it started and what motivated its long ministry? JEMS was formed in 1950 mostly by the Japanese American ministers and Christians who had a special vision and mission for the Japanese community in the United States and, as the result of years of consistent prayer, concern for Japanese everywhere. Most of the Japanese Christians in the United States were influenced by the popular conservative evangelical Christianity that was prevalent in the establishment of the first Japanese American churches; for that matter, most churches were evangelical and conservative. The zeal and initiative of the evangelical churches were popular and growing. It was this zeal that brought the first JEMS ministers together. As the result of much prayer, the affirmation was to save the lost by sharing the Gospel (good news) of God's saving grace. At the early prayer-breakfast meetings and earnest prayer meetings, the emphasis was predominantly evangelism, "winning the lost," especially the Japanese. The burden of prayer was for Japan, presumably a non-Christian nation that was in need of the Gospel of Jesus Christ. In time, the burden of prayer led to the salvation of Japanese everywhere, including South America. The major denominations were not sending Japanese American missionaries to Japan or where the Japanese were moving and settling. Some independent Japanese Americans took the initiative to go to Japan as missionaries and shared their vision with members of JEMS.

With this zeal, JEMS caught the vision to share the Gospel with Japanese everywhere. Thus the identity of JEMS—Japanese Evangelical Missionary Society. This evangelistic motivation led JEMS to develop groups on university campuses, in athletics, Japanese immigrants, Japanese language ministries, sponsoring conferences, mission tours, retreats, evangelistic meetings, musicals, and sponsoring missionaries to other countries. Of course, the Mount Hermon Conference for all ages is one of the annual events of JEMS. It was the initiative of JEMS that brought about a closer relationship with Hawai'i, with several becoming pastors of the churches in Hawai'i, and the intimate relationship that has been developed through the years.

JEMS was unique as it gave the executive secretary the opportunity to freely visit all the churches ministering to Japanese of their communities. He was able to get to know the various congregations and the pastors. This is not available to those who are settled in a church or for committed pastors. Today, 50 years later, JEMS now involves all Asians through its ministries with the local church, on college campuses, through conferences and retreats, and with many other programs and ministries. Sharing the Gospel overseas has also expanded with the development of many programs and the inclusion of South America as another mission field. Headquartered in Los Angeles, JEMS is a nonprofit, parachurch organization. It is supported by an interdenominational network of Japanese and Asian American churches and especially by individual supporters who share a faith in Jesus.

See also: Japanese American Christianity; Japanese American Religious Federation; Selma (California) Japanese Mission Church

Further Reading

"JEMS' Ministry." http://www.jems.org/about/. Accessed July 11, 2014.

MinistryWatch. Home page. www.ministrywatch.com. Accessed July 11, 2014.

NonProfitFacts. "Japanese Evangelical Ministry Society (Los Angeles, California)." Tax-Exempt Organizations in California. www.nonprofitfacts.com. Accessed July 11, 2014.

Paul M. Nagano

JAPANESE GARDENS

The Japanese garden is predicated upon the idea of an experience wherein art and nature merge seamlessly. Soteriologically the concept of the garden extends out of the temple complex, as it does historically from the courtly palaces. The interplay between Pure Land and Zen traditions in and around medieval Kyoto produced a number of landscape gardens that were not only formulative but are to this day exemplary—as with the renowned Saihō-ji temple gardens, which were altered to fit the more meditative aspects of Zen in the Muromachi period (1336–1573). From that time especially, the idea of the garden has generally taken the aspect of an aid to contemplation (and enlightenment); and it is often attached to other cultural practices, such as the tea ceremony (*chanoyū*). Although they are preeminently physical and experiential, the image of the garden is also important— occupying as it does the main subject of many works of art

Statue of a seated Buddha in a Japanese garden, San Francisco, California. (Martin Lehmann/ Dreamstime.com)

due to the associations with nature, beauty, and spiritual experience. Although certain core aspects may be found in different gardens—landscape in miniature, suggestions of rustication, concepts of transience, as well as the strategic use of stones and plant life—there are seven types of gardens that are commonly distinguished:

- *chisen-shoyū-teien* (pond garden, also as *shinden-zukuri-teien*)
- *jōdo-teien* (the Paradise Garden)
- *kare sansui* (dry landscape, literally, dry mountain water)
- *cha niwa* (the tea garden, also as *roji niwa*—dewy ground garden)
- *kaiyū-shiki-teien* (the stroll garden)
- *tsubo niwa* (the courtyard garden; miniature versions are known as *hakoniwa*, small boxed garden)
- the hermitage garden

The first of these, introduced from China, suggests the excursions that take place from the main building (the *shinden*) across the lake by boat ride. The next four (*jōdo-teien, kare sansui, cha niwa,* and *kaiyū-shiki-teien*) are mentioned below. *Tsubo niwa*, known for their small size and enclosed space, were developed from inner courtyard gardens and today form the basis for many urban architectural gardens found in temples and businesses alike. Bamboo and stone lanterns are commonly used, and the emphasis is on an immaculate area of natural, calming respite that is, however, not usually entered. Finally, the hermitage garden was typically created around an architectural work for the purpose of inspiration. Here, also, the emphasis is on a microcosm of the (natural) world. By far the most prominent of these is Shisen-dō (now a temple), built by the Confucian scholar and landscape architect Jozen Ishikawa (1583–1672)—known also for its main hall, Shizen-no-ma (Poets' Room), which houses the work and images of 36 classical Chinese poets.

There are perhaps more contemporary American and global adaptations of the Japanese garden than can be counted or classified, though the prevalence of domestic examples—especially along the West Coast of the United States—should be mentioned. Journals, books, video, and new media (including the Internet) have prolonged the intellectual and practical life of the Japanese garden in recent years, especially as seen in the upsurge in demand for practical skills and knowledge for their private creation. The contemporary rendition typically shares something of the traditional East Asian notion that sustained looking at beautified nature is of inherent spiritual value.

Early Japanese gardens were inspired by contact with the Chinese, and certainly the indigenous Shinto belief system—which saw in natural objects (such as stones) a profound spiritual significance—was also a major factor. The Hindu-Buddhist tradition of mythical mountains and the Daoist legend of the Isles of the Eight Immortals were also significant. Though few early structures are extant for study, the two eighth-century imperial gardens uncovered at Nara are important—one a *chisen-shoyū-teien* (pond garden), another a stream garden. By the Heian period (794–1185), the architectural *shinden* develop, as does the practice of setting stones "upright" (*ishi wo tateru*). As the aristocracy became more concerned with internal concerns and religious thought, the Buddhist associations become more entrenched, and many of the formulaic design principles can be seen at this time. The imperial gardens are famously described by Murasaki Shikibu's (ca. 978–1014 or 1025) *Tale of Genji* (*Genji Monogatari*, ca. 1005), where they are the setting for courtly life. Illustrated hand scrolls of the book from this period suggest some of the composition of the gardens. Toward the end of the Heian period, Pure Land Buddhism begins to proliferate, and with it the Paradise Garden comes into fashion as a suggestion of Amida's Paradise of the West. Among the foremost examples of these gardens is at Byōdō-in in Kyoto.

The warring of clans of the late 12th century resulted in a weakened emperor, leading to the establishment of the Kamakura shogunate in 1185 by Minamoto no Yoritomo (1147–1199). The *shogun* reestablished relations with China, and the renewed contact resulted in not only newfound interest in Song Dynasty culture but a revival in Japanese garden design. Kinkaku-ji (Rokuon-ji), erected by the third Ashikaga shogun in ca. 1398, stands as a key example of this legacy, as well as of Muromachi (1336–1573) design in general. Likely developed from a preexisting *shinden*, rocks and islands were apparently added in an elicitation of cosmology. Minimalist principles are even more apparent in the Japanese Zen rock gardens developed at this time, most famously at Ryōan-ji in Kyoto. This dry rock garden (*karesansui*) consists only of 15 stones and raked gravel (*shirakawasuna*, white river sand), emphasizing simplicity and meditative looking from a fixed point of view. Although theoretical and symbolic interpretations abound (e.g., the gravel as a sea or the rocks as the star constellation Cassiopeia), they perhaps risk missing the emphasis on abstraction and the space. Musō Soseki (1275–1351) was the Zen (Rinzai) monk who created Saihō-ji (Kōinzan Saihō-ji), known not only for its lower moss garden but also for its upper garden of (dry) rocks and "pools."

Powerful daimyos expanded their power with the 1573 overthrow of the Ashikaga shogunate; they built new castles with gardens, such as Tokushima in Shikoku. It and Sanbō-in in Kyoto share the Momoyama (1573–1615) aspect of a view from a distance with a perspective from above—as from a castle or certain view from within a building. They also feature large ponds and several paths as aspects of the stroll garden (*kaiyū-shikiteien*). At Sanbō-in, the cherry blossom festival was also a prime motivation. The tea ceremony (*chanoyu*), profoundly influenced by Sen no Rikyū (1522–1592) and the emphasis on the quality of *wabi*, called for a small garden (*cha niwa*) of a reserved, sober quality with a winding path and soft elements of color (cherry blossoms). Kobori Masakazu's (Kobori Enshū, 1579–1647) design innovations, such as the use of *O-Karikomi* (trimming shrubs in topiary fashion), beginning at this time are also noteworthy.

In the Edo period (1615–1868), the *Sukiya-zukuri* style, reflecting the tea ceremony, predominated in architecture, as at Katsura Imperial Villa where the style extended into the gardens. The architectural views opening up into the garden are important, as is the placement of the palace facing southeast (rather than the traditional south) to better view the rising moon relative to the garden plan. The references to actual (Ama no hashidate) and legendary sites are key to understanding the design. The Meiji period of the late 19th and early 20th centuries (1868–1912) saw the importation of Western ideas, such as the development of public parks and private lawns.

Contemporary versions range from the traditional, to blends of traditional and contemporary design (e.g., Shumyō Masuno), to the more dramatic—as with Tadao Ando's (1941–) Awaji Yumebutai. This "environment creation" served to restore a devastated landscape where earth was once removed to create artificial islands in Osaka Bay. The site is a part of the larger Awaji Island International Park City, which hosts a conference center and resort. The sprawling hillside gardens replace the landscape that was stripped for soil for the Kansai Airport and features strong geometric design, reflecting pools, and the spartan concrete architectural elements he is most known for.

It is difficult to generalize about all Japanese gardens, given the variety of types (as listed). Still, there are some common threads that may be gleaned in terms of artistic and philosophical concepts governing their creation. Behind the notion of the garden is an idealized vision of the natural world, and it may also be seen as a condensed experience of some aspect of the cosmos or mythological legend. These concise reproductions of greater aspects of the world lend to the garden its sense of contemplation and spiritual experience, whether it is part of a sacred site or not. Idealized nature, however, is decidedly according to East Asian conception—either as adaptation from China or in distinctly Japanese thought. Hence, plans are not laid out in a grid of predictable symmetry but are rather meant to coordinate with the irregularity of nature, as well as its element of surprise. To that end, and especially with the advent of the tea garden, the aesthetics of the Japanese garden often parallel that of *wabi-sabi*— privileging transience, imperfection, rustication, economy, and (philosophical) emptiness. Unlike so many Western gardens, the Japanese garden is at once a succinct elicitation of a larger world or truth and at the same time a continuation of it, wherein boundaries and perimeters are less distinct. Treatises on the artistic design of gardens are known from the Heian period.

With regard to garden elements, there are some common features. Water is a key element, whether it comes as a surrounding pond or running stream. For early Japanese gardens, especially, boating across the pond to experience the garden was important. Bodies of water have an important religious significance, extending to Hinduism, Shintoism, and Buddhism alike. There is also a keen distinction between wet landscape and dry landscape, even as the rock formations in a dry landscape are often orchestrated to suggest water. Stones, rocks, and gravel are another main constituent of the garden, owing also to ancient spiritual practices. The arrangement of stones in a garden is important in evoking not only harmony but also symbolism and irregularity. Sand is also used at times, and sand or gravel may be used to suggest the idea of water. Architecture is often significant not only as a setting (e.g., hermitage garden) but also in terms of a framing and contrasting element for the garden. Sometimes, as at Katsura, interior views of the outside garden are central to the design, whereas other times (such as with many tea gardens), the interior and exterior do not significantly penetrate. Architectural adornments (gates, lanterns [*tōrō*], basins [*chōzubachi*], bridges) are present relative to the specificity of the site and typically utilize natural materials, such as bamboo, wood, or stone. Certain gardens emphasize elaborate pathways and movement (e.g., *kaiyūshiki-teien*), while rock gardens may be situated for contemplation only, from a fixed point of view (e.g., Ryōan-ji). The level of greenery and color, as well as borrowed scenery (*shakkei*), will vary significantly with respect to the type of garden.

Japanese Gardens in the United States and Canada

Japanese gardens can be found throughout the United States, even in regions known for long or harsh winters (e.g., Normandale Japanese Garden, Bloomington, Minnesota), and they are particularly frequent along the West Coast. Some of the more well-known American examples include the Hagiwara Japanese Tea Garden in San Francisco's Golden Gate Park (the oldest public example in the United States); Hakone Gardens (Saratoga, California); Hayward Japanese Gardens (Hayward, California); Seiwa-en at the Missouri Botanical Garden (St. Louis); Shofuso Japanese Garden (Philadelphia); Anderson Japanese Gardens (Rockford, Illinois); Japanese Hill-and-Pond Garden, Brooklyn Botanical Garden (Brooklyn, New York); Nitobe Inazo Garden (Vancouver, British Columbia). Elements that are commonly found in the gardens of Japan can be found in these American iterations—such as stone lanterns, ponds, and winding pathways. Moreover, these gardens help to articulate to American audiences some of the aesthetic principles that have informed their Japanese ancestors: asymmetry, naturalness, and austerity.

In addition to the above public spaces, Japanese garden design is ubiquitous in Hawaiʻi, the West Coast states, and other locales with a Japanese community. The liberal use of stone and sand, manicured pine trees, maples, azaleas, camellias, and moss are popular features in the front yards of many homes. The impact of Japanese garden design can be attributed in large part to the lack of employment opportunities to Japanese immediately after the end of World War II. Unable to secure employment, many earned a living tending lawns and designing gardens.

See also: Japanese Gardens

Further Reading

Kuitert, Wybe. *Themes in the History of Japanese Garden Art.* Honolulu: University of Hawaiʻi Press, 2002.

Levick, Melba. *Japanese-Style Gardens of the Pacific West Coast.* New York: Rizzoli, 1999.

Oster, Maggie. *Reflections of the Spirit: Japanese Gardens in America.* New York: Dutton Studio Books, 1993.

Larry M. Taylor

JŌDO SHŪ (PURE LAND SECT)

Jōdo Shū traces its beginnings as the first independent school of Pure Land Buddhism in Japan to when its founder Hōnen (also known as Hōnen-bō

Genkū, 1133–1212) left the Tendai monastic center of Mount Hiei in 1175 to spread his teachings to the general populace. The Pure Land denomination known today as Jōdo Shū was established by one of Hōnen's main disciples, Shōkō-bō Benchō (1162–1238), who founded the Chinzei branch in Kyushu in the south, and his disciple Ryōchū (1199–1287), who formed the branch in the Kanto (present-day Tokyo) region. The sect welcomed a period of great prosperity under the patronage of the shogun Tokugawa Ieyasu (1543–1616), who in 1590 selected Chion-in in Kyoto and Zōjō-ji in Edo (present-day Tokyo) to be the family's temples. Today, Jōdo Shū has approximately 7,000 temples, of which Chion-in is the grand head temple (*sōhonzan*). The head temples (*daihonzan*) are Zōjō-ji (Tokyo), Kurodani Konkaikōmyō-ji (Kyoto), Hyakumanben Chion-ji (Kyoto), Shōjōke-in (Kyoto), Zendō-ji (Kurume), Kōmyō-ji (Kamakura), and Zenkō-ji Daihongan (Nagano).

Life and Teachings of Hōnen

Hōnen was born in Mimasaka Province (now Okayama Prefecture) in 1133 as the only child of the provincial lord Uruma no Tokikuni. According to the official 48-volume illustrated biography, *Hōnen Shōnin gyōjō ezu* (translated by Coates and Ishizuka as *Hōnen, the Buddhist Saint: His Life and Teaching*, 1925), compiled by Shunjō in 1141, when Hōnen was nine, his father Tokikuni was assassinated by a political rival, Akashi no Sadaakira. On his deathbed, Tokikuni was said to have told his son not to avenge his death but to become a monk and pray for his and his enemy's deliverance. The Daigo-edition Hōnen biography, however, mentions that Hōnen had already left for Enryaku-ji Temple on Mount Hiei before his father passed away. In either case, Hōnen was ordained in 1147 and devoted himself to the study of the Tendai teachings. In 1175, at the age of 43, Hōnen abandoned other forms of practice and devoted himself exclusively to repeating the *nembutsu*—"*Namu Amida Butsu*" (Homage to Amida Buddha). In 1198, at the request of his patron and disciple, the former regent Kujō Kanezane (1149–1207), Hōnen composed *Senchaku hongan nembutsu shū* (Passages on the Selection of the Nembutsu in the Original Vow), in which he systematically laid out the teaching of *nembutsu* and established the basis for Jōdo Shū.

Hōnen taught that the Pure Land path (*Jōdo mon*) was the most expedient means for attaining enlightenment in the age of *mappō* (degenerate or latter Dharma). To this end, he emphasized the importance of faith in Amida (Skt. Amitābha) Buddha and continuously chanting the *nembutsu*. The accessibility of the *nembutsu* teaching attracted people from all walks of life, regardless of gender, social class, or education level. The popularity of Hōnen's teaching, however, alarmed the entrenched Buddhist orthodoxy and eventually led to his expulsion from Kyoto. In 1207, at the age of 75, Hōnen accepted his exile to Shikoku as a way to spread his teaching. Though pardoned later that same year, he was not permitted to return to the capital until 1211. On the 23rd day of the first month of 1212, Hōnen authored his final testament, *Ichimai kishōmon* (The One-Page Document), which stated the essence of his *nembutsu* teaching. Two days later, on the 25th day, Hōnen passed away at the age of 80.

Hōnen's teachings had a major impact on Japanese Buddhism. Over his lifetime, Hōnen had some 200 disciples and many more followers of all classes and walks of life. Among the most prominent of his disciples were Shōkū (1177–1247), whose followers established the Seizan branch of Jōdo-shū, and Shinran (1173–1263), whose descendants founded Jōdo Shinshū. Also, as the leading figure advocating exclusive adherence, Hōnen greatly influenced subsequent Buddhist reformers during the Kamakura period such as Nichiren (1222–1282), who promoted the exclusive recitation of the title of the *Lotus Sūtra* (*Namu Myōhōrengekyō*), and Dōgen (1200–1253), who promoted the sole practice of Zen meditation.

Jōdo Shū in Hawai'i

Overseas activity for Jōdo Shū started in the late 19th century with the rise of Japanese immigration to Hawai'i. Learning of the hardships of the immigrant workers in the sugar plantations, Rev. Ikawa Takuzen (n.d.) expressed an interest in establishing an overseas mission and solicited the help of the chief abbot Hino Reizui (1818–1896) and other influential leaders of the sect in 1893. In the same year, Rev. Shiraishi Gyōkai (1854–1927) led the effort to raise funds for the Hawai'i Missionary Group (*Hawai'i senkyō kai*) through the head temple Zōjō-ji in Tokyo. In March 1894, Rev. Matsuo Taijō (1868–1898) arrived in Hawai'i, followed by Rev. Okabe Gakuō (1866–1922) in May of that year. The two pioneering ministers traveled throughout the islands offering spiritual solace. In November 1896, Okabe began raising funds to build the first Japanese Buddhist temple in the Hamakua area on the island of Hawai'i. Rev. Tanaka Makaen (1893–1905) arrived in March 1898 and led the effort to build a second Jōdo Shū temple, the Laupahoehoe Jōdo Buddhist Assembly Hall, to serve its congregation of 662 members in the following year.

By the early 20th century, Jōdo Shū had quickly established 16 temples (8 on the island of Hawai'i, 3 on Maui, 3 on O'ahu, and 2 on Kaua'i). In 1902, temples were established in Olaa (present-day Kurtistown) and Kapaau (present-day Kohala) on the island of Hawai'i. The Kohala temple built the first and only *sutra* repository—an architectural feature of the traditional Japanese temple complex—in the entire state for the *Shukusatsu Daizōkyō*, an unabridged, reduced-sized set of the complete *sūtra* collection. In 1903, the Laupahoehoe temple became the headquarters for the Hawai'i Overseas Mission. Rev. Shimizu Shinjun (d. 1919), later the first bishop, recognized the need for the headquarters to be in the burgeoning capital of Honolulu and had a new temple constructed at South and King Streets in 1907. The current head temple, the Jōdo Mission of Hawai'i (also known as the Betsuin, or branch headquarters), located at 1429 Makiki Street, Honolulu, was built in 1936.

Three more temples were established on the island of Hawai'i in the towns of Hakalau and Wainaku in 1905, and another in Hawi in 1909. In 1910, Koloa Jōdo Mission became the first Jōdo Shū temple on the island of Kaua'i, and Puunene Jodo Mission (relocated to Kahului in 1969) became the first on Maui. The following year, Hilo Meisho-in was established on the island of Hawai'i. Temples were also founded in Haleiwa, O'ahu; in Lahaina, Maui; and in Kapaa, Kaua'i, in 1912. The community in Wailuku, Maui, built their temple in 1914. The devotees of Ewa, O'ahu, formed a worship community in 1916 and met at a temporary facility until building a temple in the following year. The Ookala community on the island of Hawai'i founded a missionary center and Japanese school in 1920.

In addition to the temples, these communities established 18 Japanese-language schools and various Buddhist associations such as Seinenkai (youth group) and Fujinkai (women's group). The temples also served as a community gathering place for social and cultural programs. With the outbreak of World War II, the priests were interned and the mission was temporarily suspended. The U.S. Army requisitioned some of the temple buildings and shuttered others. Services were also prohibited since no more than five people of Japanese ancestry were allowed to gather.

In December 1945, the interned priests returned to Hawai'i, where they resumed their activities in spite of the significant challenges in rebuilding their community due to the scattering and loss of members. In the 1970s, several temples disbanded due to the loss of employment of many of their members who worked in sugar cane and pineapple plantations.

Today, the Hawai'i Council of Jōdo Missions consists of 13 temples with approximately 1,000 families. Although membership has greatly declined, members continue to enjoy fellowship at various temple functions including Sunday services and in statewide organizations, such as the Laypersons' Association, Fu jinkai (Women's Association), and YBA (Young Buddhists' Association). The different temples and organizations each contribute to the community in their own way such as *imon* (visitations to elderly homes and centers), participating in community cleanup, and cooperating in community service work programs for juveniles.

Jōdo Shū in North America

The history of Jōdo Shū in North America began in 1936 with the arrival of the Rev. Nozaki Reikai Nozaki (1901–1978) in Los Angeles from Honolulu.

However, the outbreak of World War II disrupted his ministry. After the end of the war, in October 1950, the community established a temple at 2003 Jefferson Boulevard. Archbishop Shiio Benkyō (1876–1971), abbot of Zōjō-ji, led the celebration for the dedication service. In 1972, Chief Abbot Kishi Shinkō (1889–1979) was the lead celebrant for the 35th anniversary of the establishment of the North American ministry in tandem with the 800th anniversary of the founding of Jōdo Shū.

In the late 1980s, Jōdo Shū North America Buddhist Missions relocated to Little Tokyo in Los Angeles into a newly built facility with the support of the Jōdo Shū–affiliated Bukkyō University in Kyoto. The first floor houses the Bukkyō University–LA Extension, while the temple is located on the second floor. The Japanese artist Koiwai Shūhō (1920–2007) created and donated the paintings of the state flowers of the United States and the national flower of Japan that adorn the ceiling of the second-floor sanctuary. On June 28, 1992, Chief Abbot Nakamura Koryu (1906–2008) led the dedication celebration of the new temple.

The Jōdo Shū North America Buddhist Missions facility is a center of worship, learning, research, and publication. In 1995, the temple instituted the Los Angeles Seminar, a program to nurture Jōdo Shū ministers for the 21st century. The continuing focus of the seminar is to familiarize participants to the religious and cultural pulse of the United States by visits to churches and social welfare facilities and through home stays. Eight seminars have been held thus far. Of the 40 participants, five have elected to become overseas missionaries. In autumn of 1996, Jōdo Shū North America Buddhist Missions together with Bukkyō University–LA Extension hosted the first joint seminar of the three Jōdo Shū overseas ministerial districts Hawai'i, United States, and Brazil. In 2007, Jōdo Shū North America Buddhist Missions celebrated its 70th anniversary in conjunction with the 15th anniversary of the construction of its current facility in Little Tokyo. That same year, Bukkyō University–LA Extension published *Teachings of Hōnen*, an English translation of *Hōnen Shōnin gohōgo* (*Hōnen Shōnin sayings*). In 2012, the Los Angeles temple hosted the 800th Grand Memorial Service of Hōnen Shōnin, which was officiated by Chief Abbot Itō Yuishin (1931–) from Chion-in. During the winter of 2012, the Los Angeles Temple held *Gojū sōden*, a three-day Fivefold Transmission retreat, in which 50 participants received certificates of completion issued by Chion-in temple.

Beliefs

[R]ecite single-heartedly and exclusively the name of Amida Buddha while walking, standing, sitting, or lying down, without regard for length of time, and to engage in the recitation of nembutsu without cessation throughout one's life. This is called the rightly established practice because it is in accordance with the essential vow of Amida Buddha.

Inspired by the above passage from *Guan wuliang shou jing zhuo* (*Kanmuryōjukyō sho*; *Commentary on the Meditation Sūtra*) by Shandao (Zendō, 613–681), Hōnen laid the foundations for the single practice of *nembutsu* recitation (*shōmyō nembutsu*) and exclusive devotion to Amida Buddha. In his *magnum opus, Senchaku hongan nembutsu shū*, Hōnen systematized the basis for an independent Pure Land, Jōdo Shū tradition, by drawing upon the Indian and Chinese Pure Land patriarchs. Indian patriarchs Nāgārjuna (ca. 150–250 CE) and Vasubandu (ca. 400–500 CE) provided buddhological justification for single-practice recitation of the *nembutsu* and single-minded devotion to Amida Buddha; and his Chinese predecessors clarified such key notions as Original Vow, the nature of Amida Buddha, Other Power, and recitation of the *nembutsu*. From Shandao, Hōnen identified the Three Pure Land *Sūtras* (*Jōdo sanbukyō*).

Hōnen drew upon Shandao's conclusions from the *Daśabhūmikavibhāṣa Śāstra*, in which Nāgārjuna asserted that, in addition to long years of discipline and study (Path of the Sages), faith (Easy Path, also known as the Pure Land) is a legitimate *upāya* (expedient means) method for attaining enlightenment. Vasubandhu provided additional support for Pure Land devotion in the *Sukhāvatīvyūhopadeśa*, where he listed chanting the name Amida among four other forms of meditation. Hōnen looked to the Chinese Dharma master Danluan, who in his commentary on Vasubandhu's *Sukhāvatīvyūhopadeśa* (Chinese, *Wangsheng lun chu*; Japanese, *Jōdo ronchū*), equated the name of Amida with ultimate reality, thus attributing to it the power to break through ignorance that bound sentient beings to *saṃsāra*. This, in turn, lends support to the efficacy of Amida Buddha's Vow or Other Power to embrace all beings who recite his name to effectively transcend the duality between the devotee and the goal of *Nirvāṇa* or enlightenment.

Drawing from these spiritual predecessors, Hōnen advocated the simple practice of vocalizing the *nembutsu* or reciting "*Namu Amida Butsu*" to save all beings in the age of *mappō*. By chanting *nembutsu*, the devotee would be welcomed by Amida Buddha at death to the Pure Land, where enlightenment could be most effectively realized. Thus, Hōnen encouraged the development of deep faith in Amida and the continual recitation of *nembutsu* until one's last moment.

Practices
The central practice of Jōdo Shū devotees is *shōmyō nembutsu* or the continuous recitation of Amida Buddha's name, "*Namu Amida Butsu*." Services at most temples include the traditional form of chanting (see, for example, the Daily Prayer

from the Jōdo Shū North America Buddhist Missions, http://english.jodoshuna .org/prayer/daily-prayer/), followed by the recitation of the Golden Chain and the Eightfold Path and the singing of Hōnen's poem *Tsukikage* (Moonlight) and English *gathas* or hymns. Sermons are offered in Japanese and/or English, or both. Some temples also hold monthly *obetsuji* or special *nembutsu* chanting sessions. Like most other Japanese Buddhist sects in the United States, Jōdo Shū has adopted the practice of Sunday services and installation of pews.

Jōdo Shū temples serve as spiritual centers as well as places of cultural and community gatherings. Annual observances include New Year's service, Gyokie (Hōnen's memorial service), Nehan-e (Nirvana Day service), Ohigan-e (spring and autumn equinox services), Hanamatsuri (Buddha's birthday service; "Buddha Day" in Hawai'i), Mother's and Father's Day services, Obon (commemoration for the deceased), Ojūya (literally, 10-night [chanting of *nembutsu*]), Jōdo-e (Buddha's Enlightenment service), and Joya-e (New Year's Eve service).

See also: Buddhist Churches of America; Higashi Honganji; Honpa Hongwanji Mission of Hawai'i; Japanese American Religions; Nichiren Shōshū; Rinzai Zen; Soka Gakkai; Sōtō Zen

Further Reading

Andrews, Allan A. "Hōnen and Popular Pure Land Piety: Assimilation and Transformation." *Journal of the International Association of Buddhist Studies* 17, no. 1 (1994): 96–110.

Blum, Mark L. *The Origins and Development of Pure Land Buddhism: A Study and Translation of Gyōnen's* Jōdo Hōmon Genrushō. New York: Oxford University Press, 2002.

Maya Hara and Jodo Tanaka

JUDO IN AMERICA

Judo is a Japanese martial art that is practiced in the United States and throughout the world. Judo means the "gentle way," and students are instructed in the complementary philosophies of maximum efficiency and minimum effort and mutual welfare and benefit. Judo is an empty-handed combat sport with a focus on throws, takedowns, grappling, pins, and chokes. Judo techniques involve either disrupting an attacker's kuzushi (balance) and making him or her susceptible to being thrown or, when on the ground, causing an attacker to submit to a pin or choke. Judo is not only a martial art but is a competitive sport and is one of only two martial arts included in the Olympic Games. Currently, there are 6 million practitioners in 30 countries around the world.

The founder of judo is Dr. Jigoro Kano (1860–1938). Kano began his early training in the Japanese martial art of Jujitsu but because that art was quickly declining in popularity in Japan, Kano was forced to seek out other arts and eventually merged what he studied into his own practice of judo. In 1880, Kano opened his first judo school and in 1882 it was named the Kodokan. Kano meant for judo to be a competitive sport, though he also believed it to be much more than a sport or even a martial art. Like many other devout practitioners, Kano saw judo as a way of life.

Judo as self-defense and exercise is applicable and available to people of all genders, ages, and sizes. In competition, weight, gender, age, and rank are factors that determine eligible opponents. In class, students often rotate partners and the practice can be adjusted to be complementary with a focus on learning rather than competition. However, regardless of the structure, rank is always observed and lower-ranked students must respect and defer to senior students. Similar to most Asian martial arts, students wear belts around their training uniforms (gi) to designate their rank. Belt color rankings for middle-ranked students may differ among schools and for children and adults. However, a white belt is always the first belt and black signifies the beginning of the higher levels. Currently, 10th degree is the highest black belt awarded.

Judo classes are often composed of many elements that culminate in a type of sparring called *randori* (free practice). Students often begin training by practicing rolls, falls, and escape techniques that they will need in competition or randori. Judo has both standing and ground components. Much of judo is also composed of partner exercises. Standing practice includes not only actual throws but also body-fitting techniques that emphasize the correct positioning for getting one's partner off balance and susceptible to being thrown. Ground practice includes techniques that focus on pinning or choking a partner until he or she must tap or risk serious injury.

Judo's inclusion as a demonstration sport for men in the 1932 Olympic Games was the beginning of its introduction to the world. In 1964, judo became an official Olympic medal event for men. Women's Olympic judo followed much later. It was a demonstration event in the 1988 games and finally a medal event in 1992. However, before being an official Olympic medaling event, judo made its first worldwide appearance in 1956 at the World Judo Championships. Currently, the World Judo Championships are still held in every year when an Olympics is not occurring.

Though practiced worldwide, judo's highest-ranking students and teachers are primarily from Japan and all but one are men. Only one woman in the history of judo has achieved a 10th degree black belt. On July 28, 2011, at the age of 98, Sensei Keiko Fukuda of San Francisco, California, was awarded the 10th degree rank and the title of Shihan (Grandmaster). Fukuda Sensei began judo in her teens and continued her training and teaching into her adult years. Instead of a traditional life of marriage and family, Fukuda gave her life to judo and eventually left Japan to pursue teaching opportunities in California. She eventually traded her Japanese citizenship for American citizenship.

Fukuda Sensei's advancement in judo was challenging both on the mat and within judo governing organizations. Though judo was welcoming of a few high-ranking females, there were rules against women advancing past fifth degree black belt. Though she was a former teacher at Dr. Kano's school, the Kodokan, and was one of the top women in the world in the art, she was forced to wait almost two decades to be promoted from fifth to sixth degree black belt. It was not until 1972 when the sexist rules outlining women's promotions in the art were revised.

A moving documentary about Fukuda Sensei's life in judo premiered in March 2012 at the San Francisco International Asian American Film Festival. The film, *Mrs. Judo: Be Strong, Be Gentle, Be Beautiful*, focuses on Fukuda's life as a woman who both sacrificed for her love of judo and challenged sexism and adversity to recognize her full potential. The city of San Francisco where Fukuda Sensei lived for over 40 years recognizes August 19 as Keiko Fukuda Day. Mayor Willie Brown named the day for Fukuda Sensei in 2001 after she was promoted to ninth degree black belt. Fukuda Sensei died February 9, 2013.

See also: Aikido in America; Martial Arts

Further Reading

Flying Carp Productions. "Mrs. Judo: Be Strong, Be Gentle, Be Beautiful." Romer, Yuriko Gamo. http://www.flyingcarp.net/2009/04/be-strong/. Accessed June 18, 2012.

JudoInfo: Online Dojo. "Jigoro Kano." Ohlenkamp, Neil. http://judoinfo.com/kano4.htm. Accessed June 18, 2012.

Watson, Brian. *Judo Memoirs of Jigoro Kano*. Bloomington, IN: Trafford Publishing, 2008.

Valerie Lo

KONKŌKYŌ/THE KONKO FAITH

Konkōkyō (the Konko faith) is a belief system characterized by an accepting and nonjudgmental view of humanity. It teaches belief in a divine parent (called *Tenchi Kane No Kami*) who is the life and energy of the universe—indeed *is* the universe—as well as a loving parent who wishes only the happiness and well-being of all human beings, the children. "*Kami*" is the term most frequently used for this entity. A core teaching of Konkōkyō is that Kami and humans exist in a relationship of interdependence or "mutual fulfillment" known as *aiyokakeyo*: Tenchi Kane No Kami fulfills humanity and humanity fulfills Tenchi Kane No Kami. In this relationship, humans are exhorted to cultivate an attitude of sincere gratitude for Kami's blessings received daily, both large and small. This principle of *aiyokakeyo* encompasses the fundamental nature and workings of the universe, which includes the dynamic, synergistic, and loving relationship between Kami and humanity.

By extension, human beings also exist in relationships of mutual dependence with each other and with the larger social and natural world. They are therefore encouraged to help each other and take care of the world they live in. Other notable features of Konkōkyō include respect for and appreciation of other belief systems, an absence of rigid dogma, and a personalized, customized approach to advising individuals and ministering to believers. Realizing happiness, peace of mind, and divine blessings by living in harmony with Kami, as well as helping others to do so—these are important spiritual goals for a Konko believer.

In 1919 the first two associations of Konko believers in Seattle were formed, followed by the establishment of the Konko Church of Seattle in 1928—the first Konko church in North America. Propagation in Hawai'i and in Los Angeles started in 1926 with the formation of believers' groups. By the start of World War II there were seven churches on the West Coast of the United States and two in Hawai'i. The ministers of the churches in the continental United States, viewed as leaders of the Japanese American community, were all detained by the U.S. government as enemy aliens during World War II. Most spent the war years in federal detention separated from their families, who were themselves interned in 10 War Relocation Centers/concentration camps for the duration of the war.

After the war, Japanese American churches and temples of all faiths gradually reestablished themselves in their prewar communities as well as in new locations. Four more Konko churches were established in Hawai'i, and two more in the continental United States. Two churches were established in Canada as well. Finally, the churches on the continent were incorporated as the Konko Churches of North America (KCNA) in 1969, and 1971 saw the incorporation of the Konko Missions in Hawai'i (KMH). Four more churches have been added in recent years for a total of 15 in North America.

Konkōkyō is also found in other parts of the world. Brazil has seven churches and a propagation hall, and there has been a Konkōkyō Activities Center in Asunción, Paraguay, since 1996. There is also a Konkōkyō Seoul Activity Center and faith gatherings in Europe. It is estimated that followers of Konkōkyō currently number approximately 400,000 worldwide.

Beliefs

Konkōkyō is a belief system that focuses on helping individuals to attain happiness and peace of mind in their daily lives through an appreciation of their relationship with Kami. It does not attempt to answer such questions as how or why the universe was created, what are the details of the afterlife, or the "problem of evil." Konkōkyō is concerned with this life and with helping people to find solutions for their problems through the teachings of the founder.

As mentioned in the Introduction, Konkōkyō teaches the belief in a deity called Tenchi Kane No Kami (or Kami), who is described somewhat impersonally as "the universe," its life, forms, and energy. At the same time, Kami is also described as a loving parent whose earnest wish is for everyone's happiness and well-being. This is one of several profound mysteries at the heart of the Konko faith. Believers are encouraged to develop an intimate, personal relationship with this divine parent, always looking to Kami, conversing with Kami through prayer and *toritsugi* meditation, becoming "one with Kami." The divinity that is worshipped in Konkōkyō is therefore both the impersonal universe—earth, the heavenly bodies, the forces of nature, physical laws both known and as yet undiscovered—as well as a very personal, caring, and nonjudgmental deity who is the ideal loving parent, both mother and father.

The parent–child model may help explain another mystery of Konkōkyō, the teaching that humans exist in a relationship of interdependence or "mutual fulfillment" (*aiyokakeyo*) with Kami, as already mentioned. Believers are taught that human beings certainly need Kami, as children need their parents, but Kami needs them as well and is dependent on their happiness and well-being to be fulfilled as Kami, as the divine parent. The analogy— though imperfect—is that, in an ideal familial relationship, human parents are emotionally and psychologically fulfilled as parents by the happiness, well-being, and love of their children.

There is an important corollary to this principle of *aiyokakeyo*, namely, that human beings also exist in a relationship of interdependence with each other and also with nature. People are therefore called upon to look after one another and care for the human and natural world around them.

Furthermore, the personal, parental deity of Konkōkyō is not an "other" who is external to and separate from the individual. All humans are born with a part of Kami within them, and one of the goals of followers of Konkōkyō is to bring to life this divinity within. The goal of believers is not to "go to heaven" or to be otherwise rewarded in the afterlife. Rather, it is to awaken the *kami* or divinity that is already within them and to live a life consistent with their mutually dependent relationship with the divine parent and with the human and natural world.

An important manifestation of the divine parent's love for humanity is the concept of *okage*, or blessings. There are grand blessings on a large scale, such as the very fact of life itself; others may seem mundane and often taken for granted, such as being able to eat when hungry. Some may seem small at first but turn out to be quite significant; others may not seem to be blessings at first—quite the contrary, in fact—yet turn out to be life-changing. Believers are encouraged to cultivate an "attitude of gratitude," to realize blessings in every aspect of life. They are also taught to pray earnestly and sincerely to Kami in gratitude for blessings and to ask for continuing divine favors.

Belief in the power of prayer to realize blessings—provided it is based on the right attitude—is fundamental to Konkōkyō. Believers are taught that if they pray selflessly, with gratitude, humility, and sincerity, the prayer will be answered and blessings granted, though maybe not in the manner requested. There are also stories told of miraculous cures of illness after sincere, intense prayer by the minister and/or the believer. A less dramatic, though no less important, benefit of prayer is the peace of mind that believers report when they pray wholeheartedly, do their best, and then trust the outcome to Kami. Ultimately, the goal of prayer is said to be a state of mind in which the believer is in a continuous conversation with Kami—constantly aware of Kami, grateful for even the smallest blessing, and becoming one with Kami.

As to the source of these blessings, Kami is of course the ultimate source. Yet, paradoxically, blessings are also to be found within people's own hearts. This is the profound message of the *Tenchi Kakitsuke*, the revelation that encapsulates the core teachings of Konkōkyō. The *Tenchi Kakitsuke* exhorts believers to "Pray sincerely, with all your heart" to Tenchi Kane No Kami; at the same time, "Kami's blessings begin within / Hearts grateful and caring, in harmony and joy." That is, blessings both come from Kami and already reside within the believer's heart, a heart that is joyful and grateful, cares about others, and exists in harmony with Kami and the world.

Although the focus of Konkōkyō is more on this life than on the details of the afterlife, it does teach that the spirit lives on after death. Humans are born with bodies from nature and spirits from Kami. Upon death, the body returns to nature and the spirit to Kami. The spirits of those who have passed away are called *mitama*, and they continue to intercede with Kami on behalf of those who call on them. For many believers, the idea that a beloved relative or friend who has died is still with them, though unseen, and will help them navigate the many vicissitudes of life—this is a most comforting teaching. Those who have small altars at home will often display photographs of such loved ones and pray to and for their *mitama* spirits as part of their daily prayer routine. This honoring of and looking to the deceased is a characteristic shared by many belief systems in the world. The founder's *mitama*, his "eternal spirit" called Ikigami Konkō Daijin, holds a special place in the faith, second only to that of Tenchi Kane No Kami. In fact, many believers pray to Tenchi Kane No Kami through Ikigami Konkō Daijin.

Another feature of the Konko faith is a great tolerance of other belief systems. This is not unusual in Japan, which has not had the history of religious strife that has plagued many other parts of the world. But given the world we live in today, Konkōkyō's welcoming stance toward other faiths is a characteristic worth mentioning.

Konkōkyō also has few specific, absolute rules. Believers are exhorted to pray with true sincerity, to apologize for irreverences, and to give thanks for blessings. They are further encouraged to be continuously aware of Kami, of the workings of Kami in their daily lives, and of what is expected of them in their mutually dependent relationships with Kami and the human and natural world around them. Beyond that, however, if asked specific questions about appropriate behavior, a minister may give very different, even seemingly contradictory, advice to two people with similar problems. This absence of dogmatism and absolutes—a positive characteristic for many believers—also makes it challenging to explain Konkōkyō succinctly and, by extension, to propagate it. For some believers, it is frustrating that a faith that in their view is so open-minded, inclusive, and positive in its approach and teachings also has difficulty expanding its reach precisely because of these qualities.

Practices

Central to the practice of the Konko faith is *toritsugi* mediation, in which a believer asks a minister to intercede with Tenchi Kane No Kami on his or her behalf, to act as a kind of "go-between." The request may be related to something consequential, such as a serious illness or a difficult personal relationship. It may be more mundane, such as a request for prayers for a safe journey. Some requests for *toritsugi* mediation may be to give thanks for the positive outcome of a previous request. In every case, the minister's duty is to listen compassionately, pray on the believer's behalf, and provide guidance and/or comfort, as appropriate. In doing so, the minister calls on his or her understanding of the teachings as well as on the support of the eternal spirit of the founder, Ikigami Konkō Daijin.

This very individualized way of ministering to people extends to the head of the Konko faith. Thousands of believers travel to Konkōkyō headquarters annually and are able to access directly the spiritual leader of the faith, referred to as Konkōsama. The current leader is the great-great-grandson of the founder. Most, though not all, Konko churches in Japan are also handed down within the minister's family. Although this was also the practice earlier in North America, it is less so today.

Although individual *toritsugi* mediation is at the heart of Konko faith practice, churches also hold regular services, generally followed by fellowship and the sharing of a meal. In spring and autumn, there are special memorial services dedicated to *mitama*, the spirits of those who have died. Another service in spring is designated the Tenchi Kane No Kami Grand Ceremony honoring Kami; in fall, the Ikigami Konkō Daijin Grand Ceremony honors the eternal spirit of the founder.

Believers make offerings to express gratitude for *toritsugi* mediation or for blessings received, as well as on the occasion of a service. In the case of monetary offerings, there is no designated amount, not even a "suggested donation." It is entirely up to the individual and what she or he feels moved to give.

Many external elements of Konkōkyō reflect its early association with Shinto. For example, the vestments and headgear worn by ministers during services, as well as the wooden staff they hold, are very similar to those used by Shinto priests. In other respects, Shinto elements have been modified or adapted for use in Konkōkyō rituals. In the Konko faith, the start and end of prayers is marked by four hand claps; visitors to Shinto shrines typically clap twice. For every service, the Konkōkyō minister prepares a special written prayer that is read aloud in solemn tones. This is similar to Shinto practice.

Since the postwar years, Konkōkyō has been shedding the external trappings of Shinto. One of the most important of such changes has been the replacement of the old prayers, which had been taken verbatim from Shinto ritual and echoed passages from ancient Japanese texts. They did not convey Konkōkyō teachings or beliefs very well. The new prayers, which are more closely aligned with Konkōkyō beliefs, came into common use in North American churches in the 1980s. Some North American churches include the older prayers to this day. New, original prayers and practices continue to be created to reflect the needs of a heterogeneous North American society.

Conclusion

Konkōkyō was one of several belief systems that were founded in mid-19th century Japan and whose early, formative years coincided with the turbulent decades of the late Tokugawa and early Meiji periods. Being a relatively young belief system, it has not yet had the kind of thoroughgoing discussion and debate about its teachings and role in the world that older religious traditions have had. It has also been bound geographically and culturally to Japan for most of its first hundred years. Nevertheless, it continues to evolve as an institution and faith community in Japan, North America, and elsewhere, its goal being to expand beyond its ethnic roots and serve the spiritual needs of all. It will be interesting to see how the Konko faith navigates its way beyond the Japanese immigrant and Japanese American communities and adapts its messages to a very different culture from that of its birthplace.

See also: Japanese American Religions

Further Reading

Fukuda, Yoshiaki. *Live with Faith: Being a Konko Believer*. San Francisco: Konko Church of San Francisco, 2007.

Konko Kyo's 50 Years in America. San Francisco: Konko Churches of America and Konko Missions in Hawai'i, 1976.

Material Resource Committee, Konko Churches of North America

MAHIKARI (TRUE LIGHT)

Established in 1959 by Okada Yoshikazu (1901–1974), Mahikari (True Light) is a spiritual organization that, after a split in 1978, exists as two separate groups, Sekai Mahikari Bunmei Kyōdan (Church of the World True-Light Civilization) and Sūkyō Mahikari (Sūkyō True Light). Despite the separation, the groups largely share the belief and practice established by Okada, which teaches that certain spiritual principles underlie the world and humans can attain greater happiness by attuning themselves to these principles. The core practice for connecting with these spiritual principles is giving and receiving Divine Light energy, transmitted through the palm, which produces physical, psychological, and spiritual benefits. Although the primary focus of light-giving is to help others and foster one's own personal growth, it is not restricted to humans. Light may be given to any sentient or nonsentient being and overall increases the connection of humans to their environment.

The North American headquarters of Sūkyō Mahikari are in Rancho Santa Margarita, California. It operates 23 centers in major U.S. cities as well as Canada and Puerto Rico. Current membership for the North American Region is 10,000. Sekai Mahikari Bunmei Kyōdan's main centers are in California, New York, and Kentucky. It also operates a traveling minister system where leaders visit remote locations.

Belief and Practice

In his writings, Okada presented a cosmology that consisted of a supreme god, Su God, which created everything and shared its spirit with the creation. Su God is the head of a group of gods related to the sun. This group withdrew and placed the world under the rule of lesser gods related to the moon. During this time the world became more materialistic, ignoring spiritual realities, and various problems arose until ultimately a time would come when "Su God would reveal himself and return the world to its pristine form, ushering in a new civilization of spirit characterized by health, peace, and prosperity. To prepare humankind for the advent of this radical change, Su God chose Okada Kōtama as the *Sakigake no meshia* . . . the harbinger Messiah of the new age who urges people to undergo the great 'cleaning' and so become the *tanebito* . . . the 'seed people,' of the new civilization."

This cosmological-eschatological vision of the need for universal purification grounds Mahikari's core notion of the importance of *mihikari* or "Divine Light" that proceeds from Su God and purifies and eliminates problems, including physical and spiritual illnesses, moral and relational problems, or material and financial wants. It is also referred to as *mahikari* or "True Light." The significance of True Light motivates the core practice of Mahikari, *okiyome*, the activity of dispensing Divine Light through one's hand onto any object that needs healing. This light is believed to purify the body from possessing spirits and from "toxins," poisonous material accumulated in the body. The whole world is seen as needing purification, so the ritual can be performed on any object, sentient or nonsentient. Essential to effective *okiyome* is wearing a special amulet called an *omitama* that is given to new members at the end of the initiatory three-day course. After the basic three-day course, intermediate and advanced courses are offered to deepen one's understanding and practice. Although *okiyome* is what Mahikari is best known for, the practice of transmitting divine energy through the hand is not unique to it. The activity also exists in the spiritual traditions of Sekai Kyūseikyō and Oomoto. The extent to which these earlier groups influenced the formation of Mahikari is debated.

For Mahikari, then, all physical, psychic, emotional, and social problems are rooted in conflict in the spiritual realm. In addition to Su God and the lesser spirits under it, there are other personal spirits and impersonal forces. Ancestral spirits play an important role, and maintaining a good relationship with them through daily offerings is emphasized. Impersonal forces include the notion of *ki*, which can refer to a feeling in a place, a psychological or bodily state, or a vital essence that permeates and unites the cosmos, as well as *kotodama*, the spiritual power of words, *reihasen*, "cords of spiritual vibrations," and *reiha* or *hinami*, "spirit waves." Mahikari also endorses a view of reincarnation.

Rather than seeing itself as exclusive of other religions or spiritual traditions, Mahikari is quite inclusive, claiming to be the fulfillment of what other religious traditions pointed to. Okada Yoshikazu insists that "all religions are basically one, belief is basically one, mankind is basically one, and the earth is originally one," but adds that the importance of the historical religions lies only in their function as "breaks" to prevent mankind's total deviation from God's plan. They will be superseded in due time by the *sūkyō*. In this way, Mahikari does not require that new members reject their previous beliefs or practices. But although Mahikari sees itself as universally relevant and more than just a local Japanese spiritual tradition, this has presented challenges. Although Mahikari's emphasis on solving immediate, practical problems has been very attractive to Western audiences, other features resist adaptation to new contexts and inevitably produce a certain foreignness. It is the correct performance of the ritual and the exact pronunciation of the prayers that brings about the desired results. Both the teachings and the rituals are, moreover, believed to be divinely revealed, and thus not subject to change. The ways both Sūkyō Mahikari and Sekai Mahikari Bunmei Kyōdan negotiate this balance between cultural particularity and global adaptation will certainly impact their continued relevance in the future.

See also: Japanese American Religions

Further Reading

Broder, Anne. "Mahikari in Context: Kamigakari, Chinkon kishin, and Psychical Investigation in Ōmoto-lineage Religions." *Japanese Journal of Religious Studies* 35, no. 2 (2008): 331–362.

Cornille, Catherine. "Mahikari." In *Encyclopedia of New Religious Movements,* edited by Peter B. Clarke, 383–385. New York: Routledge, 2006.

Cornille, Catherine. "The Phoenix Flies West: The Dynamics of the Inculturation of Mahikari in Western Europe." *Japanese Journal of Religious Studies* 18, nos. 2–3 (1991): 265–285.

Peter L. Doebler

MARTIAL ARTS

The martial arts from different Asian countries have become popular in the United States, and are practiced more as a sport than as a spiritual or character-building pursuit. Among the Japanese and Japanese Americans, one of the more popular martial arts is judo, which translates as the "gentle way." Yoshitsugu Yamashita is credited with introducing judo to the United States in 1903. Yamashita was a student of Jigoro Kano, the father of modern judo. Kano had taken elements of jujitsu, which focused on breaking bones and dislocating joints, and transformed it into judo, a martial arts form that taught participants how to defend themselves in unarmed combat without purposely injuring the opponent.

During the early 1900s, Japanese immigrant parents enrolled their American-born children in judo or kendo, the way of the sword, as a means to teach physical and moral character. Most judo dojos were built next to Japanese-languages schools. Because the Japanese immigrants had limited resources, they improvised the dojos. Sometimes the walls and roofs were merely corrugated tin. For flooring, immigrant women sewed together canvases and packed it tight with sawdust. In the United States, kendo was first practiced among urban male elites. In contrast to judo, which required nothing more than the purchase of a judo-gi (uniform), kendo required equipment such as the shinai (bamboo) or bokuto (wooden) sword, and a protective helmet and body

Among the Japanese and Japanese Americans, one of the more popular martial arts is judo, which translates as the "gentle way." (Anna Jurkovska/Dreamstime)

armor. Sometimes, those who could not afford the equipment practiced with a rolled-up newspaper. However, by the 1930s, kendo had become popular among Japanese Americans, thanks largely to the formation of the Hokubei Butokukai, or North American Martial Virtue Society.

In Japan, kendo became closely associated with Japanese militarism in the late 1930s. As a result, when the United States entered World War II, the government quickly rounded up kendo instructors in the United States. After Japan's surrender in 1945, the U.S. occupying forces banned kendo in Japan until 1950.

In recent years, kendo has attracted interest from younger Japanese Americans as well as from non-Japanese. Along with kendo, naginata, a long pole sword, has also become popular. Karate became popular in the United States after U.S. soldiers were stationed in Okinawa during and after World War II. Karate developed in the Ryūkyū Islands, which became Okinawa after Japan's annexation of the Ryūkyū Kingdom in 1879. Starting from the 1960s, Hollywood movies popularized the word "karate," which started to refer to any generic Asian martial arts. The Karate Kid movie series in the 1980s further popularized the word.

See also: Aikido in America; Judo in America

Further Reading

Azuma, Eiichiro. "Social History of Kendo and Sumo in Japanese America." In *More Than a Game: Sport in the Japanese American Community*, edited by Brian Niiya. Los Angeles: Japanese American National Museum, 2000.

Svinth, Joseph. "Judo." In *Encyclopedia of Japanese American History*, edited by Brian Niiya. Los Angeles: Japanese American National Museum, 2001.

Martha Nakagawa

MATSURI

Matsuri is a Japanese expression that refers to religious and seasonal festivals. Related to the verb *matsuru*, meaning to supplicate, enshrine, or worship, originally matsuri were rituals that honored various deities (*kami*) and the spirits of deceased ancestors; rituals also were performed to placate angry *kami* and spirits. In the early history of Japan, these rituals were performed by the head of the community. As such, matsuri predates the introduction of Buddhism to Japan.

Matsuri come in various types and sizes, ranging from small ad-hoc rituals to pacify land deities (*jichin-sai*), to familyoriented events such as Hina-matsuri (the Doll Festival, for the healthy growth of girls, celebrated on March 3), to much bigger communal seasonal festivals. Major large-scale festivals include Kamo-matsuri, popularly known as Aoi-matsuri, and Gion-matsuri, held in May and July respectively in Kyoto, and Tanabata-matsuri, which takes place in Sendai in August. These matsuri attract a large number of tourists from across the country and abroad. Many such traditional matsuri are related to agricultural cycles and involve Shinto rituals performed by Shinto priests (*shinshoku*) and shrine maidens (*miko*) to supplicate and give thanks to the *kami*. Deities are often carried around in the *mikoshi*, a portable shrine, which normally marks the climax of the matsuri. This is followed by communal feasting with Japanese liquor (*sake*, or *omiki* in this specific context), which has been first offered to the *kami*, and dancing.

Major Buddhist matsuri include Hanamatsuri, celebrated on April 8, that commemorates the birth of the historical Buddha (Śākyamuni) in the Mahāyāna tradition. Originally an agricultural ritual, Natsu-matsuri, the "summer festival," is now associated with the Buddhist Obon (or simply *bon*) period. During the Obon season, the spirits of the ancestors return to visit the homes where they formerly lived to be with their progeny. Obon is an occasion to prepare the ancestral altar with special delicacies and flowers to welcome the spirits. Often a priest will be invited for a memorial service. At the end of their three-day visit, the ancestral spirits are given a special send-off. The residents of Kyoto commemorate their return with *Gozan-no-okuri-bi*, a set of five large "sendoff" fires made on the mountainsides on August 16.

In the United States the Japanese community celebrates Hanamatsuri and Obon-matsuri as major Buddhist events. In addition to these traditional services, the matsuri is an occasion to highlight Japanese culture within the larger U.S. community. Thus, the San Francisco Sakura-matsuri held in April is a festive occasion for the various arts and performing organizations to showcase their respective expertise. It is an occasion for enthusiasts of *ikebana* (flower arrangements), *shodō* (calligraphy), and *sumi-e* (ink painting) to exhibit their work. *Buyō* (traditional dance), *koto*, *samisen*, and *shakuhachi* performances are also featured. Other Japanese community–sponsored events take on such names as Nikkei-matsuri, Daruma-matsuri, Akimatsuri, and Haru-matsuri. These matsuri are no longer reminders of their agricultural origins, but are occasions for community solidarity and festivity.

See also: Cherry Blossom Festival; Obon (Urabon)

Further Reading

Joya, Mock. *Things Japanese*. Tokyo: Tokyo News Service, 1963.
Sugimoto, Etsuko Inagaki. *A Daughter of the Samurai*. Rutland, VT: Tuttle, 1966.
Varley, Paul. *Japanese Culture*. Honolulu: University of Hawai'i Press, 2000.

Kieko Obuse

NICHIREN SHŌSHŪ

Nichiren Shōshū is a sect of Nichiren Buddhism that experienced great success in the United States from the 1960s to the 1980s. This success was due in large part to its close connection with the lay organization Soka Gakkai, known as Nichiren Shōshū of America (NSA) until the two split in 1991. Since the division, Nichiren Shōshū has maintained a modest presence in the United States. There are currently six temples in the greater metropolitan areas of San Francisco, Los Angeles, Hawai'i, Chicago, New York, and Washington, D.C.

Beliefs and Practices

One of the distinguishing features of Nichiren Shōshū is that it traces its origin to Nikkō (1246–1333), one of Nichiren Daishōnin's (1222–1282) disciples. Nikkō is credited with building the temple at Taiseki-ji at the foot of Mount Fuji. The temple houses the primary object of reverence, the Dai-Gohonzon, a wooden *maṇḍala* inscribed by Nichiren with the name of the *Lotus Sūtra* in Chinese characters and Nichiren's signature. Nichiren Shōshū places emphasis on the importance of the priesthood and highlights its ability to trace a direct line back to Nikkō. This continual priestly lineage, passed down from one high priest to the next, is known as *kechimyaku sojo*, or "Heritage of the Law."

Nichiren Shōshū documents describe this as follows: "The Heritage of the Law refers to the master (the Buddha) selecting a single disciple whom he considers to be most suited for his successor and entrusting him with the essence of Buddhism in its entirety. The transmission of the Heritage of the Law is of utmost importance, since the Law would be lost no matter how outstanding the teacher if he had no successor to follow him. . . . Nichiren Shōshū is the only orthodox sect which has handed down the Daishonin's teaching correctly in such an unbroken line" (Nichiren Shōshū, 63). This emphasis on the priesthood also supports a sharp delineation between the priesthood and the laity (*hokkeko*) within Nichiren Shōshū, a fact that becomes particularly relevant for the conflict with Soka Gakkai.

Also unique to Nichiren Shōshū is the belief that Nichiren Daishōnin was the "Original (True) Buddha, the fundamental master of all Buddhas" (Nichiren, 1). This is based on the conviction that Śākyamuni Buddha taught the idea of *Mappō*, a coming time when belief in Buddhism would decline and a more perfect Buddha would appear. Nichiren Shōshū identifies this Buddha as Nichiren and as a consequence renders all previous versions of Buddhism moot.

A final unique feature of Nichiren Shōshū is its belief that the Dai-Gohonzon is what makes enlightenment possible and that it is the sole object of reverence for all people. It identifies other Nichiren-based groups as having either confused objects of worship, such as statues of Shakyamuni Buddha or "counterfeit" Gohonzons. These groups include the Nichiren shū sect based at Mt. Minobu, which the Buddhist Church of America is based on, Risshō Kōsei-kai, Reiyūkai, and Soka Gakkai. Again, from Nichiren Shōshū's perspective it is the unbroken priestly lineage that can guarantee the authenticity and efficaciousness of the Dai-Gohonzon. As a result of this commitment to the Dai-Gohonzon, *tozan* (pilgrimage) to Taiseki-ji is an essential practice.

History

When considering the history of Nichiren Shōshū in the United States it is difficult to separate it from the history of Soka Gakkai. This is because until 1991 Nichiren Shōshū entrusted Soka Gakkai—at the time Nichiren Shōshū of America (NSA)—with guiding Nichiren Shōshū adherents outside of Japan.

In conjunction with NSA efforts, Nichiren Shōshū's early appearance in the United States was via immigrant communities, especially Japanese women who had married American servicemen. This was followed by explosive growth in the 1960s and 1970s through intensive proselytization efforts known as *shakubuku* as well as cultural changes that made Nichiren Shōshū more accessible to non-Japanese, such as using English at meetings. However, at the same time, within NSA there was progressively a less militant commitment to the absolute uniqueness of Nichiren Shōshū in contrast to other traditions.

The tremendous expansion of Soka Gakkai globally and its changing methods and activities distanced it from the Nichiren Shōshū priesthood. Ultimately this led to Nichiren Shōshū cutting off all relations with Soka Gakkai and its members on November 28, 1991. After this formal separation NSA changed its name to Soka Gakkai International while those who left SGI and stayed loyal to the Nichiren priesthood adopted the name Nichiren Shōshū Temple. While there were numerous variables involved in the split, Nichiren Shōshū's distinct emphasis on the importance of the priesthood played a major role. While Soka Gakkai has gone in a much more progressive direction focused on environmental and social issues, Nichiren Shōshū has consolidated and focused on its core beliefs and traditions, believing that these will ensure true success in the future.

See also: Buddhist Churches of America; Higashi Honganji; Honpa Hongwanji Mission of Hawai'i; Japanese American Religions; Jōdo Shū (Pure Land Sect); Rinzai Zen; Soka Gakkai; Sōtō Zen

Further Reading

Hurst, Jane. *Nichiren Shoshu Buddhism and the Soka Gakkai in America: The Ethos of a New Religious Movement*. New York: Garland, 1992.

Snow, David A. *Shakubuku: A Study of the Nichiren Shōshū Buddhist Movement in America, 1960–1975*. New York: Garland, 1993.

Peter L. Doebler

OBON (URABON)

Urabon or simply Obon, the Japanese variant of the Sanskrit *Ullambana*, is a Buddhist service of gratitude offered to the ancestors. Its origins are obscure, but many scholars trace it to the tale of Jaratkāru, who appears in the Indian epic *Mahābharata* (I, 13–14; 45–48). According to this account, Jaratkāru chances upon a large pit over which a number of persons are suspended upside down by a single root of grass that was being gnawed at by a rat. He learns that they are the ancestral spirits of his deceased father and ancestors. They find themselves in their predicament, not by their doing, but because Jaratkāru, who chose to become an ascetic and celibate, would leave no heirs and thus end the family linage. Moved, Jaratkāru promises to marry and produce an heir. Buddhists reworked the story by featuring Maudglyāna, one of Buddha's 10 great disciples, who rescues his mother from *preta*, the realm of hungry ghosts. *Preta* is the second lowest of six *gatis* or realms through which beings transmigrate. The lowest is hell, the others in ascending order are: (3) the animal realm, (4) the *asuras* (constantly fighting demigods) realm, (5) the human realm, and (6) the *deva* or heavenly realm.

The *Nihon Shoki* (Chronicles of Japan) reports that Obon was first observed during the reign of Emperor Saimei on the 15th day of the seventh lunar month in 656. The court sponsored a service in 733 and annually thereafter. The Japanese evolved Obon into a three-day festival of great joy, because they believed and still believe that their ancestors return from their spiritual abode to be with their progeny. Prior to the introduction of Buddhism, the Japanese celebrated *tama matsuri* or the "welcoming of the spirits festival." Observed twice annually, at the end of the year and at the end of summer, this indigenous celebration welcomed the ancestral spirits of the fields, water, and other nature deities to solicit their assistance for good planting conditions and abundant harvests. The Obon celebration was eventually absorbed into the summer *tama matsuri* festival, and the end of year festival was abandoned.

Reminiscing about her childhood during the early 20th century in *A Daughter of the Samurai*, Etsuko Inagaki Sugimoto describes the preparations her grandmother and mother took to welcome the ancestral spirits at Obon. They made special offerings and placed them on the *butsudan* (family altar), where the ancestral tablets were placed. She writes of her anticipation as follows: "Like all children I always looked forward with pleasure to [the] visit of the ancestors, but after Father's death, I felt a deep personal interest, and my heart was beating with excitement, as the family met at the shrine."

When it was time for the ancestral spirits to return at dawn on the fourth day of their three-day visit, the family placed offerings and a lantern in a miniature canoe fashioned from a pampas mat. The offerings would sustain their visitors and the lantern would light the way. They hurried to the river, floated the offering-filled canoe, and watched it drift downstream. This ritual is still observed in a number of locations in Japan. In Hawai'i *toro nagashi* or floating of the lantern has become a community event that coincides with Memorial Day.

Obon is a major service; and *hatsu obon* or first obon refers to the first service for those families who lost loved ones during the past year. For these families, the service is especially poignant. The return of the ancestral spirits is an occasion for great joy that is expressed through the *bon odori* or *bon* dance. Typically the *yukata*-clad dancers circle around a *yagura*, a wooden scaffold on which the musicians and singers provide the music. The late summer "Bon season" is an important part of the present-day culture and life of Hawai'i and North America. Buddhist temples use the occasion to highlight Japanese cultural arts with exhibits and a food bazaar. The Ghost Festival is the Chinese counterpart of the Bon Festival.

See also: Buddhist Churches of America; Matsuri

Further Reading

Matsunaga, Daigan, and Alicia Matsunaga. *Foundations of Japanese Buddhism*. 2 vols. Los Angeles: Buddhist Books International, 1974.

Menon, Ramesh, trans. *The Mahābhārata: A Modern Rendering.* New Delhi: Rupa, 2004.
Sugimoto, Etsuko Inagaki. *A Daughter of the Samurai.* Rutland, VT: Charles E. Tuttle, 1966.

Ronald Y. Nakasone

OKINAWAN (RYŪKYŪAN) SPIRITUAL CULTURE

The spiritual culture of the Okinawan (Ryūkyūan) people (or *Uchinaanchu* as they refer to themselves in their native tongue) residing in Hawai'i and the continental United States is a complex blend of archaic indigenous shamanic and animistic beliefs and ancestral veneration that has been reinforced and honed by centuries of interaction with Chinese faith traditions, especially Confucianism, and with Japanese Buddhism. The belief that they share the world with innumerable disembodied spirits and that their identity is linked to their genealogy is formalized in family, kin group, and community rituals.

Okinawans in Hawai'i and the Continental United States

The exodus of Okinawans from their homeland was prompted in large part by the demand for cheap labor after the end of the African slave diaspora, Japanese imperial designs after World War I, and post–World War II U.S. military strategy. Statistics published by the Okinawan Prefectural Government reveal that between 1899 and 1911, 13,335 Okinawans sought work overseas, mostly as agricultural laborers. Of this number 10,250 settled in Hawai'i and 863 migrated directly to the continental United States. At the end of World War I, Japanese entrepreneurs recruited Okinawan laborers to populate and work in the newly acquired League of Nations–mandate territories once held by Germany in the southeast and northeast Pacific. Further, the 1920 collapse of world sugar prices and the subsequent loss of employment forced many Okinawans to seek work abroad. Okinawans migrated to South and East Asia (21,047) and to South America (31,243) between 1927 and 1940. By 1940, 75,318 persons, approximately 15 percent of the population, had migrated overseas.

In the aftermath of vanquishing the Japanese defending the island of Okinawa, the U.S. military requisitioned prime farmland, much of which it still holds. Additionally, after 1946 more than 180,000 out of an estimated 332,000 Okinawans and their descendants living abroad were repatriated back to war-shattered Okinawa and its outlying islands. This large influx of people resulted in a lack of employment opportunities that prompted a second wave of migration. Between 1948 and 1993 most of the 17,714 Okinawan immigrants ventured to South America. Many Okinawan women also left as brides of U.S. servicemen stationed on Okinawa. Interest in emigration waned after the late 1960s with the growing prosperity of Japan and as overseas immigrants began returning to Japan and Okinawa.

At the present, the two largest concentrations of Okinawans in the United States reside in Hawai'i and greater Los Angeles, where approximately 50,000 and 15,000 persons, respectively, claim to be Okinawan. These communities include first-, second-, third-, fourth-, and even fifth-generation persons of Okinawan descent, each with varying degrees of affiliation with their ancestral homeland.

Beliefs and Practices

The basis for Okinawan spiritual culture can be extrapolated from the *Omoro-sōshi*, an anthology of 1,553 shamanic poems that preserves the earliest aspirations and memories of the Okinawan people. From these poems we learn that the ancient Okinawans believed that they shared the world with innumerable animate and inanimate spirits, and that they had, and still have, great reverence for their elders and ancestors and for the wisdom they acquired from their life experiences. This reverence, evident in the ritual expression of their spiritual culture, is reinforced by Confucian notions of filiality.

First and foremost is the prominent presence of the *ubutidan* (Japanese, *obutsudan*), the ancestral altar that enshrines the *tōtōmē* or *ifee* (Japanese, *ihai*), memorial tablets of successive generations of ancestors in the main room of a traditional home. The *futuki* (Japanese, *hotoke*) or ancestral spirits are believed to reside in memorial tablets and thus are able to observe the daily comings and goings of their progeny. The living attend to their ancestors through regular offerings and by reporting births, marriages, and other significant events. The 1st and 15th days of each lunar month are set aside for formal rituals. Before merrymaking, relatives visiting from abroad will approach the ancestral altar.

In addition, the numerous tombs that can be seen on hillsides and beach-fronts also speak of the Okinawan respect for their ancestors. Families make periodic pilgrimages to the family tomb, in which the remains of successive generations are interred. Special effort is made to visit the site on *usīmīsai* or "spring equinox festival" that is observed during the third lunar month, a custom adopted from the Chinese observance of *Qingming*. On this occasion, the family will clean the grave site and repair the tomb, before conducting a service and sharing a meal at the site. Another important rite is *ubun*, which is observed on the 13th, 14th, and 15th days of the seventh lunar month that corresponds to the Japanese Buddhist Obon. On this occasion the family prepares the ancestral altar with a festive array of offerings to welcome the ancestral spirits on the 13th day. On the 15th day, the family sends off their ancestors to their spiritual abode, *nirai-kanai*. Memorials that mark the anniversary of death are also occasions for family rituals. These rituals reinforce family solidarity and an individual's awareness of his or her place among the generations. The oldest person of the family, usually a female, is the lead celebrant; a professional ritual specialist is not required. These family-oriented rituals contrast with Japanese custom that normally requires the services of a Buddhist cleric.

In addition to offering incense and *uchikabi*, the burning of ritual money, in traditional Okinawa the women would prepare special dishes that typically include *rafuté* (glazed pork); deep-fried tofu and sweet potatoes, stewed *gobo* (burdock), turnip, and *konbu* (pork wrapped in kelp); *kamaboku* (fish cake); and *mochi* (rice cakes). These dishes are arranged in neat rows in an *ujū*, multitiered lacquered boxes or arranged on a plate. Confectionery, fruits, stalks of sugar cane, and *awamori* (Okinawan *sake*) are also offered. Recently, these traditional offerings have been replaced by other celebratory dishes and liquors. At the end of the service, these offerings are consumed. Families in Hawai'i and the continental United States have simplified the food offerings and rarely share meals at the grave site. They often return home or retreat to a restaurant to share a meal.

Diasporic Okinawan families and communities continue the reverence for their ancestors by observing many of these traditional rituals, albeit in different guises. Children are constantly reminded of the sacrifices of their immigrant forebears by regular private and community memorial services. I have not come across nor have I made any formal survey of Okinawan households, but personal observation and anecdotal evidence suggest that most Okinawan families have an ancestral altar and make regular offerings but do not mark the traditional fortnightly rituals with any particular observance. Offerings to the ancestors are observed on New Year's Day, memorial rites that mark the anniversary of death, and other days of family significance. Families also make an effort to visit the grave sites on Memorial Day, Mother's Day, and Father's Day, which are American observances. The anniversaries of deaths, birthdays, and the Buddhist Obon are also occasions to visit grave sites.

Most recently, many Okinawa prefectural organizations sponsor Irei no hi or Day to Honor the Departed Spirits for those who perished during the Battle of Okinawa. Irei no hi, June 23, marks the formal end of the Battle of Okinawa.

Additionally, Okinawan families honor their elders with a series of late life celebrations. *Kajimaya* or the 97th birthday is especially celebratory. *Kajimaya* is based on the Chinese 12-year zodiac cycle. The first birthday is celebrated with great fanfare; thereafter the 13th, 25th, 37th, 49th, 61st, 73rd, and 85th birthdays are especially auspicious. Some Okinawan communities sponsor a special party to celebrate the longevity of their elders in conjunction with Kei-rō no hi or Respect for the Aged Day, a recently established Japanese national holiday on the third Monday of September. These late life celebrations together with the mortuary rites and memorial observances underscore the belief that the corporeal and spiritual constitute a continuum. With the end of corporeal life, the individual continues his or her spiritual life.

"Sister-Protector," Ritual Sites

Okinawans carried many portable aspects of their traditional spiritual culture to their new homes, but not the formal structure and rituals of the national faith that was headed by the office of the *chifijin* (Japanese, *kikoeogimi*), or national priestess. The office was established by Shō Shin (1465–1527; r. 1477–1526), the third monarch of the second Shō Dynasty. The *chifijin* appointed the regional and local priestesses, *nuru* (Japanese, *noro*), who in turn supervised the village *nīgami* (Japanese, *ne-gami* or root deity) and other subordinate functionaries.

Okinawans believe females to be spiritually gifted, an idea that can be traced to ancient Ryūkyū, when the islands consisted of consanguineous settlements centering on a founding family. At this time the expression *kami* or deity was synonymous with *fu* or "mother," whom the ancients associated with *kan'unna* or "female deity." These designations—*kami*, *fu*, and *kan'unna* (Japanese, *kami onna*) are rooted in the belief that women were more in tune with the unseen spiritual world, and thus better able to tap its resources and to communicate with beings dwelling in that realm. The spiritual power of the female is personified in the personality of the *unarigami* or "sister-protector," who shields the male members of her family from harm. For their part, the men labor to provide the material needs of the family and attend to matters outside the family. This sister–brother partnership provided the rationale for Ryūkyūan polity and the establishment of the office of the *chifijin ganashii mee* who together with the king shared the responsibility for ensuring the well-being and prosperity of the nation. This dual sovereignty system—a partnership of the highest spiritual and secular authorities—is celebrated in Ryūkyūan creation myths and folklore and is still operative in all levels of present-day Okinawan society and its overseas communities.

During the Ryūkyū Kingdom the *chifijin* conducted rituals of thanksgiving, offered prayers for peace, and observed memorials for the royal ancestors to ensure the well-being of the king and the nation. However, the 1879 Japanese annexation and the forcible exile of King Shō Tai (r. 1848–1879) and his court to Tokyo essentially dismantled the office. The chief-priestess, a daughter of Shō Iku (r. 1835–1847), chose to remain behind; her sacerdotal responsibilities were too important to abandon. Although the last *chifijin* died in 1944, memories of nationhood continue through the *munchū*, the family clan. Most significant is the *Agari umāi* or Eastern Pilgrimage. Once led by the *chifijin*, it recalls the mythical origins of the Ryūkyūan people. Two of the most revered sites are Haiinju and Ukinju, artesian springs that watered the first rice field. Indeed, even today, families and individuals observe *kā umāi* or "well pilgrimage" in and around their village to honor and give thanks to the water *kami* (spirit) from which their ancestors drew life-giving water. Revered well sites are referred to as *uganju* and are essential aspects of the indigenous animistic tradition.

Another important site is the *utaki* or sacred grove. The *utaki* is associated with the burial site of the founding family—*nīya* (Japanese, *neya*) or root house of the traditional village. Located in the hills or nearby woods, the focal point of an *utaki* is the *ibi*, a stone representing common ancestral spirits. On the *utaki's* grassy clearing the *nuru* (Japanese, *noro*) or local priestess or priestess leads the rites of *umatī* (Japanese, *matsuri*) that coincide with planting and harvesting. One of the more significant rites is *gungwati umatī* that celebrates the rice harvest. The temperate climate in the southern islands allows for this festival to be celebrated on the 15th day of the fifth lunar month.

Interestingly, the office of the *chifijin* did not include the *yuta* or shaman in the state sacerdotal hierarchy system. The *yuta* is recognized at an early age by the community and by other *yutas* to be endowed with shamanic (*saadakaumari*) and paranormal powers (*kamidari*). It appears that the *yuta's* nonrational powers of clairvoyance and prognostication, and her ability to traverse the spiritual realms and communicate with the unseen could not be quantified, and thus was beyond state control. Perhaps it is for these reasons that Shō Shōken (1617–1675) and Saion (1682–1761), chief councillors during the kingdom, deemed the *yuta's* powers to be irrational and superstition. They issued decrees to ban their activities. The Japanese also attempted to exterminate the *yuta* in the early 20th century. But these attempts failed. The *yuta* still enjoys great popularity, probably because she can divine the needs of the ancestral spirits, remind the living of those ritual responsibilities they may have forgotten, and identify auspicious days for marriage, travel, starting a new venture, and other important undertakings. The *yuta* is the only spiritual personality that has been active in the overseas Okinawan community.

See also: Okinawa and Okinawans

Further Reading

Nakasone, Ronald Y., ed. *Okinawan Diaspora*. Honolulu: University of Hawai'i Press, 2002.

Sakihara, Gary K. "Okinawan Household Survey." In *Uchinanchu: A History of Okinawans in Hawai'i*. Honolulu: University of Hawai'i/United Okinawan Association of Hawai'i, 1981.

Sakihara, Mitsugu, ed. *Uchinanchu: A History of Okinawans in Hawai'i*. Honolulu: University of Hawai'i/United Okinawan Association of Hawai'i, 1981.

Tamamori, Terunobu, and John C. James. *Okinawa: Society and Culture*. Naha: Bank of Ryūkyūs International Foundation, 2000.

Ronald Y. Nakasone

PILGRIMAGE TO INTERNMENT SITES

Since 1969, sizable pilgrimages to the Manzanar and Tule Lake internment sites have been regularly scheduled and organized by the Manzanar and Tule Lake committees, respectively. Intermittent pilgrimages, ranging from personal visits to large groups, have also been made to most of the 10 internment sites, including Poston (Arizona), Minidoka (Idaho), and Heart Mountain (Wyoming). The Manzanar Pilgrimage has its roots in the compassion of two religious leaders, Rev. Sentoku Maeda, a Buddhist priest, and his friend, Rev. Shoichi Wakahiro, a Christian minister. Every year after Manzanar closed in November 1945, they would return to the Eastern Sierras of California to the Manzanar cemetery, protected by the I-REI-TO (Soul Consoling Tower) obelisk, with a small group of Issei on Memorial Day to pray for the dead who were without family to do so. In 1969, the energies and struggles of the civil rights and redress movements converged with this practice of remembrance. To the young Sansei students and their friends in the Asian American studies movement, Rev. Maeda suggested the pilgrimage to help release the stories of their Nisei parents and led their religious ceremonies, initiating the present-day annual tradition of the Manzanar Pilgrimage. At the same time, the

Buddhist priests from the Los Angeles area light incense before a memorial ceremony at the Manzanar National Historic Landmark near Lone Pine, California, 2002. About 1,000 people took part in a pilgrimage at the site to mark the 60th anniversary of the executive order that sent Americans of Japanese descent to the internment camp at Manzanar and to other camps during World War II. (AP Photo/Joe Cavaretta)

Tule Lake Pilgrimage originated when Asian American students from northern California organized the first pilgrimage to its site in Newell, California, near the Oregon border, bringing together students, community activists, and former "internees."

Pilgrimages to the former sites of Japanese American detention during World War II were a catalyst for the Japanese American community, enabling a space for the intergenerational community to come to terms with long-buried emotions and to realize that a great injustice had been done by the U.S. government. The euphemistic terms of "evacuation" and "relocation" implied a situation of natural disaster rather than the forced removal of all persons of Japanese ancestry—citizens and noncitizens—who lived in California, the western parts of Oregon and Washington, and the southern part of Arizona, the designated military security zone of exclusion. Highlighting the essence of the redress movement, which was healing the wounds through confronting the injustice, not simply receiving monetary payment, the process of renewing collective memory on the pilgrimages and days of remembrance garnered the emotional commitment to engage in the campaign for redress. Yet after the passage of the Civil Liberties Act of 1988, which granted the nation's apology and a symbolic payment of $20,000 to survivors, the pilgrimages and days of remembrance continue to this day in response to the continued spiritual need for the healing of the wounds of both persons and communities, and the deepening of compassion toward others in a similar situation today. They are spiritual practices of remembrance, honoring ancestors, healing, and hope that are now shared by a diverse intercultural and intergenerational community. As a way of inhabiting shadowed ground, the pilgrimages reclaim them as sites of suffering and hope and are journeys that evoke layers of meaning, memory, mourning, healing, and ongoing commitment for reconciliation and justice. They are expressive of a cultural cosmology that highlights the relatedness of all beings and seeks to restore relationships broken by historical injuries.

See also: Executive Order 9066; Internment, World War II; Kooskia Internment Camp; Manzanar Children's Village (1942–1945); Post–World War II Redress; World War II

Further Reading

The Manzanar Committee. *The Manzanar Pilgrimage: A Time for Sharing.* Los Angeles: The Manzanar Committee, 1981.

Joanne Doi

RINZAI ZEN

Rinzai Zen-shū is the Japanese lineage of the Chinese Linji Chan (Zen) School, which was founded during the Tang Dynasty (607–918) by Linji Yixuan (Japanese, Rinzai Gigen, d. 867). Zen was introduced to Japan as early as the

Nara period (647–794), but it did not take root until Myōan Eisai (1141–1215) returned from his second trip to China, where he received his *inka* (seal of Dharma succession) from Xuan Huichang (n.d.), a Linji master. He returned in 1191. After overcoming resistance to establishing a new Buddhist tradition, in 1202 he founded Kenninji Temple in Kyoto. Originally trained as a Tendai (Chinese, Tianti) monk, Eisai combined Zen meditation with Tendai rituals. His successors, Shūhō Myōchō (Daitō Kokushi, 1283–1337) and Musō Soseki (1275–1351), evolved Rinzai Zen into a distinctively Japanese institution. During the Muromachi period (1336–1573) the purveyors of Rinzai melded Zen ideas (such as emptiness, transiency, and selflessness) with Japanese aesthetic sensibilities (asymmetry, simplicity, spontaneity, "agedness," and tranquility) to give rise to the Higashiyama culture. Much of what is commonly understood to be traditional Japan—*chadō*, *ikebana*, *Noh* drama, *sumi-e* painting, architecture with its distinctive *washitsu* (Japanese-style room) with its distinctive *fusuma* (sliding panels), *tatami* (straw mats), *shoji* (paper screens), *tokonoma* (decorative alcove), and *karesansui* (dry landscaping)—emerged at this time. After this burst of creative activity, Rinzai entered a period of stagnation until Hakuin Ekaku (1681–1769) revived the tradition through his *kōan* training methods that serve as the framework for modern Rinzai Zen practice.

Today Rinzai is not a single organized body. Rather, it is divided into 14 branches identified by their head temples, of which half are based in Kyoto. The largest and most influential is the Myōshinji branch, founded in 1342 by Kanzan Egen Zenji (1277–1360). The other 13 branches are Nanzenji and Tenryūji, both founded by Musō Soseki; Daitokuji, founded by Shūhō Myōchō; Tōfukuji, founded by Enni Ben'en (1202–1280); Kenninji, Kenchōji, Engakuji, Kokutaiji, Kōgakuji, Eigenji, Hōkōji, Shōkokuji, and Buttsūji.

These 14 temples are organizational divisions that arose from temple history and teacher–student lineage and do not represent sectarian divide or difference in fundamental practice. These head temples preside over approximately 6,000 temples, 40 monasteries, and one nunnery. The Myōshinji, with approximately 3,500 temples and 19 monasteries, has one temple in Hawai'i.

At the time of its founding in 1932 by Rev. Okamoto Nanshin, the Paia Myōshinji Rinzai Zen Temple on Maui was the only Rinzai temple in the United States and its territories. A native of Okinawa, Okamoto was educated and trained in Kyoto. Before immigrating to Hawai'i, he was the abbot of Torinji Temple on Ishigaki Island. Rev. Oshiro Kiyoshi, a native of Tomigusuku, Okinawa, who succeeded Okamoto, was instrumental in rebuilding the temple after the 1946 tsunami. With a membership of approximately 130 families, the temple serves the spiritual needs of the Okinawan community. The temple is also a venue for Okinawan (Ryūkyūan) culture.

The first Rinzai master to address an American audience was Shaku Soyen (1869–1919), who spoke at the 1893 Chicago World Parliament of Religions. Before returning to Japan, he spent nine months in the San Francisco area, where he established a small *zendō* at the home of Alexander and Ida Russell, where he led *zazen* meditation sessions and lectured. Shaku was followed by Rev. Senzaki Nyozen (1876–1958), who taught at various sites in California until his death in 1958. Senzaki's friend and colleague Okamoto of the Paia temple translated and published his *On Zen Meditation* in 1938. Another Rinzai pioneer was Rev. Sasaki Shigetsu, better known by his clerical name, Sokei-an (1882–1945), who was active in New York. In 1931, his small group was incorporated as the Buddhist Society of America, later renamed First Zen Institute of America. One of his most active supporters was Ruth Fuller Everett, an American socialite and the mother-in-law of Alan Watts (1915–1973). Shortly before his death in 1945, Sokei-an and Everett wed and she took the name Ruth Fuller Sasaki (1892–1967). Some of the more prominent recent Rinzai Zen teachers include Rev. Sasaki Kyosan Jōshū (1907–2014), who founded the Mt. Baldy Zen Center in California, and Rev. Shimano Eidō Tai (1932–), who established the Dai Bosatsu Zendō Kongōji in New York state. Rev. Ōmori Sōgen (1904–1994) founded Daihonzan Chōzen-ji, the first Rinzai headquarters temple established outside of Japan, in Honolulu.

Beliefs and Practices

Zen emphasizes that the truth and reality of Buddhism resides in the enlightenment of Śākyamuni Buddha and that all beings have the potential for attaining a similar experience. The realization of this potential is not to be found in the written documents, no matter how sacred, but through *zazen* or sitting meditation, *koan* practice, and *samu* (physical labor). The goal of Zen is *kenshō*, "seeing one's true nature"; it is an expression that is often used interchangeably with satori, "comprehension" or "understanding." *Kenshō* is the initial insight or awakening, not full enlightenment; it is the portal to a lifetime of post*kenshō* training aimed at deepening this insight through the activities of daily life.

In contrast to Dōgen's Sōtō Zen tradition that emphasized *zazen*, Hakuin employed *koan* (Chinese, *kongan*) practice. The *koan* is a pedagogical device designed to prod, heighten, and test a student's understanding of the Zen experience. *Koans* are often framed in the form of a "riddle" that forces a student to confront the limits of rationality and ordinary logic. Consider the following *koan* by Hakuin. Clapping his hands, he queries, "This is the sound of two hands clapping. What is the sound of one hand clapping?" The *koan* is an examination that does not call for a doctrinal or rational response. It does not ask the student for his or her opinion or judgment. If the student had attained an understanding of the basis of the *koan*, he or she would respond appropriately, either verbally and/or with some action. The encounter between teacher and student is direct and immediate. When the student's mind (understanding) meets the teacher's mind, the Dharma is transmitted. Case Six of the *Mumonkan* recalls the moment at Mt. Gṛdhrakuta (Vulture Peak) when Śākyamuni Buddha lifted a flower to those who had gathered to receive his teachings. Everyone was silent. Mahākāśyapa broke into a broad smile. Whereupon Śākyamuni said, "I possess the true Dharma eye, the marvelous mind of Nirvana, the true form of the formless, the subtle Dharma Gate, independent of words and transmitted beyond doctrine. This I entrust to Mahākāśyapa."

A thousand years later Bodhidharma (ca. fifth–sixth century), the transmitter of Zen from India to China, explained the meaning of Zen: "A special transmission outside the scriptures, [that is] not to be founded upon words and letters; By pointing directly to [one's] mind It lets one see into [one's own true] nature [Buddhahood]."

In *koan* practice, should the student's response be unsatisfactory, the teacher will ask the student to wrestle with it during *zazen* meditation and in the course of daily life. By forcing the student to realize the limits of language and rationality, the exercise prods the student to tap and release the Buddha-mind to transform his or her basis for life. After the initial *kenshō* experience, the student must continue to deepen the realization and make it visible in every thought, word, and act. Every event is an opportunity and every object replete with the lesson of the Buddhadharma. The Zen life is one of increasing authentic spontaneity with maturity. Such spontaneity can be seen in the drawings and calligraphy of Hakuin, who revealed his deepening stations of spiritual maturity.

The idea of *samu* or engaging in spiritual exercises beyond the meditation hall can be traced to Baizhang Huaihai (720–814), who coined the famous maxim: "No work, no food." Baizhang expected Zen monks to approach agricultural and all manner of manual labor with the same attitude as sitting meditation. Work is much more than simply working in the fields: it is a spiritual exercise. Through work, a practitioner takes charge of his or her spiritual exercises and contributes to the welfare of the community.

Contributions

As noted above, the impact of Rinzai Zen on the early immigrant experience has been largely confined to the Okinawan American community on Maui. However, it has had a broad and deep impact on the arts. D. T. Suzuki's (1870–1966) lectures at Columbia University in the early 1950s and his writings influenced many artists, poets, writers, and composers. In the mid-1950s, writers associated with the Beat Generation took a serious interest in Zen, including Joyce Johnson (1935–), Jack Kerouac (1922–1969), Allen Ginsberg (1926–1997), Kenneth Rexroth (1905–1982), and Ruth Weiss (1928–). In 2009, "The Third Mind: American Artists Contemplate Asia, 1860–1989" at the New York City Guggenheim Museum showcased the impact of Zen influences on such abstract expressionists as Franz Kline (1910–1962), Sam Francis (1923–1994), Phillip Guston (1913–1980), Robert Motherwell (1915–1991), Jackson Pollack (1912–1956), David Smith (1906–1965), and Mark Toby (1890–1976). These artists drew inspiration from the expressive spontaneity of *Zenga* (Zen paintings) and Zen-inspired calligraphers such as Morita Shiryū (1912–1998) and Inoue Yu'ichi (1916–1985). Composer John Cage (1912–1992), who also attended Suzuki's lectures, came away with the idea that the purpose of art is "to wake people up." To this end he composed *4'33"*, a piece in which the performer sits in front of a piano without playing a note for 4 minutes and 33 seconds.

The performance is bracketed by the performer lifting and closing the piano lid. The ambient sounds from the audience provide the "sounds" of the piece. The "unusual" performance forced the audience to appreciate silence or "no-sound." The Zen idea of immediacy provided a rationale for minimalism, an art and design movement that set out to expose the essence of an object by eliminating all nonessential features and concepts.

See also: Sōtō Zen

Further Reading

Dumoulin, Heinrich. *Zen Buddhism: A History*. Vol. 2: *Japan*. New York: Macmillan, 1990.
Suzuki, Daisetz T. *Zen and Japanese Culture*. New York: Pantheon Books, 1959.

Ronald Y. Nakasone

SELMA (CALIFORNIA) JAPANESE MISSION CHURCH

Selma Japanese Mission Church (1917–2011) was a unique 94-year experiment in Buddhist–Christian interfaith cooperation and sharing among the farming community of Selma, California. Much of the initial motivation and detail for this experiment has been lost and must be extrapolated from the recollections of interviewees who recalled the memories of their predecessors, as well as from oblique references found in scattered documents. The following narrative sketches the shared experiences and vision of one interfaith community.

A Shared Past

Japanese immigrants began settling in California's San Joaquin (Central) Valley during the early 1900s, in response to the need for agricultural laborers. These hardworking immigrants quickly established their own farms and businesses, including a *Nihonmachi* (Japanese business district) on the south side of the town of Selma. As the Japanese community grew, so did their need to share community resources. Selma Issei (first-generation Japanese) were deeply committed to a single group serving the Japanese community. Upon arriving in town, new Japanese immigrants, regardless of religion, would be visited by representatives of the settled Japanese community, Buddhist and Christian, and asked to lend financial support. After a decade of fund-raising, sufficient donations were assembled to purchase a Japanese community center in Selma.

In 1916, the Selma Japanese community established a committee of Buddhist and Christian Japanese residents to locate and secure a suitable venue for a community center that could be used for religious and cultural events. They selected the former Christian Church of Selma on Whitson Street between Second and Third Streets. The building and property were purchased for $400. Full conveyance of the property was transferred on February 5, 1917, to six U.S.-born Nisei (second-generation) minors, whose Japanese-born parents were prohibited from owning land. The original owners were children from both Buddhist and Christian families.

In 1938, the community group incorporated with the state of California as the not-for-profit Selma Japanese Mission Church. Due to discrimination and to appear as innocuous as possible, Japanese Buddhists in the United States regularly adopted names and practices that conformed to mainstream religious practices and perceptions. The use of the expression "church" (from the Greek *kuriakos* meaning "belonging to the Lord," which designated a Christian place of worship) was one such adjustment. "Church" is not synonymous with *bukkyōkai* (literally, Buddhist association), which is the proper expression for a Buddhist temple. The Selma Japanese Mission "Church" was neither a Christian nor a Buddhist organization, rather, it was a nonreligious community group founded by Japanese immigrants. Within the organization, however, were two religious fellowships: one for local Japanese Buddhists and one for local Japanese Christians.

The Selma Japanese Mission Church's building remained unused and vacant for the duration of World War II, while persons of Japanese ancestry, Buddhist and Christians alike, were forcibly sent to relocation camps. The Selma Japanese Mission Church reopened in 1946 when members from both the Christian and Buddhist fellowships returned home. The first religious programs each fellowship held were religious classes for their children.

In 1954, the church sold the property to Friis Hansen and Company. Proceeds from the sale, along with donations from the membership, were used to purchase a two-and-a-half-acre parcel at 2415 Floral Avenue and to erect a new facility. Construction began on a new, larger facility in April 1955 across from the cemetery. The new building was dedicated on February 11, 1956. During the ensuing years, membership declined as founders of the Selma Japanese Mission Church passed away and their descendants left local farms and settled elsewhere—often moving out of agricultural work. In 2011, the building and land were sold to the Thomas-Robinson Funeral Home. The proceeds were divided by the number of surviving members, to be distributed directly to religious nonprofits. Among the Buddhist fellowship members, most funds were given to the Fresno Betsuin Buddhist Temple and their membership was transferred to the temple in Fresno upon closure of the Selma Japanese Mission Church. Within the Selma Christian fellowship, many members chose to donate their portion of the proceeds to the United Japanese Christian Church of Clovis in gratitude for years of providing clergy support, while a few donated to local Protestant Christian churches where they now held membership.

Sharing Spaces

Members of the Selma Japanese Mission Church shared resources, space, and experiences in unique ways. First and foremost the fellowships shared worship and religious education space. Members of the church were welcome to attend either or both Buddhist and Christian worship services and religious instruction classes for children, which were held independently on different days of the week.

Evening worship services were conducted by Fresno clergy from the Buddhist temple and the Japanese-member Christ United Methodist Church (which merged with the Japanese Congregational Church in 1990 to become the United Japanese Christian Church of Clovis). After both worship services, held on different nights of the week, family and friends remained for fellowship and a potluck meal.

Memorial services for members of the Selma Japanese Mission Church, whether a member of the Buddhist or Christian fellowship, featured a special arrangement. Both fellowships would offer a traditional memorial service led by their clergy, one after another. At Buddhist memorial services members from the Selma Christian Fellowship would represent the Christian community during the Buddhist incense offering ritual. Between services the altars were changed. Following the last service everyone enjoyed a shared communal meal.

The Selma Japanese Mission Church on Whitson Street was the venue for the local chapter of the Young Buddhists of America, the Selma Buddhist Club, and the Selma Women's Association, which began in 1924 as the Bisaka Club, to meet and to host events. Clergy from the Fresno temple provided worship leadership and support for Buddhist fellowship members.

In 1929, Japanese youths from Selma First Methodist Church, supported by Edith Tsuruda of the national Methodist Church's Board of Missions and Lola Brown of the Selma Methodist Church, organized a Japanese Christian fellowship in Selma for Protestant Christian Japanese living in the area who had been attending churches further away. Clergy from Fresno's Christ United

Methodist church provided worship leadership, Bible study, and pastoral care; the Selma Methodist Church and Selma Baptist Church assisted with Sunday school teachers and support for youth groups. The Selma Fellowship participated in regional Methodist events such as the Fresno Japanese Methodist Epworth League. In January 1941, Christ Methodist Church started the Fresno Nisei Church held on Sunday evenings. Youths would gather in different locations in the greater Fresno area. On the third Sundays, they met in Selma.

After the attack on Pearl Harbor both fellowships ceased meeting. Programming at the church for both the Buddhist and Christian communities was reactivated in the summer of 1946. After World War II, a joint Buddhist–Christian Memorial Day Service was held annually in Selma, a still common practice among Japanese Americans nationwide. The interfaith ritual eulogized the local Christian and Buddhist Japanese American servicemembers who died during World War II. In later years the annual service honored veterans, deceased members of the military and their relatives, and all ancestors. Memorial plaques honoring deceased servicemembers were placed on the walls of the church.

The facility on Floral Avenue was fully shared by members of the Selma Japanese Mission Church, Buddhist and Christian alike. The rectangular building included an entryway, a main hall with a stage, meeting rooms used for classes, a kitchen, and bathrooms. A Buddhist altar was permanently placed in the main hall; it was enclosed behind sliding doors when not in use. A portable altar with its attendant cross and candles would be carried in for Christian services. In 1956, a few months after moving into the new property, the Christian fellowship asked the board of the interfaith Selma Japanese Mission Church to purchase a cross, candleholders, offering plates, and a purple cloth to be used in their worship services, as well as during the annual interfaith Memorial Day Services. The request was approved by the multifaith board. Since its inception, the Selma Japanese Mission Church was a Japanese community group that pulled leadership from both the Christian and Buddhist fellowships.

Sharing Experiences

As was true in many Japanese immigrant communities, Christian and Buddhist children learned their ancestral language together. The Whitson Street facility hosted a *Nihongakko* (Japanese-language school) that drew students from Selma and beyond. The first students were transported to and from class in Yoshinhei Torii's horse-drawn buggy. The first graduating class in 1918 included 11 students. The school operated through 1941.

Nisei (second-generation Japanese) recall attending both Buddhist and Christian Sunday school classes, which were held weekly on Sundays. Childhood exposure to both religions created strong bonds between neighbors and led to interfaith marriages.

The church's annual springtime picnic, a highlight of the year for the local Japanese community, included fun and games for persons of all ages. The Selma Japanese Mission Church also sponsored a Tencho Setsu (Japanese Culture Festival) in November. And there were movie nights featuring Japanese films projected onto sheets in lieu of a projection screen. At these events and other cooperative events Christians and Buddhists worked side by side to plan and implement events. All funds raised were used for the church, the broad organization that hosted both the Buddhist and Christian fellowships. They understood themselves to be a Japanese community first, and Buddhist or Christian second.

Shared Vision

With declining membership in both the Buddhist and Christian fellowships, members questioned the future of the Selma Japanese Mission Church. In 2011, it was decided to sell the property and close the church. Members of the Buddhist fellowship moved their memberships to the Fresno Betsuin Buddhist Temple. Their Japanese altar was given to the temple. Members of the Christian fellowship chose to move their memberships to area congregations, most opting to join the United Japanese Christian Church in Clovis.

On March 16, 2014, during the United Japanese Christian Church's "Year of Heritage," an 81-inch-tall granite Japanese pagoda lantern located in the church's Japanese Garden and a shorter lantern located at the entrance to the church were dedicated to honor Selma's Japanese interfaith community. During the dedication service all attendees pledged their commitment to keep the story of this interfaith community alive as the youth presented surviving members with symbols of appreciation. One of the members recalled that this was a community "that got along just fine" and all hoped their multifaith experiment would be tried again.

See also: Japanese American Christianity; Japanese American Religions

Further Reading

Buddhist Churches of America, ed. *Buddhist Churches of America, 75 Year History, 1899–1974.* Vol. 1. Chicago: Nobart, 1974.

United Japanese Christian Church. "History of the Selma Mission Church." In *The Focal Point.* Clovis, CA: United Japanese Christian Church, August 2012. Reprinted from *Fresno Betsuin Buddhist Temple (1901–1986).* Fresno: Fresno Betsuin Buddhist Temple, 1986, 94–95.

United Japanese Christian Church. "History of the UJCC: How We Got Here." www.ujcclife.com. Accessed September 30, 2013.

United Japanese Christian Church. "Selma Christian Fellowship: 1929–Present." In *This Is My Story, This Is "Our Song"; United Japanese Christian Church. 100th Anniversary of Christ United Methodist Church and 85th Anniversary of Japanese Congregational Church.* Clovis, CA: United Japanese Christian Church, 1993.

Kathryn M. Schreiber

SHIN BUDDHIST MUSIC

Jōdo Shinshū, one of the largest Pure Land denominations of Buddhism in Japan, is represented in the United States by several different communities, the largest of which is the Buddhist Churches of America (BCA), a national umbrella organization with more than 60 affiliated communities across the country. The BCA traces its history back to the late 1800s when a number of Shin priests were sent by their parent organization, the Nishi Hongwanji in Kyoto, to minister to the needs of Japanese migrant workers who had been immigrating to both Hawai'i and the mainland United States for some decades. They quickly established the Buddhist Mission of North America, which was renamed the Buddhist Churches of America during the internment of Japanese Americans during World War II. The organization continues to serve the needs of the Japanese American community while reaching out, as it has for most of its history, to the larger American Buddhist population. Thus, American Shin Buddhism can be seen as negotiating a space between their historical Japanese roots and attempts to acculturate to normative American religious customs. This dual nature of American Shin Buddhism is perhaps clearest in its music.

Shin Buddhist music in the United States can be roughly divided into four broad categories:

1. *Shōmyō* or chanting *Sūtras* and other sacred texts
2. *Gāthā* or hymns
3. *Taiko* ensembles
4. *Gagaku* or classical Japanese court music

The last two categories, *taiko* and *gagaku*, are not, strictly speaking, Shin Buddhist music. That is to say, they are not limited to a Shin Buddhist context but are instead part of the larger world of classical Japanese music. In the case of taiko, for example, the term itself merely refers to Japanese drums, and the style of taiko music most commonly found in the United States traces its roots to the post–World War II taiko revival in Japan, which was imported to the United States via Saiichi Tanaka in the late 1960s. It was during this time that Sansei (third-generation) Japanese Americans were beginning to formulate a specifically Asian American identity against the backdrop of the civil rights era, and taiko served as a way to challenge the stereotype of the "passive Asian" while claiming a connection to their Japanese roots. It was not long, however, before taiko became popular outside of the Japanese American community, and today most taiko ensembles are pan–Asian American in character.

Gagaku, classical Japanese court music played with traditional instruments such as the *biwa, koto*, and *shō* (mouth organ), is also not limited to the Shin Buddhist context where it is sometimes referred to as *hōraku* (lit. Dharma music). Like taiko, gagaku has become increasingly popular in the Japanese American context more recently, perhaps reflecting a desire to reconnect with individuals' Japanese roots. Both taiko and gagaku are performed at special occasions or festivals, most notably during Obon festivals where large taiko ensembles accompany the Obon dance to celebrate and memorialize the dead. Moreover, to the extent that both taiko and gagaku are not limited to the Shin Buddhist context, nor indeed to a strictly Japanese American context, the remainder of this entry will focus instead specifically on Shin Buddhist music.

Ritual Context for Shin Buddhist Music

The vast majority of BCA-affiliated and other American Shin Buddhist communities hold a weekly worship service at a local temple. This is a clear departure from normative Shin Buddhist temple practice in Japan where Shin Buddhists generally only attend temple services during large holidays or festivals and the resident priest or minister will instead visit members' homes to perform specific rituals, memorials, and rites. In the United States, owing to a tendency to adapt to normative Protestant Christian standards, Shin Buddhists attend weekly Sunday services, a service that provides the ritual context for the communal chanting of texts and singing of songs.

Whereas the Sunday service varies from temple to temple across the United States, its most basic form is as follows. The service begins with the ringing of a large *kansho* bell located somewhere outside the main worship hall or *hondo*. The ringing of the bell calls the *sangha* community members to gather in the *hondo* where they will presently be joined by the minister and his or her assistant minister. A lay member of the community will serve as officiant, directing the congregation to the texts that will be chanted or sung. Generally, the community will begin by chanting a shorter *Sūtra*, followed by taking refuge in the Three Treasures (the Buddha, the Dharma, and the *sangha*), singing a *gāthā*, and listening to the minister deliver a Dharma talk, or sermon. There may be a second chant or song sung following this sermon, and at some point before, during, or after the service, members are expected to *ōshoko* (offer incense) at the main altar. On most Sundays, there is a small social gathering following the service.

Shōmyō Sutra Chanting

At least once during the service, *sangha* members will collectively chant a *Sūtra* text. There are a limited number of texts specific to the Jōdo Shinshū tradition: selections from the so-called Three Pure Land *Sūtras*; commentarial literature by Jōdo Shinshū patriarchs such as Shandao and Nāgārjuna; and devotional poems (*wasan*) written by the tradition's founder, Shinran Shonin. Some texts, such as the *San Butsu Ge*, are chanted more frequently or on specific occasions such as a memorial service or holiday. And, of course, throughout the service, members will recite the *nembutsu*, a short, mantra-like phrase in praise of the Buddha Amida, "*namu-amida-butsu*." Reciting the *nembutsu* often precedes the *Dharma* talk, for example, and is a part of most of the *Sūtra* chants as well. Historically, Shin Buddhists were known for spontaneously chanting the *nembutsu* during ritual observances, a phenomenon that is not as common in contemporary practice.

Shōmyō, or the chanting of Buddhist sacred texts, has a long history in Japan that borrows heavily from Chinese styles of musical chanting, which in turn may be based on ancient Indian traditions. The Japanese style that American Shin Buddhists have inherited is based on a pentatonic scale of five basic notes. *Sūtras* are generally chanted in their classical Japanese readings at a steady rhythmic pace with one syllable per beat in sets of five or seven. A minister will lead the *sangha* through the chant, and most texts have a specific section for the cantor to chant solo with response from the congregation. Generally, time is marked by the striking of bells, gongs, or an *ōdaiko* drum. As mentioned, reciting the *nembutsu* during or immediately after a chant is common.

Whereas Shin Buddhist ministers are given extensive training in the proper way to chant their tradition's sacred texts, lay members rarely receive such guidance apart from their relationships with local ministers. As a result, participation in the communal chanting of texts varies across different local communities, reflecting individuals' comfort with the classical chanting style. Moreover, as Shin Buddhism developed in North America over the course of the 20th century, attempts were made to render the classical Japanese style of chanting into contemporary English, often through direct translations of the *Sūtras*. Hence, it is common to see in service books traditional Japanese musical notations with English translations beneath them. This in some sense can be read as the community making explicit attempts to relearn its tradition in response to the process of Americanization that may have distanced it from its Japanese roots. However, some Buddhist leaders have questioned the utility of direct translation, noting that this, too, is based on the Protestant Christian assumption that textual exegesis is more important than psychological or spiritual development; that is, it may be more important to *perform* the chant than to intellectually understand its content.

American Gāthā

In addition to chanting sacred texts, services are marked with the singing of hymns or *gāthā*. In the American Shin context, these hymns most closely resemble Protestant Christian hymns in genre and style. However, their complex and nuanced history is worth deeper exploration than the simple assumption of linear acculturation from Japan to the West. Many *gāthā* were written at the turn of the 20th century; others are centuries-old Japanese folk songs or modern adaptations of Shinran Shonin's *wasan* set to Western-style music. Still others are more contemporary works composed over the past few decades. And *gāthā* have been composed by Japanese, Japanese American, and Euro-American Buddhists alike.

The most widely used collection of Shin Buddhist *gāthā* today is the *Shin Buddhist Service Book* compiled in 1994 by the BCA Department of Education. (The book also contains the *Sūtras* regularly chanted as well as notes on temple services and etiquette.) The *Service Book* contains 68 *gāthā*, as well as instrumental and choral music compositions, roughly evenly divided between English and Japanese. Whereas several songs were composed specifically for the creation of the *Service Book*, the book also includes a substantial number of *gāthā* from previous volumes, songs written, composed, or set to modern Western music as early as the 1890s. Like the chanting of sacred texts, some songs are more popular than others, and some are sung only on special occasions. For example, "In Lumbini's Garden," a song composed by Paul Carus in the early 1900s, is regularly sung on Hanamatsuri to celebrate the birth of the historical Buddha. The song "White Ashes," based on an epistle written by 15th-century Shin Buddhist reformer Rennyo Shonin with music by American composer Lou Harrison, is often sung during memorial services.

It should also be noted that the *Service Book* by no means represents the extent of contemporary American Shin Buddhist *gāthā* or musical repertoire. Most temples, in addition to standard BCA service books, have their own local collections of songs culled from other Shin Buddhist collections or compositions by local musicians. Moreover, many temples have talented musical members who compose original songs in a variety of genres for Sunday services, which may never be written down or recorded. In sum, *gāthā* creates a space within the service for individuals to creatively express their own Buddhist identities and share these expressions with the community as a whole.

Conclusion

The Shin Buddhist experience in the United States is closely linked to the Japanese American experience, an experience that has been marked by World War II internment. Internment and racial prejudice has forced the community to carefully negotiate a specifically Japanese as well as American identity, and one can see tension within the community to hold fast to its Japanese roots while creatively engaging and adapting to normative white American cultural customs. Ritualized music is one space where this tension is sharply on display.

Attempts to translate Japanese *Sūtras* and other sacred texts into modern English for the purpose of ritual chanting have generally failed. The pentatonic scale of these chants does not lend itself naturally to English, and as mentioned above there is a sense that the value in such chanting is not intellectual understanding but spiritual practice. Furthermore, ritual practices can be slow to change; generally, rituals are performed because they have always been performed, in this way, and ritualists are resistant to adapt them too far from their assumed "right" method. Thus, the chanting of Shin Buddhist sacred texts can be read as an attempt by the community to retain its specifically Shin Buddhist and Japanese identity.

The history of American Shin, however, does not end with its Japaneseness. The community has consistently engaged with non–Japanese Americans, engagement that has had significant influence on the ritual life of the community. This is self-evident in the singing of Shin Buddhist songs and *gāthā*. Not only is the music itself performed in a style imported to Japan and Jōdo Shinshū from Western European sources, but many of the songs sung were themselves written or composed by non-Japanese converts to the tradition. When the most recent service book was compiled, an attempt was made to exclude *gāthā* that were "too Christian" or whose popularity had waned. It is interesting to note that the attempt was not to create a more "Japanese" collection but rather a more "Buddhist" collection, suggesting then that the community embraced songs and compositions that fulfilled this objective regardless of their source. Contemporary music makers similarly eschew rigid ethnic categorizations, and thus *gāthā* and other Shin Buddhist songs can be seen as the antithesis to *Sūtra* chanting: a space for creative and innovative expressions of Shin Buddhist practice and faith.

See also: Jōdo Shū (Pure Land Sect)

Further Reading

Ama, Michiro. *Immigrants to the Pure Land: The Modernization, Acculturation, and Globalization of Shin Buddhism*. Honolulu: University of Hawai'i Press, 2011.

Mitchell, Scott A. "Sunday Morning Songs." *The Pure Land* 22 (2006): 127–138.

Terada, Yoshitaka. "Shifting Identities of Taiko Music in North America." *Senri Ethnological Reports* 22 (2001): 37–59.

Wells, Keiko. "Shin Buddhist Song Lyrics Sung in the United States: Their History and Expressed Buddhist Images (2), 1936–2001." *Tokyo daigaku taiheiyō* 3 (2003): 41–64.

Scott A. Mitchell

SHINTO

Shinto, the indigenous spirituality of the Japanese, refers to an outlook and life-style grounded in a sentiment of the innate sacred nobility of the natural world and every animate and inanimate denizen who is part of it. The sacredness that animates all existences is referred to as *kami*, who are present everywhere, especially in auspicious objects and beings. This belief is so deeply interwoven into the fabric of society and culture that even those Japanese who profess not to hold such sentiments readily participate in its domestic and communal rituals. Domestic or family rituals include such milestones as births, coming-of-age celebrations, weddings, and other felicitous occasions. Yearnings for safe childbirth, success in examinations and business, and luck in finding a soul-mate merit a visit to the shrine or other sacred sites. The origins of *matsuri* or festivals are linked to a community's collective experience that includes plant-ing and harvesting, and mitigating the causes of disease and natural calamities. Matsuri also emerged from guilds. Fisherfolk not only celebrate good catches, but also conduct rituals for safe passage while at sea. The overriding sentiment underlying these rituals is a sincere gratitude for the gifts that nature provides to nourish life and well-being; and for the assistance of mythical and personal ancestors for safe passage through this world.

Shinto in Hawai'i

Japanese immigrants to Hawai'i carried with them their Shinto culture, where it became an essential component in the spiritual and cultural life of the com-munity. However, because its rituals and symbols supported the ideology of imperial Japan, shrines and devotees experienced U.S. government and soci-etal pressure during and immediately after World War II. These and other factors led to the closure of many shrines and the dismantling of their orga-nization, which resulted in the loss of their records and memories. Maeda Takakazu estimates that Japanese immigrants established at least 59 shrines, a number culled from newspapers, magazines, newsletters, diaries and other unpublished sources, and oral history. This number does not include shrines erected in the cane fields that asked for abundant harvest, or shrines at harbors from which fishermen set out to sea, or shrines erected in private homes and gardens. These once numerous shrines have long vanished.

Today on Maui only a handful of the larger shrines with institutional links to Japan are active: Konpira Jinsha, Lāhainā Daijingu, and the Wailuku Izumo Taisha. Mau'i Jinsha was established by Rev. Matsumura Masahoin 1915, who arrived from the Big Island a year earlier. Matsumura returned to Japan in 1936; he was succeeded by Rev. Koakutsu Hatsuhiko. Six years later, he was replaced by Rev. Masao Arine Masao, a Maui boy who went to Japan in 1941 to receive formal training. While studying he met his future wife, Torako Yamauchi,

The Tea House in the Japanese Tea Garden in Golden Gate Park, San Francisco, California. This Japanese Tea Garden is the oldest public Japanese garden in the United States and displays important elements of the Shinto religion in its design, including embracing nature as a spiritiual practice. (Vampy1/Dreamstime)

a Waipahu girl who had returned to Hiroshima with her mother and sister when she was seven. Less than six months after their return to Hawai'i, Pearl Harbor was attacked. As U.S. citizens, they at first avoided internment. However, Rev. Arine was later interned at the military camp in Haiku, Maui. After Arine's death in 1972, his wife assumed the responsibilities of Mau'i Jinsha and the Ebisu Kotohira Jinsha. Rev. Torako Arine continued to offer services one Sunday each month until 2013, when she was 99. She died May 16, 2014. In 1978 the shrine was placed on the National Register of Historical Places. The architect Takata Ichirō designed a traditional *nagare*-style shrine; it was constructed without the use of nails by Tomokiyo Sei'ichi and Takada Ichisaburō, first-generation immigrants.

Of the five shrines that once served Kaua'i, only markers remain. One such marker is on the grounds of the Kapa'a Sands resort. The four active shrines on O'ahu are Daijingu Temple, Hawai'i Kotohira Jinsha–Hawai'i Dazifu Tenmangu, Hawai'i Izumo Taishakyō, and Ishizuchi Jinja. Many of the shrines in Hawai'i are associated with shrines of the homeland of the immigrants. The recently established Tsubaki America and Tsubaki Kannagara Jinja are not part of the early Japanese immigrant experience.

In addition to their spiritual functions, Shinto shrines and priests served as purveyors of Japanese culture and identity. Much like the Buddhist temples, shrines built Japanese-language schools and offered a venue for festivals and other community activities. Kotohira Jinsha sponsored a Japan-Hawai'i Goodwill Sumo Tournament in 1956 between the All Japan High School Champions and Hawai'i Sumo Champions.

Beliefs and Practices

The *Kojiki*, *Nihongi*, and other ancient documents reveal that all manner of animate beings and inanimate things owe their existence to *kami*, a noble and sacred spirit that infuses life and vitality. Although *kami* may be everywhere and in all objects such as rocks and trees, and all beings, including humans, the Japanese normally identify *kami* with awe-inspiring natural phenomena and personalities who have demonstrated exceptional accomplishments. Perhaps the most famous natural *kami* is Mt. Fuji. Jimmu (ca. 660–585 BCE), the first emperor, and Emperor Meiji (1866–1912) have been deified as *kami*. Ancestral spirits are also referred to as *kami*. The above-mentioned Kato Jinsha deified the spirit of Kato Kiyomasa, a warlord of Higo during the Azuchi-Momoyama era (1568–1615).

Consistent with the belief that humanity shares and interacts with the world, and its denizens are sacred, the Shinto "lifestyle" is one of gratitude for the blessings bestowed by *kami* and to their ancestral spirits. Such a lifestyle is demonstrated through a sincere relationship with *kami* and through affection toward and cooperation with others that share the world. The devotee is expected to observe the proper ritual offerings and prayers, to make pilgrimages to sacred sites, and to remember to make sacrifices to their deceased ancestors. Neglect of any or all rituals can and often will invite *wazawai* (misfortune, calamity, curse). The *kami* in turn responds in a manner that is appropriate to the devotee's reverence or neglect thereof. A visit to the family grave or sponsoring a simple service is often enough to mollify a neglected ancestral *kami*. Traditionally *wazawai* was thought to be a form of *tsumi* (pollution, misfortune) that needed to be exorcised by *harae*, physical and/or spiritual purification, before the individual was allowed to reenter the community.

Shrines are also established to appease angry spirits. Daizifu Tenmangu, for example, was built to pacify the *goryō* (angry and vengeful spirit) of Sugawara no Michizane (845–903), who was ousted from his position as the minister of the right, the second-highest political post at the court. After his exile and subsequent death, the capital, Kyoto, was ravaged by a series of natural calamities and those who engineered his ouster suddenly died. In an effort to pacify his spirit, Michizane was posthumously pardoned, promoted in rank, and enshrined as Tenman, Kitano Daimyōjin, the highest rank of a *tenjin* or heavenly personality. These actions mollified Michizane's spirit; he is now honored as a *kami* of learning and literature. His shrine at the Kotohira Jinsha-Daizifu Tenmangu is frequented by students wishing for success in their educational pursuits. The practice of appeasing vengeful spirits continued during the early immigrant experience. Alarmed at the number of drownings of children and fishermen in 1913, Yamaguchi Susumu carved an image of Jizō to pacify vengeful spirits that lurked in and around Kawaihapai Bay, Mokuleia, Oʻahu.

Jizō (*Kṣitigarbha*) is a Buddhist spiritual hero, not a Shinto *kami*, but in the popular Japanese mind, he is identified with Sae no Kami, who is often seen in thoroughfares that lead into villages. In the *Kojiki*, Sae no kami stands watch on the boundary that divides the world of the living from that of the dead. Jizō is certainly the most appropriate *kami* for safeguarding from drowning. In his Buddhist guise, Jizō promised Śākyamuni Buddha that he would traverse the six hells and assist those in suffering until the future Maitreya appears. Jizō continues to fulfill his promise; the vengeful spirits that once lurked in the bay have since been pacified; drownings have ceased. The image was moved to the Wahiawa Ryūsenji temple in 2004.

It is not possible to build a shrine to mollify every vengeful spirit, but it is possible to control them through *harae*, a general expression for purification ceremonies designed to counter misfortune and pollution and restore ritual purity. Washing hands before approaching the *kami* is a form of *harae*. Before a bout, sumo wrestlers sprinkle salt to purify the ring of spirits that may be lurking nearby. New homes and new undertakings are blessed to avoid misfortune. Salt is sprinkled at the entryway after returning home from a funeral. This ritual prevents the spirit of the deceased, who may have followed the mourner home, from entering the house. Death is a form of *kegare* or pollution or defilement. *Kegare* from death still has considerable force in the Japanese community. If a death in the family has occurred, the traditional New Year pilgrimage to the shrine is forgone and New Year greeting cards are not sent.

In addition to appealing for protection, Japanese appeal to *kami* for protection from misfortune. *Yakudoshi* or "age of bad luck" is widely observed by Japanese in Hawai'i. The 42nd year for men and the 33rd for women are especially dangerous. In Japanese the numeral 4 is pronounced *shi* and 2 is voiced *ni*. Forty-two or *shini* in a different context means "to die." The number 33 is pronounced *sanzan*, which in a different situation can mean "disaster." Men and women who come of age can mitigate or even avoid the misfortunes of *yakudoshi* by visiting a shrine and/or sponsoring a large party. The present usage of the expression possesses little of its former meaning. The *kanji* or ideogram pronounced *yaku* means "misfortune" or "bad luck"; but the *kanji* for "duty" or "responsibility" is also pronounced *yaku*. Originally, *yakudoshi* marked an auspicious milestone that called for a celebration of longevity (*toshi iwai*). A person reaching a *yakudoshi* age underwent rituals of purification by abstinence and confinement and engaged in some sacred activity.

The *matsuri* or festivals that punctuate the calendar year are expressions of joy and gratitude, and celebrate the agricultural cycle and mark coming of age milestones and other events specific to the community. These celebrations, especially the planting and harvest *matsuri*, are shared by the entire community, regardless of faith affiliation. Some of the more important observances are *hatsumode, momo no sekku, tango no sekku, tanabata,* and *shichi-gosan. Hatsumōde* is the first visit to the shrine in the New Year. The devotee recommits him- or herself to a life of gratitude and asks *kami* for health and prosperity for him- or herself and for the family. Celebrated in early February, *setsubun* marks the first day of spring according to the lunar calendar. *Momo no sekku* marks the blooming of the peach blossoms; the third day of the third month is Girl's Day. *Tango no sekku* is the season of the iris; the fifth day of the fifth month is Boy's Day. *Tanabata* or star festival celebrates the meeting of the deities Orihime and Hikoboshi (represented by the stars Vega and Altair, respectively) who meet only once a year on the seventh day of the seventh lunar month. On this occasion wishes are written on color strips of paper and hung on bamboo sprays. *Shichi-go-san* (Seven-Five-Three) marks the rite of passage for girls five to seven years of age, and boys three to five years of age. On November 15th, children wearing traditional kimonos visit the shrines to pray for health and for protection against misfortune.

Miyamairi is the custom of bringing a newborn to a shrine a month after birth. On this visit the priest blesses the child and wards off any pollutants. Shrines also provide, for a fee, *omamori*, amulets to hang on the car's rearview mirror for protection from accidents. There are amulets imbued with the spirit of a protector *kami* to ensure protection of the home from fire and other calamities, safe childbirth, success in business, and luck in finding love. Priests often perform purification rituals at the construction of a new home. They are called to exorcise homes from the pollution of death or bless a new venture.

Although the shrine is a sacred site where the *kami* can be invited and where the people can experience its presence, traditional Japanese families maintain a *kamidana* or home shrine where daily offerings are made. Families often place images of *shichifukujin*, the seven *kamis* of good fortune, and other symbols on the *kamidana* to ensure longevity, happiness, and luck. But perhaps the most ubiquitous presence of the Shinto lifestyle is the Japanese obsession with cleaning, especially during the waning days of December. The home must be spotless to welcome the New Year.

See also: Japanese American Religions

Further Reading

Cali, Joseph, and John Dougill. *Shintō Shrines, A Guide to the Sacred Sites of Japan's Ancient Religion.* Honolulu: University of Hawai'i Press, 2013.

Herbert, Jean. *Shintō: At the Fountain-head of Japan.* London: George Allen & Unwin, 1967.

Michael Maricio

SOKA GAKKAI

Soka Gakkai International (SGI) is a lay Buddhist organization with roots in Nichiren Buddhism, particularly Nichiren Shōshū Established in the United States in the early 1960s, it existed under the name Nichiren Shōshū of America (NSA) until 1991, after which it changed its name to Soka Gakkai International–USA (SGIUSA). Of the so-called New Japanese Religions, Soka Gakkai has become the largest and most ethnically diverse. According to the organization's own estimates there are currently 126,806 members in the United States. According to information obtained from SGI-USA headquarters, California had the largest membership in 2013, claiming 37,655 members.

Beliefs and Practices

Soka Gakkai was a lay association of the Nichiren Shōshū sect until 1991 and its beliefs and practices generally adhere to the main teachings of Nichiren Buddhism. Nichiren Buddhism was founded by the former Tendai priest Nichiren Daishōnin (1222–1282). Nichiren viewed the *Saddharma Puṇḍarīka* or *Lotus Sūtra* as the most important of Buddhist teachings, particularly the idea that the Buddha-nature is already within all sentient beings and that enlightenment can be attained through the wisdom of the *Lotus Sūtra*. Individual enlightenment in turn engenders social peace. Nichiren taught that three great secret laws of Buddhism would appear in a period when the Buddha Dharma was in decline, known as *mappō*. The three laws were the importance of the *Dai-Gohonzon*, the *daimoku*, and the *kaidan*.

Daimoku is both the phrase "*Nammyōhō-renge-kyō*," variously translated as "I devote myself to the Mystic Law of the *Lotus Sūtra*" or "hail to the wonderful Dharma *Lotus Sūtra*," and the activity of invoking the phrase through chant.

The *Dai-Gohonzon* is a wooden *maṇḍala* inscribed late in life by Nichiren with the name of the *Lotus Sūtra* in Chinese characters and Nichiren's signature surrounded by the names of individuals representing various life conditions, ranging from demons, teachers, and heavenly kings to bodhisattvas and Buddhas. The object of highest veneration in Nichiren Shōshū Buddhism, it is housed at the head temple, Taisekiji, at the foot of Mt. Fuji. It is thought to embody the Dharma and also to embody Nichiren, who, as an incarnation of the eternal Buddha, infused his enlightenment into his original *gohonzons*. A copy of the *Dai-Gohonzon*, a *gohonzon*, is given to the adherent in a formal ceremony, *gojukai*, and is placed on the home altar. Saying the *daimoku* in front of the *gohonzon* is known as *shodai* and is considered to be highly efficacious for the realization of one's own true nature and for the attainment of supreme enlightenment. Practitioners may also engage in *gangyo*, the exercise of reading sections of the *Lotus Sūtra*, especially the 2nd chapter and the 16th chapter, emphasizing the teachings of the inherent Buddha-nature of all sentient beings and that Buddhahood is attained from within rather than externally. Chanting the *daimoku* before the *gohonzon* thus constitutes the core practice of Soka Gakkai and is the means to bring about spiritual transformation in the individual or, as the second president Josei Toda called it, "human revolution." Practice brings one into harmony with the basic rhythm of the Dharma that underlies the universe, enabling individuals to face the challenges of their own lives and to realize, according to the organization's Web site, "one's unique life purpose." Then through individual change social and global change can begin.

Finally, Nichiren taught that the *kaidan*, the most important Buddhist sanctuary, would appear in the age of *mappō*. Nichiren Shōshū has identified Taisekiji temple as the *kaidan*, and as a result pilgrimage to Taisekiji has always been essential. Since the occlusion of the group by Nichiren Shōshū in 1991, Soka Gakkai members have been prohibited from entering Taisekiji.

Although chanting the *daimoku* continues to be the core practice of Soka Gakkai, the break with Nichiren Shōshū has led the organization into more progressive directions, prioritizing lay leadership, especially among women and minorities. Although Nichiren Shōshū, and Nichiren Buddhism in general, claim exclusivity, Soka Gakkai has shown a greater tolerance for other faith positions. The overall emphasis now is on personal, social, and global peace and prosperity, starting with the individual, and a firm belief in the possibilities for happiness and peace in this world, rather than one to come. SGI-USA currently engages in numerous cultural, educational, and social initiatives including advocating for peace and disarmament, ecological sustainability, human rights, and intercultural and interfaith dialogue.

History

The history of Soka Gakkai can be easily organized according to its three presidents: Tsunesaburo Makiguchi (1871–1944), Josei Toda (1900–1958), and Daisaku Ikeda (1928–). Founded by Makiguchi in 1937, Soka Gakkai originally started as Sōka Kyōiku Gakkai (Value Creation Education Society). Focused on Makiguchi's ideas of progressive education that stressed individual initiative, benefit, and critical thought, at first the organization had no connection to Nichiren Shōshū. After his own conversion to Nichiren Shōshū, Makiguchi practiced chanting with others in his education club. Although there was no formal association between the two, Makiguchi's education advocacy and his faith commitments became more connected to the point that he and other Sōka Kyōiku Gakkai leaders were imprisoned in 1943 for treason due to their opposition to State Shintoism. Makiguchi died in prison in 1944. His close disciple Josei Toda was released in 1945 and would become Sōka Kyōiku Gakkai's second president in 1951.

It was Toda who, after the war, shifted the organization's focus from education to spiritual practice, supported by his religious vision informed by Nichiren's idea of *kosen-rufu*, a term that connotes both the conversion of the world to true Buddhism and a utopian vision of a world peace and harmony. In 1951, he changed the name to Soka Gakkai and formally made the organization a lay association of Nichiren Shōshū, placing members under the authority of the Nichiren priesthood and giving them access to priest services such as weddings and funerals. The association between Soka Gakkai and Nichiren Shōshū would provide mutual benefits for many years, giving Soka Gakkai institutional legitimacy and providing Nichiren Shōshū with new members, financial resources, and contemporary relevance. At the time of Toda's death in 1958 the movement had experienced phenomenal growth in Japan thanks to its aggressive form of proselytization known as *shakubuku*.

Daisaku Ikeda became president of Soka Gakkai in 1960. Under his leadership the organization would grow considerably in its membership, geographic coverage, and variety of activities. While *shakubuku*-style proselytization continued, Soka Gakkai also extended its reach through cultural and political institutions. Ikeda established the Soka Gakkai Culture Bureau in 1961, which produced public-image friendly projects such as the Tokyo Fuji Art Museum, the Min-On Concert Association, and Soka Schools. Politically, Soka Gakkai became active in 1955, sponsoring candidates and eventually forming its own party, Komeito, in 1964. The close association of a "religious" group with a political party caused controversy and eventually Soka Gakkai formally separated itself from Komeito. Such a direct involvement in politics has never been a priority of SGI-USA. Perhaps most significantly, Ikeda shifted the focus of Soka Gakkai to global outreach. During the 1960s the organization expanded globally, including its establishment in the United States.

Soka Gakkai's first American members were primarily Japanese immigrants, especially Japanese women who had married American servicemembers. Through their efforts, families and friends were brought into contact with the group. In 1960, the first formal organization was founded, Soka Gakkai of America. The name was changed to Nichiren Shōshū of America. An American headquarters was established in Santa Monica, California, in the early 1960s, under the informal leadership of Masayasu Sadanaga who would later change his name to George Williams. Intensive *shakubuku* grew the organization's numbers through street solicitations, home meetings, college activities, and large cultural festivals. Through these efforts Soka Gakkai in America experienced explosive growth in the 1960s and 1970s.

Among the new religious movements that emerged from Japan in the mid-20th century, Soka Gakkai has had the most success in attracting new members, and it is also the movement that has become the least tied to Japanese ethnicity. In early stages, diversification could result in tension, such as using chairs when reciting the *Sūtra* instead of sitting on the floor, or translating key teachings into English, questioning how essential the Japanese language was for practice. Rather than being an insular means to protect one's Japanese identity, Soka Gakkai was seen as something that transcended ethnicity. Indeed, the early decision to use English at meetings is one key reason Soka Gakkai was able to reach out to non-Japanese individuals.

According to SGI-USA, they do not keep track of ethnic data anymore, but a study by Phillip Hammond and David Machacek in 1997 found that Caucasian Americans were the largest ethnic group, constituting about 42 percent of membership, while Asian Americans constituted 23 percent. There were also a significant number of African Americans and Latinos. As an international movement that encourages members to think of themselves as "global citizens," the cultural link between Soka Gakkai and Japan has been more or less severed. Indeed, sociological studies in the United States, Britain, and Australia have suggested that it is Soka Gakkai's global perspective that attracts many adherents in postindustrial societies, individuals who value a cosmopolitan outlook and self-expression. Inasmuch as SGI-USA aims to cultivate world peace and intercultural exchange, its ability to transcend association with any particular ethnic group may be viewed as a success.

The separation from Nichiren Shōshū reinforced the weakening of Soka Gakkai America's connection to its Japanese roots. As growth leveled by the end of the 1970s, outreach shifted from aggressive proselytization to a focus on social, cultural, and educational activities. At the same time there was less militant commitment to the uniqueness of Nichiren Shōshū, a position strongly advocated by Toda. In this way Ikeda recast the idea of *kosen-rufu* to mean the broad dissemination of, rather than the conversion of the world to, Nichiren Buddhism. The tremendous expansion of Soka Gakkai globally and its changing methods and activities distanced it from the Nichiren Shōshū priesthood. After this formal separation from Nichiren Shōshū the organization as a whole changed its name to Soka Gakkai International. Those who left SGI and stayed loyal to the Nichiren priesthood adopted the name Nichiren Shōshū Temple. One of the greatest obstacles posed by the break was obtaining copies of the *gohonzon* for new adherents since only the priests were authorized to consecrate additional *gohonzons* based on the original. However, SGI obtained a version transcribed by Nichikan Shonin in 1720, which serves as the basis for *gohonzons* issued today.

Overall, the break with Nichiren Shōshū has proved of little consequence, even enabling SGI-USA to pursue its progressive agenda further. Although the core practice of *daimoku* is still a central part of its identity, SGI-USA currently engages in a wide variety of cultural, educational, and social initiatives. Supporting this work are Soka Gakkai's extensive publications, particularly the weekly newspaper *World Tribune*, published since 1964, and *Living Buddhism*, a journal published since 1981 (titled *Seikyo Times* until 1997). Awareness of changing demographics is seen in the fact that subscribers to the *World Tribune* in the United States can receive language supplements in Japanese, Chinese, Korean, Thai/Cambodian, French, and Portuguese. Completely Spanish versions of both are also published, *La Tribuen del Mundo* and *Esperanza*. Finally, SGI-USA's activities extend beyond the bounds of SGI-USA proper through parainstitutions founded by Ikeda such as the Ikeda Center for Peace, Learning, and Dialogue in Cambridge, Massachusetts, and Soka University of America in Aliso Viejo, California, drawing the organization full circle back to the Nichiren Buddhist–inspired value education of Makiguchi.

See also: Japanese American Religions; Nichiren Shōshū

Further Reading

Prebish, Charles S. *Luminous Passage: The Practice and Study of Buddhism in America.* Berkeley: University of California Press, 1999.

Seager, Richard Hughes. *Buddhism in America.* New York: Columbia University Press, 1999.

Seager, Richard Hughes. *Encountering the Dharma: Daisaku Ikeda, Soka Gakkai, and the Globalization of Buddhist Humanism.* Berkeley: University of California Press, 2006.

Peter L. Doebler

SŌTŌ ZEN

Sōtōshū, a major Japanese Zen Buddhist tradition in Hawai'i and the continental United States, traces its ideological underpinnings to the insights Eihei Dōgen Zenji (1200–1253) received from Tiandong Rujing Chanshi (Japanese, Tendō Nyojō Zenji, 1163–1228), the 13th patriarch of the Chinese Caodong or Sōtō Zen linage. Dōgen returned to Japan in 1227 or 1228 and later founded Eiheiji Temple. The Japanese Sōtō tradition recognizes Dōgen, together with Keizan Jōkin Zenji (1268–1325), who established Sōjiji Temple, to be its "Two Founders." Keizan Jōkin and his disciples popularized the Sōtōshū tradition among the common people by moving away from the strict monastic discipline set forth by Dōgen. At present, there are approximately 15,000 Sōtō Zen temples throughout Japan and 30 training monasteries, including the two most important, Eiheiji and Sōjiji.

History—Hawai'i

Sōtōshū formally established itself in Hawai'i in 1903 when the Rev. Sen'ei Kawahara (?–1908) founded Taiyōji in Waipahu, O'ahu, and Rev. Ryōun Kan (1854–1917) established Zenshūji in Wahiawa, Kaua'i (the temple relocated to Hanapepe in 1977). There are currently seven other active temples. Sōtō

Mission of Hawai'i, Shōbōji Betsuin, in the heart of Honolulu, was founded in 1913. In 1921, Shōbōji became the head temple of the denomination's Hawai'i district, and its chief priest or *sōkan* became its administrative head. Ryūsenji, located in Wahiawa in central O'ahu, was established in 1904. Mantokuji Sōtō Mission of Paia, Maui, was founded in 1906. In 1914, Daifukuji Sōtō Mission was established in Kona, Hawai'i. In 1915, Taishōji was founded in Hilo, also on the island of Hawai'i. Founded in 1918, Taiheiji is located in Aiea on O'ahu. Founded in 1927, Guzeiji Sōtō Mission is the only Buddhist temple on the island of Molokai. As of 2013 these nine temples provide the spiritual needs for approximately 1,700 families who offer regular financial support.

Sōtōshū temples were originally established to serve the Japanese immigrant communities that were attached to the sugar plantations. The communities welcomed the priests, who embodied the customs and traditions of their homeland. In addition to their clerical responsibilities, the priests established Japanese-language schools and assisted the Japanese community in innumerable ways with living in a foreign country. The temples also served as community centers and venues for long-established festivals. Present-day temples and clerics continue to serve the spiritual needs of the descendants of the first immigrants with weekly Sunday services, annual rituals to celebrate important milestones in the life of the Buddha and the temples' founders. Priests lead the weekly *zazen* or sitting meditation and study sessions, and perform marriage ceremonies, funerals, and memorial services. The temples carry on as community and cultural centers, offering lessons in martial arts, flower arranging, tea ceremony, folk dancing and singing, and Japanese drums. Sōtō Mission of Hawai'i Shōbōji founded Sōtō Academy, a K–6 elementary school, where in addition to its regular curriculum, Japanese language and Kumon math are offered. The state of Hawai'i accredited the academy in 1990.

History—Continental United States

Like the Sōtō Zen temples in Hawai'i, the temples on the continental United States primarily serve the spiritual and social needs of the Japanese American community. At present, there are five Sōtō Zen temples, all in California. Founded in 1922, Zenshūji in Los Angeles has the largest membership. Sōkōji in San Francisco, the second oldest, was established in 1934. The other three are Long Beach Buddhist Church (1957), Sōzenji in Montebello (1972), and Monterey Zenshūji Soto Zen Temple in Monterey (1955). These five temples serve approximately 360 families and 43 individual members.

Sōtōshū devotees residing in and around Little Tokyo in Los Angeles invited Rev. Hōsen Isobe (1877–1953), who was at the time in Hawai'i, to establish Zenshūji Sōtō Mission. Isobe and his community faced strong anti-Japanese sentiments. Like other Japanese Buddhist temples, Zenshūji Sōtō Mission provided a refuge where the immigrant community could continue to nurture their spiritual identity and stay connected with the homeland. The community collected and sent relief aid to the victims of the 1923 Great Tokyo Earthquake. In 1924 the U.S. government passed the Immigration Act of 1924 or Johnson–Reed Act, including the National Origins Act and Asian Exclusion Act.

Responding to the Japanese attack on Pearl Harbor in 1941, President Franklin Delano Roosevelt (1882–1945) signed Executive Order 9066 incarcerating Japanese nationals and Japanese American citizens, who were believed to be threats to the national security. Zenshūji, like other Japanese Buddhist temples, warehoused the belongings of its members, who were allowed to take only two suitcases of their personal effects with them. Likewise the temples served as hostels for the returning internees while they rebuilt their lives. As a result of this dislocation, many members of the community moved away from the Little Tokyo area of Los Angeles, eroding the Zenshūji's membership and its financial base. Zenshūji celebrated the 90th anniversary of its founding in 2012.

In 1937, Zenshūji was designated as Ryōdai Honzan Betsuin Zenshūji, head temple of the North American District. With this designation its *sōkan* or head priest became the director of the Sōtō Zen Buddhism North America Office, a jurisdiction that extends from Canada to Panama. Rev. Banjō Sagumo (?–1956) served as the first director. Initially the director exerted most of his energies on the needs of the Japanese American community. However, as a result of the great interest in Zen Buddhism that emerged in the late 1950s, the director's responsibilities now include supervising more than 50 Sōtō Zen centers and more than 360 American Sōtō Zen priests scattered throughout North America.

Rev. Shunryū Suzuki (1904–1971), who served as the resident priest at Sōkōji from 1959 to 1969, played a large role in the spread of Sōtō Zen beyond the Japanese American community. Suzuki arrived in San Francisco at a most opportune moment; it was the end of the beat movement and just before the social movements of the 1960s. Persons associated with these movements were searching for alternative visions and approaches to the Vietnam War, racial discrimination, pollution, and poverty. In the meantime, D. T. Suzuki's (1870–1966) lectures and writings on Buddhism and Zen, in particular, appealed to many intellectuals and artists, who were drawn to the Zen emphasis on simple living, being in tune with nature, the nonviolent nature of Buddhism, and its art and aesthetics. Although the teaching and practice of Sōtō Zen was available at Zenshūji, Sōkōji, and other temples, they were not accessible to those who did not speak Japanese.

Shunryū Suzuki, who spoke English, attracted many beatnik and hippie types to the morning *zazen* sessions at Sōkōji; they soon outnumbered the Japanese American membership. This led to the establishment of the San Francisco Zen Center in 1962, which together with other subsequent centers provided an opportunity for persons who wanted to engage in *zazen* meditation and to learn about different aspects of Buddhist thought and culture. Today these centers offer meditation retreats, instruction for sewing robes, and meditation paraphernalia, as well as outreach opportunities in prisons, hospices, and with homeless people, based on Buddhist ideals of wisdom and compassionate practice.

These interests stand in contrast to the Japanese American devotees who grew up in the temple and for whom temple membership is a family and cultural tradition. While Obon, the festival honoring their ancestors, and the spring and autumn Ohigan are traditional Buddhist services, the Japanese American membership associate them as rituals that connect them with their ancestors and events that foster community solidarity. They associate the temple with funeral and memorial rites, and weddings and births that mark important personal and community milestones. *Shōtsuki hōyō* is a monthly service in memory of those members who passed away during the month; their names are read as part of the service.

Rev. Dainin Katagiri (1928–1990) and Rev. Hakuyū Maezumi (1931–1995) were also instrumental in spreading Sōtō Zen's teaching and practice beyond the Japanese American community. Katagiri assisted Suzuki with the establishment of the San Francisco Zen Center. In 1972, he relocated to Minneapolis, Minnesota, to establish the Minnesota Zen Meditation Center and later Hōkyōji Zen Practice Community. He returned briefly to the San Francisco Zen Center to guide it through an especially difficult period. He returned to Minnesota in 1984 where he died in 1990. He left 12 Dharma heirs (disciples who were given formal permission to be full-fledged priests). Hakuyū Maezumi is another influential figure. He founded Busshinji, also known as the Zen Center of Los Angeles, in 1968 and certified 12 Dharma heirs, ordained 68 priests, and administered the Buddhist precepts to more than 500 practitioners. Maezumi died unexpectedly while visiting Japan.

Beliefs and Practices

Dōgen Zenji was ordained at a young age; but during the course of his study, he was troubled by what seemed to be a contradiction. It appears that his question emerged from the following passage that appears in the *Mahāparinirvāṇa Sūtra* (*Nirvāṇa Sūtra*): "All living beings in their entirety have the Buddha-nature: the Tathāgata abides [in them] constantly, without changing at all." If all sentient beings possess the Buddha-nature and the Tathāgata or Buddha is present in all beings, why, then, did Śākyamuni Buddha and all previous Dharma masters need to undergo such rigorous spiritual training?

Dōgen visited many Japanese Buddhist teachers and inquired about his question, but did not receive a satisfactory answer. Finally, he was advised to go to China. After three years of intense study under Rujing Chanshi, Dōgen had a spiritual awakening. He explains in the "Busshō" (Buddha-nature) chapter in the *Shōbōgenzō* (*Treasury of the True Dharma Eye*) that the Zen student must verify for him or herself the reality and truth that indeed he or she possesses the Buddha-nature and that the Tathāgata (Buddha) resides in him or her. To this end the student must first bring forth the aspiration to awaken to his or her Buddha-nature and practice the form of meditation known as *shikantaza*.

Although often translated as "just sitting" and usually associated with sitting in meditation, *shikantaza* is not properly a practice. "Practice" implies a goal or end to be achieved. Because Buddha-nature is intrinsic, that is, it resides in each person, there is no need to engage in *zazen* meditation to realize Buddha-hood or enlightenment. This is the way it is from the viewpoint of the Dharma and for one who has verified this reality for him or herself. However, from the viewpoint of the ego-self, there is always a separation between the self and other things. According to the Sōtō Zen teaching, it is necessary to verify for oneself the nature of this reality. For this reason, it inevitably becomes necessary to start with the practice of *shikantaza*, the objective of which is to eliminate the sense of separation between the ego-self and other things. Rather than only sitting in *zazen*, this practice must be carried out in every activity that in and of itself affirms the reality of the Buddha-nature and is thus an expression of enlightenment. In the end, *shikantaza* is a description of the awakened state of someone who has let go of dualistic consciousness as well as the name of one form of *zazen*.

To be sure, sitting in *zazen* is the central practice in Sōtō Zen, but practice is not restricted to *zazen* meditation. In 1227 or 1228, the year he returned from China, Dōgen clearly states in *Fukanzazengi* (*A Universal Recommendation for Zazen*) that *zazen* is not restricted "to sitting." The goal of practice is to eliminate the illusion that one's self is separate from one's actions and that the self is separate from all things and beings. The spiritual end for Sōtō Zen is to awaken to the essential oneness of all things, beings, and events. It is to realize that every existent thing has always been, is, and will be within the causal connections of interdependence. To be aware of and live with this awareness in one's daily life is Zen realization. Dōgen summarized the essentials of this reality in "Genjōkōan" (Manifesting Suchness): "To study the Way of Buddha is to study the Self; to study the Self is to forget the ego-self; to forget the ego-self is to be enlightened by all things."

In Japan, *zazen* practice is traditionally associated with monks and nuns. Although there have always been lay persons who have practiced meditation, it is not possible for most people to engage in extended and intense *zazen* meditation. For such devotees Dōgen prescribed the *shishōbō* or four true teachings of generosity, loving speech, actions that benefit others, and mutual identification. By observing these virtues in daily life, the layperson can let go of the belief in the self and realize the self in all things. These four practices figure prominently in the *Shushōgi* (*The Meaning of Practice and Realization*), a document that was created from quotations from Dōgen Zenji's *Shōbōgenzō* at the end of the 19th century to encourage and outline the doctrine that would lead to proper living as a means to awaken to one's Buddha-nature and to affirm the Buddha in him- or herself.

Conclusion

Zenshūji and other Sōtōshū temples that serve the Japanese American community are experiencing declining membership. This is due in part to the passing of those elders who founded the temples. Those issues that prompted the founding of the temples—cultural and ethnic nostalgia, a refuge from the pressures of discrimination, and a venue for traditional events—are no longer pressing concerns. Their children and grandchildren have many other spiritual options and do not have the strong ties to Japanese culture and society that their elders once did. Whether the present membership can reconnect with the spiritual resources of Sōtōshū or rekindle its ancestral ties or remake itself to adjust to modernization to support the existence of its temples are open questions. The membership and its priests are experimenting with ways to continue to serve the needs of their Japanese American constituencies and to attract those who may wish to practice and study Zen Buddhism in such a context.

See also: Japanese American Religions; Rinzai Zen

Further Reading

Asai, Senryō, and Duncan Williams. "Japanese-American Zen Temples: Cultural Identity and Economics." In *American Buddhism*, edited by Duncan Williams and Christopher Queen, 20–35. London: Curzon Press, 1998.

Preston, David. *The Social Organization of Zen Practice: Constructing Transcultural Reality*. New York: Cambridge University Press, 1988.

Daigaku Rummé

TAIKO PERFORMANCE

Taiko is a Japanese term that refers to both a barrel-shaped drum and the art of drumming on it with two wooden sticks. As a sacred object and a musical instrument, it has taken various forms and styles in the traditional sociocultural context of Japan, such as seasonal customs and festivals in local communities, religious rituals in Shinto shrines or Buddhist temples, and professional performing arts such as Noh and Kabuki plays. Out of such a conventional, or often preindustrial, context, a new form of taiko was reinvented by young

Three female drummers in a taiko performance, 2009. The taiko movement over the years has resulted in the formation of over 100 taiko groups across North America, including Hawai'i. (Jinlide/Dreamstime)

enthusiasts in the rise of the folk "revival" movement in Japanese society in the 1960s. It took shape as a taiko-only genre, which usually takes the form of a group performance, combining several different kinds of taiko drums. Although the presentation of taiko in the conventional framework required adherence to the given rules, this emergent form of taiko has the flexibility to be adopted in a changing contemporary setting, increasing the dynamic aspects of performances. Taiko performers, in this form, typically put on the preindustrial artisan-like outfits—happi (short kimono), hachimaki (headband), momohiki (long underpants), harakake (apron), and jika-tabi (split-toed shoes with rubber soles) and emphasize manly physical postures and movements, giving martial-arts-like images of judo and karate.

The significance of the performance of taiko is its symbolic implication in popular rhetoric and imagination, in which taiko manifests the authentic "tradition" of Japanese culture, handed down from the ancient past, despite actually being a recent reconstruction. The symbolic meanings of taiko were transmitted across the Pacific and reinterpreted in Japanese American communities in the West Coast in the late 1960s as the economic and political interrelations strengthened between Japan and the United States. Taiko performance mediated Japanese and Japanese Americans, who had been separated during World War II and by the discontinuation of Japanese immigration. It brought about a festive milieu, in which Japanese and Japanese Americans interacted and reunited in the Japanese tradition.

The beginning of Japanese American taiko has been legendarily attributed to the Cherry Blossom Festival in San Francisco in 1968, in which the manly taiko performance of a newly arrived Japanese youth, Seiichi Tanaka, inspired Japanese American audiences to revitalize a then-declining community. Following his group, named San Francisco Taiko Dojo, young Japanese Americans began to organize their own taiko groups one after another. Like the pioneering group Kinnara Taiko formed in Los Angeles in 1969, many Japanese American taiko groups were affiliated with Buddhist temples, which had been the center of life for many of the prewar Japanese immigrants living on the West Coast.

Japanese American taiko groups proliferated during the 1970s and thereafter, and the taiko movement over the years has resulted in the formation of over 100 taiko groups across North America, including Hawai'i. Important to this phenomenal popularity of taiko performance among Japanese American communities are the sociohistorical contexts, particularly of the Asian American movement in the 1970s and the redress movement in the 1980s in which Japanese Americans attempted to reclaim their history in relation to the larger American society. Due to the expansive force of globalization, taiko, as a symbol of Japanese tradition, has become a locus of cultural politics, negotiation, and reconstruction of Japanese and Japanese American identity.

See also: Matsuri

Further Reading

Konagaya, Hideyo. "Taiko as Performance: Creating Japanese American Traditions." *Japanese Journal of American Studies* 12 (2001): 105–124.

Schnell, Scott. *The Rousing Drum: Ritual Practice in a Japanese Community*. Honolulu: University of Hawai'i Press, 1999.

Hideyo Konagaya

TRADITIONAL MEDICINE AND HEALING

Traditional Japanese medicine (Kampo) is an adaptation of traditional Chinese medicine that was transmitted to Japan in the seventh and eighth centuries. It was largely practiced throughout Japan until 1849 with the introduction of the smallpox vaccination, as the government speculated that its continued usage would interrupt the spread of modernization throughout Japan. It remained in decline for roughly 50 years, after which it underwent a revival. Because the government no longer perceived it as a threat to modernization, Kampo was again permitted to be practiced and eventually integrated into Japanese modern medicinal practices.

The amount of core herbs that are used is one of the distinguishing characteristics of Kampo from traditional Chinese medicine. While the Chinese system uses approximately 500 different herbs and drugs to treat the various ailments, the Japanese system uses between 100 and 200. Of these, most are of vegetable origin with only a very small number coming from animal sources. They are usually obtained from substances that are native to Japan, and thus are easy to obtain while at the same time fitting within the Japanese cultural context and identity. Further, the dosage amounts in Japan are markedly reduced from those in traditional Chinese medicine, often suggesting less than half of what might be prescribed in China.

There are a number of forms in which the herbs are administered within the Kampo system, such as capsules, tablets, teas, and a process called "moxibustion." In this process the herb (usually mugwort) is applied directly to the skin (or indirectly through the use of acupuncture) and burned. This process is considered particularly effective when the patient is suffering from chronic conditions such as depression or hyperactivity. In both moxibustion and acupuncture, the goal is to stimulate the meridians to overcome the imbalance producing the ailment.

Kampo was introduced to North America via Dr. Hong-yen Hsu, who emigrated to the United States from Taiwan. He studied pharmaceutical science in Japan and became interested in the formulas and writings of Japanese doctors. In 1975, Dr. Hong-yen Hsu established the Oriental Healing Arts Institute (OHAI) and the Brion Herbs Corporation. These two companies were created to translate Japanese Kampo texts, distribute Kampo medicines throughout North America, as well as translate Chinese texts and distribute Chinese remedies.

In North America today, there are few Kampo-specific medical practitioners outside of the Japanese communities. Due to the combining of Chinese and Japanese medicines in North America through OHAI and Brion Herbs Corporation, much of the understanding of Kampo falls under the heading of alternative medicine and is typically used in combination with other East Asian remedies. The distinguishing feature between Japanese and other East Asian forms of medicine used in North America today is typically in the application of acupuncture needles. In Kampo, the needles are inserted just below the skin to stimulate the meridians as opposed to piercing them (as in some Chinese forms of application). It is believed that this light stimulation is all that is required to achieve the desired results.

A later development in Japanese forms of treatment is Shiatsu massage. Although it was likely used prior to 1940, it was not until then that Tokujiro

Namikoshi made Shiatsu a formalized system at the Japan Shiatsu College. This is a method of massage using the thumbs or the palm of one's hands to apply pressure to the patient. The patient's nervous system is purportedly stimulated through different levels of pressure and release on particular points of the body. This method of stimulation is only recognized in Japan as a viable form of therapy, but its popularity among massage therapists in North America is growing substantially.

See also: Japanese American Religions; Aikido in America

Further Reading

Otsuka, Keisetsu. *Kampo: A Clinical Guide to Theory and Practice.* New York: Churchill Livingstone, 2010.

Rister, Robert. *Japanese Herbal Medicine: The Healing Art of Kampo.* New York: Avery Publishing Group, 1999.

Tsumira, Akira. *Kampo: How the Japanese Updated Traditional Herbal Medicine.* New York: Japan Publications U.S.A., 1991.

Christina R. Yanko

PART IV

LITERATURE, THE ARTS, POPULAR CULTURE, AND SPORTS: PEOPLE, MOVEMENTS, AND EXPRESSIONS OF IDENTITY

HISTORICAL OVERVIEW

Japanese American creative works—literary, visual, multimedia—and popular cultural expressions are all informed by their historical experience, in particular the shameful internment of Japanese Americans during World War II, and their urgent need—then and now—to claim their subjectivity as "American citizens" and be fully American. This core struggle to be Japanese and American is best illustrate by John Okada's *No-No Boy* (1957) when Ichiro Yamada says:

> No, he said to himself as he watched her part the curtains and start into the store. There was a time when I was your son. There was a time that I no longer remember when you used to smile a mother's smile and tell me stories about gallant and fierce warriors who protected their lords with blades of shining steel and about the old woman who found a peach in the stream and took it home and, when her husband split it in half, a husky little boy tumbled out to fill their hearts with boundless joy. I was that boy in the peach and you were the old woman and we were Japanese with Japanese feelings and Japanese pride and Japanese thoughts because it was all right then to be Japanese and feel and think all the things that Japanese do even if we lived in America. Then there came a time when I was only half Japanese because one is not born in America and raised in America and taught in America and one does not speak and swear and drink and smoke and play and fight and see and hear in America among Americans in American streets and houses without becoming American and loving it. But I did not love enough, for you were still half my mother and I was thereby still half Japanese and when the war came and they

Street scene in winter at the Manzanar Relocation Center, one of ten camps where Japanese American citizens and resident Japanese aliens were interned during World War II. (Library of Congress)

told me to fight for America, I was not strong enough to fight you and I was not strong enough to fight the bitterness which made the half of me which was you bigger than the half of me which was America and really the whole of me that I could not see or feel. Now that I know the taught when it is too late and the half of me which was you is no longer there, I am only half of me and the half that remains is American by law because the government was wise and strong enough to know why it was that I could not fight for America and did not strip me of my birthright. But it is not enough to be American only in the eyes of the law and it is not enough to be only half an American and know that it is an empty half. I am not your son and I am not Japanese and I am not American. (15–16)

The question and issue of loyalty became a complex and critical one: Japanese American internees had to negotiate the violation of their civil rights and their desire to support the United States, many by joining the U.S. military. How can they reconcile being loyal to a country that did not show loyalty to them and their families? This issue caused a divide among the Nisei, second-generation Japanese Americans, who wanted to prove their loyalty, and the Issei, first-generation Japanese Americans, who felt betrayed for being accused of being "disloyal." The internment camp administrators began to employ the loyalty questionnaire as a way to determine the loyalty of internees who were more than 17 years of age. It was also a means of replenishing the

442nd and 100th U.S. Army units' casualties. In a survey for Japanese American civilians from the Department of War and the War Relocation Authority (WRA) in 1943, two questions generated the most conflict:

27. Are you willing to serve in the armed forces of the United States on combat duty, wherever ordered?
28. Will you swear unqualified allegiance to the United States of America and faithfully defend the United States from any and all attack by foreign or domestic forces and foreswear any form of allegiance to the Japanese Emperor?

Questions 27 and 28 evoked anger, frustration, and resistance, most notably among young Japanese American men. Some mainland Nisei youths (Nisei from the North American continent as opposed to Hawai'i) saw no reason to fight for a government that had dispossessed them and their families of their civil rights and private property. As well, among older Japanese Americans men and women, the questions caused uncertainty because they knew about military age and gender restrictions. Question 28 asked Japanese Americans to renounce their allegiance and citizenship to Japan and its emperor, but since they were not allowed to become naturalized citizens of the United States, many feared that they would be stateless.

In some camps, leaders met to discuss how the two questions should be answered. Issei and Kibei (Japanese Americans who were born in the United States but were raised for a time in Japan) who supported Japan and wanted a way to protest the treatment of Japanese Americans since Pearl Harbor encouraged the Nisei to answer "no" to both questions. Those who qualified their answers to both questions were considered to have answered "no." Men answering "no" to both questions became known as the "No-No Boys." About 10 percent of draft-age Issei and Nisei Japanese Americans interned by the U.S. government answered "no" to both questions. The loyalty test caused strain on Japanese American families. Some simply answered "yes" to avoid being separated from their families.

In Jeanne Wakatsuki Houston's *Farewell to Manzanar* (1973), the loyalty debate forces Papa out of his barrack, isolation, and drinking. Jeanne's oldest brother, Bill, and second brother, Woodrow, or "Woody," both want to join the U.S. military and prove their loyalty. However, Papa tries to convince them not to, questioning how they can fight for a country that does not accept them, saying, "look where they have put us!" At the same time, Papa knows that his sons must answer "yes" and that his own answer would be "yes," even if it means swearing allegiance to a government that falsely imprisoned him at Fort Lincoln and denied him citizenship, and rejecting the only country where he might still have rights of a citizen.

Conflicted attitudes toward the loyalty questionnaire are further illustrated in *Farewell to Manzanar* when Papa attends a meeting to debate whether their camp should collectively answer "no-no." He is called an *inu* for opposing the measure. *Inu* means "dog," but in the context of the loyalty debate also refers to a "collaborator or informer." Papa was already considered to be an *inu* because he was released from the Fort Lincoln internment camp before others, and rumors circulated that he assisted the FBI as an interpreter, which brought him his early release. Even before Papa starts to speak, murmurs from the crowd of "*inu, inu*" erupt, and a man jumps up at the speaker's table and shouts "*inu*," which fuels a fight between him and Papa.

The loyalty question reveals the complexity of identity and what it means to be American, Japanese, and Japanese American. It highlights the psychological struggle, internal debate, and community divide that the questions vocalize. How can one negotiate and reconcile physical imprisonment, prejudice and social rejection, and assumption of disloyalty, while simultaneously being asked to give and swear loyalty to a government and country that already deemed him or her disloyal and an enemy alien? Jeanne's Papa, already dishonored and humiliated, struggles with wanting to answer "no-no," even though he would answer "yes-yes." Papa's individual internal conflicts in *Farewell to Manzanar* reflect larger internal conflicts on the question of loyalty among the internees falsely imprisoned in the camps.

Among Nisei Japanese American youths, there was a naive belief that they can overcome their physical characteristics by being and acting "more American." They wanted to escape their Japanese faces and force the world to see them as all-American. They re-created aspects of American life to shield themselves from anti-Japanese prejudice and government suspicions that they were enemy aliens with loyalty to Japan. Ironically, it was only in Manzanar and, by extension, other camps, that Japanese Americans, both Issei and Nisei, were able to freely express their American sensibilities and cultural habits of the heart.

Japanese American identity has largely been defined within simplistic theories of assimilation or cultural difference. Many sociologists have argued that Japanese Americans are one of the most assimilable ethnic groups in the United States because of perceived or real similarities between Japanese culture and Euro-American values. The model-minority stereotype, or the idea that Asian Americans are hardworking minorities who succeed in society, has largely been fueled by assimilationist theories that Japanese Americans will give up their cultural identity to gain acceptance from the dominant culture. Conversely, theories of cultural difference posit that Japanese Americans have distinctively foreign cultural values rooted in Japanese traditions. However, scholars in Asian American Studies have pointed out that inaccurate racial stereotypes are fueled by misconceptions that Asian American people are more culturally Asian than American. In reality, both theories of assimilation and cultural difference are not sufficient for explaining the spectrum of Japanese American experiences and identities.

The real and existential conflict of being Japanese and American, or rather, Japanese American is a core theme in the creative expressions of Japanese American artists during the post–World War II period, and continue to be a "source" for creative expressions. For example, contemporary American musician, rapper, guitarist, singer, songwriter, painter Michael Kenji "Mike" Shinoda's song "Kenji" tells the story of a Japanese immigrant, along with his own family, who is interned during World War II.

Although many creative expressions among Japanese American artists continue to grapple with the issues of subjectivity à la Americanness, many also draw inspiration from Japanese traditions, folklore, popular culture, and artistic styles. For example, Ken Nakazawa reworked Japanese folklore for his fantasy narrative *The Weaver of the Frost* (1927); and Henry Yoshitaki Kiyama's multilingual graphic novel *The Four Immigrants Manga* (1931) adapted Japanese comic art and social commentary.

Last, in the history of sports, many Japanese American athletes have represented the United States with honor, such as 1992 Olympic gold medalist figure skater Kristi Yonsei Yamaguchi; 1988 Olympic gold medalist in volleyball, Eric Sato; and 2008 Olympic gold medalist in the decathlon, Bryan Clay.

ASAWA, RUTH (1926–2013)

Born January 24, 1926, in Norwalk, California, Ruth Aiko Asawa was a renowned sculptor and activist in education and the arts. Asawa's parents emigrated from Japan to earn a living by growing seasonal crops. Asawa displayed talent and interest in the arts from an early age and spent her time drawing when not in school or working on the family farm.

In 1942, the 16-year-old Asawa and her family were interned during World War II, first at the Santa Anita Race Track for six months, living in horse stables, and later taken to permanent camp in Rohwer, Arkansas. During internment, Asawa continued to draw and paint and received unconventional artist training by observing and learning from several artists interned at the same camp. Asawa graduated from Rohwer High School in 1943 and went on to attend the Milwaukee State Teachers College on scholarship from the National Japanese American Student Relocation Council (NJASRC). Asawa enthusiastically studied art with the intention of becoming a schoolteacher but was ultimately dissuaded from pursuing work in a public school due to the difficulty, and potential danger, she faced as a Japanese American in securing a job. She then enrolled in the Black Mountain College, an experimental art school in North Carolina, where she studied design, color, and drawing. It was here that Asawa was encouraged by the artist and educator Josef Albers to explore the unique properties of material. Moreover, her travels to Mexico and observing indigenous artists' techniques for crocheting baskets inspired her to integrate these techniques into her wire sculptures.

In 1949, Asawa moved to San Francisco and married fellow Black Mountain College alumnus Albert Lanier. The couple had six children. Asawa continued to practice and experiment with art in her home while raising her children. Asawa first started exhibiting her work in 1951 and began to receive recognition for her crocheted wire sculptures, eventually exhibiting her work, including sculptures, paintings, and drawings, in solo and group shows across the country, including at the San Francisco Museum of Art, the Oakland Art Museum, and the Museum of Modern Art in New York. In 1965, she began receiving commissions to make public art, including Andrea, the mermaid fountain at Ghirardelli Square (1966) and the Hyatt on Union Square Fountain (1973).

Asawa also cofounded the Alvarado Arts Workshop to provide ongoing art education focused on integrating the arts and gardening to the classroom rather than the occasional art demonstration that Asawa was originally asked to teach at her children's elementary school. In 1982, Asawa worked to build the School of the Arts (SOTA) High School to educate the next generation of artists at a high standard in which students can reach their potential. In 2010, the school was renamed the Ruth Asawa SF School of the Arts. Asawa also served on the San Francisco Art Commission, California Arts Council, and the National Endowment of the Arts.

Asawa died peacefully in her home of natural causes on August 5, 2013, at the age of 87.

See also: Japanese American Artists; Noguchi, Isamu (1904–1988)

Further Reading

Asawa, R., and S. Dobbs. "Community and Commitment: An Interview with Ruth Asawa." *Art Education* 34, no. 5 (1981): 14–17.

Lanier, A., and P. Weverka. "Ruth Asawa." 2015. http://www.ruthasawa.com/. Accessed March 1, 2017.

Cynthia Mari Orozco

CLAY, BRYAN EZRA TSUMORU (1980–)

Born on January 3, 1980, in Austin, Texas, Bryan Ezra Tsumoru Clay is the son of Michele Ishimoto, a Japanese immigrant, and Greg Clay, an African American. After his parents divorced in 1985, his mother moved the family to Hawai'i. At James B. Castle High School in Kaneohe, Hawai'i, Clay participated in track and field. Skilled in most of the athletic events, he would compete in as many as six in a single meet. After graduating from high school

U.S. athlete Bryan Clay competes in the men's decathlon 110 meters hurdles race during the athletics meeting in Goetzis, Austria, 2006. (AP Photo/Kerstin Joensson)

in 1998, Clay entered Azusa Pacific University, near Los Angeles, California, where he took up the decathlon: a two-day track and field event consisting of the 100 meters, 110-meter hurdles, 400 meters, 1,500 meters, long jump, high jump, pole vault, discus throw, javelin throw, and shot put.

From 1999 to 2003, Clay competed in the decathlon with mixed success. After finishing third at the 1999 NAIA Track and Field Championships, he won the U.S. Junior Championship and the Pan-American Games Junior Championship later that year. Next year, Clay won the NAIA title. In 2001, he won the long jump at the NAIA Championships in 2001 and finished third in the decathlon at U.S. Track and Field (USATF) Championships. At the 2001 World Track and Field Championships, Clay dropped out of the decathlon competition after eight events. After defending the NAIA long jump title in 2002, he finished seventh in the decathlon at the USATF Championships that year. In 2003, Clay finished second in the USATF Championships, but did not finish the decathlon at the World Track and Field Championships, retiring after five events.

Clay enjoyed his best years in the decathlon from 2004 to 2008. At the 2004 Indoor World Track and Field Championships, he finished second in the heptathlon, the indoor equivalent of the decathlon, consisting of the 60 meters, long jump, shot put, high jump, 60-meter hurdles, pole vault, and 1,000 meters. After winning the decathlon at the 2004 USATF Championship, Clay garnered the silver medal at the Olympic Games in Athens, Greece. In successfully defending his USATF title in 2005, he established a world decathlon best of 183 feet, 3 inches (55.87 meters) in the discus throw. Clay won the decathlon at the 2005 World Track and Field Championships in the world leading score of 8,732. After finishing second in heptathlon at 2006 the Indoor World Championships, he did not finish the decathlon at the USATF Championships that year, but won a major decathlon competition, the Hypo-Meeting, in Götzis, Austria, in the world leading score of 8,677. In 2008, Clay won the heptathlon at the World Indoor Championships, the USATF Championship in a career best score of 8,832, and the gold medal at the Olympic Games in Beijing, China.

Hobbled by injuries, Clay's dominance in the decathlon declined after 2009. Absent from competition in 2009, he returned to competition in 2010, defended his title in the heptathlon at the Indoor World Track and Field Championships, and won the decathlon in Götzis in the world leading score of 8,483. After a 12th place finish in the decathlon at the 2012 USATF Championships, Clay retired from track and field. Ranked number one in the world in the decathlon three times, Clay joined Bruce Jenner, Rafer Johnson, Bob Mathis, Bill Toomey, and Dan O'Brien (with four) as the only Americans to claim that honor.

See also: Japanese American Olympians; Japanese Americans in Sports

Further Reading

"Bryan Clay." Asics. 2015. http://www.asicsamerica.com/athletes/bryan-clay. Accessed August 19, 2015.

"Bryan Clay." Olympic Sports Reference. 2000–2015. http://www.sports-reference.com. Accessed August 19, 2015.

Adam R. Hornbuckle

DESOTO, HISAYE YAMAMOTO (1921–2011)

Hisaye Yamamoto DeSoto was a master short story writer who submitted her first story for publication at the age of 14 and by age 27 had been published in a major literary magazine. Having had the self-described "addictive" experience of seeing her words in print at a young age, Yamamoto became a prolific writer with stories and essays in Japanese American and Japanese Canadian newspapers such as the *Rafu Shimpo* and *Hokubei Mainichi*, and literary magazines such as *Partisan Review, Arizona Quarterly,* and *Harper's Bazaar.* Several of her short stories appeared on Martha Foley's lists of Distinctive Short Stories for 1949, 1951, and 1960, and her story "Yoneko's Earthquake" appears in Best American Short Stories: 1952. Her short stories—"Seventeen Syllables," "The Legend of Miss Sasagawara," and "Yoneko's Earthquake"—have been widely anthologized and her work appears in *Speaking for Ourselves* (1969), *Aiiieeeee!: An Anthology of Asian American Writers* (1975), *Charlie Chan Is Dead: An Anthology of Contemporary Asian-American Fiction* (1993), and the *Heath Anthology of American Literature.* Hisaye Yamamoto received a Before Columbus Foundation's lifetime achievement award in 1986. Known for the precision of her prose and the understated emotion in her stories, Yamamoto's work is a favorite among literary scholars and commonly taught in the college classroom. In 1991, an hour-long movie, *Hot Summer Winds,* was presented by Public Broadcasting's American Playhouse; the movie was based on "Yoneko's Earthquake" and "Seventeen Syllables."

A second-generation Japanese American, Hisaye Yamamoto was born to Kanzo and Sae Tamaura Yamamoto, immigrants from Kuramoto, Japan, in Redondo Beach, California, where the couple in the author's words "eked out a living on the land" raising small profitable crops like strawberries. She had both an older and a younger brother. Hisaye Yamamoto was raised speaking Japanese until she entered kindergarten. At the age of 14, she received her first rejection notice but she also began publishing in the *Japan California Daily News* (*Kashu Mainichi*). She was an avid reader and received her associate of arts degree in European Languages and Latin from Compton Junior College.

As was the case with over 110,000 Japanese and Japanese Americans during World War II, Hisaye Yamamoto and her family were forced from their home and placed into a War Relocation Authority internment camp in Poston, Arizona, for the majority of the war. During her time in Poston, Yamamoto continued her writing, working as a reporter and publishing stories in the *Poston Chronicle*. She also became friends with playwright and short story writer Wakako Yamauchi. She was able to leave camp briefly to travel to Massachusetts to work as a cook, but then returned when her brother was killed when serving in Italy.

Following the family's release from Poston, Hisaye Yamamoto returned to Los Angeles where, from 1945 to 1948, she worked as a reporter for the *Los Angeles Tribune*, an African American newspaper. Her experience inspired an autobiographical short story, "A Fire in Fontana." In 1948, "The High Heeled Shoes, a Memoir," a story about sexual harassment, was accepted for the *Partisan Review*, and she published "Seventeen Syllables," a story based on her mother's experience, in 1949. Her artistic merit was recognized in 1950 with a John Whitney Hay Foundation Opportunity Fellowship, which allowed her to write full-time and care for her son, Paul, who she adopted in 1949. Although Hisaye Yamamoto was offered an opportunity in 1953 to study at Stanford with Yvor Winters, who admired her work, Yamamoto instead moved to Staten Island to a Catholic community work farm founded by Dorothy Day and she wrote for the *Catholic Worker* from 1953 to 1955. In 1955, she married Antony DeSoto, an Italian American, and after the couple moved to Los Angeles she gave birth to four children: Kibo, Elizabeth, Anthony, and Claude. The couple's courtship and relationship serve as the inspiration for her "Epithalamium" published in 1960. Very modest when asked about her writing, Yamamoto has noted that when asked she usually describes her occupation as a housewife.

A compilation of Hisaye Yamamoto's work, *Seventeen Syllables: 5 Stories of Japanese American Life* was first published in Japan in 1985, and 15 of her stories, *Seventeen Syllables and Other Stories*, were published in the United States in 1988. Both collections were named after her trademark short story, "Seventeen Syllables," which, in Yamamoto's lyrical and economical prose, tells the story of a young girl who watches her mother's struggle for artistic expression with an unsupportive and oppressive husband who only values the mother's manual labor. Another popular short story, "Yoneko's Earthquake," also features a young girl who observes her mother's troubled relationship with her father as she reaches adolescence. And a young female also narrates, "The Legend of Miss Sasagawara," a story about a community's reception of a new internee, a former dancer, and the dancer's reaction to her incarceration.

Hisaye Yamamoto DeSoto died in Los Angeles on January 30, 2011, at the age of 89.

See also: Hartmann, Sadakichi (1867–1944); Hirahara, Naomi (1962–); Iko, Momoko (1940–); Inada, Lawson Fusao (1938–); Japanese American Literature

Further Reading

Cheung, King-Kok. *Articulate Silences: Hisaye Yamamoto, Maxine Hong Kingston, Joy Kogawa*. Ithaca, NY: Cornell University Press, 1993.

Crow, Charles. "A MELUS Interview: Hisaye Yamamoto." *MELUS: The Society for the Study of the Multi-Ethnic Literature of the United States* 14, no. 1 (Spring 1987): 73–84.

Osborn, William P., and Sylvia A. Watanabe. "A Conversation with Hisaye Yamamoto." *Chicago Review* 39, nos. 3–4 (1993): 34–38.

Emily Morishima

FOWLER, RICKIE YUTAKA (1988–)

Rickie Yutaka Fowler was born on December 13, 1988, in Murrieta, California. His maternal grandfather, Yutaka Tanaka, is Japanese. Fowler taught himself how to play golf as a student at Murrieta Valley High School. In 2005, he won the Western Junior Tournament, his first major amateur title. Fowler, who represented the United States in its Walker Cup victory in 2007, won the Sunnehanna and the Players amateur titles that year. After graduating from high school in 2007, he entered Oklahoma State University in Stillwater and won the Fighting Illini Invitational at the University of Illinois that year. In 2008, Fowler defended the Sunnehanna title and finished the U.S. Open tied for 60th. Winner of the Ben Hogan Award as the best college player in 2008, he won all four matches in the Walker Cup and led the United States to a seven-point victory in 2009.

After the Walker Cup in 2009, Fowler debuted as a professional at the Albertsons Boise Open on the Nationwide Tour. In 2010, the PGA recognized him as its Rookie of the Year. Next year Fowler finished in a tie for second in the Bridgestone Invitational and garnered his first professional win at the Kolon Korean Open. In 2012, he won the Wells Fargo Championship in a playoff against Rory McIlroy and Darren Points. Fowler enjoyed his best year as a pro in 2014, when he finished the Masters in a tie for fifth, the U.S. Open in tie for second, the British Open in a tie for second, and the PGA Championship in a tie for third. That year he ranked eighth in earnings with over $4.8 million. Fowler, who won The Players Championship, the Deutsche Bank Championship, and the Aberdeen Asset Management Scottish Open in 2015, ranked fourth in earnings that year with over $5.7 million. In 2016, he won the Abu Dhabi HSBC Golf Championship.

See also: Japanese Americans in Sports

Further Reading

Worrall, Frank. *Rickie Fowler: Par Excellence*. London: John Blake Books, 2015.

Adam R. Hornbuckle

FUJI, PAUL TAKESHI (1940–)

Paul Takeshi Fuji, boxer, was born on July 6, 1940, in Honolulu, Hawai'i. Raised in Hawai'i, then a territory of the United States, the third-generation Japanese American, moved to Japan, where he joined the boxing gym operated by former professional wrestler Mitsuhiro Momota, better known as Rikidōzan. Trained by Eddie Townsend, also Japanese American, Fuji debuted professionally on April 14, 1964, knocking out Minoru Goto, of Japan, in the second of a six-round bout. On June 18, 1965, he challenged Nakao Sasazaki for the vacant Japanese super lightweight title, which he won in knockout in the first 45 seconds of the first round. His first loss came against Johnny Santos (John Rodriguez) in a unanimous decision after 10 rounds on November 16, 1965. Four fights later, on June 5, 1966, Fuji lost to Fel Pedranza, who knocked him out in the sixth of a 10-round fight.

After Fuji successfully defending his Japanese super lightweight title against Shigeru Ogiwara on August 25, 1966, knocking out his opponent in the second of a 10-round fight, he claimed the Oriental and Pacific Boxing Federation (OPBF) super lightweight title by knocking Rocky Alarde out in the third of a 12-round bout on September 29, 1966. Fuji claimed his first world championship belts on April 30, 1967, by knocking out Sandro Lopopolo in the second of a 15-round fight for both the World Boxing Council world super lightweight title and the World Boxing Association world super lightweight titles. On November 16, 1967, he defend his titles by knocking out Willi Quator in the fourth of a 15-round fight.

On December 12, 1968, Fuji faced Nicolino Locche, of Argentina, for the newly inaugurated World Boxing Association light welterweight, but gave up in the 10th round of the 15-round fight. He fought four more times, winning three by knockouts and one by points, before he was scheduled to face former world champion Eddie Perkins in June 1970, in a nontitle match. Claiming to have an injury, Fuji withdrew from the fight, after which the Japan Boxing Commission suspended him. He retired with a record of 34–3–1, including 29 knockouts. Fuji trains boxers in Mito, Japan.

See also: Japanese Americans in Sports

Further Reading

"Takeshi Fuji." BoxRec.com. 2013. http://boxrec.com/media/index.php/Takeshi_Fuji. Accessed August 19, 2015.

"Who Is Paul Fuji?" SecondsOut.com. 2011. http://www.secondsout.com/world-boxing -news/world-boxing-news/who-is-paul-fuji. Accessed August 19, 2015.

Adam R. Hornbuckle

FUJIKAWA, TADD (1991–)

Tadd Fujikawa was born on January 8, 1991, in Honolulu, Hawai'i. Born three months premature, he weighed only 31 ounces and was so small that his grandfather could hold him in the palm of his hand. As a result of his premature birth Fujikawa grew to 5 feet 1 inch and weighed about 150 pounds by his graduation from Moanalua High School in Honolulu in 2009.

In 2006, Fujikawa qualified for the U.S. Open as an amateur by winning the Hawai'i sectional qualifier. The youngest player in history to qualify for the tournament, he missed the final cut by nine strokes. In 2007, Fujikawa made the cut at the Sony Open, becoming the youngest player in nearly 50 years to make the cut on the PGA tour. He finished the tournament tied for 20th. Later that year, Fujikawa won the Hawai'i Pearl Open, the first amateur to win the tournament since 1992. Held annually since 1979, the Pearl Open is Hawai'i's most lucrative local golf tournament.

In 2007, Fujikawa debuted as a professional at the Reno-Tahoe Open, but failed to make the final cut. Later that year at the Albertsons Boise Open, he scored a hole-in-one on the 17th green. In 2008, Fujikawa made his first

Tadd Fujikawa during the pro-am event of the SBS Championship golf tournament in Kapalua, Hawai'i, 2010. (AP Photo/Eric Risberg)

professional cut in 12 attempts and garnered his first professional victory at the Mid-Pacific Open in Hawai'i, a tournament sponsored by the Mid-Pacific Country Club in Kailua. By defeating a mixed field of amateurs and professionals, the 17-year-old golfer became the youngest winner in the tournament's 50-year history. In 2009, Fujikawa defended his Mid-Pacific Open title for his second professional win. Later that year he won the Maui Open and finished sixth in the Hawai'i State Open. In 2010, Fujikawa, who tied for eighth in the Bolle Classic and finished fourth in the Southern Open, won the Golf Tour Championship and the Hawai'i State Open.

See also: Japanese Americans in Sports

Further Reading

Fujikawa, Tadd. PGA Profile. PGATour.com. http://www.pgatour.com/players/player .29419.html. Accessed January 15, 2017.

Adam R. Hornbuckle

FUJITA, SCOTT (1979–)

Scott Fujita, born on April 28, 1979, in Ventura, California, was adopted at six weeks of age by a third-generation Japanese American, Rodney Fujita, who was born at the Gila River Internment camp and his wife Helen. Scott, a two-sport athlete in football and basketball at Rio Mesa High School, was raised in Oxnard, California. Fujita is a 10-year veteran linebacker of the National Football League (NFL) who played for the Kansas City Chiefs, Dallas Cowboys, Cleveland Browns, and the 2010 Super Bowl champions, the New Orleans Saints.

After graduating from high school, he attended University of California, Berkeley, earning both his bachelor's and his master's degrees. He was not recruited but earned a spot on the football team through open tryouts. During his senior year, he won accolades including All-Pac 10 honorable mention and All-Pac 10 Academic Team. In 2002, Fujita entered the NFL draft and the Kansas City Chiefs selected him in the fifth round.

Although Scott Fujita is Caucasian, he is proud of his family's Japanese heritage. He is extremely close with his paternal grandparents, Nagao and Lillie Fujita. Scott's grandfather, Nagao, served in the U.S. Army with the 442nd all-Japanese Regiment Combat Team in Europe while his parents were imprisoned in the War Relocation Authority (WRA) camp in Arizona. It was in this WRA camp that Lillie gave birth to Rodney in 1943. While incarcerated, Nagao's parents could not pay the mortgage and lost all of their farmland in California. Scott was upset that he had not learned about Japanese incarceration through his formal education and conducted his own independent research on this subject.

In 2010, the NFL began investigating the New Orleans Saints for placing illegal bounties or money distributed for hard hits and knocking opposing players out of the game. There were rumors that Fujita was the main actor of "Bountygate." According to documentarian Sean Pamphilon, Fujita never took any money nor placed money into the pool, and it was Fujita who pushed the filmmaker to turn in key evidence of this program to the NFL. Commissioner Roger Goodell suspended Fujita, currently a member of the Cleveland Browns, for three games for his role in Bountygate. Fujita appealed this decision, but on June 8, 2012, arbitrator Stephen Burbank supported Goodell's power as commissioner to discipline players. In December 2012, a report by former NFL commissioner Paul Tagliabue declared that Fujita did not engage in "conduct detrimental to the league," and vacated his suspension.

See also: Japanese Americans in Sports

Further Reading

"Scott Fujita: Bio." http://www.scottfujita.com/bio/. Accessed September 12, 2012.

Terumi Rafferty-Osaki

GAINES, COREY YASUTO (1965–)

Corey Yasuto Gaines was born on June 1, 1965, in Los Angeles, California, to an African American father and a Japanese mother. He played guard on the basketball team at Saint Bernard High School in Playa del Rey, California. After graduating from high school, Gaines played guard on the basketball teams at the University of California, Los Angeles, from 1983 to 1986, and Loyola Marymount University, from 1987 to 1988. In three seasons with the Bruins, he scored 336 points, including 88 from the free throw line; maintained a field goal percentage of 48.4 percent and a free throw percentage of 68.2 percent. In one season at Marymount, Gaines scored 540 points, including 122 from the free throw line; maintained a field goal percentage of 51.8 percent and a free throw percentage of 67.8 percent.

As the 65th pick overall in the 1988 National Basketball Association (NBA) draft, 6-foot 3-inch, 195-pound Gaines was selected by the Seattle Supersonics in the third round. He played five seasons in the NBA with four different teams, the New Jersey Nets from 1988 to 1989; the Philadelphia 76ers from 1989 to 1990 and from 1994 to 1995; the Denver Nuggets from 1990 to 1991; and the New York Knicks from 1993 to 1994. In 80 NBA games, Gaines maintained a 42.4 percent field goal percentage, making 92 of 217 field goal attempts. He posted a 73.6 percent free throw percentage, completing 53 of 72 attempts from the charity stripe. Gaines also grabbed 12 offensive and 57 defensive rebounds, assisted in 247 shots, had 39 steals, and blocked 72 shots.

When not playing in the NBA, Gaines played for teams in the Continental Basketball Association, World Basketball League, National Basketball League, Europe, Israel, and Japan. Continental Basketball Association teams included the Quad City Thunder from 1988 to 1989, the Omaha Racers from 1989 to 1990, the Yakima Sun Kings from 1990 to 1991 and 1992 to 1993, and the La Crosse Catbirds from 1993 to 1993. In 1989 he played for the Calgary 88s of the World Basketball Association and, in 1992, the Montreal Dragons of the National Basketball League. Gaines played for Scavolini Pesaro in Italy in 1994; Galatasaray in Turkey in 1995; Mash J. Verona in Italy in 1996; Hapoel Eilat, in Israel in 1996; Japan Energy Griffins in 1997; and Maccabi Rishon LeZion, in Israel in 1999.

Gaines joined the Long Beach Jam of the NBA Developmental League in 2003, and after one season as a player became an assistant coach in 2004. After serving as head coach for the Jam in 2005, Gaines became an assistant coach for the Phoenix Mercury of the Women's National Basketball Association in 2006. Promoted to head coach in 2007, he directed the Mercury to its second WNBA title in 2009. Appointed general manager in 2011, Gaines left the Phoenix Mercury in 2013 and became an assistant head coach for the Phoenix Suns of the NBA. After the Suns replaced its entire coaching staff following the appointment of a new interim head coach in 2013, Gaines continued to work for Phoenix as a new player developmental coach and returned to the position of assistant coach in 2015.

See also: Japanese Americans in Sports

Further Reading

"Corey Gaines." Basketball-Reference.com. http://www.basketball-reference.com/players /g/gaineco01.html. Accessed January 15, 2017.

"Corey Gaines." SR/College Basketball. http://www.sports-reference.com/cbb/players /corey-gaines-1.html. Accessed January 15, 2017.

Adam R. Hornbuckle

GORMAN, MIKI "MICHIKO" SUWA (1935–2015)

Miki Gorman, long-distance runner, was born Michiko Suwa in 1935 in China, where her father served as an officer and physician in the Japanese army occupying Manchuria. She grew up, however, in Tokyo with two younger twin brothers. During World War II, the Suwa family left Tokyo to escape the Allied bombing raids that destroyed the city. After Japan surrendered in 1945, she resumed attending school, walking six miles a day because there was no other means of transportation.

Hired to work as a nanny for the family of a U.S. military officer, Suwa moved to Carlisle, Pennsylvania, in 1963. After arriving on a student visa, she attended secretarial college, married a local businessperson, Michael Gorman, and became a U.S. citizen. In the late 1960s, Gorman moved to Los Angeles with her husband. To get out of the house and expand her social circle, her husband encouraged her to join the Los Angeles Athletic Club (LAAC). Gorman, who stood five feet and half an inch and weighed 86 pounds, believed that exercise, especially running, would increase her appetite so she would gain weight by eating more.

Soon after taking up running, Gorman began competing in long-distance races. After competing several times in an annual 100-mile race held indoors at the LAAC, she ran the Culver City Marathon in 1973, winning the 26.2-mile

Michiko Gorman is hugged by supporters as she became the first woman to finish in the Boston Marathon, 1974. She completed the marathon in record time for women entrants that year. (AP Photo)

race in 2:46:36, six seconds short, at that time, of the world's best time of 2:46:30 established by Adrienne Beames of Australia in 1971. Since then, however, the International Association of Athletics Federations has recognized Gorman's time as an official world's best, because Beames's performance came on a short course. In 1974, the LAAC sent Gorman to compete in the Boston Marathon, which she won in the course record time of 2:47.11. After finishing second to Kim Merritt at Boston in 1976, she won the New York City marathon in the course record time of 2:39:11, which would remain the fastest time of her competitive career. In 1977, Gorman won the Boston Marathon, in 2:48:43, and the New York City Marathon, in 2:43:10, making her the only runner, male or female, to have won Boston and New York in the same year. In 1978, she established a world record of 1:15:58 for the half marathon in Pasadena, California.

Gorman retired from competition in 1982. She died of cancer at the age of 80 in Bellingham, Washington.

See also: Japanese Americans in Sports

Further Reading

Bakoulis, Gordon. "Miki Gorman." *Runner's World*, October 1, 2001. http://www.runner sworld.com/elite-runners/miki-gorman. Accessed August 19, 2015.

"Miki Gorman." The National Distance Running Hall of Fame. Class of 2005 Nominees. 2010. http://www.distancerunning.com/news/class_05.html. Accessed August 19, 2015.

Adam R. Hornbuckle

HARADA, TSUNEO "CAPPY" (1921–2010)

Tsuneo "Cappy" Harada was born in Santa Maria, California. A lifelong athlete, he competed in high school and semipro baseball, ultimately scouting for the San Francisco Giants. In high school, he played in exhibition games against future Hall of Famers Ted Williams, Bob Lemon, and Jackie Robinson.

Harada was scouted by the St. Louis Cardinals before World War II broke out. Harada joined the military intelligence service and was shipped out to help the United States in the Pacific theater campaigns. Wounded twice, he continued with the U.S. military for 10 years during the occupation of Japan. Harada was placed in charge by Gen. Douglas MacArthur with reestablishing Japanese athletics to help build morale. Harada focused on baseball and resurrected professional baseball and the national High School Baseball Tournament at Koshien.

In 1949, Harada arranged a baseball goodwill tour of Lefty O'Doul and the San Francisco Seals in Japan. In 1951 and 1953, the Joe DiMaggio All-Stars and the New York Giants also brought Major League Baseball stars to Japanese ballparks. A highlight of Harada's time spent in Japan was hosting DiMaggio and his wife, actress Marilyn Monroe, on their honeymoon to Japan in January 1954. With Harada's assistance, the Yankee Clipper squeezed in some batting clinics for Japanese baseball players.

From 1951 to 1954, Harada became a special adviser to the Tokyo Giants of the Japanese Baseball League (JBL). Under Harada, the Giants took four straight JBL championships. He also pioneered a two-league format and adopted a World Series–style playoffs in Japan.

In 1965, Harada was named general manager of the Lodi (California) Crushers, now called the Rancho Cucamonga Quakes, in California League Class A (affiliate of the Los Angeles Angels of Anaheim since 2001). The team was a minor league affiliate of the Chicago Cubs (1966–1968), and Harada was the first Nisei (second-generation Japanese American) to be named a general manager in professional baseball. In 1966, he was named executive of the year by the *Sporting News* and the National Association of Professional Baseball.

For over 20 years, Harada worked for the San Francisco Giants as a special assistant in the scouting and player personnel department. He also worked with player development, basic business operations, and trans-Pacific scouting.

Harada is credited with signing the first Japanese player to a Major League contract, left-handed pitcher Masanori Murakami. He was acquired by the Giants from Japan's Nankai Hawks in 1964. Murakami played two seasons and had a career record of 5 wins and 1 loss. Between the 1970s to the late 2000s, Harada served as an adviser to Major League Baseball. Harada died of heart failure on June 5, 2010, at the age of 88 in California.

See also: Japanese Americans in Baseball

Further Reading

Fitts, Robert. *Remembering Japanese Baseball: An Oral History of the Game.* Carbondale: Southern Illinois University Press, 2005.

Mukai, Gary. *Diamonds in the Rough: Baseball and Japanese-American Internment.* Stanford, CA: Stanford Program on International and Cross-Cultural Education (SPICE), 2004.

Nakagawa, Kerry Yo. *Through a Diamond: 100 Years of Japanese American Baseball.* San Francisco: Rudi Publishing, 2001.

Kerry Yo Nakagawa

HARTMANN, SADAKICHI (1867–1944)

Art critic, poet, and dramatist Sadakichi Hartmann was born in 1867 on Dejima Island in the harbor of Nagasaki, Japan, to Carl and Osada Hartmann. After his mother's death in 1868, Hartmann was sent to be raised by his paternal grandmother and rich uncle in Hamburg, Germany, where he learned about European literature, art, and upper-class deportment. When forced to attend the German Imperial Naval Academy, Hartmann decamped to Paris. Disappointed, his father sent him to live with poorer relatives in Philadelphia, Pennsylvania, in 1882. Hartmann worked as a lithographic stippler, perfume peddler, and negative retoucher among other odd jobs, but he continued his education by reading at libraries and bookstores. An aspiring poet, Hartmann visited Walt Whitman in nearby Camden, New Jersey, intermittently over a period of seven years. Although Whitman became annoyed at Hartmann for allegedly misquoting him, he saw much promise in Hartmann's poetry. In the 1880s and 1890s Hartmann worked in the United States and Europe as a journalist with specialties in art and literature.

As an art critic, Hartmann championed photography as a fine art form, explained the significance of particular artists like Eduard Steichen and James Whistler, and introduced Japanese art to western audiences. In Alfred Stieglitz's journal *Camera Work*, Hartmann, writing under the name "Sidney Allan," elucidated the difficulty and artistry involved in photography and advocated for using everyday scenes in New York as subjects. Hartmann lauded Steichen's and Whistler's works for their technical accomplishment and suggestivism, the latter quality of which he identified as "one of the leading characteristics of Japanese art." His book *Japanese Art* (1904) was considered one of the best introductions to the field of its time.

In his poetry Hartmann combined Japanese artistic ideals with what he learned from American writers like Walt Whitman and Symbolist writers like Stéphane Mallarmé. *Naked Ghosts* (1898) and *Drifting Flowers of the Sea* (1904) combine Whitman's vocabulary of nautical and natural images with the Symbolists' philosophy of poetry as a means of transport to other worlds—inner and outer. In *My Rubáiyát* (1913), Hartmann joined a craze for imitating Edward FitzGerald's English translation of the Persian *Rubáiyát of Omar Khayyám*. Hartmann's version is written in sestets instead of quatrains, however, and rails against war and capitalism as barriers to living the simple life that Khayyám's poem celebrates. As early as 1898, Hartmann wrote haiku and tanka in English, and his 1904 essay "The Japanese Conception of Poetry" may have influenced modernist writers like Ezra Pound who were searching for inspiration in Chinese and Japanese literary traditions. Hartmann's work in Japanese poetic forms culminated in *Japanese Rhythms* (1933). Interestingly, Hartmann chose to employ end-rhyme in his haiku and tanka, which limited his word choice but enabled him to make his work more familiar to a Western readership.

Not averse to experimentation, Hartmann was perhaps boldest in his dramatic productions. For instance, he wrote plays like *Christ,* whose sexual content offended upholders of blue laws in Massachusetts and got him jailed in 1893. And, in 1902, he pioneered "perfume concerts" in which he transported audiences on a "trip to Japan in sixteen minutes" with the aid of giant electric fans and various odors. He conducted such concerts himself, gave readings of his plays, and even acted in Douglas Fairbanks's *Thief of Bagdad* (1924), playing the role of the Court Magician.

Hartmann spent his waning years in a shack on the Morengo Indian Reservation near Banning, California. In 1942, some locals considered his star-gazing suspicious and the FBI interviewed him, but he avoided internment. Hartmann died in 1944. For many years his work and influence on modernist art and literature were forgotten, but thanks to the efforts of scholars since the 1970s, his reputation is increasing. Recently, members of the Japanese American community have begun to call him an "Issei pioneer."

See also: Japanese American Artists; Japanese American Literature

Further Reading

Hartmann, Sadakichi. *Sadakichi Hartmann: Collected Poems*, edited by Floyd Cheung. Stroud, UK: Little Island Press, 2016.

Weaver, Jane Calhoun. *Sadakichi Hartmann: Critical Modernist*. Berkeley: University of California Press, 1991.

Floyd Cheung

HAYAKAWA, SESSUE "KINTARO" (1886–1973)

Sessue Hayakawa was an actor, producer, director, playwright, and scriptwriter whose lengthy career extended from the early days of Hollywood cinema in the 1910s through the 1960s. He performed in a broad range of venues and genres—from silent film and theater to television—in the United States, Japan, France, England, and Germany. At times, his status as a transnational actor was a locus of cultural and sociopolitical friction between the United States and Japan.

Sessue was born Hayakawa Kintarō, the second son and the youngest of five children in a well-to-do family with a fishing business in Nanaura village

Actor, director, and writer Sessue Hayakawa beagn his career in silent films of the early 20th century and remained professionally active into the 1960s. (John Springer Collection/Corbis via Getty Images)

in Minamibōsō-gun, Chiba Prefecture. Sessue's aspiration to become a naval officer was cut short after he failed a health examination at a preparatory school for the Imperial Japanese Naval Academy. In 1907, shortly after returning from the school to his village, Sessue traveled to the United States to attend the University of Chicago. He enrolled in the Home Studies Department, where he studied political economy for just over one year. Sessue next settled in Los Angeles, where he worked at various temporary jobs, including performing on the stage of Fujita Tōyō's theater troop in Little Tokyo.

Sessue's career as a Hollywood film actor began shortly before he married the already established Japanese American Hollywood actress Aoki Tsuru (1890–1961) in 1914, and his matinee idol status flourished thereafter, making him the first non-Caucasian Hollywood star. However, in 1922, when anti-Japanese immigrant sentiment was growing in intensity, Sessue left Los Angeles for New York, after which he appeared on stage and screen in the United States, France, England, and Germany before returning to Japan in 1930. Apart from living in Paris from 1936 until 1949, Sessue lived in Japan until his death in 1973, when he left behind a second wife, Watanabe Shizuko, as well as a son and two daughters, all born outside of marriage.

Sessue's long and prolific career as an Asian diaspora actor has important implications for understanding the nature and history of racial performativity, as well as the status of thespians as cultural and sociopolitical agents. His career can be said to have echoed changes in Western images of Japan and of the Asian Other, as well as in so-called Orientalist thinking in the West, in Japan, and within Japanese society in the United States at various junctures in the early to mid-20th century. Particularly notable in this regard are his roles in two of his best-known films: *The Cheat* (1915) and *The Bridge on the River Kwai* (1957). In *The Cheat*, Sessue fueled Western imaginations with his portrayal of a mysterious Japanese antiques dealer who seduces and subjects a Caucasian woman to sadistic violence. Sessue, who performed the role in an expressionless style characteristic of Japanese kabuki acting, drew much criticism in Japan—where *The Cheat* has never been shown publicly—as well as among the Japanese diaspora for portraying this and other brutal and villainous Japanese characters. By contrast, in *The Bridge on the River Kwai*, a film that marks a turning point in "mainstream" postwar Anglo-American perceptions of Japan, Sessue plays Col. Saitō, the aged, stoic, and honorable officer and symbol of a defeated army and nation. This role earned Sessue an Academy Award nomination in the category of Best Supporting Actor.

See also: Ishigo, Estelle (1899–1990); Japanese Americans in Film; Takei, George Hosato (1937–)

Further Reading

Marchetti, Gina. *Romance and the "Yellow Peril": Race, Sex and Discursive Strategies in Hollywood Fiction.* Berkeley and Los Angeles: University of California Press, 1993.

Miyao, Daisuke. *Sessue Hayakawa: Silent Cinema and Transnational Stardom.* Durham, NC: Duke University Press, 2007.

Richie, David. *A Hundred Years of Japanese Film: A Concise History, with a Selective Guide to DVDs and Videos.* New York: Kōdansha USA, 2012.

Midori Tanaka Atkins

HIRAHARA, NAOMI (1962–)

Born on May 12, 1962, in Pasadena, California, Naomi Hirahara is the daughter of Isamu and Mayumi Hirahara. She attended Stanford University and graduated with a degree in international relations and had the opportunity to study at the Inter-University Center for Advanced Japanese Language Studies in Tokyo and volunteer in Ghana, West Africa. For nine years, Hirahara worked as a reporter and editor of the *Rafu Shimpo*, a Japanese American newspaper based in Los Angeles during the redress and reparations movement (a pivotal moment in history for Japanese Americans) and the Los Angeles riots. In 1996,

Hirahara left the newspaper to pursue other writing endeavors and attended Newman University in Wichita, Kansas, as a Milton Center Fellow in creative writing. After the completion of the program, Hirahara returned to California and began to write and publish her own work, even establishing her own small press, Midori Books. Currently, Hirahara resides in Southern California with her husband, Wes, where she leads a number of writing workshops. She is also an active member of her church and serves on the board of the Southern California chapter of the Mystery Writers of America.

Although Hirahara is best known for her beloved character Mas Arai and his subsequent and often reluctant detective adventures, she began writing nonfiction that focused mostly on marginalized or little-known Japanese American history. Hirahara's nonfiction is region-specific and illuminates local history that is important to particular community formations in Southern California. For instance, *Green Makers: Japanese American Gardeners in Southern California* (2000) examines the history of this group of Japanese Americans who struggled against discrimination and faced economic limitations as they labored to keep their communities green and beautiful. Hirahara has also authored two biographies for the Japanese American National Museum: *An American Son: The Story of George Aratani, Founder of Mikasa and Kenwood* (2000) and *A Taste for Strawberries: The Independent Journey of Nisei Farmer Manabi Hirasaki* (2003). In addition to her accounts of these two influential Japanese American community members, she compiled the reference book, *Distinguished Asian American Business Leaders* (2003), which highlights the lives of 96 businesspersons whose stories are informative as well as inspiring. In 2004, she coauthored *Silent Scars of Healing Hands: Oral Histories of Japanese American Doctors in World War II Detention Camps*, which looks at how these men and women provided medical assistance to fellow internees with limited equipment, technology, and funds. She also released the book, *A Scent of Flowers: The History of the Southern California Flower Market* (2004) that examines the contributions of ethnic families to this particular industry through their personal stories and photographs.

Hirahara's first mystery, *Summer of the Big Bachi* (2004) took her 15 years to conceptualize, research, and complete. Her novel follows Mas Arai, a Kibei Hibakusha gardener turned sleuth who is forced to remember his traumatic past as a Hiroshima atomic bomb survivor as he searches for a person from that past. Kibei refers to a Japanese American who was born in the United States but grew up in Japan whereas Hibakusha refers to a Hiroshima atomic bomb survivor. Mas is loosely based on Hirahara's own father who was born in California but taken to Japan as an infant; he was only miles away from the epicenter of the atomic bomb but survived. At the end of the war, he returned to California and became a gardener and landscaper much like the fictional Mas. Hirahara weaves this particular history into her novel because it was not only an important part of her own family's personal story but one that has remained silent within the community. Although Hirahara did not expect to continue with Mas's character, *Summer of the Big Bachi* is the first of the current four in the Mas Arai series—which may be continued. The second of the series, *Gasa-Gasa Girl* (2005) follows Mas who stumbles upon a murder when he visits his daughter who is in need of his help. *Snakeskin Shamisen* (2006) won an Edgar Allan Poe Award in 2007 for the category of Best Paperback Original and highlights the Okinawan community in South Bay, California. The fourth in the series is *Blood Hina* (2010), whose mystery revolves around the disappearance of an ancient Japanese doll display that Mas must solve when the blame is placed upon his friend. Hirahara has also written a young adult novel, *1001 Cranes*, about a young girl who is living through her parents' divorce but strengthening her own relationships to family and friends through the tradition of origami.

See also: Japanese American Literature

Further Reading

Hirahara, Naomi. "About Naomi." www.naomihirahara.com. Accessed September 16, 2012.

Ko, Nalea J. "Bringing Back Mas Arai." Pacific Citizen. www.pacificcitizen.org. Accessed September 16, 2012.

Wendi Yamashita

HIRASHIMA, HIROTO "HIRO" (1910–2007)

Hiroto "Hiro" Hirashima, bowler, was born on July 11, 1910, on Honolulu, Hawai'i. For nearly all of his adult life, he worked as a letter carrier for the United States Postal Service. An avid bowler, Hirashima's opportunities to compete in tournaments were very limited because of restrictive racial policies toward Japanese Americans, which increased during World War II. Participation in tournaments sanctioned by the American Bowling Congress (ABC) was entirely unavailable to Japanese Americans, as well as other minorities, because membership in the ABC was open to Caucasians only. Organized in New York in 1913, the ABC set the standards for bowling in the United States, permitting only white males to participate in the organization.

After the ABC abandoned its "whites only" membership policy in 1950, Hirashima took the lead in organizing Japanese American bowling teams to compete in tournaments. His major accomplishment was organizing nine teams to compete in the ABC Tournament in Seattle in 1954. Encouraged by the ABC to increase minority involvement in the sport, Hirashima was elected to the ABC board of directors in 1963. The first minority elected to the board, he served for over 30 years.

Hirashima founded the Hawai'i State Bowling Association and the Oahu Bowling Association. Honored as an ABC life member in 1995, he was inducted into the United States Bowling Congress Hall of Fame as an ABC Pioneer that same year. Hirashima was inducted into the Hawai'i Sports Hall of Fame in 1999. He died on November 23, 2007, in Kaneohe, Hawai'i.

See also: Japanese Americans in Sports

Further Reading

Adamski, Mary. "Hiroto 'Hiro' Hirashima / 1910–2007: Bowler Knocked Down Pins and Racial Barriers." *Star Bulletin*, December 20, 2007, http://archives.starbulletin .com/2007/12/20/news/story10.html. Accessed January 15, 2017.
"Japanese-American Pioneer Hiroto Hirashima Dies." BowlingDigital.com. http://www .bowlingdigital.com/bowl/node/3467. Accessed January 15, 2017.

Adam R. Hornbuckle

HIRAYAMA, SATOSHI "FIBBER" (1930–)

Satoshi "Fibber" Hirayama was an all-star Japanese American baseball player who began his serious baseball days as a 12-year-old farm boy in Exeter, California. During World War II, his family was relocated with thousands of other Japanese Americans to Poston, Arizona, site of Internment Camp Number Two. When there, he played sandlot football and moved on to organized baseball within the camp's 32-team league.

Hirayama refined and developed his baseball skills with the competitive nature of camp ball. After the war, his family returned to California's San Joaquin Valley. He finished high school and received a scholarship to play baseball at Fresno State College. There he lettered in football and baseball. His incredible base path speed led to two records that stood for more than 40 years: 76 stolen bases in a season and 5 stolen bases in one game.

With speed on the base paths and a strong arm in the outfield, his world-class skills earned him a contract from the Stockton Ports, a farm team of the St. Louis Browns. He became one of the first Japanese Americans from Fresno to play professional baseball. But one year later Uncle Sam called; from 1953 to 1955, Hirayama continued his baseball days as a soldier at Fort Ord. Many of his teammates went on to Major League clubs.

After being discharged, Hirayama signed with the Hiroshima Carp in the Japanese Baseball League. Both Hirayama and fellow teammate Kenshi Zenimura were received with incredible fanfare and popularity. They were the first mainlanders to play in Japan. More than 100,000 fans showed up at the Hiroshima train station to greet these two U.S. ballplayers. Hirayama became a two-time All-Star and competed in Japanese-MLB All-Star games against future Hall of Famers like Mickey Mantle, Whitey Ford, and Stan Musial.

Hirayama played for Hiroshima for 10 years, and later became a scout for the Carp organization in Japan and in the Dominican Republic. During his career, Hirayama exemplified the competitive spirit of a young Nisei who rose to many of life's challenges. He pioneered baseball in California and abroad in Japan. He truly is one of the game's great ambassadors and a legend in Japanese American baseball history.

See also: Japanese Americans in Baseball; Japanese Americans in Sports

Further Reading

Felton, Todd, and Bill Knowlin, eds. *When Baseball Went to War*. Chicago: Triumph Books, 2008.

Mukai, Gary. *Diamonds in the Rough: Baseball and Japanese-American Internment*. Stanford, CA: Stanford Program on International and Cross-Cultural Education (SPICE), 2004.

Nakagawa, Kerry Yo. *Through a Diamond: 100 Years of Japanese American Baseball*. San Francisco: Rudi Publishing, 2001.

Kerry Yo Nakagawa

HIROSHIMA

Hiroshima is an American contemporary jazz band founded in Los Angeles in 1974. They are best known for being pioneers in Asian American jazz by including Japanese instrumentation such as the shakuhachi, the koto, and taiko drums into their music.

Founding

The band was originally founded by Daniel Kuramoto (band leader and wind instruments), June Okida Kuramoto (koto), Johnny Mori (percussion), Dave Iwataki (keyboards), Danny Yamamoto (drums), and Peter Hata (guitar). With the exception of June Okida Kuramoto, who immigrated to the Crenshaw district of Los Angeles from Saitama Prefecture in Japan at the age of 6, the other original members were Japanese Americans born in the United States and each identify as part of the Sansei generation. Alluding to the band's unique Japanese American political identity, they adopted their name after the Japanese city that was struck by an American atomic bomb in 1945.

Although many Japanese American stage bands existed before, during, and immediately after World War II, these bands all tended to play covers of popular songs instead of original compositions. When Hiroshima began in the mid-1970s, they attributed much of their inspiration to the changing social climate

Pioneers in Asian American fusion, the band Hiroshima blends traditional Japanese instrumentation with American music stylings. (Paul Natkin/Getty Images)

following the Vietnam War, the desegregation of the American South, and the growing movements toward peace and diversity.

Hiroshima is directly connected to the Asian American movement of the late-1960s. Band leader Daniel Kuramoto was the first chairman of the Asian American Studies Program at California State University, Long Beach, and was also involved with Visual Communications, the first Asian American film organization. In 1974, Hiroshima was featured in Duane Kubo's "Cruisin' J-town," a 30-min documentary and seminal work of Asian American cinema. Some of the band's earliest performances targeted popular Japanese American community groups of the time, including AADAP, the Amerasia Bookstore, and the Little Tokyo Service Center.

Some of Hiroshima's early influences include a wide variety of artists such as Carlos Santana and Earth, Wind, and Fire, but their sound is perhaps most often characterized by June Okida Kuramoto's unique blend of classically trained koto technique with non-Japanese melodic patterns, accompanying instruments, and rhythms.

Critical Acclaim

Hiroshima's self-titled debut album was released in 1979 on Arista Records, featuring the single "Roomful of Mirrors." In 1981, they became the first Asian

American Grammy nominee when their song "Winds of Change" received a nomination for Best R&B Instrumental Performance. They won the Soul Train Music Award for Best Jazz Album in 1988 for *Go*. In 1989, they created and produced the musical drama "Sansei" at the Mark Taper Forum in Los Angeles. Also, Hiroshima was chosen to be the opening act of Miles Davis's 1990 world tour.

Hiroshima received their second Grammy nomination in 2010 when *Legacy* was nominated for Best Pop Instrumental Album. The band released its 20th album *Songs with Words* in 2015, and remains active as of 2017. The current principal band members include three founding musicians Daniel Kuramoto, June Okida Kuramoto, and Danny Yamamoto, as well as Kimo Cornwell (keyboard), and Dean Cortez (bass guitar). Besides their contributions toward challenging the public perceptions of Asian Americans as musicians, the band continues to stretch the boundaries of jazz fusion and new-age music.

See also: Iijima, Chris (1948–2005); Japanese American Hip-Hop; Nagano, Kent (1951–); Shinoda, Michael Kenji "Mike" (1977–)

Further Reading

Cruisin' J-Town. Dir. Duane Kubo and Daniel Valdez. Visual Communications, 1974.

"Jazz Monthly Feature Interview Hiroshima." Interview by Jonathan Widran. Jazz Monthly.com. 2013.

Lornell, Kip, and Anne K. Rasmussen. *The Music of Multicultural America: Performance, Identity, and Community in the United States*. Jackson: University Press of Mississippi, 2016.

Dean Ryuta Adachi

IIJIMA, CHRIS (1948–2005)

Chris Iijima was an activist, educator, musician, and attorney who fought for social justice in Asian American and antiwar movements. In the 1970s, he and fellow musicians "Charlie" Chin and Joanne Nobuko Miyamoto formed the group the Yellow Pearl and performed songs that focused on Asian American identity. Throughout his career as a community activist and educator, Iijima fought for civil liberties and human rights.

Iijima was born to activist parents on December 19, 1948, in New York City. During World War II, his father, Takeru "Tak" Iijima, was drafted and served with Company L of the 442nd Regimental Combat Team. His mother, Kazuko Ikeda, who was originally from California, was incarcerated at the Topaz concentration camp before she was reunited with her husband in Mississippi. As Asian American activists in New York City, his parents established the civil rights organization Asian Americans for Action (Triple-A) with their son who was involved in the 1968 student protests against the Vietnam War. In 1969, Iijima graduated from Columbia University with a BA and as a member of the Yellow Pearl, he recorded the album, *A Grain of Sand: Music for the Struggle by Asians in America*. Years later, Chin and Iijima recorded another album called *Back to Back*.

After working for a number of years as a school teacher in New York, Iijima attended New York University School of Law and obtained a JD in 1988. Upon graduation from law school, he clerked for the U.S. District Court for the Southern District of New York before working at a law firm in New York City. After working at the New York University School of Law and Western New England College School of Law, Iijima obtained a position at the University of Hawai'i at Mānoa's William S. Richardson School of Law in 1998 where he worked as the director of the Pre-Admission Program that admits and supports students from historically underserved communities.

Iijima passed away on December 31, 2005, at the age of 57 after battling a rare blood disease. He was survived by his parents, wife Jane Dickson, sons Alan and Christopher, and sister Lynne. Services were held in Hawai'i and across the country in remembrance of the many lives he touched.

See also: Hiroshima; Japanese American Hip-Hop; Nagano, Kent (1951–); Shinoda, Michael Kenji "Mike" (1977–)

Further Reading

A Song for Ourselves. Documentary film. Directed by Tadashi Nakamura. Downtown Community Media Center, 2009. 35 minutes.

Fujimori, Leila. "UH Law Professor was Asian-American Activist." *Honolulu Star-Bulletin*, January 17, 2006.

Kelli Y. Nakamura

IKO, MOMOKO (1940–)

When she was but two years old, Momoko Iko was forced to leave her Wapato, Washington, home along with her parents to relocate to the Heart Mountain Internment camp in Wyoming. After their release in 1945, the family had to move to New Jersey to start a living as migrant laborers. It was here that the young Iko was exposed to heartfelt stories from other displaced Japanese who congregated frequently at her home. The family eventually settled in Chicago.

Momoko Iko started writing when at Northern Illinois University and completed her undergraduate degree in English at the University of Illinois at Urbana-Champaign in 1961. She went on to complete her MFA degree from the University of Iowa. Iko's initial attempts at writing were confined to prose and poetry. She initially concentrated on personal essays that included a prose poem entitled "And There Are Stories, There Are Stories."

Iko happened to see a call for plays in a notice advertising the submission of plays for a playwriting contest sponsored by the East West Players. Out of this inspiration came her first play *Gold Watch* (1972), which premiered at the Inner City Cultural Center, Los Angeles, under the direction of Bernard Jackson. The play is one of the first literary pieces that spoke against the abuse of power and the shame of incarceration. The play deals with the issue of forced relocation and the consequent results of what happened to the Japanese American community after Pearl Harbor. Not only does the play address prewar issues among the Japanese community but also it examines the Kibei, the American-born children of Japanese immigrants who were sent away to Japan to be educated. The varied nature of their allegiances and dilemma did pose a problem for them, given the context that they were living in. The direct and indirect effects of the internment camps pervaded many facets of Japanese American society. *Gold Watch* was shown on PBS in November 1976 with Phillip Baker Hall, Robert Ito, and Mako.

Iko has also written *Flowers and Household Gods* (1975), which centers around the Kagawa family gathering at a funeral. Here Iko examines how the family structure slowly disintegrates as individuals grow, assimilate, and move out. The structural net of the family widens and as generations grow, a crisis of identity develops. What is traditional and encompassing has been severed by the throes of the internment. Old memories are brought up and along with it a reopening of old wounds. *Boutique Living and Disposable Icons* (1987), the sequel, concentrates on a wedding 20 years later in the Kagawa household. There is a confusion of identity here followed by not only a generational difference but one of values. Her other plays include: *Boutique Living and Disposable Income* (1973) and *When We Were Young* (1974).

Iko has won numerous awards for her writing from the East West Players, The Rockefeller Foundation, the National Endowment for the Arts, and the Zellerbach Foundation.

See also: Japanese American Literature

Further Reading

Uno, Roberta, ed. *Unbroken Thread.* Amherst: University of Massachusetts Press, 1993.

Ambi Harsha

INADA, LAWSON FUSAO (1938–)

A third-generation Japanese American (Sansei) born in Fresno, California, on May 26, 1938, Lawson Fusao Inada is a well-known poet, writer, activist, and educator. At the age of four, Inada and his family were forcibly relocated to the Fresno County Fairgrounds and later incarcerated at an internment camp in

Jerome, Arkansas, before finally arriving at Amache, Colorado. After the war, the Inada family returned to Fresno and luckily enough were able to resume their business, the Fresno Fish Market, because it and their home had been looked after by their neighbors. At the age of 18, Inada met jazz singer Billie Holiday at one of her shows and instantly became inspired to write poetry. Inada took classes at Fresno State University and eventually attended the University of Iowa's Writers' Workshop. In Iowa, he met his wife Janet and they have two grown children, Miles and Lowell. Inada also received his MFA from the University of Oregon and began teaching at Southern Oregon University where he remains an emeritus professor of English. Inada has received many awards and honors including the Guggenheim Fellowship in 2004, the American Book Award for Legends from Camp (1992), and the Oregon Book Award for another collection of poetry, *Drawing the Line* (1997). Inada has also served as chair of the National Steinbeck Center and judge for the National Book Award in Poetry. And from 2006 to 2010, Inada was appointed the fifth Oregon poet laureate, whose role is to foster the art of poetry, encourage literacy and learning, address central issues relating to the humanities and heritage, and reflect on public life in Oregon. The Oregon poet laureate must provide public readings and partake in numerous public events to not only share their work but to inspire others to engage in poetry as a creative expression.

Inada articulates poetry as a way to express himself and finds it not only therapeutic to write poetry but to share it with others. Although his poems are very personal and about particular experiences (often internment), Inada believes that poetry can be about finding universality or common ground that allows one to find acceptance of self and others through writing. His idea of poetry transcends the personal and is a type of communication that can even be therapeutic to the audience. For Inada, poetry is much more than words on a paper—it should be read aloud, celebrated, and shared. Inada's poetry has been published in many anthologies, but it has also been published in separate volumes including: *Before the War; Poems as They Happened* (1971), *Legends from Camp* (1993), and *Drawing the Line* (1997). In *Legends from Camp*, Inada addresses his internment memories through poetry as a way to take a hold of history and go beyond the facts. He addresses dispossession, loss, confusion, and childhood in verses that are lyrical, light, and performative despite their heavy and serious content. Inada's work is often written in this way, stemming from his past ambition to be a jazz string bass player, which he says has influenced and inspired his work. But this collection of poems is more than just about internment it also covers a variety of subjects from Inada's life: his love of jazz, Oregon, and family.

In addition to his poetry, Inada is the coeditor of two major Asian American literature anthologies, *Aiiieeeee! An Anthology of Asian American Writers* (1974) and *The Big Aiiieeeee! An Anthology of Chinese American and Japanese American*

Literature (1991) both of which highlight the importance of Asian American writing while being critical of the way the mainstream imagines Asian Americans to be. Although these anthologies focus on Japanese American and Chinese American literature, Inada and his fellow coeditors established a concrete literary history and genealogy that validated the Asian American experience. Inada is also known for reintroducing works that have been forgotten and for writing introductions to John Okada's *No-No Boy* and Toshio Mori's collection of short stories. He is also the editor of *Only What We Could Carry: The Japanese American Internment Experience* (2000), a collection that voices the struggles and emotions of internees through a variety of expression ranging from art and poetry to letters and newspaper clippings.

See also: Japanese American Literature

Further Reading

Brown, Richard. "Full Circle: An Interview with Lawson Fusao Inada." *The Museletter* 28, no. 1 (2007): 5–6.

Lawsin, Emily. "Lawson Fusao Inada." In *Japanese American History and A–Z Reference from 1868–Present*, edited by Brian Nijiya. Japanese American National Museum. New York: Facts on File, Inc., 1993.

Wendi Yamashita

ISHIGO, ESTELLE (1899–1990)

Estelle Ishigo was best known for her visual documentation of life at the Heart Mountain Relocation Center. She was one of the few whites to be incarcerated with Japanese Americans during World War II. Estelle voluntarily chose to enter Hearth Mountain in order to stay with her Nisei husband Arthur Ishigo. She authored the book *Lone Heart Mountain* (1972) and was the subject of Steven Okazaki's Academy Award–winning film *Days of Waiting* (1990).

Early Life

On July 15, 1899, Estelle Peck was born in Oakland, California, to a landscape painter father and an opera singer mother. Estelle was virtually abandoned by her parents at the age of 12, when she moved to Southern California to live with a variety of relatives and strangers, including one who would eventually rape her. While in her 20s, she enrolled in the Otis Art Institute and met an aspiring Nisei actor named Shigeharu Arthur Ishigo. Her family did not approve of this relationship due to Arthur's ethnicity, and subsequently disowned her.

In 1929, Estelle and Arthur traveled to Tijuana, Mexico, in order to be married, since antimiscegenation laws made it illegal for them to wed in California at the time. They soon settled in Hollywood, where Arthur was employed by

Paramount Studios. On December 8, 1941, just one day after the bombing of Pearl Harbor, Arthur Ishigo was fired from his job due to his ancestry. Within two weeks, Estelle herself was fired from her teaching position at the Hollywood Art Center due to her affiliation with Japanese Americans. When it became clear that all Japanese Americans on the West Coast would be sent into concentration camps, Estelle voluntarily chose to join Arthur first at the Pomona Assembly Center and ultimately at Heart Mountain, Colorado.

Life during and after World War II

A skilled artist, Estelle recorded the sights of camp in her hundreds of sketches and paintings, several of which were published in camp newspapers. In a place of veiled secrecy largely away from cameras to record the countless injustices, Estelle recorded the shocking sights taking place directly before her eyes until the final day of the concentration camp's operation. Many of her drawings have since been featured on display at museums throughout the United States.

Following World War II, the Ishigos struggled to find steady work upon returning to California. Arthur eventually gained employment in the airline industry but soon developed cancer and passed away in 1957 at the age of 55. Estelle lived in seclusion until 1972, when the California Historical Society approached her to create an exhibit of her drawings. In 1984, former Heart Mountain incarceree Bacon Sakatani found her living in a basement apartment in Los Angeles off of a $5 weekly stipend, having lost both of her legs from gangrene. Ishigo died on February 25, 1990, at a convalescent hospital in Hollywood, California.

See also: Hayakawa, Sessue "Kintaro" (1886–1973); Japanese Americans in Film

Further Reading

Days of Waiting. Dir. Steven Okazaki. Center for Asian American Media, 1990.

Hall, Vanessa. "Ishigo, Estelle." *Notable American Women: A Biographical Dictionary Completing the Twentieth Century*, vol. 5. Cambridge, MA: Harvard University Press, 2004.

Ishigo, Estelle. *Lone Hearth Mountain*. Los Angeles: Japanese American Citizens League, Hollywood Chapter, 1972.

Dean Ryuta Adachi

JAPANESE AMERICAN ARTISTS

Japanese American artists have excelled at traditional Japanese arts, Western fine arts, and modern art. Their works can be characterized by an unorthodox, often postmodern, use of techniques, symbols, and media. They utilize symbols from Japanese American religion, history, childhood memories, stereotypes, and fantasy.

Cary-Hiroyuki Tagawa arrives at the 22nd annual Critics' Choice Awards in Santa Monica, California, 2016. (Jordan Strauss/Invision/AP Photo)

The most visible Japanese American artists are models, actors, and directors. These artists excel at manipulating stereotypical images. For example, Cary Tagawa, a film actor, often portrayed yellow peril villains, but with the intensity to be taken as a serious threat instead of a comical straw man.

Other writers of plays, literature, and poetry examine the underside of Japanese American life. Playwright Philip Kan Gotanda in *After the War* described the intra- and interracial tensions of Japanese Americans in postwar San Francisco, and illustrated how dignity is difficult to maintain without a general sense of propriety and security.

After the War also highlighted Japanese American jazz, which was in place before internment. Jazz, taiko (drumming), and hip-hop have expressed the psychic impact of internment on the community. Miya Masaoka (jazz koto) painted the barren landscape of an internment camp in "Topaz Reflections." Anthony Brown (jazz drums) and San Jose Taiko teamed up in Big Bands behind Barbed Wire to express the energy of the memory of internment, while Mike Kenji Shinoda (hip-hop) put himself in the place of those interned in "Kenji." Artist and musician Mike Shinoda—a.k.a. Fort Minor—painted the cover of the Fort Minor album *The Rising Tied*, as well as creating a shoe line. Shinoda and other painters in oils, watercolors, comics (manga), and graffiti contrast the circular and angular, expressing the duality of being silent and disturbed. Well before internment, Henry Kitayama (manga) drew about the open racism in the United States, and during internment Mine Okubo (manga) illustrated the lack of space and privacy of internment. Similarly, after internment, Chizuko Judy Sugita de Queiroz (watercolors) painted her internment memories, contrasting life with industrial imprisonment.

Gardeners and landscape architects have beautified the homes and churches of Japanese Americans with a mixture of plants symbolic of religious themes, the unity of all life, serenity, community, a connection to an idealized Japan, and success in agriculture. They have been employed often by non-Japanese who desired an "oriental" garden in their homes, hotels, and city parks. Thus, gardeners have excelled at stereotypical Japanese images as well as authentic representations of Japanese American history.

Sculptors, including rock gardeners, illustrate traces of the past. There are sculptors in metal, plaster, wood (including furniture), paper (origami and gift wrapping), and flowers (ikebana). For example, Ruth Asawa combined wood, paper, and metal sculpture in her fountains in San Francisco's Japantown; these fountains combine the shapes and tactileness of origami with the flowing lines of wooden baskets. Thus, the fountains bring together the experiences of learning to fold origami with Asawa's childhood memories of the flowing impressions of her feet dragging behind the back of a pickup truck.

See also: Asawa, Ruth (1926–2013); Noguchi, Isamu (1904–1988)

Further Reading

Creef, Elena Tajima. *Imaging Japanese America: The Visual Construction of Citizenship, Nation, and the Body*. New York: New York University Press, 2004.

Hirasuna, Delphine. *The Art of Gaman: Arts and Crafts from the Japanese American Internment Camps, 1942–1946*. Berkeley, CA: Ten Speed Press, 2005.

Brett Esaki

JAPANESE AMERICAN HIP-HOP

Several Japanese Americans have been involved in the hip-hop cultural movement. Although hip-hop and its several forms trace its roots to African Americans in New York City during the early 1970s, it subsequently spread to several ethnic communities throughout the country and even the world.

Lyrics Born

In 1993, rapper Tsutomu "Tom" Shimura released "Send Them" under the stage name Asia Born. "Send Them" was released as a double A side EP by the underground hip-hop label Solesides, coupled with "Entropy" by DJ Shadow.

Although "Entropy" received more critical acclaim than "Send Them," the success of this EP raised awareness of Shimura's rapping abilities.

Shimura was born in Tokyo in 1972 to a Japanese father and an Italian mother. At the age of two, his family moved to Salt Lake City, Utah, and ultimately to Berkeley, California, where he discovered hip-hop. While a student at University of California, Davis, Shimura was a DJ at the college radio station KDVS. He adopted the stage name Asia Born in reference to his birthplace. However, in 1995, he switched to the Lyrics Born moniker in order to stress his lyrical dexterity above his ethnic heritage.

Shimura later partnered with rapper Lateef the Truth Speaker to form the duo Latyrx. Their debut LP *The Album* was released in 1997 and would go on to sell over 100,000 copies. In 2003, Shimura released his first studio album as Lyrics Born, *Later That Day* under the Quannum Projects label. This album included the single "Callin' Out," which was featured in several films, video games, and even a Diet Coke advertisement campaign.

Key Kool

In 1995, Key Kool and Rhettmatic were the first specifically Asian American rap group to release a widely recognized hip-hop album. Key Kool is the stage name of Kikuo Nishi, a third-generation Japanese American from Torrance, California, partnered with Filipino DJ Rhettmatic of the Universal Zulu Nation Rock Steady Crew and World Famous Beat Junkies to release their first album *Kozmonauts*. One of Nishi's earliest exposures to hip-hop was through Steve Yano, a fellow Japanese American who sold hip-hop records at Southern California swap meets during the 1980s. Yano coincidentally played an important role in the development of the pioneering rap group N.W.A., when he introduced Dr. Dre to Eazy-E.

Nishi attributes his passion for rap music from the first time he heard "Rapper's Delight," the seminal 1979 track by The Sugarhill Gang. He began breakdancing in sixth grade, followed soon after by experimenting with turntables and eventually writing his own rhymes. Around 1989, he began rapping with a group called the United Nations Committee under the Rhyme Syndicate collective, led by rapper-turned-actor Ice-T. Through this exposure, Nishi partnered with a Mexican Samoan rapper named Intellect and signed a record deal. The record label believed that there was no market for an Asian American rapper, and thus chose to focus on Intellect's Latino heritage. Nishi eventually withdrew from the label without releasing an album.

On *Kozmonautz*, Key Kool and Rhettmatic included the song "Reconcentrated," which deals with the concentration camp experience of Japanese Americans. Nishi was also a founding member of the hip-hop group The Visionaries, as well as President of Up Above Records, which he cofounded with his manager Doug "Papadoug" Kato, DJ Rhettmatic, and the World Famous Beat Junkies.

Mike Shinoda

Michael Kenji Shinoda first rose to prominence as a member of Linkin Park. Shinoda was born in Southern California to a third-generation Japanese American father and a white mother. Although Linkin Park is generally classified as a rock band, Shinoda's rapping and Korean American Joe Hahn's inclusion as the band's turntablist helped popularize the growing wave of hip-hop rock in the late 1990s.

In 2004, Shinoda formed a hip-hop group called Fort Minor. On their debut album *The Rising Tied*, the group included the song "Kenji," which also addresses the Japanese American incarceration experience that his family faced. As a producer, Shinoda has worked directly with many notable rappers including Jay-Z, Lupe Fiasco, and the X-Ecutioners. Besides his musical endeavors, he is an active visual artist and has even showcased his work at the Japanese American National Museum in Los Angeles.

Other Notable Contributions to Hip-Hop by Japanese Americans

The first Asian American rap group to earn a number one song on the *Billboard* Hot 100 chart was Far East Movement with "Like a G6" in October 2010. One of the founding members of the group, Kevin Nishimura (stage name: Kev Nish), is a half–Japanese American, half–Chinese American from Los Angeles. Far East Movement has produced songs with a number of famous hip-hop, pop, and electronic musicians including Flo Rida, Snoop Dogg, Lil Jon, Ryan Tedder, Justin Bieber, Skrillex, Afrojack, and Marshmello.

Shing02 is the stage name for rapper, producer, and activist Shingo Annen. Annen was born in Tokyo, Japan, in 1975, and moved to the San Francisco Bay Area at the age of 15. His first single "A Day Like Any Other" featured fellow underground rappers El-P, Murs, and Yeshua Da Pond. Unlike most other Japanese American rappers, Annen often raps in both English and Japanese. He has collaborated with musicians such as Nujabes, Tokimonsta, Ken Ishii, Kero One, and Emi Meyer. In 2007, he developed the Vestax Faderboard musical instrument in collaboration with Vestax and Korg.

Although American hip-hop music and culture have long been visible in Japan, a small number of Japanese hip-hop artists have achieved limited success in the United States. Some examples include DJ Honda (turntablist and producer), Hikaru Utada (R&B singer raised in New York), Crystal Kay (R&B singer born to an African American father and Korean mother and raised on an American Navy base), and the Teriyaki Boyz (produced by Kanye West, DJ Premier, The Neptunes, and others).

Besides rappers, another notable Japanese American with ties to hip-hop culture is artist Gajin Fujita, whose work combines Japanese elements and techniques with Latino-styled graffiti. Fujita was born in 1972 to Japanese immigrant parents and raised in the Boyle Heights neighborhood of Los Angeles.

See also: Hiroshima; Iijima, Chris (1948–2005); Nagano, Kent (1951–); Shinoda, Michael Kenji "Mike" (1977–)

Further Reading

Asakawa, Gil. *Being Japanese American: A JA Sourcebook for Nikkei, Hapa . . . & Their Friends*. Berkeley, CA: Stone Bridge Press, 2004.

Donohue, Marlena. "Gajin Fujita." ArtScene, 2002. http://artscenecal.com/ArticlesFile /Archive/Articles2002/Articles0902/GFujitaA.html. Accessed January 15, 2017.

Hirano Culross, Mikey. "A Long, Legendary Reach." *Rafu Shimpo,* September 26, 2014. http://www.rafu.com/2014/09/a-long-legendary-reach/. Accessed January 15, 2017.

Pang, Angela. "Lyrics Born: Japanese-Italian Rapper Is Lyrically Born." Solesides, 2006. http://www.solesides.com/lyrics-born-japaneseitalian-rapper-is-lyrically-born.html. Accessed January 15, 2017.

Weiss, Jeff. "Far East Movement Hits the Dancefloor." *Los Angeles Times,* December 25, 2009. http://latimesblogs.latimes.com/music_blog/2009/12/far-east-movement-hits -the-dance-floor.html. Accessed January 15, 2017.

Yokota, Ryan Masaaki. "Key Kool: Nikkei on the Down Side." Buddhahead Productions, 2002. http://www.buddhahead.org/writing/features_010094.htm. Accessed January 15, 2017.

Dean Ryuta Adachi

JAPANESE AMERICAN LITERATURE
Early Japanese Immigrant Writers

Since their arrival in the United States, people of Japanese descent have been writing about issues of identity, nationality, and ethnicity. While the harsh conditions under which the first immigrants lived—including language barriers, hard work, and racist propaganda—made literature not a first priority, the Issei still wrote poems and stories that were mostly published in Japanese-language newspapers.

As one of these early authors, Carl Sadakichi Hartmann (1867–1944), who had a German father and a Japanese mother, came to the United States at the age of 15. He wrote prolifically about European and Japanese art and literature and published various collections of poetry, among them *Drifting Flowers of the Sea and Other Poems* (1904), *My Rubáiyát* (1913), and *Japanese Rhythms* (1915). Etsu Inagaki Sugimoto (1874–1950), who arrived in the United States in 1898, authored a number of novels that were set in Japan and were supposed to explain Japanese culture to an American audience. Sugimoto is most acclaimed for her autobiographical novel, *A Daughter of the Samurai* (1925). Yonejirō (Yone) Noguchi (1875–1947), who lived in the United States between 1893 and 1904 and is the father of famous sculptor Isamu Noguchi (1904–1988), is most well-known for his poetry but also published two novels, *The American Diary of a Japanese Girl* (1902) and *The American Letters of a Japanese Parlor Maid* (1905). Ayako Tanaka Ishigaki's (1903–1996) memoir, *Restless Wave: My Life in Two Worlds* (1940), is one of the first books written in English by a woman of Asian descent and the author's only book in English. She came to the United States in 1926 at the age of 23 at a time when Asian immigration was illegal. Ishigaki's immigration was possible through a visa that she was granted for staying with relatives, who held diplomatic status, in Washington, D.C. When she left her family and moved to New York, she became an undocumented alien. As a journalist and feminist activist, Ishigaki wrote more than 20 books in the United States and Japan on the exploitation of workers and women. Bunichi Kagawa (1904–1981), who immigrated in the 1920s, published his poetry collection, *Hidden Flame*, in 1930. He lived in the Tule Lake internment camp during World War II where he helped with the publication of the literary magazine, *Tessaku*, which was printed in Japanese.

Nisei Literature

Nisei, second-generation Japanese Americans, first started publishing their work in community newspapers like *Kashu Mainichi* and *The New World—Sun*. The Nisei community also circulated literary magazines like *Reimei*, which was inaugurated in 1931. With the 1932 poem "Japanese American" by Chiye Mori, Nisei writing turned more overtly toward politics with a critique of U.S. and Japanese legislation and policies. At the same time, generational and cultural issues within the Japanese American community remained important topics. Taro Katayama's short story "Haru" (1933), for example, explores, through the eyes of the main character, Haru, generational differences among the Issei and Nisei and discusses arranged marriages as a controversial matter. Perhaps the most well-known Nisei writer before World War II was Toshio Mori (1910–1980). His short story collection *Yokohama, California* was supposed to be published in 1942 but did not appear until 1949 because of the outbreak of the war. Stories like "The Woman Who Makes Swell Doughnuts" and the title story, "Yokohama, California," depict daily life in the Japanese American community. Mori's characters are not exoticized (like most depictions of people of Asian descent in U.S. popular culture and literature at the time), but they are invested in Japanese American values and emphasize the community's humanity.

The internment during World War II suppressed the wider publication of Japanese American writing; but Nisei kept producing literary work and published it in three literary magazines. The *Tulean Dispatch* at Tule Lake, California, *The Pen* at Rohwer, Arkansas, and the *Trek* at Topaz, Utah, disseminated stories and poems about camp life and issues of identity and equality. Because these journals were controlled by the government, direct political criticism was infrequent. Authors still included cultural and political critique in more subversive ways. Toyo Suyemoto (1916–2003), a poet, memoirist, and librarian, for example, wrote poems like "Gain" (1942) and "Topaz, Utah" (published after she revisited the camp site) that critically engaged with conditions in the internment camps. Journalist Mary Oyama (1907–1994) wrote extensively on racism, integration, and marriage. Her article "My Only Crime Is My Face" (1943), for example, appeared in *Liberty* magazine and analyzed the internment as a social injustice based on racist prejudices and xenophobia.

Once the internment period ended, Nisei writers had to put their literary aspirations on hold due to economic need and persistent struggles with discrimination in finding housing and employment after relocation. Many Nisei, however, published in Japanese American newspapers like the *Rafu Shimpo* in Los Angeles and the *Hokubei Mainichi* in San Francisco. Likely because they did not experience mass internment, Japanese Americans in Hawai'i were able to produce a larger amount of longer texts. Shelley Ota's (1911–1987) novel *Upon Their Shoulders* (1951), possibly the first published novel by a Japanese American, recounts the lives of two Japanese American families in Hawai'i who lose some of their members to the internment. Margaret Harada's novel *The Sun Shines on the Immigrant* (1960) is a variation of the rags-to-riches storyline with a Japanese American male immigrant protagonist that ends shortly before World War II. Kazuo Miyamoto (1897–1988), who served as a physician in a mainland internment camp, deals more critically with his community's trauma in his novel *Hawai'i: End of the Rainbow* (1964), which focuses on the experiences of two interned Issei.

Of the Nisei writers on the mainland United States, Hisaye Yamamoto (1921–2011) is likely the best known. Her short stories explore issues of gender, race, generational differences, relationships between mothers and daughters, and multiculturalism. Some of her most widely disseminated stories are "Seventeen Syllables" (1949), a tale about the relationship between a Nisei daughter who is absorbed in her adolescence and her Issei mother who struggles with her unhappy marriage, and "Yoneko's Earthquake" (1951), which also takes a critical look at marriage through the eyes of a disillusioned Issei wife who engages in an affair with a Filipino worker. Yamamoto, as one of very few Japanese American mainland authors, wrote about the internment immediately after the abandonment of the camps. In "The Legend of Miss Sasagawara" (1951), she scrutinizes the support among members of the Japanese American community through the account of an aging ballet dancer whose loyalty is questioned by her fellow inmates in camp. Miné Okubo (1912–2001) expressed her experiences in the Tanforan detention facility in her illustrated memoir, *Citizen 13660* (1946), through a mix of drawings and text. In 1953, Monica Sone's (1919–2011) memoir, *Nisei Daughter*, was published, recalling her Nisei childhood in Seattle and the prejudice that the community encountered, her family's internment at Minidoka, and her life after resettlement and struggles with creating a Nisei identity. Although Okubo and Sone relied on their own memories for their works, John Okada (1923–1971) took a fictional approach to writing *No-No Boy* (1957). The novel tells of the aftermath of the internment through the perspective of Ichiro Yamada, who had refused to serve in the U.S. Army and to pledge allegiance to the U.S. government, which led to his imprisonment. The book starts shortly after his release from prison and investigates the fragmentation and healing within the postwar Japanese American community. In the genre of poetry, Yasuo Sasaki (1911–2008), a physician, activist, and editor of the magazine *Reimei*, brought out *Ascension* (1968) and *Village Scene/Village Herd* (1986).

The mid-1970s redress movement encouraged more Nisei to write about their lives in confinement. Jeanne Wakatsuki Houston (1934–) and her husband James Houston (1933–2009), who, as a Caucasian, did not experience internment, coauthored *Farewell to Manzanar* (1973). The memoir begins with Jeanne Houston's childhood in California, goes into detail with her family's detention at Manzanar, describes their lives after relocation first to Long Beach and later a berry farm in San Jose, and ends with Houston's visit of the camp ruins in 1972. Through the character of Houston's troubled father, *Farewell* explores Issei men's helplessness during the internment period and beyond. Yoshiko Uchida's (1921–1992) autobiography, *Desert Exile: The Uprooting of a Japanese-American Family* (1982), too, focuses especially on the Issei generation and how they dealt with the xenophobia and betrayal that they experienced. Her novel *Picture Bride* (1987) follows the journey of Hana, a young Japanese woman who leaves for the United States with high hopes of a good life with her new husband, whom she has never met. Upon arrival, she realizes that living conditions are much harsher than she anticipated, and they only deteriorate when she and her husband are put into an internment camp. Besides these works, Uchida is mostly known as an author of children's books. Milton Murayama's (1923–2016) *All I Asking for Is My Body* (1975) is set in Hawai'i and deals with plantation politics and dynamics in the 1930s and 1940s. In the realm of drama after the internment, Wakako Yamauchi (1924–) is well-known for her play *And the Soul Shall Dance* (1982), which focuses especially on gender relations in the Japanese American community and Issei women's isolation and strength during the internment. Mitsuye Yamada's (1923–) *Camp Notes* (1976), a collection of poems and stories, analyzes the injustice her community experienced during their internment in Minidoka. Her second book, *Desert Run* (1988), includes similar themes and particularly emphasizes sexism and racism.

Sansei Authors

Among Sansei poets, Lawson Fusao Inada (1938–) caused a stir with *Before the War: Poems as They Happened* (1971), the first collection of poetry by a Japanese American printed by a major American publisher. In his work, Inada experiments with new literary styles to express his community's identity. Poet Janice Mirikitani (1941–) does not shy away from difficult topics either and explores racism and the webbed connections of different forms of oppression in her collections *Awake in the River* (1978) and *Shedding Silence* (1987). One of her most famous poems that expresses these concerns is entitled "Japs" (1978). Other Sansei poets who have received national attention are Juliet Kono (1943–) with her collection *Hilo Rains* (1988) and Garrett Kaoru Hongo (1951–) with *Yellow Light* (1982) and *The River of Heaven* (1988). David Mura (1952–) became first known through his poems, especially those in *After We Lost Our Way* (1989). He also wrote a memoir, which is called *Turning Japanese* (1991). In both works, he adds a decidedly postmodern edge to Sansei literature. Kimiko Hahn's (1955–) poems explore female subjectivity and desires. Among other compilations, she published *The Narrow Road to the Interior* (2006) and *Toxic Flora* (2010).

In the sphere of Sansei drama, Philip Kan Gotanda's (1951–) plays, like *Song for a Nisei Fisherman* (1993) and *The Wash* (1990), portray family dynamics. Velina Hasu Houston's (1957–) drama deals with cross-cultural and cross-racial issues. She received special attention for *Tea* (1988), a play that depicts the lives of Japanese war brides in the United States.

In terms of short story telling, Sylvia Watanabe (1953–) published *Talking to the Dead* in 1992, a collection of stories exploring life in a small Hawai'ian village. The short narratives of David Mas Masumoto (1954–) in *Silent Strength* (1984) negotiate the connections between geographic location, community, and identity. And Ruth A. Sasaki's stories in *"The Loom" and Other Stories* (1991) negotiate Japanese American lives in San Francisco after the internment.

Sansei novels became more transnational than Nisei works. For example, Karen Tei Yamashita's (1951–) novels *Through the Arc of the Rainforest* (1990) and *Brazil Maru* (1992) are set in Brazil, which hosts the largest Japanese diaspora. Ruth Ozeki (1956–), who has an American father and a Japanese mother, comments in *My Year of Meats* (1998) on both Japanese and American culture and unites two women across the globe through a cooking show. Novelist Julie Shigekuni published *A Bridge between Us* in 1995, *Invisible Gardens* in 2003, and *Unending Nora* in 2008. All of her works have female protagonists and revolve around intergenerational relationships and female sexual desire.

Lois-Ann Yamanaka (1961–), a Hawai'ian poet and novelist, uses Pidgin English in her creative work to point to ongoing racial issues, like in her novel *Wild Meat and the Bully Burgers* (1996). *The Floating World* (1989) by Cynthia Kadohata (1956–), who won the U.S. National Book Award in 2013, underlines the diversity of Japanese American experiences in the 1950s. Kadohata mostly works on children's and young-adult literature. Her book *Weedflower* (2006), for instance, tells the story of her father's life in the Poston internment camp. Mitchiko Kakutani (1955–), who has won the Pulitzer Price for her writing, has worked as a literary critic for the *New York Times* since 1983.

See also: DeSoto, Hisaye Yamamoto (1921–2011); Hartmann, Sadakichi (1867–1944); Hirahara, Naomi (1962–); Iko, Momoko (1940–); Inada, Lawson Fusao (1938–); Kogawa, Joy (1935–); Mori, Toshio (1910–1980); Mura, David (1952–); Murayama, Milton (1923–2016); Okada, John (1923–1971); Otsuka, Julie (1962–)

Further Reading

Yogi, Stan. "Japanese American Literature." In *An Interethnic Companion to Asian American Literature,* edited by Kink-Kok Cheung, 125–155. Cambridge, UK: Cambridge University Press, 1997.

Zhang, Benzi. "Japanese American Literature." In *New Immigrant Literatures in the United States. A Sourcebook to Our Multicultural Literary Heritage,* edited by Alpana Sharma Knippling, 125–141. Westport, CT: Greenwood Press, 1996.

Ina C. Seethaler

JAPANESE AMERICAN OLYMPIANS

Since the end of World War II, 34 Japanese Americans have participated in the Olympic Games. Of these, 21 were men and 13 were women. Further, 23 participated in the Summer Olympic Games and 11 participated in the Winter Olympics. Of the Summer Olympians, eight competed in judo, four in swimming, three in volleyball, two in fencing, two in weightlifting, one in gymnastics, one in handball, one in platform diving, and one in track and field. As for Winter Olympians, five competed in ice dancing, four in figure skating, one in short-track speed skating, and one in snowboarding. Although most of the Japanese American Olympians have represented the United States, two have represented Japan, and one has represented Georgia.

Fourteen Japanese Americans have won a total of 29 Olympic medals, including 10 gold medals, 10 silver medals, 9 bronze medals. The most successful Japanese American Olympian is Apolo Anton Ohno, a short-track speed skater, who won eight medals from 2002 to 2010. His medal winning performances include gold medals in the 1,500 meters in 2002 and the 500 meters in 2006; silver medals in 1,000 meters in 2002 and 1,500 meters in 2010; and bronze medals in the 1,000 meters in 2006, 5,000-meter relay in 2006, 1,000 meters in 2010, and 5,000-meter relay in 2010. Ohno also finished 11th in the 500 meters in 2002; 4th in the 5,000-meter relay in 2002; 8th in the 1,500 meters in 2006; and 8th in the 500 meters in 2010. Ohno is the most decorated American winter Olympic athlete.

Five other Japanese Americans have won more than one Olympic medal. Ford Hiroshi Konno, a swimmer, won four medals from 1952 to 1956. His medal winning performances include gold medals in the 1,500-meter freestyle and the 4 × 200-meter freestyle relay in 1952; and silver medals in the 400-meter freestyle and 4 × 200-meter freestyle relay in 1956. Konno's gold medal performance resulted in Olympic records of 18:30.3 in the 1,500 meters and 8:31.1 in the 4 × 200-meter freestyle relay. Tamio "Tommy" Kono, a weightlifter, won three medals from 1952 to 1960. In 1952, he won the gold medal in the lightweight class division, setting an Olympic record of 362.5 kilograms. In 1956, Kono won the gold medal in the light-heavyweight division, lifting a world record of 447.5 kilograms. In 1960, he won the silver medal in the middleweight division with a 427.5-kilogram lift. Bryan Ezra Tsumoru Clay, a track and field athlete, won two medals from 2004 to 2008. In 2004, he won the silver medal in the decathlon, and, in 2008, he won the gold medal in the decathlon. Eric Anthony Terou Sato, a volleyball player, won two medals from 1988 to 1992. In 1988, he won a gold medal, and, in 1992, he won a bronze medal. Evelyn Tokue Kawamoto, a swimmer, won two bronze medals in the 400-meter freestyle and the 4 × 100-meter relay in 1952.

Eight athletes have won one Olympic medal. Yoshinobu "Yoshi" Oyakawa, a swimmer, won the gold medal in the 100-meter backstroke in the Olympic record time of 1:05.4 in 1952. He also finished eighth in the 100-meter backstroke in 1956. Kristine Tsuya "Kristi" Yamaguchi, a figure skater, won the gold medal in the singles competition in 1992. Harold Toshiyuki Sakata, a weightlifter, won the silver medal in the light-heavyweight division in 1948. Richard Tsugio "Sonny" Tanabe Jr. a swimmer, won a silver medal in the 4x200-meter freestyle relay in 1956. Kevin Yoshimi Asano, a judoka, won a silver medal in the extra-lightweight division in 1988. Tamari Miyashiro, a volleyball player, won the silver medal in 2012. Peter Jonathan Westbrook, a fencer, won the bronze medal in the individual sabre in 1984. Liane Lissa Sato, a volleyball player, won a bronze medal in 1992.

Eighteen Japanese Americans have competed in the Olympics without winning medals. Kyoko Ina, a figure skater, finished ninth in mixed pairs in 1994, fourth in mixed pairs in 1998, and fifth in mixed pairs in 2002. Rena Inoue, a figure skater, seventh in mixed pairs in 2006. Haley Dyan Ishimatsu, a diver, finished 14th in the platform and 5th in the platform team in 2008. Teimoc Jonston-Ono, a judoka, finished 13th (tie) in the middleweight division in 1976. Paul Kuniaki Maruyama, a judoka, finished fifth (tie) in the lightweight division in 1964. Sayaka Matsumoto, a judoka, finished 13th (tie) in the extra-lightweight division in 2008. Mirai Aileen Nagasu, a figure skater, finished fourth in the singles in 2010. George Nonomura, a fencer, finished 14th in the team competition in 1988. Liliko Ogasawara, a judoka, finished seventh (tie) in 1996. Kenneth Kenji Okada, a judoka, finished 19th (tie) in 1972. Antonio M. "Tony" Okada, a judoka, finished 35th (tie) in the extra-lightweight division in 1992. Rodney Kenji "Rod" Oshita, handball, finished 9th in team handball in 1984 and 12th in 1988. Makoto Douglas Sakamoto, a gymnast, finished 20th in the all-around and was part of the U.S. team that finished 7th in 1964, and in 1972, he finished 10th in the all-around. Alex Hideo and Maia Harumi Shibutani, ice dancing, finished ninth in the mixed pairs in 2014. Taylor Takata, judo, finished ninth (tie) in the half-lightweight division in 2008. Graham Watanabe, a snowboarder, finished 31st in boardercross in 2006 and 18th in 2010.

Three athletes have represented nations other than the United States. Rena Inoue, a figure skater, finished 14th in mixed pairs in 1992, 18th in singles in 1994 representing Japan. Allison Lynn Reed, ice dancer, finished 22nd in mixed pairs representing Georgia in 2010. Cathy Reed and Chris Reed, ice dancers, finished 17th in mixed pairs 2010, 21st in mixed pairs in 2014, and 5th in mixed team in 2014 representing Japan.

See also: Japanese Americans in Sports

Further Reading

Sports Reference/Olympic Sports. Sports Reference.com. http://www.sports-reference.com/olympics/. Accessed January 15, 2017.

Wallechinsky, David, and Jaime Loucky. *The Complete Book of the Olympics: 2012 Edition.* London: Aurum Press, 2012.

Adam R. Hornbuckle

JAPANESE AMERICANS IN BASEBALL

Baseball has been a significant aspect of Japanese American life since the height of Japanese immigration to the United States and its Pacific territories in the late 19th and early 20th centuries. The Issei, the first generation of Japanese immigrants to the United States, established baseball teams and leagues. Their children, the Nisei, embraced baseball as a way to maintain and preserve Nikkei culture and tradition, but also as a way to join the American mainstream. Baseball, one of several sports played by Japanese Americans, uplifted the community in the face of limited economic and social opportunities reinforced by racial prejudice. Baseball became especially important to Japanese Americans during internment, when the U.S. government held tens of thousands of them in military administered concentration camps during World War II; the sport offered not so much a diversion to pass the time but a mechanism to maintain their community, a sense of dignity, and self-worth. In the decades after the war, baseball facilitated the reconstruction of the Japanese American community, which gradually overcame much of the prejudice of the Issei era. Moreover, the late 20th and early 21st centuries witnessed a proliferation of Japanese Americans entering major league baseball.

Modern baseball developed from a variety of bat and ball games played in North America during the 1830s and 1840s. Known as "town-ball," "round-ball," and "base-ball," these games involved hitting the ball with a bat and running a series of bases. In 1845, Alexander Cartwright of the New York Knickerbockers Athletic Club standardized and codified the rules of the game. In 1846, the first official baseball game played according to the "Knickerbocker Rules" occurred between the New York Nine and the Knickerbockers in Hoboken, New Jersey, in which the Nine won 23–1. A baseball craze, which developed in New York City in the 1850s, swept across the nation and led to the formation of many amateur and semiprofessional teams. In 1869, the Cincinnati Red Stockings emerged as the first fully professional team. From 1871 to 1875, the National Association of Professional Base Ball Players marked the first professional league. Major League Baseball, as it is presently known, originated with the formation of the National League in 1876, followed by the American League in 1901.

In the 1870s, Japan embraced baseball first as a loosely organized fitness and recreational activity to an organized sport. In 1872 Horace Wilson, a Civil War veteran, hired by the Japanese government as a foreign adviser to assist in the modernization of the Japanese education system following the Meiji Restoration in 1868, introduced baseball to students at the Kaisei Academy in Tokyo. A professor of English, Wilson thought playing baseball would improve the physical fitness of his students. Interest in baseball swept the academy and soon teams of students and foreign instructors began playing each other. However, the impetus for organized baseball in Japan did not come from Wilson's endeavors, but from those of Hitaoka Hiroshi of the Meiji Ministry of Engineering, who learned about baseball during a visit to the United States in 1871. In baseball, with its emphasis on rule and order, Hiroshi recognized a game fit for the modern society which Japan sought to establish through its recent reforms. He returned to Japan with baseballs and bats and, in 1878, established the Shimbashi Athletic Club, Japan's first organized baseball team. Professional teams did not appear until the 1920s.

In the decades following the Meiji Restoration, Japanese immigrated to Hawai'i and the western United States in significant numbers. Increased property taxes to finance the industrial reforms, the seizure of land for industrial expansion, and increased competition for economic resources led many

Japanese to look elsewhere for economic and social opportunities. For many, the sugar plantations of Hawai'i offered particular promise and, by 1896, over 24,000 Japanese, nearly a quarter of the nation's population had immigrated to Hawai'i. Although Japanese immigrants brought baseball with them, the sport already had gained a foothold on the islands through the establishment of the Young Men's Christian Association by American religious missionaries and other organizations interested in "Americanizing" indigenous Hawai'ians. One the other hand Japanese Christian ministers like Takie Okumara, used baseball to promote and preserve Japanese culture. In the 1890s, Japanese formed teams that became part of the Hawai'ian Baseball League, which also included teams consisting of Chinese, Portuguese, Filipinos, and Hawai'ians. Hawai'ian Sugar Planters Association formed baseball teams consisting of their workers. Second-generation Nisei formed the Japanese Ancestry League. Hawai'i offered exposure to other cultures for the American college teams that played there.

Just as the need for labor on sugar plantations drew Japanese to Hawai'i, so did employment opportunities offered by the railroads, sawmills, mines, and farms of the western United States. Although immigration to America started in the mid-19th century, it peaked in the 1890s; the Japanese population exceeded 24,000 in 1900, with more than 10,000 in California alone. Chirua Obata, an 18-year-old artist, who immigrated to San Francisco in 1903, established the Fuji Athletic Club, the first Japanese baseball team in California in 1904. After the 1906 San Francisco earthquake, Japanese dispersal throughout northern California resulted in baseball organizing in San Jose in 1910, Sacramento in 1912, and Oakland in 1915. About 19,000 Japanese had settled in Southern California, with the majority in Los Angeles. The Japanese American Association promoted participation in sports and, by 1915, enough interest in baseball led to the creation of the Southern California Japanese Baseball League. Compared to California, Japanese settlement in the Pacific Northwest was small with only 8,000 to 9,000, but interest in baseball was just as keen. The Seattle Mikados, established in 1907, rose to prominence in the region. Its star player, Frank Tokichi Fukada, a 1906 immigrant, organized the Cheery Team in 1909, which became a social club, known as the Asahi Club, in 1912. Later Fukada coached youth baseball teams in Portland, but an organized team never fully emerged.

As Japanese American baseball took shape in the western United States, Japanese immigration faced serious challenges. Anti-Japanese nativism in California public schools led to the Gentlemen's Agreement of 1907, in which the U.S. government agreed not to restrict the immigration of wives, children, and parents, and to avoid legal discrimination against Japanese American children in California schools, so long as the Japanese government agreed to curtail immigration of skilled and unskilled workers to the United States. This unofficial agreement remained in effect until President Calvin Coolidge signed into law the

Immigration Act of 1924, which included the Asian Exclusion Act that banned further Asian immigration to the United States and denied immigrants already in the country the opportunity to become American citizens. Without a chance to garner citizenship, first-generation Japanese immigrants, the Issei, realized that the future success of Japanese in America depended upon the Nisei, the first generation of Japanese born in the United States. Although Japanese America families wanted their children to absorb the values of America culture, they also wanted them to retain the spirit of what it meant to be Japanese.

In the late 1920s, baseball provided the Nisei with a bridge between Japanese and American culture. Issei baseball pioneer Frank Fukada took his best players to Japan to compete in their ancestral land, thinking it would provide them with a broader appreciation of the values shared by Japanese and American cultures. Another Issei who recognized the importance of baseball bridging cultures was Kenichi Zenimura, who had immigrated to Fresno in 1920. Born in Hiroshima in 1900, Zenimura grew up in Hawai'i where he led his high school to the island school baseball championship. In Fresno, he assembled a baseball league consisting of 10 teams that regularly played against teams of Mexican American semiprofessionals, Negro League clubs, and Pacific Coast League teams. In 1924, Zenimura took the best players from his teams to play against Waseda University in Japan. The Fresno Athletic Club concluded its 1927 barnstorming tour of Japan with a game against the Philadelphia Royal Giants of the Negro Leagues. The game demonstrated the athletic skill shared by the Nisei and African Americans with their Caucasian counterparts at a time when racial segregation created separate leagues in the United States. Also the barnstorming games elevated the play of the Japanese at a time when many wanted to establish a professional league in Japan.

By the mid-1930s, baseball had become an institution in the Japanese American community, as baseball teams formed in the first decade of the 20th century now had a substantial history. In addition to the established teams, new ones formed to fulfill the needs of the burgeoning Nisei population. In California, the Japanese American community in cities such as San Francisco and Sacramento had increased by more than 4,000 to 6,000 since 1900. The increase in teams with the increased population permitted Nisei teams to compete among themselves rather than against Caucasian, African American, and Mexican American teams as did the Issei. Improvements in the roads throughout northern California, resulting from New Deal construction projects, facilitated their competition by linking the communities. Baseball's institutionalization within the Japanese American community underscored its importance in fostering loyalty, honesty, and courage—virtues common to both Japanese and American cultures. In contrast to European immigrants who settled in the eastern United States, the Japanese brought baseball with them, they did not adopt the sport as part of their initiation into becoming Americans.

In the late 1930s, baseball provided Japanese Americans with one of many institutional havens to escape racial discrimination. Although *Nihonmachis* or "Little Tokyos" had flourished since the arrival of Japanese immigrants to the western United States in the early 1900s, they took on greater significance in the decade following the implementation of the Immigration Act of 1924. By then the burgeoning Nisei population had increased to such an extent that the Japanese American community retreated from the American mainstream and looked to itself to provide services. At that time the New Deal Works Progress Administration built baseball parks across the country, Japanese Americans built their own, financed without federal or local resources. Closely associated with churches or farms, the baseball parks offered a safe place for them to play their games. Churches, farms, businesses, schools, and baseball parks offered spaces in which Japanese Americans could pursue their activities without discrimination. Some Nisei, like Tadashi Henry Wakabayashi, returned to Japan to play professional baseball.

Baseball provided the Japanese American community with an instrument to endure and overcome the significant challenges that confronted them during the 1940s. On December 7, 1941, Japan launched a surprise air attack on Pearl Harbor, Hawai'i, home of America's Pacific Fleet, destroying eight battleships, 188 aircraft, and killing 2,403 American servicemembers and civilians. The United States declared war on Japan the following day and, on February 19, 1942, President Franklin D. Roosevelt signed Executive Order 9066, which ordered the deportation or internment of Japanese Americans for the duration of the war. Within six weeks, nearly 130,000 Japanese Americans had been relocated from their homes in the western United States to 10 militarily run internment camps across nine western and southern states. Kenichi Zenimura, who transformed Fresno into a significant hub for Japanese American baseball in the 1920s, led the organization of baseball teams and leagues within the internment camps. Baseball teams were formed for men and women of all ages and levels of skill. At the camp near Gila River, Arizona, Zenimura organized 32 teams alone and, in 1944, persuaded War Relocation Authority officials to permit a team of "all-stars" from the camp near Granada, Colorado, to travel to Arizona to play the "all-stars" in Gila River and Poston. Much more than a mere diversion, baseball provided internees with opportunities for lively play, competition, and entertainment as well as the means to preserve and reinforce their cultural traditions.

In the late 1940s through the 1960s, baseball facilitated the integration of Japanese Americans back into the American mainstream. Upon their initial return to their hometowns, many Japanese Americans encounter significant hostility and rebuke. For many baseball was the last thing on their minds, as they wanted to rebuild their homes and businesses. On the other hand, for those like Kenichi Zenimura, who had promoted baseball in Fresno in the

1920s and 1930s and in the internment camps in the 1940s, the reestablishment of baseball in Fresno and northern California was very important, especially in mending the fissures between the Japanese American and Caucasian communities. This period marked the decline of Japanese American baseball as an insulated Nikkei institution as skilled Nisei and Sansei began to play on integrated teams and leagues. Skilled players, like Kenshi and Kenso Zenimura, sons of Kenichi Zenimura, played baseball at Fresno State College and then went on to professional careers in Japan. Perhaps the most notable of these expatriates was Nisei Wallace Kaname "Wally" Yonemine, who not only played, coached, and managed professional baseball in Japan but also became the first Japanese American to play professional football with the San Francisco 49ers in 1947.

Since the late 1960s, Japanese American baseball players have competed in major league baseball. Mike Lum, who joined the Atlanta Braves in 1967, became the first individual of Japanese descent to play in the major leagues. Born in Hawai'i to an American father and a Japanese mother, he was adopted and raised by a Chinese couple. Lum, who played in the major leagues until 1981, became the first Japanese American to play on a World Series championship team, the Cincinnati Reds in 1976. Some baseball historians consider Ryan Kurosaki, who pitched in six games for the St. Louis Cardinals in 1975, the first Japanese American to play in the major leagues because of his unadulterated Nikkei heritage. Lenn Sakata played second base from 1977 to 1987, claiming a World Series title with the Baltimore Orioles in 1983. Atlee Hammaker pitched from 1981 to 1995, including an All-Star appearance in 1983, the year he led the National League in earned run average. Don Wakamatsu, who debuted as a catcher with the Chicago White Sox in 1991, became the first Japanese American manager with the Seattle Mariners in 2009. Other Japanese American players include Shane Victorino, Brandon League, Jeremy Guthrie, Travis Ishikawa, and Kurt Suzuki.

See also: Japanese Americans in Sports

Further Reading

Franks, Joel S. *Asian Pacific Americans and Baseball: A History.* Jefferson, NC: McFarland, 2008.

Nakagawa, Kerry Yo, *Through a Diamond: 100 Years of Japanese American Baseball.* San Francisco: Rudi Publishing, 2001.

Rader, Benjamin. *Baseball: A History of America's National Game.* Urbana: The University of Illinois Press, 1992.

Regalado, Samuel O. *Nikkei Baseball: Japanese American Players from Immigration and Internment to the Major Leagues.* Urbana: The University of Illinois Press, 2013.

Adam R. Hornbuckle

JAPANESE AMERICANS IN FIGURE SKATING

Japanese American have participated with much success in figure skating since the 1980s.

Kristi Yamaguchi

Kristi Yamaguchi was the first Japanese American to achieve success as a figure skater. Born on July 12, 1971, in Hayward, California, she started skating at the age of six and began competing as a teenager. Her first major competition resulted in a fifth place finish in the pairs section of the U.S. Junior Figure Skating Championships in 1985. Next year, she and her partner Rudy Galindo won the national junior championship and finished fifth at the World Junior Championships. Yamaguchi and Galindo finished fifth in the senior U.S. Figure Skating Championships and third in the World Junior Figure Skating Championships in 1987. Next year they won the World Junior Figure Skating Championship. In 1989, they won the U.S. Figure Skating Championship and finished fifth in the World Figure Skating Championships. They won the U.S. Figure Skating Championship and finished fifth in the World Figure Skating Championships in 1990.

Yamaguchi, who entered singles competition in 1988, placed 10th in the U.S. Figure Skating Championships, but won the World Junior Figure Skating singles title that year. In 1989, she skated to second place at the U.S. Figure Skating Championships, but finished sixth in the World Figure Skating Championships. In 1990, Yamaguchi finished second in the U.S. Figure Skating Championships and fourth in the World Figure Skating Championships. After finishing second for a third time at the U.S. Figure Skating Championships in 1991, she won the World Figure Skating Championship, Goodwill Games, Nations Cup, and Skate America. At the World Figure Skating Championships, she led an American sweep of the medals, with Tonya Harding in second, and Nancy Kerrigan in third. In 1992, Yamaguchi won the U.S. Figure Skating Championship, the Olympic Games, and the World Figure Skating Championship.

Rena Inoue

Born in Nishinomiya, Japan, on October 17, 1976, Rena Inoue is a Japanese American singles and pairs skater. She began skating in Japan before moving to train in the United States in 1996. Inoue won the singles competition in the Japanese Junior Championships in 1991 and 1993, and finished second in 1992 and 1993. Competing in the senior Japanese Championships, she won the pairs competition in 1991 and 1992 with Tomoaki Koyama. In 1991, Inoue and Koyama finished 15th in the pairs competition at the World Championships.

Next year they finished 14th in the pairs competition at the Olympic Games. Competing as a single in 1994, Inoue finished second in the senior Japanese Championships, 18th in the Olympic Games, and 13th in the World Championships. In 1997, she finished second in the singles competition at the World Student Games and, in 1999, second in the singles competition at the Japanese Championships.

In 2000, Inoue began skating in pairs competitions with John Baldwin Jr. of the United States. Coached by Baldwin's father, a former world-class figure skater, the pair finished 11th in the U.S. Championships in 2001, improving to 4th in 2002, 3rd in 2003, and finally winning the national title in 2004. After she became a U.S. citizen in 2005, Inoue and Baldwin finished second in the national championships that year and claimed the national championship in 2006. That year they also won the Four Continents competition, finished fourth in the World Championships, and finished seventh in the Olympic Games. In the latter, Inoue and Baldwin became the first figure skating pair to successfully execute the throw triple axel in international competition. They continued skating through 2010, finishing second in 2007 and 2008, third in 2009 and 2010 in the U.S. Championships, and third in the Four Continents in 2007. No longer competing, Inoue and Baldwin are now married and have a family.

Kyoko Ina

Born in Tokyo, Japan, on October 11, 1972, Kyoko Ina grew up in New York, as her family moved to the United States in 1980. Born into an athletic family, her grandfather, Katsuo Okazaki, competed as a long-distance runner in the 1920s and represented Japan in the Olympic Games in 1924. Her grandmother, Shimako Okazaki, played tennis and represented Japan at Wimbledon. Her mother, Yoshi Ina, competed as a swimmer and a sculler.

Beginning to skate at the age of four, Ina finished seventh in the singles competition at the Japanese Junior Figure Skating Championships and eighth in the singles competition at the World Junior Figure Skating Championships in 1987. She won the singles section of the U.S. Junior Figure Skating Championships in 1989. Continuing to compete as single through 1997, Ina began competing in pairs competition with Jason Dungjen in 1991. After several second- and third-place finishes in the Champions Series Cup tournaments, they won the Karl Schäfer Memorial in 1997. That year Ina and Dungjen finished fourth in the World Championships. Next year, they finished fourth in the Olympic Games.

In 1999, Ina began skating with John Zimmerman. After finishing second in the pairs competition of the U.S. Figure Skating Championship in 1999, they won the title from 2000 to 2002. Ina and Zimmerman finished fifth in the Olympic Games in 2002 and finished third in the World Figure Skating Championships that year, for their best performance in that tournament. After retiring from competition in 2002, they performed with the Stars on Ice tour. In 2010, Ina participated in the second season of the Battle of the Blades with Kelly Chase, a retired professional hockey player.

Cathy and Chris Reed

Cathy Reed (1987–) and Chris Reed (1989–) are an American-born ice dancing pair who compete for Japan. Born in Kalamazoo, Michigan, their mother is Japanese and their father is American. In 2004, they finished 10th in the novice division of the Eastern Sectionals of the U.S. Figure Skating Championships. Next year, the Reeds placed fifth in the novice division of the Eastern Sections but won the novice division in the North Atlantic Regionals. In 2006, they won the novice division in both the Eastern Sectionals and the U.S. Championships.

In 2007, the Reeds began to compete for Japan. In that year, they finished second in ice dancing at the Japanese Figure Skating Championships. From 2008 to 2011 and from 2013 to 2015, the Reeds won the national ice dancing title. In World Championship competition, the Reed's achieved their best performance in 2011, when they finished 13th. In World Championship team competition they have finished third twice in 2013 and 2014. Their record in the Olympic Games is a 17th place in 2010 and 21st place finish in 2014. The Reeds contributed to Japan's fifth place finish in the ice dancing team competition in the Olympic Games in 2014.

Allison Reed

Allison Reed, born on June 8, 1994, in Kalamazoo, Michigan, is the younger sister of Cathy and Chris Reed. She began skating at the age of four and competed as a singles skater until joining Otar Japaridze, of the Republic of Georgia, as an ice dancer. They trained in Mount Laurel, New Jersey, with Evgeni Platov, a former Russian ice dancer. Reed and Japaridze represented Georgia in the Olympic Games in 2010, where they finished 22nd. Their best performance that year came at the Pavel Roman Memorial competition, in which they finished ninth. Other finishes in 2010, included 19th at the European Figure Skating Championships and 21st at the World Figure Skating Championships. In 2011, Reed and Japaridze finished 7th in the European Championships, 18th in the World Championships, 4th in the Golden Spin of Zagreb, and 2nd in the Ice Challenge.

In 2012, Reed began competing for Israel with Belarussian expatriate Vasili Rogov. In 2013, they finished 12th in the Nebelhorn Trophy competition, 7th in the Golden Spin of Zagreb, 10th in the Pavel Roman Memorial, and 23rd in the World Championships. Next year, Reed and Rogov finished 18th in Nebelhorn Trophy competition, 24th in the European Championships, 7th in the Golden Spin of Zagreb, 10th in the U.S. Classic, 6th in the Ukrainian

Open, and 30th in the World Championships. In 2015, they finished 6th in the Nebelhorn Trophy competition, 16th in the European Championships, 20th in the World Championships, and 5th in the Finlandia Trophy competition.

Mirai Aileen Nagasu

Born in Montebello, California, on April 16, 1993, Mirai Aileen Nagasu is the daughter of Japanese immigrants, who own a Japanese restaurant in Arcadia. She began skating at the age of five, inspired by Kim Yuna, of South Korea, Michelle Kwan, of the United States, and Mao Asada, of Japan. In 2003, Nagasu finished fifth in the juvenile level of the Southwest Pacific Regionals. Next year in the intermediate level, she finished fourth in the Southwest Pacific Regionals. Nagasu won the intermediate level in the Southwest Pacific Regionals in 2005. After a fifth place finish in the novice level in the Southwest Pacific Regionals in 2006, she won the Pacific Coast Sectional Junior title in 2007. That year Nagasu also won the Southwest Pacific Regional and U.S. Junior Championships and placed second in the World Junior Championships. In 2008, she defended her U.S. Junior title, and placed third at the World Junior Championships. That year Nagasu also finished third in the Japan Open and won the Junior Grand Prix Final.

In 2009, Nagasu began participating in senior-level competition. That year, she finished fifth in the U.S. Championships, second in 2010, third in 2011, seventh in 2012 and 2013, third in 2014, and fifth in 2015. Nagasu finished fourth in the Olympic Games and seventh in the World Championships in 2010.

Alex Hideo and Maia Harumi Shibutani

Alex Hideo and Maia Harumi Shibutani, ice dancers, were born on April 25, 1991, in Boston, Massachusetts, and on July 20, 1994, New York, New York, respectively. Their father, Chris Shibutani, is an anesthesiologist who works as an investment banker, and, their mother, Naomi, who was born in Japan, is a former concert pianist. The Shibutanis began figure skating in 1998, when Alex was eight years old and Maia was four years old. They skated as singles until 2003 when their parents took them to the World Figure Skating Championships in Washington, D.C. Captured by the ice dancing competition, Alex and Maia decided to become an ice dancing pair themselves.

The Shibutanis began ice dancing in 2004, competing on the juvenile level, the lowest competitive level in the U.S. Figure Skating testing structure. In 2005, they won the ice dancing competition at the North Atlantic Regional Championships, which qualified them to compete in the U.S. Junior Championships that year, in which they won the silver medal. Moving up to the intermediate level in 2006, the Shibutanis won the ice dancing competition at both the Southwestern Regional Championships and the Junior Championships that year. As novice competitors in 2007, they won the ice dancing competition at both the Midwestern Regional Championships and the Junior Championships. In 2008, the Shibutanis finished third at the Midwestern Regional Championships and fourth in the Junior Championships. Next year, they finished second in both the Junior Championships and the Junior World Figure Skating Championships. In Junior Grand Prix competition in 2009, they won in France and Spain but finished fourth in the Junior Grand Prix final. In 2010, their last year competing as juniors, the Shibutanis won the Junior Championships and the United States and Croatian Grand Prix, finished third in the Junior Grand Prix Final, and finished fourth in the Junior World Figure Skating Championships.

In 2011, the Shibutanis began competing in the senior level. In that year, they finished second in the U.S. Figure Skating Championships and third in the World Figure Skating Championships. In 2011, they finished second in the Four Continents Championships and third in Skate America. Next year, they finished second in the U.S. Figure Skating Championships, second in the Finlandia Trophy, fourth in the Four Continents, fourth in the Chinese Grand Prix Cup, fifth in the Grand Prix Final, won the Grand Prix NHK Trophy. In 2013, they finished third in the U.S. Figure Skating Championships, eighth in the World Figure Skating Championships, fourth in the Four Continents, fourth in the Russian Grand Prix, and third in the Grand Prix NHK Trophy. In 2014, they finished third in the U.S. Figure Skating Championships, Grand Prix NHK Trophy, and Grand Prix Skate America. At the 2014 Olympic Games, they finished ninth, and at the World Figure Skating Championships, they finished sixth. In 2015, they finished second in the U.S. Figure Skating Championships, second in the Chinese Grand Prix and U.S. Grand Prix. They finished third in the Four Continents and won the Ondrej Nepela Trophy. They finished fifth in the World Figure Skating Championships.

See also: Japanese American Olympians; Japanese Americans in Sports

Further Reading

"Kristi Yamaguchi." Biography.com. http://www.biography.com/people/kristi-yamaguchi-20950449. Accessed January 15, 2017.

Wallechinsky, David, and Jaime Loucky, *The Complete Book of the Winter Olympics, 2014 Edition*. Hertford, NC: Crossroad Press, 2013.

Adam R. Hornbuckle

JAPANESE AMERICANS IN FILM

Japanese Americans technically indicate Americans with Japanese ancestry and Japanese with the U.S. citizenship through naturalization, and occasionally include permanent residents. However, Hollywood sometimes employs Japanese actors and actresses whose residency are not limited in the United States. This tendency is particularly notable in the 21st century. Regardless of citizenship and residency, this entry attempts to introduce both Japanese and Japanese Americans who have been influential on the history of "Japanese Americans in Film."

Japanese Americans along with other Asian Americans faced to racism that reduced acting opportunities in films. It was not an uncommon practice that white actors and actresses put makeup, so-called "yellow face," and played Asian characters. One of the infamous examples is Mickey Rooney's role, Mr. Yunioshi, in *Breakfast at Tiffany's* (1961). The Japanese character, who is buck-toothed and comically angry, emphasizes misconceptions of Japanese in racialized contexts. Additionally, this kind of stereotype promotes the false image of Japanese and Japanese Americans through the medium of film.

While "yellow faces" reduced employment opportunities for Japanese Americans, they also encouraged actors to play stereotypes and negative images. However, it does not necessarily mean that Japanese Americans agreed with the intensions of film productions. Japanese Americans as a racial minority who have fewer acting opportunities than mainstream Americans have to compromise at some point to play these stereotypes.

Japanese American Actors and Actresses

Sessue Hayakawa (1889–1973) is the first Japanese actor who rose to stardom in the silent film era of Hollywood. Born in Japan, Hayakawa immigrated to the United States in 1907 first as a manual laborer. Hayakawa who had never had acting experience appealed to a Japanese theater company in Little Tokyo, Los Angeles, to give him a chance to act. Hayakawa adapted a play, *The Typhoon*, written by Hungarian Melchior Lengyel, which depicts a Japanese spy who strangles a French lover and ultimately dies. Aoki Tsuruko (1892–1961), who already debuted in *The Oath of Tsuru* (1913) and got married to Hayakawa in 1914, persuaded film director Thomas H. Ince to watch the play. Ince recruited Hayakawa and made films on Japan at the time when whites played Asian roles with "yellow face." Hayakawa often played Asian villain roles, one of which was *The Cheat* (1915) made him a star, yet initially created antagonism against him in the Japanese American community. In the early 1920s, Hayakawa could not get away from anti-Japanese sentiments symbolized as a murder attempt on him. Hayakawa left Hollywood and moved his career to Broadway and eventually Europe. The French film, *La Bataille* (1923) on the Russo-Japanese War, which Hayakawa played, became sensational although it was not well accepted in Japan because of sympathetic tones with Europeans. In 1930, after establishing his career in France and England, Hayakawa moved back to Japan and appeared in films and plays. Hayakawa lived in France in the midst of World War II and moved back to the United States again with an invitation to costar with actor Humphrey Bogart in the film *Tokyo Joe* (1949). While acting in both the

United States and Japan, Hayakawa played Col. Saito in the film *The Bridge on the River Kwai* (1956) that made him a nominee as a supporting actor in the Academy Awards.

The next generation of Japanese American actors and actresses after Sessue Hayakawa's stardom was coincidentally born in a short span between the late 1920s and the early 1930s: Miyoshi Umeki (1929–2007), Pat Morita (1930–2005), Mako Iwamatsu (1933–2006), and James Shigeta (1933–2014). They began to establish their acting careers in the post–World War II period. The Cold War politics, which changed the U.S.–Japan relationship from enemy to ally, stimulated the emergence of the Japanese Americans in Hollywood. Although acting opportunities for Japanese Americans were still limited, a number of interracial romance films created acting opportunities for them.

Miyoshi Umeki (1929–2007) gained her popularity through such interracial romance films. Born in Otaru of the northern part of Japan, Umeki established her career as a jazz singer under the stage name Nancy Umeki before moving to Hollywood. In the United States, she contracted with Mercury Records and released two albums in 1956 and 1958. Her debut film in Hollywood was *Sayonara* (1958), an adaptation of James Michener's novel that took the stage in postwar Japan. Umeki played Japanese woman named Katsumi who gets married to American G.I. Joe (Red Buttons) but ends with their tragic suicides as a contrast with another couple played by Marlon Brando and Miiko Taka. Umeki received an Oscar for the supporting role as the first Asian. With the success, Umeki joined Broadway musical *Flower Drum Song* (1958) with costar Pat Suzuki. Playing Chinese immigrant Mei Li, Umeki was nominated for a Tony Award as Best Leading Actress in a Musical. In 1961, the film version of the musical was released with Umeki as Mei Li and James Shigeta as her love interest, Wang Ta. Although she appeared in a couple more films, Umeki was seen more in TV dramas. In the TV sitcom, *The Courtship of Eddie's Father* (1969–1972), Umeki played Japanese housekeeper Mrs. Livingston for which she was nominated as Best Supporting Actress in the Golden Globe Awards.

Hawai'ian-born Sansei or the third-generation Japanese American James Shigeta (1929–2014) became famous for his leading roles in interracial romance films, as he received a Golden Globe Award for New Star of the Year in 1960. In *The Crimson Kimono* (1959), Detective Joe Kojaku played by Shigeta wins over Christine Downes (Victoria Shaw) in the wake of a love triangle with his colleague, Charlie Bancroft (Glenn Corbett). *Bridge to the Sun* (1961) portrays an interracial couple, Japanese Hidenari Terasaki (Shigeta) and his American wife Gwen (Carroll Baker) caught up in the height of antagonism between the two countries. Interracial couples of Asian women and white men have been common in the American mainstream; however, Shigeta played roles opposing white women and broke the stereotypical feminized image of Asian Americans.

Actor Pat Morita is best remembered for his roles in *Happy Days* and *The Karate Kid*. (AP Photo)

Both Mako Iwamatsu, better known by his first name, and Pat Morita were nominated for the Academy Awards and the Golden Globe for their supporting roles in *The Sand Pebbles* (1966) and *The Karate Kid* (1984), respectively. Born in Japan as a son of a well-known painter Yashima Taro (1908–1994), Mako immigrated to the United States after World War II, following his parents who left for Japan because of the opposition to Imperial Japan. After joining the U.S. Army in the early 1950s, he changed his career to acting. Facing limited career opportunities as a racial minority in show business, in 1965, Mako cofounded the East West Players in Los Angeles as a theatrical space for Asian Americans. Mako's name is seen on the Hollywood Walk of Fame. Meanwhile, born in California, Pat Morita went through hardships during his childhood before becoming well known for his role, karate teacher Keisuke Miyagi, in *The Karate Kid* film series. During his childhood, Morita was hospitalized because of tuberculosis for nine years and was sent to an internment camp in Gila, Arizona, directly from a hospital. Starting his show business career as a stand-up comedian at the age of 30, he appeared in numerous comedy series on TV as well as films since the late 1970s.

Like Pat Morita, George Takei (1937–) was interned during his childhood at Rohwer camp in Arkansas. Born in California, Takei started his career as a voice-over actor in show business in the late 1950s. After acting in various TV series, Takei was chosen for his now best-known role, Hikaru Sulu, in sci-fi TV series *Star Trek* in 1966. The original Star Trek TV series (1966–1969; 1973–1974) expanded its venue to motion pictures (in 1979, 1982, 1984, 1989, 1991) and has had a long-running popularity. Alongside his acting career, Takei advocates for human rights and LGBT communities. His community activism for the equal rights has been profoundly affected by his childhood experience at internment camps during World War II, and he created a Broadway musical based on that experience.

In the turn of the 21st century, Japanese actors who have already established their career in Japan internationally work in Hollywood. Their backgrounds, in terms of citizenship and residence, are different from those of Japanese Americans. Yet, their reputation in Hollywood cannot be negated in the contexts of Japanese Americans in films because of the shared ethnic backgrounds for which they are regarded as one group in the mainstream. For example, Ken Watanabe (1959–), who has been well known in Japanese TV dramas and films since the middle of the 1980s, was nominated for Best Supporting Actor in the Academy Awards for his role in *The Last Samurai* (2003). Likewise, Rinko Kikuchi became a Supporting Actress nominee for the Academy Awards for *Babel* (2006).

Japanese American Filmmakers

The first Japanese American filmmaker who won Academy Award is Jimmy T. Murakami (1933–2014) for *The Magic Pear Tree* (1968) under the category of animated short film. More than a decade later, the first Japanese American feature film, *Hito Hata: Raising the Banner* (1980), directed by Duane Kubo and Robert A. Nakamura, was released, which is also the first full-length Asian American film. Kubo and Nakamura along with Alan Ohashi and Eddie Wong cofounded a Los Angeles based nonprofit organization, Visual Communications, to advocate the equal opportunity for Asian Americans in the film industry. *Hito Hata* premiered by the organization narrates that Issei or the first-generation Japanese American Oda (Mako) recollects his life before being interned at a camp during World War II.

Aside from *Hito Hata*, Japanese Americans began to direct films since the late 1980s. The majority of the filmic style has been documentary especially on social justice. Renee Tajima-Peña's (1958–) documentary film, *Who Killed Vincent Chin?*, brings an attention to the Asian American community in terms of racial solidarity against hate crimes. Through the documentary film, *History and Memory: For Akiko and Takashige* (1991), Rea Tajiri (1958–) approaches her parents' experiences at an internment camp. Later, Tajiri directs *Strawberry Fields* (1997), a road movie of Sansei teenager Suzy (Irene Kawai) who visits a camp site where her grandfather was once interned, by cowriting with Canadian Japanese novelist Kerri Sakamoto (1960–). Likewise, Chris Tashima (1960–) received the Academy Award for Live Action Short Film for *Visas and Virtue* (1997) that is based on a true story of Japanese diplomat Sugihara Chinue who issued transit visas for Jews to escape from Nazis during World War II.

Steven Okazaki (1952–) is four-time Oscar nominee for his documentary works. He won an Oscar for the short documentary film, *Days of Waiting: The*

Life & Art of Estelle Ishigo (1990), based on Caucasian Ishigo's life story who decided to be interned with her Japanese American husband at a camp. Okazaki captures people whose lives were impacted by political injustice: *Unfinished Business* (1986) on Fred Korematsu, Minoru Yasui, and Gordon Hirabayashi, who fought against Executive Order 9066 that forced Japanese Americans to internment camps; *The Mushroom Club* (2006) on the atomic bomb survivors in Hiroshima; and *The Conscience of Nhem Em* (2009), on Em's adolescent years during the Khmer Rouge when he had to take ID photos of prisoners before they were killed.

Feature films by Japanese American directors appeared in the middle of the 1990s, 15 years after the first one, *Hito Hata*, was released. In *Picture Brides*, Kayo Hatta (1958–2005) depicts Issei plantation workers in Hawai'i centering on women's lives. Desmond Nakano (1953–) directs *White Man's Burden* (1995), casting John Travolta as a factory worker, Louis Pinnock, whose life was turned down because of a false accusation by African American boss, as well as *American Pastime* (2007), which portrays Japanese American lives at an internment camp in Topaz, Utah, during World War II.

In the 21st century, Japanese American directors of mixed heritage emerged. For example, Paul Mayeda Berges (1968–) of Japanese and Basque descents began his career in documentary on the Japanese American community and has numerous collaborations with his spouse, Indian British director Gurinder Chadha (1960–), including *Bend It Like Beckham* (2002) and *The Mistress of Spices* (2005). Cary Fukuyama (1977–) of Japanese and Swedish descents directed *Sin Nombre* (2009) about a Mexican juvenile caught up with gang life and *Jane Eyre* (2010), the adaptation of Charlotte Brontë's novel.

See also: Hayakawa, Sessue "Kintaro" (1886–1973); Ishigo, Estelle (1899–1990); Takei, George Hosato (1937–)

Further Reading

Miyao, Daisuke. *Sassue Hayakawa: Silent Cinema and Transnational Stardom*. Durham, NC: Duke University Press, 2007.

Ono, Kent A., and Vincent Pham. *Asian Americans and the Media*. 1st ed. Cambridge: Polity, 2008.

Yuki Obayashi

JAPANESE AMERICANS IN SPORTS

Sports have been an integral part of Japanese American life since the Japanese first immigrated to the United States and its Pacific Territories in the late 19th century. Initial Japanese immigrants, the Issei, brought their own sportive traditions with them to the United States, transplanting them in their adopted

United States' Erik Shoji, left, and his brother Kawika Shoji on the bench during a men's preliminary volleyball match against Canada at the 2016 Summer Olympics in Rio de Janeiro, Brazil. (AP Photo/Jeff Roberson)

land. Their children, the Nisei, adopted the sports and games common to the United States, while maintaining an interest in their sporting traditions. Although sports provided Japanese Americans with an avenue to assimilation into mainstream American life, they also enabled them to maintain a sense of what it meant to be Japanese, especially in the face of limited economic and social opportunities reinforced by racial prejudice. Sports and recreation proved to be especially important to Japanese Americans during internment, when the U.S. government held hundreds of thousands of them in military administered concentration camps during World War II; sports functioned more than just as a diversion to pass the time, but as a mechanism to maintain their community and tradition. After the war, Japanese Americans increasingly became part of the American sporting mainstream, making significant contributions to amateur and professional sports and representing the United States successfully in international competition, especially in the Olympic Games.

Japanese immigration to Hawai'i and the western United States began in the decades following the Meiji Restoration of 1868, which reinstated imperial rule and initiated a sweeping modernization movement, including land reform and industrialization. Japan's rush to modernization led to increased competition for social and economic resources, causing many Japanese to look elsewhere for opportunities. The need for labor overseas, especially the sugar plantations of Hawai'i and the railroads, sawmills, mines, and farms of the western United States, encouraged Japanese to immigrate to these locations. The initial wave of Japanese immigrants experienced harsh working conditions, strenuous physical labor, irregular and seasonal employment, and racial prejudice. Anti-Asian sentiment reached a threshold in the United States during the late 1880s, resulting in the passage of the Chinese Exclusion Act of 1892, which forced many Chinese to return to China, leaving the remaining immigrants to form close-knit segregated and self-sustaining communities. In the early 1900s, Japanese immigrants faced similar challenges. In 1907, the "Gentlemen's Agreement" between the governments of Japan and the United States ended the immigration of Japanese unskilled workers, but permitted the immigration of businesspersons, students, and spouses of Japanese immigrants already in the country. In 1922, the Ozawa Supreme Court decision upheld the ban on naturalization of Issei and, in 1923, the Alien Land Act of 1913 was evoked to prevent them from acquiring agricultural land. Finally, the Asian Exclusion Act, part of the broader Immigration Act of 1924, banned Japanese immigration to the United States.

Beginning in the late 1890s, Japanese immigrants brought sumo wrestling to Hawai'i and the United States. Sumo wrestling exhibitions highlighted holiday picnics, community celebrations, and ceremonial occasions. These sumo "crazes" often featured prominent Japanese *sumotori* (sumo wrestlers) who toured throughout Hawai'i and the western United States. Japanese immigrant communities held sumo tournaments to commemorate important occasions, ranging from the emperor's birthday to American independence on the Fourth of July. Toyomori Hosokawa ranked as one of the leading *sumotori* of the Issei era. He immigrated to California in 1924, before the enactment of the federal law ending Japanese immigration, and settled in the Sacramento Delta area. Hosokawa, who wrestled under the nickname Toshuzan, won numerous local tournaments and represented his community in competitions throughout California. His death from pneumonia in 1930 inspired a memorial tournament drawing the top sumo wrestlers of the area.

Besides sumo wrestling, the Issei transplanted their passion for baseball in their communities. Developed in the United States during the 1830s and 1840s, baseball became a popular sport in Japan during the 1870s. Japanese learned the game from American educators and Japanese who had returned to Japan after visiting or studying in the United States. By the height of Japanese immigration to Hawai'i and the United States, baseball had gained great popularity, with the organization of teams and leagues. Japanese immigrants in California established teams in San Francisco in 1904, San Jose in 1910, Sacramento in 1912, Oakland in 1915, Los Angeles in 1915, and Fresno in the 1920s. Issei baseball enthusiast, Kenichi Zenimura spearheaded the growth of baseball in Fresno; he assembled a baseball league consisting of 10 teams, which regularly played against teams of Mexican American semiprofessionals, Negro League clubs, and Pacific Coast League teams. The Seattle Mikados sparked the organization baseball teams in the Pacific Northwest in 1907, followed by the Cheery Team in 1909, later known as the Asahi Club in 1912. Japanese immigrants in Portland played baseball but did not establish formal teams.

In the late 1920s and 1930s, the second generation of Japanese Americans, known as the Nisei became particularly enamored by sumo, judo, and kendo. These traditional combative sports, which involved much skill and discipline, contributed to the Nisei's increasing awareness and association with Japan. The best Japanese *sumotori*, *judoka* (practitioners of judo), and *kendōka* (practitioners of kendo) came to America to demonstrate the latest techniques, while younger *sumotori, judoka,* and *kendōka* competed against their Nisei peers. Japanese American sumo, judo, and kendo groups traveled to Japan, sponsored by prominent Issei businessmen and associations. At this time, several Nisei pursued professional careers in sumo, including Sadaji "Fukunishiki" Fukuyama of Sacramento, who went to compete in Japan in 1934, but returned to America when he turned 21, to avoid being drafted into the Japanese military. Coloradoan Harley "Toyonishiki" Ozaki, the most successful Nisei sumotori in Japan, became the first foreigner to achieve *sekitori*, a ranking in one of the top two divisions of professional sumo.

In the late 1920s, sports provided both the Issei and the Nisei with a bridge between Japanese and American cultures. In addition to sumo, judo, and kendo, Japanese Americans competed in baseball, basketball, and football. Participation in traditionally American sports provided the Nisei with a way to demonstrate their assimilation into the American mainstream and excel in an area in which one achieved success according to ability rather than race and ethnicity. For the Issei, their children's participation in segregated leagues ensured that they would be interacting with peers from other Japanese American communities. Issei baseball pioneer, Kenichi Zenimura, who believed baseball provided a bridge between American and Japanese culture, regularly took teams of the best players from Fresno on barnstorming tours of Japan to facilitate cultural engagement. Not only men and boys participated in sports, but Nisei women as well in basketball and softball leagues. In an era when vigorous sporting activity is deemed by the larger society as inimical to femininity for women of all races and ethnicities, Japanese American women were playing ball with the approval of the leaders of the Nikkei community.

As sports afforded Japanese Americans with an avenue to assimilate into the American mainstream, sports also provided a safe haven from the prejudice institutionalized by the court decisions and federal immigration law of the 1920s. *Nihonmachis* or "Little Tokyos" took on great significance in the

1930s, as many became self-sustaining communities that did not look outside for goods and services, including federal assistance from New Deal programs to build sports and recreation parks. Japanese Americans built their own parks often associated with churches or farms, which offered them safe spaces where they could pursue their activities without discrimination and ridicule. During the decade baseball players like Tadashi Henry Wakabayashi, a Hawai'ian Nisei who pitched for two Japan teams in the late 1930s through the 1950s, returned to Japan to play professional baseball. A strong sense of Japanese nationalism developed in the insulated Japanese American communities. During the 1932 Summer Olympic Games, held in Los Angeles, Japanese Americans followed the Japanese contingent of 131 athletes closely. The Los Angeles *Rafu Shimpo*, the local Japanese American newspaper, published articles celebrating Japanese accomplishments. The Japanese won 18 medals, including 7 gold medals, 7 silver medals, and 4 bronze medals; the total medal count ranked fifth among the 37 teams competing in the Olympic Games. In swimming, the Japanese won 5 gold, 5 silver, and 2 bronze medals for a total of 12, their largest in a single sport. Chūhei Nambu, Japan's best individual performer, won the gold medal in the triple jump and the bronze medal in the long jump. In the triple jump, he established a world record of 15.72 meters (51 feet 7 inches).

Although Japanese American enclaves provided their inhabitants refuge from discrimination and hostility, they caused many in the Caucasian community to question their loyalty and national preference. White suspicion surfaced at a time when Japan began to exert itself militarily in Manchuria in 1931, allying with Nazi Germany in 1936, and invading China in 1937 and French Indochina in 1940. On December 7, 1941, Japan attacked American and British interests in Asia and the Pacific, including Pearl Harbor, Hawai'i, home of America's Pacific Fleet, destroying several battleships, hundreds of aircraft, and killing over 2,000 American servicemembers and civilians. The United States declared war on Japan the following day and, on February 19, 1942, President Franklin Delano Roosevelt signed Executive Order 9066, which ordered the deportation or internment of Japanese Americans for the duration of the war. Within six weeks, nearly 130,000 Japanese Americans had been relocated from their homes in the western United States to militarily run internment camps across nine western and southern states. With regard to sports, Japanese Americans replicated the activities they had enjoyed before the war, holding sumo tournaments, establishing baseball, basketball, and football teams, and many other types of sporting activities. Kenichi Zenimura, who had led barnstorming tours of Nisei baseball teams in Japan in the 1920s, led the organization of baseball teams and leagues within the internment camps, and convinced officials to permit a team of "all-stars" from Colorado to the "all-stars" in Arizona. Much more than a mere diversion, sports provided internees with opportunities for lively play, competition, and entertainment as well as the means to preserve and reinforce their cultural traditions.

Not all Japanese Americans, however, competed in sports behind the barbed wire fences of the internment camps. Before the outbreak of World War II, Soichi Sakamoto, a high school biology teacher formed the "Three Year Swim Club" in Maui in 1937. The name of the club reflected the goal of the team, which was to qualify for the U.S. Olympic team for the 1940 Olympic Games in three years. An ambitious goal considering that Sakamoto had no prior experience coaching swimming, but many of the athletes became dominant performers. His first successful swimmer, Keo "Casey" Nakama claimed 27 U.S. Amateur Athletic Union (AAU) national titles from 1939 to 1945. During World War II, Nakama earned degrees from Ohio State University in Columbus, won National Collegiate Athletic Association (NCAA) titles in the 440-yard and the mile freestyle races, and played second base on the baseball team in 1943 and 1944. Wataru "Wat" Misaka, who led Ogden High School in Utah to the state basketball championship in 1940 and a regional championship in 1941, played at Weber State from 1941 to 1943 and at the University of Utah from 1943 to 1944 before serving in a U.S. Army intelligence unit in 1945. Misaka returned to the University of Utah in 1946 and led the Utes to a 19–5 record and a 49–45 victory over the University of Kentucky in the National Invitational Tournament in 1947.

After World War II, Japanese Americans used sports to integrate back into the American mainstream. Upon their initial return to their hometowns, many Japanese Americans encounter significant hostility and rebuke. For many, sports were the last thing on their minds, as they wanted to rebuild their homes and businesses. Kenichi Zenimura, who had promoted baseball in the 1920s and 1930s as a bridge of cultural understanding, led the reestablishment of baseball in Fresno and northern California to mend the fissures between the Japanese American and Caucasian communities. On the other hand, professional wrestling promoters seeking to capitalize on the communications media of television, encouraged Japanese American performers to exploit the lingering wartime animosity to their advantage. To the chants from the audience of "kill the Jap!," Hawai'ian born wrestler Masaru "Charlie" Iwamoto, who wrestled as "Mr. Moto," would enter the ring wearing a kimono, clogs, and small black round glasses. Other performers who exploited cultural stereotypes included George "The Great Togo" Okumura and Harold "Tojo Yamamoto" Watanabe. Outside the ring, these entertainers often required police protection as angry Caucasian mobs threaten to attack them. After a match in Florida, an angry veteran attacked Iwamoto with a stick while eating in a coffee shop. Newspaper editors, such as Larry Tajiri of the *Pacific Citizen*, argued that the wrestlers' actions provoked needless prejudice and violence against the Japanese American community.

In the late 1940s and 1950s, Japanese Americans contributed to the rise of the United States as a contender in international Olympic-style weightlifting. In 1948, Bob Hoffman, owner of York Barbell Company, coached the U.S. Olympic weightlifting team, which consisted of Japanese Americans, including Toshiyuki "Harold" Sakata, who won a silver medal in the light-heavyweight class. Sakata's Olympic teammate Kotaro Emerick Ishikawa, who had moved to California from Hawai'i in 1940 to train as a weightlifter and ended up detained in the internment camp near Tule Lake, California, finished sixth in the featherweight class. While imprisoned, Ishikawa organized a weightlifting club in the camp, continued to lift, and after his release won AAU Championships as a bantamweight in 1944 and 1945, as a featherweight in 1946 and 1947, and a bronze medal in the featherweight class at the 1947 World Championships. Tamio "Tommy" Kono, who patterned himself after Ishikawa, won gold medals in the lightweight class at the 1952 Olympic Games and in the light-heavyweight division at the 1956 Olympic Games and a silver medal in the middleweight division at the 1960 Olympic Games.

In the 1950s, judo became a championship level sport in the United States and in the Olympic Games. Japanese American Yosh Uchida, who coached an informal judo team at San Jose State University for several years, led a movement to have judo recognized as a national level championship sport by the AAU in 1953. That year San Jose State sponsored the first AAU championship and, in 1962, Uchida organized the first NCAA judo championship. After claiming the first NCAA title in 1962, San Jose State won 28 of the next 31 intercollegiate titles. Judo debuted as an Olympic sport in Tokyo, Japan, in 1964. That year Uchida coached the U.S. Olympic judo team, which consisted of San Jose State *judoka* Paul Kuniaki Maruyama, who finished tied for fifth in the lightweight division. Silver medalist in the middleweight class at the 1963 Pan American Games, Maruyama won AAU titles in the lightweight class in 1966, 1970, and 1975, and coached the 1980 and 1984 Olympic teams. Other Japanese Americans who have won medals in international judo competition include Keith Nakasone, who garnered gold in the 1979 Pan American Games, and Kevin Asano, who claimed a silver medal in the extra-lightweight class at the 1988 Olympic Games.

Beginning in the late 1980s, Japanese Americans achieved success in winter sports. Kristi Yamaguchi became an acclaimed figure skater, first in pairs competition and then in singles. In 1988, she and her partner, Rudy Galindo, won the pairs competition in the World Junior Figure Skating Championship. In 1989, they won the first of two consecutive U.S. Figure Skating Championships. Yamaguchi, who began competing in singles completion in 1988, won the first of two World Figure Skating Championships in 1991, and the U.S. Figure Skating Championship and the Olympic Games in 1992. Other Japanese American figure skaters include Kyoko Ina, Rena Inoue, Allison Reed,

Cathy Reed, Chris Reed, and Mirai Aileen Nagasu. Siblings Alex Hideo and Maia Harumi Shibutani excel in ice dancing. The most successful Japanese American in winter sports is Apolo Anton Ohno, a short-track speed skater, who dominated the sport from 1999 to 2010. In that time, he won 21 World Championship medals, including 8 golds, 7 silvers, and 6 bronzes, from 1999 to 2009. In the Olympic Games, Ohno garnered eight medals, including two golds, two silvers, and four bronzes, from 2002 to 2010. He is the most decorated American winter Olympic athlete.

Since the end of World War II, Japanese Americans have made significant achievements in professional sports. In 1947, Wallace Kaname "Wally" Yonemine became the first Japanese American to play professional football with the San Francisco 49ers of the All American Football Conference, a precursor of the National Football League (NFL). In 1951, he began a 26-year career playing and managing professional baseball in Japan. University of Utah basketball standout Wataru "Wat" Misaka, who played for the New York Knicks from 1947 to 1948, became the first Japanese American to enter the Basketball Association of America, the forerunner of the National Basketball Association (NBA). Other Japanese Americans who have played in the NBA include Corey Gaines from 1988–2004, Rex Walters from 1993–2003, and Robert Swift from 2004–2011. Michael Ken-Wai Lum, the adopted son of a Hawai'ian Chinese couple, joined the Atlanta Braves in 1967, to become the first Japanese American to play Major League Baseball. Don Wakamatsu, who debuted as a catcher with the Chicago White Sox in 1991, became the first Japanese American manager with the Seattle Mariners in 2009. Ann Kiyomura, who defeated Martina Navratilova for Wimbledon junior singles title in 1973 and teamed with Kazuko Sawamatsu to win Wimbledon women's doubles title in 1975, played professional tennis from 1973 to 1984. Johnnie Morton and Haruki Robert Nakamura played in the NFL from 1994 to 2005 and 2008 to 2013, respectively. Lenore Muraoka Rittenhouse played professional golf from 1980 to 2001, as have Tadd Fujikawa and Rickie Yutaka Fowler since 2007 and 2009, respectively. Thoroughbred horse racing jockey Corey Nakatani has competed since 1990.

See also: Clay, Bryan Ezra Tsumoru (1980–); Fowler, Rickie Yutaka (1988–); Fuji, Paul Takeshi (1940–); Fujikawa, Tadd (1991–); Fujita, Scott (1979–); Gaines, Corey Yasuto (1965–); Gorman, Miki "Michiko" Suwa (1935–2015); Harada, Tsuneo "Cappy" (1921–2010); Hirashima, Hiroto "Hiro" (1910–2007); Hirayama, Satoshi "Fibber" (1930–); Japanese American Olympians; Japanese Americans in Baseball; Japanese Americans in Figure Skating; Kono, Tamio Tommy (1930–2016); Misaka, Wataru "Wat" (1923–); Nakamura, Haruki Robert (1986–); Walters, Rex Andrew (1970–); Yamasaki, Lindsey Brooke (1980–); Yonamine, Wallace Kaname "Wally" (1925–2011); Zenimura, Kenichi (1900–1968)

Further Reading

Niiya, Brian, ed. *More Than Just a Game: Sport in the Japanese American Community*. Los Angeles: Japanese America National Museum, 2000.

Regalado, Samuel O. *Nikkei Baseball: Japanese American Players from Immigration and Internment to the Major Leagues*. Urbana: The University of Illinois Press, 2013.

Staples, Bill, Jr. *Kenishi Zenimura: Japanese American Baseball Pioneer*. Jefferson City, NC: McFarland Press, 2011.

Adam R. Hornbuckle

JAPANESE IMMIGRANT PRESS

Japanese immigrants (Issei) had a remarkable penchant for organizing the ethnic press. Both on the U.S. mainland and in Hawai'i, a large number of newspapers and periodicals have been published, and major concentrations of Issei populations such as San Francisco, Los Angeles, Seattle, and Honolulu had at least two major vernacular dailies from the beginning of the 20th century through December 1941. Despite the wartime incarceration of Japanese Americans, the postwar years saw the revival of the ethnic press whereas the main readership shifted from the immigrant to the American-born generation. Yet, Japanese-language vernaculars have continued to occupy an important place in contemporary Japanese America as the influx of postwar newcomers from Japan still necessitates their presence.

The history of the Japanese ethnic press began as soon as the first group of immigrant intellectuals arrived in San Francisco around 1886. Having escaped the Japanese government's suppression of the People's Rights movement, Issei political exiles used mimeographed newspapers called *Shinonome* (*Dawn*) and *Shin Nippon* (*New Japan*) as the venue to condemn Tokyo's antidemocratic policy. These political newspapers frequently changed names, but they continued to be published, albeit in very small circulation, in San Francisco from 1886 through 1894. Initially, they carried mostly news items and commentaries on Japanese politics. Yet, as mimeographed weeklies gave way to lithographed dailies around 1892, they began to print more "local" reports relating to Japanese immigrant society and exclusionist agitation. The first immigrant daily was called the *Soko Shimbun* (*San Francisco News*), whose name subsequently changed to the *Soko Shimpo* (*The San Francisco Daily*) in 1893 and *Soko Jiji* (*San Francisco Times*) in 1895. Published from 1893 to 1895, another lithographed daily titled *Kinmon Nippo* (*Golden Gate News*) had four to six pages with a regular subscription of about 70.

Around 1895, Japanese immigrant press transformed from a medium of political advocacy to an important institution of ethnic community. The first typeset daily, *Shin Sekai Shimbun* (*New World Daily*), started its operation in May

1894 with circulation of 80 (increased to 200 by 1897). By 1899, it expanded from a six-page to an eight-page newspaper with growing subscriptions, for the *Shin Sekai* attracted readership from Buddhists and nationalistic segments of early Japanese America. Opponents of these groups, like Christians, American-educated intellectuals, and entrepreneurs, supported rival newspapers, which subsequently merged into the *Nichibei Shimbun* (*Japanese American News*) in April 1899. Until the mass incarceration of Japanese Americans in the spring of 1942, these two dailies remained the most important vernacular press, whose influence reached through much of California and as far east as the Rocky Mountain states. In 1922, the *Nichibei Shimbun* acquired a bankrupt daily and renamed it as the *Rafu Nichibei* (*Los Angeles Japanese American*), which continued to publish until 1931.

Southern California saw the publication of the first regional vernacular *Rafu Shimpo* (*Los Angeles Japanese Daily News*) in 1904. Similar to its northern California counterpart, the local Japanese immigrant community sustained a number of newspapers according to divided political interests and internal factionalism. During the decade following the birth of the *Rafu Shimpo*, a number of vernaculars came and went, and by 1920 there were four major Japanese dailies in the area. The post–World War I recession reconfigured the discursive and business landscape in Southern California, consolidating four-way competition into rivalry between the *Rafu Shimpo* and *Rafu Nichibei*. After the latter was liquidated in 1931, some of its staff writers collaborated with other immigrants who had been critical of a collusion between the *Rafu Shimpo* and local Japanese association leadership to establish the *Kashu Mainichi* (*Japan California Daily News*) in Los Angeles.

Seattle was another home for some of the earliest vernacular newspapers. Starting in 1897, a succession of short-lived mimeographed weeklies came out, but bitter rivalries within the local Japanese community provided a background for the publication of three major dailies known as the *Hokubei Jiji* (*North American Times*), *Asahi Shimbun*, and *Taihoku Nippo* (*Great Northern Daily News*). Although the *Asahi Shimbun* had a short life of 10 years after 1905, the *Hokubei Jiji* and *Taihoku Nippo*, published in 1902 and 1910, respectively, survived as major Japanese dailies of the Pacific Northwest until the early months of 1942.

In the continental United States, there were other regional newspapers. In the Pacific Northwest, the *Oshu Nippo* began its operation in Portland, Oregon, in 1904, and the *Takoma Shuho* (*Tacoma Japanese Times*) eight years later. In California, around 1907, the *Ofu Nippo* (*Sacramento Daily News*) and *Chuka Jiho* (*Japanese Times of Central California*) were published in Sacramento and Fresno to serve the local populations. The Japanese fishing community of Terminal Island had its own *Minami Engan Jiho* (*Southern Coast Herald*) since 1915. All these regional newspapers survived until Japan's bombing of Pearl Harbor.

The Rocky Mountain region constituted a vibrant site for early Japanese immigrant discursive formation when thousands of mining and railroad workers lived in Utah, Colorado, Wyoming, and parts of Nebraska. Between 1907 and 1914, three major dailies emerged, but their influence waned as the local laboring population diminished after the immigration exclusion of the mid-1920s. Although the printing of the *Kakushu Jiji* (*Colorado Times*) of Denver decreased from daily to three times a week, the *Utah Nippo* of Salt Lake City absorbed its Ogden rival, *Rakki Jiho*, in 1927. The *Kakushu Jiji* and *Utah Nippo*, however, became important outlets of information during the Pacific War when all major West Coast Japanese American newspapers were shut down.

New York City was an important hub of international merchants, immigrant intellectuals, artists, and political activists, as well as some Issei domestic workers. An elite segment of prewar New York Japanese formed an exclusive society, which had shored up small weeklies since 1897. Published in 1900 and 1911, respectively, the *Nichibei Jiho* (*Japanese American Commercial News*) and *Nyuyoku Shinpo* provided Issei with news reports relating to local Japanese affairs and U.S.–Japan trade.

With the increase of second-generation Japanese Americans (Nisei), the 1920s saw a rise in bilingualism in the Japanese immigrant press. The first vernacular newspaper that included an English-language section was the *Nichibei Shimbun* of San Francisco, which attempted to mold a separate public opinion among American-born citizens. Because existing anti-Japanese legislation used the Issei's legal status as unnaturalizable aliens as the basis of racial discrimination, Abiko Kyutaro, the publisher of the *Nichibei Shimbun*, anticipated that Nisei citizens would overcome institutionalized racism as long as the ethnic community nurtured their leadership and elevated their overall quality. For Abiko, inserting English pages into his daily was as much an educational endeavor for his ethnic posterity as it was a shrewd business decision to tap into a neglected new readership. Other major dailies, like the *Shin Sekai*, *Rafu Shimpo*, *Taihoku Nippo*, and *Kashu Mainichi*, followed suit through the late 1920s and 1930s, employing Nisei editors and writers for the English sections. Reflecting the diverging viewpoints between Issei and Nisei, the Japanese and English pages sometimes revealed different assertions and varying focuses. To cater to the unique challenge and interests of Nisei youngsters, James Sakamoto of Seattle took it upon himself to start an all-English Nisei weekly titled the *Japanese American Courier* in 1928. Starting from October 1929, the *Pacific Citizen* was also published in English as the weekly organ of the Japanese American Citizens League (JACL).

Other notable developments in the Japanese immigrant press included the publication of trade papers, religious journals, and political organs. In the mid-1910s, the Japanese Agricultural Association of California issued a monthly titled the *Kashu Chuo Nokai Geppo* for the benefit of Issei farmers in the Golden State. In Southern California, the local Japanese farm federation printed a weekly, which later expanded into the *Beikoku Sangyo Nippo* (*Japanese Industrial Daily*). On a religious front, the Buddhist Mission of America issued the monthly *Beikoku Bukkyo* (*American Buddhism*) between 1901 and 1918. Though much smaller in circulation, Issei leftists and radicals of California and Washington put forth newspapers and periodicals under various titles. Between 1926 and 1941, one stream of such a publication transformed itself from the *Kaikyusen* (*Class Struggle*) to the *Zaibei Rodo Shimbun* (*Japanese Worker in America*), and from the *Rodo Shimbun* (*Rodo Shimbun*) to the *Doho* (*Doho*). During the 1930s, these leftist papers were shipped to Japan as well under the auspices of the American Community Party. In Seattle, local Japanese labor activists and leftists published the *Rodo* (*Labor*) semimonthly from 1920.

Hawai'i

Despite the longer history of Japanese immigration to the islands, Hawai'i lagged behind California in the formation of vernacular press. Combined with the dominance of government-sponsored contract laborers between 1885 and 1892, the dearth of an intellectual class explained the difference between the two population hubs of early Japanese America. In Hawai'i, the first mimeographed paper appeared in 1892, and other short-lived weeklies with various names. Many early papers tended to serve the cause of Japanese labor activism, as they offered a forum for expressing discontent for exploitation by both sugar planters and Japanese emigration companies, as well as mistreatment by immigration officials. Published in 1894, the *Hawai'i Shimpo*, Hawai'i's first Japanese typeset daily, played a major role in ethnic mobilization around these issues, though it flip-flopped on the 1909 Oahu Strike by opposing mass labor action against sugar planters. Often characterized as a "red paper," the *Hawai'i Nichi Nichi Shinbun* was especially active in the area of labor struggle on the eve of the 1904 plantation strikes.

By 1912, Hawai'i's Japanese came to have two major dailies in Honolulu in accordance with political, religious, and temperamental divides within the ethnic community. Initially known as the *Yamato Shimbun* in 1895, the *Nippu Jiji*'s prominence stemmed from its dogged support of the massive Japanese strike of 1909, which resulted in the arrest and detention of its publisher Soga Yasutaro. Subsequently, however, the *Nippu Jiji* tended to take a more "conciliatory" position on the questions of racism and discrimination than its rival, the *Hawai'i Hochi,* that was published by Makino Kinzaburo in 1912. In contrast to *Nippu Jiji*'s penchant for interracial cooperation and its call for assimilation, the *Hawai'i Hochi* often confronted instances of overt racism head-on. The community-wide test case against Hawai'i's foreign language school laws is a case in point. Whereas the *Nippu Jiji* disapproved of such an action out of its desire to work with Hawai'i's Haole leaders and Japanese diplomats, the

Hawai'i Hochi stood behind Issei parents, teachers, and community leaders, who decided to bring a lawsuit against the territorial government, a suit that ended in a historic victory at the U.S. Supreme Court in 1927. The rivalry between the two papers continued through the prewar years. Just as in California and Washington, the *Nippu Jiji* and the *Hawai'i Hochi* carried both Japanese and English sections after the 1920s.

Because of the problem of accessibility, Hawai'i's Japanese community outside the island of Oahu supported a number of regional newspapers that continued operation until the outbreak of the Pacific War. In Hilo, a town of eastern Hawai'i, the *Hawai'i Shokumin Shimbun* began daily publication in 1909, and from 1914 to 1941 it was known as the *Hawai'i Mainichi*. The *Kona Hankyo* (*Kona Echo*) served the residents of western Hawai'i since as early as 1897. The islands of Kaua'i and Maui had the *Kaua'i Shimpo* and the *Maui Shimbun* established in 1904 and 1915, respectively.

Wartime and Postwar Years

During the Pacific War, all West Coast newspapers were put out of commission as Japanese Americans were removed from the area to War Relocation Centers. Outside of the military exclusion zone, the *Utah Nippo* of Salt Lake City, the *Colorado Times*, and the newly established *Rocky Shimpo* of Denver rapidly increased circulation because many internees and resettlers subscribed to them. Along with the JACL's *Pacific Citizen*, each relocation center also issued a bilingual newspaper that carried official U.S. government reports and camp affairs. In Hawai'i, the *Nippu Jiji* and the *Hawai'i Hochi* remained in business, though with more Americanized names as the *Hawai'i Times* and the *Hawai'i Herald*, respectively. Except for the *Rocky Shimpo* and camp newspapers, all of the Rocky Mountain and Hawai'ian vernaculars continued their operations after 1945.

The postwar years saw not only the revival of major dailies in the Pacific Coast states but also the emergence of new vernaculars in other parts of the continental United States. In Los Angeles, the *Rafu Shimpo* and the *Kashu Mainichi* resumed publication in 1946 and in 1947, whereas another bilingual daily titled the *Shin Nichibei Shimbun* (*New Japanese American News*) was formed under the partnership of local Issei and Nisei businesspersons and community leaders. In San Francisco, former employees and supporters of the *Nichibei Shimbun* organized the *Nichibei Jiji* (*Nichi Bei Times*) in 1946, and a lineal descendant of the prewar *Shin Sekai* appeared in the name of the *Hokubei Mainichi*. Seattle had only one daily called the *Hokubei Hochi* (*North American Post*), which was a successor of the *Hokubei Jiji*. Meanwhile, because many resettlers made the Midwest and the East their new home after release from the internment camps, there emerged the *Chicago Shimpo* and the *Hokubei Shimpo* of New York in 1945.

In contemporary Japanese America, the ethnic press still offers an important site for discursive and identity formation even though generation shift and easy information access have made many newspapers vulnerable to a shrinkage of readership. Currently, the *Rafu Shimpo, Nichi Bei Jiji, North American Post, Chicago Shimpo, Hawai'i Herald,* and *Pacific Citizen* are still present, albeit in various formats. There are also a myriad of new regional vernaculars and free papers in many cities with a sizable Japanese population.

See also: Abiko, Kyutaro (1865–1936); *Nichibei Shimbun (Japanese American News)*

Further Reading

Ebihara, Hachiro. *Kaigai Hoji Shimbun Zasshishi.* Tokyo: Gakuji Shoin, 1936.
Ichioka, Yuji. *The Issei: The World of the First Generation Japanese Immigrants, 1885–1924.* New York: Free Press, 1988.

Eiichiro Azuma

JAPANESE TRANSNATIONAL IDENTITY

Transnationalism refers to the condition of being connected to multiple nation-states at the same time. These connections must be real, lived ties—not simply imagined or historical linkages. Transnational ties can be studied and observed in terms of political, economic, cultural, and social dimensions.

Japanese transnational identities may overlap with, but are analytically distinguishable from, Japanese American ethnic identities. Japanese American ethnic identities are the ways in which ethnic Japanese in the United States identify with their Japanese heritage. These identities are rooted in the histories and experiences of Japanese Americans in the United States. Some of these ethnic identities may take on transnational forms, when Japanese Americans identify with contemporary Japanese society and culture. But ethnic identities are not necessarily transnational, as Japanese Americans may identify with the Japanese cultural forms that migrants in the early 20th century brought with them and these are not necessarily the same as contemporary forms that one would find in Japanese society today.

Japanese transnational identities linked to Japan and the United States can be conceived of in two major ways: Japanese migrating from Japan and Japanese Americans developing ties or migrating to Japan. Alternatively, Japanese transnational identities can be separated into three generational groups: first-generation Japanese who migrate abroad; second-generation Japanese Americans who are born in the United States but grow up connected to Japan; and third-, fourth-, and later-generation Japanese Americans who develop connections to Japan later in life and usually not through familial connections.

Japanese Migrating from Japan and Japanese Americans Developing Ties or Migrating to Japan

Japanese migrants from Japan to the United States have been able to maintain ties to both countries in ways that facilitate transnationalism. These linkages have taken different shapes in different time periods. In the prewar period (1880s to 1940s), Japanese migrants adapted and integrated into the neighborhoods in the United States where they resided. Although participating in local U.S. communities, they also maintained ties to Japan through reading Japanese newspapers, sending letters to family and friends in Japan, and joining Japanese organizations to keep informed about happenings in Japan. Many sent money back to Japan, and some traveled to Japan for family and business reasons.

In the postwar period (since World War II) technological advancements have made it much easier and less expensive to maintain connections with people in faraway places. In addition to previous forms of communication such as postal letters and telephone calls by landline, Japanese migrants in the United States can now stay connected to people in Japan via the Internet. Although previous waves of emigrants had to rely on printed forms of newspapers and other documents sharing news from Japan, recent migrants can now access newspapers online, as well as see Japanese television news programs to view news almost instantly as it is reported. Many Japanese television programs and films are also available online, as well as for rent or purchase at video stores in larger urban areas in the United States.

Many U.S.-born Japanese Americans go to Japan and live there as exchange students, to teach English, or for other study or work, including training in martial and other cultural arts, such as Japanese tea ceremony, kimono-wearing, ikebana (flower arranging), and Japanese calligraphy. These Japanese Americans are what social scientists call "ethnic return migrants"—the descendants of emigrants born and raised outside of the homeland who migrate "back" (though this movement is often their first time going to or living in the homeland).

Japanese Migrants in the United States Maintain Ties to Japan

First-generation Japanese migration abroad and the resulting Japanese transnational identities that emerge can be thought of in at least three ways, which often overlap. Although Issei refers to first-generation Japanese migrants generally, in the United States, this term is usually associated more specifically with prewar Japanese migration that mostly took place from the late 1800s to the early 1900s.

The postwar migration of Japanese to the United States can be separated into two subgroups, based on whether or not they settle in the United States; these are the second and third types of first-generation Japanese transnational identities. One of these groups of Japanese emigrants is the Shin-Issei: the "new" Issei who have migrated since World War II. This group comes from diverse backgrounds; at one end are "war brides" who come from lower socioeconomic backgrounds and married U.S. soldiers then migrated to the United States with them, and at the other end are more highly educated Japanese who migrated with more financial resources as part of the post-1965 wave of more skilled Asian migrants.

The third group of Japanese emigrants can be called "overseas Japanese." This group includes Japanese businesspersons (and their families) who are temporarily stationed abroad for work, college students from Japan, and "creative" or "lifestyle migrants" who are pursuing work as artists. Shin-Issei implies ultimate Japanese settlement in the United States, whereas "overseas Japanese" does not necessarily imply settlement in the United States.

The terminology used to describe first-generation Japanese migrants reflects differing national perspectives. Issei means first generation and implies the first generation of Japanese to settle outside of Japan; it is commonly used to describe these migrants in the nations in which they settle. Meanwhile, from a Japanese perspective, any Japanese nationals overseas (regardless of eventual settlement) would be considered "overseas Japanese."

Japanese Return Migrants in Japan

Japanese of various ages have migrated abroad (as overseas Japanese) then returned to Japan. The language and culture that they learn when outside of Japan continues to influence their identity once they return to Japan. Japanese returnees usually lack the "Japanese common sense" that is expected of mainstream Japanese in Japan, even though they are Japanese citizens who typically were raised by two parents who are Japanese citizens. For children, this is because they grew up in other countries, and for adults this is because they have lived abroad for so long that their way of thinking and acting has changed.

Japanese who have lived abroad and were primarily socialized as children in non-Japanese contexts before returning to Japan are commonly referred to as "Japanese returnees" or kikokushijo. These children are often teased upon their return for eating uncommon lunch foods at school in Japan (e.g., peanut butter and jelly sandwiches), and for dressing and speaking in atypical Japanese ways.

Japanese who have been educated or have worked abroad as adults (i.e., from college age on) would not be considered "Japanese returnees" or kikokushijo. There is no particular term in Japanese to describe this group but academics would classify them as "return migrants" who are different from "Japanese returnees" because their experience abroad was of their own choosing, thus making for different dynamics of adaptation and acculturation.

Second-Generation Japanese American Transnationalism

Japanese Americans born in the United States may also develop ties to Japan and identify transnationally. Even if brought up and based in the United States, when exposed to contemporary Japanese culture and society on an ongoing basis, second-generation Japanese Americans may learn to identify with Japan.

For prewar Nisei (second-generation Japanese Americans) brought up in the 1900s, it was less common for those raised completely in the United States to identify transnationally; rather, Nisei transnationalism would refer to Kibei Nisei who were born in the United States and raised partly in Japan before returning to the United States.

In the postwar period, Shin-Nisei or the "new" Nisei generation are transnational in new ways. They are the children of postwar Shin-Issei as discussed earlier. With increasing globalization, this newer wave of second-generation transnationalism is shaped by parents (who have the financial resources) regularly taking the children to Japan to visit relatives and friends, speaking Japanese at home, observing Japanese religious practices, celebrating Japanese cultural holidays (e.g., celebrating Boy's Day or Girl's Day, Japanese New Year), reading Japanese books and newspapers, belonging to Japanese organizations (e.g., organizations based on Japanese prefectures), watching Japanese television shows and films (e.g., NHK news from Japan broadcast on local networks, renting videos of Japanese TV dramas), and actively participating in Japanese community events.

Later-Generation Transnationalism

Japanese Americans born and raised in the United States, with parents from the United States, are also developing transnational ties and identifications with Japan. Sansei (third-generation) and later generations may not grow up with much of a connection to contemporary Japanese society through their parents, but with increasing transnational flows of people and information, they are exposed to contemporary Japanese people and culture through Japanese/Japanese American community events, anime, martial and other cultural arts, and through working and living in Japan. Japanese Americans in Hawai'i, even more than those from the U.S. mainland, may interact with Japanese tourists and students, increasing their knowledge of contemporary Japan. Through their families, later generation Japanese Americans are exposed to bits of Japanese society and culture; these cultural forms, however, are older, from the Meiji period of the late 1800s and early 1900s when the prewar Issei left Japan (not the contemporary period), and lower class, as this first migrant wave was predominantly composed of peasants and farmers. For this group, developing a Japanese transnational identity is different from (yet sometimes overlaps with) a Japanese American ethnic identity. A Japanese American ethnic identity could be transnational or not, depending on whether or not it entails the creation of new ties to contemporary Japan.

See also: Kibei; Shin-Issei/Shin-Nisei Identity

Further Reading

Kanno, Yasuko. *Negotiating Bilingual and Bicultural Identities: Japanese Returnees Betwixt Two Worlds.* Mahwah, NJ: L. Erlbaum, 2003.

Kurotani, Sawa. *Home Away from Home: Japanese Corporate Wives in the United States.* Durham, NC: Duke University Press, 2005.

White, Merry. *The Japanese Overseas: Can They Go Home Again?* Princeton, NJ: Princeton University Press, 1992.

Jane H. Yamashiro

KIBEI

Kibei are second-generation Japanese Americans born in the United States who lived for some time in Japan, either for education or economic reasons, and then returned to the United States. "Kibei" translates literally to mean a person who "returned to America." As these generational labels tend to be rooted in a historical time period, Kibei generally refers to those who came of age in the 1930s and 1940s. Set apart from their fellow second-generation Nisei peers because of their time in Japan, Kibei often felt alienated from the Japanese American community as well as from the white American majority. During World War II, differences between Kibei and other Nisei heightened tensions around issues of Americanization, loyalty, and Japanese culture. As members of the second generation who went to live in Japan, but then returned to the United States, Kibei do not fit neatly into a more unidirectional and linear model of American immigration. Their increased familiarity with Japan complicates the Japanese American Citizens League (JACL)'s early postwar ethnic success story of the melting pot and narrative of Japanese acculturation and assimilation to Anglo-white normative U.S. society.

Having lived in Japan, Kibei were more likely to speak Japanese as their primary language, more familiar with Japanese culture, and less likely to be acculturated to American customs than other Nisei. Because of their racial difference, Kibei often struggled to find employment outside of the Japanese American community, but also faced marginalization from their Nisei peers for being "too Japanese" and community leaders stereotyped the entire group of Kibei as ruining the second generation's exemplary record by engaging in criminal activities.

Kibei were internally varied based on their age, length of time spent in Japan, and whether they were educated in Japan during a more politically progressive or more militaristic and authoritarian periods. To establish a sense of community, Kibei established their own organizations, such as the literary Kibei Club in Los Angeles, and the Kibei Citizens Council of San Francisco, which had a counterpart in Los Angeles.

As they were more sympathetic to Japanese culture and language, Kibei were also politically distinct from other Nisei. They were less likely to favor the "100% Americanization" promoted by the explicitly patriotic JACL in the lead-up to World War II. Kibei also tended to be more sympathetic to, or at least less openly opposed to, Japanese militarism in the Pacific.

The outbreak of war between the United States and Japan in 1941 highlighted these differences within the second generation. U.S. government officials, who already viewed Japanese Americans as a whole with suspicion of disloyalty to the United States, viewed Kibei with particular suspicion. Cmdr. Kenneth D. Ringle, assistant district intelligence officer for the Eleventh Naval District in Los Angeles in 1940, viewed the Kibei as extremely dangerous, loyal to Japan, and possibly planted in the United States for the purpose of espionage by the Japanese government. Likewise, Col. Cross of the U.S. Army viewed the Kibei and their Issei parents with suspicion, questioning why they had sent their children to be educated in Japan if not for reasons of cultural and political indoctrination.

During internment in the War Relocation Authority (WRA) camps, Kibei earned a reputation as "troublemakers." The Kibei were less likely to support the JACL's strategy of cooperating with government authorities to prove their loyalty, with the notable exception of Karl Yoneda, a Kibei who was active with the Communist Party. According to the Western Defense Command officials, the Kibei were responsible for stirring up trouble and violently threatening others who otherwise would have been more acquiescent.

The WRA also described the protest and unrest at Manzanar on December 6, 1942, as an aberration in the otherwise peaceful context of the camps, and their corrective action after the uprising mostly targeted Kibei. On the previous day, Fred Tayama, JACL leader, was beaten by a group of unidentified men and was recovering in the hospital. Though he was unable to make a positive identification, several Kibei labeled as "malcontents" were arrested. In particular, Harry Ueno seemed to have been targeted for arrest because of his efforts at organizing a Kitchen Workers' Union and having recently accused WRA officials of stealing sugar and meat from camp rations. In response, Joe Kurihara, a Nisei from Hawai'i, spoke before a large crowd of demonstrators, some of whom demanded the release of Ueno. Others stormed the hospital to attack Tayama again. In the chaos that followed, troops threw teargas grenades and fired into the unarmed crowd. Two internees were killed and at least 10 others were injured. Joe Kurihara, Harry Ueno, and 14 others, all Kibei except for Kurihara, were sent to an isolation camp for "troublemakers." Whereas camp authorities attribute most of the unrest to a group of Kibei provocateurs, other accounts by historians detail a broader context of strife, mistrust, internal tensions, and dissatisfaction felt by Japanese Americans toward being held in WRA camps.

To rehabilitate the public image of Japanese Americans and facilitate their ultimate resettlement outside of the camps, government officials and JACL leaders drew upon negative stereotypes of the Kibei to blame them as the cause of tension and unrest. In addition to the isolation camps, WRA officials launched an effort to sort the "loyal" from the "disloyal" and issued a loyalty questionnaire in January 1943. Dillon Myer, director of the War Relocation Authority, referred to the Kibei as "bad" and "social outcasts" when justifying the removal of "troublemakers" from the mainstream camp population and their segregation in the Tule Lake camp. In some cases, WRA officials noted that they had misclassified some who had never been to Japan as Kibei solely because they had been involved in the attacks and that Kibei status was conflated with being a "troublemaker."

Overall, Kibei were more likely to have been classified as "disloyals" and segregated in Tule Lake, especially those from agricultural, Buddhist, and non-college educated background. They were also more likely to have responded negatively to Questions 27 and 28 on the questionnaire, which asked if they would serve in the military and if they would forswear allegiance to the emperor of Japan. Paradoxically, Kibei were overrepresented both in the Tule Lake Segregation Center for those deemed "disloyal" and in the Military Intelligence Service (MIS), for the same Japanese language skills that made them seem potentially subversive were also useful for U.S. military intelligence purposes.

See also: Japanese American Citizens League; Japanese Transnational Identity; Shin-Issei/Shin-Nisei Identity

Further Reading

Hosokawa, Bill. *Nisei: The Quiet Americans*. New York: William Morrow, 1969.

Takahashi, Jere. *Nisei/Sansei: Shifting Japanese American Identities and Politics*. Philadelphia: Temple University Press, 1997.

Yoneda, Karl. *Ganbatte: Sixty-Year Struggle of a Kibei Worker*. Los Angeles: Asian American Studies Center, UCLA, 1983.

Katie Furuyama

KOGAWA, JOY (1935–)

An accomplished novelist and poet, Joy Kogawa is best known for the novel *Obasan*. Scholars agree that Joy Kogawa's novel about the internment of Japanese Canadians, *Obasan* (1981), is a seminal book for its treatment of the unlawful incarceration of 21,000 Japanese Canadians in labor and detention camps in British Columbia during World War II. *Obasan* tells the story of one family and their wartime experiences from the viewpoint of Naomi Nakane,

Writer Joy Kogawa is best known for her novel *Obasan*, which highlighted the struggle of Japanese Canadians for redress following World War II. (Bernard Weil/Toronto Star via Getty Images)

a third-generation Japanese Canadian school teacher raised by her fraternal uncle and aunt (obasan). The death of the uncle who raised her sparks Naomi's mental journey through her memories as she comes to terms with her childhood experience of the war and her mother and father's absence. Naomi's memories are combined with excerpts from Naomi's activist aunt Emily Kato's diaries, newspaper clippings, and government documents Kogawa again follows the family and the Japanese Canadian struggle for redress in the novel, *Itsuka* (1992).

Although Shizue Takashima's memoir was the first book published about the Canadian internment, Kogawa's *Obasan* has a significant readership in Canada and America and is a favorite among scholars. *Obasan* earned the Books in Canada First Novel Award, the Canadian Authors Association Book of the Year Award, the Before Columbus Foundation Book Award, and the American Library Association's Notable Book Award. It was also included in the Literary Review of Canada's 2006 list of top 100 books.

Joy Nozomi Nakagawa was born in Vancouver, British Columbia, on June 6, 1935, to Gordon and Lois Nakayama, an Anglican clergyman and kindergarten teacher, respectively. During World War II, the Nakayama family was forced to move to Slocan detention camp in the southeastern interior of British Columbia and their property, except for personal items, was confiscated by the Canadian government. A 1986 study estimated that Japanese Canadians lost $443 million in property and wages. Conditions in the camps were poor—the Red Cross facilitated supplemental food shipments from Japan to the camps during the war and the Canadian government spent one-third the per capita amount spent by the American government on its internees. Following the war, Japanese Canadians were given the option of going to Japan or moving east of British Columbia. Joy Nakagawa and her family moved to Coledale, Alberta. When in Alberta, Joy Nakagawa studied at the University of Toronto and began teaching elementary school in Coledale. She then enrolled in the Anglican Women's Training College and Conservatory of Music in Toronto transferring the next year to another music school in Vancouver. She married David Kogawa in 1957. After having two children together, Gordon and Diedre, and living in British Columbia, Saskatchewan, and Ottawa, the couple divorced in 1968, the same year Kogawa published her first book of poetry, *Splintered Moon*. She worked for the Office of the Prime Minister in Ottawa while writing poetry. Joy Kogawa was active in the Canadian movement for redress, so much so that she stopped writing *Itsuka* during that time and instead took notes. Excerpts from *Obasan* were read aloud in the House of Commons in 1988 when the redress settlement was announced. The government of Brian Mulroney offered a formal apology, a payment of $21,000 to the survivors, and the reinstitution of citizenship for those who were deported to Japan.

Kogawa is a prolific author and poet who published numerous books of poetry and prose including: *The Splintered Moon* (1968), *A Choice of Dreams* (1974), *Jericho Road* (1977), *Six Poems* (1978), *Obasan* (1981, republished as *Naomi's Road* in 1986), *Woman in the Woods* (1985), *Itsuka* (1992 republished as *Emily Kato* in 2005), *The Rain Ascends* (1995), *A Song of Lilith* (2000), *A Garden of Anchors: Selected Poems* (2003), and the illustrated children's book *Naomi's Tree* (2008). She is the recipient of a number of honorary degrees and awards: Member of the Order of Canada (1986), a Ryerson Polytechnical Institute Fellowship, an LLD from the University of Lethbridge (1991), a LittD from the University of Guelph (1992), an LLD from Simon Fraser University (1993), an Urban Alliance Race Relations Award (1994), a Grace MacInnis Visiting Scholar Award (1995), a Lifetime Achievement award from the Association of American Studies (2001), a LittD from the University of British Columbia (2001), Member of the Order of British Columbia (2006), a George Woodcock Lifetime Achievement award (2008), and the Order of the Rising Star from Japan (2010).

See also: DeSoto, Hisaye Yamamoto (1921–2011); Hartmann, Sadakichi (1867–1944); Hirahara, Naomi (1962–); Iko, Momoko (1940–); Inada, Lawson Fusao (1938–); Japanese American Literature; Mori, Toshio (1910–1980); Mura, David (1952–); Murayama, Milton (1923–2016); Okada, John (1923–1971); Otsuka, Julie (1962–)

Further Reading

Cheung, King-Kok. *Articulate Silences: Hisaye Yamamoto, Maxine Hong Kingston, and Joy Kogawa*. Ithaca, NY: Cornell University Press, 1993.

Hsu, Ruth Y., and Joy Kogawa. "A Conversation with Joy Kogawa." *Amerasia Journal* 22, no. 1: 199–216.

Kogawa, Joy. "What Do I Remember of the Evacuation." *Chicago Review* 42 (1996): 3.

Emily Morishima

KONO, TAMIO "TOMMY" (1930–2016)

Tamio "Tommy" Kono was the dominant U.S. weightlifter of the Cold War era (1947–1991), and one of the most successful Asian American athletes of all time. He won gold medals in weightlifting in the 1952 and 1956 Olympics, and a silver medal in the 1960 Olympics.

Between 1953 and 1959, he won eight consecutive world weightlifting championships, and at one point, he held world records in four different weight classes. During the same years, he also won the physique titles of Mr. Universe three times and Mr. World once.

After retiring from competitive lifting in 1964, Kono coached the Mexican weightlifting team in preparation for the 1968 Mexico City Olympics and the West German weightlifting team in preparation for the 1972 Munich Olympics. From 1972 to 1976, he served as head coach for the U.S. men's Olympic team, and, finally, he served as head coach for the U.S. women's Olympic team from 1987 to 1990.

Kono's philosophy could be summarized as follows: (1) Things could be worse, so be grateful for what you have. (2) Take care of your equipment. (3) Success is the result of good technique, carefully done. (4) Approach the bar (and life) as a challenge rather than as something to be beaten.

Tamio Kono died at age 85 in Honolulu, Hawai'i.

See also: Japanese American Olympians; Japanese Americans in Sports

Further Reading

Tommy Kono Bands and Power Hooks Website. http://tommykono.com/. Accessed December 10, 2012.

Joseph R. Svinth

MISAKA, WATARU "WAT" (1923–)

Wataru "Wat" Misaka, basketball player, was born on December 21, 1923, in Ogden, Utah. His father, who worked as a barber, left Hiroshima, Japan, in the early 1900s. After the death of his father in 1939, the Misaka family considered returning to Hiroshima but decided to remain in Ogden despite the discrimination. Misaka started playing basketball as a student at Ogden High School. A skilled ball handler and shooter, he led the Tigers to the state championship in 1940 and a regional championship in 1941.

After the United States declared war in 1941, most of the Japanese Americans living in Utah were relocated to the internment camp in Topaz, Utah. However, the Misaka family was allowed to remain in Ogden because of the family's reputation. After graduating from high school in 1941, he entered Weber College (now Weber State University) in Ogden. As a member of the basketball team,

Misaka led Weber to two junior college championships.

After graduating from Weber College in 1943, Misaka entered the University of Utah to study engineering. He played on the basketball team, which received invitations to play in both the National Collegiate Athletic Association (NCAA) and National Invitation Tournament (NIT) basketball championship tournaments in 1944. Utah chose to play in the NIT because then it was the most prestigious of the national tournaments. Utah lost to the University of Kentucky in the first round. Utah replaced Arkansas in the NCAA tournament and won the tournament, by defeating Dartmouth College 40–42. Two weeks later, Utah defeated St. Johns, the NIT champion, by the score of 43–36.

After the end of the 1944 college basketball season, Misaka

Former University of Utah and New York Knicks basketball player Wat Misaka at home in Bountiful, Utah, 2008. The son of Japanese immigrants, Misaka played in an era when most players on the court were of European descent and America was at the height of the anti-Japanese sentiment of World War II. (AP Photo/Douglas C. Pizac)

was drafted into the U.S. Army. He used his Japanese language skills as a member of an intelligence unit that surveyed Hiroshima, which had been destroyed by the first atomic weapon deployed in combat, and interviewed survivors of the explosion. Misaka met his uncle, who still lived in the family home, which stood in the shadow of a hill that shielded it from the atomic blast.

In 1946, Misaka returned to the University of Utah to resume study. Rejoining the basketball team, he led Utah to a 19–5 record and a 49–45 victory over the University of Kentucky in the NIT in 1947. Misaka defended Kentucky's top scorer, Ralph Beard, holding him to one point.

Selected by the New York Knicks in 1947 Basketball Association of America draft, Misaka debuted as the first non-Caucasian player in professional basketball in 1947. He played in three games and scored seven points before being cut from the team because, as Misaka believes, the Knicks had too many guards. He declined an offer to play with the all-black Harlem Globetrotters and returned to the University of Utah to complete his degree in engineering.

Misaka graduated from the University of Utah in 1948, began working for an engineering firm in Salt Lake City, married and had two children. Inducted into the Utah Sports Hall of Fame in 1999, Misaka was featured in *More Than a Game: Sport in the Japanese American Community*, an exhibit at the Japanese American National Museum in Los Angeles in 2000. A documentary film, *Transcending: The Wat Misaka Story* premiered in 2008 about his basketball career and status as first non-Caucasian player in professional basketball.

See also: Japanese Americans in Sports

Further Reading

Boyer, Edward J. "A Story of Japanese American Athletes." *Los Angeles Times*, March 4, 2000. http://www.webcitation.org/6Dyu3is8d. Accessed August 19, 2015.

Vecsey, George. "Pioneering Knick Returns to Garden." *New York Times*, August 11, 2009. http://www.nytimes.com/2009/08/11/sports/basketball/11vecsey.html?_r=0. Accessed August 19, 2015.

Adam R. Hornbuckle

MORI, TOSHIO (1910–1980)

Author Toshio Mori was born on March 20, 1910, in Oakland, California. As Japanese Asian Americans, Mori and his family were subjected to internment during World War II at the Topaz Relocation Center in Utah under U.S. Executive Order 9066.

Although the internment experience had a great influence on Mori's style of writing, he is generally known for the diversity of his short stories, only a handful of which deal specifically with internment. In this way, Mori is recognized as one of the first celebrated Japanese and Asian American short story writers of post–World War II United States.

Mori's writing style was also influenced by a number of his contemporary authors including Sherwood Anderson, Stephen Crane, Ernest Hemmingway, and William Saroyan. Indeed, literary scholars have cited the parallel contributions of both Sherwood Anderson and Toshio Mori to the development of American literary modernism.

Mori is perhaps best known for his book *Yokohama, California,* a compilation of short stories about the colorful world of Japanese and Asian American communities in pre–World War II California. In a telling example of the anti-Japanese sentiment after the United States entered World War II, the release of Mori's book was scheduled for 1941 but was postponed until 1949, well after the war had ended. Mori would go on to write two other books, *The Chauvinist and Other Stories* (1979) and *The Woman from Hiroshima* (1980). Critics have commended Mori for his ability to approach storytelling through an impassioned sense of historical reality and humor.

Although several of Mori's biographers have noted that he aspired to be an artist, a professional athlete, or even a Buddhist missionary, he instead spent much of his life running a flower nursery by day and freelance writing by night. In 1947, Mori married Hisayo Yoshiwara and fathered a son. Toshio Mori died on April 12, 1980.

See also: Japanese American Literature

Further Reading

Mori, Toshio. *Unfinished Business: Selected Works of Toshio Mori.* Berkeley, CA: Heyday Books, 2000.
Mori, Toshio. *Yokohama, California.* Seattle: University of Washington Press, 1985.

Salvador Jimenez Murguia

MURA, DAVID (1952–)

A third-generation Japanese American (Sansei), David Mura is a performance artist and writer who engages in multiple genres. His published works include several collections of poetry, one novel, two memoirs, and numerous plays and essays. Much of Mura's writing explores the intricate and complex interconnections between race, history, memory, Asian American masculinity, and sexuality, extending and complicating issues that have been addressed by earlier generations of Asian American male authors such as Carlos Bulosan, Frank Chin, and Shawn Wong.

Born David Uyemura in June 1952, Mura spent most of his childhood and young adult life with his family in the suburbs of Chicago in a primarily Jewish community. His father, Tom Mura, who worked as a reporter for the International News Service (INS), changed the family name from Uyemura to Mura when David was seven years old to get "better bylines" at his job as Tom found that most people had difficulty pronouncing his Japanese last name. David Mura's parents both lived in internment camps during World War II, and they have been reluctant to discuss their experiences in the camps with their children. As a writer, Mura explores the roots and implications of his parents' silence toward the camps and tries to excavate and reimagine that part of his family history that has been buried. Mura's writings demonstrate how the history of the internment continues to impact contemporary Japanese American life.

The discovery of a *Playboy* magazine in his parents' closet when he was in junior high marks the beginning of David Mura's exploration of the connections between race and sexuality. Mura's critique of the ways in which Asian American men have been emasculated by the dominant culture and his desire to articulate the connection between the history of the internment camp and the formation of his sexuality and desire as a Sansei constitute some of the central themes of his writing.

Mura received his BA from Grinnell College and an MFA in creative writing from Vermont College. Much of his college years and the beginning of his graduate career were marked by his addiction to pornography, binge drinking, and bouts of depression, as he struggled with his self-image as a Japanese American man. Mura recounts these experiences in his 1996 memoir *Where the Body Meets Memory: An Odyssey of Race, Sexuality and Identity*.

In 1984, Mura received a U.S./Japan Creative Artist Exchange Fellowship while working as an arts administrator for the Writers-in-the Schools program in Minnesota. His one-year fellowship in Japan resulted in the publication of his first memoir: *Turning Japanese: Memoirs of a Sansei*, which won the Josephine Miles Book Award from the Oakland PEN and was listed among the New York Times Notable Books of Year in 1991.

Mura has written three collections of poetry. The first, *After We Lost Our Way*, won the 1989 National Poetry Series Contest. His second collection, *The Colors of Desire*, published in 1995, won the Carl Sandburg Literary Award from the Friends of the Chicago Public Library. His third book of poetry, *Angels for the Burning*, was published in 2004. Mura has also published the chapbook, *A Male Grief: Notes on Pornography & Addiction*, and a collection of critical essays entitled *Song for Uncle Tom, Tonto & Mr. Moto: Poetry & Identity* was published by the University of Michigan Press in its Poets on Poetry series in 2002. With the publication of his first novel *Famous Suicides of the Japanese Empire* in September 2008, Mura's work continues to illuminate the relationship between discourses of race, masculinity, and desire.

As a performance artist and playwright, Mura has worked with African American writer Alex Pate. Together they have created and performed a multimedia performance piece, Secret Colors, which depicts their lives as men of color and explores Asian American–African American relations. A film adaptation of this piece, *Slowly, This,* was broadcast in the PBS series ALIVE TV in July/August 1995. Mura has also been featured on the PBS series, *The Language of Life*. His other performance pieces and plays include, *Relocations: Images from a Sansei, Silence & Desire,* and *After Hours.*

Mura has received a Lila Wallace-Reader's Digest Writers' Award, a U.S./Japan Creative Artist Fellowship, two NEA Literature Fellowships, two Bush Foundation Fellowships, four Loft-McKnight Awards, several Minnesota State Arts Board grants, and a Discovery/The Nation Award.

Aside from his writing career, Mura is also a teacher and has an active presence in various literary and artistic communities. He has taught at the University of Minnesota, St. Olaf College, the University of Oregon, the Loft Literary Center, and the Voices of the Nation Association writers' conference. He cofounded the Asian American Renaissance, an Asian American arts organization and served as its artistic director. Currently, he teaches at Hamline University, VONA (Voices of the Nation Association), and the Stonecoast MFA program. Mura frequently gives readings and presentations at educational institutions, businesses, writers' conferences and other organizations throughout the United States. David Mura currently resides in St. Paul, Minnesota, with his wife and their three children.

See also: Japanese American Literature

Further Reading

David Mura Official Website. http://davidmura.com/. Accessed August 10, 2010.
Mura, David. *Turning Japanese: Memoirs of a Sansei*. New York: Anchor, 1991.
Mura, David. *Where the Body Meets Memory: An Odyssey of Race, Sexuality and Identity*. New York: Anchor, 1997.

Nan Ma

MURAYAMA, MILTON (1923–2016)

Milton Murayama was an American Nisei author and playwright, and a pioneer in local Hawai'ian literature. He was the author of *All I Asking for Is My Body* (1975), *Five Years on a Rock* (1994), *Plantation Boy* (1998), and *Dying in a Strange Land* (2008). He also wrote and produced two plays, *Yoshitsune* (1977) and an adaptation of *All I Asking for Is My Body* (1989). Murayama was one of the first writers to transcribe pidgin and Japanese in English-language literature. His work has been given a considerable amount of critical attention within Asian American studies and Hawai'ian local literature.

Murayama was born in 1923 in Laihana, Hawai'i, to a Japanese family that emigrated from Kyushu, Japan. When he was a child, his family moved to a sugar plantation camp in Pu'ukoli'i, a small town made up of several hundred workers and their families, which doesn't exist today. His experiences in that environment provide much of the content for his novels.

Following his graduation from Lahailuna High School in 1941, Murayama enrolled in the University of Hawai'i. Though he initially enlisted and served in the Territorial Guard, in the aftermath of Pearl Harbor, like other Japanese Americans, he was discharged. Yet, this act did not prevent Murayama from volunteering to serve in the U.S. Army's Military Intelligence Service (MIS) in 1944. As a native speaker of Japanese, he acted as a translator in the China-Burma-India Theater, where he completed a tour in Taiwan to aid in the surrender and repatriation of Japanese troops.

Upon his return to the United States in 1946, Murayama completed his BA in English and philosophy from the University of Hawai'i in 1947. Under the G.I. Bill, he completed his MA in Chinese and Japanese at Columbia University in 1950. Following his graduation, he moved to Washington, D.C., and worked at the Armed Forces Medical Library from 1952 to 1956. To facilitate his writing, which he felt he needed to invest more time in, he moved to San Francisco, where he worked first at the public library and then at the U.S. Customs Office as an import specialist. Murayama is retired and currently lives in San Francisco with his wife, Dawn.

At Columbia, he began to write creatively, simultaneously completing his master's thesis and "I'll Crack Your Head Katsun," a short story that would later become the first chapter of *All I Asking for Is My Body*. The story was first published in the *Arizona Quarterly* in 1959, and then in *The Spell of Hawai'i*, an anthology of Hawai'ian literature, in 1968. Despite the positive reception of the short story, Murayama had difficulty securing a publisher for the full-length novel, *All I Asking for Is My Body*. Publishers were wary to issue the book, which made risky narrative moves such as wide use of pidgin and transcribed Japanese, and dealt heavily with local Hawai'ian issues that publishers did not find marketable. After nearly three decades of failing to find a publisher, Murayama and his wife incorporated Supa Press and published the novel in 1975. *All I Asking for Is My Body* proved the fears of established publishing houses wrong when it became a huge success. It won the American Book Award from the Before Columbus Foundation in 1980 and the Hawai'i Award for Literature in 1991. In 1989, Murayama adapted the novel into a play performed by the Kuma Kahua theater company. The novel has since become a classic in the Asian American canon, as representative of prewar Japanese American plantation life in Hawai'i. It is currently reprinted by University of Hawai'i Press.

Murayama's four novels, *All I Asking for Is My Body, Five Years on a Rock, Plantation Boy,* and *Dying in a Strange Land* all feature the Oyama clan, who struggle with the plantation society in which they live and must negotiate the incommensurability of Japanese and American culture. To write his novels, Murayama developed a system of transcribing pidgin, which he believed was critical in understanding the local Hawai'ian experience.

All I Asking for Is My Body follows the struggles of Kiyoshi Oyama as he grows up in the prewar Hawai'ian plantation society. The novel underscores economic and ethnic conflict within the socially hierarchized plantation community composed of Portuguese, Spanish, Japanese, and Filipino families. The predominant source of tension in the novel arises in the choices Kiyoshi must make between social mobility and ethnic loyalty—a trope central in many diasporic narratives that is reproduced and further developed in all of Murayama's subsequent novels.

Five Years on a Rock, published in 1994, approaches Kiyoshi's conflict through the mother's eyes. Though the Oyama boys feel that they are at constant odds with their parents, whom they view as a source of oppression and old-fashioned traditions that conflict with American ideals, Sawa Oyama's narrative demonstrates that the Japanese "disease" of gaman (patience, perseverance) can become a means of survival. The positive aspects of gaman are further illustrated in

1998, with *Plantation Boy*, which tells Toshio's bildungsroman tale mediated by gaman: by working hard and persevering with Japanese ideals, Toshio is able to realize his dream of finally leaving the plantation.

Rounding out the Oyama family saga is *Dying in a Strange Land*. Published in 2008, Murayama's capstone novel traces the Oyamas' diasporic journey from Japan to Hawai'i to the mainland as they continue to strive with ethnic transformation and self-formation.

Murayama's work captures the complexity of Hawai'i's complicated past, rendering history in the present within a remarkable archive that documents the Japanese American fight for upward mobility and self-making. From the grueling work and poverty of Hawai'i's plantation society to the systemic racism that pervades the modern mainland, Murayama's work simultaneously documents Japanese American experience and provides an incisive cultural critique.

Milton Murayama died at the age of 93 in 2016.

See also: DeSoto, Hisaye Yamamoto (1921–2011); Hartmann, Sadakichi (1867–1944); Hirahara, Naomi (1962–); Iko, Momoko (1940–); Inada, Lawson Fusao (1938–); Japanese American Literature; Kogawa, Joy (1935–); Mori, Toshio (1910–1980); Mura, David (1952–); Okada, John (1923–1971); Otsuka, Julie (1962–)

Further Reading

Murayama, Milton. *All I Asking for Is My Body*. Honolulu: University of Hawai'i Press, 1988.

Murayama, Milton. *Dying in a Strange Land*. Honolulu: University of Hawai'i Press, 2008.

Murayama, Milton. *Five Years on a Rock*. Honolulu: University of Hawai'i Press, 1994.

Murayama, Milton. *Plantation Boy*. Honolulu: University of Hawai'i Press, 1998.

Krystal Shyun Yang

NAGANO, KENT (1951–)

Kent Nagano is a conductor of symphonic and operatic music with extensive engagements in North America and Europe.

Nagano was born in Berkeley, California, in 1951 to Japanese American parents and grew up in Morro Bay in the Central Coast of California. He began piano lessons with his mother, who was a microbiologist and a pianist; he also learned the clarinet and the koto. During the 1950s and 1960s, he received musical training through California's public school system, in which a Georgian-born musician infused students with music in the style of European conservatories.

Nagano studied sociology and music at the University of California, Santa Cruz (receiving his BA in 1974). During this time he had intended to pursue a law degree and a career in international relations, and he was involved in the civil rights, antiwar, and other social movements. Nagano chose to pursue music after having studied composition with Grosvenor Cooper and Roger Nixon. He then studied conducting and piano at San Francisco State University (receiving his MM in 1976) and at the University of Toronto.

From the beginning of his musical training and career, Nagano has been deeply grounded in opera. His first employment as a conductor was with the Opera Company of Boston, where he apprenticed under Sarah Caldwell from 1977 to 1979 and learned the operatic repertoire and métier in the German tradition. During his Boston years, he worked as an assistant conductor to Seiji Ozawa at the Boston Symphony Orchestra and played a key role in the world premiere of Olivier Messiaen's opera, Saint Francois d'Assise. This was the beginning of Nagano's long association with Messiaen, who became his mentor and collaborator. Nagano has championed Messiaen's music, claiming that its beauty and challenging complexity address universal nature and religious thought that stand over and against time

In 1978, Nagano became the music director of the Berkeley Symphony Orchestra. With his strong connection to the San Francisco Bay Area community and his strong artistic vision, especially his association with the music of Messiaen, Nagano turned the Berkeley Symphony Orchestra into a progressive force in the West Coast music scene over the next three decades.

Much of the next phase of Nagano's career was based in Europe. He was the music director of the Lyons Opéra from 1988 to 1998; associate principal guest conductor of the London Symphony Orchestra from 1990 to 1998; and music director of the Hallé Orchestra in Manchester from 1992 to 2000. Nagano is renowned for his mastery of late 19th- and 20th-century music. During his tenure in Lyons he performed and recorded rare repertoire, including Poulenc's *Dialogues des Carmélites*, Martinu's *Les trois souhaits*, Prokofief's *The Love for Three Oranges*, Debussy's *Rodrigue et Chimène*, Busoni's *Doktor Faust*, Carlisle Floyd's *Susannah*, and the first recording of Strauss's *Salomé* with the original French text by Oscar Wilde. In 2000, he conducted the premiere of John Adams's nativity oratorio *El Niño* at the Théâtre du Châtelet in Paris. During Nagano's appointment at the Hallé Orchestra, some criticized him for his emphasis on contemporary works that led to expensive programming, and he was blamed for the orchestra's near-bankruptcy. In 2000, he became the chief conductor of the Deutches Sinfonieorchester in Berlin and served in this position until 2006.

Nagano was appointed principal conductor of the Los Angeles Opera in 2000. His first performance of Lohengrin was set against the terrorist attacks on September 11, 2001. He was named the Los Angeles Opera's first music director in 2003. He stepped down from the position in 2006 to take up two new posts as music director of the Bayerische Staatsoper in Munich and the Montréal Symphony Orchestra.

Nagano's extensive recordings represent a range of works in both established and contemporary repertoire, including works by John Adams, Bartók, Beethoven, Bernstein, Britten, Bruchner, Mahler, Milhaud, Prokofiev, Ravel, Schoenberg, Stravinsky, and Zemlinsky.

As a strongly identified Californian and Japanese American, Nagano has been involved in artistic projects that deal with the ethnic and the regional communities. In 2005, he led a performance of *Manzanar: An American Story* at Royce Hall at UCLA. This musical work told the story of Japanese American internment during World War II and addressed issues of human rights and civil rights. The project involved three composers, including Japanese-born Naomi Sekiya and playwright/director Philip Kan Gotanda; U.S. senator Daniel Inouye, actors John Cho and Martin Sheen, and figure skater Kristi Yamaguchi served as narrators; and local musical organizations such as the American Youth Symphony, the Santa Monica College Chamber Choir, and the Manzanar Youth Choir were part of the production. Nagano believed that this was an important project in keeping alive the historical memory of the Japanese American internment and addressing contemporary issues of civil liberties. The work critically depicted the difficulties faced by the immigrant and the Nisei generations while illustrating the complexity, diversity, and hybridity of the Japanese American experience through narrative and musical devices.

Although Nagano is thus strongly identified with his Japanese American background and involved in issues of social justice, as a classical musician he firmly believes that factors such as ethnic or national identity are secondary to his artistic goals, stressing the importance of assimilating oneself into the culture and language of the music. "This art form (of classical music) has too much tradition to respect. One needs to embrace the responsibility to assimilate, evolve, and improve. Only by doing so, one can evolve to a different level," he said in an interview. At the same time, Nagano has considered it important as a music director to be aware of trends in popular culture and has collaborated with musicians in other genres, such as rock musician Frank Zappa and avant-pop artist Björk.

Nagano is married to Japanese pianist Mari Kodama, and they have one daughter.

See also: Hiroshima; Iijima, Chris (1948–2005); Japanese American Hip-Hop; Shinoda, Michael Kenji "Mike" (1977–)

Further Reading

Kent Nagano Official Website. http://www.kentnagano.com. Accessed July 5, 2012.
Yoshihara, Mari. *Musicians from a Different Shore: Asians and Asian Americans in Classical Music*. Philadelphia, PA: Temple University Press, 2007.

Mari Yoshihara

NAKAMURA, HARUKI ROBERT (1986–)

Haruki Robert Nakamura, professional football player, was born on April 18, 1986, in Elyria, Ohio. He is the youngest of four children of Ryozo and Karen Nakamura. His father, an eighth-degree black-belt in judo and former coach of the Japanese judo Olympic team, immigrated to the United States to teach judo. His mother, an American, a fourth-degree black belt in judo, worked as an X-ray technician. His parents met while Ryozo taught judo in Rhode Island, and both competed in national and international judo competitions.

Nakamura's father, who died in 1991, discouraged his sons from playing football because of the potential for serious injury. Nevertheless, Nakamura began playing football at the age of 10. His older brother, Yoshi, a state high school wrestling champion, completed the application and release forms. Despite objections from his mother, Nakamura went to play football at St. Edward High School, an all-boys Catholic school in the Cleveland suburb of Lakewood. Playing both as a wide receiver and defensive back, he contributed significantly in the team's runner-up finish in the 2003 Ohio Division I playoffs. After earning second-team "All-Ohio" honors as a defensive back as a

Carolina Panthers' Haruki Nakamura (43) runs onto the field during player introductions before an NFL football game against the Miami Dolphins in Charlotte, North Carolina, 2012. (AP Photo/Mike McCarn)

senior, Nakamura graduated in 2004. Nakamura accepted an athletic scholarship to play football at the University of Cincinnati.

Nakamura joined the Baltimore Ravens of the National Football League in 2008, as the 206th draft pick in the 10th round. Playing four seasons at Baltimore, from 2008 to 2011, in which he forced one fumble, and posted 18 tackles, including 10 solo tackles. In 2010, Nakamura made an interception against the Kansas City Chiefs, in Baltimore's 30–7 wild card win. In 2012, he joined the Carolina Panthers, intercepting two passes for 39 yards, and completing 28 tackles, of which 11 were solo. After sustaining a concussion in the 2013 preseason, the Panthers placed him on injured reserve and later released him.

Since June 2011 Nakamura has been married to Jamie Pentaudi.

See also: Japanese Americans in Sports

Further Reading

Nakamura, Haruki. Cincinnati Bearcats, The Official Athletics Site of the University of Cincinnati. http://www.gobearcats.com/sports/m-footbl/mtt/nakamura_haruki00.html. January 15, 2017.

Nakamura, Haruki. Sports Reference/College Football. http://www.sports-reference.com/cfb/players/haruki-nakamura-1.html. January 15, 2017.

Adam R. Hornbuckle

NAKATANI, COREY (1970–)

Corey Nakatani, thoroughbred jockey, was born on October 21, 1970, in Covina, California. He is the one of 10 children of Roy and Marie Nakatani. His father, a Japanese American, was born in an internment camp during World War II.

A high school wrestling champion, Nakatani, aged 16, became interested in thoroughbred horse racing after visiting the Santa Anita Park in Arcadia, California, after a wrestling tournament. Soon he began working for Roger Stein, a horse trainer at Santa Anita, cleaning out stalls and walking horses. Within a week, Nakatani expressed interest in becoming a jockey, and with the help of Stein began working on a thoroughbred horse farm owned by Tony Matos. Later he broke and galloped horses for retired jockey Johnny Longden and his son, Eric Longden. In 1988, Nakatani graduated from jockey school in Castaic, California, and won his first race that year aboard Blue King in Caliente, Mexico. In 1989, he became thoroughbred horse racing's leading apprentice jockey.

In his first decade of racing, Nakatani won 34 major races. In 1990, he won the first of three Hollywood Derbies, with the others in 1993 and 1996. That year Nakatani won the first of Hollywood Turf Cup Stakes, with the others in 1998 and 2010. In 1991, he won the first of two Kentucky Oats; the other in 1996. In 1994, he won the first of five Eddie Read Handicaps. In 1995, he won the first of four John C. Mabee Handicaps. In 1996, he won the first of 10 Breeder's Cup races, including three consecutive Breeder's Cup Sprint races from 1996 to 1998.

Nakatani won his 3,000th race on May 29, 2006, when he guided Shakin N Dancin to victory in the ninth race at Hollywood Park in Inglewood California. In 2006, he ranked sixth among U.S. jockeys with 145 wins on 738 mounts, with earnings of $14,001,900. In 2011, he finished second in the Kentucky Derby in Lexington, his best finish in 17 races.

See also: Japanese Americans in Sports

Further Reading

Dulay, Cindy Pierson. "Corey Nakatani." http://horseracing.about.com/od/jockeys/p /aanakatani.htm. January 15, 2017.

"Jockey Profile: Corey S. Nakatani." Equibase.com. http://www.equibase.com/profiles /Results.cfm?type=People&searchType=J&eID=1339. January 15, 2017.

Adam R. Hornbuckle

NOGUCHI, ISAMU (1904–1988)

Japanese American artist Isamu Noguchi was born in Los Angeles to Japanese poet Yone Noguchi and Leonie Gilmoure, a writer and teacher. The two never married; upon visiting Japan in 1907, Leonie discovered that Yone was already married with a Japanese wife and family. Throughout their lives, the relationship between father and son was tense. After attending school in Japan, 13-year-old Isamu was sent to the states and enrolled in the progressive Interlaken School at Indiana. The school closed shortly after his arrival, though Interlaken's director, Edward Rumley, provided for Isamu to remain in the United States to complete high school. Isamu interned briefly with the sculptor Gutzon Borglum, known for sculpting Mt. Rushmore—though Borglum concluded that Isamu would never be a sculptor. While studying premed at Columbia University, he began taking free art courses at the Leonardo da Vinci School in New York. There he developed a talent for sculpting portrait busts, providing him a meager living. It was during this time that he adopted his Japanese name, abandoning his mother's maiden name.

Throughout his life, Isamu felt caught between two cultures—not fully accepted in either. Yet he later expressed how fortunate he had been to grow up in Japan. "I don't mean to belittle other places," He said, "but one is much more aware of nature in Japan—not a vast panorama of nature but its details: an insect, a leaf, a flower."

During the 1920s, Isamu met a number of influential figures, including Japanese choreographer Michio Ito, architect Buckminster Fuller, and artist

Constantin Brancusi, all of whom aided the young artist in formulating his own distinctive approach to art. Brancusi, whom Isamu worked with in France while on a Guggenheim fellowship, was of particular importance. Though they did not speak a common language, Isamu recognized that Brancusi's approach to materials was much like the Japanese, avoiding unnecessary decorations or additions to sculpture, but rather drawing on the unique qualities inherent in the materials themselves.

In many ways, he approached his everyday life from the standpoint of continuous artistic expression, and as such, made invaluable contributions to the study and understanding of Japanese American folklore. While maintaining studios in Japan and the United States, his work touched on many areas, from furniture and decorative arts to large-scale gardens, fountains, and sculpture. His influence on the decorative arts is felt to this day. As a prolific and eclectic artist, his work avoids classification toward a distinct signature style. There are, however, common themes that reappear in his sculptures of the 1960s, such as Sunken Garden (Yale University, 1963) or Sky Viewing Sculpture (Western Washington University, 1969); works that draw on the square, the triangle, and the circle, elements common to calligraphy and that denote concepts of the universe. His work also draws on Zen Buddhist aesthetics, such as Black Sun (Seattle, 1969), a large irregular black granite circle that transforms the rigidness of stone into a glistening and calligraphic freeform expression.

See also: Asawa, Ruth (1926–2013); Japanese American Artists

Further Reading

Duus, Masayo. *The Life of Isamu Noguchi.* Princeton, NJ: Princeton University Press, 2000.

John Handley

OKADA, JOHN (1923–1971)

John Okada, an Asian American novelist, was born on September 23, 1923, in Seattle. As Japanese Americans Okada and his family were subjected to internment in Minidoka, Idaho, during World War II under U.S. Executive Order 9066. It was Okada's memory of this internment camp experience that informed his dual consciousness about an identity as both a descendant of Japan and an American resident.

Although Okada was well aware of the injustices of internment, he also recognized the value of his American citizenship and chose to enlist in the U.S. Air Force. After being discharged in 1946, he attended the University of Washington, where he earned a bachelor's degree in English. He would later go on to earn a master's degree from Columbia University in English and another bachelor's degree from the University of Washington in library science. In 1950, Okada married Dorothy Arakawa and later fathered two children. He died on February 20, 1971.

Okada is best known for his 1957 novel *No-No Boy*, published first in Japan by Charles E. Tuttle. In *No-No Boy*, Okada tells the story of a young Japanese American man named Ichiro Yamada, whose life is deeply affected by his decision to answer "no" to two controversial questions that were part of a 1943 "Leave Clearance Application Form"—an official document used to discharge residents of the internment camps. Where the first of these two controversial questions asks about the respondent's willingness to serve in the U.S. Armed Forces, the second question generally asks if the respondent will forswear any allegiance to the Japanese emperor.

The controversy surrounding these two questions refers to their vague and misleading content that was administered to respondents who had just experienced internment, many of whom were harboring suspicions about the implications of their answers. Some believed that answering "yes" to the first question might have volunteered them for active duty or draft, while answering yes to the second question might have assumed that one would have already had allegiance to the Japanese emperor and thus would have confirmed this premise. Those like Okada's Ichiro Yamada character who are confused, conflicted, or even betrayed by these questions responded in the negative to both, becoming No-No Boys.

Okada's novel was largely overlooked until the mid-1970s when it was rediscovered and celebrated by Japanese American communities. Literary critics have argued that Okada himself was distraught over the initial reception of *No-No Boy*, yet his sole work is now considered a classic of Asian American literature. As evidence of this legacy, in 2010 Timescape Arts Group honored Okada by releasing Ken Narasaki's stage adaptation of *No-No Boy* at Miles Memorial Playhouse in Santa Monica, California.

See also: Japanese American Literature

Further Reading

Okada, John. *No-No Boy*. Seattle: University of Washington Press, 1979.
Wang, Qun. "'Double Consciousness,' Sociological Imagination, and the Asian American Experience." *Race, Gender & Class: Asian American Voices* 4 (1991): 88–94.

Salvador Jimenez Murguia

OTSUKA, JULIE (1962–)

Julie Otsuka wrote the best-selling novel, *When the Emperor Was Divine*, depicting the internment of a Japanese American family during World War II. Since the novel's publication in 2002, the book has gained a wide readership and has become a favorite among high school and college educators. *When the Emperor Was Divine* tells one family's story from the father's arrest following Pearl Harbor, through the mother and children's incarceration in a War Relocation Authority internment camp in Topaz, Utah, to the family's release and reunification with the father following his release from a federal prison camp. The novel has few historical details and instead focuses intently on the inner turmoil of each family member as they endure their separation and imprisonment during the war and as they attempt to rebuild their lives upon their release; each of the chapters in the novel focuses on a different family member, each of whom remains nameless in the novel. Beautifully written with understated emotion, the novel is lauded for its psychological realism and the universality of its characterization.

American writer Julie Otsuka after she was awarded a French literary prize for foreigners in Paris, 2012. (AP Photo/Thibault Camus)

For Otsuka, the unlawful incarceration of over 110,000 Japanese and Japanese Americans during World War II was a subject that haunted her artistic imagination as she began the novel during her stint in the MFA program at Columbia University. Her grandfather's arrest by the Federal Bureau of Investigation, and her mother, uncle, and grandmother's imprisonment at Topaz provided the loose inspiration for the novel. Years before she began the novel in the 1980s, Otsuka read through her grandmother's collection of her grandfather's letters and postcards to his family, which had been censored. Although inspired by her family's experience, the novel is fictional and the result of many months of research reading through oral histories, newspapers, and other sources, as her family did not often discuss their wartime experiences especially as she was growing up.

Julie Otsuka was born on May 15, 1962, in Palo Alto, California, and grew up in the state. Her father, a Japanese immigrant, worked as an aerospace engineer, and her mother, a second-generation Japanese American, worked as a lab technician. She has two younger brothers. Otsuka graduated from Yale University in 1984. She pursued a career as a painter before moving to New York City where she began writing. In 1999, she received her MFA from Columbia University and had several chapters of *When the Emperor Was Divine* completed by then. The book manuscript was finished in 2001 and published a year later.

See also: Japanese American Literature

Further Reading

Duncan, Andres. "Julie Otsuka." http://www.indiebound.org/author-interviews/otsuka julie. Accessed September 18, 2012.

Otsuka, Julie. *When the Emperor Was Divine*. New York: Alfred A. Knopf, 2003.

Palitz, Cordelia. "Q & A with Julie Otsuka." http://www.studlife.com/news/2009/09/16 /qa-with-julie-otsuka/. Accessed September 18, 2012.

Emily Morishima

SHIN-ISSEI/SHIN-NISEI IDENTITY

The word "shin" in "Shin-Issei" and "Shin-Nisei" translates to "new" in the Japanese language. Issei meaning "first generation" and Nisei meaning "second generation" are borrowed from the popular language of Japanese diaspora around the world. What is "new" about these immigrants and their offspring is that they were part of the second wave migration, post–World War II. Shin-Issei immigrants include those who are known as "war brides," wives of U.S. military men, as well as any Japanese who immigrated to the United States after the 1965 Immigration and Nationality Act, which repealed the 1924 National Origins Act.

Context for Migration

The newcomer Japanese population is relatively low when compared to other post-1965 Asian immigration. However, the recent U.S. Census shows that Japanese newcomers make up as much as 30 percent of the Japanese American population in certain states such as New York, Illinois, Washington, and Hawai'i. This confirms that certain parts of the United States are still popular destination places for Japanese emigration.

Japanese newcomers enter the United States with various motives. After the war, people may have left Japan because of widespread famine and the war-torn environment. However, unlike the new wave of Chinese immigrants who heavily relied on the "family reunification clause" of the 1965 Immigration Reform Act, which allowed them to be with their naturalized children, spouse, or siblings, the new wave of Japanese immigrants typically had no relatives living in the United States and had to find other ways for legal entry.

One of the major forces of migration was the global economic restructuring of the postwar era. Particularly during the 1980s, Japan experienced a huge economic boom in which the value of the yen skyrocketed. This provided the outward push for Japanese capitalism, and, consequently, multinational corporations set up headquarters in places like Torrance, California, operated by Japanese expatriates. Most of these male expatriates, along with their wives and children, usually came for two- to five-year periods on work visas, but some of them have remained or returned later, changing their status to more permanent forms such as "green cards" (permanent residency card) or obtained American citizenships, often with employer sponsorship.

Japan also went through massive reforms in education as part of its globalization efforts in which the study-abroad experience, traditionally limited to upper-class elites during the Meiji era, was now being promoted to average citizens. Soon, Japan became one of the top nations in issuing student visas. Similarly, with the rising value of the yen, tourism was a new popular form of entertainment. Some of these Japanese migrant students and tourists became immigrant newcomers for one reason or another, including securing qualifying employment and marriage to American citizens. Although there are no data that clearly show what percentage of Japanese immigrants first entered on visa-status as opposed to immigrant-status, it has been noted by some that post-1965, more Japanese came as "nonimmigrants" before adjusting their status to permanency. In Canada, Nobuko Chubachi found that most Japanese Canadian immigrants actually went through "gradual immigration" in which they took a step-by-step process, experiencing "the West" typically first through a travel, student, or work visa before finally deciding to immigrate permanently. It is highly likely that most Japanese in the United States also came first on visas before becoming permanent residents.

Japanese immigrants have low rates of naturalization when compared to other Asian immigrant groups. According to the 2009 U.S. Census, only 38 percent of Japanese foreign born in California became naturalized citizens. When compared to the 69 percent of Chinese and 67 percent of Filipinos who have naturalized, Japanese immigrants are not becoming American citizens. This may be attributed to many factors such as national pride, security of benefits, and/or economic and political stability of Japan. The census also shows that Japanese female immigrants are more likely to naturalize than their male counterparts. This may be attributed to the fact that Japanese women marry American citizens more often as compared to marriages of Japanese men to American women.

The children of the Shin-Issei immigrants, the Shin-Nisei, are U.S. citizens by birth. As children of Japanese nationals, many Shin-Nisei also have Japanese citizenship by bloodline. Currently, Japan does not recognize dual-citizenship and thus, lawfully, Shin-Nisei must choose which nationality to keep. However, because Japan does not enforce this regulation, many Shin-Nisei have been able to keep both citizenships, hiding their American passport from Japanese immigration officials.

Identity Formation

The Shin-Issei and Shin-Nisei identities are strongly influenced by the socio-cultural and historical context of their local regions. For example, in areas such as California where ethnic resources (Japanese language schools, supermarkets, Japanese restaurants, travel agencies, banks, newspapers) are abundant because of the long history of Japanese and Japanese American communities, Shin-Issei and Shin-Nisei are able to maintain their Japanese lifestyles in America. On the other hand, if a Japanese newcomer and their children live their lives in less ethnic regions of the United States, their connection to Japan and Japanese language and culture will be limited, though not entirely cut off thanks to new modes of communication and affordable travel.

Particularly in California, a majority of the Shin-Issei and Shin-Nisei are bilingual and bicultural because of the availability of transnational resources such as language institutions and cultural products, ranging from Japanese television to hair and beauty products. For instance, in Southern California, because of the high number of expatriate families whose children must ease back into Japan at a later point in life, the Japanese government established the Asahi Gakuen, a formal Japanese language school that teaches based on a curriculum comparable to the one followed in Japan. Through language, the Shin-Nisei are inculcated Japanese values and traditions. Therefore, within these ethnic-rich areas, the Shin-Nisei individuals embody a highly transnational identity that navigates between what it means to be Japanese and what it means to be American.

Partly because of this strong dual identity as Japanese and as Americans, Shin-Nisei's place within the old-timer Japanese American spaces is sometimes questioned. Growing up among Yonsei and Gosei Japanese Americans, Shin-Nisei's understanding of their ethnic identity may conflict with those understood as traditionally Japanese American. For instance, many Shin-Nisei do not have a culture of playing J-league basketball, learning odori, or participating in Nisei week although more and more of these activities and events are being inclusive of the new wave of immigrants and their children.

In conclusion, Shin-Issei and Shin-Nisei identity, like all other forms of identity, are fluid and situational. Their identity formation depends heavily on the regional, social, and historical context in which they are raised as well as how close they identify with their Japanese side. No one description of identity can capture the diverse and dynamic nature of Shin-Issei and Shin-Nisei identity, and their ever-changing ethnic identity must be understood within the context of the larger local and global trends.

See also: Japanese Transnational Identity; Kibei

Further Reading

Chubachi, Nobuko. 2009. "Gender and Construction of the Life Course of Japanese Immigrant Women in Canada." PhD dissertation, Queen's University, Canada, 2009.

Kameyama, Eri. 2012. "Acts of Being and Belonging: Shin-Issei Transnational Identity Negotiations." Master's thesis, University of California, Los Angeles, 2012.

Machimura, Takashi. "Living in a Transnational Community within a Multi-ethnic City: Making a Localized 'Japan' in Los Angeles." In *Global Japan: The Experience of Japan's New Immigrant and Overseas Communities*, edited by Roger Goodman, Ceri Peach, Ayumi Takenaka, and Paul White. New York: Psychology Press, 2003.

Eri Kameyama

SHINODA, MICHAEL KENJI "MIKE" (1977–)

Michael Kenji "Mike" Shinoda is a Japanese American multi-instrumentalist, record producer, and rapper for the alternative rock group Linkin Park. Shinoda was born in Agoura Hills, California, in 1977, and established a musical side project from 2003–2006 called Fort Minor. The Fort Minor project was primarily formed to highlight his rap and hip-hop creative energies that were rather limited within the Linkin Park framework. Consequently, he does not incorporate musical elements, including melodies, instruments, and vocals indicative of traditional or contemporary Japanese music. Still, Fort Minor includes one vestige of Japanese American history involving cultural ties with World War II.

Shinoda's Japanese American ancestry is poignantly illustrated in the song "Kenji," from Fort Minor's 2005 *The Rising Tied* album. The song details the life of his family before, during, and after internment at Manzanar during World War II. Manzanar was a large Japanese American internment camp located in Owens Valley near Lone Pine, California, that housed over 100,000 individuals in 1942. "Kenji" is an anthem or a voice for Japanese Americans everywhere. It encapsulates the racial tensions, violence, and paranoia between Japanese and Americans before, during, and after World War II.

"Kenji," which is Shinoda's middle name, is also a Japanese word for "wise" or "healthy." In the song, Kenji serves as a symbol of hope for survival in the midst of impossible living conditions. The authenticity of the song is highlighted by soundbites from an interview with actual Shinoda family members. The cross-generational lyrics help bridge the gap between elders and youth across social, historical, and cultural spectrums. The crossroads of Japanese ancestry and American hip-hop music provide an inspirational and nostalgic examination of early American history, international relations, music, and war.

See also: Hiroshima; Iijima, Chris (1948–2005); Japanese American Hip-Hop; Nagano, Kent (1951–)

Further Reading

Fort Minor. *The Rising Tied.* 2005. CD.

Seaver, Morley. "Mike Shinoda (Linkin Park, Fort Minor)." http://www.antimusic.com /morley/05/FortMinor.shtml. Accessed January 15, 2010.

Matthew J. Forss

TAKEI, GEORGE HOSATO (1937–)

George Hosato Takei (1937–) is a Japanese American actor and activist. Takei's most famous role was that of Hikaru Sulu, pilot of the *USS Enterprise* on the original *Star Trek* series, which aired from 1966 to 1969, as well as related films and spin-off television shows.

Born April 20, 1937, in Los Angeles, California, Takei's mother had been born in California; his father had emigrated from Yamanashi Prefecture in Japan. With the United States' entry into World War II after Pearl Harbor, the forced relocation and internment of Japanese Americans began, and the Takei family was first held at the Santa Anita racetrack assembly center before being relocated to the Rohwer War Relocation Center in Arkansas. Eventually, the Takei family was relocated again to California, this time the Tule Lake War Relocation Center in California.

At the end of the war, the Takei family returned to the Los Angeles area, where George Takei graduated from Los Angeles High School. He then enrolled at the University of California, Berkeley, before transferring to the University of California, Los Angeles (UCLA). He received his BA and MA in theater from UCLA in 1960 and 1964, respectively.

While attending UCLA, Takei launched his acting career, which was challenging because of the lack of good roles for Asian Americans. The prevailing racism and Orientalism, which still persist in Hollywood today, limited opportunities for Asian American actors. His early television roles included *Playhouse 90*, *The Twilight Zone*, and *Mission: Impossible*, while he appeared in several movie roles, including playing a South Vietnamese Army officer in *The Green Berets*. His deep distinctive voice and resonant delivery also won him numerous voice-over roles and would be his trademark for years to come.

However, Takei's most famous role, the one that would launch his lifelong career, was that of Hikaru Sulu, helmsman of the *USS Enterprise* on the original

Star Trek series. The cast of *Star Trek* was revolutionary for being so inclusive and diverse, and the vibrant fan culture that developed from the franchise has long been a fixture at comic book conventions.

After *Star Trek*, Takei became active in local Los Angeles politics, running for City Council in 1972 and serving on the board of directors for the Southern California Rapid Transit District from 1973 to 1984. He continued to record voice-overs and act, appearing the TV series *Heroes* as well as a variety of commercials and public service announcements. Leveraging his talents and visibility, George Takei continues to be active in many important social causes, including the Japanese American Citizens League and the Japanese American National Museum in Los Angeles.

A chance meeting at an off-

Actor George Takei's most famous role was that of Hikaru Sulu, helmsman of the USS *Enterprise* on the original *Star Trek* series, which aired from 1966 to 1969, as well as related films and spin-off television shows. (Sbukley/Dreamstime.com)

Broadway show led to the development of the Broadway musical *Allegiance*, a fictionalized account of Japanese American internment inspired by Takei's internment experience. Although taking liberties with some historical facts for dramatic effect, the musical captured many enduring themes facing Japanese Americans during and after World War II, including generational gaps and the difficulties of remaining loyal to a country that treated its people as dangerous enemy aliens. Set at the Heart Mountain Relocation Center in Wyoming, *Allegiance* ran on Broadway in 2015–2016, starring Takei himself and famed Filipina Broadway performer Lea Salonga.

In the hostile, antigay climate of Gov. Arnold Schwarzenegger's California, Takei became an outspoken advocate of LGBT rights, coming out in a 2005 interview discussing his long-term relationship with partner Brad Altman, whom he married in 2008. Takei often directly confronts other public figures and celebrities on both traditional and social media. For example, Takei's response to NBA Tim Hardaway's admission of homophobia went viral in 2007, while Takei's Facebook page and continued public activity keeps him in the spotlight. *To Be Takei*, a highly regarded documentary about his love and his life, premiered at Sundance in 2014.

Recent controversies stem from the Syrian refugee crisis and terrorist attacks in Europe starting in 2015: as right-wing politicians and pundits have advocated a ban on all Muslims in the United States. Not without controversy, Takei spoke out against this ban, drawing parallels to Japanese internment.

Takei's lifetime of activism on behalf of both Japanese American and LGBT communities has not gone unnoticed: He has received numerous awards, including the Order of the Rising Sun from Japan and awards from the American Humanist Association, the Gay & Lesbian Alliance against Defamation, and the Japanese American National Museum, complementing the star on the Hollywood Walk of Fame Takei received in 1986.

See also: Hayakawa, Sessue "Kintaro" (1886–1973); Ishigo, Estelle (1899–1990); Japanese Americans in Film

Further Reading

Takei, George. *To the Stars: The Autobiography of George Takei*. New York: Pocket Books, 1994.

To Be Takei. Directed by Jennifer M. Kroot. Starz Digital Media, 2014.

Yvette M. Chin

WALTERS, REX ANDREW (1970–)

Rex Andrew Walters, basketball player and coach, was born on March 12, 1970, in Omaha, Nebraska. His father is American and his mother is Japanese. Walters grew up in San Jose, California, where he played basketball at Piedmont Hills High School and Independence High School.

After graduating from Independence High School in 1988, Walters earned an athletic scholarship to play basketball at Northwestern University in Evanston, Illinois. He played two seasons at Northwestern, scoring 542 points for an average of 10.4 points per game. In 1990, Walters transferred to the University of Kansas. In two seasons in Lawrence, he scored 1,064 points for an average of 15.6 points a game, and led Kansas to the Final Four in the NCAA men's college basketball championship tournament in 1993.

In 1993, the New Jersey Nets of the National Basketball Association (NBA) selected Walters, a 6-foot 4-inch, 190-pound shooting and point guard in the first round of the NBA draft, the 16th pick overall. After three seasons, New Jersey traded him to the Philadelphia 76ers. Walters played three seasons in Philadelphia before joining the Miami Heat in 1997. He retired from the NBA in 2000. That year he played for Club Baloncesto in León, Spain, and the Kansas City Knights of the American Basketball Association. In 2001, Walters played one season for Club Baloncesto Gran Canaria in Las Palmas, Canary Islands. In 2002, he returned to Kansas City for one more season.

After retiring from professional basketball in 2003, Walters began coaching college basketball. In 2003, he became an assistant coach at Valparaiso University in Indiana. Walters joined Florida Atlantic University in Boca Raton as an assistant coach in 2005, and became the head coach in 2006. In 2008, he became the head coach at the University of San Francisco in California.

See also: Japanese Americans in Sports

Further Reading

Chu, Bryan. "USF Hires Rex Walter." *SFGate*, April 15, 2008. http://www.sfgate.com/sports/article/USF-Hires-Rex-Walters-3287292.php. Accessed August 19, 2015.

"Rex Walters." Basketball Reference. 2000–2015. http://www.basketball-reference.com/players/w/waltere01.html. Accessed August 19, 2015.

Adam R. Hornbuckle

YAMASAKI, LINDSEY BROOKE (1980–)

Lindsey Brooke Yamasaki, basketball player, was born on June 2, 1980, in Oregon City, Oregon. She is one of three children of Syd and Kriss Yamasaki. Her father is Japanese and mother is American. Yamasaki played basketball at Oregon City High School. She led the basketball team, nicknamed the Pioneers, to four consecutive Oregon state championships from 1995 to 1998. Oregon City finished number one in the *USA Today* national rankings for three years. Yamasaki, who graduated from high school in 1998, was one of the most sought after recruits in college basketball. Named a Women's Basketball Coaches Association All-American, she participated in the WBCA High School All-America Game, in which she scored 16 points, and earned recognition as the Most Valuable Player.

Yamasaki earned an athletic scholarship to Stanford University in California. As a senior, she led the team to the 2002 PAC-10 regular season championship based on an undefeated regular season with 18 victories. Stanford made the National Collegiate Athletics Association Championship tournament in each of the four seasons Yamasaki played for the team. In four years at Stanford, she averaged 3.9 points per game, 44.3 percent field goal percentage, 38.9 percent 3-point field goal percentage. At the 2001 World University Games in Beijing, China, Yamasaki averaged 6.9 points in the tournament, which resulted in the United States defeating China, 87–67, for the gold medal. She graduated with a bachelor's degree in urban studies in 2002.

In the 2002 Women's National Basketball Association draft, the Miami Sol selected Yamasaki 29th overall, the 13th pick in the second round. That year, she played 15 games for the Sol, averaging 3.5 points per game. In 2003, Yamasaki joined the New York Liberty in 2003 and averaging 0.7 points in 24 games. That year, she also played for the Botas Spor of the Turkish Women's Basketball League, leading the team to the league championship. In 2004, Yamasaki played briefly for the Chicago Blaze of the National Women's Basketball Association. In 2005, she played for the San Antonio Silver Stars and Ceyhan Belediye Spor of the Turkish Women's Basketball League. In 2006, she played for the San Jose Spiders. That year she joined the Seattle Storm but was soon released.

After retiring from professional basketball in 2006, Yamasaki coached volleyball at Palo Alto High School, leading her teams to two De Anza League Championships. At that time, she also served as the director of the Palo Alto Volleyball Club. In 2007, Yamasaki coached a high school basketball team at the Japanese Cultural and Community Center of Northern California for a Japanese Exchange Program that traveled to Japan. In 2008, she was named as the first head coach of the first ever Women's Basketball Team at the Academy of Art University in San Francisco.

See also: Japanese Americans in Baseball

Further Reading

"2008–2009 Women's Basketball Coaching Staff." Academy of Art University. 2015. http://academyartathletics.com/coaches.aspx?rc=9&path=wbball. Accessed August 19, 2015.

Adam R. Hornbuckle

YONAMINE, WALLACE KANAME "WALLY" (1925–2011)

Wallace Kaname "Wally" Yonamine, football and baseball player, was born on June 24, 1925, in Olawalu, Hawai'i. His father, Matsusa, a native Okinawan, immigrated to Maui to work on the sugar plantations. His mother, Kikue, whose parents emigrated from Hiroshima, was born on Maui.

Yonamine began playing football in high school in Maui, but transferred to Farrington High School in Honolulu because the school recruited him for his extraordinary running skill. As a 5 foot 9 inch, 188-pound fullback, he led the Generals to the Hawai'ian high school championship. Yonamine, who took the name Wallace while in high school, was drafted into the U.S. Army during World War II after graduation in 1943. Stationed at the Schofield Barracks in Oahu, he spent most of his time playing football and baseball. Once discharged from military service after the war, Yonamine turned down a football scholarship from Ohio State University to join the Hawai'ian Warriors, a semiprofessional football team. His play for the Warriors impressed mainland professional scouts, who signed him to a two-year contract with the fledgling San Francisco 49ers of the All-American Football Conference. Yonamine, the first Asian American to play professional football, carried the ball 19 times for 74 yards and caught three passes for 40 yards in 1947. An off-season wrist injury while playing baseball ended his football career.

Wally Yonamine, the first non-Japanese national to play professional baseball in Japan after World War II, poses with baseball gear in Honolulu, 1998. (AP Photo/Ronen Zilberman)

In the late 1940s, Yonamine played amateur and semiprofessional baseball in Hawai'i. His batting and field skills caught the attention of Lefty O'Doul, manager of the San Francisco Seals, a minor league team, and adviser to the Yomiuri Giants of the Nippon Professional Baseball League. Yonamine played one year for a Seals affiliate in Salt Lake City before taking O'Doul's advice to play professional baseball in Japan. In 1951, he joined the Yomiuri Giants, becoming the first American to play for a Japanese professional baseball team. Yonamine played for Giants until 1960, during which time they won the Japanese Series eight times. Playing for the Chunichi Dragons from 1961 to 1962, he led them to the series title in 1961. Yonamine managed the Chunichi Dragons from 1972 to 1977.

Initially reviled by Japanese fans for being an American, especially with the war still fresh in their minds, Yonamine won them over with his championship playing style. His accolades include Central League MVP in 1957, 7 Best Nine Awards from 1952 to 1958, 11 All-Star teams, and 3-time batting champion. Inducted into the Japanese Baseball Hall of Fame in 1994, Yonamine is the only American admitted as a player. Nicknamed the "Nisei Jackie Robinson" for integrating Japanese baseball, he died on February 28, 2011, in Honolulu.

See also: Japanese Americans in Baseball

Further Reading

Fitts, Robert K. *Wally Yonamine: The Man Who Changed Japanese Baseball*. Lincoln: University of Nebraska Press, 2008.

Song, Jaymes. "'Nisei Jacki Robinson' Dies at Age 85." *Washington Post*, March 1, 2011. http://www.washingtonpost.com/wp-dyn/content/article/2011/03/01/AR20110 30105741.html. Accessed August 19, 2015.

Adam R. Hornbuckle

ZENIMURA, KENICHI (1900–1968)

During his lifetime, Kenichi Zenimura was known as "The Dean of the Diamond" and with his passing he has come to be recognized as "The Father of Japanese American Baseball." Many baseball historians believe he earned this title for his remarkable career as a player (excelled at all positions), manager (of Japanese American league teams and Caucasian teams in the Twilight Leagues), and international ambassador of the game.

Born in Hiroshima, Japan, in 1900, Zenimura moved to Hawai'i just before his seventh birthday. He was introduced to the game of baseball in the islands and began competitive play at the age of 12. He attended Mills High School (now Mid-Pacific University) and played with the semipro Hawai'ian Asahi between 1915 and 1920. He mastered the sport and served as a player and captain of the Mills High team that won back-to-back island championships in 1918 and 1919. In early 1920, Zenimura moved to Fresno, California, where he worked at a small restaurant and as a mechanic. He immediately joined the newly founded Fresno Athletic Club Japanese American baseball team and would eventually establish a 10-team Nisei league. He managed, coached, and played competitively until he was 55 years old.

Zenimura crossed the chalk lines of discrimination and played for the semipro Fresno Twilight Leagues. Later his all-star team, the Fresno Athletic Club, became so dominant that when Ruth and Gehrig arrived in town on a barnstorming tour in 1927, several Nikkei players, including Zenimura, the "Nisei Babe Ruth" Johnny Nakagawa, the "Nisei Rogers Hornsby" Harvey Iwata, and Fred Yoshikawa, were invited to play.

Zenimura's teams dominated such college clubs as Stanford, St. Mary's, the University of Southern California, and Fresno State during exhibition play. Internationally, he organized six-month tours in 1924, 1927, and 1937 to Japan, Korea, and Manchuria. These goodwill all-stars compiled a 40–8–2 record over the "Big Six" universities in Japan.

In addition to organizing barnstorming tours to Japan, Zenimura was instrumental in the negotiations that led to Babe Ruth's visit to Japan in 1934. Several years earlier (in 1927) Zenimura also helped arrange a barnstorming tour to Japan for the Negro-league All-Star Philadelphia Royal Giants, led by Hall of Famers Biz Mackey and Andy Cooper. Japanese baseball historian Kazuo Sayama argues that it was the Royal Giants tour in 1927 and not Ruth's visit in 1934 that inspired the formation of the Japanese Professional Baseball League in 1936.

During World War II, the Zenimura family was sent to two internment camps, one in the horse stalls at the Fresno fairgrounds, and later the desert wastelands in Gila River, Arizona. In both locations, baseball stadiums were constructed under the guidance of Kenichi's baseball vision. He organized a 32-team league and also coached and played on the team that won the camp championship. Zenimura field was much more than a ballpark, it was a sacred location that bonded the thousands of wartime internees and gave Japanese Americans a sense of pride, hope, and normalcy, making life bearable during their unjust incarceration. With the closing of Butte Camp at Gila River, Zenimura field officially closed on November 10, 1945.

Following the war, the Zenimura family returned to Fresno. He organized and coached the Fresno Nisei baseball team that won two state Nisei Championships and climaxed their performance in 1950 by winning the national Nisei championship in Fresno.

Zenimura's sons, Kenshi and Kenso, as well as Fibber Hirayama benefited from the solid fundamentals taught to them by coach Zenimura. The trio starred at Fresno State College and all went on to play professionally in Japan for the Hiroshima Carp.

Kenichi Zenimura was the chief organizer, manager, coach, and captain of one of California's most fierce and competitive ball clubs in the Central Valley. He became the first Japanese American elected to the Fresno Athletic Hall of Fame in 1979. Zenimura continued to scout players and arrange goodwill tours to Hawai'i and Japan until his death on November 13, 1968.

During the 18th Annual Cooperstown Symposium on Baseball and American Culture (2006), a campaign was launched to establish a permanent exhibit for Japanese American Baseball in the National Baseball Hall of Fame, as well as the enshrinement of the first Japanese American player. The campaign proposes that the first Japanese American player enshrined with a plaque in Cooperstown is Kenichi Zenimura, "the Father of Japanese American Baseball." In 2006, Zenimura was honored in the Baseball Reliquary, a nonprofit, educational organization "dedicated to fostering an appreciation of American art and culture through the context of baseball history," funded in part by a grant from the Los Angeles County Arts Commission. The wartime experience of Kenichi Zenimura inspired the character of Kaz Nomura, the patriarch in the major motion picture *American Pastime* released in 2007.

See also: Japanese Americans in Baseball; Japanese Americans in Sports

Further Reading

Mukai, Gary. *Diamonds in the Rough: Baseball and Japanese-American Internment*. Stanford, CA: Stanford Program on International and Cross-Cultural Education (SPICE), 2004.

Staples Jr., Bill. *Zenimura: Dean of the Diamond*. Jefferson, NC: McFarland & Company, 2011.

Bill Staples Jr. and Kerry Yo Nakagawa

PRIMARY DOCUMENTS

THE TREATY OF KANAGAWA,
MARCH 31, 1854

The Treaty of Kanagawa, also known as the Perry Convention, was the first treaty between the United States and Japan. It was also the latter's first treaty with a Western nation and marked the end of Japan's period of isolation (1639–1854). This document set the tone for the tension-filled Japan–U.S. relationship in the 20th century.

With the support of leaders such as Oda Nobunaga, Catholic missionaries were able to foster a thriving community of converts in 14th-century Japan. However, after Nobunaga's death, his successor, Toyotomi Hideyoshi, launched the antiforeign, anti-Christian policy that culminated in the Tokugawa exclusion edicts. Japan's closed-door policy was fully implemented by the third Tokugawa shogun, Iemitsu in 1639. It was forcibly brought to an end in 1854 with the signing of the Treaty of Kanagawa.

As the United States began to expand beyond its continental boundaries and become heavily involved in maritime trade, it became increasingly determined to bring Japan's two-century-old policy of self-imposed isolation to a close. In 1953, U.S. President Millard Fillmore sent Commo. Matthew C. Perry to Tokyo with the latest steam-powered warships to pressure the Tokugawa government into an agreement that would protect the rights of American whalers, provide for coaling ports, and create a trade relationship. Perry successfully secured two coaling ports and protection for American whalers. In 1858, the U.S. consul achieved Perry's final objective: establishing a commercial treaty.

The United States of American and the empire of Japan, desiring to establish firm, lasting and sincere friendship between the two nations, have resolved to fix, in a manner clear and positive by means of a treaty or general convention of peace and amity, the rules which shall in future be mutually observed in the intercourse of their respective countries; for which most desirable object the President of the United States has conferred full powers on his commissioner, Matthew Calbraith Perry, special ambassador of the United States to Japan and the august sovereign of Japan has given similar full powers to his commissioners, Hayashi-Daigaku-no-kami, Ido, Prince of Tsus-Sima; Izawa, Prince of Mmimasaki; and Udono, member of the Board of Revenue.

And the said commissioners after having exchanged their said full powers and duly considered the premises, have agreed to the following articles:

ARTICLE I

There shall be a perfect, permanent and universal peace, and a sincere and cordial amity, between the United States of American on the one part and between their people, respectfully, (respectively,) without exception of persons or places.

ARTICLE II

The port of Simoda, in the principality of Idzu and the port of Hakodadi, in the principality of Matsmai are granted by the Japanese as ports for the reception for American ships, where they can be supplied with wood, water, provisions and coal, and other articles their necessities may require, as far as the Japanese have them. The time for opening the first named port is immediately on signing this treaty; the last named port is to be opened immediately after the same day in the ensuing Japanese year . . . .

ARTICLE III

Whenever ships of the United States are thrown or wrecked on the coast of Japan, the Japanese vessels will assist them, and carry their crews to Simoda or Hakodadi and hand them over to their countrymen appointed to receive them. Whatever articles the shipwrecked men may have preserved shall likewise be restored and the expenses incurred in the rescue and support of Americans and Japanese who may thus be thrown up on the shores of either nation are not to be refunded.

ARTICLE IV

Those shipwrecked persons and other citizens of the United States shall be free as in the other countries and not subjected to confinement but shall be amenable to just laws.

ARTICLE V

Shipwrecked men and other citizens of the United States, temporarily living at Simoda and Hakodadi, shall not be subject to such restrictions and confinement as the Dutch and Chinese are at Nagasaki but shall be free at Simoda to go where they please within the limits of seven Japanese miles from a small island in the harbor of Simoda, marked on the accompanying chart hereto appended; and shall in like manner be free to go where they please at Hakodadi, within limits to be defined after the visit of the United States squadron to that place.

ARTICLE VII

It is agreed that ships of the United States resorting to the ports open to them, shall be permitted to exchange gold and silver coin and articles of goods for other articles of goods under such regulations as shall be temporarily established by the Japanese government for that purpose. It is stipulated, however, that the ships of the United States shall be permitted to carry away whatever articles they are unwilling to exchange.

ARTICLE X

Ships of the United States shall be permitted to resort to no other ports in Japan but Simoda and Hakodadi, unless in distress or forced by stress of weather.

ARTICLE XI

There shall be appointed by the government of the United States consuls or agents to reside in Simoda at any time after the expiration of eighteen months from the date of the signing of this treaty; provided that either of the two governments deem such arrangement necessary.

ARTICLE XII

The present convention, having been concluded and duly signed, shall be obligatory, and faithfully observed by the United States of America, and Japan and by the citizens and subjects of each respective power; and it is to be ratified and approved by the President of the United States, by and with the advice and consent of the Senate thereof, and by the august Sovereign of Japan, and the ratification shall be exchanged within eighteen months from the date of the signature therefore, or sooner if practicable.

In faith, whereof, we, the respective plenipotentiaries of the United States of America and the empire of Japan aforesaid have signed and sealed these presents.

Done at Kanagawa, this thirty-first day of March, in the year of our Lord Jesus Christ one thousand eight hundred and fifty-four and of Kayei the seventh year, third month and third day.

Source: Hunter Miller, ed. *Treaties and Other International Acts of the United States of America.* Volume 6. Washington, DC: Government Printing Office, 1942.

Document 2

SHEBATA SAITO, APPLICATION FOR U.S. CITIZENSHIP, JUNE 27, 1894

Shebata Saito, a Japanese man, applies for U.S. citizenship, but U.S. circuit courts refuse the request after concluding that a native of Japan is ineligible for the Naturalization Act because it is restricted to only "aliens being free white persons." This case predates the Takao Ozawa case (1922) by nearly three decades.

In re Saito.
(Circuit Court, D. Massachusetts. June 27, 1849.)
Aliens—Naturalization of Japanese
A native of Japan, of the Mongolian race, is not entitled to naturalization, not being included within the term "white persons" in Rev. St. § 2169.

Application by Shebata Saito for naturalization.
J. Henry Taylor, for applicant.
Colt, Circuit Judge. This is an application by a native of Japan for naturalization.

The act relating to naturalization declares that "the provisions of this title shall apply to aliens being free white persons, and to aliens of African nativity and to persons of African descent." Rev. St. § 2169. The Japanese, like the Chinese, belong to the Mongolian race, and the question presented is whether they are included within the term "white persons."

These words were incorporate in the naturalization laws as early as 1802. . . . At that time the country was inhabited by three races, the Caucasian or white race, the Negro or black race, and the American or red race. It is reasonable, therefore, to infer that when congress, in designating the class of persons who could be naturalized, inserted the qualifying word "white," it intended to exclude from the privilege of citizenship all alien races except the Caucasian. . . .

Whether this question is viewed in the light of congressional intent, or of the popular or scientific meaning of "white persons," or of the authority of adjudicated cases, the only conclusion I am able to reach, after careful consideration, is that the present application must be denied.

Application denied.

Source: The Federal Report, Volume 61. Cases Argued and Determined in the Circuit Courts of Appeals and Circuit and District Courts of the United States (June–August 1894). St. Paul, MN: West Publishing, 1894.

Document 3
REPORT ON INCOMING JAPANESE STEAMER *HONGKONG MARU*, MARCH 20, 1900

As Japanese immigrants arrived in the United States via San Francisco in the early 1900s, ship logs with passenger listings were maintained. The passage below records the arrival of a Japanese steamer containing 246 Japanese and 111 Chinese passengers on the SS Hongkong Maru *on March 20, 1900.*

JAPANESE ARE POURING INTO SAN FRANCISCO

The Toyo Kisen Kaisha's steamer *Hongkong Maru* arrived from the Orient late Wednesday night and was sent into quarantine yesterday morning. As soon as Dr. Kinyoun learned that the plague was dying out in Honolulu he allowed the cabin passengers to land.

The vessel was held for fumigation, however, and will probably dock to-day. . . .

In the steerage the Japanese mail boat has three Europeans, 246 Japanese and 111 Chinese passengers. The influx of Japanese into California has been something wonderful of late.

Every steamer from the Orient brings them into the United States in hundreds, and in consequence every vessel from the Sound has her steerage crowded with them. The *Walla Walla* brought in over a hundred, while the *City of Puebla*, due here Sunday, has near two hundred aboard.

The demand for Japanese labor has increased with leaps and bounds within the last few months. The Highbinder Wars among the Chinese have paralyzed that class of labor, and the "little brown men" from Japan are wanted in their place. On its face, however, it looks very much like contract labor coming into California.

Source: Hongkong Maru. Passenger Lists: San Francisco 1800s. The Maritime Heritage Project, San Francisco 1846–1899. http://www.maritimeheritage.org/

Document 4
ANTI-JAPANESE CAMPAIGN, *SAN FRANCISCO CHRONICLE*, MAY 7, 1900

The first large-scale anti-Japanese protest takes place in San Francisco. It was organized by various labor groups. By 1905, the San Francisco Chronicle *conducted an anti-Japanese campaign, warning of the invasion of Asiatics and the peril the state will face as a result.*

CONVENTION MEETS TODAY TO PROTEST AGAINST JAPS

Delegates from labor organizations and civic and commercial bodies from all over the Convention proposed by the union labor interests of San Francisco. The convention is recognized as the most important held in California since the convention to protest against the unrestricted immigration of Chinese and will have a strong bearing upon the anti-Asiatic agitation which is gaining ground all over the country.

Delegates from Labor and Civic Bodies All Over State to Attend

The meeting of the Anti-Japanese Convention at Lyric Hall this afternoon will mark an important epoch in the history of San Francisco, of California, and in fact of the whole country. No movement of recent years has been more important to the vital interests of the country than the agitation against the unrestricted immigration of a non-assimilative horde of Asiatics.

While the labor unions, the wage-earners of California, have taken the initiative in the movement, the question is one which affects every American, irrespective of occupation or affiliation. It is an admitted fact that the Japanese form a more dangerous element than the Chinese or the most undesirable immigrants from any other part of the globe. That assemblage will be a representative one admits of no doubt. Almost every organization having the welfare of the community at heart will be represented by duly accredited delegates.

Source: "Convention Meets Today to Protest against Japs." *San Francisco Chronicle*, May 7, 1905.

Document 5
THE ASIATIC EXCLUSION LEAGUE MEETING, MAY 14, 1905

The Asiatic Exclusion League is established in San Francisco by 67 labor unions. Eventually over 200 labor unions joined the league to restrict Asian immigration to the United States. The Asiatic Exclusion League met at Council Hall, 316 14th St., San Francisco, California, on January 5, 1908, to discuss concerns about "the invasion of the Pacific Coast, especially California, by Japanese laborers, together with the methods used by them in gaining admission to the mainland of the United States."

THE JAPANESE INVASION

The fruits of the various Chinese Restriction Acts were enjoyed by the people of the Pacific Coast for a very short time because, immediately following the decrease in the number of Chinese coolies, another evil closely followed upon their retreating footsteps. This evil—the Japanese—crept in so easily, so gradually, so secretly, that its danger was not fully recognized by the people at large until after the year 1890. It is true that in the middle eighties, industrial strife had been precipitated by the employment of large numbers of Japanese in the Coast shipping and mines of British Columbia, and it was hoped that the defeat of the ship owners by the Coast Seamen's Union would cause the elimination of that class of labor from among us. The hope was vain. The daily press, from time to time, would call attention to the arrival of Japanese laborers, but they would quietly move to the farming districts where they attracted but little attention, until the white laborers who had been in the habit of obtaining employment throughout the interior, were confronted with, to them, an appalling condition—seeking employment and being refused the same, while gangs of Japanese were busily engaged performing the work which had formerly, and of right, been performed by the actual and prospective American citizen.

Source: Proceedings of the Asiatic Exclusion League, San Francisco: Organized Labor Print, January 1908, 10.

Document 6
PRESIDENT THEODORE ROOSEVELT'S EXECUTIVE ORDER, MARCH 14, 1907

The Gentlemen's Agreement of 1907–1908 between the United States and Japan, arose as a solution to a situation instigated by the segregationist policies of the San Francisco Board of Education. On October 11, 1906, the San Francisco Board of Education ordered the segregation of all Asian children into separate public schools. Because Chinese children were already restricted to segregated schools, it was understood that the order targeted the Japanese population. Roughly 93 ethnic Japanese students were ordered to attend the racially segregated Chinese school. The Chinese school was located in an area that had been devastated by the San Francisco earthquake and fires of that year. All but two families objected and refused to send their children to the segregated school. Some families retained an Issei (first-generation Japanese) attorney to file a legal challenge to the segregation order.

Both the Theodore Roosevelt administration and the Japanese foreign ministry were aware of their delicate political relationship and worked to ensure its stability despite the brewing crisis in San Francisco and growing anti-Japanese sentiment in California. The Gentlemen's Agreement presented itself as a compromise for both nations: in exchange for rescinding the San Francisco segregation order, the Japanese government agreed to restrict the immigration of Japanese laborers to the continental United States. Returning laborers, and parents, wives, and children of laborers already residing in the United States, were allowed to immigrate.

Although the Roosevelt administration intended the executive agreement to curb the growing Japanese population, it actually led to a steady increase in numbers. As part of the agreement, all Issei residents of the United States were required to register with the Japanese foreign ministry. With the assistance of the Japanese consulate general, community leaders organized Japanese associations to help with the bureaucratic processes of registration. They also assisted in processing applications to bring Japanese women into the United States as "picture brides." As a result of this loophole, the Issei were able to form families and escape the extreme gender imbalance that plagued the Chinese community.

THEODORE ROOSEVELT EXECUTIVE ORDER

Whereas, by the act entitled "An Act to regulate the immigration of aliens into the United States," approved February 20, 1907, whenever the President is satisfied that passports issued by any foreign government to its citizens to go to any country other than the United States or to any insular possession of the United States or to the Canal Zone, are being used for the purpose of enabling the holders to come to the continental territory of the United States to the detriment of labor conditions therein, it is made the duty of the President to refuse to permit such citizens of the country issuing such passports to enter the continental territory of the United States from such country or from such insular possession or from the Canal Zone;

And Whereas, upon sufficient evidence produced before me by the Department of Commerce and Labor, I am satisfied that passports issued by the Government of Japan to citizens of that country or Korea and who are laborers, skilled or unskilled, to go to Mexico, to Canada and to Hawai'i, are being used for the purpose of enabling the holders thereof to come to the continental territory of the United States to the detriment of labor conditions therein;

I hereby order that such citizens of Japan or Korea, to-wit: Japanese or Korean laborers, skilled and unskilled, who have received passports to go to Mexico, Canada, or Hawai'i, and come therefrom, be refused permission to enter the continental territory of United States.

It is further ordered that the Secretary of Commerce and Labor be, and he hereby is, directed to take, thru the Bureau of Immigration and Naturalization such measures and to make and enforce such rules and regulations as may be necessary to carry this order into effect.

Theodore Roosevelt
The White House,
Signed March 14, 1907.

Source: CIS Presidential Executive Orders and Proclamations, EO-589, March 14, 1907. Microfiche, Law Library of Congress, Washington, D.C.

Document 7
JAPANESE "PICTURE BRIDES," *EVENING BULLETIN,* DECEMBER 20, 1910

Japanese "picture brides" arrive in the United States. The Gentlemen's Agreement of 1907 stopped the issuance of passports to Japanese laborers wanting to go to America or Hawai'i. However, a loophole in the agreement allowed wives and children of Japanese laborers already residing in the United States to emigrate. As a result of the loophole, many Japanese picture brides were able to migrate to Hawai'i and the United States.

San Francisco. Dec. 13.—Of the thirty Japanese "picture brides" who arrived on the Chiyo Maru on Friday, thirteen met disappointment on the eve of matrimony.

When they were taken to the hospital at Angel Island to undergo an examination for the hookworm disease the brides made no objection. It was afterward learned that they thought this ceremony was but a part of the American marriage service, as they had been instructed that the department required brides who had been wedded by the photograph method to be married here according to the local customs.

But when thirteen of them were informed that they were victims of the hookworm disease, which, according to the American law, would prevent their meeting their picture husbands and necessitates their departure, there was great lamentation.

Fortunately for the brides a section of the revised statues was discovered that permits aliens certified by medical examiners to be held for treatment when this course seems advisable "to meet the ends of justice and humanity."

So the picture brides will remain on Angel Island until they are cured, or pronounced incurable, paying $1.25 a day for the Government as a hospital fee. When Dr. Glover pronounces the happy word they will be allowed to join their waiting husbands.

Source: "Nippon Brides Have Hookworm." *Evening Bulletin,* December 20, 1910.

Document 8
THE WEBB ACT (ALIEN LAND ACT OF 1913), MAY 19, 1913

California State legislature passed the Webb Act, or Alien Land Act. This act prohibits "aliens ineligible to citizenship" from buying land or leasing it for longer than three years. In 1913, five antialien land bills were introduced in the California assembly and two in the senate. Despite the Japanese government's protest and U.S. Secretary of State William Jennings Bryan's cross-country trip to pressure California's lawmakers not to pass the legislation, Gov. Hiram Johnson signed the bill into law on May 19, 1913.

Although the Alien Land Law of 1913 prohibited "aliens ineligible for citizenship" from owning land and possessing long-term land leases, it was understood that it was meant to exclude Japanese immigrants from land ownership in California. Issei families navigated around the law, with some purchasing land through a white intermediary, and others forming corporations to purchase land on behalf of the immigrants. Many families chose to purchase land in the name of their U.S.-born citizen children. Although the Alien Land Law of 1913 prohibited long-term land leases of more than three years, this practice actually increased, as European American landowners realized larger financial returns from farms cultivated by Japanese tenants.

§ 1. All aliens eligible to citizenship under the laws of the United States may acquire, possess, enjoy, use, cultivate, occupy, transfer, transmit and inherit real property, or any interest therein, in this state, and have in whole or in part the beneficial use thereof, in the same manner and to the same extent as citizens of the United States, except as otherwise provided by the laws of this state.

§ 2. All aliens other than those mentioned in section one of this act may acquire, possess, enjoy, use, cultivate, occupy and transfer real property, or any interest therein, in this state, and have in whole or in part the beneficial use thereof, in the manner and to the extent, and for the purposes prescribed by any treaty now existing between the government of the United States and the nation or country of which such alien is a citizen or subject, and not otherwise. . . .

§ 7. Any real property hereafter acquired in fee in violation of the provisions of this act by any alien mentioned in Section 2 of this act, . . . shall escheat as of the date of such acquiring, to, and become and remain the property of the state of California. . . .

The intent of the law was to restrict land ownership by Japanese immigrants. However, by assigning ownership of land to second-generation children, born in the United States and thus citizens, or by the use of extended leases, the law could be evaded. The result was Proposition 1 on the California ballot in 1920:

Proposition 1: Permits acquisition and transfer of real property by aliens eligible to citizenship, to same extent as citizens except as otherwise provided by law; permits other aliens, and companies, associations and corporations in which they hold majority interest, to acquire and transfer real property only as prescribed by treaty, but prohibiting appointment thereof as guardians of estates of minors consisting wholly or partially of real property or shares in such corporations; provides for escheats in certain cases; requires reports of property holdings to facilitate enforcement of act; prescribes penalties and repeals conflicting acts.

Source: The Statutes of California and Amendments to the Codes Passed at the Fortieth Session of the Legislature, 1913. Sacramento: Superintendent of State Printing, 1913.

Document 9
IMMIGRATION ACT OF 1917, FEBRUARY 5, 1917

On February 5, 1917, the U.S. Congress passed the Immigration Act of 1917. The most stringent law to date, it established a literacy requirement for immigrants over 16 years of age and restricted the entry of "undesirables" from other countries including idiots, alcoholics, poor, criminals, beggars, any person suffering attacks of insanity, aliens who have a physical disability that will restrict them from earning a living in the United States, polygamists, anarchists, prostitutes, and contract laborers. The Immigration Act of 1917 restricted immigration of anyone born in a geographically defined "Asiatic Barred Zone" excluding the Japanese and Filipinos. The Gentlemen's Agreement already restricted immigration of Japanese laborers, and the Philippines was an American colony so they were considered American nationals and had unrestricted entry. On December 14, 1916, President Woodrow Wilson had vetoed the act, but Congress overrode his veto. The act prohibited immigration from all of Asia and India by drawing an imaginary line from the Red Sea in the Middle East all the way through the Ural Mountains: people living east of the line were not allowed entry to the United States. This act also includes a literacy test requirement. Immigrants from China and Japan were not named because they were already excluded from the United States through the Chinese Exclusion Act of 1882 and Gentlemen's Agreement of 1907. The "Barred Zone" Act was amended in 1946, with the enactment of the Luce-Celler Bill. At that time, Asian Indians were allowed to enter the United States, but the quota was set at 100 persons per year.

CHAP. 29. An Act to regulate the immigration of aliens to, and the residence of aliens in, the United States.

Be it enacted by the Senate and House of Representatives of the United States of America in Congress assembled, That the world "alien" wherever used in this Act shall include any person not a native-born or naturalized citizen of the United States; but this definition shall not be held to include Indians of the United States not taxed or citizens of the island under the jurisdiction of the United States . . . *unless otherwise provided for by existing treaties, persons who are natives of islands not possessed by the United States adjacent to the Continent of Asia, situate south of the 20th parallel latitude north, west of the 160th meridian of longitude east from Greenwich, and north of the tenth parallel of latitude south, or who are natives of any country, province, or dependency situate on the Continent of Asia west of the 110th meridian of longitude east from Greenwich and east of the 50th meridian of longitude east from Greenwich and south of the fiftieth parallel of latitude north, except that portion of said territory situate between the fiftieth and the sixty-fourth meridians of longitude east from Greenwich and the twenty-fourth and thirty-eighth parallels of latitude north, and no alien now in any way excluded from, or prevented from entering, the United States shall be admitted to the United States.* The provision next foregoing, however, shall not apply to persons of the following status or occupations: Government officers, ministers or religious teachers, missionaries, lawyers, physicians, chemists, civil engineers, teachers, students, authors, artists, merchants, and travelers for curiosity or pleasure, nor to their legal wives or their children under sixteen years of age who shall accompany them or who subsequently may apply for admission to the United States, but such person or their legal wives or foreign-born children who fail to maintain in the United States a status or occupation placing them within the excepted classes shall be deemed to be in the United States contrary to law, and shall be subject to deportation as provided in section nineteen of this Act. . . .

Source: The Statutes at Large of the United States of America, Volume XXXIX, Part I. Washington, DC: Government Printing Office, 1917.

Document 10
TAKAO OZAWA V. UNITED STATES, NOVEMBER 13, 1922

Takao Ozawa v. United States was a landmark Supreme Court case that denied the right to naturalization for all Issei (first-generation Japanese immigrants). Under the

Nationality Acts of 1790 and 1870, federal law had restricted the right of naturaliza-
tion to aliens who were either, "free white" or of "African nativity and descent." Oza-
wa's argument rested in the ambiguity of the term, "white," which he claimed could
apply to Japanese immigrants who were physically, "whiter" than many Southern and
Eastern Europeans who had become naturalized citizens.

Takao Ozawa himself was a Japanese immigrant who had come to the United States
as a minor in 1894. He attended the University of California before moving to the
Territory of Hawai'i in 1906 when the Great Earthquake in San Francisco disrupted
his studies.

By the time he applied to become a naturalized citizen, Ozawa had lived in the
United States for 20 years. He was the model of an assimilated immigrant: he spoke
English at home with his wife and children, belonged to a Christian church, worked
for an American company, and did not drink, smoke, or gamble. When he applied for
naturalization, Ozawa did not ask for the support of the Japanese American Citizens
League or Japanese immigrant organizations.

When the U.S. district court in northern California denied Ozawa's application,
he took his case to the U.S. District Court in Hawai'i, where he again was rebuffed.
Ozawa appealed and his case was referred to the U.S. Supreme Court in 1917.

Justice George Sutherland wrote the unanimous opinion upholding the lower court
ruling that Ozawa was racially "ineligible for citizenship" because he was "not Cau-
casian." In other words, in 1922 the Court determined that racial origins, rather than
skin color, were what mattered in defining who was eligible for naturalization.

Mr. Justice SUTHERLAND delivered the opinion of the Court.

The appellant is a person of the Japanese race born in Japan. He applied, on
October 16, 1914, to the United States District Court for the Territory of Hawai'i
to be admitted as a citizen of the United States. His petition was opposed by
the United States District Attorney for the District of Hawai'i. Including the
period of his residence in Hawai'i appellant had continuously resided in
the United States for 20 years. He was a graduate of the Berkeley, Cal., high
school, had been nearly three years a student in the University of California,
had educated his children in American schools, his family had attended American churches and he had maintained the use of the English language in his
home. That he was well qualified by character and education for citizenship is
conceded. . . .

The question then is: Who are comprehended within the phrase 'free white
persons'? Undoubtedly the word 'free' was originally used in recognition of the
fact that slavery then existed and that some white persons occupied that status.
The word, however, has long since ceased to have any practical significance and
may now be disregarded.

The determination that the words 'white person' are synonymous with the
words 'a person of the Caucasian race' simplifies the problem, although it does

not entirely dispose of it. Controversies have arisen and will no doubt arise again in respect of the proper classification of individuals in border line cases. The effect of the conclusion that the words 'white person' means a Caucasian is not to establish a sharp line of demarcation between those who are entitled and those who are not entitled to naturalization, but rather a zone of more or less debatable ground outside of which, upon the one hand, are those clearly eligible, and outside of which, upon the other hand, are those clearly ineligible for citizenship. . . .

The appellant, in the case now under consideration, however, is clearly of a race which is not Caucasian and therefore belongs entirely outside the zone on the negative side. A large number of the federal and state courts have so decided and we find no reported case definitely to the contrary. These decisions are sustained by numerous scientific authorities, which we do not deem it necessary to review. We think these decisions are right and so hold.

Source: Takao Ozawa v. United States, 260 U.S. 178 (1922).

Document 11
HIDEMITSU TOYOTA V. UNITED STATES, MAY 25, 1925

The U.S. Supreme Court in Hidemitsu Toyota v. United States *rules that a "person of the Japanese race, born in Japan, may not legally be naturalized." In 1922, the U.S. Supreme Court confirmed in* Takao Ozawa v. United States *that Japanese immigrants were not eligible to become naturalized citizens. Takao Ozawa immigrated to the United States in 1894 as a student, graduated from Berkeley High School and then attended the University of California, Berkeley. He was a self-described "assimilated" American who primarily spoke English in his home. In October 1914, Ozawa applied for citizenship in the U.S. District Court in Hawai'i. The court rejected his application on the grounds that he was of the Japanese race, and not white. Ozawa filed a lawsuit that gradually made its way to the U.S. Supreme Court. The court's ruling in November 1922 declared that first-generation Japanese Americans, or natives of Japan, the Issei, are ineligible of becoming naturalized citizens. Hidemitsu Toyota tested whether service in America's armed forces during World War I made him eligible for naturalization. Toyota enlisted in the Coast Guard in 1913 and served during wartime. He petitioned for naturalization under a 1918 act allowing alien war veterans who had been honorably discharged to become naturalized citizens. Toyota's naturalization bid was successful, but the government filed to revoke his citizenship in the First Circuit Court of Appeals. The Supreme Court upheld that decision and contended that there was no reason to enlarge the categories of aliens eligible for naturalization under existing statutes.*

Mr. Justice BUTLER delivered the opinion of the Court.

Hidemitsu Toyota, a person of the Japanese race, born in Japan, entered the United States in 1913. He served substantially all the time between November of that year and May, 1923, in the United States Coast Guard Service. This was a part of the naval force of the United States nearly all of the time the United States was engaged in the recent war. He received eight or more honorable discharges, and some of them were for service during the war. May 14, 1921, he filed his petition for naturalization in the United States District Court for the District of Massachusetts. The petition was granted, and a certificate of naturalization was issued to him. This case arises on a petition to cancel the certificate on the ground that it was illegally procured. Section 15, Act of June 29, 1906, c. 3592, 34 Stat. 596, 601 (Comp. St. § 4374). It is agreed that if a person of the Japanese race, born in Japan, may legally be naturalized under the seventh subdivision of section 4 of the Act of June 29, 1906, as amended by the Act of May 9, 1918, c. 69, 40 Stat. 542 (Comp. St. 1918, Comp. St. Ann. Supp. 1919, § 4352), or under the Act of July 19, 1919, c. 24, 41 Stat. 222 (Comp. St. Ann. Supp. 1923, § 4352aaa), Toyota is legally naturalized. The District Court held he was not entitled to be naturalized, and entered a decree canceling his certificate of citizenship. 290 F. 971. An appeal was taken to the Circuit Court of Appeals, and that court under section 239, Judicial Code (Comp. St. § 1216), certified to this court the following questions: (1) Whether a person of the Japanese race, born in Japan, may legally be naturalized under the seventh subdivision of section 4 of the Act of June 29, 1906, as amended by the Act of May 9, 1918; and (2) whether such subject may legally be naturalized under the Act of July 19, 1919. The material provisions of these enactments are printed in the margin.

Source: Toyota v. United States, 268 U.S. 402 (1925).

Document 12
EXECUTIVE ORDER 9066, FEBRUARY 19, 1942

The bombing of Pearl Harbor by Japanese forces on the morning of December 7, 1941, marked a bitter turning point in Japanese American history. President Franklin D. Roosevelt signed Executive Order 9066 in February 19, 1942, authorizing the exclusion of Japanese—including Okinawan—Americans from the West Coast. The order granted the federal government the ability to create military zones, including the authority to remove individuals—mostly American citizens and residents of Japanese descent—from areas that there deemed threats to national security. Immediately after Pearl Harbor, the Federal Bureau of Investigation (FBI) identified and captured Japanese

American community leaders from California, Oregon, and Washington—states that were designated critical zones of national security. These early detainees, arrested by the FBI as early as December 1941, were sent to facilities such as the Department of Justice internment camp in Santa Fe, New Mexico, Crystal City, Texas, and Fort Missoula, Montana. They were held without bail, without being formally charged, and without knowing what crime they were being accused of committing.

Now, therefore, by virtue of the authority vested in me as President of the United States, and Commander in Chief of the Army and Navy, I hereby authorize and direct the Secretary of War, and the Military Commanders whom he may from time to time designate, whenever he or any designated Commander deems such action necessary or desirable, to prescribe military areas in such places and of such extent as he or the appropriate Military Commander may determine, from which any or all persons may be excluded, and with respect to which, the right of any person to enter, remain in, or leave shall be subject to whatever restrictions the Secretary of War or the appropriate Military Commander may impose in his discretion. The Secretary of War is hereby authorized to provide for residents of any such area who are excluded therefrom, such transportation, food, shelter, and other accommodations as may be necessary, in the judgment of the Secretary of War or the said Military Commander, and until other arrangements are made, to accomplish the purpose of this order. The designation of military areas in any region or locality shall supersede designations of prohibited and restricted areas by the Attorney General under the Proclamations of December 7 and 8, 1941, and shall supersede the responsibility and authority of the Attorney General under the said Proclamations in respect of such prohibited and restricted areas.

I hereby further authorize and direct the Secretary of War and the said Military Commanders to take such other steps as he or the appropriate Military Commander may deem advisable to enforce compliance with the restrictions applicable to each Military area hereinabove authorized to be designated, including the use of Federal troops and other Federal Agencies, with authority to accept assistance of state and local agencies.

I hereby further authorize and direct all Executive Departments, independent establishments and other Federal Agencies, to assist the Secretary of War or the said Military Commanders in carrying out this Executive Order, including the furnishing of medical aid, hospitalization, food, clothing, transportation, use of land, shelter, and other supplies, equipment, utilities, facilities, and services.

This order shall not be construed as modifying or limiting in any way the authority heretofore granted under Executive Order No. 8972, dated December 12, 1941, nor shall it be construed as limiting or modifying the duty and responsibility of the Federal Bureau of Investigation, with respect to the investigation of alleged acts of sabotage or the duty and responsibility of the Attorney General and the Department of Justice under the Proclamations of December 7 and 8, 1941, prescribing regulations for the conduct and control of alien enemies, except as such duty and responsibility is superseded by the designation of military areas hereunder.

Franklin D. Roosevelt
The White House,
February 19, 1942.

Source: Executive Order 9066, February 19, 1942; General Records of the United States Government; Record Group 11; National Archives. https://www .archives.gov/historical-docs/todays-doc/?dod-date=219. Accessed January 13, 2017.

Document 13
EXECUTIVE ORDER 9102, MARCH 18, 1942

On March 18, 1942, President Roosevelt issued Executive Order 9102, establishing the War Relocation Authority (WRA) for the purposes of relocating Japanese Americans named in Order 9066. In total, 112,000 Japanese Americans were forced to leave their homes and property and move into government detention facilities euphemistically called "Assembly Centers" and "Relocation Centers." They were sent to 10 camps located in far-flung regions, each housed 10,000 to 20,000 Japanese Americans: Rohwer and Jerome, Arkansas; Gila River and Poston, Arizona; Manzanar and Tule Lake, California; Amache, Colorado; Minidoka, Idaho; Topaz, Utah; and Heart Mountain, Wyoming.

EXECUTIVE ORDER 9102 ESTABLISHING THE WAR RELOCATION AUTHORITY

By virtue of the authority vested in me by the Constitution and statutes of the United States, as President of the United States and Commander in Chief of the Army and Navy, and in order to provide for the removal from designated areas of persons whose removal is necessary in the interests of national security, it is ordered as follows:

1. There is established in the Office for Emergency Management of the Executive Office of the President the War Relocation Authority, at the head of which shall be a Director appointed by and responsible to the President.

2. The Director of the War Relocation Authority is authorized and directed to formulate and effectuate a program for the removal, from the areas designated from time to time by the Secretary of War or appropriate military commander under the authority of Executive Order No. 9066 of February 19, 1942, of the persons or classes of persons designated under such Executive Order, and for their relocation, maintenance, and supervision.

3. In effectuating such program the Director shall have authority to
   (a) Accomplish all necessary evacuation not undertaken by the Secretary of War or appropriate military commander, provide for the relocation of such persons in appropriate places, provide for their needs in such manner as may be appropriate, and supervise their activities.
   (b) Provide, insofar as feasible and desirable, for the employment of such persons at useful work in industry, commerce, agriculture, or public projects, prescribe the terms and conditions of such public employment, and safeguard the public interest in the private employment of such persons.
   (c) Secure the cooperation, assistance, or services of any governmental agency.
   (d) Prescribe regulations necessary or desirable to promote effective execution of such program, and, as a means of coordinating evacuation and relocation activities, consult with the Secretary of War with respect to regulations issued and measures taken by him.
   (e) Make such delegations of authority as he may deem necessary.
   (f) Employ necessary personnel, and make such expenditures, including the making of loans and grants and the purchase of real property, as may be necessary, within the limits of such funds as may be made available to the Authority.

4. The Director shall consult with the United States Employment Service and other agencies on employment and other problems incident to activities under this Order.

5. The Director shall cooperate with the Alien Property Custodian appointed pursuant to Executive Order No. 9095 of March 11, 1942, in formulating policies to govern the custody, management, and disposal by the Alien Property Custodian of property belonging to foreign nationals removed under this Order or under Executive Order No. 9066 of February 19, 1942; and may assist all other persons removed under either of such Executive Orders in the management and disposal of their property.

6. Departments and agencies of the United States are directed to cooperate with and assist the Director in his activities hereunder. The Departments of War and Justice, under the direction of the Secretary of War and the Attorney General, respectively, shall insofar as consistent with the national interest provide such protective, police, and investigational services as the Director shall find necessary in connection with activities under this Order.

7. There is established within the War Relocation Authority the War Relocation Work Corps. The Director shall provide, by general regulations, for the enlistment in such Corps, for the duration of the present war, of persons removed under this Order or under Executive Order No. 9066 of February 19, 1942, and

shall prescribe the terms and conditions of the work to be performed by such Corps, and the compensation to be paid.

8. There is established within the War Relocation Authority a Liaison Committee on War Relocation, which shall consist of the Secretary of War, the Secretary of the Treasury, the Attorney General, the Secretary of Agriculture, the Secretary of Labor, the Federal Security Administrator, the Director of Civilian Defense, and the Alien Property Custodian, or their deputies, and such other persons or agencies as the Director may designate. The Liaison Committee shall meet at the call of the Director and shall assist him in his duties.

9. The Director shall keep the President informed with regard to the progress made in carrying out this Order, and perform such related duties as the President may from time to time assign to him.

10. In order to avoid duplication of evacuation activities under this Order and Executive Order No. 9066 of February 19, 1942, the Director shall not undertake any evacuation activities within military areas designated under said Executive Order No. 9066, without the prior approval of the Secretary of War or the appropriate military commander.

11. This Order does not limit the authority granted in Executive Order No. 8972 of December 12, 1941; Executive Order No. 9066 of February 19, 1942; Executive Order No. 9095 of March 11, 1942; Executive Proclamation No. 2525 of December 7, 1941; Executive Proclamation No. 2526 of December 8, 1941; Executive Proclamation No. 2527 of December 8, 1941; Executive Proclamation No. 2533 of December 19, 1941; or Executive Proclamation No. 2537 of January 14, 1942; nor does it limit the functions of the Federal Bureau of Investigation.

Source: Executive Order 9102, Franklin D. Roosevelt. Available via the National Park Service. https://www.nps.gov/manz/learn/historyculture/historic-documents .htm

Document 14
YASUI V. UNITED STATES, JUNE 21, 1943

The Supreme Court rules in Yasui v. United States *declaring that Congress in enacting Public Law 77-503 authorized the implementation of Executive Order 9066 and provided criminal penalties for violation of orders of the Military Commander.*

Yasui v. United States (1943)
Argued May 11, 1943
Decided June 21, 1943

Syllabus
MR. CHIEF JUSTICE STONE delivered the opinion of the Court.

This is a companion case to *Hirabayashi v. United States, ante*. . . decided this day.

The case comes here on certificate of the Court of Appeals for the Ninth Circuit, certifying to us questions of law upon which it desires instructions for the decision of the case. § 239 of the Judicial Code as amended, 28 U.S.C. § 346. Acting under that section, we ordered the entire record to be certified to this Court so that we might proceed to a decision as if the case had been brought here by appeal.

Appellant, an American-born person of Japanese ancestry, was convicted in the district court of an offense defined by the Act of March 21, 1942. The indictment charged him with violation, on March 28, 1942, of a curfew order made applicable to Portland, Oregon, by Public Proclamation No. 3, issued by Lt. Gen. J. L. DeWitt on March 24, 1942. 7 Federal Register 2543. The validity of the curfew was considered in the *Hirabayashi* case, and this case presents the same issues as the conviction on Count 2 of the indictment in that case. From the evidence, it appeared that appellant was born in Oregon in 1916 of alien parents; that, when he was eight years old, he spent a summer in Japan; that he attended the public schools in Oregon, and also, for about three years, a Japanese language school; that he later attended the University of Oregon, from which he received A.B. and LL.B degrees; that he was a member of the bar of Oregon, and a second lieutenant in the Army of the United States, Infantry Reserve; that he had been employed by the Japanese Consulate in Chicago, but had resigned on December 8, 1941, and immediately offered his services to the military authorities; that he had discussed with an agent of the Federal Bureau of Investigation the advisability of testing the constitutionality of the curfew, and that, when he violated the curfew order, he requested that he be arrested so that he could test its constitutionality.

The district court ruled that the Act of March 21, 1942, was unconstitutional as applied to American citizens, but held that appellant, by reason of his course of conduct, must be deemed to have renounced his American citizenship. 48 F.Supp. 40. The Government does not undertake to support the conviction on that ground, since no such issue was tendered by the Government, although appellant testified at the trial that he had not renounced his citizenship. Since we hold, as in the *Hirabayashi* case, that the curfew order was valid as applied to citizens, it follows that appellant's citizenship was not relevant to the issue tendered by the Government, and the conviction must be sustained for the reasons stated in the *Hirabayashi* case.

But as the sentence of one year's imprisonment—the maximum permitted by the statute—was imposed after the finding that appellant was not a citizen, and as the Government states that it has not and does not now controvert his citizenship, the case is an appropriate one for resentence in the light of these circumstances. See *Husty v. United States*, 282 U.S. 694, 282 U.S. 703. The conviction will be sustained, but the judgment will be vacated and the cause remanded to the district court for resentence of appellant, and to afford that court opportunity to strike its findings as to appellant's loss of United States citizenship.

So ordered.

Source: Yasui v. United States, 320 U.S. 115 (1943).

Document 15
PROCLAMATION 4417—"AN AMERICAN PROMISE," RESCISSION OF EXECUTIVE ORDER 9066, FEBRUARY 19, 1976

On this day, President Gerald Ford rescinds Executive Order 9066, 34 years after World War II. After World War II, Japanese Americans worked hard to restore their lives and recover from the devastation of having been imprisoned without due process and charged with any crimes. Many did not want to talk about their experiences. Nisei became notorious for keeping their wartime experiences from their Sansei children. However, it is the Sansei generation who will fight for their rights, and the rights of their elders to be recognized and treated as fully American!

The social and political climate during the postwar period was one of civil rights and ethnic pride. While the Japanese American Citizens League (JACL) was disparaged for cooperating with the U.S. government in all of their policies during World War II, lawyers and lobbyists for the JACL worked diligently to overturn laws banning interracial marriage, legalizing segregation, and restricted rights to citizenship and immigration based on race.

AN AMERICAN PROMISE

By the President of the United States of America

A Proclamation

In this Bicentennial Year, we are commemorating the anniversary dates of many of the great events in American history. An honest reckoning, however, must include a recognition of our national mistakes as well as our national achievements. Learning from our mistakes is not pleasant, but as a great philosopher once admonished, we must do so if we want to avoid repeating them.

February 19th is the anniversary of a sad day in American history. It was on that date in 1942, in the midst of the response to the hostilities that began on December 7, 1941, that Executive Order No. 9066 was issued, subsequently enforced by the criminal penalties of a statute enacted March 21, 1942, resulting in the uprooting of loyal Americans. Over one hundred thousand persons of Japanese ancestry were removed from their homes, detained in special camps, and eventually relocated.

The tremendous effort by the War Relocation Authority and concerned Americans for the welfare of these Japanese-Americans may add perspective to that story, but it does not erase the setback to fundamental American principles. Fortunately, the Japanese-American community in Hawai'i was spared the indignities suffered by those on our mainland.

We now know what we should have known then—not only was that evacuation wrong, but Japanese-Americans were and are loyal Americans. On the battlefield and at home, Japanese-Americans—names like Hamada, Mitsumori, Marimoto, Noguchi, Yamasaki, Kido, Munemori and Miyamura—have been and continue to be written in our history for the sacrifices and the contributions they have made to the well-being and security of this, our common Nation.

The Executive order that was issued on February 19, 1942, was for the sole purpose of prosecuting the war with the Axis Powers, and ceased to be effective with the end of those hostilities. Because there was no formal statement of its termination, however, there is concern among many Japanese-Americans that there may yet be some life in that obsolete document. I think it appropriate, in this our Bicentennial Year, to remove all doubt on that matter, and to make clear our commitment in the future.

Now, Therefore, I, Gerald R. Ford, President of the United States of America, do hereby proclaim that all the authority conferred by Executive Order No. 9066 terminated upon the issuance of Proclamation No. 2714, which formally proclaimed the cessation of the hostilities of World War II on December 31, 1946.

I call upon the American people to affirm with me this American Promise— that we have learned from the tragedy of that long-ago experience forever to treasure liberty and justice for each individual American, and resolve that this kind of action shall never again be repeated.

In Witness Whereof, I have hereunto set my hand this nineteenth day of February in the year of our Lord nineteen hundred seventy-six, and of the Independence of the United States of America the two hundredth.

Gerald R. Ford

Source: Gerald R. Ford: "Proclamation 4417—'An American Promise,'" February 19, 1976. Ford Library Museum.gov. https://fordlibrarymuseum.gov /library/speeches/760111p.htm. Accessed January 17, 2017.

Selected Bibliography

Adachi, Nobuko. "Emigrants from Japan." In *Japan at War: An Encyclopedia*, edited by Louis Perez. Santa Barbara, CA: ABC-CLIO, 2013.

Allen, Helena. *The Betrayal of Liliuokalani: Last Queen of Hawaii 1838–1917*. Honolulu: Mutual Publishing, 1982.

Almaguer, Tomas. *Racial Fault Lines: The Historical Origins of White Supremacy in California*. Berkeley: University of California Press, 1994.

Alonso, Karen. *Korematsu v. United States: Japanese American Internment Camps*. Berkeley Heights, NJ: Enslow Publishers, 1998.

Ancheta, Angelo. *Race, Rights, and the Asian American Experience*. New Brunswick, NJ: Rutgers University Press, 1998.

Asakawa, Gil. "Minoru Yasui." *Densho Encyclopedia*. 2017. http://encyclopedia.densho .org/Minoru_Yasui/. Accessed January 13, 2017.

Asher, Robert, and Charles Stephenson, eds. *Labor Divided: Race and Ethnicity in United States Labor Struggles, 1835–1960*. Albany: State University of New York Press, 1990.

Auslin, Michael. *Negotiating with Imperialism: The Unequal Treaties and the Culture of Japanese Diplomacy*. Cambridge, MA: Harvard University Press, 2004.

Azuma, Eiichiro. "Racial Struggle, Immigrant Nationalism, and Ethnic Identity: Japanese and Filipinos in the California Delta." *Pacific Historical Review* 67, no. 2 (May 1998): 163–199.

Bailey, Paul. *City in the Sun: The Japanese Concentration Camp at Poston, Arizona*. Los Angeles: Westernlore Press, 1971.

Bangarth, Stephanie. *Voices Raised in Protest: Defending Citizens of Japanese Ancestry in North America, 1942–49*. Vancouver: University of British Columbia Press, 2008.

Bannai, Lorraine. *Enduring Conviction: Fred Korematsu and His Quest for Justice*. Seattle: University of Washington Press, 2015.

Blair, Doug. "The 1920 Anti-Japanese Crusade and Congressional Hearings." Seattle Civil Rights & Labor History Project. University of Washington. http://depts .washington.edu/civilr/Japanese_restriction.htm. Accessed October 26, 2016.

Blussé, Leonard. *Visible Cities: Canton, Nagasaki, and Batavia and the Coming of the Americans*. Cambridge, MA: Harvard University Press, 2008.

Bowman, John Stewart, ed. *Columbia Chronologies of Asian History and Culture*. New York: Columbia University Press, 2000.

Buchanan, Paul. *Race Relations in the United States: A Chronology, 1896–2005*. Jefferson, NC: McFarland & Company, 2005.

Burgan, Michael. *The Japanese American Internment: Civil Liberties Denied*. Minneapolis, MN: Compass Point Books, 2007.

Castelnuovo, Shirley. *Soldiers of Conscience: Japanese American Military Resisters in World War II.* Westport, CT: Greenwood Press, 2008.

Chan, Sucheng. *Asian Americans: An Interpretive History.* New York: Twayne, 1991.

Chang, Derek. *Citizens of a Christian Nation: Evangelical Missions and the Problem of Race in the Nineteenth Century.* Philadelphia: University of Pennsylvania Press, 2010.

Chaurasia, R. S. *History of Japan.* New Delhi: Atlantic Publishers, 2003.

Chen, C. Peter. "Japan's Surrender (14 Aug 1945–2 Sep 1945)." World War II Database. 2017. http://ww2db.com/battle_spec.php?battle_id=13. Accessed January 13, 2017.

Cheng, Cindy I-Fen. *Citizens of Asian America: Democracy and Race during the Cold War.* New York: New York University Press, 2013.

Chin, Gabriel, and Rose Villazor, eds. *The Immigration and Nationality Act of 1965: Legislating a New America.* Cambridge, UK: Cambridge University Press, 2015.

Cuison Villazor, Rose. "Rediscovering *Oyama v. California*: At the Intersection of Property, Race, and Citizenship." *Washington University Law Review* 87, no. 5 (2010): 979–1042.

Daniels, Roger. *Asian America: Chinese and Japanese in the United States since 1850.* Seattle: University of Washington Press, 1988.

Daniels, Roger. *The Politics of Prejudice: The Anti-Japanese Movement in California and the Struggle for Japanese Exclusion.* Berkeley: University of California Press, 1962.

Daniels, Roger, Sandra Taylor, Harry Kitano, and Leonard Arrington. *Japanese Americans: From Relocation to Redress.* Seattle: University of Washington Press, 1992.

Danley, Sharon Yamato. "Japanese Picture Brides Recall Hardships of American Life." *Los Angeles Times,* May 11, 1995. http://articles.latimes.com/1995-05-11/news/cb -64865_1_picture-bride. Accessed October 14, 2016.

Davidson, Sue. *A Heart in Politics: Jeannette Rankin and Patsy T. Mink.* Seattle, WA: Seal Press, 1994.

Dickinson, Frederick R. "Japanese Empire." In *Encyclopedia of the Age of Imperialism, 1800–1914,* edited by Carl C. Hodge. Westport, CT: Greenwood Press, 2008.

Dickinson, Frederick R. *War and National Reinvention: Japan in the Great War, 1914– 1919.* Cambridge, MA: Harvard University Press, 1999.

Dower, John. *Embracing Defeat: Japan in the Wake of World War II.* New York: W. W. Norton & Company, 2000.

Dudden, Alexis. *Japan's Colonization of Korea: Discourse and Power.* Honolulu: University of Hawai'i Press, 2004.

Easton, Stanley, and Lucien Ellington. "Japanese Americans." *Multicultural America,* 2011. http://www.everyculture.com/multi/Ha-La/Japanese-Americans.html. Accessed June 11, 2014.

Fryer, Heather. "The Japanese American Experience: History and Culture." In *Asian American History and Culture: An Encyclopedia,* edited by Huping Ling and Allan Austin. Armonk, NY: M. E. Sharpe, 2010.

Fujikane, Candance, and Jonathan Okamura, eds. *Asian Settler Colonialism: From Local Governance to the Habits of Everyday Life in Hawai'i.* Honolulu: University of Hawai'i Press, 2008.

Fujita-Rony, Thomas. "Poston (Colorado River)." *Densho Encyclopedia*. 2017. http://encyclopedia.densho.org/Poston (Colorado_River)/. Accessed August 1, 2017.

Fukuda, Moritoshi. *Legal Problems of Japanese-Americans: Their History and Development in the United States*. Tokyo: Keio Tsushin Company, 1980.

Gallagher, Charles, and Cameron D. Lippard, eds. *Race and Racism in the United States: An Encyclopedia of the American Mosaic*. Westport, CT: Greenwood, 2014.

Gardiner, C. Harvey. *Pawns in a Triangle of Hate: The Peruvian Japanese and the United States*. Seattle: University of Washington Press, 1981.

"Gentlemen's Agreement." History.com. http://www.history.com/topics/gentlemens-agreement. Accessed October 14, 2016.

Gesensway, Deborah, and Mindy Roseman. *Beyond Words: Images from America's Concentration Camps*. Ithaca, NY: Cornell University Press, 1988.

Girdner, Audrie, and Anne Loftis. *The Great Betrayal: The Evacuation of the Japanese-Americans during World War II*. New York: Macmillan, 1969.

Glenn, Evelyn Nakano. *Issei, Nisei, War Bride: Three Generations of Japanese American Women in Domestic Service*. Philadelphia, PA: Temple University Press, 1986.

Griffiths, Ben. "Commodore Perry's Expedition to Japan." http://www.grifworld.com/perryhome.html#who. Accessed October 6, 2016.

Haney López, Ian. *White by Law: The Legal Construction of Race*. New York: New York University Press, 1996.

Harth, Erica. *Last Witnesses: Reflections on the Wartime Incarceration of Japanese Americans*. New York: Palgrave MacMillan, 2001.

Hasegawa, Atsuko, and Nancy Shiraki. *Hōsha: A Pictorial History of Jōdo Shinshū in Hawaii*. Honolulu: The Hawai'i Federation of Honpa Hongwanji, 1989.

Hatamiya, Leslie. *Righting a Wrong: Japanese Americans and the Passage of the Civil Liberties Act of 1988*. Stanford, CA: Stanford University Press, 1993.

Hawaii Nikkei History Editorial Board, compiler. *Japanese Eyes, American Heart: Personal Reflections of Hawaii's World War II Nisei Soldiers*. Honolulu: Tendai Educational Foundation, 1998.

Hawaiian Planters' Record vol. 61, Nov. 3, 2009. Kunia: Hawaii Agriculture Research Center. Available at http://www.harc-hspa.com/uploads/2/6/1/7/26170270/hawnplant_-_new_edit_9-12-11.pdf. Accessed October 11, 2016.

The Hawai'ian Sugar Planters' Association Plantation Archives. University of Hawai'i at Manoa. http://www2.hawaii.edu/~speccoll/hawaiihspa.html. Accessed October 11, 2016.

Hing, Bill Ong. *Defining America through Immigration Policy*. Philadelphia, PA: Temple University Press, 2004.

Hing, Bill Ong. *Making and Remaking Asian America through Immigration Policy: 1850–1990*. Stanford, CA: Stanford University Press, 1993.

Hirabayashi, Gordon, James Hirabayashi, and Lane Ryo Hirabayashi. *A Principled Stand: The Story of* Hirabayashi v. United States. Seattle: University of Washington Press, 2013.

Hirobe, Izumi. *Japanese Pride, American Prejudice: Modifying the Exclusion Clause of the 1924 Immigration Act*. Stanford, CA: Stanford University Press, 2001.

Hosokawa, Bill. *Colorado's Japanese Americans from 1886 to the Present*. Boulder: University Press of Colorado, 2005.

Hosokawa, Bill. *JACL in Quest of Justice: The History of the Japanese American Citizens League*. New York: William Morrow, 1982.

Houston, Jeanne Wakatsuki, and James Houston. *Farewell to Manzanar*. New York: Bantam Books, 1978 (reprint New York: Houghton Mifflin, 2000).

Howard, John. *Concentration Camps on the Home Front*. Chicago, IL: University of Chicago Press, 2008.

Hune, Shirley, and Gail Nomura, eds. *Asian/Pacific Islander American Women: A Historical Anthology*. New York: New York University Press, 2003.

Ichioka, Yuji. "The Early Japanese Immigrant Quest for Citizenship: The Background of the 1922 Ozawa Case." *Amerasia Journal* 4, no. 2 (1977): 1–22.

Ichioka, Yuji. *The Issei: The World of the First Generation Japanese Immigrants, 1885–1924*. New York: The Free Press, 1988.

Inada, Fusao, ed. *Only What We Could Carry: The Japanese American Internment Experience*. Berkeley, CA: Heyday Books, 2000.

Irons, Peter. *Justice at War: The Story of the Japanese American Internment Cases*. Berkeley: University of California Press, 1993.

Japanese American Citizens League. https://jacl.org/asian-american-history/. Accessed October 13, 2016.

Japanese American Citizens League (JACL). *The Japanese American Experience: Lesson in American History. Curriculum and Resource Guide*. 5th ed. 2011. https://jacl.org/wordpress/wp-content/uploads/2015/01/covers.pdf. Accessed January 17, 2017.

Japanese Emigration to Brazil. "Chapter 1 before the Beginning: Early History of Japanese Emigration." National Diet Library. Japan. 2014. http://www.ndl.go.jp/brasil/e/s1/s1_1.html. Accessed October 8, 2016.

Jiobu, Robert M. *Ethnicity & Assimilation: Blacks, Chinese, Filipinos, Japanese, Koreans, Mexicans, Vietnamese, and Whites*. Albany: State University of New York Press, 1988.

Kawakami, Barbara. *Picture Bride Stores*. Honolulu: University of Hawai'i Press, 2016.

Kawakami, Barbara F. *Japanese Immigrant Clothing in Hawaii 1885–1941*. Honolulu: University of Hawai'i Press, 1993.

Kanstroom, Daniel. *Deportation Nation: Outsiders in American History*. Cambridge, MA: Harvard University Press, 2007.

Kessler, Lauren. *Stubborn Twig: Three Generations in the Life of a Japanese American Family*. New York: Random House, 1993.

Kikumura, Akemi. *Issei Pioneers: Hawaii and the Mainland, 1885–1945*. Honolulu: University of Hawai'i Press, 1993.

Kim, Hyung-chan, ed. *Asian Americans and the Supreme Court: A Documentary History*. Westport, CT: Greenwood Press, 1992.

Kim, Hyung-chan, ed. *Distinguished Asian Americans: A Biographical Dictionary*. Westport, CT: Greenwood Press, 1999.

Kimura, Yukiko. *Issei: Japanese Immigrants in Hawai'i*. Honolulu: University of Hawai'i Press, 1988.

Kurashige, Lon. *Japanese American Celebration and Conflict: A History of Ethnic Identity and Festival, 1934–1990*. Berkeley: University of California Press, 2002.

Kurashige, Lon. *Two Faces of Exclusion: The Untold History of Anti-Asian Racism in the United States.* Chapel Hill: University of North Carolina Press, 2016.

Lai, Eric, and Dennis Arguelles, eds. *The New Face of Asian Pacific America: Numbers, Diversity, & Change in the 21st Century.* San Francisco, CA: AsianWeek, 2003.

Lee, Jonathan H. X. *History of Asian Americans: Exploring Diverse Roots.* Westport, CT: Greenwood, 2015.

Leighton, Alexander H. *The Governing of Men: General Principles and Recommendations Based on Experience at a Japanese Relocation Camp.* Princeton, NJ: Princeton University Press, 1946.

Luther, Claudia. "Fred Korematsu Obituary." *Los Angeles Times*, April 1, 2005.

Lyon, Cherstin. *Prisons and Patriots: Japanese American Wartime Citizenship, Civil Disobedience, and Historical Memory.* Philadelphia, PA: Temple University Press, 2011.

Matsumoto, Valerie. *Farming the Home Place: A Japanese American Community in California, 1919–1982.* Ithaca, NY: Cornell University Press, 1993.

McClain, Charles. "Tortuous Path, Elusive Goal: The Asian Quest for American Citizenship." *Asian American Law Journal* 2, article 3 (January 1995).

McKenzie, Roderick. *Oriental Exclusion: The Effect of American Immigration Laws, Regulations and Judicial Decisions upon the Chinese and Japanese on the American Pacific Coast.* New York: J. S. Ozer, 1971.

Meyer, Evelene. *Wakamatsu Tea and Silk Farm Colony.* North Charleston, SC: CreateSpace Independent Publishing, 2016.

Mink, Patsy. *Congresswoman Patsy T. Mink.* Washington, DC: Congress of the United States, House of Representatives, 2001.

Muller, Eric. *Free to Die for Their Country: The Story of the Japanese American Draft Resisters in World War II.* Chicago, IL: University of Chicago Press, 2001.

Murray, Alice. *Historical Memories of the Japanese American Internment and the Struggle for Redress.* Stanford, CA: Stanford University Press, 2008.

Nakasone, Ronald, ed. *Okinawan Diaspora.* Honolulu: University of Hawai'i Press, 2002.

Neu, Charles. *An Uncertain Friendship: Theodore Roosevelt and Japan, 1906–1909.* Cambridge, MA: Harvard University Press, 1967.

Niiya, Brian, ed. *Japanese American History: An A-to-Z Reference from 1868 to the Present.* New York: Facts on File, 1993.

Nishimoto, Richard. *Inside an American Concentration Camp: Japanese American Resistance at Poston, Arizona.* Tucson: University of Arizona Press, 1995.

Nishimoto, Richard, and Lane Ryo Hirabayashi. *Inside an American Concentration Camp: Japanese American Resistance at Poston, Arizona.* Tucson: University of Arizona Press, 1995.

Nishimura, Arthur. "The Buddhist Mission of North America 1898–1942: Religion and Its Social Functions in an Ethnic Community." In *North American Buddhists in Social Context,* edited by Paul David Numrich. Leiden: Brill, 2008.

Odo, Franklin, ed. *The Columbia Documentary History of the Asian American Experience.* New York: Columbia University Press, 2002.

Odo, Franklin. *No Sword to Bury: Japanese Americans in Hawai'i during World War II.* Philadelphia, PA: Temple University Press, 2004.

Okihiro, Gary. *American History Unbound: Asians and Pacific Islanders.* Berkeley: University of California Press, 2015.

Okihiro, Gary. *Cane Fires: The Anti-Japanese Movement in Hawaii, 1865–1945*. Philadelphia, PA: Temple University Press, 1991.

Ohikiro, Gary. *Common Ground: Reimagining American History*. Princeton, NJ: Princeton University Press, 2001.

Okihiro, Gary. *Margins and Mainstreams: Asians in American History and Culture*. Seattle: University of Washington Press, 1994.

Okihiro, Gary, and David Drummond. "The Concentration Camps and Japanese Economic Losses in California Agriculture, 1900–1942." In *Japanese Americans: From Relocation to Redress*, edited by Roger Daniels, Sandra Taylor, Harry Kitano, and Leonard Arrington. Seattle: University of Washington Press, 1992.

"Organic Act." Hawaiian Independence. http://www.hawaii-nation.org/organic.html. Accessed October 12, 2013.

Perez, Louis, ed. *Japan at War: An Encyclopedia*. Santa Barbara, CA: ABC-CLIO, 2013.

Preserving California's Japantowns. "Oxnard." http://www.californiajapantowns.org /oxnard.html. Accessed October 12, 2016.

Rawitsch, Mark. *The House on Lemon Street: Japanese Pioneers and the American Dream*. Boulder: University Press of Colorado, 2012.

Rawitsch, Mark. *No Other Place: Japanese American Pioneers in a Southern California Neighborhood*. Riverside: University of California Riverside, Department of History, 1983.

Reeves, Richard. *Infamy: The Shocking Story of the Japanese American Internment in World War II*. New York: Henry Holt and Company, 2015.

Robinson, Greg. *By Order of the President: FRD and the Internment of Japanese Americans*. Cambridge, MA: Harvard University Press, 2001.

Robinson, Greg. *A Tragedy of Democracy: Japanese Confinement in North America*. New York: Columbia University Press, 2009.

Scott, James Brown. "Japanese and Hindu Naturalization in the United States." *The American Journal of International Law* 17, no. 2 (April 1923): 328–330.

Shumsky, Neil Larry. *The Evolution of Political Protest and the Workingmen's Party of California*. Columbus: Ohio State University Press, 1992.

Shurtleff, William, and Akiko Aoyagi, compilers. *History of Soybeans and Soyfoods in Japan, and in Japanese Cookbooks and Restaurants Outside Japan (701 CE to 2014)*. Lafayette: Soyinfo Center, 2014.

Simpson, Kelly. "Japanese Picture Brides: Building a Family through Photographs." KCET, August 1, 2012. https://www.kcet.org/shows/departures/japanese-picture -brides-building-a-family-through-photographs. Accessed October 14, 2016.

Spickard, Paul. *Almost All Aliens: Immigration, Race, and Colonialism in American History and Identity*. New York: Routledge, 2009.

Spickard, Paul R. "The Nisei Assume Power: The Japanese-American Citizen's League, 1941–1942." *Pacific Historical Review* 52 (May 1983): 147–174.

Starr, Kevin. *Endangered Dreams: The Great Depression in California*. Oxford, UK: Oxford University Press, 1996.

Starr, Kevin. *Golden Dreams: California in an Age of Abundance, 1950–1963*. Oxford, UK: Oxford University Press, 2009.

Takahashi, Jere. *Nisei/Sansei: Shifting Japanese American Identities and Politics*. Philadelphia, PA: Temple University Press, 1997.

Takaki, Ronald. "Ethnicity and Class in Hawaii: The Plantation Labor Experience, 1835–1920." In *Labor Divided: Race and Ethnicity in United States Labor Struggles, 1835–1960*, edited by Robert Asher and Charles Stephenson. Albany: State University of New York Press, 1990.

Takaki, Ronald. *Issei and Nisei: The Settling of Japanese America*. Langhorne, PA: Chelsea House Publishing, 1994.

Takaki, Ronald. *Pau Hana: Plantation Life and Labor in Hawaii*. Honolulu: University of Hawai'i Press, 1983.

Takaki, Ronald. *Strangers from a Different Shore: A History of Asian Americans*. rev. ed. Boston: Little, Brown, 1998.

"*Takao Ozawa v. US*." FindLaw.com. http://caselaw.findlaw.com/us-supreme-court/260/178.html. Accessed October 26, 2016.

Tamura, Eileen. *In Defense of Justice: Joseph Kurihara and the Japanese American Struggle for Equality*. Urbana: University of Illinois Press, 2013.

Tateishi, John. *And Justice for All: An Oral History of the Japanese Detention Camps*. Seattle: University of Washington Press, 1984.

Tichenor, Daniel. *Dividing Lines: The Politics of Immigration Control in America*. Princeton, NJ: Princeton University Press, 2002.

Toji, Dean S. "The Rise of the Nikkei Generation." In *The New Face of Asian Pacific American: Numbers, Diversity & Change in the 21st Century*, edited by Eric Lai and Dennis Arguelles. San Francisco, CA: AsianWeek, 2003.

"*Toyota v. United States* 268 U.S. 402 (1925)." Justia U.S. Supreme Court. https://supreme.justia.com/cases/federal/us/268/402/case.html. Accessed November 10, 2016.

Treat, Payson. *Japan and the United States 1853–1921*. Stanford, CA: Stanford University Press, 1928.

Uchida, Yoshiko. *Picture Bride: A Novel*. Seattle: University of Washington Press, 1987.

Uchida, Yoshiko. *The Invisible Thread*. New York: Simon & Schuster, 1991.

Van Sant, John E. *Pacific Pioneers: Japanese Journeys to America and Hawaii, 1850–1880*. Urbana: University of Illinois Press, 2000.

Wang, Frances Kai-hwa. "The Untold Stories of Internment Resisters." NBC News. http://www.nbcnews.com/news/asian-america/uclas-suyama-project-document-japanese-american-resistance-internment-during-world-n321426. Accessed January 14, 2017.

Williams, Duncan Ryuken, and Tomoe Moriya. *Issei Buddhism in the Americas*. Urbana: University of Illinois Press, 2010.

List of Contributors

Dean Ryuta Adachi
California State University, East Bay

Midori Tanaka Atkins
School of Oriental and African
Studies
University of London

Eiichiro Azuma
University of Pennsylvania,
Philadelphia

Alfred Bloom
University of Hawai'i
Honolulu, Hawai'i

Floyd Cheung
Smith College
Northampton, Massachusetts

Yvette M. Chin
Independent Scholar
Boston, Massachusetts

Linda Sun Crowder
California State University, Fullerton

Peter L. Doebler
Graduate Theological Union
Berkeley, California

Joanne Doi
Maryknoll Sisters Integration
Program
Chicago, Illinois

Michael M. Ego
University of Connecticut,
Stamford

Rachel Endo
College of Saint Mary
Omaha, Nebraska

Brett Esaki
Georgia State University
Atlanta, Georgia

Matthew J. Forss
Independent Scholar
Omro, Wisconsin

Katie Furuyama
University of California, Irvine

John Handley
Graduate Theological Union
Berkeley, California

Maya Hara
Independent Scholar

Ambi Harsha
University of California, Santa
Barbara

Jeanette Yih Harvie
University of California, Santa
Barbara

James A. Hirabayashi
San Francisco State University

Lane Ryo Hirabayashi
University of California, Los Angeles

Kevin Hogg
Mount Baker Secondary School
Cranbrook, British Columbia,
Canada

Adam R. Hornbuckle
Independent Scholar
Spring Hill, Tennessee

Daniel H. Inouye
Queens College, City University New
York

Eri Kameyama
University of California, Los Angeles

Hideyo Konagaya
Waseda University
Tokyo, Japan

Jonathan H. X. Lee
San Francisco State University

Valerie Lo
University of Hawai'i, Manoa

Nan Ma
Independent Scholar
Woodinville, Washington

Material Resource Committee
Konko Churches of North America
San Francisco, California

Michael Maricio
Independent Scholar

Valerie J. Matsumoto
University of California,
Los Angeles

Scott A. Mitchell
Institute of Buddhist Studies
Berkeley, California

Barbara Lynne Rowland Mori
California Polytechnic State
University,
San Luis Obispo

Lauren S. Morimoto
Sonoma State University,
California

Emily Morishima
Western Governors University
Salt Lake City, Utah

Sean Morton
Brock University
St. Catharines, Ontario,
Canada

Salvador Jimenez Murguia
Miyazaki International College
Kiyotake, Miyazaki, Japan

Paul M. Nagano
American Baptist Minister

Kerry Yo Nakagawa
Founder, Nisei Baseball Research
Project
Fresno, California

Martha Nakagawa
Journalist and Freelance Writer

Kelli Y. Nakamura
Kapi'olani Community College
Honolulu, Hawai'i

Ronald Y. Nakasone
Graduate Theological Union
Berkeley, California

Kesaya E. Noda
Independent Scholar
Plainfield, New Hampshire

Yuki Obayashi
University of California, Santa Cruz

Kieko Obuse
Mahidol University
Bangkok, Thailand

Ruby Toshimi Ogawa
Bunkyo University
Chigasaki City, Japan

Cynthia Mari Orozco
California State University,
Long Beach

Lori Pierce
DePaul University
Chicago, Illinois

Vincent Kelly Pollard
University of Hawai'i, Manoa

Terumi Rafferty-Osaki
American University
Washington, D.C.

David Alan Rego
Independent scholar

Greg Robinson
Université du Québec À Montréal
Montreal, Canada

Daigaku Rummé
Zenshuji Soto Temple
Los Angeles, California

Noriko Sanefuji
Smithsonian National Museum of
American History
Washington, D.C.

Kathryn M. Schreiber
United Church of Christ

Ina C. Seethaler
Coastal Carolina University
Conway, South Carolina

Bill Staples Jr.
Nisei Baseball Research Project
Chandler, Arizona

Joseph R. Svinth
Independent Scholar
Tumwater, Washington

Isao Takei
Nihon University
Tokyo, Japan

Aiko Takeuchi-Demirci
Stanford University
Palo Alto, California

Jodo Tanaka
Jodo Shu North America Buddhist
Missions

Larry M. Taylor
Center for Art, Religion, and
Education
Guerneville, California

Richard Tennes
Honpa Hongwanji Mission of
Hawaii

Kathleen A. Tobin
Purdue University Calumet
Hammond, Indiana

Yoko Tsukuda
Seijo University
Tokyo, Japan

Priscilla Wegars
Independent Scholar
Moscow, Idaho

Lily Anne Yumi Welty
University of California, Santa
Barbara

Megan White
University of California, Santa
Barbara

Ken Yamada
Jodo Shinshu Otani Ha
Berkeley, California

Jane H. Yamashiro
University of Southern California

Jeffrey T. Yamashita
University of California, Berkeley

Wendi Yamashita
University of California, Los Angeles

Krystal Shyun Yang
Brown University
Providence, Rhode Island

Christina R. Yanko
Jodo Shinshu Buddhist Temple of
Canada

Grace J. Yoo
San Francisco State University

Mari Yoshihara
University of Hawai'i, Manoa

About the Editor

Jonathan H. X. Lee, PhD, is an associate professor of Asian American studies at San Francisco State University. He received his doctorate in religious studies from the University of California at Santa Barbara in 2009. He is the founder of the Asian American Religious Studies section for the American Academy of Religion, Western Region (AAR/WR) conference. His work has been published in *Peace Review: A Journal of Social Justice*; *Nidan: International Journal for the Study of Hinduism*; *Chinese America: History & Perspectives—The Journal of the Chinese Historical Society of America*; *Empty Vessel: The Journal of the Daoist Arts*; *Spotlight on Teaching/American Academy of Religion*; *Asia Pacific Perspectives*; *Pacific World: Journal of the Institute of Buddhist Studies*; *JATI: Journal of Southeast Asian Studies*; *Amerasia Journal*; and other journals and anthologies, both nationally and internationally. His published works include ABC-CLIO's *Encyclopedia of Asian American Folklore and Folklife* (2011); *Encyclopedia of Asian American Religious Cultures* (2015); *History of Asian Americans: Exploring Diverse Roots* (2015); and *Chinese Americans: History and Culture of a People* (2016). In addition, he is author of *Cambodian American Experiences: Histories, Communities, Cultures, and Identities* (2010, reprint 2015); *Asian American Identities and Practices: Folkloric Expressions in Everyday Life* (2014); *The Age of Asian Migration: Continuity, Diversity, and Susceptibility,* volume 1 (2014); and *Southeast Asian Diaspora in the United States: Memories and Visions, Yesterday, Today, and Tomorrow* (2015). He has published extensively on Chinese, Cambodian, Vietnamese, Chinese-Southeast Asian, and Asian American histories, folklore, cultures, and religions. Currently, Lee serves as editor-in-chief of *Chinese America: History & Perspectives*, a peer-review journal published by the Chinese Historical Society of America.

Index

Note: Page numbers in **bold type** indicate main encyclopedia entries; page numbers in *italics* indicate photographs.